THE YEARBOOK

OF

EDUCATION LAW

2001

Edited by

CHARLES J. RUSSO

University of Dayton

EDUCATION LAW ASSOCIATION
DAYTON, OHIO

Copyright © 2001

by

EDUCATION LAW ASSOCIATION
300 COLLEGE PARK
DAYTON, OHIO 45469
Phone: 937-229-3589
Fax: 937-229-3845
http://www.educationlaw.org

Library of Congress Catalog Card Number 52-2403

ISBN 1-56534-102-3

PRINTED IN U.S.A.

ABOUT THE EDITOR

Charles J. Russo is a Professor in the Department of Educational Administration, School of Education and Allied Professions, and a Fellow in the Center for International Programs at the University of Dayton, Dayton, Ohio. Dr. Russo is a Past President of the Education Law Association. Among other publications, he is a co-author of *The Law of Home Schooling* (1994) and *Special Education Law: Issues & Implications for the '90s* (1995). Dr. Russo has been a member of the Editorial Advisory Committee of West's *Education Law Reporter* since 1987 and was appointed to the Editorial Advisory Committee in 1996. He is a past regional reporter for the *School Law Reporter* and author of the *Law Review Digest* in *ELA Notes*. He has authored more than 200 articles and presented numerous papers at national and international conferences, including his ongoing activity in Bosnia.

CONTRIBUTORS

F. King Alexander
Assistant Professor
University of Illinois
Champaign, Illinois

Judith Adkison
Associate Dean
University of North Texas
Denton, Texas

William E. Camp
Professor
University of North Texas
Denton, Texas

William Bradley Colwell
Associate Professor
Education Law and Public Policy
Southern Illinois University - Carbondale
Carbondale, Illinois

Jay Cummings
Associate Professor
University of North Texas
Denton, Texas

David L. Dagley
Associate Professor
Educational Leadership and Policy Studies
University of Alabama - Tuscaloosa
Tuscaloosa, Alabama

Jan DeGroof
Professor
Interuniversitair Centrum
Voor Onderwijsrecht
President, European Association for Education Law and Policy
Antwerpen, Belgium

William J. Evans, Jr.
Teacher and Administrator
Smithtown Central School District
Smithtown, New York

Dennis J. Farrington
Professor
University of Stirling
Stirling, Scottland

Scott Ellis Ferrin
Assistant Professor
Department of Educational Leadership and Foundations
Adjunct Professor of Law
Brigham Young University
Provo, Utah

Rick Allen Griffin
Brigham Young University
Provo, Utah

Neville Harris
Professor of Law
School of Law, Social Work and Social Policy
John Moores University
Liverpool, United Kingdom

Johnetta Hudson
Associate Professor
University of North Texas
Denton, Texas

Anwar (Andy) N. Khan
Professor Emeritus of Legal Studies
Athabasca University
Alberta, Canada and
Visiting Professor of Business Law
Murdoch University, Murdoch
Perth, Australia

Katherine Lindsay
Faculty of Law
University of Newcastle
Newcastle, NSW, Australia

Ralph D. Mawdsley
Professor of Educational Administration
Department of Counseling, Administration,
  Supervision and Adult Learning
Cleveland State University
Cleveland, Ohio

Scott C. McLeod
Assistant Professor
University of Minnesota
Minneapolis, Minnesota

Izak Oosthuizen
Faculty of Education
Pu Vir Cho
Potchefstroom, South Africa

Allan G. Osborne, Jr.
Principal
Snug Harbor Community School
Quincy, Massachusetts

Hilde Penneman
European Association for Education Law and Policy
Interuniversitary Centre for Education Law
Antwerpen, Belgium

Paul Rishworth
Faculty of Law
University of Auckland
Auckland, New Zealand

Charles J. Russo
Professor, Department of Educational Leadership
School of Education and Allied Professions and
Adjunct Professor, School of Law
University of Dayton
Dayton, Ohio

Linda A. Sharp
Associate Professor
Sport Admnistration
School of Kinesiology and Physical Education
Univeristy of Northern Colorado
Greeley, Colorado

Douglas Stewart
Senior Lecturer
School of Professional Studies - Kelvin Grove Campus
Queensland University of Technology
Brisbane, Queensland, Australia

Paul W. Thurston
Professor
Department of Educational Organization and Leadership
University of Illinois
Champaign, Illinois

CONTENTS

2 - PUPILS
Jay Cimmings, Johnetta Hudson, Bill Camp and Judith Adkison

3 - BARGAINING
Scott McLeod

4 - STUDENTS WITH DISABILITIES
Allan G. Osborne, Jr.

5 - TORTS
William J. Evans, Jr.

6 - SPORTS
Linda A. Sharp

7 - HIGHER EDUCATION
F. King Alexander and Paul W. Thurston

8 - STUDENTS IN HIGHER EDUCATION
Brad Colwell

9 - FEDERAL AND STATE LEGISLATION
David L. Dagley

10 - EDUCATION RELATED
Scott Ellis Ferrin and Rick Alan Griffin

11 - INTERNATIONAL LAW

HIGHER EDUCATION IN GREAT BRITIAN
Dennis J. Farrington

GREAT BRITIAN K-12
Neville Harris

NEW ZEALAND
Paul Rishworth

SOUTH AFRICA
Izak Oosthuizen

1
EMPLOYEES

Ralph D. Mawdsley

Introduction

This year's chapter reviews almost 160 cases involving employees in public and nonpublic K-12 schools. While the Supreme Court did not address any cases involving K-12 employees, this chapter cites precedent-setting rulings from past years where appropriate. The chapter excludes cases focusing primarily on procedural matters. As in past years, the section with the largest number of cases concerns dismissal, nonrenewal, demotion, and discipline along with school board compliance with district and state policies.

Discrimination in Employment

Discrimination claims can arise under state or federal statutes. Even so, most lawsuits identifying state law as a claim also invoke federal law, if for no other reason than that states tend to follow federal law in interpreting their own anti-discrimination statutes. However, states may also act under their own statutes to protect categories that may be the same or different from those under federal law.

Federal nondiscrimination statutes are divided into two broad groups: those prohibiting discrimination in employment and those outlawing it in educational institutions receiving federal financial assistance. The employment statutes include Title VII of the Civil Rights Act of 1964,[1] which prohibits discrimination on the basis of race, color, religion, sex, and/or national origin; the Age Discrimination Act in Employment Act of 1967 (ADEA)[2] which forbids discrimination against persons forty years of age or older; the Americans with Disabilities Act of 1990 (ADA)[3] which is aimed at preventing discrimination by state and local governments on the basis of disabilities in employment and in public accommodations; and the Family and Medical Leave Act (FMLA)[4] which affords employees the right to extended leave for personal and family medical needs and illnesses.

Anti-discrimination statutes which are predicated on receiving federal financial assistance include Section 504 of the Rehabilitation Act of 1973,[5] which prohibits discrimination on the basis of disabilities; Title IX of the Educational Amendments of 1972,[6] which forbids gender discrimination; and Title VI of the Civil Rights Act of 1964, which outlaws discrimination on the basis of race, color or national origin. Remedies for discrimination can

---

[1] 42 U.S.C. § 2000 *et seq.*
[2] 29 U.S.C. § 621 *et seq.*
[3] 42 U.S.C. § 12101 *et seq.*
[4] 29 U.S.C. § 2611 et *seq.*
[5] 29 U.S.C. § 794.
[6] 20 U.S.C. § 1681.

also be pursued under two other federal laws that can apply to both employment and non-employment situations. Section 1981 of the Civil Rights Act of 1866[7] prohibits discrimination on the basis of national origin and race in the making of contracts. Section 1983 of the Civil Rights Act of 1871,[8] which contains no discriminatory categories of its own, is a vehicle for seeking damages for violations of federal constitutional and statutory rights.

Frequently, discriminatory claims involve more than one category. For example, in an ongoing saga involving the Chicago Public Schools, an appellate court in Illinois court held that 188 of 700 teachers who were not reassigned to their former schools during a reconstitution were entitled to certain information used in the assignment process. The court agreed with the teachers that information such as interview questions and criteria used in determining who conducted the interviews was relevant in evaluating whether reassignments were discriminatorily based on gender and race.[9]

A federal trial court in Colorado sustained a school board's dismissal of an employee for poor performance in a suit alleging both race and sexual harassment discrimination. Even though the former employee's supervisor had not investigated her alleged claims of sexual harassment, and falsely testified that he had not known about it, the court reasoned that district officials could discharge the employee for her poor performance rather than take the time to investigate her harassment claim. The court noted that the supervisor's failure to address the harassment did not affect the legitimacy of the basis for her dismissal in observing that "[p]reference of existing grounds [for discharge] is not the equivalent of pretextual grounds."[10]

Occasionally, discriminatory claims arise under state law. In Minnesota, an appellate court affirmed the validity of a school board's anti-nepotism policy which prohibited any of its employees from being directly supervised by a spouse or family member. In upholding the board's refusal to consider the plaintiff for a position where she would have been supervised by her husband, the court found that the policy was a bona fide occupational qualification.[11]

In a significant case involving burden of proof in a discrimination retaliation case, the Second Circuit distinguished between the knowledge of a school board and that of supervisory personnel. In vacating and remanding a grant of summary judgment that had been entered on behalf of a board in

---

[7] 42 U.S.C. § 1981.
[8] 42 U.S.C. § 1983.
[9] Chicago Sch. Reform Bd. of Trustees v. Illinois Educ. Labor Rel. Bd., 734 N.E.2d 69 [147 Educ. L. Rep. 662] (Ill. App. Ct. 2000).
[10] Torrence v. Cherry Creek Sch. Dist. No. 5, 119 F. Supp.2d 1135, 1139 [148 Educ. L. Rep. 883] (D. Colo. 2000).
[11] Belton-Kocher v. St. Paul Sch. Dist., 610 N.W.2d 374 [144 Educ. L. Rep. 731] (Minn. Ct. App. 2000).

New York, the court ascertained that a teacher who filed a retaliation claim after she was denied an administrative position and subsequently received poor performance evaluations by her supervisors was entitled to a new trial. The court rejected the board's argument that it should not be liable since, even though it knew of the teacher's retaliation claim, none of the supervisors who had evaluated her knew that the claim had been filed. The court contended that the knowledge level required for a prima facie case under the burden shifting requirements of a retaliation claim contained in *McDonnell Douglas Corporation v. Green*[12] applied to the board, not to its agents.[13]

The Seventh Circuit, in reversing a directed verdict in favor of a school board in Wisconsin, clarified one of the evidentiary issues in a Title VII suit, namely the nature of evidence that is admissible to prove whether a plaintiff was treated differently from other similarly situated persons. The court commented that the time frame for similarly situated comparisons can apply to a period of ten months after a plaintiff ceased to be an employee. The court permitted the plaintiff, a black employee with a disability, to introduce testimony that two white employees with disabilities, who, like him, were unable to do the work required by their job descriptions, were temporarily assigned to other jobs, an option that he was not given. The court was of the opinion that "[t]he last date of the allegedly discriminatory conduct is not a bright line beyond which the conduct of the employer is no longer relevant in a discrimination case."[14]

Race

Claims of discrimination can fail for a number of reasons. Among the most common reasons are failure to satisfy the elements of a prima facie case and inability to prove that a school board's decision was pretextual. The four elements are that the plaintiff is a member of a protected class; that the plaintiff is qualified for the job applied for; that the plaintiff was rejected despite his qualifications; and, that the position went to an equally qualified or less qualified person who was not a member of plaintiff's class. A white substitute teacher in Florida unsuccessfully filed a title VII race discrimination claim against a board that hired a black female instead of him. In granting the board's motion for summary judgment, a federal trial court decided that the plaintiff failed on the fourth element since he did not apply for the

---

[12] 411 U.S. 792 (1973).
[13] Gordon v. New York City Bd. of Educ., 232 F.3d 111 [148 Educ. L. Rep. 735] (2d Cir. 2000).
[14] Freeman v. Madison Metropolitan Sch. Dist., 231 F.3d 374, 382 [148 Educ. L. Rep. 629] (7th Cir. 2000).

position filled by the black female in the year in which she was hired. The court pointed out that the plaintiff's application for the preceding year was for a job in a middle school, while the position at issue was in a new magnet school.[15]

In a case from Minnesota, the Eighth Circuit affirmed that a superintendent's stray comments, perceived by a discharged Native American as discriminatory, did not constitute direct evidence of a discriminatory animus. The court was satisfied that the superintendent's alleged remarks about pitching a tent, scrubbing Indian ponies, and a Native American student sleeping in a locker so as not to be late to school, did not establish the existence of a racially motivated decision where the teacher had numerous opportunities to rectify her tardiness over a two-year period.[16]

A federal trial court in Mississippi decided that a black applicant for a job as a high school principal failed to demonstrate that a board's reason for selecting a white applicant was motivated by discriminatory animus. In granting the board's motion for judgment as a matter of law, the court was of the view that the applicant did not overcome the board's reason based on a disagreement over the amount of credit to be given on a rating form for his work experience and academic achievement.[17] Similarly, a white applicant in Indiana for a job as an administrative aide failed to prove that his not being hired based on his past performance was pretextual. The court indicated that statements by school officials that the jobs were reserved for blacks and women were not discriminatory even though white males filled only two of the fifty-three positions.[18]

Employees who are able to meet the requirements of a prima facie case will, at the minimum, be entitled to a trial on the merits and, if successful, a damages award. In such a case, a federal trial court in Illinois was convinced that a white tenured teacher, who was demoted to a job as a permanent substitute teacher as part of a high school's drastic remediation process, stated a claim under title VII and section 1983 for race discrimination. In rejecting the school board's motion for summary judgment, the court ascertained that it could not ascertain a nondiscriminatory reason why the white

---

[15] Anthony v. School Bd. of Hillsborough County, 92 F. Supp.2d 1317 [143 Educ. L. Rep. 832] (M.D. Fla. 2000).
[16] Clearwater v. Independent Sch. Dist. No. 166, 231 F.3d 1123 [148 Educ. L. Rep. 728] (8th Cir. 2000).
[17] Hardy v. Simpson County Sch. Dist., 87 F. Supp.2d 637 [142 Educ. L. Rep. 900] (S.D. Miss. 1999).
[18] Rayl v. Ft. Wayne Community Schs., 87 F. Supp.2d 870 [142 Educ. L. Rep. 925] (N.D. Ind. 2000).

teacher was demoted and similarly situated black teachers were retained. The court also refused to grant qualified immunity to the board and the administrators who were involved in the demotion.[19]

In Florida, a black former maintenance employee was awarded front and back pay after being dismissed for committing a lewd conduct offense three years prior to his being hired as an electric motor repair master. A federal trial court judged that the former employee stated a prima facie case since a white employee who committed a similar offense was granted rehabilitation.[20]

Claims of racial discrimination, like gender, can involve harassment. A black female teacher in Tennessee unsuccessfully alleged race and gender harassment for hostile environment discrimination by a male co-worker where the building principal, on receiving her complaint, promptly called a meeting, chastised the co-worker, and issued a formal letter of reprimand. The court believed that employer liability under title VII for co-worker harassment occurs only where an employer's response manifests indifference or unreasonableness. The court posited that the behavior of the co-worker was not severe or pervasive, not physically threatening or humiliating, and did not unreasonably interfere with the teacher's work performance.[21]

Sex

A hostile work environment is one of the most frequent grounds for gender-based claims. In order to render a school board liable for the actions of a co-worker, a claimant must establish, as part of a prima facie case, that gender was the basis for the harassment. In such a case, the Eleventh Circuit affirmed a grant of summary judgment in favor of a school board in Florida against a claim by a married, male teacher that verbal and physical actions by an unmarried female teacher, with whom he taught and with whom he had carried on a one-year sexual relationship, were not the basis for a harassment claim. The panel agreed with the trial court that the female's harassment was "motivated not by [the plaintiff's] male gender, but rather by [her] contempt for him following their failed relationship; [the plaintiff's] gender was merely coincidental."[22]

---

[19] Mohr v. Chicago Sch. Reform Bd. of Trustees, 99 F. Supp.2d 934 145 Educ. L. Rep. 280] (N.D. Ill. 2000).
[20] Silvera v. Orange County Sch. Bd., 87 F. Supp.2d 1265 [142 Educ. L. Rep. 966] (M.D. Fla. 2000).
[21] Anderson v. Memphis City Schs. Bd. of Educ., 75 F. Supp.2d 786 [140 Educ. L. Rep. 677] (W.D. Tenn. 1999).
[22] Succar v. Dade County Sch. Bd., 229 F.3d 1343, 1345 [148 Educ. L. Rep. 95] (11th Cir. 2000).

In a complex sexual harassment claim, the Seventh Circuit upheld not only a grant of summary judgment in favor of a school board in Indiana under title VII and section 1983, but also a $25,000 punitive damages award against a principal under section 1983. The court maintained that even if a principal cannot be considered an employer for purposes of title VII, he can be liable individually under section 1983. The court acknowledged that while the board's actions had not risen to the standard of deliberate indifference to warrant liability, the principal's conduct toward the teacher-plaintiff met the section 1983 requirement because the law regarding sexual harassment was well establishment the time of his conduct. In addition, the court upheld an award of joint and several liability for $67,000 attorney fees on the theory that since the board lacked a policy regarding sexual harassment, the litigation resulted in its adopting one.[23]

School board liability for gender-based discriminatory conduct depends on the knowledge of board members. Title IX liability for sexual abuse or harassment against an employer requires actual notice of a hostile environment as well as knowledge by a supervisor who has remedial power to hire, fire, and discipline an alleged harasser; such knowledge is sufficient to impute notice to an employer. In such a case from Ohio, a federal trial court refused to dismiss a claim where genuine issues of material fact existed as to whether school officials' awareness of discriminatory behavior by a teacher could be imputed to the board.[24]

Liability under title IX depends on whether school officials have demonstrated deliberate indifference to complaints. A federal trial court in Georgia declared that parents of a middle school student raped by a school custodian on school premises did not have a title IX claim for damages where the principal, upon hearing of the rape, investigated the claim and discharged the custodian. The court explained that damages are available under title IX only where a school official with actual knowledge of sexual discrimination fails to respond in a manner that amounts to deliberate indifference.[25]

As witnessed by a case from Virginia, a school board's failure to have the requisite knowledge can result in liability for a school administrator but not a board. A federal trial court upheld a $350,000 title IX damages award against a principal but vacated a $700,000 award against a board. The judge agreed with the jury that the principal acted with deliberate indifference in

---

[23] Molnar v. Booth, 229 F.3d 593 [148 Educ. L. Rep. 54] (7th Cir. 2000).

[24] Massey v. Akron City Bd. of Educ., 82 F. Supp.2d 735 [141 Educ. L. Rep. 1104] (N.D. Ohio 2000).

[25] Sherman v. Helms, 80 F. Supp.2d 1365 [141 Educ. L. Rep. 689] (M.D. Ga. 2000).

failing to investigate complaints of sexual abuse of a former student by a teacher who later sexually abused the plaintiff. According to the court, the fact that the former student was an adult did not diminish the principal's deliberate indifference where she chose not to report the sexual abuse to the police when it occurred ten years earlier. Further, the court ruled that the principal satisfied the deliberate indifference standard when, in seeking advice of the board's executive director of personnel regarding her suspicions about the teacher's inappropriate relationships with students, she failed to mention that she saw the plaintiff sitting on the teacher's lap in a classroom. The court concluded that the board was not liable because no one high enough in its chain of command, including the superintendent, knew about the abusive acts.[26]

A case from Illinois illustrates the importance of title VII's filing requirement. In granting a school board's motion for summary judgment, a federal trial court decreed that a high school music teacher who alleged that his male principal sexually harassed him with comments and physical contact failed in his title VII harassment claim where he had not filed his complaint within 300 days of the last alleged discriminatory act. The teacher also unsuccessfully alleged constructive discharge where his principal showed him a single offensive photograph and engaged in unspecified conduct. The court refused to find that the employment conditions were so intolerable so as to force a person to resign.[27]

At the same time, the 300 day filing requirement does not necessarily apply to the admission of evidence. A federal trial court in New York entered some helpful evidentiary clarifications in a case regarding a school district custodial employee's allegation of sexual harassment by a school maintenance worker. As to the plaintiff's title VII claim, the court commented that evidence that the maintenance worker sexually harassed the custodial worker was admissible even though the conduct occurred more than 300 days prior to the plaintiff's filing an administrative complaint. In addition, the court wrote that evidence indicating that the board allowed the worker to resign, rather than terminate his employment or begin disciplinary proceedings against him, was admissible as to whether the board had a policy of protecting harassers from dismissal.[28]

Besides the legal remedy of damages, courts have authority to award a number of equitable remedies, including reinstatement, if possible. In a case where continued hostility continued to exist among employees, a federal

---

[26] Baynard v. Lawson, 112 F. Supp.2d 524 [147 Educ. L. Rep. 136] (E.D. Va. 2000).

[27] Cross v. Chicago Sch. Reform Bd. of Trustees, 80 F. Supp.2d 911 [141 Educ. L. Rep. 662] (N.D. Ill. 2000).

[28] Peck v. Hudson City Sch. Dist., 100 F. Supp.2d 118 [145 Educ. L. Rep. 317] (N.D.N.Y. 2000).

trial court in Iowa refused to award reinstatement as a remedy. Instead, the court ordered three years full front pay and three years part-time pay.[29]

Age

A key element in any discrimination claim is meeting the requisite burden of proof. In a case from Connecticut, the federal trial court rejected a teacher's discrimination claim where he offered no evidence that the board's reason for selecting a younger person of the same race and gender was pretextual. Although the plaintiff disagreed with the board's assessment of his teaching qualifications and the quality of his application materials, the court stated that he was required to prove more than that he would have been a good employee.[30]

In a case from Maine, the federal trial court contended that a former high school librarian with shoulder tendonitis who was discharged for inability to work with her supervisor, failed to state causes of action under ADEA or ADA. Noting that inability to get along with a supervisor represents a legitimate, nondiscriminatory reason for discharge, the court interpreted the supervisor's comment to the plaintiff, that she wanted to "trade" her in for "two twenty-fivers," as insufficient to establish age discrimination.[31]

A plaintiff can succeed in an age discrimination claims by presenting sufficient evidence to counter a school board's motion for summary judgment. In New York, a federal trial court held that a teacher who was not hired for five positions that were filled by younger candidates was entitled to go to trial under the ADEA. The court discerned that despite the board's claim that the plaintiff's lack of interview skills was sufficient to articulate a legitimate, nondiscriminatory reason, genuine issues of material fact precluded granting its motion for summary judgment.[32]

In a case from Alabama filed by a former principal of a parochial school, a federal trial court agreed with the administrator's allegation that school officials' proffered nondiscriminatory reasons for his nonrenewal were pretextual because they were subjective. The court observed that the school's claim that the principal's leadership skills were inadequate was

---

[29] Prine v. Sioux City Community Sch. Dist., 95 F. Supp.2d 1005 [144 Educ. L. Rep. 239] (N.D. Iowa 2000).

[30] Lopos v. Ruocco, 99 F. Supp.2d 207 [146 Educ. L. Rep. 125] (D. Conn. 2000).

[31] Ridge v. Cape Elizabeth Sch. Dist., 77 F. Supp.2d 149 [140 Educ. L. Rep. 923] (Me. 1999).

[32] Gavigan v. Clarkstown Cent. Sch. Dist., 84 F. Supp.2d 540 [142 Educ. L. Rep. 179] (S.D.N.Y. 2000).

offset by a seven-year history without admonitions or reprimands and his ability to offer alternative explanations for the school's specific examples of supposedly weak leadership.[33]

Disparate impact discrimination claims are not easy to prove. A sixty-four year-old unsuccessful applicant for a high school teaching position in Connecticut failed in his disparate impact claim when a younger female was hired in his stead. The federal trial court asserted that evidence that the school district had a significantly lower percentage of male teachers than the statewide population of male teachers was insufficient to overcome its nondiscriminatory reason based on an interview. Although the plaintiff's qualifications on paper were comparable to those of the person who was hired, the court reflected that "there is nothing in title VII or the ADEA that required defendants to base their hiring decision solely upon objective 'paper' credentials and overlook subjective factors gleaned from the applications and interviews."[34]

Occasionally, the legality of early retirement plans designed to encourage employees with the greatest number of years of service to retire are contested. A federal trial court in Missouri determined that an early retirement benefit plan that decreased lump-sum payments to retirees solely on the basis of age facially violated the ADEA. The court uncovered direct evidence of the plan's discriminatory treatment in its purpose to provide a better "age blend" and create a younger working staff.[35]

Disability

An issue that does not generally arise is whether a school is subject to a lawsuit as an employer. In a case of first impression, a federal trial court in the District of Columbia was of the opinion that a Catholic parish and school in the Washington, D.C., archdiocese cannot be sued for alleged violations of the ADA. The court reasoned that since the parish and school were unincorporated divisions of the archdiocese and were incorporated by Congress as a corporation sole, they could not be sued by the EEOC. The court added that although federal procedure allows unincorporated associations to be sued, this does not extend to unincorporated divisions of a corporation.[36]

---

[33] Shook v. St. Bede Sch., 74 F. Supp.2d 1172 [140 Educ. L. Rep. 628] (M.D. Ala. 1999).

[34] Byrnie v. Town of Cromwell Pub. Schs., 73 F. Supp.2d 204, 213 [140 Educ. L. Rep. 560] (D. Conn. 1999).

[35] Equal Employment Opportunities Comm'n v. Hickman Mills Consl. Sch. Dist. No. 1, 99 F. Supp.2d 1070 [145 Educ. L. Rep. 287] (W.D. Mo. 2000).

[36] Equal Employment Opportunities Comm'n v. St. Francis Xavier Parochial Sch., 77 F. Supp.2d 71 [140 Educ. L. Rep. 913] (D.D.C. 1999).

School boards won a number of disability cases involving a wide range of issues based on the proposition that a plaintiff cannot recover without demonstrating that a disability affects a major life function. In Wyoming, the federal trial court contended that a fourth grade teacher in a parochial school who had several hip surgeries and might have needed additional operations failed to state an ADA claim where her contract was nonrenewed for poor performance. In dismissing the teacher's claim, the court decided that she failed to establish that she was substantially limited in a major life function. Even though the teacher was in pain, the court was convinced that since she was able to carry out her teaching functions, she was not disabled within the meaning of the ADA.[37]

A disability claim may relate to prior conduct that a person alleges is protected under the ADA. In a case from Ohio, the Sixth Circuit upheld a school board's refusal to hire a bus driver who, several years earlier, was involved in a beer-drinking incident at an elementary school. The driver had alleged that the board's choice not to hire him violated the ADA because it acted based on his record of alcohol impairment. The court pointed out that the prior on-the-job drinking incident provided the board with a legitimate, nondiscriminatory reason for not employing him as a bus driver: "[t]he plaintiff cannot force [the] defendant to hire him as a school bus driver when there is a serious risk that he may again drink on the job, have an accident and kill a group of school children."[38]

At some point, an employee may engage in conduct that prompts an employer to order the individual to undergo mental testing. The Sixth Circuit upheld a school board's suspension of a tenured teacher in Michigan who refused to undergo an ordered mental and physical fitness-for-duty examination. The court, in rejecting the teacher's ADA claim that the order treated him as having a disability, agreed that the board had reason to believe that he could not perform his job functions since he engaged in disruptive and abusive verbal outbursts, shoved papers in the faces of individual board members, and refused to stop speaking at board meetings when the board president asked him to do so. The court ascertained that although an employer's discretion to order employees to undergo post-hiring mental or physical examinations is limited, it is supportable where a reasonable person would inquire whether an employee is still capable of performing his job.[39]

---

[37] Brown v. Holy Name Church, 80 F. Supp.2d 1261 [141 Educ. L. Rep. 669] (D. Wyo. 2000).
[38] Martin v. Barnesville Exempted Village Sch. Dist. Bd. of Educ., 209 F.3d 931 [143 Educ. L. Rep. 731] (6th Cir. 2000).
[39] Sullivan v. River Valley Sch. Dist., 197 F.3d 804 [140 Educ. L. Rep. 127] (6th Cir. 1999).

Like other alleged discrimination claims, employers may act based on nondiscriminatory reasons. The Fifth Circuit affirmed a grant of summary judgment in favor of a school board in Louisiana over a librarian's claims that it failed to accommodate his hearing disability. The court agreed that the librarian was given a lateral transfer to a library position with less pay because several positions were eliminated, not due to his disability.[40]

The federal trial court in Puerto Rico permitted the non-renewal of the contract of a teacher in a Catholic school despite his claim that this occurred in violation of ADA because he was HIV-positive. In granting the school's motion for summary judgment, the court was persuaded that officials acted on nondiscriminatory basis such as the plaintiff's tardiness, problems managing students, and disrespect for monastic life.[41]

In Michigan, a federal trial court upheld the state Department of Education's refusal to issue a bus driver endorsement to a person whose leg was amputated below the knee. In rejecting the plaintiff's equal protection claim, the court was of the view that since, pursuant to *City of Cleburne v. Cleburne Living Center,*[42] a disability is not a suspect class, the Department presented a rationally related legitimate state interest in protecting school children. The court also rejected the plaintiff's ADA claim because the Department was not his employer and his section 1983 charge since Congress created a private cause of action through the ADA which rendered a section 1983 suit unnecessary.[43]

A federal trial court in Pennsylvania rejected a school board's motion for summary judgment where a former secretary demonstrated that her disability was connected to a major life function. Although not disputing that the former secretary's bipolar disorder qualified as a disability, the board claimed that her condition did not affect a major life function. In its opinion, the court referenced an earlier case from the Third Circuit which maintained that "thinking" could be a major life function.[44]

Courts can be called upon to evaluate whether reception of disability benefits disqualifies a person from bringing a disability discrimination claim. The federal trial court in Massachusetts posited that a high school field hockey coach with a panic disorder presented a justiciable claim under the ADA after she was dismissed. In denying a school board's motion for

---

[40] Allen v. Rapides Parish Sch. Bd., 204 F.3d 619 [142 Educ. L. Rep. 44] (5th Cir. 2000).

[41] Velez Cajigas v. Order of St. Benedict, 115 F. Supp.2d 246 [147 Educ. L. Rep. 928] (D. Puerto Rico 2000).

[42] 473 U.S. 432 (1985).

[43] Porter v. Ellis, 117 F. Supp.2d 651 [148 Educ. L. Rep. 283] (W.D. Mich. 2000).

[44] Taylor v. Phoenixville Sch. Dist., 113 F. Supp.2d 770 [147 Educ. L. Rep. 558] (E.D. Pa. 2000).

summary judgment, the court found that the coach's being awarded Social Security benefits for her disability did not necessarily disqualify her from an ADA claim. The court also dismissed the coach's claim against a husband and wife for their alleged role in encouraging school officials to terminate her contract in explaining that individuals cannot be liable under the ADA.[45]

An appellate court in New Jersey's interpretation of a state anti-discrimination law raised an interesting proof issue for individuals alleging disability discrimination. The court reversed an earlier grant of summary judgment in favor of a school board and superintendent after a jury rendered a verdict of discriminatory treatment by the latter. The court agreed that the plaintiff-vice-principal, whose contract was not renewed, produced sufficient evidence that the basis for the board's action was her recurrence of breast cancer. The court was satisfied that the vice- principal produced sufficient evidence from which a jury could conclude that the superintendent reacted with resentment, anger, and hostility to her recurrence of breast cancer.[46]

Substantive Constitutional Rights

This section discusses First Amendment constitutional rights and those associated with liberty and property interests under the Fifth and Fourteenth Amendments. Cases involving states are brought under the Fourteenth Amendment while those involving the federal government are brought pursuant to the Fifth Amendment.

Speech

In a case of first impression, the Ninth Circuit ruled that a school board in California that created a bulletin board for Gay and Lesbian Awareness month did not have to permit a teacher to post material that officials contended opposed its multicultural purpose. Even though faculty and staff could add material to the bulletin board, a teacher's material was removed because it contained items condemnatory of homosexuality. In affirming a grant of summary judgment in favor of the board against the teacher's claim that it violated his right to free speech, the court agreed that since the bulletin board was a nonpublic forum and represented the views of only the district, officials could limit the views that it wanted to present. Contrary to

---

[45] Lemire v. Silva, 104 F. Supp.2d 80 [146 Educ. L. Rep. 161] (D. Mass. 2000).
[46] Blume v. Denville Township Bd. of Educ., 756 A.2d 1019 [146 Educ. L. Rep. 771] (N.J. Super. Ct. App. Div. 2000).

other cases where private speech is permissible in a limited public or public forum, the court declared that this was a "a case of the government itself speaking."[47]

In a similar case, a federal trial court in Virginia rejected the claims of an English teacher that a principal's order directing him to remove a pamphlet from his room containing a list of banned books violated his right to free speech. In denying the teacher's request for injunctive relief, the court upheld the school board's alternative free speech theories. Under one theory, the court judged that since the pamphlet could be considered part of the curriculum, its being posted was not protected free speech. Alternatively, the court acknowledged that even if the pamphlet represented a matter of public concern, the board had a countervailing interest in promoting approved community values that outweighed the teacher's right to engage in such speech.[48]

One of the common themes in free speech cases is whether an employer has retaliated against an employee for comments that he or she has made. A trial court in Connecticut granted a principal's motion for summary judgment over a free speech damages claim under section 1983. The court decided that the principal's criticism of a teacher's handling of a parent's complaint about comments that the teacher made about immigration in class did not arise to the level a free speech claim. The court offered that the teacher neither suffered any damage nor was criticized for the content of her classroom remarks. Rather, the court wrote that the principal's remarks were directed at the teacher's interaction with a parent and that it did not rise to the level of protected free speech.[49]

Conversely, the Third Circuit, in reversing a grant of summary judgment in favor of a school board in Pennsylvania in a free speech retaliation case, found that a teacher presented sufficient facts to go to trial. The court stated that there were sufficiently disputed facts as to whether the teacher's being arrested for allegedly removing materials from the school without permission was in response to her advocating multicultural awareness.[50]

The most frequently litigated issue is whether an employee's comments are protectable free speech because they raise a question of public concern. Generally, employees have a difficult time making such a claim. A federal trial court in Texas held that an assistant superintendent's comments about a

---

[47] Downs v. Los Angeles Unified Sch. Dist., 228 F.3d 1003, 1110 [147 Educ. L. Rep. 855] (9th Cir. 2000).

[48] Newton v. Slye, 116 F. Supp.2d 677 [148 Educ. L. Rep. 179] (W.D. Va. 2000).

[49] Sivek v. Baljevic, 758 A.2d 473 [147 Educ. L. Rep. 203] (Conn. Super. Ct. 1999).

[50] Merkle v. Upper Dublin Sch. Dist., 211 F.3d 782 [144 Educ. L. Rep. 83] (3d Cir. 2000).

board's failure to comply with testing procedures did not qualify as a matter of public concern since it primarily concerned her role as an employee. The court decided that since the administrator who assigned the plaintiff to a new position in charge of textbooks and janitorial services could not reasonably know whether her speech was protected, he was entitled to qualified immunity.[51] Similarly, the Fifth Circuit noted that a principal in Texas who resigned at the end of the first year of a two-year contract failed to prove that the board retaliated against her after she wrote several memos regarding the school's activity fund. The court agreed with the board's contention that the principal's complaints about its failure to address alleged defamatory charges concerning her handling of the fund amounted to negotiations to be released from her contract. The court observed that "speech rises to the level of public concern when an individual speaks primarily as a citizen rather than as an employee."[52] The court asserted that although the complaints about the activity fund had some element of public concern, the principal's memoranda primarily related to the preservation of her job.

According to a federal trial court in Ohio, a track coach who recommended that one of his distance runners drink a cola with caffeine as a performance enhancing substance prior to competing could not claim that his remarks were protected by free speech. In upholding his being relieved of his coaching duties and being placing him on administrative suspension, the court found that his remarks were not on a matter of public concern. Even though the coach claimed that his removal was based on inaccurate information, the court reflected that the test for public concern is what the administrator who ordered the coach's removal "reasonably thought that [the coach] had said to [the student], without respect to what he may have actually said."[53]

Association

The federal trial court in Connecticut determined that an elementary school social worker who was dismissed for living with a non-custodial father of two children to whom she provided social services stated a First Amendment claim to intimate association. The court remarked that the social worker's interests had to be balanced against those of the school board in promoting the efficiency of public services it performs and in achieving its goals as effectively and efficiently as possible. In ruling for the board on the

---

[51] Rodriguez v. Laredo Indep. Sch. Dist., 82 F. Supp.2d 679 [141 Educ. L. Rep. 1080] (S.D. Tex. 2000).

[52] Bradshaw v. Pittsburgh Indep. Sch. Dist., 207 F.3d 814, 816 [143 Educ. L. Rep. 65] (5th Cir. 2000).

[53] Schul v. Sherard, 102 F. Supp.2d 877, 886 [145 Educ. L. Rep. 1016] (S.D. Ohio 2000).

association claim, the court found persuasive the city director of health's reasonable belief that the social worker might have violated the ethics code, brought discredit upon municipal service, and hindered other social workers in the performance of their work.[54]

Privacy

The cases concerning privacy addressed a wide range of issues. In a case of first impression, the Seventh Circuit affirmed in part that a teacher in Illinois whose employment contract was not renewed because he refused to sign an authorization waiving his privilege of confidentiality for attorney-client communications had a right of privacy claim against the school board. While the waiver did not violate the Sixth Amendment's protection of right to counsel, the court noted that a broad release of confidential information violated the teacher's privacy right where the board did not have a basis for requiring the information and there were no safeguards against misuse or further disclosure.[55]

A second privacy case concerned parent information provided to a classroom teacher. A federal trial court in Louisiana contended that a teacher violated the privacy rights of a mother by revealing the contents of a letter, concerning the exclusion of her son from school activities, that she received from the parent to the media. Even though the letter was released after the mother announced her candidacy for a city council position and although it contained items of general social and political concern about which the parent may have spoken, the court was convinced that its contents did not constitute a matter of public concern. The court ascertained that since the letter was an education record under FERPA, the teacher violated federal law by releasing it without the mother's consent.[56]

In yet another privacy claim involving a classroom, a teacher unsuccessfully tried to prevent board members and school officials from viewing an unauthorized videotape of her classroom performance that was made by two students without her knowledge. Even though California's Education Code provides sanctions against persons who make classroom recordings without consent, the court pointed out that classroom teaching did not violate the confidential communication provision of the Penal Code. The court maintained that state law neither implies an exclusionary rule nor do

---

[54] Kelly v. City of Meriden, 120 F. Supp.2d 191 [148 Educ. L. Rep. 925] (D. Conn. 2000).

[55] Denius v. Dunlap, 209 F.3d 944 [143 Educ. L. Rep. 736] (7th Cir. 2000).

[56] Warner v. St. Bernard Parish Sch. Bd., 99 F. Supp.2d 748 [145 Educ. L. Rep. 257] (E.D. La. 2000).

state privacy statutes prohibit use of illegally obtained videotape record-ings of teacher classroom performances in disciplinary proceedings. The court reasoned that since teacher communications in a classroom are not confidential, no teacher should have reasonable expectation of privacy.[57]

An appellate court in Georgia, in an unusual privacy case, affirmed that a teacher's guilty plea for violating the state's sodomy law could be vacated because the statute violated the state constitution. The court posited that under state law at that time, acts of sodomy between a teacher and a student over the age of fourteen (the student here was fifteen and seventeen at the times of the acts) were not criminal as long as they were consensual, unen-forced, private, and noncommercial. As a footnote, it is worth noting that Georgia has since amended its sodomy statute to change the legal age of consent to sixteen.[58]

In a Connecticut case involving the state's Freedom of Information Act, an appellate court remanded an order of the Freedom of Information Com-mission calling for the disclosure of a superintendent's performance evaluation. The court directed the Commission to afford the superintendent the opportunity to prove whether the disclosure would have caused an invasion of her personal privacy so as to be exempt under the Act.[59]

Substantive Due Process

Substantive due process issues involve allegations that rules or their enforcement are unreasonable. West Virginia's highest court upheld, under a rational basis test, a state statute that compensated some principals, but not others, for attending a mandatory Principal's Academy. The court ac-knowledged that the statute's distinguishing between long-term and short-term contract employees was rational in light of significant discretion given county school boards in making personnel decisions and in the state's interest in having all principals attend the Academy to provide a thorough and efficient system of free schools.[60]

A substantive due process claim is similar to one under equal protec-tion. A federal trial court in New York rejected a claim that a school board's dismissal of a part-time teacher under its anti-nepotism policy violated equal protection where the district superintendent was the teacher's husband.

---

[57] Evens v. Superior Ct., 91 Cal.Rptr.2d 497 [140 Educ. L. Rep. 332] (Cal. Ct. App. 1999).

[58] State v. Eastwood, 535 S.E.2d 246 [147 Educ. L. Rep. 1112] (Ga. Ct. App. 2000).

[59] Chairman, Board of Educ. of Town of Darien v. Freedom of Information Comm'n, 760 A.2d 534 [148 Educ. L. Rep. 393] (Conn. Ct. App. 2000).

[60] Carvey v. West Virginia State Bd. of Educ., 527 S.E.2d 831 [143 Educ. L. Rep. 1077] (W. Va. 1999).

The teacher alleged that the board acted arbitrarily and irrationally because fifty-seven other employees in the district had family members employed in the district who were not dismissed. In granting the board's motion for summary judgment, the court commented that, even if arbitrary and irrational, the board's enforcement of its policy did not represent an equal protection violation absent an allegation of improper motive.[61]

Procedural Due Process

Procedural due process focuses on fair treatment. Unlike substantive due process that considers the fairness of rules or statutes, procedural due process addresses the fairness of the process available to a person charged with violating a rule or statute. The most common procedural rights are those associated with notice and hearing. Both the Fifth and Fourteenth Amendments provide that a person's liberty and property rights cannot be abridged without due process of law. At the same time, liberty and property rights can also be considered substantive rights to the extent that they create protected substantive constitutional rights such as a parent's right to direct the education of his or her child(ren) and the right of bodily integrity.

Liberty and Property Interests

Property rights consider whether a person has an entitlement in a position that cannot be changed without according the individual procedural due process. In a case from Texas, an appellate court affirmed that a teacher with a one-year contract has no protected property interest in its renewal even though the school board, at her hearing, violated its own policy by placing a one-hour limit on her presentation of evidence.[62] Similarly, an appellate court in Louisiana amended, and affirmed, and order that since a former non-tenured teacher's aide lacked a property right in continued employment, she was only entitled to the due process set forth in the board's policies regarding the dismissal of non-tenured employees.[63]

In Connecticut, the federal trial court granted a school board's motion for summary judgment in a case involving the reassignment of a middle school teacher to a high school after the board unsuccessfully attempted to terminate her contract. The court judged that the board did not violate the

---

[61] Payne v. Huntington Union Free Sch. Dist., 101 F. Supp.2d 116 [145 Educ. L. Rep. 387] (E.D.N.Y. 2000).
[62] Stratton v. Austin Indep. Sch. Dist., 8 S.W.3d 26 [140 Educ. L. Rep. 1049] (Tex. App. 1999).
[63] Scott v. Ouachita Parish Sch. Bd., 768 So. 2d 702 [147 Educ. L. Rep. 1135] (La. Ct. App. 2000).

teacher's due process rights because she lacked a constitutionally protected property right to remain in the same school teaching the same
subjects.[64] In like manner, the Seventh Circuit affirmed that the reassignment of a school principal in Illinois to administrative duties in the central
office at the same pay and benefits did not deprive him of a property interest
in continued employment.[65]

Procedural rights can depend on the nature of an alleged property right.
An appellate court in Kansas reversed in favor of a board in writing that
teachers with extended that allowed them to teach summer school, as well as
during the regular year, had minimal property rights when it chose to eliminate the summer school teaching assignments. Despite the teachers' claim
that they did not receive an adequate pre-termination hearing, the court
offered that since they were only entitled to, and received, notice of the
board's action, its reasons for acting, and an opportunity to respond, their
property right claim was properly dismissed.[66]

Claims of liberty violations concern stigmatization of a person's reputation and, if successful, entitle the individual to a name-clearing hearing. The
federal trial court in Colorado granted a school board's motion to dismiss a
dispute over published statements about teachers in a charter school whose
were not renewed, that the school experienced problems, and that its administrator intended to return the school to normalcy. In concluding that the
statements did not have the kind of reputational content warranting a name-
clearing hearing, the court observed that at best, the remarks related to
neglect of duties and insubordination that are not stigmatizing.[67]

Not unusually, both property and liberty interests can be raised in the
same case. A federal trial court in Wisconsin declared that a principal, whose
duties were substantially curtailed, based on parental complaints, did not
have her property or liberty interests violated. The court was of the view
that since the principal had no statutory right to perform the duties from
which she had been relieved, she had no protectable property interest and
that the board did not violate her liberty interests when a district administrator stated publicly that parents in her school raised concerns about lack of
trust involving dishonesty attributed to the principal. In addition, the court
discerned that the release of a letter written to the board about the principal

---

[64] Gordon v. Nicoletti, 84 F. Supp.2d 304 [142 Educ. L. Rep. 169] (D. Conn.
2000).
[65] Bordelon v. Chicago Sch. Reform Bd. of Trustees, 233 F.3d 524 [149 Educ.
L. Rep. 133] (7th Cir. 2000).
[66] Baughman v. Unified Sch. Dist., 10 P.3d 21 [147 Educ. L. Rep. 1094] (Kan.
Ct. App. 2000).
[67] Brammer-Hoelter v. Twin Peaks Charter Academy, 81 F. Supp.2d 1090 [141
Educ. L. Rep. 762] (D. Colo. 2000).

did violate a liberty interest where the disclosure was probably mandated under the state's freedom of information law.[68]

According to the federal trial court in Puerto Rico, the brief two month suspension with pay of a tenured elementary school teacher pending an investigation of allegations of sexual and physical abuse of a student did not raise property and liberty interests. The court was satisfied that since teacher was suspended for a relatively time, after which she was reinstated without suffering a financial loss, her constitutional rights were not violated.[69]

Aspects of Notice

Notice of charges are important if a person charged with an offense is to be able to prepare a response. A federal trial court in Ohio believed that a teacher whose employment was wrongfully terminated was entitled to $107,000, plus $24,000 in benefits for the period of time that she was out of work before being reinstated by the school board. The court added that the teacher was entitled to $37,000 in attorneys' fees, even though all of these expenses were paid by the Ohio Education Association (OEA) and, by agreement with her attorneys, any such fee awards would go to OEA. The court considered this an egregious case not only because the board failed to provide the teacher with pre-termination notice and an opportunity to respond bust also since it had not borne its burden of proof that she failed to mitigate damages.[70]

Notice claims frequently raise statutory rather than constitutional issues, even though both can be present in the same case. An appellate court in Colorado, in upholding the dismissal of an assistant principal, decreed that a state statute's provision that notice of charges for dismissal be sent by certified mail is not required by the due process clause. The court interpreted due process as only requiring a party to receive actual notice reasonably calculated to provide the individual with an opportunity to present his or her objections.[71]

A federal trial court in Illinois granted a school board's motion for summary judgment where a teacher whose contract was terminated filed a claim

---

[68] Ulichny v. Merton Community Sch. Dist., 93 F. Supp.2d 1011 [143 Educ. L. Rep. 882] (E.D. Wis. 2000).

[69] Santiago v. Fajardo, 70 F. Supp.2d 72 [140 Educ. L. Rep. 150] (D. Puerto Rico 1999).

[70] McDaniel v. Princeton City Dist. Bd. of Educ., 114 F. Supp.2d 658 [147 Educ. L. Rep. 611] (S.D. Ohio 2000).

[71] Feldewerth v. Joint Sch. Dist. 28-J, 3 P.3d 467 [145 Educ. L. Rep. 769] (Colo. Ct. App. 1999).

for wrongful discharge after he was not provided with an explanation of its action. The court asserted that within the broad reforms instituted in the Chicago Public Schools, the board had discretion in laying off tenured teachers.[72]

As reflected by a case from Missouri, state statutes may clarify the kind of notice a teacher is entitled to. An appellate court upheld the non-renewal of the contract a preschool teacher with a valid teaching certificate who alleged that she had not received the notice required under the state's Teacher Tenure Act. The court agreed with the school board that since the Act applied only to teachers with certificates for grades K-12, in order for the notice requirement to have applied to the plaintiff, she would have had both to possess a teaching certificate and be teaching in one of the K-12 grades.[73]

Aspects of Hearing

One of the aspects of a hearing is an employee's utilization of an attorney. An appellate panel in New York affirmed the reversal of a hearing officer's denying a tenured teacher the opportunity to consult with his attorney during adjournments in his disciplinary hearing. The hearing, which involving five days of cross-examination of the teacher over a ten-week period, resulted in his dismissal. In upholding the teacher's claim that he was denied a due process right to a fair hearing, the court explained that a tenured teacher's property right in his position affords him due process hearing rights similar to those in criminal cases.[74] Conversely, the Supreme Court of South Dakota affirmed that a teacher was not denied due process when a school board refused to permit her and her attorney to attend an executive session. During the session the board only received an administrator's recommendation not to renew the teacher's contact but did not take new evidence against her. The court agreed that the board acted properly since it needed to receive these recommendations if it was to fulfill its statutory duty to prepare written notice and reasons for dismissal.[75]

The Tenth Circuit held that a teacher in Oklahoma, at her dismissal hearing, had a due process right to cross-examine individuals who provided information to the school board in affidavits. The court followed its own precedent in noting that while cross-examination is not required in every

---

[72] Chandler v. Board of Educ. of City of Chicago, 92 F. Supp.2d 760 [143 Educ. L. Rep. 822] (N.D. Ill. 2000).

[73] Sealey v. Board of Educ., 145 S.W.3d 597 [143 Educ. L. Rep. 1091] (Mo. Ct. App. 1999).

[74] Elmore v. Plainview-Old Bethpage Cent. Sch. Dist., Bd. of Educ., 708 N.Y.S.2d 713 [144 Educ. L. Rep. 1022] (N.Y. App. Div. 2000).

[75] Wuest v. Winner Sch. Dist. 59-2, 607 N.W.2d 912 [142 Educ. L. Rep. 1040] (S.D. 2000).

hearing, it is where "charges depriving a plaintiff of her livelihood by attacking her morality and fitness as a teacher are sufficiently serious."[76]

A federal trial court in Ohio ruled that a hearing must provide a person with a protectable property with an opportunity to respond to charges. The federal court contended that a school board's failure to provide a tenured teacher with an opportunity to respond to three of five charges against her in a pre-dismissal hearing violated her due process rights as set forth by the Supreme Court.[77] The court indicated that under such circumstances, due process includes an opportunity to be heard before a person's property rights can be ended.[78]

Hearings may encounter due process problems when they are not conducted in a reasonably prompt manner. In Illinois, a federal trial court remarked that a teacher/coach who was punished with a thirty-day suspension following the drowning death of a student was denied his due process rights to a reasonably prompt hearing where the school board reassigned him for ten months without providing a hearing. Despite the board's claim that it was concerned of its liability for retaliation against the teacher if he returned to his school pending a hearing, the court was of the opinion that once the board determined the punishment should be suspension rather than dismissal, it no longer had an interest in refusing to return him to a teaching position, albeit perhaps at another building.[79]

Individuals conducting a hearing are expected to be impartial. A teacher in Mississippi whose claim for disability benefits was denied won her appeal where members of the Public Employees' Retirement System Board, which rejected her claim, also sat on the Appeals Committee which reviewed, and upheld, its earlier action. An appellate court found that the conflict of interest cast serious doubt on the integrity of the process by denying the teacher administrative proceedings "conducted in a fair and impartial manner."[80] However, the Sixth Circuit, in a case from Kentucky, affirmed the dismissal of teachers' requests for a preliminary injunction challenging their transfer to other schools, allegedly for their speech on a matter of public concern. The teachers claimed that their pre-transfer hearing was biased because the school board had stated that the transfers would become effective at 5:00 p.m. on the day of the hearing, regardless of the outcome. The court was convinced

---

[76] McClure v. Independent Sch. Dist. No. 16, 228 F.3d 1205 [147 Educ. L. Rep. 892] (10th Cir. 2000).

[77] McDaniel v. Princeton City Sch. Dist. Bd. of Educ., 72 F. Supp.2d 874 [140 Educ. L. Rep. 275] (S.D. Ohio 1999).

[78] Cleveland Bd. of Educ. v. Loudermill, 470 U.S. 532 (1972).

[79] Townsend v. Vallas, 99 F. Supp.2d 902 [145 Educ. L. Rep. 263] (N.D. Ill. 2000).

[80] Burns v. Public Employees Retirement Sys. of Miss., 748 So. 2d 181, 183 [141 Educ. L. Rep. 405] (Miss. Ct. App. 1999).

that bad faith or bias in conjunction with the hearing could be raised in post-deprivation hearings.[81]

Administrative hearings, such as those conducted by school boards, can operate with more relaxed rules than might apply in court. Under state law, an appellate court in Texas affirmed that a dismissed teacher's statutory right to a hearing was not altered when the school board failed to review a hearing examiner's decision before voting to terminate her contract. The court ascertained that the board's error was harmless since its members reviewed the examiner's fifty-three findings of fact.[82]

In Mississippi, an appellate court upheld dismissal of a teacher where much of the evidence was based on hearsay. The court pointed out that even though state law prohibited a non-renewal based solely on hearsay, the school principal provided testimony based on his observations of the teacher's handling of children and of his conversations with parents.[83]

Dismissal, Nonrenewal, Demotion, and Discipline

Many of the cases in this section involve state courts interpreting state laws. Although constitutional rights can be at issue, courts most frequently are called upon to evaluate whether school boards have accorded employees the rights found in state statutes.

Generally, reassignment of an employee pending disciplinary proceedings over alleged wrongdoing implicates no due process constitutional rights and, absent state statutory language to the contrary, is within the authority of a superintendent.[84] However, the Eleventh Circuit, in reversing a grant in favor of a school board in Georgia, posited that a reassignment involving reduction in pay, prestige, or responsibility could be a title VII violation.[85]

Disciplinary proceedings instituted when an employee alleges a violation of a state's whistleblower statute represent a difficult balancing of a board's right to operate well-run schools with the public's interest to know. The federal trial court in Connecticut rejected a board's motion for summary judgment where a school business manager claimed that he was dismissed in retaliation for reporting suspected violations of law. The court commented

---

[81] Leary v. Daeschner, 228 F.3d 729 [147 Educ. L. Rep. 824] (6th Cir. 2000).

[82] McGilvray v. Moses, 8 S.W.3d 761 [141 Educ. L. Rep. 377] (Tex. App. 1999).

[83] Doty v. Tupelo Pub. Sch. Dist., 751 So. 2d 1212 [142 Educ. L. Rep. 1109] (Miss. Ct. App. 1999).

[84] Gray v. Crew, 699 N.Y.S.2d 408 [140 Educ. L. Rep. 344] (N.Y. App. Div. 1999).

[85] Hinson v. Clinch County, Georgia Bd. of Educ., 231 F.3d 821 [148 Educ. L. Rep. 702] (11th Cir. 2000).

that since the plaintiff stated a prima facie claim for a violation of the state's whistleblower act and the board responded with a non-retaliatory reason for eliminating his position, he was entitled to a trial over whether the board's reason was pretextual.[86]

Courts usually grant school boards considerable discretion in imposing an appropriate penalty for inadequate performance. Occasionally, though, as in New York, a court can revise a penalty. An appellate court judged that the dismissal of a school custodian with twelve years of experience for three violations of adequately cleaning rooms was "so disproportionate to the offense as to shock one's sense of fairness."[87] Instead, the court remanded the dispute to the board to impose a penalty the would not exceed suspension without pay for up to a maximum of twelve months.

Disciplinary action can implicate privacy concerns. The Supreme Judicial Court of Massachusetts noted that a superintendent's report regarding discipline of a teacher for writing inappropriate comments on student papers could not be disclosed under the state's public records law. The court acknowledged that since the report was personal information under the public record law, it was exempt from disclosure.[88]

Although reinstatement is frequently a remedy in discipline cases, it may not be available when violations of public policy are at stake. In Massachusetts, an appellate court reversed an arbitrator's reinstatement of a teacher with twenty-five years of experience who was dismissed for three acts of physical force against students. The court maintained that reinstatement is not possible where state laws prohibiting corporal punishment demonstrate "a clearly defined public policy protecting students against physical harm."[89]

Unprofessional Conduct, Unfitness, Willful Neglect of Duty

Courts have sustained disciplinary actions involving a variety of kinds of misconduct. The Supreme Court of Mississippi upheld the non-renewal of the of two teachers based on allegations by the state's Department of Education regarding noncompliance with testing procedures. The court declared that teachers failed to meet their burden of refuting the department's evidence supporting irregularities in the testing.[90]

---

[86] Ritz v. Town of East Hartford, 110 F. Supp.2d 94 [147 Educ. L. Rep. 79] (D. Conn. 2000).

[87] Brown v. Murphy, 713 N.Y.S.2d 798 [147 Educ. L. Rep. 1048] (N.Y. App. Div. 2000).

[88] Wakefield Teachers' Ass'n v. School Comm. of Wakefield, 731 N.E.2d 63 [145 Educ. L. Rep. 462] (Mass. 2000).

[89] School Dist. of Beverly v. Geller, 737 N.E.2d 873, 879 [148 Educ. L. Rep. 461] (Mass. Ct. App. 2000).

[90] Buck v. Lowndes County Sch. Dist., 761 So. 2d 144 [145 Educ. L. Rep. 1118] (Miss. 2000).

In New York, an appellate court confirmed a school board's dismissal of a school bus driver who consumed beer on school property, attended a driver safety workshop after doing so, and drove her car in a reckless manner upon her return to school. However, the court granted the driver's request for backpay during the period of time between the board's original action and her subsequent dismissal following remittal.[91]

An appellate court in Florida upheld the dismissal of a teacher whose misconduct in school was so severe as to impair her effectiveness. During one memorable class day, the teacher had two students in the office reporting an in-class theft, two others out of class being searched for stolen property, one so intoxicated that two adults had to carry him from class, and three trying to hide contraband. The court concluded that the teacher's loss of classroom control met the statutory definition of ineffectiveness.[92]

In the first of two cases involving the use of evidence from criminal proceedings, the Supreme Court of Tennessee affirmed the dismissal of a teacher who plead guilty to sexual battery under a plea arrangement whereby, after one year, his record would be expunged. The court reasoned that even if a school board could not use information covered by the expungement order, it could rely on information reported in the local newspaper and an admission made to its Personnel Director that was developed prior to entry of the expungement order.[93]

An appellate court in Florida affirmed that a teacher's contract can be non-renewed for statements made at a criminal trial, even though he was found not guilty. The court agreed with school officials that since a teacher is a role model even inaccurate statements as to what happened during his arrest could be used to demonstrate his impaired effectiveness.[94]

A case from Louisiana reveals the unfortunate consequences that can occur to a well-meaning teacher who reports the suspected theft of a handgun from his car in the school's parking lot to his supervisor. After the teacher also reported the theft to local police, the school board used both reports as the basis for his dismissal for willful neglect. The court affirmed that a teacher can be discharged for willful neglect on the basis of "general knowledge concerning the responsibilities and conduct of teachers."[95]

---

[91] Collins v. Parishville-Hopkinton Cent. Sch. Dist., 710 N.Y.S.2d 728 [146 Educ. L. Rep. 357] (N.Y. App. Div. 2000).

[92] Walker v. Highlands County Sch. Bd., 752 So. 2d 127 [142 Educ. L. Rep. 1116] (Fla. Dist. Ct. App. 2000).

[93] Canipe v. Memphis Schs. Bd. of Educ., 27 S.W.3d 919 [147 Educ. L. Rep. 1115] (Tenn. 2000).

[94] Purvis v. Marion County Sch. Bd., 766 So. 2d 492 [147 Educ. L. Rep. 740] (Fla. Dist. Ct. App. 2000).

[95] Howard v. West Baton Rouge Parish Sch. Bd., 770 So. 2d 441, 443 [149 Educ. L. Rep. 278] (La. Ct. App. 2000).

Evaluating whether a teacher engaged in misconduct can involve using the appropriate standard of review. Maine's highest court upheld an arbitrator's reversal of a teacher's dismissal for using excessive force in disciplining a student. Using a clear and convincing standard, the arbitrator discerned that the school board failed to establish that the misconduct occurred. The court rejected the argument that applying a clear and convincing standard stripped the board of its statutory mandate to provide a safe learning environment and to protect itself from civil liability.[96]

A case connecting disciplinary action to employee benefits suggests that school boards need a broader knowledge than simply state law about dismissals. A federal trial court in Pennsylvania was satisfied that a former teacher raised triable issues of fact as to whether he could be dismissed for misconduct involving sexual assault of a student where criminal charges were dismissed. The court believed that the teacher also raised a question as to whether the board failed to notify him about the termination of medical benefits since federal law required it to do so where a person is not dismissed for "gross misconduct."[97]

Duty

Immorality

Immorality can concern inappropriate personal contact between an employee and students. Generally, the termination of of employees who engaged in inappropriate sexual relationships with students are upheld. An appellate court in Indiana affirmed that a school board was justified in dismissing a teacher on a continuing contract for inappropriate behavior with a female student. Among the items of objectionable conduct that the court observed were that the teacher gave the student a cookie without giving any to other children, keeping a comment written on the blackboard by another student stating that the teacher loved the female student, and putting comments on the student's quizzes that were unrelated to the work.[98] Similarly, an appellate court in Oklahoma affirmed the dismissal of a female special education teacher for moral turpitude based on her having had a romantic relationship with a seventeen-year-old male student that included hugging and public

---

[96] Union River Valley Teachers' Ass'n v. Lamoine Sch. Comm., 748 A.2d 990 [143 Educ. L. Rep. 558] (Me. 2000).
[97] McKnight v. School Dist. of Philadelphia, 105 F. Supp.2d 438 [146 Educ. L. Rep. 187] (E.D. Pa. 2000).
[98] Hierlmeier v. North Judson-San Pierre Bd. of Sch. Trustees, 730 N.E.2d 821 [144 Educ. L. Rep. 1024] (Ind. Ct. App. 2000).

kissing. The court upheld the admission of testimony of a student who, fifteen years earlier, had sexual relations with the teacher for the purpose of impeaching her testimony that she had not had improper relations with minors.[99]

Moral turpitude can also involve conduct between a teacher and a principal. An appellate panel in Oklahoma upheld a trial court's reversal of a school board's dismissal of a career teacher for falsely claiming that his principal purchased pornographic material uncovered in a school dumpster. Both courts agreed that the board failed to prove moral turpitude where the teacher contacted the seller of the material and was given the principal's name as the purchaser but was unaware that another employee had confessed to buying the material.[100]

As reflected in a case of first impression from Illinois, immoral conduct can affect an employee's retirement benefits. An appellate court affirmed that a former school principal who was drawing retirement from the state retirement system could have his pension revoked after he pleaded guilty to six counts of aggravated criminal sexual abuse involving his molestation of two boys. The court asserted that since the statute authorizing revocation was unambiguous, the former principal's convictions fit within the statutory language of being "connected with," "related to," and "arose out of" his "service as a teacher."[101]

Immorality in a religious school can take on an expanded meaning. The Supreme Court of Montana affirmed that a counselor in a Catholic school who was living with a man to whom she was not married failed to present a marital status discrimination claim under state law. In upholding a grant of summary judgment for the school in support of its termination of the counselor's contract, the court agreed that since her conduct violated Catholic teachings on morality, and no discrimination was present, her claim was meritless.[102]

In a case limited by its facts, an appellate court in Maryland mandated that a teacher who was accused of sexual abuse, sexual harassment, and sex discrimination could proceed with a defamation suit against female students on the track team that he coached. The teacher filed suit after he was suspended for four months, reprimanded, and transferred to another school

---

[99] Andrews v. Independent Sch. Dist. No. 57, 12 P.3d 491 [148 Educ. L. Rep. 1061] (Okla. Civ. App. 2000).
[100] Hawzipta v. Independent Sch. Dist. No. 1-004 of Noble County, 13 P.3d 98 [149 Educ. L. Rep. 250] (Okla. Ct. App. 2000).
[101] Goff v. Teachers' Retirement Sys. of State of Ill., 713 N.E.2d 578 [141 Educ. L. Rep. 275] (Ill. App. Ct. 1999).
[102] Parker-Bigback v. St. Labre Sch., 7 P.3d 361 [146 Educ. L. Rep. 1129] (Mont. 2000).

without the opportunity under state statute or school board procedures to request a hearing to contest the charges prior to his being disciplined.[103] The court was of the view that public policy did not require that the students' complaints be treated as absolutely privileged.

Incompetence

As illustrated by a case from the Supreme Court of Connecticut, incompetence relates to a variety of kinds of employee conduct. The court affirmed the dismissal of a tenured teacher who was employed as an assistant principal on the ground that she supervised a single strip search of fifth and sixth female students. In deciding that the state's standard for incompetence was whether an individual's overall performance falls below a requisite standard, the court agreed that the teacher's behavior fell below it in light of the school board's policy prohibiting strip searches.[104]

The Supreme Court of New Mexico held that not all employee misconduct fits a state's definition of incompetence. The court reversed a school board's dismissal of a teacher who was arrested for driving while intoxicated and resisting arrest. The court decreed that the misdemeanors did not involve moral turpitude, did not relate to his competence as a teacher, and represented disparate treatment regarding how other teachers with substantially similar conduct were handled.[105]

An appellate court in New York court upheld dismissal of an employee for excessive absences. The court agreed that the employee's absences supported a finding of incompetence and that dismissal was not so disproportionate so as to be shocking to one's sense of fairness.[106]

Compliance with School Board Policies and State Statutes

An appellate court in New Jersey followed a state statute by confirming a school board's dismissal of a tenured teacher after a criminal conviction for assaulting a student. The court ascertained that the statute clearly gave such authority to boards and that the forfeiture was mandatory from the date of conviction.[107]

---

[103] Flynn v. Reichardt, 749 A.2d 197 [143 Educ. L. Rep. 585] (Md. Ct. App. 2000).

[104] Rogers v. Board of Educ. of the City of New Haven, 749 A.2d 1173 [143 Educ. L. Rep. 968] (Conn. 2000).

[105] *In re* Termination of Kible, 996 P.2d 419 [143 Educ. L. Rep. 382] (N.M. 1999).

[106] McKinnon v. Board of Educ. of North Bellmore Union Free Sch. Dist., 709 N.Y.S.2d 104 [145 Educ. L. Rep. 1100] (N.Y. App. Div. 2000).

[107] State v. Ercolano, 762 A.2d 259 [149 Educ. L. Rep. 174] (N.J. Super. Ct. App. Div. 2000).

State laws generally have time limits for complying with certain requirements. A thirty-one year veteran teacher in Alabama who was appointed as an acting principal lost her challenge to a school board's decision in October to return her to teaching when she failed to appeal her reassignment within the statutory fifteen days. Even though state law accords hearing rights to a tenured teacher promoted to an administrative position, that court affirmed that it can only be asserted with a timely claim.[108]

An appellate court in Illinois affirmed that a local school council's failure to appoint a new principal within the ninety day statutory limitation did not deprive a principal who was appointed beyond the ninety days of his position. Even though the ninety-day provision was expressed as "shall," the court considered the selection period as directory, not mandatory.[109]

State laws frequently require evaluation of employees. West Virginia's highest court reversed an earlier order reinstating a principal whose contract had not been renewed. The court broadly interpreted a state statute that evaluations required a notice of deficiencies and a remediation plan. The court judged that the plaintiff's receiving several memoranda noting that he was frequently not at work on time satisfied the statute.[110]

An appellate court in Ohio reinstated a school board's non-renewal of the contract of a limited contract teacher since it was satisfied that the building principal complied with the state's teacher evaluation statute. The court determined that the principal performed two in-class observations and filed written reports including specific recommendation for improvement.[111]

Oral contracts can limit remedies available to an employee who has been dismissed. An appellate court in Indiana affirmed the dismissal of a director of information services whose position was eliminated. The court rejected the director's claim that his oral contract was breached since under Indiana law, he lacked even an enforceable oral contract because the school board had not approved a written employment contract during his almost six years on the job.[112]

---

[108] Coley v. Alabama State Tenure Comm'n, 766 So. 2d 846 [147 Educ. L. Rep. 748] (Ala. Civ. Ct. App. 2000).
[109] Chicago Sch. Reform Bd. of Trustees v. Martin, 723 N.E.2d 731 [144 Educ. L. Rep. 379] (Ill. App. Ct. 1999).
[110] Baker v. Board of Educ., County of Hancock, 534 S.E.2d 378 [147 Educ. L. Rep. 376] (W. Va. 2000).
[111] McComb v. Gahanna-Jefferson City Sch. Dist. Bd. of Educ., 720 N.E.2d 984 [139 Educ. L. Rep. 1037] (Ohio Ct. App. 1998).
[112] Rockwell v. MSD Southwest Allen County, 737 N.E.2d 829 [148 Educ. L. Rep. 455] (Ind. Ct. App. 2000).

Reduction-in-force and Involuntary Leaves of Absence

Removal of employees for other than disciplinary reasons present unique statutory issues. Virtually all states have statutes regulating the procedures to be used in laying-off employees in non-disciplinary situations. In some states, the statutes can be modified by collective bargaining .

Necessity for Reduction-in-force

An appellate court in Kentucky explained that a teacher whose contract was not renewed had a state law right to challenge the board's written reason for terminating her contract, namely that there was a decline in student enrollment. The court added that if the board's reason was untrue, the non-renewal of her contract would be rendered void and of no effect.[113]

Elimination of Position

The Supreme Court of Ohio ruled that a collective bargaining agreement permitting school boards to abolish non-teaching positions and to lay off such personnel did not extend to individuals whose work was outsourced. The court indicated that since the state's collective bargaining statute created job security for non-teaching personnel, elimination of positions and outsourcing was permissible only where the agreement manifested a clear intent to achieve such a result.[114]

According to the Supreme Court of Arkansas, a school board's eliminating the jobs of two teachers, thereby resulting in their discharges, did not deprive them of a right to a hearing. The court affirmed that under state law, discharges of a mandatory type, such as those resulting from financial decisions to eliminate a job, do not entitle discharged employees to a hearing.[115]

Realignment/Reassignment

In Minnesota, an appellate court affirmed that a teacher on unrequested leave of absence, who declined a school board's offer of employment in the middle of the year because she was under contract elsewhere, was not entitled to that position under the Teacher Tenure Act when her contract ended.

---

[113] Kidd v. Board of Educ. of McCreary County, 29 S.W.3d 374 [148 Educ. L. Rep. 509] (Ky. Ct. App. 2000).
[114] State *ex rel.* Ohio Ass'n of Pub. Sch. Employees/AFSCME v. Batavia Local Sch. Dist. Bd. of Educ., 729 N.E.2d 743 [144 Educ. L. Rep. 689] (Ohio 2000).
[115] Stephens v. Arkansas Sch. for the Blind, 20 S.W.3d 397 [146 Educ. L. Rep. 566] (Ark. 2000).

The court held that the Act which provides teachers with the most seniority to the right of first refusal does not compel a board to delay filling an open position.[116]

Call-back Rights

The Supreme Court of Appeals of West Virginia reversed a school board's decision to fill a vacant position with a non-employee rather than a former teacher whose name was on a recall list. The court concluded that a state statute, which required hiring former teachers on the recall list over non-employees, prevailed over the board's claim that the nonemployee was better qualified. The court thus ordered the board to place the former teacher in the position with back pay and benefits.[117]

In New York, an appellate court affirmed that a teacher who retired lost his statutory right of recall. Once the teacher retired, the court was of the opinion that he was not entitled to be placed on a preferred eligibility list even though his former position was abolished.[118]

Contract Disputes

School boards frequently act on employee contracts in a manner that does not fit into other categories in this chapter. Some of the cases in this section implicate general principles of contract law while others involve interpretation of state statutes.

Board Policies and Contract Stipulations

An appellate court in Indiana court affirmed the dismissal of a breach of contract claim filed by a non-permanent teacher whose contract was not renewed on the ground that since non-tenured teachers have no right to continued employment, their rights exist only with regard to a contract entered into for a given year. The court was satisfied that the reason given by the school board for not renewing the teacher's contract due to the insufficient quality of instructional contribution, met the requirement of state law that permitted "any reason considered relevant to the school corporation's interest."[119]

---

[116] Shaner v. Independent Sch. Dist. No. 2884, 604 N.W.2d 803 [141 Educ. L. Rep. 299] (Minn. Ct. App. 2000).

[117] Board of Educ. of County of Mercer v. Owensby, 526 S.E.2d 831 [143 Educ. L. Rep. 1065] (W. Va. 1999).

[118] Morehouse v. Mills, 702 N.Y.S.2d 406 [141 Educ. L. Rep. 1162] (N.Y. App. Div. 2000).

[119] North Miami Educ. Ass'n v. North Community Schs., 736 N.E.2d 749, 757 [148 Educ. L. Rep. 445] (Ind. Ct. App. 2000).

In the first of two cases dealing with compensation issues, the Supreme Court of North Dakota affirmed that a teacher who taught music and physical education was not entitled to additional compensation due to the unavailability of specialist teachers who were occupied with musical rehearsals and play days. The court noted that since teachers never received extra compensation in such situations, it was not its function to amend the work agreement.[120]

Relying on the principles of equitable estoppel and promissory estoppel, the Supreme Court of Wyoming reversed a grant of summary judgment that had been entered on behalf of a school board in a dispute over a teacher salary schedule that allegedly exceeded the one agreed on in the union contract. The court rejected the board's claim that it should have been able to reduce teacher salaries where genuine issues of material fact existed as to whether the teachers had a breach of contract claim because the board had ratified the higher salaries.[121]

In the first of three cases addressing retirement issues, the Supreme Court of Alaska was called upon to resolve whether a school board's motion to offer retirement incentives to teachers with seniority was a contract offer. The dispute arose after six teachers notified the board of their intention to retire early before administrators realized that they had erroneously calculated the financial effect of the incentives. In reversing a grant of summary judgment in favor of the teachers, the court remarked that genuine issues of material fact existed as to whether the retirement incentives constituted a contract offer.[122]

An appellate court in Indiana declared that a principal who submitted a letter of intention to retire to his board of education and accepted an administrative position in another district was entitled to severance pay of $57,453 under his collective bargaining agreement. The court acknowledged that although the agreement under which the principal claimed severance pay expired prior to submission of his letter, the new agreement was not signed until after he retired. As such, the court wrote that until the new agreement was approved, the board was bound by the terms of the preceding contact.[123]

---

[120] Mandan Educ. Ass'n v. Mandan Pub. Sch. Dist. No. 1, 610 N.W.2d 64 [143 Educ. L. Rep. 1054] (N.D. 2000).

[121] Wells v. Board of Trustees of Laramie County Sch. Dist. No. 1, 3 P.3d 861 [145 Educ. L. Rep. 785] (Wyo. 2000).

[122] Copper River Sch. Dist. v. Traw, 9 P.3d 280 [147 Educ. L. Rep. 681] (Alaska 2000).

[123] Crawford County Community Sch. Corp. v. Enlow, 734 N.E.2d 685 [146 Educ. L. Rep. 851] (Ind. Ct. App. 2000).

In Texas, an appellate court pointed out that two school officials who voted against a school employee's retirement annuity, after promising to provide one in writing, were entitled to official immunity against a fraud claim. The court stated that since official immunity applies to discretionary actions, and the vote became discretionary when the promissory letter was written, there was a question as to its enforceability without board approval.[124]

A substitute teacher in Washington who was dismissed after two weeks unsuccessfully claimed that she was a permanent employee based on statements by a coordinator of special services. In affirming the dismissal of the teacher's complaint, an appellate court agreed that the coordinator's question as to whether she still wanted the job and telling her to call the principal did not form the basis for promissory estoppel. The court contended that even if the coordinator had representative authority, the teacher knew that a contract required action by the board.[125]

In Illinois, an appellate court posited that a former high school principal who was discharged at the end of the first year of his four-year contract was entitled to damages for the three remaining years of his contract but not to reinstatement. The court relied on a standard clause used in the contract which explicitly asserted that it expires at the end of the stated term and did not create contractual rights or expectancy beyond that date.[126]

As reflected by a case before the Supreme Court of Idaho, while at-will contracts normally do not provide due process rights prior to termination, they may be present in ancillary agreements. The court maintained that a school bus driver whose at-will contract was terminated was entitled to a fair and impartial hearing under his collective bargaining agreement where he alleged that the board violated public policy by retaliating against him for his union activities.[127]

Administrative Regulations and Statutory Provisions

The largest number of cases in this section concerned retirement benefits. Six suits from New York involved attempts by employees to gain retroactive membership in the state retirement system. Employees in these cases frequently claim that they had not been properly notified of their right

---

[124] Lopez v. Trevino, 2 S.W.3d 472 [140 Educ. L. Rep. 417] (Tex. Civ. App. 1999).

[125] McCormick v. Lake Washington Sch. Dist., 992 P.2d 511 [141 Educ. L. Rep. 352] (Wash. Ct. App. 1999).

[126] Eddings v. Board of Educ. of City of Chicago, 712 N.E.2d 902 [141 Educ. L. Rep. 255] (Ill. App. Ct. 1999).

[127] Roberts v. Board of Trustees, Pocatello Sch. Dist. No. 25, 11 P.3d 1108 [148 Educ. L. Rep. 502] (Idaho 2000).

to join the retirement system. In the first action, a school board successfully rebutted a claim when it presented evidence of a standard practice of advising all newly hired teachers of their eligibility.[128] Another court upheld a board's denial of retroactive membership for a school nurse had been a member of the retirement system but took time off to raise a family since it provided supporting evidence to its claim that officials gave the nurse information regarding her eligibility when she returned to work.[129] In yet another district, a teacher was unsuccessful where an appellate court decided that since her testimony that the board had not advised her of eligibility for participation in the retirement system was vague, equivocal, incomplete and inconsistent, the board was entitled to a finding that her statements were not credible.[130]

At the same time, some teachers in New York obtained retroactive membership in the state retirement system. In three separate cases, teachers prevailed where they were able to establish that a school board had no official policy or procedure informing employees of the option to join;[131] that a board either could not produce materials regarding membership or evidence that they had been actually delivered;[132] and, that school officials could provide only vague and conclusory allegations regarding a board's standard practices in notifying teachers about the system.[133]

The final case in this section from New York involved a statute that prohibits employees who transfer within three years of retirement from combining time credited in two state retirement systems. An appellate court affirmed, but modified, a judgment that did not bar a teacher's attempt, one year before his retirement, to combine his prior service in the State and Local Employees' Retirement System, with thirty-one years of current service in the State Teachers' Retirement System. The court interpreted the statute as only applying to teachers who changed jobs, not to those who transferred service credits.[134]

---

[128] Liebert v. Board of Educ. for Scotia-Glenville Cent. Sch. Dist., 704 N.Y.S.2d 352 [142 Educ. L. Rep. 477] (N.Y. App. Div. 2000).

[129] Capone v. Board of Educ. of Layette Cent. Sch. Dist., 697 N.Y.S.2d 895 [139 Educ. L. Rep. 1006] (N.Y. App. Div. 1999).

[130] French v. Board of Educ. for South Glens Falls Cent. Sch. Dist., 706 N.Y.S.2d 510 [143 Educ. L. Rep. 620] (N.Y. App. Div. 2000).

[131] Nesenoff v. Board of Educ. of Syosset Cent. Sch. Dist., 705 N.Y.S.2d 602 [143 Educ. L. Rep. 337] (N.Y. App. Div. 2000).

[132] Pershyn v. Board of Educ. of Uniondale Union Free Sch. Dist., 703 N.Y.S.2d 223 [142 Educ. L. Rep. 463] (N.Y. App. Div. 2000).

[133] Serio v. Board of Educ. of Valley Stream Union Free Sch. Dist. No. 13, 703 N.Y.S.2d 232 [142 Educ. L. Rep. 465] (N.Y. App. Div. 2000).

[134] Guido v. New York State Teachers' Retirement Sys., 699 N.Y.S.2d 697 [140 Educ. L. Rep. 705] (N.Y. 1999).

Cases from other states involved issues regarding eligibility in retirement systems. An appellate court affirmed that two auxiliary services teachers who taught in a private, nonsectarian school were not "teachers" who were qualified for membership in the Ohio State Teachers' Retirement System. The court reasoned that since the teachers never worked in a public school and were not subject to a board's supervision over their performance in the private school, they were not entitled to membership.[135] Similarly, in the first of two cases from Massachusetts, an appellate court affirmed the denial of a teacher's request to purchase creditable retirement service for his nonpublic school service because his entitlement to receive Social Security benefits for this teaching disqualified him from being able to purchase retirement service.[136]

The Supreme Judicial Court of Massachusetts affirmed that a change of retirement benefits for part-time service could not be done retroactively. The court ascertained that since part-time teachers had a contractual expectation to benefits, the state retirement board could not unilaterally alter that relationship.[137]

In Connecticut, an appeals court reversed a determination of a city retirement board, commenting that teachers who resigned from a school system and were later rehired were entitled to reinstatement to the retirement system. The court was convinced that the board's creation of a statute of limitations barring teachers from reinstatement exceeded its express authority under the city's code.[138]

An appellate court affirmed that former employees of the Minnesota Federation of Teachers (MFT) who received state retirement benefits after retiring from the MFT, but who continued to work for a new merged union, were subject to the statutory re-employed-annuitant earnings. The court decreed that the purpose of the statute was to impose the same limitation on union employees as existed for teachers.[139]

Four cases dealt with issues relating to compensation. The Supreme Court of Ohio affirmed that a state statute requiring long-term substitute teachers be paid a salary not less than the minimum on the current salary

---

[135] State *ex rel.* State Teachers' Retirement Bd. v. West Geauga Local Sch. Dist. Bd. of Educ., 722 N.E.2d 93 [140 Educ. L. Rep. 743] (Ohio Ct. App. 1998).
[136] Dube v. Contributory Retirement Appeal Bd., 733 N.E.2d 1089 [146 Educ. L. Rep. 414] (Mass. Ct. App. 2000).
[137] Madden v. Contributory Retirement Appeal Bd., 729 N.E.2d 1095 [144 Educ. L. Rep. 721] (Mass. 2000).
[138] Alexander v. Retirement Bd. of City of Waterbury, 750 A.2d 1139 [144 Educ. L. Rep. 318] (Conn. Ct. App. 2000).
[139] McDermott v. Minnesota Teachers Retirement Fund, 609 N.W.2d 926 [143 Educ. L. Rep. 1049] (Minn. Ct. App. 2000).

schedule does not require a school board to give credit for years of experience and level of education. The court offered that the statute, in only requiring a minimum salary, permits a board to hire full-time substitute teachers at the bachelors level with no credit for experience or education.[140]

In New York, an appellate court affirmed that a superintendent whose contract was terminated was not entitled to the cash value of his unused vacation days. The court was of the view that the superintendent failed to prove that the school board acted to prevent his using the vacation days during his last year.[141]

An appellate court in Massachusetts affirmed that only wages earned as a salary could be calculated in determining retirement benefits. As such, the court rejected a claim by a former driver's education teacher that his benefits should include hourly wages earned before and after school.[142]

In a case interpreting Texas' state minimum salary law, an appellate court affirmed that a school board can reduce the amount of its local supplement when the state minimum is raised as long as a teacher's salary is not less than the previous year. The court rejected a teacher's argument that a local supplement that had been in place for the preceding eight years amounted as an implied or de facto agreement.[143]

The first of two cases where employees prevailed in claims for workers' compensation was in Louisiana. An appellate court affirmed the claim of an elementary school teacher who alleged that being jostled on a bus while on a field trip exacerbated a back injury.[144]

In an expansive treatment of "work-related" for purposes of qualifying for workers' compensation benefits, an appellate court in Oregon ruled that criticisms by students and parents may provide a basis for benefits. Although the court remanded the dispute to the Workers' Compensation Board for a determination of whether a disciplinary letter was the basis for a teacher's depression, and eventual resignation, it concluded that a broad range of incidents, including slashed tires on her car and suspicious activity by teenagers near her home, could be characterized as work-related.[145]

---

[140] Antonucci v. Youngstown City Sch. Dist. Bd. of Educ., 722 N.E.2d 69 [140 Educ. L. Rep. 740] (Ohio 2000).

[141] Gratto v. Board of Educ. of the Ausable Valley Cent. Sch. Dist., 711 N.Y.S.2d 574 [146 Educ. L. Rep. 365] (N.Y. App. Div. 2000).

[142] Hallett v. Contributory Appeals. Bd., 725 N.E.2d 222 [142 Educ. L. Rep. 510] (Mass. 2000).

[143] Weslaco Fed. of Teachers v. Texas Educ. Agency, 27 S.W.3d 258 [147 Educ. L. Rep. 730] (Tex. App. 2000).

[144] McCartney v. Orleans Parish Sch. Bd., 743 So. 2d 821 [139 Educ. L. Rep. 1078] (La. Ct. App. 1999).

[145] Liberty Northwest Insur. Corp. v. Shotthafer, 10 P.3d 299 [147 Educ. L. Rep. 713] (Or. Ct. App. 2000).

As reflected in a case from Indiana, not all worker compensation claims were upheld. An appellate court affirmed the denial of the request for worker's compensation filed by the widow of a school bus driver shot and killed by another worker at the parking site for school buses. In discerning that the shooting arose out of a prior animosity unrelated to the driver's work, the court agreed that since his death did not arise out of his employment, his widow not entitled to benefits.[146]

One of the statutory issues addressed by courts is whether employees were eligible for disability benefits. The Supreme Court of New Jersey held that a media specialist, who was assaulted while reporting early for work, was entitled to receive accidental disability retirement benefits. The court observed that since the injury met the statutory requirement of occurring during, and as a result of, the performance of her regular or assigned duties, the specialist was not disqualified because the assault occurred outside the building at a time earlier than teachers normally reported to work. The court added that the specialist's attempting to enter the school building was necessary to her being able to perform her assigned work.[147]

In a second case from New Jersey, a former teacher prevailed in her claim that the state Board of Trustees of Teachers' Pension and Annuity Fund (TPAF) improperly refused to consider her application for accidental disability retirement. The court indicated that since the former teacher notified the TPAF in 1995 that she was receiving workers' compensation benefits, it could not deny her 1997 claim for disability retirement on the ground that she withdrew her retirement contributions since it failed to advise her in 1995 that she was required to continue paying into the fund. The court reflected that without this information, the former teacher had been denied a choice whether to continue making contributions.[148]

Not all disability claims were successful. A physical education teacher in Florida with a permanent disability unsuccessfully sought in-line-of-duty retirement benefits. In affirming the denial of the teacher's claim, an appellate court agreed with the State Retirement Commission that the teacher was unable to prove that her disability resulted from a job-related injury when she later suffered three other injuries that were not work-related.[149]

---

[146] Conway v. School Dist., City of East Chicago, 734 N.E.2d 594 [146 Educ. L. Rep. 844] (Ind. Ct. App. 2000).
[147] Kaspar v. Board of Trustees of Teachers' Pension Annuity Fund, 754 A.2d 525 [146 Educ. L. Rep. 224] (N.J. 2000).
[148] Outland v. Board of Trustees of Teachers' Pension and Annuity Fund, 741 A.2d 612 [140 Educ. L. Rep. 324] (N.J. Super. Ct. 1999).
[149] Morris v. Division of Retirement, 747 So. 2d 462 [141 Educ. L. Rep. 382] (Fla. Dist. Ct. App. 1999).

An appellate court in New Jersey interpreted regulations adopted by the TPAF and Board of Trustees of Public Employees' Retirement System (PERS), which applied to all disability retirees, regardless of age, as invalid because they exceeded the authority of the boards under state statute. The court believed that state law permitted only a five-year window for boards to assess the totality and permanency of disabilities of retirees under the age of sixty.[150]

The Supreme Judicial Court of Massachusetts, in a case on the relationship between teacher dismissal and continued eligibility for health insurance, decided that a teacher whose contract was terminated for cause was not entitled to continue coverage under a school board's health insurance. The court pointed out that while state law created a number of situations where persons no longer teaching were entitled to continued coverage, dismissal for cause was not one of them.[151]

In the first of two cases addressing state statutes dealing with eligibility for employment, the Supreme Court of Kansas declared that a teacher could not serve as a school board member in the same district in which she was employed. In reversing an earlier judgment in favor of the teacher, the court remarked that a teacher's serving as a board member was not consistent with the common law rule of incompatibility of office. The court concluded that since the teacher's contract continues, her status disqualifies her from serving on the board.[152]

The Supreme Court of Appeals of West Virginia was of the opinion that a high school principal could serve as a head varsity basketball coach in another school. The court interpreted the state statute which prohibits principals in schools with more than 170 students from being assigned to teaching duties as being inapplicable to coaching jobs.[153]

Tenure

Teachers are usually hired as probationary employees who must satisfy statutory requirements such as successfully completing a minimum number of years of teaching, in order to qualify for tenure or continuing contract status. Although state laws differ, statutes generally accord greater proce-

---

[150] New Jersey Educ. Ass'n v. Board of Trustees, Public Employees' Retirement Sys., 743 A.2d 353 [140 Educ. L. Rep. 989] (N.J. Super. Ct. 2000).
[151] Larson v. School Comm. of Plymouth, 723 N.E.2d 497 [142 Educ. L. Rep. 480] (Mass. 2000).
[152] Unified Sch. Dist. No. 501, Shawnee County v. Baker, 6 P.3d 848 [146 Educ. L. Rep. 902] (Kan. 2000).
[153] Holmes v. Board of Educ. of Berkeley County, 526 S.E.2d 310 [142 Educ. L. Rep. 1085] (W. Va. 1999).

dural due process rights to tenured teachers. In addition, since tenured teachers have a property interest in continued employment, they have an entitlement to minimal constitutional due process requirement.

Tenure Status

An appellate court in Minnesota rejected a teacher's claim that serving two years on a probationary contract entitled her to continuing contract status. The court maintained that although the teacher fulfilled the two years of service requirement while serving as a long-term substitute, she could not attain continuing contract status without first being offered and accepting a continuing contract. The court acknowledged that the superintendent had not made such an offer and that the plaintiff could not produce evidence that the school board sought to circumvent the tenure law by using long-term substitutes.[154]

The Supreme Court of Tennessee affirmed that a teacher who received notice of re-election to a fourth year contract from a school board did not qualify for permanent tenure. The court asserted that while state law provides that a teacher who is re-elected for a fourth year qualifies for tenure, this depends on a superintendent's having first notifying a board that re-election would result in an individual's receiving tenure. The court noted that since the superintendent did not provide the board with notice and the teacher did not meet the statutory requirement for tenure, his contract could be non-renewed as that of a probationary employee.[155]

Similarly, an appellate court in New York affirmed the denial of a teacher's claim that a school board resolution, granting to her tenure and due process rights under state law, was ineffective when it later rescinded the conditional tenure appointment. The court agreed with the board that tenure depended on its making an offer that the teacher accepted. The court contended that the board had not sent a letter to the teacher and that the one she received from the superintended stating the board's resolution could not substitute for board action.[156]

---

[154] Emanuel v. Independent Sch. Dist. No. 273, Edina Sch. Dist., 615 N.W.2d 415 [146 Educ. L. Rep. 860] (Minn. Ct. App. 2000).
[155] Bowden v. Memphis Bd. of Educ., 29 S.W.3d 462 [148 Educ. L. Rep. 513] (Tenn. 2000).
[156] Remus v. Board of Educ. for Tonawanda City Sch. Dist., 715 N.Y.S.2d 130 [148 Educ. L. Rep. 1009] (N.Y. App. Div. 2000).

Tenure by Default or Acquiescence

An appellate court in New York affirmed a school psychologist's claim to tenure based on estoppel after the board unilaterally extended her three-year probationary contract which ran from September 1, 1995 to September 1, 1998 to November 16, 1998 since she was absent eleven days in excess of her contractually allotted sick days due to surgery. The court ruled that while the board was entitled to extend the psychologist's contract to account for the eleven days, in doing so it unlawfully sought to deny her days of absence to which she was contractually entitled.[157]

In Washington, an appellate court affirmed that substitute teachers did not acquire continuing contract status when their board offered them four-year contracts guaranteeing them a minimum number of days. The court held that the contracts, negotiated by the board in order to address the difficulty in getting substitute teachers, fell within an exception within the state's continuing contract statute that teachers considered as replacements were not subject to rights under the statute.[158]

Certification

All states have certification or licensing requirements for a wide range of school employees, including teachers, social workers, school counselors, and bus drivers. In most states, while school boards determine an employee's job status, a state agency evaluates whether an individual should lose his or her certificate/license. In most cases, the loss of a required certificate or license also means the loss of employment.

Certification Standards

In a case with national implications, the Ninth Circuit, in a challenge by a class of Mexican-Americans, Asian-Americans, and African-Americans, affirmed that title VII applied to California's Basic Education Skills Test (CBEST). The panel also affirmed that the minimum score required in order for a person to be credentialed as a teacher was consistent with the EEOC's guidelines.[159]

Issuance of teacher or administrator certificates depends generally on satisfying prescribed requirements. An appellate court in Pennsylvania

---

[157] Maras v. Board of Educ. of City Sch. Dist of City of Schenectady, 712 N.Y.S.2d 8 [146 Educ. L. Rep. 841] (N.Y. App. Div. 2000).

[158] Moldt v. Tacoma Sch. Dist. No. 10, 12 P.3d 1042 [148 Educ. L. Rep. 1072] (Wash. Ct. App. 2000).

[159] Association of Mexican-American Educators v. State of California, 231 F.3d 572 [148 Educ. L. Rep. 639] (9th Cir. 2000).

affirmed that the State Department of Education did not abuse its discretion in refusing to issue an Administrative I certificate to an applicant who had not completed a practicum. The court agreed that the Department's refusal to accept actual work experience as a functional equivalent for the practicum requirement was within its discretion.[160]

Discretion in issuing certificates extends to protection from liability. A mother unsuccessfully sued the State of Arizona Department of Education for certifying a teacher who molested her daughter. An appellate court affirmed a grant of summary judgment in favor of the Department on the basis that the certification of teachers is a matter to which the state grants absolute immunity.[161]

States have discretion in applying certification standards to different kinds of schools. To the extent that state law requires a principal in a charter school to have an administrator's certificate, an appellate court in New Jersey affirmed that an educator in a charter school had to meet the same certification requirements as in the public schools.[162]

Decertification, Revocation, or Suspension

According to an appellate court in Illinois, the dismissal of a tenured teacher and the suspension of her teacher's certificate, after he permitted students to trade detention for electric shocks from a small engine was appropriate. The court affirmed that since the teacher's conduct was irremediable under state law, it warranted dismissal.[163]

In a protracted case that was before an appellate court in Wisconsin for the second time, the tribunal again reversed the Department of Public Instruction's revocation of the teaching license of a teacher who was tried for, but ultimately acquitted of, fatally shooting her former son-in-law while being found guilty of carrying a concealed weapon. The court found that the teacher's having shot her former son-in-law in order to protect her daughter and granddaughters from threats that he made on their lives and carrying a concealed weapon were not "immoral conduct" warranting license revocation.[164]

---

[160] Miller v. Commonwealth Dep't of Educ., 752 A.2d 451 [144 Educ. L. Rep. 998] (Pa. Commw. Ct. 2000).

[161] Doe v. State of Arizona, 7 P.3d 107 [146 Educ. L. Rep. 1117] (Ariz. Ct. App. 2000).

[162] *In re* Charter Sch. Appeal of Greater Brunswick Charter Sch., 753 A.2d 1155 [145 Educ. L. Rep. 683] (N.J. Super. Ct. App. Div. 1999).

[163] Rush v. Board of Educ of Crete-Monee Community Unit Sch. Dist. No. 201-U, 727 N.E.2d 649 [144 Educ. L. Rep. 586] (Ill. App. Ct. 2000).

[164] Epstein v. Benson, 618 N.W.2d 224 [147 Educ. L. Rep. 1059] (Wis. Ct. App. 2000).

An appellate court in California affirmed an order directing the Department of Motor Vehicles (DMV) to grant a hearing on the revocation of a bus driver's certificate for allegedly submitting an adulterated urine sample during a random drug test. The court reasoned that since the driver, who chose not to attend hearings before the school board, had not waived her right to a hearing before the DMV, she was entitled to a second hearing because it would not raise the same issue as to whether she was entitled to keep her school bus driver's certificate.[165]

Conclusion

The number of cases litigating employee issues remains fairly high. Further, the number of cases being appearing in state venues continues to exceed those decided in federal courts. Even so, the federal circuits have made some significant decisions affecting a wide range of education issues, suggesting that constitutional and federal rights affect much of what is done in K-12 education.

---

[165] Menge v. Reed, 101 Cal.Rptr. 443 [148 Educ. L. Rep. 1001] (Cal. Ct. App. 2000).

2
PUPILS

Jay Cummings, Johnetta Hudson, Bill Camp, Judith Adkison

Introduction

Federal and state courts continue to address constitutional and statutory issues relating to students in public and private schools. The courts attempt to balance the efforts of educational leaders to provide safe and orderly school environments with the requirements of meeting the constitutional and statutory protections for individuals in American schools. First Amendment rights, search and seizure, discipline, and other pupil-related issues continue to require interpretation. While addressing the substantive rights of students, the courts continue to support school boards and educational officials who follow appropriate policies and procedures. School officials are expected to be reasonable and fair in their decisions while respecting the due process rights of children and their parents when considering the appropriateness of their actions. This knowledge of consequences in legal matters surrounding the litigation explored in this chapter serves to underscore the need for balanced administrative policies when the courts intervene as guardians of constitutional and statutory protections for individuals as well as accommodating shifting societal norms that influence interpretations and case law.

Issues Relating to Public School Attendance

Compulsory Attendance

Parents in Virginia filed a civil rights action against school board members, challenging the denial of their request for a religious exemption from compulsory attendance for their children. On remand following the denial of their appeal, a federal trial court held that the parents' due process rights were not violated and that they failed to establish the existence of a civil conspiracy to deprive parents of the free exercise of religion.[1]

In the District of Columbia, a mother who was convicted of failing to have her child regularly attend school sought further review. An appellate tribunal remanded for further proceedings since the trial court relied on inadmissible evidence represented by a school form used to establish residence.[2] The court acknowledged that while the school form was admissible for the record of absences, it was inadmissible as proof of their common residence.

---

[1] Francis v. Barnes, 69 F. Supp.2d 801 [139 Educ. L. Rep. 914] (E.D. Va. 1999).
[2] Clyburn v. District of Columbia, 741 A.2d 395 [140 Educ. L. Rep. 319] (D.C. 1999).

A father in Kentucky who faced criminal charges for keeping his daughter out of school filed a malicious prosecution action against a county school board's director of pupil personnel and an elementary school principal. After a trial court entered judgment for the father, the director sought further review. An appellate court reversed and remanded with instructions for dismissal of the complaint since it was satisfied that probable cause supported charges filed against the father for violating the statute requiring compulsory school attendance for children between the ages of six and sixteen.[3] The court also ruled that the father could not maintain a malicious prosecution action against the director of pupil personnel for filing a charge against him for causing his daughter to engage in illegal sexual activity since the allegation was initiated by the county attorney's office.

In Ohio, an appellate court found that a school board's attendance policy was unreasonable since it did not distinguish between excused and unexcused absences.[4] A student who completed the school year with a 3.966 grade point average and passed all of her proficiency tests challenged the district's denial of a diploma for missing more days than allowed by the policy even though all but two of the absences were excused. The court stated that severe academic sanctions could only be applied where students were absent without excuse. Further, the court indicated that the policy of disregarding excessive absences with proof of extenuating circumstances was unreasonable when those circumstances were not defined, since it would have allowed officials to punish absentee students arbitrarily. The court ordered the board to release the student's grades with academic credit and to issue her a high school diploma.

The mother of an elementary school student in Indiana challenged a charge of violating the state's Compulsory Attendance Act after her child missed twenty-three days of school. The mother received a suspended sentence of one hundred and eighty days in jail and one year of probation. The mother's appeal claimed that the school board's attendance policy was an unconstitutional delegation of authority by the General Assembly to school corporations. An appellate court affirmed that the delegation of authority to school boards to establish attendance policies was not unconstitutional.[5]

---

[3] Collins v. Williams, 10 S.W.3d 493 [141 Educ. L. Rep. 943] (Ky. Ct. App. 1999).

[4] State *ex rel.* v. Crestwood Bd. of Educ., 731 N.E.2d 701 [145 Educ. L. Rep. 482] (Ohio Ct. App. 1998).

[5] Eukers v State, 728 N.E.2d 219 [143 Educ. L. Rep. 1029] (Ind. Ct. App. 2000).

After being expelled from a Catholic school in Massachusetts, a student who was denied admission in a public school successfully challenged the board's action. An appellate court reversed in noting that a board can consider an expulsion from another public school district but not a non-public entity in denying enrollment.[6]

Transfer of Students

In Maryland, a father filed a civil rights claim when his son was denied a transfer into a mathematics and science magnet program because he did not meet its diversity profile. Based on the compilation of student information about racial/ ethnic group membership and percentage of each group attending a particular school, the school board assigned each group a diversity category. Although the federal trial court denied the father's motion for preliminary injunction to compel his son's admittance, the Fourth Circuit reversed in deciding that the transfer policy violated the Equal Protection Clause because it failed to make a case that race was a compelling basis for such a policy.[7]

The Boston Public Schools reviewed transfers of students to a school of choice by using a formula that included the assignment of siblings, residence in the walk zone, the preference rating by applicants, priority for current students in a school, availability of seats, a child's lottery number, and a child's race or ethnicity. Students who were denied their preferred assignments sought damages on the basis that the board's action was based on race. The federal trial court in Massachusetts observed that since five students in the suit had not applied for transfers, their claims should be dismissed.[8] However, the court denied the board's motion to dismiss in regard to the other students based on its belief that injunctive relief was necessary if the assignments were the result of an unlawful plan.

In a second case from Massachusetts, the federal trial court denied an injunction to parents who challenged a board's plan for considering racial imbalance as a factor for students applying for transfers from one school to another.[9] The court explained that the successful use of racial classifications depends on the actual operation of the plan, the context in which it is used, and the purposes it served. The court rejected the parents' claims for

---

[6] Hamrick v. Affton Sch. Dist. Bd. of Educ., 13 S.W.3d 678 [143 Educ. L. Rep. 402] (Mo. Ct. App. 2000).

[7] Eisenberg v. Montgomery County Pub. Schs., 197 F.3d 123 [140 Educ. L. Rep. 88] (4th Cir. 1999).

[8] Boston's Children First v. City of Boston, 98 F. Supp.2d 111 [144 Educ. L. Rep. 938] (D. Mass. 2000).

[9] Comfort *ex rel.* Neumyer v. Lynn Sch. Comm., 100 F. Supp.2d 57 [145 Educ. L. Rep. 304] (D. Mass 2000).

relief in concluding that they were unable to show irreparable injury if the injunction were not issued, especially since they were satisfied with current placement of their children, and overcrowding of the schools was not likely to occur.

Parents of an elementary student sued a school board and officials in New York for denying their daughter a transfer from a city to a suburban school after several districts had set up an urban-suburban inter-district transfer program to reduce racial isolation and ameliorate de facto segregation. In fact, the denial of the transfer was primarily based on the girl's race. After a federal trial court granted the preliminary injunction requiring the transfer, the board appealed. The Second Circuit vacated the injunction and remanded, pointing out that the parents failed to demonstrate a likelihood of success on the merits of their claim.[10] However, the court did allow the girl to finish the current academic year at the suburban school.

The Supreme Court of Pennsylvania affirmed that a student was a resident of a school district for purposes of receiving a free, appropriate public education. The court reasoned that the student met the classic definition of residence since he lived with his mother in a leased townhouse in the school district.[11]

A public school board in Wisconsin accepted three students' applications for transfers under the open enrollment statute even though no class space was available, but denied the same exemption to a fourth student. When the student challenged the board's action, the State Superintendent of Public Instruction agreed with it but was reversed by a trial court. On further review, an appellate court affirmed that the board's denial of the one student's application because of lack of space while accepting three other students was arbitrary and unreasonable.[12]

Tuition and Fees

A school board provided a subsidy to defray the cost of a student's tuition at a private school since it did not maintain its own high school. When the student's mother purchased a house in another district to attend law school and transferred her son to a near-by public school, the original district denied him the continued support because he was no longer a resi-

---

[10] Brewer v. West Irondequoit Cent. Sch. Dist., 212 F.3d 738 [144 Educ. L. Rep. 845] (2nd Cir. 2000).

[11] In re Hearing Before Bd. of Sch. Dist., 744 A.2d 1272 [141 Educ. L. Rep. 872] (Pa. 2000).

[12] McMorrow v. Benson, 617 N.W.2d 247 [147 Educ. L. Rep. 311] (Wis. Ct. App. 2000).

dent. A trial court rejected the mother's claim that her current residence was temporary. On further review, the Supreme Judicial Court of Maine affirmed that since the mother and son did not actually live in the district, he was not entitled to the tuition subsidy.[13]

Claiming a violation of the Public School Code, residents and taxpayers in Pennsylvania secured a declaratory judgment action against a school board that planned to provide partial tuition reimbursement for children who attended private schools or non-district public schools. On further review, an appellate court affirmed that the plan was not authorized, expressly or implicitly, under the state's Public School Code.[14]

Parents challenged Florida's opportunity scholarship program which provided funds to students who attended public schools that failed for two years in a four year period so that they could attend a public school that performs satisfactorily or to pay tuition at a private school. When a trial court struck down the provision for paying private school tuition on the basis that it violated the state constitution, the State sought further review. An appellate court reversed and remanded in writing that the section of the state constitution which provides for public education to be accomplished through a system of free public schools does not explicitly or implicitly prohibit the state from paying tuition for some children to attend private schools.[15]

Private and Parochial Students

In New York, a student in a private school and his father sued the school, the local public school board, and the board's contractor for bus services to recover damages for negligence for his allegedly being sexually abused by a fellow student on a school bus. An appellate court affirmed the denial of the defendants' motions for summary judgment because unresolved questions of fact and awareness as well as questions of material fact precluded a summary judgement on the issue of punitive damages.[16]

A student at a Catholic school and his parents sued the principal, the school, and the diocese when officials suspended him for three days and recommended that he seek counseling since he engaged in sexual harass-

---

[13] Hallissey v. School Admin. Dist. No. 77, 755 A.2d 1068 [146 Educ. L. Rep. 293] (Me. 2000).
[14] Giacomucci v. S.E. Delco Sch. Dist., 742 A.2d 1165 [140 Educ. L. Rep. 976] (Pa. Commw. Ct. 1999).
[15] Bush v. Holmes, 767 So. 2d 688 [147 Educ. L. Rep. 1125] (Fla. Dist. Ct. App. 2000).
[16] David "XX" v. Saint Catherine's Ctr., 699 N.Y.S.2d 827 [140 Educ. L. Rep. 716] (N.Y. App. Div. 1999).

ment and acts of sexual violence. After removing their son from the school, the plaintiffs unsuccessfully filed suit claiming that he was overly and unfairly punished, that school officials did not follow their handbook in this matter, that he was not afforded due process, and that officials failed to punish students who pushed their son. On further review, an appellate court in Ohio affirmed in favor of the defendants on the grounds that the actions of school officials were consistent with policies outlined in their student handbook, were within the broad discretion afforded them in matters of discipline, and that the claim that the principal failed to punish other students was unsubstantiated.[17]

In Wisconsin, a private elementary school and the parents of students who attended it sued public school districts because they sought to use parental contracts instead of actual busing to transport children to school. On further review of the denial of the parents' motions for relief, an appellate court affirmed that, while the students were entitled to transportation, boards were entitled to provide it via five methods, including contracting with parents or guardians.[18]

A former student and his wife filed a claim against a priest, a church official, and the church for sexual abuse which had occurred approximately thirty years earlier. An appellate court in Missouri reversed a judgment in favor of the former student on the ground that his claims were barred by the statute of limitations despite a claim of suppressed memory of the abuse.[19] The court determined not only that the student was aware of the injury at the time but also that there was no evidence to show that he was mentally incompetent. Further, the court rejected the wife's claim for loss of consortium since the claims were barred.

In Colorado, a former student from a parochial elementary school who claimed that she was involved in a four-year sexual relationship with her teacher unsuccessfully sued the archdiocese and the school's former principal. An appellate court affirmed a grant of summary judgment in favor of the defendants on the basis that the former student failed to file her claims within the required two-year statute of limitations.[20]

---

[17] Iwenofu v. St. Luke Sch., 724 N.E.2d. 511 [142 Educ. L. Rep. 494] (Ohio Ct. App. 1999).

[18] Providence Sch. v. Bristol Sch. No. 1, 605 N.W.2d 238 [141 Educ. L. Rep. 321] (Wis. Ct. App. 1999).

[19] H.R.B. v. Rigali, 18 S.W.3d 440 [145 Educ. L. Rep. 522] (Mo. Ct. App. 2000).

[20] Sandoval v. Archdiocese of Denver, 8 P.3d 598 [147 Educ. L. Rep. 328] (Colo. Ct. App. 2000).

Substantive Rights of Students

First Amendment: Association Rights

Students who wished to form a Gay-Straight Alliance Club at a public high school in California sued a school board and individual board members under the Equal Access Act when their application was denied. A federal trial court ruled in favor of the students in stating that a public high school that allows even one non-curriculum-related student group to meet on school grounds opens the door for other non-curriculum-related groups to form and meet there.[21] The court added that under the Equal Access Act, schools that allow student groups whose purpose is not directly related to the curriculum to meet on school grounds during lunch or after class cannot deny access to other students if educational officials take exception to the content of their proposed discussions.

A high school student group in Utah with a "gay-positive" perspective challenged a policy that denied it an opportunity to meet on school premises during non-instructional time and to have access to school facilities. The federal trial court was of the opinion that the policy violated the group's Equal Access Act rights when they were denied the opportunity to meet while another non-curriculum-related student group was permitted to convene.[22] In a further action over the permissible subject matter in the school's limited public forum involving curriculum-related activities, the same court maintained that since the plaintiffs did not demonstrate how the policy had a disparate impact on their viewpoint, it did not have to examine the actual motives of board members regarding the allegations.[23]

Another federal trial court in Utah reviewed the standards governing access to a limited forum created for curriculum-related student clubs at a high school where a club proposed to examine the impact, experience, and contributions of gays and lesbians in the context of history and current events. The club argued that the official in charge of reviewing the application either misapplied the standards or added a new standard. The court granted the club's request for a preliminary injunction since there was a substantial likelihood that it would succeed on the merits of its First Amendment claim.[24]

---

[21] Colin *Ex. Rel.* Colin v. Orange Unified Sch. Dist., 83 F. Supp.2d 1135 [142 Educ. L. Rep. 138] (C.D. Cal. 2000).

[22] East High Gay/Straight All v. Board of Educ., 81 F. Supp.2d 1166 [141 Educ. L. Rep. 776] (D. Utah 1999).

[23] East High Gay/Straight Alliance v. Board of Educ., 81 F. Supp.2d 1199 [141 Educ. L. Rep. 809] (D. Utah 1999).

[24] East High Sch. Prism Club v. Seidel, 95 F. Supp.2d 1239 [144 Educ. L. Rep. 260] (D. Utah 2000).

First Amendment: Religious Rights

At issue before the Supreme Court was a challenge to a case from the Fifth Circuit over the constitutionality of a board policy in Texas which permitted student-led, student-initiated prayer at football games. The Fifth Circuit ruled that the policy violated the Establishment Clause.[25] In *Santa Fe Independent School District v. Doe*,[26] the Supreme Court affirmed that the policy and practice of allowing student-led, student-initiated prayer before football games violated the Establishment Clause since it was not private speech and was impermissibly coercive. The Court discerned that even though the board allowed two elections to choose whether the students wanted a prayer before the games and who would deliver the prayers, it did not intend to open this ceremony for indiscriminate student use. The Court posited that since the process guaranteed that minority candidates would not prevail, it effectively silenced their views, and the board could not divorce itself from the message's religious content. Finally, the Court remarked that since a game is a school sponsored event that players, band members, and cheerleaders are required to attend, it could not be seen as voluntary.

A first grade student and his mother in New Jersey unsuccessfully sued various officials in part based on a teacher's refusal to let him read a religious story to classmates and to place a religious poster on a school wall. An en banc panel of the Third Circuit affirmed that the teacher's refusal to allow the student to present religious material in class did not violate his First Amendment right of free expression.[27] However, the court afforded the plaintiffs the opportunity to amend their complaint with regard to claims arising from the poster incident.

When school officials in California refused to allow either a graduate to recite a sectarian, proselytizing valedictory speech or another student to offer a sectarian invocation at a graduation, students and others unsuccessfully sued them and the board alleging violations of their right to freedom of speech. The Ninth Circuit affirmed that the officials' refusal to allow students to deliver a sectarian prayer or sectarian proselytizing valedictory address was necessary to avoid violating the Establishment Clause and did not violate the students' free speech rights.[28]

---

[25] Santa Fe Indep. Sch. Dist. v. Doe, 168 F.3d 806 [140 Educ. L. Rep. 21] (5th Cir. 1999).

[26] 120 S. Ct. 2266 [145 Educ. L. Rep. 21] (2000).

[27] C.H. *ex rel.* Z.H. v. Oliva, 226 F.3d 198 [148 Educ. L. Rep. 585] (3rd Cir. 1999).

[28] Cole v. Oroville Union High Sch. Dist., 228 F.3d 1092 [147 Educ. L. Rep. 878] (9th Cir. 2000).

A superintendent in Florida issued a memorandum for high school graduation ceremonies in response to a request from students who wanted to have some type of brief opening and/or closing message by a classmate. The guidelines afforded students the opportunity to direct their own graduation message without monitoring or review by school officials. When speakers at ten of the seventeen high school graduation ceremonies delivered some form of religious message, other students challenged the practice as an establishment of religion and an infringement on their free exercise of religion. A federal trial court in Florida granted the board's motion for summary judgment. On further review, an en banc panel of the Eleventh Circuit affirmed that the memorandum did not violate the Establishment Clause.[29]

Taxpayers challenged the constitutionality of the voucher portion of the Ohio Pilot Scholarship Program, under which students could attend religiously affiliated non-public schools at public expense. On cross-motions for summary judgment, a federal trial court contended that since the voucher program had the impermissible effect of advancing religion by resulting in governmental indoctrination of religious beliefs or creating an incentive to attend religious schools, it violated the Establishment Clause.[30]

In North Carolina, a great grandmother who was the legal guardian of her elementary school-aged great grandson, challenged a school board's uniform policy on the basis that it violated her right to free exercise of religion. A federal trial court rejected the board's motion for summary judgment on the basis that the grandmother's hybrid-rights claim was entitled to strict scrutiny.[31] The court also granted the school officials' motions for qualified immunity in their individual capacities.

A student in Kentucky challenged a school's displays of the Ten Commandments and other religious documents, seeking to enjoin them as violating the Establishment Clause. A federal trial court, in finding that the student had a strong likelihood of success on the merits of her claim, granted the motion and ordered the removal of the displays from the school.[32]

---

[29] Adler v. Duval County Sch. Bd., 206 F.3d.1070 [142 Educ. L. Rep. 773] (11th Cir. 2000).

[30] Simmons-Harris v. Zelman, 72 F. Supp.2d 834 [140 Educ. L. Rep. 243[(N.D. Ohio 1999).

[31] Hicks v. Halifax County Bd. of Educ., 93 F. Supp.2d 649 [143 Educ. L. Rep. 861] (E.D.N.C. 1999).

[32] Doe v. Harlan County Sch. Dist., 96 F. Supp.2d 667 [144 Educ. L. Rep. 503] (E.D. Ky. 2000).

First Amendment: Freedom of Speech

Alleging that a school board in New York violated their rights to free speech and equal protection by not allowing them to use school facilities, a nondenominational children's club and its administrator unsuccessfully filed suit in a federal trial court. The Second Circuit affirmed that the policy created a limited public forum.[33] The court asserted that the limited use of school facilities was reasonable and that since the club engaged in religious instruction and prayer, officials' refusal to permit it to use them was viewpoint neutral and did not violate the Free Speech Clause.

A student in Ohio who wore Marilyn Manson shirts on successive days and was told that he could not do so, unsuccessfully filed suit claiming a violation of his First Amendment right to free speech. The Sixth Circuit upheld the board policy that prohibited students from wearing t-shirts with offensive illustrations or with drug, alcohol, or tobacco slogans to school.[34] The court, in holding that students' rights are applied in light of the special characteristics of the school environment, dismissed the First Amendment claim.

In Missouri, a high school student and his parents unsuccessfully sued their school board, alleging that when the principal disqualified him as the student body president for the unauthorized distribution of condoms attached to stickers bearing his campaign slogan, it violated his First Amendment right to free speech. The Eighth Circuit affirmed that since the election was not a public forum but a school-sponsored event in which administrators had the authority to restrict even protected individual student expression that materially and substantially interfered with the requirements for appropriate discipline in the operation of a school.[35]

A student in Georgia claimed that a school board and various officials violated his free speech and due process rights when he was suspended for three days for wearing a shirt that stated "Even adults lie." A federal trial court granted the board's motion for summary judgment in deciding that the dress code was neither overly broad nor in violation of the First Amendment and that the suspension met all procedural due process requirements.[36]

---

[33] The Good News Club v. Milford Central Sch., 202 F.3d 502 [141 Educ. L. Rep. 475] (2nd Cir. 2000).

[34] Boroff v. Van Wert City Bd. of Educ., 220 F.3d 465 [146 Educ. L. Rep. 629] (6th Cir. 2000).

[35] Henerey *ex rel.* Henerey v. City of St. Charles, 200 F.3d 1128 [141 Educ. L. Rep. 95] (8th Cir. 1999).

[36] Smith By Lanham v. Greene County Sch. Dist., 100 F. Supp.2d 1354 [145 Educ. L. Rep.. 368] (M.D. Ga. 2000).

Acting in response to racial tension between Black and White students at a high school in Kansas, a school board adopted a Racial Harassment and Intimidation policy, based on recommendations from a 350-member task force of parents, teachers and community members. When a middle school student, who was informed of the policy on several occasions, drew a confederate flag and displayed it, he was suspended for three days. The student's father unsuccessfully sued the board on the basis that the policy violated his son's rights to due process and free speech. The Tenth Circuit affirmed that the student received all of the process due him, that his suspension did not violate the Equal Protection Clause, that the policy did not violate his First Amendment right to free speech, and that the policy was neither over broad nor unconstitutionally vague.[37]

In a second case involving a Confederate flag, a student in Florida who was disciplined for displaying such a flag during class hours unsuccessfully claimed that school officials violated his First Amendment rights. The Eleventh Circuit affirmed that the administrators were working within the scope of their duty and entitled to qualified immunity since they were not the final policymakers.[38] The court also judged that since the board had not established a pervasive and well-settled policy or custom of banning the Confederate flag, it was not liable.

Sexual Abuse and Harassment by Students

When a female student with learning and hearing disabilities was allegedly raped in a school bathroom by an eleventh grade student with a lengthy history of violent and delinquent behavior, her mother unsuccessfully sued the principal and the school board for failing to maintain adequate security and for failing to warn students of his violent past. Further, a grand jury failed to indict the male for the alleged rape. The mother claimed that the grand jury's action was due to the principal's failure to contact the police or obtain medical assistance, thereby resulting in a lack of evidence that a rape occurred. The Supreme Court of Mississippi, in an interlocutory appeal, granted the defendants' motions for summary judgment on the grounds that they were entitled to statutory immunity.[39]

In the first of two cases from New York, a ninth grade student and her mother sued school officials for negligence and intentional infliction of emo-

---

[37] West v. Derby Unified Sch. Dist. No. 260, 206 F.3d 1358 [143 Educ. L. Rep. 43] (10th Cir. 2000).

[38] Denno v. School Bd. of Volusia County, Fla., 218 F.3d 1267 [145 Educ. L. Rep. 942] (11th Cir. 2000).

[39] Lincoln County Sch. Dist. v. Doe, 749 So. 2d 943 [142 Educ. L. Rep. 563] (Miss. 1999).

tional distress as well as claims for sexual discrimination and retaliation pursuant to title IX. A federal trial court dismissed the claims against the defendants in their individual capacities but denied their remaining motions for summary judgment as to the charges of negligence and violations of title IX.[40]

The mother of a second grade student filed a sexual harassment claim based on title IX against a teacher, administrator, and school board. The mother alleged that a boy in her daughter's class harassed her on a school playground by teasing, punching, and touching her private parts. A federal trial court granted the defendants' motions for summary on the basis that teasing and punching were not sexual harassment.[41] The court explained that one incident of sexual misconduct did not result in denying the child equal access to education.

In California, a student sued a classmate and school board under title IX after he was assaulted while walking home from school because of his perceived homosexuality. The student claimed that he reported the assault to school officials who failed to take steps to stop the harassment. A federal trial court rejected the board's motion to dismiss in noting that the educators' actions met the deliberate indifference element under title IX.[42]

A school board in Illinois filed an interlocutory appeal over whether a female student who was harassed by two male peers had a private right to action against it under the state constitution's gender discrimination provision. An appellate court responded that the sole mechanism for a private recovery of damages was under the Human Rights Act which does not extend to sexual harassment in primary and secondary schools.[43]

Sexual Abuse and Harassment by Employees

Male students who were sexually molested by a third grade teacher in Texas sued their school board based on section 1983 and title IX. A federal trial court granted the board's motion for summary judgment on section 1983 and dismissed the title IX claim on the basis that same sex harassment was not actionable under title IX. On further review, the Fifth Circuit affirmed

---

[40] Niles v. Nelson, 72 F. Supp.2d 13 [140 Educ. L. Rep 199] (N.D.N.Y. 1999).
[41] Manfredi v. Mount Vernon Bd. of Educ., 94 F. Supp.2d 447 [144 Educ. L. Rep. 118] (S.D.N.Y. 2000).
[42] Ray v. Antioch Unified Sch. Dist., 107 F. Supp.2d 1165 [146 Educ. L. Rep. 1036] (N.D. Cal. 2000).
[43] Teverbaugh *ex rel.* Duncan v. Moore, 724 N.E.2d 225 [144 Educ. L. Rep. 541] (Ill. App. Ct. 2000).

that since the principal's response to allegations that the teacher sexually molested the students did not amount to deliberate indifference, the board could not be liable under title IX.[44]

Five former students at a military school sued it and various officials alleging sexual harassment, abuse, and fraud. A federal trial court in Indiana dismissed the sexual harassment and abuse claims based on the statute of limitations while also granting the defendants' motion for summary judgment on the fraud claim. On further review, the Seventh Circuit affirmed that the title IX and state law claims were time-barred under the state statute of limitations and that school officials did not engage in fraud.[45]

School officials in Arkansas sought further review of the denial of their motion for qualified immunity where six minor students claimed that a teacher subjected them to verbal, physical, and sexual abuse. The Eighth Circuit reversed and remanded in stating that while the teacher did use inappropriate language with his classes, offensive language is not a constitutional violation.[46] In addition, the court declared that although physical abuse can amount to a constitutional violation if it reaches the level that shocks the conscience, none of the officials were liable because they had no notice of a pattern of such acts.

In Alabama, a high school student and her parents sued a superintendent in his individual and official capacities under title IX and the Fourteenth Amendment for violating her right to equal protection after she was allegedly sexually abused by a teacher. When the superintendent unsuccessfully made a motion for summary judgment on the basis of qualified immunity, he sought further review. The Eleventh Circuit reversed, observing that the trial court erred in not granting the superintendent's motion since there was no question of a constitutional violation.[47]

Parents and a male high school student sued a school board and various officials in Maine alleging violations of title IX, the state's human rights act, and common-law negligence arising out of his allegedly having been sexually harassed by a female teacher. The federal trial court granted the plaintiffs' motion for summary judgment on their title IX claim, noting that evidence existed that a reasonable jury could have concluded that the defendants were negligent in investigating the claims of sexual harassment.[48]

---

[44] Doe *ex rel.* Doe v. Dallas Indep. Sch. Dist., 220 F.3d 380 [146 Educ. L. Rep. 80] (5th Cir. 2000).

[45] Doe v. Howe Military Sch., 227 F.3d 981 [147 Educ. L. Rep. 507] (7th Cir. 2000).

[46] Doe v. Gooden, 214 F.3d 952 [145 Educ. L. Rep. 167] (8th Cir. 2000).

[47] Hartley v. Parnell, 193 F.3d 1263 [139 Educ. L. Rep. 95] (11th Cir. 1999).

[48] Doe v. School Admin. Dist. No. 19, 66 F. Supp.2d 57 [139 Educ. L. Rep. 399] (D. Me. 1999).

At the same time, the court denied the plaintiffs' claims that the board violated the student's equal protection rights by conducting a lesser investigation than would have occurred if the teacher were male and the student were female.

In Massachusetts, a high school student sued her school board and a coach seeking compensation and punitive damages under title IX for his admitted sexual abuse. Despite the board's having dismissed the coach, the federal trial court rejected its motion for summary judgment on the punitive damages charge in order to afford the student the opportunity to submit evidence addressing the proper elements of such a claim.[49]

When a high school student in New York sued her school board for sexual harassment by her teacher and for its negligence supervision of his behavior, the court rejected two of the board's motions for summary judgment.[50] According to the court, there were not only unresolved issues of fact regarding whether an administrator was deliberately indifferent to the student's complaints but the board had notice of the alleged discrimination. Even so, the court dismissed the claim that sought to render the board vicariously liable for the teacher's alleged misconduct since he acted out of personal reasons and not as part of his job.

In a state court in New York, a parent sued a university research foundation and school board for sexual abuse of her son by a counselor hired by the latter to administer a program to identify students who would not traditionally enter college but showed potential to succeed in college. The counselor was not an employee of the district, but met with the student behind close doors on a regular basis for a period of six months. The court dismissed claims of negligent hiring against the foundation but rejected the board's motion for summary judgment as to the negligent supervision charge since genuine issues of material fact remained as to whether the board used the same degree of care as a reasonably prudent parent.[51]

Parents of a student in Virginia who was sexually abused by his teacher sued the superintendent under section 1983 for failure to warn them that their child's teacher was accused of sexually molesting a student in the past and was suspected of inappropriate conduct with their son. A federal trial court granted the superintendent's motion for dismissal in reasoning that the parents failed to state an actionable claim for deprivation of their rights.[52]

---

[49] Canty v. Old Rochester Reg'l Sch. Dist., 66 F. Supp.2d 114 [139 Educ. L. Rep. 421] (D. Mass. 1999).

[50] Flores v. Saulpaugh, 115 F. Supp.2d 319 [147 Educ. L. Rep. 941] (N.D.N.Y. 2000).

[51] Murray v. Research Found. of State Univ., 707 N.Y.S.2d 816 [144 Educ. L. Rep. 620] (N.Y. Sup. Ct. 2000).

[52] Baynard v. Lawson, 76 F. Supp.2d 688 [140 Educ. L. Rep. 905] (E.D. Va.1999).

In a related action, when a jury awarded the student damages in his suit against the principal and school board, a federal trial court denied the principal's motion to set the verdict aside as excessive.[53] The court indicated that the award was proper since the principal showed deliberate indifference to the student by failing to act in a timely manner on reports of the teacher's prior sexual abuse of students and his inappropriate behavior in this case. Yet, the court granted the board's motion for judgment notwithstanding the verdict in pointing out that it could have been liable only if a school official with actual knowledgeof the abuse was vested by the board with both the duty to supervise the employee and the power to take action that would end such abuse and failed to do so. The court decreed that the student failed to establish that the principal had the power to dismiss or transfer the teacher.

In Ohio, students filed a civil rights action against a school board based on allegations arising from incidents of sexual abuse or harassment by a teacher. The court denied the board's motion for summary judgment in remarking that the students had a constitutional right to personal security and to bodily integrity, including the right to be free from sexual abuse or harassment by a public school employee.[54]

A former student filed section 1983 and title IX charges against a former high school teacher and school board for sexual abuse that allegedly occurred twenty-five years earlier. The federal trial court in South Dakota dismissed the claim against the board since the alleged abuse occurred before title IX was enacted.[55] The court granted the teacher's motion for summary judgment in positing that the cause of action against him could not be revived as a 1991 state statute established time limitations for civil actions arising out of sexual abuse of a child.

In Iowa, an elementary school student and her mother sued their school board for damages resulting from her having been sexually abused by a school employee. A federal trial court granted the board's motion for summary judgment in reflecting that it was not liable under title IX since there was insufficient evidence to support a finding of deliberate indifference to the employee's conduct.[56] The court was also of the view that the board was exempt on the claim of negligent hiring, retention, and supervision because state law insulated it from tort liability in the performance of discretionary functions.

---

[53] Baynard v. Lawson, 112 F. Supp.2d 524 [147 Educ. L. Rep. 136] (E.D. Va. 2000).

[54] Massey v. Akron City Bd. of Educ., 82 F. Supp.2d 735 [141 Educ. L. Rep. 1104] (N.D. Ohio 2000).

[55] Gross v. Weber, 112 F. Supp.2d 923 [147 Educ. L. Rep. 157] (D.S.D. 2000).

[56] Gordon ex rel. Gordon v. Ottumwa Community Sch., 115 F. Supp.2d 1077 [147 Educ. L. Rep. 984] (S.D. Iowa 2000).

A middle school student in Georgia and her mother sought damages from a county, school board, individual school officials, and a custodian who allegedly raped her. A federal trial court partially granted the defendants' motions for summary judgment in ruling that the Violence Against Women Act pertained only to the custodian.[57] The court also deemed that the board was not liable under title IX since there was no connection between its not providing surveillance cameras in the area where the alleged incident took place and the injury.

In Louisiana, a grandmother, acting as guardian for her grandson, unsuccessfully sued a school board, its insurer, and various officials after the child was sexually assaulted by a high school janitor. An appellate court affirmed that the board did not breach its duty to supervise elementary school students who waited at a high school for a bus to their schools and was not vicariously liable for janitor's tortuous activity.[58]

Students and their parents contested the dismissal of their civil rights claims against a school board and the estate of a deceased teacher alleging negligent supervision and retention based on his having sexually assaulted the children. An appellate court maintained that while collateral estoppel prevented the parents' claims, the statute of limitations did not bar their claims against the board and that their federal suit for damages against the estate was not an acceptable substitute for filing under the state's creditor statute.[59]

Parents unsuccessfully filed a negligence claim against a school board for failing to protect their son from a teacher, allegedly a known sexual deviant, who molested him, and against the state for granting a teaching license to a sex offender. An appellate court in Arizona affirmed the dismissal against the state on the basis that it had immunity in licensing and regulating any profession or occupation.[60]

Sexual Abuse by Other Parties

Parents in New York sued child welfare workers, a city, and others on behalf of their daughter and themselves, alleging that her removal from school and being subjected to a medical examination for signs of sexual abuse violated their due process rights and their daughter's right to be free

---

[57] Sherman *ex rel.* Sherman v. Helms, 80 F. Supp.2d 1365 [141 Educ. L. Rep. 689] (M.D. Ga. 2000).

[58] Rambo v. Webster Parish Sch. Bd., 745 So. 2d 770 [140 Educ. L. Rep. 784] (La. Ct. App. 1999).

[59] Cloud *ex rel.* Cloud v. Summers, 991 P.2d 1169 [141 Educ. L. Rep. 343] (Wash. Ct. App. 1999).

[60] Doe *ex rel.* Doe v. State, 7 P.3d 107 [146 Educ. L. Rep. 1117] (Ariz. Ct. App. 2000).

from unreasonable search and seizure. The Second Circuit affirmed that the child's due process and Fourth Amendment rights were violated. The court agreed that the defendants did not violate the substantive due process rights of the child or parents and that individual defendants were entitled to qualified immunity.[61]

Similarly, parents, individually and on behalf of their daughter, sued the Texas Department of Protective and Regulatory Services, its caseworkers and employees, teacher, and others for separating the family during an investigation of possible child abuse alleging deprivations of procedural and substantive due process of the Individuals with Disabilities Education Act (IDEA), and sexual harassment under title IX as well as and negligence and intentional torts under state law. A federal trial court granted the parents' motion for summary judgment for negligent reliance on "facilitated communications."[62]

Youths in a juvenile treatment center who alleged that they were sexually assaulted by a counselor there sued officials for negligent hiring, supervision and retention, negligent and intentional inflection of emotional distress, assault and battery and failure to report child abuse. The federal trial court in North Dakota denied the center's motions for summary judgment on all of the claims except for the intentional torts of its employee.[63] The court also granted the youths a trial regarding punitive damages.

Privacy

A student sued a school board for negligence after he was left unattended in a darkened classroom with another child who was allegedly a convicted juvenile sex offender with a history of violence and predatory sexual assaults against children. In granting the board's motion for protective order to limit the discovery of protected information, an appellate court in Colorado wrote that it had cause to believe that discovery would involve the disclosure of information normally entitled to some degree of confidentiality, including personnel records of current and former school employees, student records, and juvenile arrest and delinquency records.[64]

---

[61] Tenenbaum v. Williams, 193 F.3d 581 [140 Educ. L. Rep. 24] (2nd Cir. 1999).
[62] Morris v. Dearborne, 69 F. Supp.2d 868 [139 Educ. L. Rep. 945] (E.D. Tex. 1999).
[63] Brown v. Youth Servs. Int'l of S.D., 89 F. Supp.2d 1095 [143 Educ. L. Rep. 244] (D.S.D. 2000).
[64] Gillard v. Boulder Valley Sch. Dist. RE.-2, 196 F.R.D. 382 [147 Educ. L. Rep. 618] (D. Colo. 2000).

Where a father who was an elementary school teacher was adjudged to have sexually and physically abused his two daughters, a school board in California obtained permission to disclose juvenile court's records to the state Commission on Teacher Credentialing. On further review, an appellate court affirmed that the purpose of the law was to protect a minor's privacy, not to shield a perpetrator of sexual abuse from the consequences of his behavior.[65]

Search and Seizure

A school security guard who received information that there were drugs and/or weapons in a middle school searched student lockers. When the search led to the discovery of a folding knife and a pager in a book bag, both items that were forbidden on school property, the student unsuccessfully claimed that this violated his Fourth Amendment rights. The Court of Appeals of Maryland affirmed the legality of the search on the basis that since the student has no reasonable expectation of privacy in his locker, the search did not violate the Fourth Amendment.[66]

The parents of a high school student in New Jersey unsuccessfully sued various educators and health care providers alleging not only that their daughter was subjected to an intrusive search of her bodily fluids in violation of the Fourth and Fourteenth Amendments but also that the discussion of these results violated her privacy rights under the Ninth and Fourteenth Amendments. The Third Circuit affirmed that the state statute precluding liability for school and health care providers immunized them for alleged violations of federal law, that the testing of the student's bodily fluids in an attempt to detect the presence of drugs did not violate due process, that the actual testing was not intrusive, and that her privacy rights were not violated when the negative test results were disclosed.[67]

High school students in Louisiana alleged that police officers and a city violated their Fourth Amendment rights by having them called out of class and brought to a vice principal's office for questioning about a rumored after-school fight. A federal trial decided that since the police did not violate the students' Fourth Amendment rights, they were entitled to nominal damages. On further review, the Fifth Circuit reversed in determining that detention of students for questioning did not violate their Fourth Amendment rights since they had a significantly lesser expectation of privacy with regard to the temporary seizure of their persons than the general population and that any privacy right that they may have had did not outweigh the

---

[65] In re R. G., 94 Cal.Rptr.2d 818 [143 Educ. L. Rep. 306] (Cal. Ct. App. 2000).
[66] In re Patrick Y., 746 A.2d 405 [142 Educ. L. Rep. 401] (Md. 2000).
[67] Hedges v. Musco, 204 F.3d 109 [141 Educ. L. Rep. 1020] (3rd Cir. 2000).

board's interest in protecting its students, promoting self-discipline, and deterring violence.[68]

In the first of four cases from Indiana, students challenged a school board's random, suspicionless, drug testing policy for participants in extra-curricular activities and pupils who drove their own vehicles to school. The Seventh Circuit affirmed the use of the policy for participants in athletic and non-athletic extracurricular activities since the board demonstrated a suffi-cient governmental need to test for drugs and alcohol but not for nicotine in students who drove to the campus.[69] The court added that while it was not convinced that participants in non-athletic extracurricular activities should have been subjected to drug testing, it was bound to uphold the board's policy.

Sixth grade students sued a teacher and school board for a strip search designed to recover $38.00 that was left on a cart in a classroom. A federal trial court in Indiana granted the teacher's and board's motions for summary judgment with regard to contractual obligations, offering that an elementary guide book did not establish a contract between the school and the par-ents.[70] The court was of the opinion that the students failed to establish an equal protection violation based on his having only searched students who were from lower socio-economic status. However, the court rejected the teacher's motion for summary judgment on the claim that he violated the students' Fourth Amendment rights.

When a school police officer conducted a routine check of a girls' bath-room, she smelled cigarettes, observed two students in the same stall, confronted them, and conducted a pat down search which led to the discov-ery of a piece of paper containing marijuana. The student who possessed the paper unsuccessfully challenged her adjudication as delinquent. An appellate court in Indiana affirmed that since the pat-down search was justi-fied, it did not violate the student's Fourth Amendment rights.[71]

A juvenile in Indiana sought further review of his adjudication as a delinquent for possessing a firearm on school property, for carrying a hand-gun without a license, and for the revocation of his probation on another adjudication. On further review, the student argued that the trial court erred in admitting a gun into evidence that was discovered during a pat-down

---

[68] Milligan v. City of Slidell, 226 F.3d 652 [147 Educ. L. Rep. 429] (5th Cir. 2000).

[69] Joy v. Penn-Harris-Madison Sch. Corp., 212 F.3d 1052 [144 Educ. L. Rep. 866] (7th Cir. 2000).

[70] Higginbottom *ex rel.* Davis v. Keithley, 103 F. Supp.2d 1075 [146 Educ. L. Rep. 145] (S.D. Ind. 1999).

[71] D. B. v. State, 728 N.E.2d.179 [143 Educ. L. Rep. 1025] (Ind. Ct. App. 2000).

search. An appellate court affirmed that since the officer's pat down search of the juvenile was reasonable in light of her concern for her safety, the gun was properly admitted as evidence.[72]

The father of a middle school student sued a principal, alleging that the search of his daughter based on the suspicion that she violated the school's drinking policy contravened her Fourth Amendment rights. The federal trial court in Maine, entering judgment for the principal, commented that the search was reasonable since it led to evidence of beer drinking in the places searched, the student consented to the search, and the search was conducted in the privacy of a hallway while classes were in session.[73]

In the first of two cases from New York, a high school student who was suspected of truancy was prevented from boarding a train that was to transport her to school for class. Due to being detained and transported to school along with other students who were suspected of truancy, she sued the mayor, city, police department, and the police officer alleging violations of the Fourth Amendment and her right to equal protection. Although permitting her Fourth Amendment and equal protection claims to proceed, a federal trial court granted the police officer's claim that he was entitled to qualified immunity.[74]

Where a gym teacher allegedly confined an eighth grade student in an unlit storage closet and grabbed her arm in an attempt to get her to return a twenty-dollar bill she found on the floor, and that he thought was his, she and her parents sued the teacher and school board, claiming that the confinement was a Fourth Amendment seizure. A federal trial court in New York denied the defendants' motion for summary judgment in contending that material issues of fact existed as to whether the teacher's forcible confinement of the student was an unreasonable seizure and whether he was entitled to qualified immunity.[75] However, the court, in granting his motions for summary judgment, agreed that the teacher did not violate the student's substantive or procedural due process rights and that the board was not liable for the teacher's conduct.

A federal trial court found that a strip search of twenty-two fifth grade students in Georgia to recover $26.00 was disproportionate in relation to the harm it sought to remedy. Even in acknowledging that the search violated the Fourth Amendment, the court held that since the law was not clearly

---

[72] C.S. v. State, 735 N.E.2d 273 [147 Educ. L. Rep. 241] (Ind. Ct. App. 2000).

[73] Greenleaf *ex rel.* Greenleaf v. Cote, 77 F. Supp.2d 168 [140 Educ. L. Rep. 942] (D. Me. 1999).

[74] Colon-Berezin v. Guiliani, 88 F. Supp.2d 272 [143 Educ. L. Rep. 101] (S.D.N.Y. 2000).

[75] Bisignano v. Harrison Cent. Sch. Dist., 113 F. Supp.2d 591 [147 Educ. L. Rep. 529] (S.D.N.Y. 2000).

established at the time of the search, school officials and the board were entitled to qualified immunity.[76]

When a chief of school police was called to a high school to investigate the possibility of three truant students in an unsupervised area, they rejected his order to go to classes and made obscene gestures at him before parking their car on a city street. As the chief peered inside the vehicle, he saw a sawed-off shotgun that was partially wrapped in clothing and a shell. Additional school police opened the vehicle, recovered three guns, the sawed-off shotgun, and turned them over to the city police. The student who owned the car challenged his being convicted of various weapon offenses. An appellate court in Pennsylvania reversed in favor of the student on the basis that the school police had no authority to open the car which was parked on a city street and off school property.[77]

An assistant principal in North Carolina who was informed that a student had a gun in his book bag escorted the pupil to the school office. When the student refused to permit a search of his book bag, he was handcuffed and a security officer and dean of students assisted in the search. The search led to the discovery of a pellet gun inside the book bag. On further review of the student's adjudication as delinquent for possessing a gun on school property, an appellate court affirmed that search was legal since the principal had reasonable grounds to search the book bag and the student knowingly possessed the pellet gun at school.[78]

In the first of two cases from California, when a high school student was approached by police officers who suspected he was truant from school, they informed him that he would be cited for being truant and would be transported to school. On conducting a search of the student's backpack, the police discovered a dagger, but a trial court granted his motion to suppress the evidence. An appellate court reversed in noting that the search was lawful since it was incident to a valid arrest for truancy.[79]

A student who was declared a ward of the state for carrying a locking blade knife at school claimed that since he was detained and searched with-

---

[76] Thomas v. Clayton County Bd. of Educ., 94 F. Supp.2d 1290 [144 Educ. L. Rep. 133] (N.D. Ga. 1999).

[77] Commonwealth v. Williams, 749 A.2d 957 [143 Educ. L. Rep. 951] (Pa. Super. Ct. 2000).

[78] In re Murray, 525 S.E.2d 496 [142 Educ. L. Rep. 546] (N.C. Ct. App. 2000).

[79] In re Humberto O., 95 Cal. Rptr.2d 248 [143 Educ. L. Rep. 609] (Cal. Ct. App. 2000).

out reasonable suspicion, the evidence should have been suppressed. An appellate court in California affirmed on the ground that the security guard who detained the student had reasonable suspicion to do so.[80]

Following the denial of his motion to suppress evidence, a juvenile entered a conditional admission to carrying a deadly weapon on school premises. On further review, an appellate court in New Mexico affirmed that a school resources officer may lawfully search a student at the behest of a school official as long as the search is reasonable given the circumstances, justified at its inception, maintains the scope of its purpose, and is not overly intrusive in light of a student's age and sex.[81]

In Oklahoma, a juvenile challenged his adjudication as delinquent for unlawful possession of marijuana. An appellate court affirmed that a school official may conduct a search on school premises without a warrant when there is reasonable suspicion to believe that a school policy or the law has been or is being violated.[82]

Instructional Issues

When parents in Louisiana enjoined their school board from mandating that a disclaimer be read in all elementary and secondary classes immediately before the teaching of evolution theory, a federal trial court granted their request for attorney fees since the disclaimer constituted an establishment of religion in violation of the First Amendment. On further review, the Fifth Circuit not only affirmed but also rejected the board's motion for an en banc hearing in ascertaining that the disclaimer was not sufficiently neutral to prevent it from violating the Establishment Clause.[83]

Opponents of the Texas Assessment of Academic Skills examination challenged its being used as a requirement for high school graduation on the basis that it violated title VI regulations and the due process right of minority students. A federal trial court was of the view that while the first-time administration of the exit-level test created a legally significant adverse impact for minority students, it lacked the authority to tell the state what a well-educated high school graduate should demonstrably know. Further, in indicating that it may not review the relative merits of teacher evaluation and

---

[80] In re Randy G., 96 Cal. Rptr.2d 338 [144 Educ. L. Rep. 328] (Cal. Ct. App. 2000).

[81] In re Josue T., 989 P.2d 431 [140 Educ. L. Rep. 370] (N.M. Ct. App. 1999).

[82] F.S.E. v. State, 993 P.2d 771 [141 Educ. L. Rep. 1176] (Okla. Crim. App. 1999).

[83] Freiler v. Tangipahoa Parish Bd. of Educ., 201 F.3d 602 [141 Educ. L. Rep. 458] (5th Cir. 2000).

objective testing, the court ruled that the test did not violate either the title VI regulations or the due process right of minority students.[84]

Parents in Connecticut unsuccessfully filed educational malpractice and intentional infliction of emotional distress claims against a school board and an elementary school principal for imposing a teaching method on children that emphasized social skills at the expense of discipline and academics. An appellate court affirmed that since the parents' claim was for educational malpractice and not breach of contract, their allegations did not support the claim of malpractice.[85] However, the court reversed and reinstated the parents' claim with respect to the intentional infliction of emotional distress.

A state initiative proposed a constitutional amendment requiring all students to be taught in English as rapidly and effectively as possible while children whose primary language was other than English would participate in an English immersion program. The initiative permitted parents to seek waivers in order to permit their children to enroll in available bilingual programs while also prohibiting school boards from being required to provide bilingual programs. Prior to the election, the Supreme Court of Colorado reviewed the initiative and judged that since its provision eliminating board powers to require bilingual education was not a separate subject, it violated the single-subject requirement.[86] The court also discerned that the titles and summary of the initiative were materially defective since they failed to summarize the provision that no board could be required to offer a bilingual education program.

Miscellaneous

When a high school football player in Utah came out of a shower, was grabbed by four teammates, forcibly bound to a towel rack with highly adhesive athletic tape, and a girl that he dated was brought in to see what they did, he complained to various school officials. The student then informed the coach that he would not apologize for complaining and no longer wanted to play on the team. The coach angrily dismissed the student from the team and the remainder of the football season was canceled. The federal court in Utah dismissed the case as not significant enough to warrant time in federal court. On further review, the Tenth Circuit reversed and reinstated the claim

---

[84] GI Forum Image De Tejas v. Texas Educ. Agency, 87 F. Supp.2d 667 [142 Educ. L. Rep. 907] (W.D. Tex 2000).

[85] Bell v. Board of Educ. of West Haven, 739 A.2d 321 [139 Educ. L. Rep. 538] (Conn. App. Ct. 1999).

[86] In re Ballot Title 1999-2000 No. 258(A), 4 P.3d 1094 [146 Educ. L. Rep. 513] (Colo. 2000).

in stating that if proven, the coach, board, and various officials could be liable for the student's injuries.[87]

Inmates between the ages of sixteen and twenty-one who were incarcerated in the custody of the New York City Department of Correction filed a class action suit claiming that they were deprived of adequate general and special educational services. The youths alleged that many members of the class received little or extremely limited instruction for significant periods of time. A federal trial court directed the city to provide educational services on the basis that the IDEA applied to children who are incarcerated.[88]

When prisoners under the age of twenty-one or disabled and prisoners under the age of twenty-two sued the state asserting a right to an education, both sides sought further review. The Supreme Court of Washington asserted that the state's basic education and special education acts did not apply to the inmates.[89] The court posited that the inmates were governed by statutes providing for education of juvenile inmates and that the state met the constitutional requirements to provide for an education of children under the age of eighteen. The court concluded that the IDEA did not require the state to provide educational services to individuals over the age of eighteen who were incarcerated in adult prisons.

Parents of an elementary school student unsuccessfully sued their school board and various officials for failing to control bullies who beat their son up, alleging that their not providing protection violated his constitutional rights. A federal trial court in North Carolina granted the defendants' motions to dismiss in explaining that since the parents voluntarily withdrew their son from public school to attend a private school, they could not file a claim for deprivation of due process.[90]

In Kentucky, a fourteen-year-old student took six guns to a high school, shot and killed three female students at the end of a voluntary prayer session, and wounded five other students. When police seized the fourteen year old's computer, they discovered that he accessed computer files that were obscene, pornographic and sexually violent; he also watched a movie which portrays a student massacring his classmates. The parents of female victims then sued the makers and distributors of the video games, the movie, and the obscene internet websites alleging that the shooter's actions caused their children's deaths and loss of income. A federal trial court granted the

---

[87] Seamons v. Snow, 206 F.3d 1021 [142 Educ. L. Rep. 755] (10th Cir. 2000).

[88] Handberry v. Thompson, 92 F. Supp.2d 244 [143 Educ. L. Rep. 799] (S.D.N.Y. 2000).

[89] Tunstall *ex rel.* Tunstall v. Bergeson, 5 P.3d 691 [146 Educ. L. Rep. 528] (Wash. 2000).

[90] Stevenson *ex rel.* Stevenson v. Martin County Bd. of Educ., 93 F. Supp.2d 644 [143 Educ. L. Rep. 856] (E.D.N.C. 1999).

defendants' motions to dismiss on the grounds that they could not have reasonably foreseen that the fourteen year old would commit murder, that the thoughts, ideas and messages contained in video games, movies, and websites were not products for purposes of strict product liability, and that the parents' losses of the potential earnings of their children were not injuries to property that were sufficient to support a claim under federal racketeering statutes.[91]

When an individual sued a school board claiming that his being shot by one of its police officers violated his constitutional rights, the defendants sought to have the suit dismissed based on Eleventh Amendment immunity. The federal trial court in Nevada rejected both the board's motion in decreeing that it was not an arm of the state for Eleventh Amendment purposes and the employees' claims for Eleventh Amendment immunity.[92]

A student sued his school board, individual members, and various school employees for damages for injuries the he sustained after being sent back to class with a peer whom officials knew had previously threatened him with bodily harm. After a trial court rejected the defendants' motions for qualified immunity, they sought further review. An appellate court in New Mexico declined to address the denial of the board's motion but reversed and granted the individuals defendants' motions for summary judgment in observing that nothing in the record supported the proposition that they created or caused the danger that allegedly led to the plaintiff's being stabbed.[93]

Sanctions for Student Misconduct

Generally

African-American parents unsuccessfully filed a civil rights action against a school board and various school personnel, alleging discrimination in handling a harassment charge against him and in demoting him from first grade to kindergarten. The federal trial court in Connecticut granted the defendants' motion for summary judgment on the race discrimination claims. The Second Circuit affirmed that since that the parents failed to show that

---

[91] James v. Meow Media, 90 F. Supp.2d 798 [143 Educ. L. Rep. 500] (W.D. Ky. 2000).

[92] Herrera v. Russo, 106 F. Supp.2d 1057 [146 Educ. L. Rep. 710] (D. Nev. 2000).

[93] Sugg v. Albuquerque Pub. Sch. Dist., 988 P.2d 311 [139 Educ. L. Rep. 689] (N.M. Ct. App. 1999).

school officials acted with deliberate indifference to their son's rights, there was insufficient evidence for a reasonable jury to find that his being transferred represented intentional racial discrimination.[94]

A high school student who participated in a prank that involved breaking into and burning a portion of his high school's football field subsequently sustained a wrist injury while cutting weeds as punishment for his actions. After an appellate court reversed an earlier motion in favor of the coach who imposed the punishment, he sought further review. The Supreme Court of Georgia, in turn, reversed in favor of the coach in maintaining that absent evidence that he acted with actual malice, the coach was entitled to official immunity.[95]

When a student in an alternative school refused to comply with a school's uniform policy, refused to follow an assistant principal's directions and cursed her, he was adjudicated delinquent. On appeal, the Supreme Court of Arizona reversed in pointing out that the student's behavior did not rise to the level of criminal conduct since there was no attempt to threaten or injure any person, or disrupt the school day.[96]

In a second case from Arizona, a student was adjudicated delinquent for abuse of a teacher aide in school because he cursed at her four times while at recess. On further review, an appellate court decided not only that the statute had deleted insults from the definition of abuse but also that his words did not constitute abuse.[97] The court also reasoned that there is a difference between rude behavior and criminal conduct.

A high school student in Pennsylvania filed a civil rights action against a teacher and a school board based on the teacher's having used physical force in disciplining his disruptive or unruly behavior. A federal trial court granted the teacher's motion for summary judgment in determining that the momentary use of physical force did not shock the judicial conscience in violation of the student's right to substantive due process.[98]

In the first of three cases from Texas, a former high school student sued a school board and principal claiming that they violated his constitutional rights when he was suspended for three days, placed in an alternative education program for five days, and told that he would not graduate unless he wrote a letter of apology for taking pictures of the principal's car while it was parked in front of a female teacher's home. After the student filed suit, the

---

[94] Gant *ex rel.* Gant v. Wallingford Bd. of Educ., 195 F.3d 134 [139 Educ. L. Rep. 160] (2nd Cir. 1999).
[95] Adams v. Hazelwood, 520 S.E.2d 896 [139 Educ. L. Rep. 700] (Ga. 1999).
[96] In re Julio L., 3 P.3d 383 [145 Educ. L. Rep. 763] (Ariz. 2000).
[97] In re Paul M., 7 P.3d 131 [146 Educ. L. Rep. 1123] (Ariz. Ct. App. 2000).
[98] Kurilla v. Callahan, 68 F. Supp.2d 556 [139 Educ. L. Rep. 900] (M.D. Pa. 1999).

board permitted him to participate in graduation ceremonies only if he wrote the letters of apology or dropped the lawsuit.[99] A federal trial court rejected the board's motion for summary judgment in remarking that there were material issues of fact with regard to whether the board violated the student's rights.

The next friend of a minor student enjoined a school board's placing him in an alternative education program for disciplinary reasons. On further review, an appellate court dissolved the temporary injunctions, acknowledging that judicial review of the board's action was precluded by a statute which established the disciplinary consequences for specific conduct and the procedural due process entitlement for any student who is so punished.[100]

A high school senior basketball player in Texas who was ticketed by police officers for possessing an alcoholic beverage while attending a party was temporarily suspended from the team. After the student refused to participate in athletic exercises designed to punish him and coaches denied him the opportunity to join the school's baseball team, he and his parents enjoined officials from imposing such a punishment. On further review, an appellate court reversed on the ground that there was insufficient evidence that the student's inability to play baseball in his senior year would prevent him from obtaining an athletic scholarship to attend college.[101]

In Florida, a student sued his school board for damages alleging the excessive use of corporal punishment by school employees. A federal trial court held that since state remedies precluded it from acting, it lacked jurisdiction over the dispute.[102]

A juvenile in Indiana sought further review of his adjudication as delinquent for writing a document which described violent acts to be inflicted upon a peer that would have constituted intimidation if committed by an adult. An appellate court reversed in contending that the student's admission of authorship did not amount to a misdemeanor of intimidation or harassment.[103]

In the first of two cases from Washington, when a teacher learned that a highly emotional student revealed to friends that he had a plan to kill the principal of his school and other board employees, he challenged his adjudi-

---

[99] Riggan v. Midland Indep. Sch. Dist., 86 F. Supp.2d. 647 [142 Educ. L. Rep. 836] (W.D. Tex. 2000).

[100] Hankins v. P.H., 1 S.W.3d 352 [140 Educ. L. Rep. 407] (Tex. App. 1999).

[101] Friona Indep. Sch. Dist. v. King, 15 S.W.3d. 653 [143 Educ. L. Rep. 1106] (Tex. App. 2000).

[102] Carestio v. School Bd. of Broward County, 79 F. Supp.2d 1347 [141 Educ. L. Rep. 629] (S.D. Fla. 1999).

[103] J.T. v. State, 718 N.E.2d 1119 [139 Educ. L. Rep. 595] (Ind. Ct. App. 1999).

cation as guilty of felony harassment. An appellate court affirmed that even though the plan was originally communicated to friends, the circumstances allowed a reasonable person to fear that he might have carried it through.[104]

Similarly, a student who made statements to classmates threatening harm to his teacher sought further review of his being found guilty of intimidating a public school teacher. An appellate court in Washington affirmed that the state does not have to prove intent to carry out the threat, only intent to make the threat, and that the actual threat did intimidate the teacher.[105] However, the panel remanded for additional findings of fact as to whether the student intended to utter the threatening statements and whether they intimidated the teacher.

In Oklahoma, a student challenged a court order continuing an emergency protective order entered on behalf of a teacher after he left a voice mail message threatening to kill her husband if she continued to discipline students. The court affirmed that the teacher had standing to seek such a protective order.[106]

Suspension and Expulsion

A high school student challenged his one-year expulsion for possession of a handgun on school property in violation of the state's Safe Schools Act. The Supreme Court of Appeals of West Virginia affirmed that the mandatory one-year expulsion period in the Act is not unconstitutional and that the principal and board followed the procedures required by law before expelling the student.[107]

On receiving a report that he was drinking in the school parking lot, school officials searched a student's truck, discovered full and empty bottles of beer, and suspended him for five days for possession of alcohol. A trial court reinstated the student on the basis that educators did not provide him with the proper notice as defined in the school's handbook. On further review, the Supreme Court of Mississippi reversed in favor of the board.[108] The court indicated that while the board's action was problematic, its failure to follow the procedures in the handbook did not deny the student of any

---

[104] State v. J.M., 6 P.3d 607 [146 Educ. L. Rep. 893] (Wash. Ct. App. 2000).
[105] State v. Avila, 10 P.3d 486 [147 Educ. L. Rep. 721] (Wash. Ct. App. 2000).
[106] Spielmann v. Hayes *ex rel.* Hayes, 3 P.3d 711 [145 Educ. L. Rep. 781] (Okla. Civ. App. 2000).
[107] J. M. v. Webster County Bd. of Educ., 534 S.E.2d 50 [147 Educ. L. Rep. 351] (W. Va. 2000).
[108] Covington County v. G. W., 767 So. 2d 187 [147 Educ. L. Rep. 752] (Miss. 2000).

substantive or due processes rights and that school officials did not need a search warrant to search his truck.

The mother of a high school student in Illinois, who was expelled from school for his role in an unsuccessful plot to bring guns to school and to shoot administrators and students, appealed the dismissal of her complaint that her son was deprived of due process. The Seventh Circuit reversed in noting that the federal judiciary could assert jurisdiction over the dispute.[109]

In a second case from Illinois, high school students who were expelled for fighting in the stands during a football game sued a school board seeking a reinstatement order. According to a federal trial court, the board's adoption of a zero tolerance policy toward violence met procedural due requirements.[110]

A middle school student and his mother in Arkansas unsuccessfully challenged his expulsion based on his having had an altercation with a teacher. The Eighth Circuit affirmed that the plaintiffs' failed to establish substantive or procedural due process violations in connection with his suspension and expulsion.[111]

On the last day of classes, a high school in Oregon sponsored an activity at a local park, at which four female seniors hid in the stalls of a boys' bathroom and threw water balloons at a group of senior boys when they entered. The school board upheld the suspension of the females who were also denied the opportunity to participate in their commencement ceremony even though they did receive their diplomas. The female students unsuccessfully filed suit for damages under title IX alleging that their actions were retaliation for harassment they experienced from the senior boys. The Ninth Circuit affirmed a grant of summary judgment that had been entered on behalf of the board in agreeing that school officials could not have been liable under title IX for denying the females the opportunity to participate in the graduation ceremony.[112]

In the first of two cases from Ohio, as a deputy sheriff patrolling a high school student parking lot checking for permits placed a citation on the windshield of a car that did not have one, he noticed a gun under the front driver's seat and contacted the assistant principal's office. The student granted officials permission to search his car which led to their uncovering

---

[109] Remer v. Burlington Area Sch. Dist., 205 F.3d 990 [142 Educ. L. Rep. 689] (7th Cir. 2000).

[110] Fuller v. Decatur Pub. Sch. Bd. of Educ., 78 F. Supp.2d 812 [141 Educ. L. Rep. 531] (C.D. Ill. 2000).

[111] London v. Directors of DeWitt Pub. Schs., 194 F.3d 873 [139 Educ. L. Rep. 145] (8th Cir. 1999).

[112] Reese v. Jefferson Sch. Dist. No. 14J, 208 F.3d 736 [143 Educ. L. Rep. 450] (9th Cir.2000).

what turned out to be a plastic toy gun. After becoming belligerent and hostile, including the use of profanity and making threats, the student was expelled for his disruptive behavior and possession of a dangerous weapon. A federal trial court declared not only that the students' procedural due process rights were met but also that the school handbook's provision barring look-alike weapons was not unconstitutionally vague or overbroad.[113]

A high school student challenged his expulsion on the basis that he did not receive notice of the board's intent to expel him. Along with ordering the student's reinstatement since the board failed to comply with statutory requirements that he receive written notice of the intent to expel, a state trial court in Ohio directed school officials to expunge the expulsion from his records and permit him to attend school immediately.[114]

In Hawaii, school officials informed the parents of a high school student who was suspended for attending a school function while allegedly under the influence of alcohol that while he was subject to a maximum of ninety-two days of suspension, they would only impose a five-day penalty if they signed an agreement directing their son complete drug and alcohol counseling. In addition, the student was to be barred from participating in all athletic events for the remainder of the year, was not allowed to make up work for the classes he missed while suspended, and would be denied consideration for athletic or academic awards. The federal trial court granted the parents' request for an injunction on the basis that they were likely to prevail on the merits of their claim that their son violated a state statute prohibiting the possession of alcohol at school.[115]

A high school senior in Washington, on his own time and without school resources, created a web page characterized as the unofficial home page for the high school. The web page featured mock obituaries, an idea that was inspired by a creative writing class, and permitted visitors to vote on who would "die" next. Once the website was brought to the attention of a television station, it received negative press, and the student removed his website from the Internet. Even so, after he was suspended from school for five days, including exclusion from sports participation, the student sought a temporary restraining order on the basis that the suspension would violate his First Amendment rights and that his exclusion from school and sporting

---

[113] Turner v. South-Western City Sch. Dist., 82 F. Supp.2d 757 [142 Educ. L. Rep. 71] (S.D. Ohio 1999).

[114] Adrovet v. Brunswick City Sch. Dist. Bd. of Educ., 735 N.E.2d 995 [147 Educ. L. Rep. 277] (Ohio Com. Pl. 1999).

[115] James P. v. Lemahieu, 84 F. Supp.2d 1113 [142 Educ. L. Rep. 233] (D. Hawaii. 2000).

events was sufficient showing of irreparable injury. A federal trial court granted the student's request since it was satisfied that he showed the substantial likelihood of success on the merits and that missing school and the sporting events were irreparable injuries.[116]

In Alabama, a high school senior who was expelled for having marijuana in her car, which was parked in a school parking lot, rejected the opportunity to attend an alternative school. The student then unsuccessfully sought a preliminary injunction against various school officials. A federal trial court in Alabama wrote that a school policy providing for a range of punishment for violations did not run afoul of equal protection, that school officials did not violate the student's due process rights, and that she was afforded the opportunity to graduate on time.[117]

In the first of two cases from Pennsylvania, a mother enjoined a school board from excluding her daughter from her high school graduation ceremony after she was suspended for violating district policy by possessing alcohol at a school-sponsored event. On further review, an appellate court reversed in favor of the board.[118] The panel offered that the trial court erred in substituting its judgment for that of the board since its actions were not arbitrary, capricious, or prejudicial to the public interest.

An appellate court in Pennsylvania upheld an eighth grade student's expulsion for posting threatening and derogatory comments concerning teachers on his home website. The court was of the opinion not only that the student lacked an expectation of privacy in the website but also that his expulsion did not violate the First Amendment or his right to equal protection.[119]

In New Jersey, a high school senior who was expelled for making a false bomb threat call to the school which led to the evacuation of all students, teachers, and other personnel was adjudicated delinquent, placed on probation which included the requirements that he attend school regularly, with no excused absences and no detentions, that he maintain passing grades, and that he obtain a high school diploma. In the meantime, the board ex-

---

[116] Emmett v. Kent Sch. Dist. No. 415, 92 F. Supp.2d 1088 [143 Educ. L. Rep. 828] (W.D. Wash. 2000).
[117] Hammock ex rel. Hammock v. Keys, 93 F. Supp.2d 1222 [143 Educ. L. Rep 915] (S.D. Ala. 2000).
[118] Flynn-Scarcella v. Pocono Mountain, 745 A.2d 117 [141 Educ. L. Rep. 876] (Pa. Commw. 2000).
[119] J.S. v. Bethlehem Area Sch. Dist., 757 A.2d 412 [146 Educ. L. Rep. 794] (Pa. Commw. Ct. 2000).

pelled him from school. A state court directed the board to provide the student with a free public education until he attained his high school diploma or turned nineteen, whichever occurred first.[120]

A high school student in Maryland sought judicial review of his suspension for verbal assault on a teacher. An appellate court affirmed that the disciplinary sanctions were appropriate since the student received all of the process he was due.[121]

In Indiana, a student who was expelled three days before the end of the first semester successfully challenged the loss of all credit for the classes that he attended. An appellate court affirmed that the school board acted arbitrarily and capriciously in denying the student credit for the entire semester since he only missed three days of class.[122]

Where two high school student athletes in Florida consumed alcohol at a beach, a principal conducted an investigation and suspended them from extracurricular activities for thirty days for violating citizenship standards applicable to athletes. On further review, an appellate court affirmed the suspensions in commenting that participation in extra curricular sports activities is a privilege, not a right.[123]

Desegregation

Desegregation Plan Oversight

Following the remand of a desegregation case in New York, a federal trial court held that the school system still labored under vestiges of de jure segregation and entered a remedial order. On further review, the Second Circuit reversed in part, affirmed in part, and remanded. On rehearing, the Second Circuit reasoned that evidence that the board's curriculum and teaching techniques were insufficiently multi-cultural did not legally constitute a vestige of segregation.[124] The court stated that the alleged low teacher expectations for minority students and racial disparities in achievement test scores were not caused by prior school segregation. Further, the panel pointed

---

[120] State *ex rel.* G. S., 749 A.2d 902 [143 Educ. L. Rep. 944] (N.J. Super. Ct. Ch. Div. 2000).
[121] Mayberry v. Board of Educ. of Anne Arundel County, 750 A.2d 677 [144 Educ. L. Rep. 290] (Md. Ct. Spec. App. 2000).
[122] South Gibson Sch. Bd. v. Sollman, 728 N.E.2d 909 [144 Educ. L. Rep. 634] (Ind. Ct. App. 2000).
[123] L. P. M. v. School Bd. of Seminole County, 753 So. 2d 130 [143 Educ. L. Rep. 411] (Fla. Dist. Ct. App. 2000).
[124] United States v. City of Yonkers, 197 F.3d 41 [140 Educ. L. Rep. 70] (2nd Cir. 1999).

out that the trial court's sweeping remedy exceeded its broad power and the doctrine of municipal incapacity did deny the state's political subdivisions capacity or standing to press their cross claim against the state. However, the panel agreed that the trial court acted within its remedial authority in allocating one-half the annual costs of its previously imposed remedies to the state.

Representatives of a class of school children filed suit in state against Minnesota and various public officials alleging that a city's public schools were segregated on the basis of race and socioeconomic status due to housing and transportation policies and practices. When the suit was removed to federal court, it granted the plaintiffs' motion to return the case to a state venue. On further review, the Eighth Circuit reversed in determining that the trial court erred in remanding a properly removed case on the basis that it lacked jurisdiction.[125] As such, the panel remanded in maintaining that the claims were properly removed to federal court in order to effectuate and prevent the frustration of a consent decree that was in effect until 2002.

In Missouri, a school board sought to invalidate a sua sponte court order declaring the district unitary and dismissing a long-running desegregation case. The Eighth Circuit reversed, concluding both that the court erred in finding that the district was unitary and in dismissing the case without benefit of notice, hearing, argument, or other evidentiary presentation.[126]

An unincorporated association in Florida and two students unsuccessfully sued a school board seeking damages and injunctive relief with respect to alleged racially discriminatory practices. When a federal trial court initially dismissed the claims for injunctive relief for want of standing, the plaintiffs filed an interlocutory appeal. The court subsequently granted the board's motion for summary judgment on the students' claims for damages. On appeal, the Eleventh Circuit dismissed the association's interlocutory appeal with regard to standing and affirmed the grant of summary judgment with regard to the students' claims of disparate impact in observing that they failed to present sufficient evidence that the board acted with a racially discriminatory intent.[127]

Parents in North Carolina challenged race-based methods for admissions by a county's magnet school program. A federal trial court decided

---

[125] Xiong v. State, 195 F.3d 424 [139 Educ. L. Rep. 191] (8th Cir. 1999).

[126] Jenkins ex. rel Jenkins v. State of Mo., 205 F.3d 361 [142 Educ. L. Rep. 646] (8th Cir 2000). *See also* Jenkins v. Missouri, 216 F.3d 720 [145 Educ. L. Rep. 623] (8th Cir. 2000).

[127] Citizens Concerned About Children v. School Bd., 193 F.3d 1285 [139 Educ. L. Rep. 107] (11th Cir. 1999).

that since the county's schools had achieved unitary status, all prior injunctive orders were vacated and dissolved. Citing prohibitions against assigning children to schools or allocating educational opportunities and benefits through strict race-based lotteries, preferences, set-asides or other means, the court ruled in favor of the plaintiffs. After filing notices of appeal, the school board and plaintiffs moved for a stay and additional relief. The court denied the motions in asserting that a stay, pending appeal, was unwarranted and the clarification of the injunction was untimely.[128]

In Kentucky, parents challenged a school board's student assignment plan and racial composition guidelines on the ground that they violated equal protection. A federal trial court decreed that the desegregation order remained in effect which permitted the board to use racial classifications to prevent the re-emergence of racially identifiable schools.[129] The court added that the board's efforts to comply with its order were immune from a constitutional challenge until it was dissolved. In a continuation of the same case, parents again sought to dissolve the desegregation decree. A federal trial court granted the parents' request since the board met the requirements of an initial 1975 decree.[130] The court also reviewed the district's voluntary maintenance plan of assigning African-American students to magnet schools and struck it down as a violation of equal protection. As such, the court directed the board to admit any African-American students who were denied enrollment to a high school prior to the 2000-01 school year. Further, the court called for a new hearing on the plan but would not order an immediate change in the reassignment of students until the 2002-03 school year.

In Ohio, a school board filed two motions, one asking a federal trial court to order the state to pay for fifty percent of its educational reform plan and the second to modify its student assignment plan. The court noted that it lacked the jurisdiction to order the state to pay for the implementation of the reform plan. However, in recognizing that it did have jurisdiction over the student assignment plan, the court scheduled a conference to establish procedures for its oversight.[131]

A federal trial court dissolved a permanent injunction and relinquished jurisdiction in a long-running school desegregation case in Michigan.[132]

---

[128] Capacchione v. Charlotte-Mecklenburg Schs., 190 F.R.D. 170 [140 Educ. L. Rep 696] (W.D.N.C. 1999).

[129] Hampton v. Jefferson County Bd. of Educ., 72 F. Supp.2d 753 [140 Educ. L. Rep. 211] (W.D. Ky. 1999).

[130] Hampton v. Jefferson County Bd. of Educ., 102 F. Supp.2d 358 [145 Educ. L. Rep. 985] (W.D. Ky 2000).

[131] Brinkman v. Gilligan, 85 F. Supp.2d 761 [142 Educ. L. Rep. 353] (S.D. Ohio 1999).

[132] Davis v. School Dist. of City of Pontiac, 95 F. Supp.2d 688 [144 Educ. L. Rep. 200] (E.D. Mich. 2000).

The court ruled that the school board was not required to continue making adjustments in the racial compositions of student bodies once the duty to desegregate was completed through official action. The court was content that the board made a good faith compliance with its decree and eliminated past discrimination.

Remedies

A disagreement over the tuition owed by one district to another relating to students sent to a vocational school led to litigation in Mississippi. The dispute was initially filed in state court but was removed to federal court because the defendant district claimed that the agreement was part of an earlier desegregation order. A federal trial court disagreed in explaining that it lacked original jurisdiction in this dispute since the defendant district did not demonstrate any causal relationship between the agreement on tuition and the desegregation decree.[133]

Conclusion

The range of issues related to operational and organizational tensions between students, school boards, and educational officials strongly suggests that the judiciary is likely to remain engaged in settling disputes between students and their schools. While it is clear that shifting societal norms with respect to First Amendment rights, issues of search and seizure, discipline, attendance, sexual harassment and abuse, and instruction are resulting in increased litigation, the courts appear to be steering toward a posture that supports school boards and officials when their policies and procedures address the substantive rights of students. The interpretations and directives of both state and federal courts have been fairly consistent in pursuing a balanced course of action seeking to safeguard the rights of both school officials and students.

---

[133] Quitman Consol. Sch. Dist. v. Enterprise Sch. Dist., 105 F. Supp.2d 545 [146 Educ. L. Rep. 196] (S.D. Miss. 1999).

3
BARGAINING

Scott McLeod

The author gratefully thanks Evelyn Obeng-Darko, doctoral student in the Urban Educational Leadership Program at the University of Cincinnati, for her assistance in compiling the cases reviewed for this chapter.

Introduction

This chapter reviews litigation related to collective bargaining between school boards and their employee unions. These cases construed various federal and state statutes and are grouped according to subject matter and within subjects. Only two federal cases related to bargaining in elementary and secondary schools this year; a significant plurality of the remaining cases were from Pennsylvania and New York

Labor Organizations

Three cases dealt with practices related to assessing and collecting union fees. In a dispute over agency, or "fair share," fees, the Supreme Judicial Court of Massachusetts affirmed in part that the state Labor Relations Commission was not required to use only one formula for computing agency fees for teachers who were not members of a union.[1] Although the nonmember teachers who brought the suit asked the court to require the Commission to calculate the percentage of chargeable union expenditures to nonchargeable expenditures and then apply it to the dues amount, the court held that the Commission could appropriately calculate the agency fee for nonmember teachers by determining the total of chargeable expenses and then dividing that total by the number of bargaining unit members, even if doing so resulted in a higher fee.

In another case related to fair share fees, an appellate court in Indiana examined whether a state law prohibiting assessment of such fees to union nonmembers applied prospectively or retroactively to existing collective bargaining agreements.[2] The court ruled that since there was no express legislative indication to apply the provisions of the statute retroactively, the statute did not invalidate the provisions of the collective bargaining agreement. However, since there was a genuine issue of material fact regarding the expiration date of the agreement, the court remanded the case for further factual findings regarding the total fees owed by nonmembers.

The Supreme Court of Washington affirmed that a state statute requiring employers to obtain annual written authorization from employees for payroll deductions for political contributions did not apply to the Washington Education Association because the Association, in its role as a labor organization, was not an "employer" under the meaning of the statute.[3] The

---

[1] Belhumeur v. Labor Relations Comm'n, 735 N.E.2d 860 [147 Educ. L. Rep. 260] (Mass. 2000).

[2] New Albany-Floyd County Educ. Ass'n v. Ammerman, 724 N.E.2d 251 [142 Educ. L. Rep. 484] (Ind. Ct. App. 2000).

[3] Evergreen Freedom Found. v. Washington Educ. Ass'n, 999 P.2d 602 [144 Educ. L. Rep. 396] (Wash. 2000).

court also explained that since school boards making payroll deductions for the Association under the state Education Employment Relations and Public Employees Collective Bargaining Acts are not aware of the specific intended use of the funds, they are not legally obligated to seek annual written authorization from their employees.

As reflected by a case before the Supreme Court of Idaho, while at-will contracts normally do not provide due process rights prior to dismissal, they may be present in ancillary agreements. The court concluded that a school bus driver whose at-will contract was terminated was entitled to a fair and impartial hearing under his collective bargaining agreement since he alleged that the board violated public policy by retaliating against him for his union activities.[4]

Collective Bargaining

In the first of two cases from Pennsylvania, an appellate court declared that a school board's ratification of a tentative collective bargaining agreement and subsequent revocation of its acceptance shortly before the union voted to accept it constituted "bad faith" bargaining in violation of its obligation to reduce the agreement to writing and sign it.[5] Although the district argued that under accepted tenets of contract law the agreement was not yet a binding contract, the court was of the view that the state Public Employee Relations Act required the board not to derail the agreement in the finalization stage absent a change of circumstances justifying such an action.

Another appellate court in Pennsylvania affirmed that a school board's maintenance and custodial workers shared a sufficient community of interest with cafeteria employees to be included together in the same bargaining unit. Reasoning that perfect uniformity in conditions of employment was not required, the court indicated that the state Labor Relations Board appropriately considered such factors as "type of work performed, educational and skill requirements, pay scales, hours and benefits, working conditions, interchange of employees, grievance procedures, . . . bargaining history,"[6] and employee desire before certifying the bargaining unit. The court added that the cafeteria managers primarily performed non-supervisory functions and, they were not supervisors who could be excluded from the bargaining unit.

---

[4] Roberts v. Board of Trustees, Pocatello Sch. Dist. No. 25, 11 P.3d 1108 [148 Educ. L. Rep. 502] (Idaho 2000).
[5] Athens Area Sch. Dist. v. Pennsylvania Labor Relations Bd., 760 A.2d 917 [148 Educ. L. Rep. 398] (Pa. Commw. Ct. 2000).
[6] West Perry Sch. Dist. v. Pennsylvania Labor Relations Bd., 752 A.2d 461, 464 [144 Educ. L. Rep. 1001, 1004] (Pa. Commw. Ct. 2000).

The Court of Appeals of New York reversed an earlier judgment and decided that a school board could subcontract out its printing services to a regional Board of Cooperative Educational Services (BOCES) without engaging in the collective bargaining process.[7] Key factors in the court's rationale were that the state Commissioner of Education had the authority to approve contracts between districts and BOCES for services other than just those that are "educational" or "nurturing" and that the state-mandated timetable for boards to contract with BOCES services was extraordinarily short.

A dispute over whether a school board made a "qualified economic offer" (QEO) to its teachers union led an appellate court in Wisconsin to observe that the board's compliance with state statutory requirements created a valid QEO, even when some components of the offer were mathematically incorrect. Stating that mathematical precision was not a precondition to the existence of a QEO, the court was of the opinion that it was sufficient for the board to submit an offer to maintain fringe benefits and minimum salary increases consistent with the state Municipal Employment Relations Act.[8]

Labor

The Supreme Court of South Dakota determined that a school board breached its contract with its maintenance and custodial workers by ordering them not to come in to work during a severe winter storm despite their contractual obligations to do so. Noting that "nothing in the contract suggests that a workday for custodians can be canceled without pay if inclement weather is *too* inclement"[9] and that severe weather is "inevitable" in the state, the court was convinced that the board owed time-and-a-half overtime pay to all workers who either reported to work or made up the time missed.

The Supreme Court of North Dakota affirmed that an elementary school teacher who was required to take his class due to the "unavailability" of music and physical education teachers was not entitled to additional compensation since the school board never paid for "play day" or music rehearsals. The court commented that a board committee and union nego-

---

[7] Vestal Employees Ass'n, NEA/NY, NEA v. Public Employment Relations Bd. of State of New York, 705 N.Y.S.2d 564 [143 Educ. L. Rep. 331] (N.Y. 2000).
[8] Racine Educ. Ass'n v. Wisconsin Employment Relations Comm'n, 616 N.W.2d 504 [147 Educ. L. Rep. 291] (Wis. Ct. App. 2000).
[9] AFSCME-Local 1025 Sioux Falls Sch. Maintenance and Custodial Workers v. Sioux Falls Sch. Dist., 605 N.W.2d 811, 814-815 [141 Educ. L. Rep. 893, 896-897] (S.D. 2000).

tiators agreed that such activities were never intended to be included in the definition of "unavailability" as contained in the collective bargaining agreement.[10]

The Supreme Court of Ohio posited that it had the duty to construe the language of a collective bargaining agreement to avoid a "manifest absurdity." The court decreed that a school board could not abolish the jobs of fourteen school bus drivers and mechanics and lay them off in order to enter into a contract with a private company to perform those jobs.[11]

In a dispute over the non-renewal of the contract of a non-permanent teacher, an appellate court in Oregon affirmed that a school board did not violate its duty to reduce to writing its proposed settlement of his grievance when the teachers union never submitted a conforming written agreement constituting a valid acceptance of its settlement offer. The court judged that the board had not committed a unfair labor practice in refusing to arbitrate the teacher's grievance because a statute existed calling for the imposition of a moratorium on grievances while teachers are on programs of assistance for improvement.[12]

Unfair Labor Practices

An appellate court in Illinois affirmed that the failure of the Chicago School Reform Board of Trustees (CSRBT) to provide information requested by the teachers union constituted an unfair labor practice.[13] The dispute arose when the CSRBT chose not to reassign eighty-eight teachers as part of the reconstitution process of seven Chicago high schools. Insofar as several of the teachers who were not reassigned argued that the interview process used in making reassignments discriminated against them because of their age, race, or union activity, the union requested information about the composition of the interview teams, the questions that were asked in the interviews, and the criteria used regarding reassignment. Although the CSRBT argued that the requested information related to "class staffing and assignment," a prohibited bargaining subject, the court agreed that since

---

[10] Mandan Educ. Ass'n v. Mandan Pub. Sch. Dist. No. 1, 610 N.W.2d 64 [143 Educ. L. Rep. 1054] (N.D. 2000).

[11] Ohio Ass'n of Pub. Sch. Employees/AFSCME, Local 4, AFL-CIO v. Batavia Local Sch. Dist. Bd. of Educ., 729 N.E.2d 743 [144 Educ. L. Rep. 689] (Ohio 2000).

[12] Lane Unified Bargaining Council/SLEA/OEA/NEA v. South Lane Sch. Dist., 9 P.3d 130 [147 Educ. L. Rep. 337] (Or. Ct. App. 2000).

[13] Chicago Sch. Reform Bd. of Trustees v. Illinois Educ. Labor Relations Bd., 734 N.E.2d 69 [147 Educ. L. Rep. 662] (Ill. App. Ct. 2000).

the information instead pertained to issues of retention and discrimination it was relevant to the union's duties as the exclusive bargaining representative.

In an extremely short opinion, an appellate court in New York court affirmed that a school board did not violate its collective bargaining agreement by altering employees' working hours. Asserting that the agreement did not establish the employees' right and entitlement to specific hours of work, the court contended that the board could change their shifts to correct errors in their schedules.[14]

Alternative Dispute Resolution

As in last year's Yearbook, the greatest number of cases pertained to alternative dispute resolution. These cases tended to focus on the arbitrability of particular issues, the content and process of alternative dispute resolution, and judicial review of arbitration proceedings.

In a dispute over who should receive a group health insurance policy refund, the Supreme Court of Kansas affirmed that a teachers union was not required to exhaust administrative remedies before seeking judicial relief when the local board would not have been acting as an impartial arbiter of the claim. The court also remarked that the refund belonged to the teachers rather than the board even though the board paid the insurance premiums since the refund was a product of the subscriber teachers filing fewer and/or smaller claims than were originally anticipated.[15]

Arbitration Agreements

Three case from New York and one from Pennsylvania dealt with arbitrability. In the first, a custodian's union sued the Board of Education of the City of New York for expedited interest arbitration of the requirement that its members purchase certain supplies with funds specially allocated by the school board. An appellate court affirmed that the board had no obligation to submit the dispute to arbitration since its collective bargaining agreement with the union made no mention of such arbitration.[16]

Similarly, another New York appellate court affirmed that a school board was not required to arbitrate a grievance filed on behalf of a retired teacher

---

[14] Maineri v. Syosset Cent. Sch. Dist., 714 N.Y.S.2d 763 (148 Educ. L. Rep. 443] (N.Y. App. Div. 2000).

[15] NEA-Coffeyville v. Unified Sch. Dist. No. 445, Coffeyville Montgomery County, Kansas, 996 P.2d 821 [143 Educ. L. Rep. 388] (Kan. 2000).

[16] Board of Educ. of City of New York v. Local 891, International Union of Operating Engineers, 705 N.Y.S.2d 29 [142 Educ. L. Rep. 1020] (N.Y. App. Div. 2000).

who sought reinstatement of voluntarily-terminated retirement benefits when the bargaining agreement only allowed the union to grieve on behalf of teachers and not retirees.[17]

A third appellate court in New York held that a school board had the obligation, under its collective bargaining agreement with its teachers union, to arbitrate a grievance that a change in the company that administered the employee prescription drug plan would result in inferior coverage compared to the current plan.[18] The court decided that the specific language of the agreement mandated such arbitration even though the change was effected by the board of directors of the regional BOCES rather than the local board.

When a school board in Pennsylvania posted a vacancy for a high school girls' athletic director, it did so in such a way that only one person, the current athletic director at the high school, was eligible for the position. Consequently, the union filed a grievance on behalf of an unsuccessful applicant. An appellate court rejected the board's claim that under state case law supplemental nonprofessional employee positions cannot be covered by arbitration provisions in professional employee collective bargaining agreements. In so doing, the court maintained that the bargaining agreement in question provided the arbitrator with the authority to resolve the dispute. The court was satisfied that since the arbitrator's finding that the board did not use predetermined objective criteria and seniority considerations to fill the vacancy, despite its obligation to do so, was valid, the trial court erred in vacating the award.[19]

Proceedings and Award

Half of the cases pertaining to the content and process of alternative dispute resolutions occurred in Pennsylvania. In a New Jersey case, an appellate court overruled an adjudication by the state Public Employment Relations Commission (PERC) that all salary increment withholdings of non-teaching personnel are disciplinary in nature, regardless of the circumstances.[20] Insofar as evaluative non-disciplinary withholdings are not subject to mandatory arbitration, the court remanded the case back to the PERC to consider whether the withholdings were primarily evaluative or disciplinary.

---

[17] Odessa-Montour Cent. Sch. Dist. v. Odessa-Montour Teachers Ass'n, 706 N.Y.S.2d 771 [143 Educ. L. Rep. 998] (N.Y. App. Div. 2000).

[18] *In re* Richfield Springs Cent. Sch. Dist., 705 N.Y.S.2d 709 [143 Educ. L. Rep. 339] (N.Y. App. Div. 2000).

[19] School Dist. of City of Erie v. Erie Educ. Ass'n, 749 A.2d 545 [143 Educ. L. Rep. 595] (Pa. Commw. Ct. 2000).

[20] Randolph Township Bd. of Educ. v. Randolph Educ. Ass'n, 746 A.2d 507 [142 Educ. L. Rep. 426] (N.J. Super. Ct. App. Div. 2000).

A dispute before the Supreme Court of Pennsylvania concerned whether an arbitratorion award drew its essence from the collective bargaining agreement. Where construction of a phrase contained in the agreement, "years of service in public education," was dispositive as to whether a retired teacher was to be credited with thirty years of service and additional retirement benefits under the agreement, the court indicated that since the arbitrator properly interpreted the phrase as ambiguous he correctly relied on the board's past practice in construing the phrase. The court concluded that since the arbitrator's direction to the board to use the state Public School Employees' Retirement Code, which included maternity leave and military service in addition to actual service time, to calculate appropriate credit for service was valid, it had to treat the retiree in the same manner as other similarly-situated employees.[21]

Similarly, an intermediate appellate court in Pennsylvania affirmed that the term "furlough," as used in a collective bargaining agreement between a school board and its teachers, was ambiguous. The court was of the opinion that an arbitrator appropriately looked to the agreement's language, context, and other "indicia of the parties' intention" to construe the term as meaning that the demotions of ten teachers to part-time status was barred under the agreement's "no furlough" provision.[22]

Two other cases in Pennsylvania also concerned whether arbitration awards drew their essence from collective bargaining agreements. In the first, where a school board hired a person who was not a member of the union to be a head football coach, an appellate court affirmed that a grievance over whether the board violated a provision in the agreement requiring that all extra pay positions first be offered to union members was procedurally and substantively arbitrable since there was a dispute as to how the provision should be interpreted.[23] In the other, an appellate court affirmed that an arbitration award did not draw its essence from the collective bargaining agreement. The court declared that since the agreement explicitly preserved the school board's right to initiate and adopt policies relating to inherent management prerogatives without consultation or approval of the teachers union, the arbitrator's calling for the union's consent before implementing a new student honor roll policy was invalid.[24]

---

[21] Danville Area Sch. Dist. v. Danville Area Educ. Ass'n, PSEA/NEA, 754 A.2d 1255 [146 Educ. L. Rep. 247] (Pa. 2000).

[22] Greater Nanticoke Area Sch. Dist. v. Greater Nanticoke Area Educ. Ass'n, 760 A.2d 1214 [148 Educ. L. Rep. 410] (Pa. Commw. Ct. 2000).

[23] Penn-Delco Sch. Dist. v. Penn-Delco Educ. Ass'n, 754 A.2d 51 [145 Educ. L. Rep. 693] (Pa. Commw. Ct. 2000).

[24] Rochester Area Sch. Dist. v. Rochester Educ. Ass'n, PSEA/NEA, 747 A.2d 971 [142 Educ. L. Rep. 1011] (Pa. Commw. Ct. 2000).

In the first of two cases involving an arbitrator's ability to reinstate personnel, an appellate court in Indiana upheld an arbitrator's determination that he had no authority to reinstate a non-permanent teacher whose school board followed state-mandated procedures in not renewing her contract where state law gave the board "unfettered discretion" not to continue a nonpermanent teacher's contract.[25] Similarly, an appellate court in Illinois reasoned that since a school board's exclusive statutory power to discharge all teachers pertained to full-time substitutes, it could not delegate such authority to an arbitrator as part of a collective bargaining agreement without violating state law.[26]

Two other cases upheld the ability of arbitrators to modify disciplinary sanctions against employees. In Ohio, an appellate court noted that since an arbitrator's nullification of a school board's three-day suspension of a high school teacher for failing to report serious student misbehavior drew its essence from the collective bargaining agreement, it was appropriate. The court pointed out that since the arbitrator's comment that the teacher's "ordeal" of defending himself helped him to understand the board's concerns was not a determination in excess of the arbitrator's authority, the grievance process was sufficient discipline in and of itself.[27]

Similarly, an appellate court in Pennsylvania court upheld an arbitrator's ability to rescind a demotion and impose a five-day suspension on a painter whose overspray damaged twenty-six vehicles in a school parking lot because he failed to use protective sheeting on a windy day. The court affirmed that the agreement between the school board and the painter's union provided for the use of progressive discipline, that the painter had not previously been subject to discipline by the board, and that the agreement neither defined "progressive discipline" nor precluded the arbitrator from substituting her own disciplinary sanction for that chosen by the board.[28]

A federal trial court in Florida decreed that an African-American maintenance employee was not barred from suing his school board for racial employment discrimination in violation of title VII of the Civil Rights Act of 1964, despite losing his claim of wrongful dismissal in arbitration where none of his title VII claims were raised.[29] The employee claimed that the

---

[25] North Miami Educ. Ass'n v. North Miami Community Schs., 736 N.E.2d 749 [148 Educ. L. Rep. 445] (Ind. Ct. App. 2000).

[26] Chicago Sch. Reform Bd. of Trustees v. Illinois Educ. Labor Relations Bd., 721 N.E.2d 676 [143 Educ. L. Rep. 314] (Ill. App. Ct. 1999).

[27] Princeton City Sch. Dist. Bd. of Educ. v. Princeton Ass'n of Classroom Educators, OEA/NEA, 731 N.E.2d 186 [145 Educ. L. Rep. 471] (Ohio Ct. App. 1999).

[28] Abington Sch. Dist. v. Abington Sch. Serv. Personnel Ass'n/AFSCME, 744 A.2d 367 [141 Educ. L. Rep. 191] (Pa. Commw. Ct. 2000).

[29] Silvera v. Orange County Sch. Bd., 87 F. Supp.2d 1265 [142 Educ. L. Rep. 966] (M.D. Fla. 2000).

discrimination occurred when he was dismissed for a non-adjudicated arrest for a lewd assault of a minor child seventeen years previous while a white worker who committed a similar offense was reassigned rather than fired. Explaining that a jury could have reasonably believed that the board's reasons for distinguishing between the employees were "unworthy of credence," the court upheld a jury award of damages for back pay, front pay, interest, and its denial of compensatory damages.

Judicial Review and Enforcement of Decisions

In the first of two cases pertaining to judicial review of arbitration awards, the Supreme Judicial Court of Maine affirmed that a ten-day unpaid suspension of a teacher for use of questionable force against a student was a more appropriate disciplinary sanction than dismissal. Although the school board argued that the arbitrator's application of the heightened standard of proof of "clear and convincing evidence" to its allegation against the teacher was contrary to the state teacher dismissal law, the court was of the opinion that the arbitrator's error of law did not compel it to vacate the award.[30]

In contrast, an appellate court in Massachusetts overturned an arbitrator's reinstatement of a teacher who was dismissed for using physical force against his sixth-grade students. Recognizing the generally-accepted principle that a court may vacate an award only if an arbitrator exceeds his or her powers, the court observed that the award exceeded the arbitrator's authority because his decision offended well-established public policy against the use of physical force by teachers against students except to protect themselves or others.[31]

Labor Relations Boards and Proceedings

Two cases related to state labor relations boards and their proceedings. In the first, an appellate court affirmed that the Pennsylvania Labor Relations Board had sufficient evidence to justify its assertion that a union member was not promoted to a principalship due to anti-union animus. The court acknowledged that during her interview with the school board the plaintiff was questioned about her union involvement and the successful candidate was not.[32]

---

[30] Union River Valley Teachers Ass'n v. Lamoine School Comm., 748 A.2d 990 [143 Educ. L. Rep. 558] (Me. 2000).
[31] School Dist. of Beverly v. Geller, 737 N.E.2d 873 [148 Educ. L. Rep. 461] (Mass. App. Ct. 2000).
[32] Uniontown Area Sch. Dist. v. Pennsylvania Labor Relations Bd. *ex rel.* Uniontown Area Educ. Ass'n, 747 A.2d 1271 [143 Educ. L. Rep. 268] (Pa. Commw. Ct. 2000).

In the other case, the Supreme Court of Vermont ruled that the State Labor Relations Board erred in failing to defer to arbitration over whether a school board had the authority, under its collective bargaining agreement with its teachers and support personnel, to contract out custodial work to a private company since resolution of the dispute involved interpretation of the contract.[33]

Wages and Hours Regulations

The last three cases in this chapter pertain to state and federal wages and hours regulations. The Supreme Court of Minnesota affirmed the severance of a provision, from a state omnibus tax statute, requiring school boards to comply with the state's prevailing wage act for all construction projects in excess of $100,000. The court agreed that since the provision violated the Single Subject and Title Clause of the state constitution it could be severed from the rest of the statute.[34]

In a federal case involving the Fair Labor Standards Act (FLSA) and employees of the New York City public schools and other government agencies, the Second Circuit held that an employer with the actual practice of making impermissible pay deductions "necessarily has no intention of paying its employees on a salary basis and, therefore, cannot claim that its employees are exempt from the overtime pay requirements [of the FLSA]."[35] The court added that a determination of whether an employer actually has such a practice cannot be answered by dividing the number of impermissible pay deductions by the number of managerial employees but also must involve the consideration of factors such as the "number of times that other forms of discipline are imposed, the number of employee infractions warranting discipline, the existence of policies favoring or disfavoring pay deductions, the process by which sanctions are determined, and the degree of discretion held by the disciplining authority."[36] The court concluded that it could consider the agency employers either as separate entities or as a whole when making such a judgment and that although employees could not recover damages or back pay for violations of the FLSA prior to any applicable limitations date, it could also take any impermissible deductions that occurred before that date into account in evaluating whether an actual practice of imposing such deductions existed.

---

[33] Milton Educ. and Support Ass'n v. Milton Bd. of Sch. Trustees, 759 A.2d 479 [147 Educ. L. Rep. 633] (Vt. 2000).
[34] Associated Builders and Contractors v. Ventura, 610 N.W.2d 293 [144 Educ. L. Rep. 1040] (Minn. 2000).
[35] Yourman v. Giuliani, 229 F.3d 124, 130 [147 Educ. L. Rep. 905, 911] (2nd Cir. 2000).
[36] Id.

4
STUDENTS WITH DISABILITIES

Allan G. Osborne, Jr.

Introduction

As the United States enters the new millennium, litigation over the rights of students with disabilities continues as unabated as it had during the past two and one-half decades. As is customary, the litigation in 2000 appertained to procedural issues and contested placement decisions under the Individuals with Disabilities Education Act (IDEA).[1] Many of the procedural cases dealt with the development of Individual Education Plans (IEPs) and the IDEA's status quo provision. Most of the lawsuits on substantive issues centered on whether a school board offered a student a free appropriate public education (FAPE). As in past years, a large number of cases concerned reimbursement of legal expenses to prevailing parents in special education disputes.

Students with disabilities have rights under other laws in addition to the IDEA. Thus, lawsuits were filed under section 504 of the Rehabilitation Act,[2] the Americans with Disabilities Act (ADA),[3] and the IDEA. In most of these cases, plaintiffs alleged that students were subjected to discriminatory treatment on the basis of a disability.

Entitlement to Services

The IDEA requires school boards to provide students with disabilities with a FAPE consisting of any needed special education and related services.[4] Yet, the IDEA does not establish any substantive standards by which to judge the adequacy of those services. The IDEA provides that a child is to be afforded specially designed instruction[5] in conformance with the student's IEP.[6] The Supreme Court has held that a student with disabilities is entitled to personalized instruction with support services sufficient to permit the child to benefit from the education provided.[7] The lower courts have been cautioned not to impose their views of preferable educational methods on school districts;[8] however, frequently, they are asked to consider what level of services is required to meet the IDEA's minimum standards. Students attending private schools also are entitled to some benefits of the IDEA.[9]

---

[1] 20 U.S.C. § 1400 *et seq.*
[2] 29 U.S.C. § 794.
[3] 42 U.S.C. §§ 12101 - 12213.
[4] 20 U.S.C. §§ 1401(8) and 1412(a)(1)A).
[5] 20 U.S.C. § 1401(25).
[6] 20 U.S.C. §§ 1401(11) and 1414(d).
[7] Board of Educ. of Hendrick Hudson Cent. Sch. Dist. v. Rowley, 458 U.S. 176 [5 Educ. L. Rep. 34] (1982).
[8] *Id.*
[9] 20 U.S.C. § 1412(a)(10)(A)(i).

A federal trial court in New York issued yet another decision in a long-standing dispute over the rights of a parochial school student to receive on-site special education services. In the latest round of litigation, the court, on remand from the Second Circuit, found that the school board was not required to provide the student with the necessary services on-site.[10] The court explained that the provision of the requested services was permissive, rather than compulsory, under the 1997 version of the IDEA.

The Eighth Circuit ruled that under the 1997 IDEA Amendments, since parents in Nebraska unilaterally placed their child in a private residential facility, they had no right to an order directing a school board to provide those services a particular location.[11] The court noted that prior to being placed in the nursing facility, the student had received the requested services at home.

In a case from Nevada, the Ninth Circuit affirmed in part that the IDEA leaves discretion to the states to consider whether home education that is exempted from the state's compulsory attendance requirements constitutes an IDEA-qualifying private school.[12] In so doing, the court agreed that a student who is home-schooled is not entitled to receive publicly funded speech therapy services.

The Second Circuit affirmed that an academically gifted student in Vermont with emotional and behavioral problems was not entitled to special education.[13] The court agreed with a hearing officer who declared that the student was ineligible for services because he was performing at or above grade norms in basic skill areas.

Procedural Safeguards

The IDEA contains an elaborate system of due process safeguards to ensure that students with disabilities are properly identified, evaluated, and placed pursuant to its mandates.[14] The Act states that the parents or guardian of a child with disabilities must be provided with the opportunity to participate in the development of the IEP for and placement of their child.[15]

---

[10] Russman v. Board of Educ. of the Enlarged City Sch. Dist. of the City of Watervliet, 92 F. Supp.2d 95 [143 Educ. L. Rep. 784] (N.D.N.Y. 2000).

[11] Jasa v. Millard Pub. Sch. Dist. No. 17, 206 F.3d 813 [142 Educ. L. Rep. 750] (8th Cir. 2000).

[12] Hooks v. Clark County Sch. Dist., 228 F.3d 1036 [147 Educ. L. Rep. 870] (9th Cir. 2000).

[13] J.D. v. Pawlet Sch. Dist., 224 F.3d 60 [147 Educ. L. Rep. 39] (2d Cir. 2000).

[14] 20 U.S.C. § 1415.

[15] 20 U.S.C. §§ 1414(d)(1)(B)(i) and 1414(f).

The IDEA also requires school boards to provide written notice and obtain parental consent prior to evaluating a child[16] or making an initial place- ment.[17] Once a student has been placed in special education, a school board must provide parents with proper notice before initiating a change in place- ment.[18] Once placed, a child's situation must be reviewed at least annually[19] and the student must be reevaluated at least every three years.[20]

Under the IDEA, the parents of a student with disabilities may be entitled to an independent evaluation at public expense if they disagree with a school board's evaluation.[21] At the same time, a board may challenge a parental request for an independent evaluation in an administrative hearing, and if it turns out that the board's evaluation was appropriate, the parents are not entitled to have an independent evaluation at public expense.[22]

The IDEA stipulates that an IEP must contain statements of a student's current educational performance, annual goals and short term objectives, the specific educational services to be provided, the extent to which the child can participate in general education, the date of initiation and duration of services, and evaluation criteria to evaluate whether the objectives are being met.[23] An IEP must also include statements concerning how a child's disability affects his or her ability to be involved in and progress in the general educational curriculum along with statements regarding any modifi- cations that may be needed to allow the child to participate in the general curriculum.

Evaluation and Classification

The Seventh Circuit affirmed that a mother in Illinois who, due to her failure to cooperate by refusing to give school officials a reasonable oppor- tunity to evaluate her son, forfeited any claim for tuition reimbursement for unilaterally placing him in a private school.[24] The court rejected the mother's request because after her son was not allowed to return to a parochial school, she enrolled him in a private residential school without first giving public school personnel an opportunity to evaluate his condition.

---

[16] 20 U.S.C. § 1414(a)(1)(C).
[17] 20 U.S.C. § 1415(b)(3).
[18] 20 U.S.C. § 1415(b)(3)(A).
[19] 20 U.S.C. § 1414(d)(4)(A).
[20] 20 U.S.C. § 1414(a)(2)(A).
[21] 20 U.S.C. § 1415(b)(1).
[22] 34 C.F.R. § 300.502(b).
[23] 20 U.S.C. § 1414(d)(1)(A).
[24] Patricia P. v. Board of Educ. of Oak Park and River Forest High Sch. Dist. No. 200, 203 F.3d 462 [141 Educ. L. Rep. 986] (7th Cir. 2000).

A federal trial court in Mississippi decreed that a school board violated the IDEA by failing to provide an assessment procedure after parents had made requests to have their son evaluated.[25] The student, who had attention deficit disorder, was expelled for one year for violating the board's zero tolerance policy because he possessed a small knife.

Where school officials developed an IEP for a student who was placed in a private therapeutic treatment center after her stay there ended, her parents challenged the IEP, in part based on how the assessment was conducted. The federal district court in Maryland indicated that the parent's contention, that the student was not assessed in all areas related to her disability, was meritless.[26] The court acknowledged that evidence revealed that the board's psychologist evaluated the information provided by the parents and considered reports from the treatment center in doing so.

In a dispute involving the method by which a severely deaf student in Pennsylvania was to be re-evaluated, the Third Circuit reasoned that parents can be reimbursed for an independent evaluation only by showing that a school board's proposed evaluation would be inappropriate.[27] After a board planned to conduct the evaluation using its own personnel and a sign-language interpreter, the parents objected and obtained an independent evaluation at a school for the deaf whose personnel could communicate directly with the child via sign language. The court found that since the parents' claim, that the board's proposed evaluation was inappropriate was based on expert opinions, not statutory or regulatory language, it did not have the force of law.

Following her expulsion, the parents of a student who attended a private school sought to have her classified as disabled since a school board and independent evaluators disagreed as to whether she was seriously emotionally disturbed. A federal trial court in Tennessee, viewing the evidence as cloudy, pointed out that the preponderance of the evidence revealed that the student suffered from an emotional disturbance as defined by the IDEA because her behavior was inappropriate under normal circumstances and she exhibited behavioral problems over the course of her lifetime.[28]

---

[25] Colvin v. Lowndes County, Miss. Sch. Dist., 114 F. Supp.2d 504 [147 Educ. L. Rep. 601] (N.D. Miss. 1999).

[26] Briley v. Board of Educ. of Baltimore County, 87 F. Supp.2d 441 [142 Educ. L. Rep. 894] (D. Md. 1999).

[27] Holmes v. Millcreek Township Sch. Dist., 205 F.3d 583 [142 Educ. L. Rep. 667] (3d Cir. 2000).

[28] Johnson v. Metro Davidson County Sch. Sys., 108 F. Supp.2d 906 (M.D. Tenn. 2000).

Development of Individualized Education Programs

In a dispute challenging a proposed IEP for a student who transferred from a therapeutic treatment center, the federal trial court in Maryland observed that a school board did not commit a material procedural violation of the IDEA.[29] The court noted that although school officials had not contacted personnel from the treatment center while actually developing the IEP, they obtained data from the center and used it in formulating the IEP. Also, the court was satisfied that although a regular education teacher was not part of the team that developed the IEP, the team considered grade reports from the treatment center.

The Sixth Circuit, in a dispute involving methodology for educating a student with autism from Michigan, rejected the parents' contention that their school board was required to include an expert in the methodology they preferred on the IEP team.[30] The court affirmed that the IDEA's requirement that the IEP team include persons knowledgeable about placement options did not call for the presence of an expert in the parents' chosen methodology at the meeting.

School district personnel sometimes draft IEPs and present them for consideration and discussion at IEP conferences, a practice that the Eighth Circuit upheld in a case from Missouri. The court posited that nothing in the IDEA or its regulations prohibits school officials from coming to a meeting with tentative recommendations for an IEP.[31] The court added that the school board could not be faulted for failing to engage in an open discussion with the student's parents about placement options since they refused to participate in a discussion with school officials because they abruptly left an IEP conference when the educators made a placement recommendation that was not what they sought.

The parents of a student with disabilities claimed that school board personnel abused the IEP process through excessive meetings, misstatements of their purposes, and using them as a tool of harassment. The federal trial court in Colorado rejected the parents' claims on the basis that they failed to state a cause of action because the IDEA does not address misuse of the process.[32] On the other hand, the federal trial court in Connecticut

---

[29] Briley v. Board of Educ. of Baltimore County, 87 F. Supp.2d 441 [142 Educ. L. Rep. 894] (D. Md. 1999).
[30] Dong v. Board of Educ. of the Rochester Community Schs., 197 F.3d 793 [140 Educ. L. Rep. 116] (6th Cir. 1999).
[31] Blackmon v. Springfield R-XII Sch. Dist., 198 F.3d 648 [140 Educ. L. Rep. 519] (8th Cir. 1999).
[32] O'Hayre v. Board of Educ. for Jefferson County Sch. Dist. R-1, 109 F. Supp.2d 1284 [146 Educ. L. Rep. 1065] (D. Colo. 2000).

was convinced that a board was justified in refusing to conduct an IEP meeting at a parent's request since a large number of IEP meetings had already taken place and all of the issues raised by the parent were discussed and investigated.[33]

Change in Placement

In the first to two cases from New York, a federal trial court ascertained that once parents receive a final administrative review in their favor, the current educational placement changes in accordance with that decision.[34] The court commented that an adjudication by either a state hearing officer in a one-tiered administrative hearing system or a state reviewing officer (or panel) in a two-tiered system constitutes an agreement by the state under the status quo provision of the IDEA. At the same time, the federal trial court in Connecticut maintained that the stay put placement for a student with disabilities was the mainstream setting in which he was placed by mutual consent of his parents and school board when they could not reach agreement on an IEP.[35]

A state court in New York contended that the filing of a person in need of supervision petition by school personnel constituted a change of placement.[36] The court remarked that since the student at issue was neither charged with committing a crime nor was subject to a juvenile delinquency proceeding, the filing of the petition posed a threat to his educational program.

Minor changes to a student's IEP traditionally are not viewed as a change in placement. The Tenth Circuit held that the elimination of a certain type of occupational therapy for a student in New Mexico, known as hippotherapy, when occupational therapy itself was still provided did not contravene the IDEA.[37] Where a school board in Maryland made minor changes to a student's schedule but did not alter the goals and objectives of his IEP or change the amount of special education services he received, the federal trial court judged that a change in placement had not occurred.[38]

---

[33] Lillbask *ex rel.* Mauclaire, v. Sergi, 117 F. Supp.2d 182 [148 Educ. L. Rep. 248] (D. Conn. 2000).
[34] Murphy v. Arlington Cent. Sch. Dist. Bd. of Educ., 86 F. Supp.2d 354 [142 Educ. L. Rep. 810] (S.D.N.Y. 2000).
[35] Warton v. New Fairfield Bd. of Educ., 125 F. Supp.2d 22 [150 Educ. L. Rep. 217] (D. Conn. 2000).
[36] *In re* Beau II, 702 N.Y.S.2d 654 [142 Educ. L. Rep. 446] (N.Y. App. Div. 1999).
[37] Erickson v. Albuquerque Pub. Schs., 199 F.3d 1116 [140 Educ. L. Rep. 894] (10th Cir. 1999).
[38] Cavanagh v. Grasmick, 75 F. Supp.2d 446 [140 Educ. L. Rep. 643] (D. Md. 1999).

Similarly, the federal trial court in New Jersey wrote that a student's transfer from one high school to another, where his instructional program at the two schools was practically identical, was not a change in placement.[39]

On the other hand, substantial changes are generally treated as a change in placement. The federal trial court in New Hampshire offered that a transfer from a private residential school to a public high school program constituted a change in placement.[40] The court discerned that although the student was too old to continue at his private school, another private school would have provided an experience substantially similar to that of his previous school.

Where a school board in Maine intended for a specific placement to be only temporary, and made its intentions clearly known, the First Circuit affirmed that an interim placement does not automatically become the status quo placement.[41] The court believed that the parents and board had reached a settlement agreement whereby the child was to be placed in a private school for the remainder of the academic year. Even though the agreement specifically included a statement that the student would return to a public school at the end of the academic year, his parents contested that move. A hearing officer ordered that pending a resolution of the dispute on its merits, the child's placement was to be in a public school. After the federal trial court denied the parents' request for a preliminary injunction to maintain the student's placement at the private school, the appellate panel affirmed that, under the circumstances, the private school setting was not necessarily his then current placement.

In a case from Pennsylvania, the Third Circuit affirmed that the IDEA's status quo provision did not require a school board to implement an IEP developed in another state without considering how consistent it was with the policies and mandates of the student's new state.[42] The court declared that when a student moves from one state to another, any prior IEP need not be treated by the new state as automatically continuing in effect.

---

[39] J.S. *ex rel.* D.S. v. Lenape Reg'l High Sch. Dist. Bd. of Educ., 102 F. Supp.2d 540 [145 Educ. L. Rep. 1010] (D.N.J. 2000).

[40] Henry v. School Admin. Unit #29, 70 F. Supp.2d 52 [140 Educ. L. Rep. 139] (D.N.H. 1999).

[41] Verhoeven v. Brunswick Sch. Comm., 207 F.3d 1 [143 Educ. L. Rep. 54] (1st Cir. 1999).

[42] Michael C. v. Radnor Township Sch. Dist., 202 F.3d 642 [141 Educ. L. Rep. 495] (3d Cir. 2000).

Dispute Resolution

If parents disagree with any of a school board's actions regarding a proposed IEP or any aspect of a FAPE, they may request an impartial due process hearing.[43] Any party not satisfied with the final result of administrative proceedings may appeal to the state or federal courts;[44] however, all administrative remedies must be exhausted prior to resorting to judicial review unless it is futile to do so. While an administrative or judicial action is pending, a school board may not change a student's placement without parental consent,[45] a hearing officer's order,[46] or a judicial decree.[47]

The IDEA empowers the courts to review the record of the administrative proceedings, hear additional evidence, and "grant such relief as the court determines is appropriate" based on the preponderance of evidence standard.[48] Even so, the Supreme Court has cautioned judges not to substitute their views of proper educational methodology for that of competent school authorities.[49] Insofar as the IDEA does not contain a statute of limitations for filing suit, courts must borrow one from analogous state statutes.

In 1997 Congress amended the IDEA to insert language that provided for the resolution of disputes through a mediation process as an alternative to an adversarial proceeding.[50] Even so, it is important to recall that since mediation is voluntary, it may not be used to deny or delay a parent's right to an administrative hearing.

The IDEA is not the exclusive avenue through which parents may enforce the rights of their child(ren) with disabilities. The IDEA specifically stipulates than none of its provisions can be interpreted as restricting or limiting the rights, procedures, and remedies available under the Constitution, section 504, or other federal statutes protecting the rights of students with disabilities.[51] Lawsuits are frequently filed under section 504, the ADA, and section 1983 of the Civil Rights Act of 1871[52] in addition to the IDEA.

---

[43] 20 U.S.C. §§ 1415(f) and 1415(g).
[44] 20 U.S.C. § 1415(i)(2)(B).
[45] 20 U.S.C. § 1415(j).
[46] 20 U.S.C. § 1415(k)(2).
[47] Honig v. Doe, 484 U.S. 305 [43 Educ. L. Rep. 857] (1988).
[48] 20 U.S.C. § 1415(i)(2)(B).
[49] Board of Educ. of Hendrick Hudson Cent. Sch. Dist. v. Rowley, 458 U.S. 176 [5 Educ. L. Rep. 34] (1982).
[50] 20 U.S.C. § 1415(e).
[51] 20 U.S.C. § 1415(l).
[52] 42 U.S.C. § 1983.

Administrative Hearings

Courts continue to rule that parents must exhaust all administrative remedies prior to filing suit. A federal trial court in New York granted a school board's motion for summary judgment in finding no evidence of any exceptions to the exhaustion requirement in a case where the parent went directly to court to contest an alleged change in placement.[53] Similarly, the federal trial court in Colorado dismissed a suit in explaining that the parents' allegations did not address any of the exceptions to the exhaustion requirement and that administrative review would not have been futile.[54]

In the first of two cases from the First Circuit that arose in Rhode Island, the panel affirmed that parents withdrawal of a request for a due process hearing did not render the administrative process futile.[55] The First Circuit also affirmed that since a retaliation claim was related to the identification, evaluation, or educational placement of a student with a disability, it was subject to the exhaustion requirement.[56]

Where the father of a special education student who was expelled filed suit alleging constitutional and statutory violations, the federal trial court in Massachusetts directed him to exhaust administrative remedies because relief was available under the IDEA.[57] At the same time, the federal trial court in Connecticut dismissed a class action suit which alleged that minority students were misidentified as mentally retarded.[58] In asserting that the plaintiffs failed to exhaust administrative remedies, the court stated that claims of misidentification were the type of charges that should have been addressed in a due process hearing.

In an ongoing case from Michigan, a federal trial court once again ruled that parents, who were seeking tuition reimbursement, had to exhaust administrative remedies in a dispute over whether a school board's proposed IEP was inadequate.[59] The mother of a student in Pennsylvania who was classified as mentally retarded contested five years of her daughter's educa-

---

[53] Rabideau v. Beeckmantown Cent. Sch. Dist., 89 F. Supp.2d 263 [143 Educ. L. Rep. 202] (N.D.N.Y. 2000).

[54] O'Hayre v. Board of Educ. for Jefferson County Sch. Dist. R-1, 109 F. Supp.2d 1284 [146 Educ. L. Rep. 1065] (D. Colo. 2000).

[55] Rose v. Yeaw, 214 F.3d 206 [145 Educ. L. Rep. 140] (1st Cir. 2000).

[56] Weber v. Cranston Sch. Comm., 212 F.3d 41 [144 Educ. L. Rep. 808] (1st Cir. 2000).

[57] Demers *ex rel.* Demers v. Leominster Sch. Dep't, 96 F. Supp.2d 55 [144 Educ. L. Rep. 487] (D. Mass. 2000).

[58] Mrs. M. v. Bridgeport Bd. of Educ., 96 F. Supp.2d 124 [144 Educ. L. Rep. 491] (D. Conn. 2000).

[59] Kuszewski v. Chippewa Valley Schs., 117 F. Supp.2d 646 [148 Educ. L. Rep. 745] (E.D. Mich. 2000).

tion. After a due process hearing officer determined that the student had received an inappropriate education for two years and awarded compensatory educational services, the board sought further administrative review which reduced the compensatory education award to one year. When the mother challenged the reduction of the award, a federal trial court acknowledged that since only two years of the contested five years had been appealed, administrative remedies for the remaining three years had not been exhausted.[60]

Parents were victorious in cases where they claimed that they did not have to exhaust administrative remedies before seeking judicial relief. The Sixth Circuit indicated that where a student in Tennessee had already graduated and the only available remedy was monetary damages, proceeding through the administrative process would have been futile.[61] Similarly, the Tenth Circuit, in a case from Colorado, pointed out that exhaustion was not required where parents were not seeking relief that was available under the IDEA.[62] The federal trial court in New Hampshire was of the view that parents reasonably concluded that further efforts to pursue their claim through the administrative hearing process would be futile when the hearing officer refused to consider their claim.[63]

In the first of two cases from New York, a federal trial court noted that parents were entitled to judicial review where a state review officer failed to render an opinion in the time prescribed by law.[64] Another federal trial court in New York held that a mother was not required to exhaust administrative remedies where a school board failed to implement a hearing officer's order and she filed suit.[65] The court directed that the mother was not required to appeal the hearing officer's order because in prevailing at the hearing, she had nothing to appeal.

Administrative hearing decisions must be rendered within time lines prescribed by federal and state law. A federal trial court in North Carolina

---

[60] Kristi H. v. Tri-Valley Sch. Dist., 107 F. Supp.2d 628 [146 Educ. L. Rep. 737] (M.D. Pa. 2000).

[61] Covington v. Knox County Sch. Sys., 205 F.3d 912 [142 Educ. L. Rep. 682] (6th Cir. 2000).

[62] Padilla v. School Dist. No. 1 in the City and County of Denver, 233 F.3d 1268 [149 Educ. L. Rep. 368] (10th Cir. 2000).

[63] Henry v. School Admin. Unit #29, 70 F. Supp.2d 52 [140 Educ. L. Rep. 139] (D.N.H. 1999).

[64] Sabatini v. Corning-Painted Post Sch. Dist., 78 F. Supp.2d 138 [141 Educ. L. Rep. 510] (W.D.N.Y. 1999).

[65] R.B. *ex rel.* L.B. v. Board of Educ. of the City of New York, 99 F. Supp.2d 411 [145 Educ. L. Rep. 975] (S.D.N.Y. 2000).

refused to find a procedural violation in a case where a hearing officer issued the result later than it should have been available because the proceedings were extended due to the conduct of both parties.[66] Another federal trial court in North Carolina posited that a sixty-day limitations period prescribed by the state's Administrative Procedures Act applied to requests for due process hearings.[67]

The federal trial court in Maryland commented that experience and fairness dictate that a school board should bear the burden of proof at any administrative due process hearing over an initial IEP.[68] The court added that when a change is sought to an existing IEP, the party seeking the change should have the burden of proof.

Two courts dealt with issues regarding the jurisdiction of hearing officers to resolve complaints regarding the enforcement of settlement agreements. The Ninth Circuit affirmed that a hearing officer lacks jurisdiction to hear complaints over a previous administrative order to abide by a settlement agreement.[69] The court reasoned that issues of noncompliance with a hearing officer's order could be brought before the Compliance Office of the California Department of Education. However, the federal trial court in Connecticut observed that a hearing officer has the authority to enforce the terms of a voluntary settlement agreement.[70]

The Supreme Court of Delaware affirmed that non-attorneys cannot represent students with disabilities in due process hearings.[71] In upholding an adjudication by the Board on the Unauthorized Practice of Law, the court ascertained that although section 1415 of the IDEA is ambiguous, it could not be interpreted as granting any clear right to lay representation.

In a challenge to a hearing officer's impartiality, the federal trial court in Maine denied a motion for additional discovery.[72] The hearing officer directed a school board to pay the costs of a private school for a student who was unilaterally placed there by his parents. The board challenged the hearing officer's impartiality when it discovered that she had placed her son, who had a disability, in a private school due to dissatisfaction with the

[66] CM v. Board of Educ. of Henderson County, 85 F. Supp.2d 574 [142 Educ. L. Rep. 299] (W.D.N.C. 1999).

[67] M.E. and P.E. v. Board of Educ. for Buncombe County, 88 F. Supp.2d 493 [143 Educ. L. Rep. 493] (W.D.N.C. 1999).

[68] Brian S. v. Vance, 86 F. Supp.2d 538 [142 Educ. L. Rep. 828] (D. Md. 2000).

[69] Wyner *ex rel.* Wyner v. Manhattan Beach Unified Sch. Dist., 223 F.3d 1026 [146 Educ. L. Rep. 1000] (9th Cir. 2000).

[70] Mr. J. v. Board of Educ., 98 F. Supp.2d 226 [144 Educ. L. Rep. 956] (D. Conn. 2000).

[71] *In re* Arons, 756 A.2d 867 [146 Educ. L. Rep. 763] (Del. 2000).

[72] Falmouth Sch. Comm. v. Mr. and Mrs. B., 106 F. Supp.2d 69 [146 Educ. L. Rep. 686] D. Me. 2000).

services he received in a public school. However, the court was not convinced that there was support in the record to disqualify the hearing officer. On the other hand, a federal trial court in Louisiana judged that a student's appeal had not been given a fair hearing where one member of the review panel previously recused himself from the case citing bias in favor of the school board.[73]

Court Proceedings

In a case from Michigan, the Sixth Circuit affirmed that parents in Michigan who challenged the terms of an IEP bore the burden of proving that the recommended placement was not appropriate.[74] On the other hand, a federal trial court in West Virginia maintained that a school board should bear the burden of proof in a special education placement dispute because it had the basic obligation to provide the student with a FAPE.[75]

The Eleventh Circuit affirmed that a federal trial court was not required to hear additional evidence at the request of a school board in Georgia.[76] The panel discerned that the trial court acted well within its discretion in finding that since the admission of any additional evidence would have been cumulative, it would have undercut or unduly minimized the statutory role of the administrative process.

According to the Seventh Circuit, an issue regarding provision of services during an expulsion was moot because the student had since graduated from high school.[77] A federal trial court in Texas decided that while students' unilateral withdrawal from school could render some of their claims moot, under the record it was impossible to determine what issues, if any, could be rendered moot by reason of abandonment.[78] The federal trial court for the District of Columbia decided that a case involving a student's placement in a private school at public expense was not moot since it fell within the "capable of repetition, yet evading review" exception to the mootness doctrine.[79] The court contended that the board consistently failed to provide the parents with a required annual notice regarding their son's placement.

---

[73] Veazey v. Ascension Parish Sch. Bd., 109 F. Supp.2d 482 (M.D. La. 2000).

[74] Dong v. Board of Educ. of the Rochester Community Schs., 197 F.3d 793 [140 Educ. L. Rep. 116] (6th Cir. 1999).

[75] Board of Educ. of the County of Kanawha v. Michael M., 95 F. Supp.2d 600 [144 Educ. L. Rep. 187] (S.D. W. Va. 2000).

[76] Walker County Sch. Dist. v. Bennett, 203 F.3d 1293 [141 Educ. L. Rep. 1013] (11th Cir. 2000).

[77] Board of Educ. of Oak Park and River Forest High Sch. Dist. 200 v. Nathan R., 199 F.3d 377 [140 Educ. L. Rep. 864] (7th Cir. 2000).

[78] Eddins v. Excelsior Indep. Sch. Dist., 88 F. Supp.2d 695 [143 Educ. L. Rep. 120] (E.D. Tex. 2000).

[79] Zearley v. Ackerman, 116 F. Supp.2d 109 [147 Educ. L. Rep. 1013] (D.D.C. 2000).

The Fourth Circuit, in a case from North Carolina, affirmed that a suit filed pursuant to the IDEA is an original civil action for which a counterclaim is permitted.[80] The court believed that the judiciary in, an IDEA case, is entitled to make its own independent de novo review.

Statute of Limitations

The Eighth Circuit resolved two cases on applicable statutes of limitations. In the first, the court wrote that a claim for compensatory education was subject to the two-year statute of limitations set by the Missouri Human Rights Act because a civil rights claim was the most analogous cause of action.[81] In a case from Arkansas, the court declared that the three-year limitations period imposed by the state's general personal injury statute was most analogous to the IDEA.[82]

The federal trial court in Oregon held that the most appropriate statute of limitations in a claim for tuition reimbursement under the IDEA is that state's six-year period for actions upon a liability created by statute.[83] In Alabama, a federal trial court decreed that the appropriate statute of limitations in an action seeking the recovery of attorneys fees was the state's two-year period for actions alleging injury to the person or rights of another.[84] The Sixth Circuit explained that the statute of limitations for recovery of attorneys fees in Kentucky was the same thirty-day time frame as for judicial review of administrative proceedings.[85]

In a second case from the Sixth Circuit, the court affirmed that an action was time-barred when parents in Ohio failed to request a due process hearing in a timely fashion.[86] At the same time, the court noted that the school board's failure to prepare an IEP, as requested by the parents, before their son re-enrolled in the district constituted a separate cause of action in which they could pursue a claim.

---

[80] Kirkpatrick v. Lenoir County Bd. of Educ., 216 F.3d 380 [145 Educ. L. Rep. 573] (4th Cir. 2000).

[81] Strawn v. Missouri State Bd. of Educ., 210 F.3d 954 [145 Educ. L. Rep. 879] (8th Cir. 2000).

[82] Birmingham v. Omaha Sch. Dist., 220 F.3d 850 [146 Educ. L. Rep. 100] (8th Cir. 2000).

[83] S.V. v. Sherwood Sch. Dist., 75 F. Supp.2d 1153 [140 Educ. L. Rep. 688] (D. Or. 1999).

[84] Dickerson v. Brodgen, 80 F. Supp.2d 1319 [141 Educ. L. Rep. 684] (S.D. Ala. 1999).

[85] King v. Floyd County Bd. of Educ., 228 F.3d 622 [147 Educ. L. Rep. 814] (6th Cir. 2000).

[86] James v. Upper Arlington City Sch. Dist., 228 F.3d 764 [147 Educ. L. Rep. 840] (6th Cir. 2000).

A federal trial court in New York ruled that the four-month statute of limitations for appeals of administrative rulings applied to a suit seeking compensatory education.[87] In a mixed opinion, the court stated that while claims arising prior to one administrative adjudication were time-barred, those arising from a subsequent administrative decision were not.

In Pennsylvania, a federal trial court determined that claims for compensatory education accrue from the point that school officials knew or should have known of an IEP's failure.[88] The federal trial court in Connecticut asserted that a cause of action accrued when parents unilaterally withdrew their child from a school system since they were not only aware of the IDEA's procedural safeguards but were also aware of the alleged injury to their daughter at that time.[89]

Actions Under Other Statutes

The Ninth Circuit pointed out that a student, and his mother, in Nevada, who sought monetary damages as a result of alleged physical, emotional, and verbal inflicted by his teacher and an instructional assistant was not required to exhaust administrative remedies under the IDEA prior to filing suit.[90] The court was of the view that since such a remedy is ordinarily unavailable under the IDEA and the student was not seeking relief that was also available under the IDEA, he was not required to exhaust administrative remedies.

On the other hand, the federal trial court in Massachusetts directed parents to exhaust administrative remedies even though they were only seeking monetary damages under section 1983 because the underlying basis for the claim was a violation of the IDEA.[91] Similarly, the federal trial court in Connecticut acknowledged that claims brought pursuant to section 504 were subject to the IDEA's administrative requirements when they arose out of the same set of facts as the IDEA charges.[92]

---

[87] Butler v. South Glens Falls Cent. Sch. Dist., 106 F. Supp.2d 414 [146 Educ. L. Rep. 701] (N.D.N.Y. 2000).
[88] Kristi H. v. Tri-Valley Sch. Dist., 107 F. Supp.2d 628 [146 Educ. L. Rep. 737] (M.D. Pa. 2000).
[89] Mr. and Mrs. D. v. Southington Bd. of Educ., 119 F. Supp.2d 105 [148 Educ. L. Rep. 871] (D. Conn. 2000).
[90] Witte v. Clark County Sch. Dist., 197 F.3d 1271 [140 Educ. L. Rep. 468] (9th Cir. 1999).
[91] Frazier v. Fairhaven Sch. Comm., 122 F. Supp.2d 104 [149 Educ. L. Rep. 423] (D. Mass. 2000).
[92] Mr. and Mrs. D. v. Southington Bd. of Educ., 119 F. Supp.2d 105 [148 Educ. L. Rep. 871] (D. Conn. 2000).

Courts are divided on the issue of whether lawsuits can be filed under section 1983 based on violations of the IDEA. The federal trial court for the District of Columbia posited that parents who provided ample evidence that a school board failed to provide a timely placement, failed to pay tuition bills in a timely fashion, and failed to perform basic administrative tasks could proceed with a claim for relief under section 1983.[93] However, the Tenth Circuit reasoned that section 1983 may not be used to redress violations of the IDEA.[94]

Placement

The IDEA regulations require school boards to insure that a "continuum of alternative placements" exists to meet the needs of students with disabilities for special education and related services.[95] The continuum must range from placement in general education to a private residential facility and must also include homebound services. The placement chosen for any student must be in the least restrictive environment (LRE) for that child and removal from general education can occur only to the extent necessary to provide special education and related services.[96] All placements must be made at public expense and must meet state educational standards.[97] Each placement must be reviewed at least annually and revised if necessary.[98] The Supreme Court has found that an appropriate education is one that is developed in compliance with the IDEA's procedures and is reasonably calculated to enable a child to receive educational benefits.[99] Although states must adopt policies and procedures that are consistent with the IDEA, they may provide greater benefits than those required by the federal law. Further, if a state does establish higher standards, courts will consider those standards when evaluating the appropriateness of an IEP.[100]

---

[93] Zearley v. Ackerman, 116 F. Supp.2d 109 [147 Educ. L. Rep. 1013] (D.D.C. 2000).

[94] Padilla v. School Dist. No. 1 in the City and County of Denver, 233 F.3d 1268 [149 Educ. L. Rep. 368] (10th Cir. 2000).

[95] 34 C.F.R. § 300.551.

[96] 20 U.S.C. § 1412(a)(5).

[97] 20 U.S.C. § 1401(8).

[98] 20 U.S.C. § 1414(d)(4).

[99] Board of Educ. of Hendrick Hudson Cent. Sch. Dist. v. Rowley, 458 U.S. 176 [5 Educ. L. Rep. 34] (1982).

[100] *See e.g.*, David D. v. Dartmouth Sch. Comm., 775 F.2d 411 [28 Educ. L. Rep. 70] (1st Cir. 1985); Geis v. Board of Educ. of Parsippany-Troy Hills, Morris County, 774 F.2d 575 [27 Educ. L. Rep. 1093] (3d Cir. 1985).

Appropriate Educational Placement

When the issue involves a difference of opinion over methodologies, the courts generally side with a school board. Such was the case in a dispute from the Sixth Circuit where the parents of an autistic child in Michigan sought forty hours per week of one-on-one Lovaas-style instruction but the board proposed a placement in a public school special education program for twenty-seven and one-half hours per week that included approximately ten hours of individualized instruction.[101] In affirming an earlier judgment in favor of the board, the court observed that the parents' belief that the Lovass-style program would be best for developing their daughter's potential did not mean that it was the only appropriate program that the board could provide under the IDEA.

In a case from Missouri, where parents were also seeking funding for a private Lovaas program, the Eighth Circuit affirmed that since the child made progress in the school board's program and that school officials made substantial alterations to it under the guidance of an autism expert, it was not required to offer the placement that the parents wanted.[102] Similarly, a federal trial court in North Carolina ruled in favor of a school board where the parents were also seeking a Lovaas program since evidence indicated that the child regressed while in Lovaas therapy.[103]

The Eighth Circuit was convinced that the IDEA did not require a school board to provide the specific educational placement that the parents of a child in Missouri with severe brain injuries preferred.[104] Further, a state court in New York maintained that the addition of an after school program was not necessary for a student to receive an appropriate education.[105]

When a case involves competing methodologies, the burden is clearly on school officials to show that the program they are recommending is appropriate. A federal trial court in West Virginia decided in favor of a home-based Lovaas-type program advocated by parents where school officials failed to offer testimony showing that their proposal was generally accepted by the educational community or recognized by other educational experts.[106]

---

[101] Dong v. Board of Educ. of the Rochester Community Schs., 197 F.3d 793 [140 Educ. L. Rep. 116] (6th Cir. 1999).

[102] Gill v. Columbia 93 Sch. Dist., 217 F.3d 1027 [145 Educ. L. Rep. 894] (8th Cir. 2000).

[103] CM v. Board of Educ. of Henderson County, 85 F. Supp.2d 574 [142 Educ. L. Rep. 299] (W.D.N.C. 1999).

[104] Blackmon v. Springfield R-XII Sch. Dist., 198 F.3d 648 [140 Educ. L. Rep. 519] (8th Cir. 1999).

[105] Roslyn Union Free Sch. Dist. v. University of the State of New York, State Educ. Dep't, 711 N.Y.S.2d 582 [146 Educ. L. Rep. 369] (N.Y. App. Div. 2000).

[106] Board of Educ. of the County of Kanawha v. Michael M., 95 F. Supp.2d 600 [144 Educ. L. Rep. 187] (S.D. W. Va. 2000).

The parents' expert witnesses, on the other hand, provided clear examples of the type of instruction that the student required in light of his academic, behavioral, and social deficiencies.

The federal trial court in Maryland ascertained that a school board provided a student with a FAPE where he made what amounted to more than trivial educational progress in that program.[107] Similarly, a federal trial court in Texas offered that a student with a learning disability who essentially stayed within two grade levels of her actual grade placement had made meaningful progress.[108]

In another case from Texas, the Fifth Circuit affirmed that despite parental claims that school officials failed to implement all aspects of their son's IEP, he received a FAPE.[109] Insofar as the court was satisfied that school officials followed significant provisions of the student's IEP and he received an educational benefit, it judged that the party challenging an IEP must show more than de minimis failure to implement all of its elements.

The fact that a school board does not already have a program in place for a child is not fatal as long as school personnel are prepared to develop and implement one. The parents of a student from Maryland with a severe language disability who removed her from the public schools and enrolled her in a private school later claimed that the board did not deliver the program called for in her IEP. In rejecting the parents' claim, the federal trial court found evidence revealing that the board was sufficiently prepared to implement the student's IEP.[110]

According to a federal trial court in Indiana, progress must be gauged in relation to a student's potential.[111] Where a student with a severe learning disability but significant potential made no transferable progress in three years in a public school program, the court discerned that a proposed IEP consisting of essentially the same services was not reasonably designed to provide him with educational benefit. Similarly, the Second Circuit concluded that a student in New York did not receive a FAPE where his performance had not improved in spite of his receiving special education services.[112]

---

[107] Cavanagh v. Grasmick, 75 F. Supp.2d 446 [140 Educ. L. Rep. 643] (D. Md. 1999).

[108] Socorro Indep. Sch. Dist. v. Angelic Y., 107 F. Supp.2d 761 [146 Educ. L. Rep. 744] (W.D. Tex. 2000).

[109] Houston Indep. Sch. Dist. v. Bobby R., 200 F.3d 341 [141 Educ. L. Rep. 62] (5th Cir. 2000).

[110] Carnwath v. Grasmick, 115 F. Supp.2d 577 [147 Educ. L. Rep. 955] (D. Md. 2000).

[111] Nein v. Greater Clark County Sch. Corp., 95 F. Supp.2d 961 [144 Educ. L. Rep. 214] (S.D. Ind. 2000).

[112] M.S. *ex rel.* S.S. v. Board of Educ. of the City Sch. Dist. of the City of Yonkers, 231 F.3d 96 [148 Educ. L. Rep. 606] (2d Cir. 2000).

The Eighth Circuit commented that a student from Missouri, who received an education in which communication skills were not a priority in spite of evaluations over the years calling for an intensive need for a language-based program that adequately considered her deafness, had not received an appropriate education.[113] The court remanded the case for a consideration of an appropriate remedy.

A federal trial court in California contended that a school board is required to offer a single, specific placement rather several options.[114] The court wrote that providing a variety of placements put an undue burden on the parent to eliminate potentially inappropriate placements and made it more difficult for a mother to elect whether to accept the board's offer.

Least Restrictive Environment

Implementing the IDEA's least restrictive environment mandate can be challenging when a student is of preschool age. Opportunities for full inclusion are limited because not all school systems offer preschool programs for students who are not disabled. In fact, many school systems create programs that use a reverse approach where students who are not disabled are enrolled in a preschool special education class for the purpose of providing special education students with the opportunity to associate with peers who are not disabled. The Third Circuit modified its LRE test[115] for such hybrid situations. Under the court's latest ruling, a hybrid program can satisfy the IDEA's LRE mandate under only two circumstances: where education in a regular classroom, with supplementary aids and services, cannot be achieved satisfactorily or where a regular classroom is not available within a reasonable commuting distance of the child's home.[116]

---

[113] Strawn v. Missouri State Bd. of Educ., 210 F.3d 954 [145 Educ. L. Rep. 879] (8th Cir. 2000).

[114] Glendale Unified Sch. Dist. v. Almasi, 122 F. Supp.2d 1093 [149 Educ. L. Rep. 477] (C.D. Cal. 2000).

[115] In *Oberti v. Board of Educ. of the Borough of Clementon Sch. Dist.*, 995 F.2d 1204 [83 Educ. L. Rep. 1009] (3d Cir. 1993) the court adopted a two-part test for assessing compliance with the LRE requirement: whether education in the regular classroom, with the use of supplementary aids and services, can be achieved satisfactorily; and if a placement outside of the regular classroom is necessary, whether the school has mainstreamed the child to the maximum extent appropriate. This test was originally proposed by the Fifth Circuit in Daniel R.R. v. State Bd. of Educ., 874 F.2d 1036 [53 Educ. L. Rep. 824] (5th Cir. 1989).

[116] T.R. and E.M.R. v. Kingwood Township Bd. of Educ., 205 F.3d 572 [142 Educ. L. Rep. 656] (3d Cir. 2000).

Private Facilities

A federal trial court in New York ordered a school board to pay for college courses for a student with disabilities where there was no other alternative.[117] Under the terms of a settlement agreement, school officials tried, but were unable, to locate a residential facility that would accept the student. However, since the student was accepted at a college that offered a program for individuals with learning disabilities, the court declared that although he was in a college and not a high school did not mean that it could not provide him with the educational services he needed to obtain a high school diploma. The court posed the issue as whether funds could be disbursed under the IDEA for college courses where the intent was to apply credit for them toward the acquisition of a high school diploma.

In Maryland, the federal trial court indicated that a student who had good academic achievement and superb musical talents but significant social difficulties required a private placement.[118] The court supported an administrative law judge's conclusions that the student needed stability in her learning environment, was frightened by unfamiliar situations, was confused in a large school setting, and required a differentiated level of instruction that was not provided in the proposed public school setting.

The mother of a student with disabilities in Connecticut unsuccessfully charged that school officials placed her son in a private facility in retaliation for her having exercised her statutory right to a hearing. The trial court held not only that the private school was highly specialized and was very appropriate for the child since it had the services he required but also that he would have received little or no benefit from inclusion.[119]

Related Services

The IDEA requires school boards to provide related, or supportive, services to students with disabilities if they are needed to assist children in benefitting from their special education programs.[120] The IDEA specifically mentions transportation and such developmental, supportive, and corrective services as speech pathology, audiology, psychological services,

---

[117] Sabatini v. Corning-Painted Post Area Sch. Dist., 78 F. Supp.2d 138 [141 Educ. L. Rep. 510] (W.D.N.Y. 1999).

[118] Board of Educ. of Montgomery County v. Hunter, 84 F. Supp.2d 702 [142 Educ. L. Rep. 189] (D. Md. 2000).

[119] Lillbask *ex rel.* Mauclaire v. Sergi, 117 F. Supp.2d 182 [148 Educ. L. Rep. 248] (D. Conn. 2000).

[120] 20 U.S.C. § 1401(a)(22).

physical therapy, occupational therapy, recreation (including therapeutic recreation), social work services, counseling services (including rehabilitation counseling), orientation and mobility services, medical services (for diagnostic or evaluative purposes only), and early identification and assessment as related services.[121] The Supreme Court has declared that related services need be provided only to students receiving special education and only those services that are necessary for the child to benefit from special education must be incorporated into the IEP.[122] The only limit on what can be considered a related service is that medical services are exempted unless they are specifically for diagnostic or evaluative purposes.

A state appellate court in New York affirmed that a school board was not required to provide a child with transportation to a private after school program.[123] The court noted that since the board had not denied the student access to its after school program and that an alternative after school program was not required for the child to receive educational benefit, the board was not obligated to provide transportation to the private after school program.

A federal trial court in California determined that a student who had delays in all areas of development required two hours of occupational therapy services a week instead of just the one hour proposed in her IEP.[124] The court was of the view that the student's intensive needs required services which focused on improving her dressing and eating deficits.

Discipline

When first enacted, there were no provisions in the IDEA specifically referring to discipline; however, disciplinary sanctions as applied to students with disabilities were frequently the source of litigation. In the past, courts mandated that the IDEA's change in placement and status quo provisions were applicable to the disciplinary process. More specifically, in *Honig v. Doe*,[125] the Supreme Court found that students in special education settings cannot be expelled for disciplinary infractions that are manifestations of their disabilities.

---

[121] *Id.*

[122] Irving Indep. Sch. Dist. v. Tatro, 468 U.S. 883 [18 Educ. L. Rep. 138] (1984).

[123] Roslyn Union Free Sch. Dist. v. University of the State of New York, State Educ. Dep't, 711 N.Y.S.2d 582 [146 Educ. L. Rep. 369] (N.Y. App. Div. 2000).

[124] Glendale Unified Sch. Dist. v. Almasi, 122 F. Supp.2d 1093 [149 Educ. L. Rep. 477] (C.D. Cal. 2000).

[125] 484 U.S. 305 [43 Educ. L. Rep. 857] (1988).

When Congress amended the IDEA in 1997, it included specific provisions dealing with discipline for the first time.[126] These provisions codified some of the prior case law and helped to clarify some grey areas that still existed. One of the new provisions allows school administrators to transfer a student to an interim alternative setting for up to forty-five days for possession of weapons or drugs.[127] The 1997 amendments also made it clear that educational services must continue during an expulsion period.[128]

Honig and current language of the IDEA make it clear that school officials are not without recourse in disciplining students with disabilities. Students in special education placements may be temporarily suspended, and are subject to other normal disciplinary sanctions. If necessary, school officials may seek the intervention of a hearing officer or court pending completion of administrative due process hearings if it can be shown that a student is dangerous and educators cannot reach an agreement with the child's parents concerning a proper placement. *Honig* and the IDEA also allow school officials to use normal disciplinary sanctions, such as suspensions of ten days or less, that do not result in a change in placement for students in special education placements.

In Texas, a federal trial court supported a school board's transfer of a pupil with disabilities to an alternative education program after he sexually assaulted another student.[129] The student, in consort with a nondisabled peer, ripped the pants of the female student. When the school's evaluation team acknowledged that this act was not a manifestation of the student's disability, it recommended that he be assigned to an alternative education facility for the remainder of the school year. The court explained that the team's disciplinary response was entirely appropriate given the facts and that when faced with such conduct, school officials were justified in taking stern and aggressive remedial action.

A federal trial court in New York observed that a school district's summer school disciplinary policy, which gave principals discretion to impose disciplinary sanctions with no right to appeal, did not meet the minimal requirements of the IDEA.[130] The case arose as a result of a class action suit filed on behalf of several students with disabilities who were required to complete the summer school program for promotion to the next grade but were suspended for disciplinary infractions. The court reasoned that school

---

[126] 20 U.S.C. § 1415(k).

[127] 20 U.S.C. § 1415(k)(1).

[128] 20 U.S.C. § 1412(a)(1)(A).

[129] Randy M. v. Texas City ISD, 93 F. Supp.2d 1310 [144 Educ. L. Rep. 106] (S.D. Texas 2000).

[130] LIH *ex rel.* LH v. New York City Bd. of Educ., 103 F. Supp.2d 658 [145 Educ. L. Rep. 1031] (E.D.N.Y. 2000).

officials had not made any attempt to evaluate whether the misconduct was a manifestation of each student's disability. The court added that since the summer school program was intrinsically related to the students' ability to receive FAPEs, it was subject to the IDEA's disciplinary procedures.

The federal trial court in Connecticut believed that a student whose parents expressed concern over his poor performance and requested evaluations in the past was entitled to the protections of the IDEA for students facing disciplinary actions.[131] The court pointed out that under these circumstances, school personnel had knowledge that the student was a child with a disability even though he was not classified when he misbehaved.

In Mississippi, where a student with attention deficit disorder faced expulsion for possession of a small Swiss Army knife, a federal trial court asserted that his parents failed to establish that he had a disability.[132] However, the court further maintained that since his parents failed to establish that the student did not have control of his conduct when he brought the knife to school or that he did not comprehend the school's disciplinary rules, he was not subject to the IDEA's stay put provision.

Remedies

If a school board fails to provide a student with a disability with a FAPE, the courts are empowered to grant such relief as they deem appropriate.[133] The relief frequently involves reimbursement of costs borne by parents in unilaterally obtaining appropriate services for their child. The Supreme Court has ruled that school boards may be required to reimburse parents for costs incurred in providing their child with special education and related services if they prevail in having their chosen placement deemed appropriate.[134] In an amendment to the IDEA, essentially codifying those rulings, reimbursement awards may be limited if parents do not provide a school board with prior notice of their dissatisfaction with their child's placement and their intent to enroll the child in a private school.[135] Reimbursement is allowed even if the parents chosen facility is not state approved as long as it offers an otherwise appropriate education.[136] Awards of compensatory

---

[131] J.C. v. Regional Sch. Dist. No. 10, 115 F. Supp.2d 297 [147 Educ. L. Rep. 935] (D. Conn. 2000).

[132] Colvin v. Lowndes County, Mississippi Sch. Dist., 114 F. Supp.2d 504 [147 Educ. L. Rep. 601] (N.D. Miss. 1999).

[133] 20 U.S.C. § 1415(i)(2)(A).

[134] Burlington Sch. Comm. v. Department of Educ., Commonwealth of Mass., 471 U.S. 359 [23 Educ. L. Rep. 1189] (1985).

[135] 20 U.S.C. § 1412(a)(10)(C)(ii).

[136] Florence County Sch. Dist. Four v. Carter, 510 U.S. 7 [86 Educ. L. Rep. 41] (1993).

education services have been made in cases where parents did not have the financial means to obtain private services while the litigation was pending.

In 1986 Congress passed the Handicapped Children's Protection Act to allow parents who prevail in a suit pursuant to the IDEA to recover their legal expenses.[137] In 1990 Congress passed legislation specifically abrogating the states' Eleventh Amendment immunity to suits in the federal courts for actions that occurred after October 30, 1990.[138] These amendments to the IDEA were passed in response to Supreme Court holdings that the original Act did not allow for the recovery of attorney fees by prevailing parents[139] and did not specifically abrogate the states' sovereign immunity.[140]

Damages

A federal trial court in New York remarked that compensatory and punitive damages are not included in the IDEA's authorization for relief as the judiciary determines is appropriate.[141] Even so, the court refused to bar a student's section 1983 claim for damages as a matter of law, stating that the Second Circuit had not yet resolved the question of whether damages are available under section 1983 for IDEA violations. Interestingly, another federal trial court in New York ascertained not only that monetary damages are available under section 1983 for IDEA violations but also that the Act expressly contemplated such claims.[142]

Tuition Reimbursement

The Seventh Circuit affirmed that a mother in Illinois who unilaterally enrolled her son in a private school, without first giving her school board the opportunity to evaluate him and make a placement recommendation, forfeited the right to be reimbursed for that placement.[143] Similarly, the Fifth

---

[137] 20 U.S.C. § 1415(i)(3)(B) *et seq.*

[138] 20 U.S.C. § 1403.

[139] Smith v. Robinson, 468 U.S. 992 [18 Educ. L. Rep. 148] (1984).

[140] Dellmuth v. Muth, 491 U.S. 223 [53 Educ. L. Rep. 792] (1989).

[141] Butler v. South Glens Falls Cent. Sch. Dist., 106 F. Supp.2d 414 [146 Educ. L. Rep. 701] (N.D.N.Y. 2000).

[142] R.B. *ex rel.* L.B. v. Board of Educ. of the City of New York, 99 F. Supp.2d 411 [145 Educ. L. Rep. 975] (S.D.N.Y. 2000).

[143] Patricia P. v. Board of Educ. of Oak Park and River Forest High Sch. Dist. No. 200, 203 F.3d 462 [141 Educ. L. Rep. 986] (7th Cir. 2000). *See also* L.K. *ex rel.* J.H. v. Board of Educ. for Transylvania County, 113 F. Supp.2d 856 [147 Educ. L. Rep. 566] (W.D.N.C. 2000).

Circuit posited that parents in Texas who enrolled their dyslexic child in a private school without their board's consent were not entitled to reimbursement after a federal trial court upheld the board's IEP.[144]

Parents of a child with dyslexia in Indiana sought further review after a trial court and hearing officer agreed that they were not entitled to tuition reimbursement for unilaterally enrolling their son in a private school. The Seventh Circuit affirmed that the parents were not entitled to reimbursement since the public school placement was appropriate.[145]

In a second case from the Seventh Circuit, the court affirmed the denial of a parental request for reimbursement for a hospital placement in Indiana based on their claim that her unstable psychological condition necessitated the hospitalization and rendered her unable to handle the residential placement recommended in her IEP.[146] Agreeing that the student was admitted to the hospital for almost exclusively medical reasons rather than educational purposes, and that the services she received were medical, not educational, the court deemed that reimbursement was not warranted.

Although the Second Circuit wrote that a school board in New York failed to offer a student a FAPE, it denied reimbursement because it was not satisfied that the private placement chosen by the parent was appropriate.[147] The court discerned that tuition reimbursement is only available for an appropriate placement.

In another case from the Second Circuit, the court remanded an earlier judgment in commenting that the federal trial court in Connecticut erred by not considering whether either of the placements proposed in the student's IEP were adequate.[148] The court denied reimbursement for counseling because parents had failed to raise the issue until eight months after the child's treatment ended. On remand, the trial court found that one of the programs offered by the school board, although not as desirable as the private school, would have been adequate.[149]

---

[144] Houston Indep. Sch. Dist. v. Bobby R., 200 F.3d 341 [141 Educ. L. Rep. 62] (5th Cir. 2000).

[145] Linda W. v. Indiana Dep't of Educ., 200 F.3d 504 [141 Educ. L. Rep. 86] (7th Cir. 1999).

[146] Butler v. Evans, 225 F.3d 887 [147 Educ. L. Rep. 53] (7th Cir. 2000).

[147] M.S. *ex rel.* S.S. v. Board of Educ. of the City Sch. Dist. of the City of Yonkers, 231 F.3d 96 [148 Educ. L. Rep. 606] (2d Cir. 2000).

[148] M.C. *ex rel.* Mrs. C. v. Voluntown Bd. of Educ., 226 F.3d 60 [147 Educ. L. Rep. 69] (2d Cir. 2000).

[149] M.C. *ex rel.* Mrs. C. v. Voluntown Bd. of Educ., 122 F. Supp.2d 289 [149 Educ. L. Rep. 434] (D. Conn. 2000).

A federal trial court in Indiana awarded partial reimbursement to parents who selected a private school that provided their son with an appropriate education even though they failed to notify their school board in writing of their intent to enroll him there at public expense.[150] In addition, the court offered that the board failed to provide the student with a FAPE.

In California, a federal trial court awarded partial reimbursement to a parent who had not fully cooperated with a school board.[151] The parent unilaterally enrolled her daughter in a private school that did not have any personnel certified to provide special education services. Although the court indicated that the private school provided activities that were appropriate for the child's mental age, it reduced the reimbursement award since the parent's lack of cooperation frustrated the board's attempts to design a program for the student.

Parents in New Hampshire were awarded tuition reimbursement after the federal trial court concluded that the private school that they chose was more closely analogous to the child's previous private school placement than a public school program proposed by the board.[152] The parents obtained a preliminary injunction placing their son in their chosen facility since he was no longer able to attend his previous school because of his age and the parties could not agree on a new placement.

In awarding tuition reimbursement for a private school placement, the federal district court in Maryland defined the term "removal" as used in the IDEA's prior notice requirements as the actual physical removal of a student from a public school.[153] The court added that if a child is enrolled in a private school during a summer recess, the ten business days start for notice purposes from the beginning of the school year.

A federal trial court in Tennessee granted parents' request for tuition reimbursement where they were faced with the option of placing their child in a private school where she would have been educated in a highly structured environment or placing her in a public school where she would not have been in such a setting.[154] The school board had determined that the student was not eligible for special education even though she was eventu-

---

[150] Nein v. Greater Clark County Sch. Corp., 95 F. Supp.2d 961 [144 Educ. L. Rep. 214] (S.D. Ind. 2000).

[151] Glendale Unified Sch. Dist. v. Almasi, 122 F. Supp.2d 1093 [149 Educ. L. Rep. 477] (C.D. Cal. 2000).

[152] Henry v. School Admin. Unit #29, 70 F. Supp.2d 52 [140 Educ. L. Rep. 139] (D.N.H. 1999).

[153] Sarah M. v. Weast, 111 F. Supp.2d 695 (D. Md. 2000).

[154] Johnson v. Metro Davidson County Sch. Sys., 108 F. Supp.2d 906 (M.D. Tenn. 2000).

ally declared to be seriously emotionally disturbed. In granting tuition reimbursement, the court offered that equity prevented the reimbursement of costs accrued prior to the point when the board had the opportunity to evaluate the child.

In a consolidated action from Illinois, the Seventh Circuit explained that the state was not required to pay a portion of court ordered tuition reimbursement.[155] In two cases where school boards were ordered to pay tuition reimbursement, they sought to have the state pay a portion of the award.[156] The court noted that since the boards received their share of the federal special education appropriation, they had to provide services out of that share.

Compensatory Services

The Supreme Court of Appeals of West Virginia approved a special master's recommendation directing a school board to provide a student with special education services for two years beyond the time that it was statutorily required to do so to compensate for past deficiencies in its delivery of services.[157] The court accepted the special master's finding that the board did not fully perform its legal obligations under the student's IEP and that its efforts to make up the omitted services had fallen short.

A federal trial court in New York rejected a school board's motion for summary judgment where parents asked for compensatory education due to its alleged failure to provide their son with an appropriate education.[158] The court asserted that questions of fact existed as to whether the board violated the IDEA by declassifying the student and not providing special education services for a period of six years.

---

[155] Board of Educ. of Oak Park and River Forest High Sch. Dist. No. 200 v. Kelly E., 207 F.3d 931 [143 Educ. L. Rep. 70] (7th Cir. 2000).
[156] T.H. v. Board of Educ. of Palatine Community Consol. Sch. Dist. 15, 55 F. Supp.2d 830 [137 Educ. L. Rep. 555] (N.D. Ill. 1999); Board of Educ. of Oak Park and River Forest High Sch. Dist. No. 200 v. Illinois State Bd. of Educ., 21 F. Supp.2d 862 [130 Educ. L. Rep. 726] (N.D. Ill. 1998).
[157] State of West Virginia *ex rel.* Justice v. Board of Educ. of the County of Monongalia, 539 S.E.2d 777 (W. Va. 2000).
[158] Butler v. South Glens Falls Cent. Sch. Dist., 106 F. Supp.2d 701 [146 Educ. L. Rep. 701] (N.D.N.Y. 2000).

Attorneys Fees

The Ninth Circuit affirmed an award of attorneys fees for representation at IEP meetings called pursuant to an order resulting from a favorable decision in a complaint resolution proceeding.[159] In its analysis, the court believed that Congress intended that attorneys fees could be awarded in cases involving complaint resolution proceedings as well as impartial due process hearings.

The first of two cases from the Third Circuit, both of which originated in Pennsylvania, was filed by parents of a severely deaf student who requested a due process hearing to raise concerns about the child's sign-language interpreter. Rather than subject himself to a hearing, the interpreter requested, and was granted, a transfer to another position. The parents then sought attorneys fees. Using the catalyst theory, the court was of the view that the parents were entitled to such an award because the interpreter's departure was motivated by their legal action.[160] However, the court observed that the parents' attorney failed to properly support her hourly rate and the fee breakdown in her billing records was out of line with what was reasonable for an attorney of her level of experience. Further, the court questioned the amount of time the attorney claimed for exploring the interpreter's qualifications and indicated that the litigation was needlessly protracted. As such, the court reduced the requested amount accordingly.

In the second case, the Third Circuit affirmed an award of fees for representation at an IEP meeting specifically called to make a final attempt at settlement.[161] The court agreed that the IEP meeting had been convened as a result of an impending hearing.

The federal trial court in New Jersey refused to order attorneys fees where a school board acceded to the parents' request to transfer their son from one high school to another.[162] Although the parents had received the request they sought, the court judged that the transfer was not one that would have affected the student's learning.

In a case from Illinois, the Seventh Circuit denied an award of attorneys fees where parents received only interim relief on the basis that it does not qualify a party for attorneys fees.[163] The Seventh Circuit also denied a fee

---

[159] Lucht v. Molalla River Sch. Dist., 225 F.3d 1023 [147 Educ. L. Rep. 61] (9th Cir. 2000), *aff'g* 57 F. Supp.2d 1060 [138 Educ. L. Rep. 183] (D. Or. 1999).

[160] Holmes v. Millcreek Township Sch. Dist., 205 F.3d 583 [142 Educ. L. Rep. 667] (3d Cir. 2000).

[161] Daniel S. v. Scranton Sch. Dist., 230 F.3d 90 [149 Educ. L. Rep. 17] (3d Cir. 2000).

[162] J.S. D.S. v. Lenape Reg'l High Sch. Dist. Bd. of Educ., 102 F. Supp.2d 540 [145 Educ. L. Rep. 1010] (D.N.J. 2000).

[163] Board of Educ. of Oak Park and River Forest High Sch. Dist. 200 v. Nathan R., 199 F.3d 377 140 Educ. L. Rep. 864] (7th Cir. 2000).

award for parents in Indiana who had only limited success in administrative hearings.[164] The court acknowledged that in order to prevail in litigation, one must win on the merits and not just score tactical victories in interlocutory skirmishes.

A section of the 1999 District of Columbia Appropriations Act that imposed caps on both the hourly rate and the total amount of compensation the District could pay lawyers of parents who prevailed in proceedings under the IDEA was at issue in Washington, D.C. The federal appeals court affirmed that this provision was constitutional since capping fees would produce additional resources for direct educational services.[165]

In the first of three cases from Connecticut, a school board unsuccessfully challenged an award of attorneys fees by a federal magistrate, arguing that the judge considered success on issues not formally raised in the written request for a due process hearing. The federal trial court awarded fees, pointing out that the magistrate properly considered success on issues that were litigated by the parties even though they were not formally raised in the request for a due process hearing.[166]

Another federal trial court in Connecticut reduced a requested fee award to reflect the partial success achieved by parents.[167] The court further reduced the award because entries in the attorney's time records lacked sufficient specificity.

In the final suit from Connecticut, the federal trial court was convinced that parents who succeeded in having an expulsion hearing canceled and their child being granted special education services were entitled to attorney fees because the record was clear that they had obtained all the relief they sought.[168] The court added that the pressure of a suit was a material factor in bringing about a settlement.

A federal trial court in North Carolina awarded fees but reduced the requested amount in maintaining that the parents sought excessive fees in

---

[164] Linda W. v. Indiana Dep't of Educ., 200 F.3d 504 [141 Educ. L. Rep. 86] (7th Cir. 1999).

[165] Calloway v. District of Columbia, 216 F.3d 1 [145 Educ. L. Rep. 555] (D.C. Cir. 2000).

[166] N.S. *ex rel.* P.S. and P.S. v. Stratford Bd. of Educ., 97 F. Supp.2d 224 [144 Educ. L. Rep. 897] (D. Conn. 2000).

[167] Mr. J. v. Board of Educ., 98 F. Supp.2d 226 [144 Educ. L. Rep. 956] (D. Conn. 2000).

[168] J.C. v. Regional Sch. Dist. No. 10, 115 F. Supp.2d 297 [147 Educ. L. Rep. 935] (D. Conn. 2000).

a simple matter which the school board settled with little resistance and quickly agreed to pay a reasonable amount of attorneys fees.[169] The court adjusted the lodestar downward by 10% to sanction the plaintiffs for over-reaching and to deter such conduct in the future.

Other IDEA Issues

A state court in Pennsylvania upheld a school board's decision to deny a parental request for a student with Downs Syndrome to participate in graduation ceremonies even though he was not graduating that year. The court conceded that there was no language in the IDEA or state special education regulations that granted a student with a disability the right to participate in a graduation ceremony if he had not yet met the requirements for graduation.[170]

State Laws

Special education is governed by state and federal law. While each state's special education statutes must be consistent with the IDEA, differences do exist. Although most states have legislation similar in scope to the IDEA, several have requirements that go beyond the IDEA's provisions. Some states have higher standards of what constitutes an appropriate education and/or stricter procedural requirements. In other instances, state laws establish procedures for special education program implementation that are not explicitly covered by federal law. Federal and state courts frequently are called upon to interpret those provisions.

A state appellate court in New Jersey ruled that fairness dictated that two school districts bear equally the costs of a child's special education where the parents were divorced and had joint legal custody.[171] The court remarked that the child lived with each parent on alternate weeks but the parents lived in different school districts.

---

[169] AD *ex rel.* SD and JD v. Board of Pub. Instruction of the City of Asheville, 99 F. Supp.2d 683 [145 Educ. L. Rep. 245] (W.D.N.C. 1999).

[170] Woodland Hills Sch. Dist. v. S.F., 747 A.2d 433 [142 Educ. L. Rep. 990] (Pa. Commw. Ct. 2000).

[171] Somerville Bd. of Educ. v. Manville Bd. of Educ., 752 A.2d 793 [144 Educ. L. Rep. 1007] (N.J. App. Div. 2000).

Discrimination Under the Rehabilitation Act, Section 504/b

Section 504 of the Rehabilitation Act of 1973, as amended, provides that "[n]o otherwise qualified individual with a disability . . . shall, solely by reason of her or his disability be excluded from participation in, be denied the benefits of, or be subjected to discrimination under any program or activity receiving [f]ederal financial assistance. . . ."[172] Section 504 effectively prohibits any recipient of federal funds from discriminating against individuals with disabilities in the provision of services or employment. Section 504 applies to any agency that receives federal funds, not just schools.

A person is considered to have a disability under section 504 if he or she has a physical or mental impairment that substantially limits one or more of the person's major life activities, has a record of such an impairment, or is regarded as having such an impairment.[173] Major life activities are "functions such as caring for oneself, performing manual tasks, walking, seeing, hearing, speaking, breathing, learning, and working."[174] The Supreme Court has held that an individual is otherwise qualified for purposes of section 504 if he or she is capable of meeting all of a program's requirements in spite of the disability.[175] If a person is otherwise qualified, a recipient of federal funds is expected to make reasonable accommodations for the individual's disabilities unless doing so would create an undue hardship.[176]

Students

Elementary and Secondary

Students with disabilities at the elementary and secondary level have rights under section 504 as well as the IDEA. Often students and their parents file suits that present claims under both statutes. Frequently, the claims proffered under one statute are identical or similar to the claims stated under the other law; even so, sometimes distinct claims are brought under section 504.

Where a student in Kentucky with hemophilia and hepatitis B had a notation in his medical records that he should not participate in activities

---

[172] 29 U.S.C. § 794.
[173] 29 U.S.C. § 706(7)(B).
[174] 34 C.F.R. § 104.3(j)(2)(ii).
[175] School Bd. of Nassau County v. Arline, 480 U.S. 273 [37 Educ. L. Rep. 448] (1987); Southeastern Community College v. Davis, 442 U.S. 397 (1979).
[176] 34 C.F.R. § 104.12(a).

which would put him at increased risk for physical injury, he challenged the actions of school officials who put his status as a player on the basketball team on hold until they could seek medical direction and clearance for physical activities from his doctor. The Sixth Circuit affirmed that the educators acted reasonably since they were obligated to limit the risk of exposure to a contagion to others as well as limiting any injury the student might suffer.[177]

The Second Circuit, in a suit from Vermont, affirmed that section 504 does not require a public school board to provide students with disabilities with a potential maximizing education.[178] Rather, the court posited that the law only requires reasonable accommodations to give students with disabilities the same access to the benefits of a public education as their pees who are not disabled. The court concluded that the school board provided an appropriate education to an academically gifted student who had emotional and behavioral problems.

According to a federal trial court in Indiana, there was no evidence of a causal link between a student's disability and his not being selected for a basketball team.[179] The court explained that while the student had a section 504 alternative learning plan, he was not selected for the basketball team because the coach did not think that he had the requisite skill level.

Higher Education
The Eighth Circuit affirmed the dismissal of a suit filed by a medical student with dyslexia in Iowa who was expelled from medical school for failing too many multiple-choice tests.[180] The court found that the medical school had done all that was necessary to modify its testing procedures to accommodate the student.

In an ongoing dispute, a federal trial court in Virginia declared that a student with a learning disability was not disabled under either section 504 or the ADA.[181] The court indicated that the record showed that the student had a history of scholastic success in spite of his learning disability and that his learning disorder did not restrict his ability to learn in comparison to the average person in the general population.

In another on-going dispute regarding the National Collegiate Athletic Associations's (NCAA) athletic eligibility rules, the federal trial court in

---

[177] Doe v. Woodford County Bd. of Educ., 213 F.3d 921 [145 Educ. L. Rep. 887] (6th Cir. 2000).
[178] J.D. v. Pawlet Sch. Dist., 224 F.3d 60 [147 Educ. L. Rep. 39] (2d Cir. 2000).
[179] Doe v. Eagle-Union Community Sch. Dist., 101 F. Supp.2d 707 [145 Educ. L. Rep. 413] (S.D. Ind. 2000).
[180] Stern v. University of Osteopathic Med. and Health Servs., 220 F.3d 906 [146 Educ. L. Rep. 108] (8th Cir. 2000).
[181] Betts v. Rector and Visitors of the Univ. of Va., 113 F. Supp.2d 970 [147 Educ. L. Rep. 573] (W.D. Va. 2000).

New Jersey decreed that there were still unresolved material issues of fact regarding whether a student with a learning disability was a qualified individual based on his physical attributes and football skills.[182] The court added that the NCAA had not carried its burden of showing that its treatment of special education courses under the core course requirement was essential or necessary to its goal of ensuring that student-athletes would succeed academically in their first year of higher education.

Other Section 504 Issues

A federal trial court wrote that the three-year statute of limitations applicable to California disability statutes was appropriate in an action filed under section 504.[183] The court reasoned that the state statute was not just analogous, but was virtually identical to section 504 and the ADA.

In New York, where the mother of a student with disabilities sued for damages, a federal trial court determined that she alleged sufficient facts to support her allegations of bad faith and misjudgment.[184] The court contended that the mother's allegations included the failures to take any action to implement the student's IEP, to develop an interim service plan promptly after the student's suspension, to implement the interim service plan, and to implement a hearing officer's order. In a second case from New York, a federal trial court ascertained that evidence that school officials failed to develop IEPs and developed several inappropriate IEPs, which resulted in a failure to provide special education services, if proven, could constitute deliberate indifference to the fact that a student's rights were being violated.[185] The federal trial court in New Jersey also noted that monetary damages are available under section 504 in cases of intentional discrimination because there can be no question either as to the recipient's obligations under the act or that it was aware of those obligations.[186]

In an *en banc* decision, the Eighth Circuit affirmed that Arkansas was not immune from a section 504 lawsuit under the Eleventh Amendment.[187]

---

[182] Bowers v. National Collegiate Athletic Ass'n, 118 F. Supp.2d 494 [148 Educ. L. Rep. 760] (D.N.J. 2000).
[183] Kramer v. Regents of the Univ. of Cal., 81 F. Supp.2d 972 [141 Educ. L. Rep. 755] (N.D. Cal. 1999).
[184] R.B. *ex rel.* L.B. v. Board of Educ. of the City of N.Y., 99 F. Supp.2d 411 [145 Educ. L. Rep. 975] (S.D.N.Y. 2000).
[185] Butler v. South Glens Falls Cent. Sch. Dist., 106 F. Supp.2d 414 [146 Educ. L. Rep. 701] (N.D.N.Y. 2000).
[186] Bowers v. National Collegiate Athletic Ass'n, 118 F. Supp.2d 494 [148 Educ. L. Rep. 760] (D.N.J. 2000)
[187] Jim C. v. United States of Am., 235 F.3d 1079 [150 Educ. L. Rep. 34] (8th Cir. 2000).

The court ruled that the requirements imposed on the states in regard to section 504 were comparable to the ordinary quid pro quo that the Supreme Court has repeatedly approved since the states are offered federal funds for some activities, but, in return, must meet certain federal requirements. The court further reflected that the state had the choice to either give up federal aid to education or agree that it can be sued under section 504 and that such a choice was not unconstitutionally coercive.

Americans with Disabilities Act

The Americans with Disabilities Act (ADA),[188] which was enacted in 1990, is designed to prohibit discrimination against persons with disabilities in a wide range of activities sponsored by private as well as public entities. The ADA's greatest impact is on the private sector; however in as much as many of its provisions apply to public entities and are similar in scope to those of section 504, lawsuits filed under the ADA should interest consumers of education law. Generally, compliance with section 504 results in compliance with the ADA; however, several provisions of the ADA addressed loopholes in section 504 and codified judicial interpretations of the Rehabilitation Act. Many lawsuits that arise in the public sector are now brought on the basis of the ADA as well as section 504. In most of these cases, the disposition for both laws is identical. Cases that were discussed in the section 504 part of this chapter that were resolved in the same way as under the ADA are not being repeated in this section.[189]

Students

A federal trial court in Georgia commented that the NCAA's minimum academic scores are an essential eligibility requirement.[190] The court was of the view that a judicially-ordered waiver of those academic standards would negate the requirements and compromise the educational purpose of the NCAA. The court concluded that the ADA does not require the abandoning the NCAA's minimum eligibility requirements.

---

[188] 42 U.S.C. § 12101 *et seq.*
[189] Kramer v. Regents of the Univ. of Cal., 81 F. Supp.2d 972 [141 Educ. L. Rep. 755] (N.D. Cal. 1999); Doe v. Woodford County Bd. of Educ., 213 F.3d 921 [145 Educ. L. Rep. 887] (6th Cir. 2000), R.B. *ex rel.* L.B. v. Board of Educ. of the City of New York, 99 F. Supp.2d 411 [145 Educ. L. Rep. 975] (S.D.N.Y. 2000), Betts v. Rector and Visitors of the Univ. of Va., 113 F. Supp.2d 970 [147 Educ. L. Rep. 573] (W.D. Va. 2000); Bowers v. National Collegiate Athletic Ass'n, 118 F. Supp.2d 494 [148 Educ. L. Rep. 760] (D.N.J. 2000).
[190] Cole v. National Collegiate Athletic Ass'n, 120 F. Supp.2d 1060 [148 Educ. L. Rep. 935] (N.D. Ga. 2000).

Other ADA Issues

A federal trial court in Washington ruled that the ADA does not apply to the NCAA since it is not a place of public accommodation insofar as the organization only regulates the eligibility and membership criteria of its member institutions and their student athletes.[191] Conversely, the federal trial court in New Jersey held that title III of the ADA did apply to the NCAA as that organization was an operator of a place of public accommodation.[192] The court found that the NCAA had not presented any evidence that its control did not exist such that it could not be considered an operator of a place of public accommodation.

Conclusion

The 1997 amendments to the IDEA figured more prominently in litigation during 2000 than it had in the previous years since its enactment. In particular, the 1997 amendments were a fctor in several suits involving the provision of special education services to students placed in private schools by their parents, special education students facing disciplinary sanctions, and parents seeking tuition reimbursement for unilateral private school placements.

Courts are split on the issue of whether section 1983 can be used to redress violations of the IDEA. This leaves unsettled the question of whether damages are an available remedy for a school district's failure to provide a student with a FAPE. While the majority of courts have refused to award damages under the IDEA itself, some cases suggest that they may be available under section 1983 for IDEA violations

---

[191] Matthews v. National Collegiate Athletic Ass'n, 79 F. Supp.2d 1199 [141 Educ. L. Rep. 619] (E.D. Wash. 1999).
[192] Bowers v. National Collegiate Athletic Ass'n, 118 F. Supp.2d 494 [148 Educ. L. Rep. 760] (D.N.J. 2000)

5
TORTS

William J. Evans, Jr.

Introduction

Tort law offers remedies to individuals for harm caused by the unreasonable conduct of others. This chapter examines cases brought by or on behalf of students, school employees, and, in some instances, visitors on school grounds. Tort actions resulting from interscholastic sports are discussed in Chapter 6, Sports.

Negligence

Negligence is the most common tort committed by school personnel. A tort can arise when an improper act, or failure to act, causes injury to another. At the same time, an individual cannot be liable for a tort unless there is a causal relationship between the alleged conduct and the injury. When an injured party claims that a tort has occurred, the behavior of school personnel is measured against what a reasonable and prudent professional of similar training and experience would, or should, have done in the same or similar circumstances.

Where school officials allegedly failed to identify a student's medical problem as scoliosis, her parents filed a negligence action claiming that they failed to conduct a mandatory screening. An appellate court in New York affirmed a grant of summary judgment in favor of the school board on the ground that the statutory requirement that schools conduct periodic scoliosis screening was not enforceable by a private right of action.[1] The court added that the allegation that the board assumed a special relationship with the student by participating in the screening program was insufficient to raise a claim for common law negligence.

Injuries

Schools are responsible for having safe and healthy environments in which learning can take place. The following cases are divided into categories according to where or how an injury was sustained and when sovereign or statutory immunity was not used as the defense.

---

[1] Uhr v. East Greenbush Cent. Sch. Dist., 698 N.Y.S.2d 609 [140 Educ. L. Rep. 336] (N.Y. App. Div. 1999).

Off School Property and After School Hours

In the first of three cases from New York, an appellate court affirmed a grant of summary judgment in favor of a school where a student sued for injuries he sustained while roller skating.[2] The court refused to impose liability on the school since the accident occurred off of school premises, out of the custody and control of school authorities, and after the student passed into the custody and control of his mother.

An elementary school student and his parents unsuccessfully sought recovery for injuries that he suffered when he was slashed across the face by a peer with a razor . An appellate court in New York affirmed that since there was no evidence that the student was under the control and custody of school officials at the time of the altercation, they did not owe him a duty of adequate supervision.[3]

In the third case, another student unsuccessfully sued a school board for injuries he sustained in a fight with the cousin of a peer with whom he had an on-going dispute. In affirming a grant of summary judgment in favor of the board, an appellate court in New York could not find any evidence that a teacher knew of the plan to attack the student. The court was satisfied that school officials' custody of the student ceased when he passed out of the area of their authority and entered the subway station where he was attacked.[4]

When a booster club member hemmed the uniform pants of a high school band member so that he could march with the band, the student unsuccessfully filed suit after he tripped and was injured when the tape failed to work. An appellate court in Louisiana affirmed the dismissal of the student's suit on the ground that the booster's actions were not "abuse of a minor" for the purposes of the three year prescriptive period and the injury was caused by an accident arising from the mechanics of inanimate objects.[5]

En Route to and From School

When an eight-year-old student was sexually assaulted by a janitor as she waited for her school bus on high school property, she and her family unsuccessfully sued the school board for damages. An appellate court in Louisiana affirmed that since it was not foreseeable that a high school jani-

---

[2] Ruiz v. Life Skills Sch., 700 N.Y.S.2d 456 [141 Educ. L. Rep. 289] (N.Y. App. Div. 1999).

[3] Winter v. Board of Educ. of the City of N.Y., 704 N.Y.S.2d 142 [142 Educ. L. Rep. 472] (N.Y. App. Div. 2000).

[4] Bertrand v. Board of Educ. of City of N.Y., 707 N.Y.S.2d 218 [144 Educ. L. Rep. 608] (N.Y. App. Div. 2000).

[5] Woods v. St. Charles Parish Sch. Bd., 750 So. 2d 1168 [142 Educ. L. Rep. 585] (La. Ct. App. 2000).

tor would molest an elementary school student on the high school campus when she was unsupervised by either a teacher, assistant principal or principal, the board was not liable.[6] The court further remarked that the board was not at fault since the custodian's act was not employment rooted because it was not incidental to the performance of his duties.

In a second case from Louisiana, a student who was wheelchair bound recovered damages for injuries that he sustained after he was transferred to his school bus and it backed into an automobile. An appellate court affirmed that the student was entitled to damages since his injury was causally related to the accident.[7]

When the grandmother of a student who was suspended from riding a school bus boarded it to discuss the sanction with the driver and fell as she was getting off, she unsuccessfully filed a negligence action against the driver, school board, and its insurer. An appellate court in Georgia affirmed that since the bus was engaged solely in transporting children and teachers to and from school and was not a common carrier, the grandmother's being on board did not make her a passenger for the purposes of her negligence action.[8]

A student and her mother unsuccessfully brought a personal injury action against a school bus driver for injuries that she allegedly sustained while riding the bus. On further review, the District of Columbia Court of Appeals reversed a grant of summary judgment that had been entered on behalf of the bus driver and remanded the dispute for trial.[9] The court held that testimony of a medical expert was sufficient to allow a jury to conclude that the student suffered a discrete injury, in the form of migraine headaches, as a result of the bus accident.

In New York, an eight-year-old student who was struck by a car five to ten minutes after he departed from his school bus challenged a grant of summary judgment in favor of the bus service and driver. An appellate court affirmed in refusing to declare the place where the student was discharged as unsafe.[10] Additionally, the court noted that the school board had a rule according to which a regular education child may be left unattended at a bus stop.

---

[6] Rambo v. Webster Parish Sch. Bd., 745 So. 2d 770 [140 Educ. L. Rep. 784] (La. Ct. App. 1999).
[7] Marshall v. Caddo Parish Sch. Bd., 743 So. 2d 943 [139 Educ. L. Rep. 1085] (La. Ct. App. 1999).
[8] Hancock v. Bryan County Bd. of Educ., 522 S.E.2d 661 [140 Educ. L. Rep. 1042] (Ga. Ct. App. 1999).
[9] McLeish v. Beachy, 746 A.2d 892 [142 Educ. L. Rep. 431] (D.C. 2000).
[10] Guadalupe v. Franklin, 703 N.Y.S.2d 175 [142 Educ. L. Rep. 457] (N.Y. App. Div. 2000).

A school board in Ohio contested the denial of its motion to dismiss an action brought by a student with a disability who was injured as she was getting off of a school bus. An appellate court affirmed that since an aide failed to secure the student in her chair when assisting her from the bus, she presented a justiciable claim despite the board's attempted defense of sovereign immunity.[11]

The mother of a child who was assaulted while riding a school bus challenged the dismissal of her suit which claimed that school board personnel willfully and wantonly assigned her son to the same bus as a child who had previously assaulted him. An appellate court affirmed that since such an assignment is a discretionary act, the board and its personnel were statutorily immune from liability.[12]

When a student suffered brain and spinal injuries after being chased into the street near his bus stop, a school board sought further review of its being declared negligent with regard to the placement of the bus stop. An appellate court in Arizona affirmed that since the bus stop was placed on a busy street, rather than in a subdivision, the board was the proximate cause of the child's injuries because such a situation was foreseeable and unreasonable.[13]

School Settings During School Hours

A high school student who was attacked by a classmate successfully sued the school board for its failure to supervise employees who were unable to prevent the attack even though she had been harassed for several months and her school bus driver had reported this to the principal. On further review, the Supreme Court of Appeals West Virginia denied the board's challenge of a $250,000 award in favor of the student because it did not agree that the amount was excessive in light of her injuries and evidence of negligence on the part of the defendants.[14]

In the first of three cases from Mississippi, a student unsuccessfully sued a teacher who responded that she was acting within the course and scope of her employment when she administered excessive corporal punishment. The Supreme Court of Mississippi affirmed that the state's Tort Claim

---

[11] Groves v. Dayton Pub. Schs., 725 N.E.2d 734 [142 Educ. L. Rep. 514] (Ohio Ct. App. 1999).

[12] D.M. v. National Sch. Bus Serv. Inc., 713 N.E.2d 196 [141 Educ. L. Rep. 263] (Ill. Ct. App. 1999).

[13] Warrington v. Tempe Elementary Sch. Dist. No. 3, 3 P.3d 988 [146 Educ. L. Rep. 508] (Ariz. Ct. App. 2000).

[14] Spaulding v. Mingo County Bd. of Educ., 526 S.E.2d 525 [144 Educ. L. Rep. 420] (W. Va. 1999).

Act provides that no employee can be personally liable for acts that occur within the course and scope of his or her duties.[15]

A kindergarten student who was restrained and fondled by fellow pupils during recess sought further review of the dismissal of his damages action against his church-owned school. The Supreme Court of Mississippi affirmed that the allegations were insufficient to support a claim of mental anguish by the child's parents since they had not witnessed the incident. However, the court reversed a grant of summary judgment on the negligent supervision part of the claim that had been entered on behalf of the school because there were material issues of fact as to foreseeability and breach of duty by school personnel.[16]

When a middle school student injured her teeth as she hit the back of a chair during a classroom skit, her mother challenged a grant of summary judgment in favor of the board in their negligence action. The Supreme Court of Mississippi, in examining a video tape of the incident, indicated that since there was no "horseplay" and the teacher was present supervising the activity, it was an unfortunate but unforeseeable accident.[17]

In the first of seven cases from New York, a school board contested the denial of its motions for summary judgment when a student filed a negligence action against it and a classmate who allegedly pushed him. An appellate court affirmed that material issues of fact precluded granting the board's motion as to whether school employees failed to provide adequate supervision over the students in their charge and whether the plaintiff's injuries were proximately related to the absence of adequate supervision.[18]

A student unsuccessfully filed a personal injury action against a school board for injuries that he sustained when he fell from a playground swing. An appellate court in New York affirmed a grant of summary judgment in favor of the board in observing that the student's sudden, unforeseeable, unsuccessful attempt to perform a backflip dismount from a moving swing while his teacher's back was turned was the sole proximate cause of his injuries.[19]

Following a meeting with school officials, as a mother, her son, and two relatives exited a school cafeteria, they encountered a student who fired a

---

[15] Duncan v. Chamblee, 757 So. 2d 946 [144 Educ. L. Rep. 1089] (Miss. 2000).
[16] Summers v. St. Andrew's Episcopal Sch., 759 So. 2d. 1203 [145 Educ. L. Rep. 830] (Miss. 2000).
[17] Jones v. Jackson Pub. Schs., 760 So. 2d 730 [145 Educ. L. Rep. 845] (Miss. 2000).
[18] Maucher v. South Huntington Union Free Sch. Dist., 698 N.Y.S.2d 307 [139 Educ. L. Rep. 1017] (N.Y. App. Div. 1999).
[19] Ascher v. Scarsdale Sch. Dist., 700 N.Y.S.2d 210 [140 Educ. L. Rep. 724] (N.Y. App. Div. 1999).

revolver wounding her son and killing one of the relatives. The families then unsuccessfully filed suit against the school board alleging negligent supervision. An appellate court in New York affirmed the dismissal of the claims since it was of the opinion that there was no evidence that school officials had sufficiently specific knowledge or notice of the dangerous third party conduct at issue.[20]

A parent sued a university research foundation and school board for sexual abuse of her son by a counselor hired by the latter to administer a program to identify students who would not traditionally enter college but showed potential to succeed in college. The counselor, who was not an employee of the board, met with the student behind close doors on a regular basis for a period of six months. A trial court in New York court dismissed claims of negligent hiring against the foundation but rejected the board's motion for summary judgment as to the negligent supervision charge since genuine issues of material fact remained as to whether school officials used the same degree of care as a reasonably prudent parent.[21]

When a child lost the use of an eye after being hit by a twig thrown by a peer with whom he was engaging in friendly horseplay, he sued the school board for negligent supervision. In response to cross appeals by both parties, an appellate court in New York affirmed that questions of fact as to whether the student assumed the risk of injury precluded the board's motion for summary judgment. The court further affirmed that any lack of supervision, where the incident lasted less than a minute and involved students with no history of such activities, was not the proximate cause of the child's injury.[22]

A school board contested the denial of its motion for summary judgment in a negligent supervision claim filed by a tenth-grade student who was injured as he attempted to break up a fight between two fifth-grade students. An appellate court in New York reversed in favor of the board it explaining that it could not be liable for the thoughtless or careless act by which one student may injure another.[23]

In the final case from New York, a school board challenged the denial of its motion for summary judgment where a student who was injured in an altercation with another child sued to recover damages for personal injuries.

[20] Billinger v. Board of Educ. of Amityville Union Free Sch. Dist., 706 N.Y.S.2d 178 [143 Educ. L. Rep. 616] (N.Y. App. Div. 2000).
[21] Murray v. Research Found. of State Univ. of N.Y., 707 N.Y.S.2d 816 [144 Educ. L. Rep. 620] (N.Y. Sup. Ct. 2000).
[22] Convey v. City of Rye Sch. Dist., 710 N.Y.S.2d 641 [146 Educ. L. Rep. 350] (N.Y. App. Div. 2000).
[23] Hernandez v. Christopher Robin Academy, 714 N.Y.S.2d 518 [147 Educ. L. Rep. 1057] (N.Y. App. Div. 2000).

In reversing, an appellate court decided that the board was not liable for the second student's actions because they could not have been reasonably anticipated.[24]

A high school student in Indiana who was severely beaten by peers while in a school parking lot sought further review of a grant of summary judgment in favor of the board and the private security company responsible for safeguarding the lot. An appellate court partially reversed in asserting that since school officials' knowledge of instances of criminal activity in the parking lot made the beating foreseeable, they were not relieved of their duty to supervise the safety of students by hiring the security company. At the same time, the court pointed out that the security company did not owe the student a duty to protect him as a third-party beneficiary to the contract between it and the board.[25]

In Arkansas, a high school student who accidentally amputated four fingers on his right hand in a vocational class while operating a table saw which had its safety guard removed and his parents unsuccessfully sued a school board alleging negligence and the tort of outrage. An appellate court affirmed a grant of summary judgment in favor of the board in positing that the plaintiffs did not support their claim of outrage.[26]

A student injured his head during recess and his mother contested the damages award that they received in their personal injury action against a school board. An appellate panel in Louisiana affirmed not only that the award was sufficient but also that the trial court did not err in failing to assign comparative fault to the student and his classmate as the two children attempted to move a tether ball pole which struck the plaintiff student in his head, thereby causing his injury.[27]

In School Buildings and On School Grounds

A student who broke his forearm while using a springboard in a school gymnasium appealed a grant of summary judgment in favor of the school board in his damages action. The Supreme Court of Kansas reversed in favor of the student in deciding that the gymnasium was an "open area" and public property within the meaning of the state Tort Claims Act.[28] Further,

---

[24] Johnsen v. Carmel Cent. Sch. Dist., 716 N.Y.S.2d 403 [149 Educ. L. Rep. 592] (N.Y. App. Div. 2000).

[25] King v. Northeast Security, Inc., 732 N.E.2d 824 [146 Educ. L. Rep. 388] (Ind. Ct. App. 2000).

[26] Brown v. Fountain Hill Sch. Dist., 1 S.W.3d 27 [140 Educ. L. Rep. 393] (Ark. Ct. App. 1999).

[27] LaBouisse v. Orleans Parish Sch. Bd., 757 So. 2d 866 [144 Educ. L. Rep. 1082] (La. Ct. App. 2000).

[28] Jackson v. Unified Sch. Dist. 259, Sedgwick County, 995 P.2d 844 [142 Educ. L. Rep. 1066] (Kan. 2000).

the court remanded the case for a determination as to whether the gymnasium was intended or permitted to be used for recreational purposes which would provide the board with an exception to liability.

In the first of five cases from New York, a high school student who was injured in a school parking lot when the car he was sitting on was put in motion by another pupil contested a grant of summary judgment in favor of the school board in his damages action. An appellate court affirmed that alleged inadequate supervision was not a proximate cause of the student's injuries since they were brought about by the result of the spontaneous and unforeseeable act of the other pupil.[29]

The estate of a thirteen-year-old student who died after falling through a school's skylight challenged the dismissal of its wrongful death action. An appellate court in New York affirmed the dismissal since there were no claims that the skylight was in any way defective or in an unobservable dangerous condition.[30] The court reasoned that even though children had been known to play on the roof occasionally, stepping on the skylight was an extraordinary occurrence which need not have been guarded against.

Where a student claimed that an accumulation of water on school steps caused him to fall and injure himself, a school contested the denial of its motion for summary judgment. An appellate court in New York dismissed in favor of the school in writing that there was no evidence that officials had actual or constructive notice of the hazard, meteorological reports for the date of the injury showed cloudless conditions, and the deposition of a peer who was standing next to the plaintiff when he fell stated there was no water on the steps.[31]

A student who was injured when he slipped and fell in the hallway of his junior high school unsuccessfully filed a damages action against his school board. An appellate court in New York affirmed that the board was not liable since there was no proof that the specific substance on which the student allegedly slipped was in the hall for a sufficient length of time to permit staff to discover and remedy the condition.[32]

In the final case from New York, a pedestrian sued a school board for injuries she sustained when she tripped and fell over the curb divider in a high school parking lot. On further review of the denial of the board's

---

[29] Castle v. Board of Coop. Educ. Serv. of Putnam and Westchester Counties, 703 N.Y.S.2d 203 [142 Educ. L. Rep. 459] (N.Y. App. Div. 2000).
[30] Clifford v. Sachem Cent. Sch. Dist., 707 N.Y.S.2d 133 [143 Educ. L. Rep. 1006] (N.Y. App. Div. 2000).
[31] Leo v. Mt. St. Michael Academy, 708 N.Y.S.2d 372 [144 Educ. L. Rep. 626] (N.Y. App. Div. 2000).
[32] Rivera v. City of N.Y., 713 N.Y.S.2d 196 [147 Educ. L. Rep. 238] (N.Y. App. Div. 2000).

motion for summary judgment, an appellate court affirmed that although the pedestrian had stepped over a white divider on her way into the building, there were issues of fact as to whether the hazard was readily observable when cars were closely parked together.[33]

A pedestrian and his wife challenged a grant of summary judgment in favor of a school board in his negligence action to recover for injuries that he sustained after he slipped and fell on an icy patch on a school sidewalk. An appellate court in Minnesota affirmed that the board was not liable since the icy patch was caused when an accumulation of shoveled snow melted, ran onto the sidewalk, and froze and that to require it to place the snow where it could not run in such a fashion was likely to be physically impossible and if attempted, prohibitively expensive.[34]

The mother of a child who was injured in a fall from playground equipment sought further review of a jury verdict in favor of the school board in her suit for gross negligence. An appellate court in Kentucky reversed in declaring that since evidence of industry standards for playground equipment was relevant, the mother was prejudiced by its exclusion from trial.[35]

Where a police officer who was on routine patrol in a middle school fell from a retaining wall and crushed his ankle, he challenged a grant of summary judgment in favor of the board on his premises liability claim. An appellate court in Florida reversed in ascertaining that not only was the board's failure to erect a guardrail or illuminate the area not shielded by governmental immunity but also that there were issues of fact as to whether the officer had prior knowledge of the unprotected ledge.[36]

Negligence Defenses

School boards, administrators, and/or teachers involved in negligence actions have a number of defenses available ranging from common law sovereign immunity to more affirmative defenses. The motivation behind common law immunity is to limit the flow of public money to private citizens because such payments detract from the educational functions of the schools. Affirmative defenses bar recovery by parties whose behavior in some way caused their injuries.

---

[33] O'Leary v. Saugerties Cent. Sch. Dist., 716 N.Y.S.2d 424 [149 Educ. L. Rep. 594] (N.Y. App. Div. 2000).

[34] Otis v. Anoka-Hennepin Sch. Dist. No. 11, 611 N.W.2d 390 [144 Educ. L. Rep. 748] (Minn. Ct. App. 2000).

[35] Elledge v. Richland/Lexington Sch. Dist. Five, 534 S.E.2d 289 [147 Educ. L. Rep. 372] (S.C. Ct. App. 2000).

[36] Green v. School Bd. of Pasco County, 752 So. 2d 700 [143 Educ. L. Rep. 408] (Fla. Dist. Ct. App. 2000).

Immunity

Common Law (Governmental Immunity)

In the twenty reported cases involving an immunity defense, plaintiffs were successful only six times. Following his threats against a classmate, an assistant principal warned a student about the consequences of fighting. After the student seriously injured a classmate during a fight, the latter child's parents unsuccessfully filed a negligent supervision claim against the assistant principle and school board. The Supreme Court of Alabama affirmed that the assistant principal was entitled to discretionary function immunity from the tort claim.[37] Specifically, the court was convinced that the assistant principal was protected by immunity since he was acting within the scope of his authority in considering what disciplinary action he should have taken against the student who made the threat and was performing a discretionary function when he discerned that the child had not violated school board policy in a way that required him to notify law-enforcement officials and to suspend the aggressive student.

The Supreme Court of Mississippi reversed the dismissal of a suit in which a student sued a school board for negligently supervising, monitoring, and failing to provide a safe environment.[38] In acknowledging that the student was beaten and sexually assaulted on leaving an after-school detention, the court remanded the case for trial in contending that the board's failure to provide ordinary care relieved it of the shield of sovereign immunity.

The Supreme Court of Rhode Island vacated and remanded a case involving a cheerleader who was injured during practice as she attempted a new maneuver. As a member of the cheerleading squad, the court found that the student was an identifiable person to whom the school board owed a special duty because an injury of the type that she sustained was sufficiently foreseeable. According to the court, whether the maneuver involved the doctrine of assumption of risk was a matter for trial.[39]

Where a kindergarten student was killed when he was pinned against an ambulance by a golf cart as an unsupervised child started a second cart that was used in a annual safety demonstration sponsored by a city, a jury

---

[37] Carroll *ex rel.* Slaught v. Hammett, 744 So. 2d 906 [140 Educ. L. Rep. 777] (Ala. 1999).

[38] L.W. v. McComb Separate Mun. Sch. Dist., 754 So. 2d 1136 [143 Educ. L. Rep. 1138] (Miss. 1999).

[39] Schultz v. Foster-Glocester Reg'l Sch. Dist., 755 A.2d 153 [146 Educ. L. Rep. 256] (R.I. 2000).

apportioned fault at sixty-six percent for the city and thirty-four percent for the school board. On appeal, the Supreme Court of Iowa affirmed that the board was not entitled to immunity since it breached its duty to supervise insofar as officials did not exercise ordinary care in implementing one of its policies for field trips.[40]

In Connecticut, a student who was struck in the head by a door opened by a teacher challenged a grant of summary judgment in favor of the school board. An appellate court reversed in favor of the student on the basis that the identifiable person-imminent harm exception to governmental immunity for discretionary acts performed by municipal employees was applicable.[41]

Where a motorist who was involved in a collision with a school teacher sued the teacher and school board, an appellate court in Michigan reversed the denial of the teacher's motion to amend her answer to add the defense of governmental immunity.[42] An appellate court decreed that since the teacher was acting in the course of her employment and within the scope of her authority while driving between schools, she could present an immunity defense.

Statutory Immunity

The estate of a student who was shot and killed by a peer in the hallway of his high school unsuccessfully filed a wrongful death action against a school board. The Supreme Court of South Carolina, in examining the supervision provided by school officials, held that since school officials exercised slight care, they were covered by a gross negligence exception to the Tort Claims Act.[43]

After a female student with learning and hearing disabilities was allegedly raped in a school bathroom by a male peer with a lengthy history of violent and delinquent behavior, her mother unsuccessfully sued the principal and the school board for failing to maintain adequate security and for failing to warn students of his violent past. Further, a grand jury failed to indict the male for the alleged rape. The mother claimed that the grand jury's action was due to the principal's failure to contact the police or obtain medical assistance, thereby resulting in a lack of evidence that a rape oc-

---

[40] City of Cedar Falls v. Cedar Falls Community Sch. Dist., 617 N.W.2d 11 [147 Educ. L. Rep. 671] (Iowa 2000).

[41] Colon v. City of New Haven, 758 A.2d 900 [147 Educ.. Rep. 209] (Conn. Ct. App. 2000).

[42] Backus v. Kauffman, 605 N.W.2d 690 [141 Educ. L. Rep. 887] (Mich. Ct. App. 1999).

[43] Etheredge v. Richland Sch. Dist. One, 534 S.E.2d 275 [147 Educ. L. Rep. 368] (S.C. 2000).

curred. The Supreme Court of Mississippi, in an interlocutory appeal, granted the defendants' motions for summary judgment on the ground that they were entitled to statutory immunity.[44]

Following a school-sponsored band concert, a student who was injured trying to avoid an altercation involving his friend contested a grant of summary judgment in favor of a school board. On further review, the Supreme Court of Mississippi reversed in ruling that since the board's statutory duty to control and discipline students was ministerial rather than discretionary, the State Tort Claims Act's exception from liability for failure to exercise a discretionary function did not apply. The court further believed that whether administrators and teachers were entitled to sovereign immunity was a question of fact for trial.[45]

The Supreme Court of Nebraska affirmed a verdict against a school board and teacher on the basis that their negligent supervision was the proximate cause of a student's injuries.[46] The court agreed that discretionary function exception of the Tort Claims Act did not apply to allowing an inexperienced welding student to wear an untreated cotton shirt or the teacher's failure to provide him with a leather apron.

In Indiana, a middle school student challenged a grant of summary judgment in favor of his school and the state Department of Natural Resources in his damages action seeking to recover for injuries resulting from the at-home explosion of a shotgun shell after he attended a lecture on the parts of a shell by a conservation officer . An appellate court affirmed that school officials did not owe the student a duty for injuries that he sustained in the at-home accident. The court also agreed that the Department was entitled to statutory immunity because the conservation officer could not have foreseen the intervening negligent act of the student's striking the shell with a hammer and his father's leaving live ammunition unsupervised at home.[47]

A ten year-old child with a disability and his parents contested the dismissal of their damages action arising out of injuries that he sustained when the stroller that that he was sitting on was in the doorway to a closet.

---

[44] Lincoln County Sch. Dist. v. Doe, 749 So. 2d 943 [142 Educ. L. Rep. 563] (Miss. 1999).

[45] Lang v. Bay St. Louis/Waveland Sch. Dist., 764 So.2d 1234 [146 Educ. L. Rep. 1166] (Miss. 1999).

[46] Norman v. Ogallala Pub. Sch. Dist., 609 N.W.2d 338 [143 Educ. L. Rep. 629] (Neb. 2000).

[47] Mangold v. Indiana Dept. of Natural Resources, 720 N.E.2d 424 [139 Educ. L. Rep. 1021] (Ind. Ct. App. 1999).

An appellate panel in Colorado affirmed that a trial court's failure to conduct a hearing before dismissing the suit was not an abuse of discretion.[48]

In the first of five cases from Illinois, a high school student who was injured in a physical education swimming class supervised by a substitute teacher unsuccessfully alleged negligence and willful and wanton misconduct on the part of the board. The Supreme Court of Illinois affirmed that "public entity" immunity protected the board since the state's Tort Immunity Act extended to the student's claim.[49]

The parents of a student who was injured in physical education class while performing a maneuver off to the side, by herself, which was not part of the proscribed curriculum, unsuccessfully filed a damages action against the school board. An appellate court in Illinois affirmed that the board was statutorily immune from charges of failure to supervise and the improper use of public property.[50]

In Illinois, the mother of a child with a developmental disability who was sexually assaulted by a peer on a school bus contested the dismissal of her negligence action against the school board and transit company. An appellate court affirmed that the mother failed to prove that board officials acted in a willful and wanton manner with knowledge that male students were likely to commit sexual assaults but chose not to prevent them from doing so.[51]

When a woman was injured after she fell off of an access ramp as she left a school graduation ceremony, a school board sought further review of the denial of its motion for dismissal based on statutory immunity. An appellate court noted that since the ramp was not recreational public property, it did not come within the scope of the law for which immunity could be granted. However, the court remarked that absent a record of reports that the ramp was unsafe, and its having met all appropriate safety standards, board officials did not engage in willful and wanton conduct.[52]

A motorist who was injured in a collision with a high school student who was driving home from school unsuccessfully sued a school board alleging willful and wanton conduct by officials who permitted the student to drive home early due to inclement weather. On further review, an appellate

---

[48] Padilla v. School Dist. No. 1 of City and County of Denver, 1 P.3d 256 [144 Educ. L. Rep. 753] (Colo. Ct. App. 1999).
[49] Henrich v. Libertyville High Sch., 712 N.E.2d 298 [144 Educ. L. Rep. 347] (Ill. 1998).
[50] Grandalski v. Lyons Township High Sch. Dist. 204, 711 N.E.2d 372 [141 Educ. L. Rep. 245] (Ill. Ct. App. 1999).
[51] A.R. *ex rel.* v. Chicago Bd. of Educ., 724 N.E.2d 6 [144 Educ. L. Rep. 532] (Ill. Ct. App. 1999).
[52] Capps v. Belleville Sch. Dist. No. 201, 730 N.E.2d 81 [145 Educ. L. Rep. 733] (Ill. Ct. App. 2000).

court in Illinois reversed in declaring that the choice of school personnel whether to create an exception to the existing procedure for one student was not made at the planning level since it did not involve the formulation of principles to achieve a common public benefit and was not an exercise of discretion protected by immunity.[53]

The parents of a student who drowned while attending a junior high school function at a university supervised by his teachers challenged a grant of summary judgment in their wrongful death action against the university, school board, and various employees. An appellate court in Texas affirmed that the mandatory duty of school employees to supervise students involved the exercise of judgment or discretion for which they were afforded statutory immunity.[54]

In the first of two cases from Ohio, the parents of a second-grade student who was struck by a car as he walked home from school contested a grant of summary judgment in favor of their school board. An appellate court was of the view that while a principal, teacher, and the board breached their duty to safeguard the student, the educators' acts were not so reckless as to preclude their motion for statutory immunity. At the same time, the court decided that those same acts and omissions were not exercises of discretion that entitled the board to the same protection.[55]

The parents of a first grade student who was sexually assaulted by older students who asked her to come to the rear of a school bus sought further review of a grant of summary judgment in their negligence action against the school board. An appellate court in Ohio affirmed that the board was not liable since the child's injuries were not caused by the driver's negligent operation of the bus that would have brought them under an exception to tort liability in connection with the performance of a governmental function.[56]

Notice of Claim

Plaintiffs were successful in filing late notice of claim in the first two of the six reported cases, both of which were from New York. Parents of an elementary school student who was injured when he fell from a swing at a

---

[53] Harrison v. Hardin County Community Unit, 730 N.E.2d 61 [145 Educ. L. Rep. 726] (Ill. Ct. App. 200).

[54] Williams v. Chatman, 17 S.W.3d 694 [144 Educ. L. Rep. 775] (Tex. App. 1999).

[55] Addis v. Howell, 738 N.E.2d 37 [148 Educ. L. Rep. 473] (Ohio Ct. App. 2000).

[56] Doe v. Dayton City Sch. Dist. Bd. of Educ., 738 N.E.2d 390 [148 Educ. L. Rep. 1026] (Ohio Ct. App. 1999).

school playground sought further review of the denial of their claim to file a late notice of claim. An appellate court reversed in reasoning that the limitations period for the injured infant did not apply to the parents.[57]

In New York, an appellate court affirmed that the mother of a child who was allegedly mistreated by a teacher was allowed to file a late notice of claim.[58] The panel agreed that the trial court properly exercised its discretion since the mother had contacted school officials shortly after she learned of the incidents involving her son and their investigation of the teacher had uncovered similar instances occurring over the course of three years.

A special education coordinator unsuccessfully sued an educational unit alleging sexual harassment and intentional infliction of emotional distress. The Supreme Court of North Dakota affirmed that in light of his claim that a stroke impaired his ability to remember events that formed the basis for his claim, the coordinator failed to establish that he was entitled to relief.[59]

A student at a school for the blind sought further review of the dismissal of her suit for injuries she sustained in a wheelchair incident. The Supreme Court of Mississippi reversed and remanded in observing that the student's sending notice to the State Superintendent, rather than to the head of one of the branches of the State Education Department, substantially complied with the Act's requirement to notify the "chief executive officer" of the governmental entity.[60]

In South Dakota, a former student filed section 1983 and title IX charges against a high school teacher and school board for sexual abuse that allegedly occurred twenty-five years earlier. The federal trial court dismissed the claim against the board since the alleged abuse occurred before title IX was enacted.[61] The court granted the teacher's motion for summary judgment in positing that the cause of action against him could not be revived as a 1991 state statute established time limitations for civil actions arising out of sexual of a child.

A former student from a parochial elementary school who claimed that she was involved in a four-year sexual relationship with her teacher unsuc-

---

[57] Blackburn v. Three Village Cent. Sch. Dist., 705 N.Y.S.2d 53 [142 Educ. L. Rep. 1022] (N.Y. App. Div. 2000).

[58] Drodzal v. Rensselaer City Sch. Dist., 716 N.Y.S.2d 435 [149 Educ. L. Rep. 597] (N.Y. App. Div. 2000).

[59] Follman v. Upper Valley Special Educ. Unit., 609 N.W.2d 90 [143 Educ. L. Rep. 623] (N.D. 2000).

[60] Jones v. Mississippi Sch. For the Blind, 758 So. 2d 428 [144 Educ. L. Rep. 1103] (Miss. 2000).

[61] Gross v. Weber, 112 F. Supp.2d 923 [147 Educ. L. Rep. 157] (D.S.D. 2000).

cessfully sued the archdiocese and the school's former principal. An appellate court in Colorado affirmed a grant of summary judgment in favor of the defendants in indicating that the former student failed to file her claims within the required two-year statute of limitations.[62]

Educational Malpractice

A father who was investigated regarding the possible abuse of his child unsuccessfully sued school officials claiming that they recklessly injured him by improperly instructing his child about proper and improper touching. An appellate court in Connecticut affirmed a grant of summary judgment in favor of school officials on the claim for reckless instruction in explaining that a charge of improper curriculum was essentially an unrecognizable claim for educational malpractice.[63]

Liability Insurance

Where a school board's business automobile insurer sought to establish that its policy did not provide primary coverage and that it did not owe a duty to defend or indemnify a teacher for an accident that occurred while she was driving her own car in the course and scope of her duties, her own insurance company challenged a ruling that it was the primary source of her coverage. An appellate court in Illinois reversed in pointing out that since the legislature did not intend to eliminate school boards' mandatory duty to defend their employees for damages claims, despite the language of the board's insurance policy, it did provide primary coverage for the claim.[64]

In Kentucky, a school board's automobile insurer sought a determination that the board's liability policy provided coverage for an accident where a student was struck by a truck as she exited her school bus. An appellate court affirmed that since the injuries that the student suffered as she crossed the street under the protection of the school bus's warning lights and stop arm constituted "use of the bus," they were within the coverage of the automobile policy.[65]

---

[62] Sandoval v. Archdiocese of Denver, 8 P.3d 598 [147 Educ. L. Rep. 328] (Colo. Ct. App. 2000).
[63] Vogel v. Maimonides Academy of Western Conn., 754 A.2d 824 [145 Educ. L. Rep. 1084] (Conn. Ct. App. 2000).
[64] County Mut. Ins. Co. v. Teachers Ins. Co., 727 N.E.2d 1047 [144 Educ. L. Rep. 590] (Ill. Ct. App. 2000).
[65] Hartford Ins. Co. v. Kentucky Sch. Bds., 17 S.W.3d 525 [144 Educ. L. Rep. 769] (Ky. Ct. App. 2000).

The parents of an elementary school student sued a school board and an assistant principal after their daughter was struck by a vehicle while in route to her bus stop. The location of the bus stop had been moved five months earlier in response to a claim that several boys had assaulted the student at her prior stop. An appellate court in North Carolina reversed the denial of the board's motion for summary judgment in asserting that the doctrine of sovereign immunity was applicable to the charges of negligent supervision and constructive fraud in reference to the actions of the assistant principal who changed the bus stop. The court concluded that since the board's commercial umbrella policy did not cover the student's injuries, it did not waive the board's and assistant principal's governmental immunity from suit.[66]

With the knowledge and approval of his school board, a teacher rented a city-owned theater for the production of a class presentation at which a student was injured. After the parties reached a settlement with the general liability insurer that covered the city, board, and teacher, the excess insurer sought to limit its liability. An appellate court in Minnesota found that the teacher's having purchased private excess insurance was not valid and collectible insurance that should have been taken into account when considering the extent of the board's waiver of its liability limits.[67]

Employee Injuries

The widow of a school maintenance worker who was killed when he came in contact with a high voltage electrical line on a high school baseball field challenged a judgment in favor of a city and the electrical utility company in her wrongful death action. The Supreme Court of Indiana vacated and remanded in favor of the widow in writing that material issues of fact remained as to whether the defendants were involved in the design of electrical transmission facility and whether they owed a duty of care to the school employee.[68]

After being assaulted by a parent at an open school event, an assistant principal contested the dismissal of his suit against a school board and principal to recover for physical and emotional injuries. An appellate court in New York affirmed the dismissal on the basis that the assistant principal failed to show that the defendants owed her a special duty. The court added

---

[66] Herring v. Winston-Salem/Forsyth County Bd. of Educ., 529 S.E.2d 458 [144 Educ. L. Rep. 1062] (N.C. Ct. App. 2000).
[67] City of Red Wing v. Ellsworth Community Sch. Dist. 617 N.W.2d 602 [147 Educ. L. Rep. 683] (Minn. Ct. App. 2000).
[68] Butler v. City of Peru, 733 N.E.2d 912 [146 Educ. L. Rep 406] (Ind. 2000).

that the assistant principal's claims of emotional distress based on the parent's being allowed to enter her office were too remote and speculative to support recovery.[69]

In a second case from New York, when a school custodian sued a catering company in an attempt to recover for injuries he sustained when he slipped and fell on a greasy substance in a school kitchen, a trial court dismissed the company's third-party action. An appellate court reversed in precluding summary judgment since there were unresolved issues of fact as to whether employees of the company created the hazard.[70]

A teacher who was injured in an altercation with another teacher unsuccessfully sued a school board for her injuries. On further review, an appellate court in Louisiana affirmed a grant of summary judgment in favor of the board in contending that it was not vicariously liable for the teacher's intentional torts.[71]

Two months after a high school secretary slipped and fell on an icy sidewalk leading into a school, she gave birth to a premature child that died shortly thereafter. The secretary unsuccessfully filed wrongful death and survival actions against the school board. On further review, the District of Columbia Court of Appeals affirmed that a reasonable juror could have found that the premature birth and death of the child was caused by factors other than the secretary's slip and fall.[72]

Workers' Compensation

When an assistant principal sought compensation for injuries he sustained while driving to work, an appellate court reversed a finding of the Workers' Compensation Commission that his injury arose out of the course of his employment. On further review, the Supreme Court of South Carolina, in turn, reversed in stating that the going and coming rule was inapplicable since the injury occurred on school premises. The court reasoned that since the assistant principal's car skidded on an icy road behind the school and came to rest on its football practice field, he sustained a compensable injury while on the employer's premises.[73]

---

[69] Johnson v. New York City Bd. of Educ., 704 N.Y.S.2d 281 [142 Educ. L. Rep. 474] (N.Y. App. Div. 2000).

[70] Hopkins v. Statewide Indus. Catering Group, 710 N.Y.S.2d 81 [145 Educ. L. Rep. 755] (N.Y. App. Div. 2000).

[71] Affeltranger-Cheramie v. Zachary, 757 So. 2d 751 [144 Educ. L. Rep. 1079] (La. Ct. App. 2000).

[72] Newell v. District of Columbia, 741 A.2d 28 [140 Educ. L. Rep. 303] (D.C. 1999).

[73] Aughtry v. Abbeville County Sch. Dist. #60, 533 S.E.2d 885 [147 Educ. L. Rep. 349] (S.C. 2000).

An appellate court in Indiana affirmed the denial of the request for worker's compensation filed by the widow of a school bus driver who was shot and killed by another worker at the parking site for school buses. In discerning that the shooting arose out of a prior animosity unrelated to the driver's work, the court agreed that since his death did not arise out of his employment, his widow not entitled to benefits.[74]

In Louisiana, an elementary school teacher who injured her back on a field trip when the school bus in which she was riding repeatedly hit potholes in the road recovered workers' compensation. On further review, an appellate court affirmed that since the teacher established that her injury was work-related, she was entitled to medical expenses and attorney fees.[75]

An appellate court in Oregon ascertained that criticisms by students and parents may provide a basis for workers' compensation benefits. Even though it remanded the dispute to the Workers' Compensation Board for a determination of whether a disciplinary letter was the basis for a teacher's depression, and eventual resignation, the court was convinced that a broad range of incidents, including slashed tires on her car and suspicious activity by teenagers near her home, could be characterized as work-related.[76]

Defamation/Intentional Infliction of Emotional Distress

A teacher contested a grant of summary judgment in her defamation suit against another teacher with whom she shared chaperone duties on a school trip. At issue was a letter that the second teacher sent to a principal outlining the plaintiff's alleged improper actions on the trip. The Supreme Court of New Jersey affirmed in favor of the defendant in holding that the letter was entitled to substantial First Amendment protection because it involved a matter of public concern, namely the welfare of children entrusted to the care of a teacher.[77]

A teacher sued her principal, assistant principal, and school board alleging intentional infliction of emotional distress, tortious interference with a contract, and breach of contract after she resigned following discussions

---

[74] Conway v. School City of East Chicago, 734 N.E.2d 594 [146 Educ. L. Rep. 844] (Ind. Ct. App. 2000).

[75] McCartney v. Orleans Parish Sch. Bd., 743 So. 2d 821 [139 Educ. L. Rep. 1078] (La. Ct. App. 1999).

[76] Liberty Northwest Ins. Corp. v. Shotthafer, 10 P.3d 299 [147 Educ. L. Rep. 713] (Or. Ct. App. 2000).

[77] Rocci v. Ecole Secondaire Macdonald-Cartier, 755 A.2d 583 [146 Educ. L. Rep. 283] (N.J. 2000).

related to her supervision of students and general mental health. The Supreme Court of Connecticut affirmed that since the teacher did not suffer any actual loss as a result of the conduct of the principal and his assistant, there was no basis to her claim for tortious interference with contract.[78]

In Maryland, a high school teacher/coach who was suspended and reprimanded after two female members of his cross-country team falsely accused him of sexual misconduct in an attempt to get a different coach sought further review of the dismissal of his defamation and tortious interference with his economic relationship action against the students and their parents. An appellate court, in reversing in favor of the teacher, decided that under the circumstances, the student's complaints were not absolutely privileged despite the strong public interest that they and their parents should be protected from suit for reporting a teacher's alleged sexual misconduct.[79]

A former student filed a due process claim under section 1983 for sexual molestation along with state law claims for assault and intentional infliction of emotional distress. The federal trial court in Maine denied the teacher's motion for summary judgment with regard to the emotional distress claim in believing that his alleged acts of touching were so extreme and outrageous as to preclude granting his request.[80]

Former employees of an early childhood education program filed a defamation suit against their director for comments that he made about them to television reporters. On further review of the denial of the director's motion for summary judgment, an appellate court in Texas reversed in his favor.[81] The court reasoned that since the director's remarks were incident to or within the scope of his employment, he was not liable.

A high school teacher challenged the dismissal of her suit against students for intentional infliction of emotional distress which alleged that they produced and distributed a newsletter which contains threats not only on her life but also to rape and kill her children. An appellate court in Florida reversed in acknowledging that the students' conduct was so outrageous and extreme that it went beyond all possible bounds of decency.[82]

---

[78] Appleton v. Board of Educ. of Stonington, 757 A.2d 1059 [146 Educ. L. Rep. 1097] (Conn. 2000).

[79] Flynn v. Reichardt, 749 A.2d 197 [143 Educ. L. Rep. 585] (Md. Ct. App. 2000).

[80] Hinkley v. Baker, 122 F. Supp.2d 57 [149 Educ. L. Rep. 416] (D. Me. 2000).

[81] Enriquez v. Khouri, 142 S.W.3d 458 [142 Educ. L. Rep. 1102] (Tex. App. 2000).

[82] Nims v. Harrison, 768 So. 2d 1198 [148 Educ. L. Rep. 518] (Fla. Dist. Ct. App. 2000).

Constitutional Torts

Eight of the reported cases involved allegations of sexual abuse or misconduct of students by school employees, four of which involved such allegations between students. Parents of a student in Virginia who was sexually abused by his teacher sued a superintendent under section 1983 for failure to warn them that their child's teacher was accused of sexually molesting a student in the past and was suspected of inappropriate conduct with their son. A federal trial court granted the superintendent's motion for dismissal in noting that the parents failed to state an actionable claim for deprivation of their rights.[83] In a related action, when a jury awarded the student damages in his suit against a principal and a school board, a federal trial court denied the principal's motion to set the verdict aside as excessive.[84] The court decreed that the award was proper since the principal showed deliberate indifference by failing to act in a timely manner on reports of the teacher's prior sexual abuse of students and his inappropriate behavior in this case. The court granted the board's motion for judgment notwithstanding the verdict in explaining that it could have been liable only if a school official with actual knowledge of the abuse was vested by the board with both the duty to supervise the employee and the power to take action that would end such abuse and failed to do so. The court concluded that the student failed to establish that the principal had the power to dismiss or transfer the teacher.

Student Initiated Cases

Parents in New York sued child welfare workers, a city, and others on behalf of their daughter and themselves, alleging that her removal from school and being subjected to a medical examination for signs of sexual abuse violated their due process rights and her right to be free from unreasonable search and seizure. On further review of a trial court's granting motions for summary judgment on various issues for both parties, the Second Circuit affirmed that while welfare workers violated the child's due process and Fourth Amendment rights, they were entitled to immunity. The court agreed that the defendants did not violate the substantive due process rights of the child or parents and that individual defendants were entitled to qualified immunity.[85]

---

[83] Baynard v. Lawson, 76 F. Supp.2d 688 [140 Educ. L. Rep. 905] (E.D. Va.1999).
[84] Baynard v. Lawson, 112 F. Supp.2d 524 [147 Educ. L. Rep. 136] (E.D. Va. 2000).
[85] Tenenbaum v. Williams, 193 F.3d 581 [140 Educ. L. Rep. 24] (2nd Cir. 1999).

As punishment for talking in gym class, a middle school student in Texas whose coach ordered him to perform one hundred "squat thrusts" suffered internal injuries for which he unsuccessfully filed suit alleging that this violated his due process rights. The Fifth Circuit affirmed the dismissal of the claim on the ground that the teacher's conduct did not violate substantive due process and that state law provided adequate remedies.[86]

The mother of a mentally impaired student in Michigan unsuccessfully filed a title IX action against the school board and various officials following the alleged sexual abuse and rape of her daughter. The Sixth Circuit affirmed a grant of summary judgment in favor of the defendants in positing that state law entitled the superintendent to absolute immunity and that other school officials were entitled to immunity because their conduct did not rise to the level of gross negligence.[87] The court also observed that the student lacked a private right of action against the teacher and school officials in their individual capacities since only recipients of federal funds could be held liable for damages under title IX.

When a high school student in Tennessee was expelled after a knife, which had been placed in his car by a friend, was uncovered as he was attending a school function, a school board and various officials sought further review of the denial of their motion for summary judgment in his suit to recover compensation for his having been expelled. The Sixth Circuit, in affirming in favor of the student, rejected the board's arguments that since safety is not only important but also because it is difficult to evaluate a pupil's state of mind that it did not have to try to ascertain whether he knowingly possessed the weapon before taking steps to expel him.[88]

In Kentucky, a school board challenged the denial of its motion for judgment as a matter of law where a female high school student alleged that she was the target of peer sexual harassment which she and her mother repeatedly reported to school authorities from the time she was a sixth grader. The Sixth Circuit affirmed that there was evidence sufficient to establish that school officials violated title IX because they were deliberately indifferent to harassment which was both persistent and severe.[89]

When, after the last day of classes, a high school in Oregon sponsored an activity at a local park, four female seniors hid in the stalls of a boys bathroom and threw water balloons at a group of senior boys when they

---

[86] Moore v. Willis Indep. Sch. Dist., 233 F.3d 871 [149 Educ. L. Rep. 337] (5th Cir. 2000).

[87] Soper *ex rel.* Soper v. Hoben, 195 F.3d 845 [139 Educ. L. Rep. 807] (6th Cir. 1999).

[88] Seal v. Morgan, 229 F.3d 567 [148 Educ. L. Rep. 34] (6th Cir. 2000).

[89] Vance v. Spencer County Pub. Sch. Dist., 231 F.3d 253 [148 Educ. L. Rep. 616] (6th Cir. 2000).

entered. The school board upheld the suspension of the females who were also denied the opportunity to participate in their commencement ceremony even though they did receive their diplomas. The female students unsuccessfully filed suit claiming damages under title IX alleging that their actions were in retaliation for harassment they experienced from the senior boys. The Ninth Circuit affirmed a grant of summary judgment that had been entered on behalf of the board in agreeing that school officials could not have been liable under title IX for denying the females the opportunity to participate in the graduation ceremony.[90]

A student in Florida who was disciplined for displaying a Confederate Flag during class hours unsuccessfully claimed that school officials violated his First Amendment rights. The Eleventh Circuit affirmed that the administrators were working within the scope of their duty and entitled to qualified immunity since they were not the final policymakers. The court pointed out that since the board had not established a pervasive and well-settled policy or custom of banning the Confederate flag, it also was not liable.[91]

Three students unsuccessfully sued a school board and principal along with a former teacher who, they alleged, violated title IX when he sexually molested them. The Eleventh Circuit affirmed a grant of summary judgment in favor of the board and principal on the basis that another student's complaint about the teacher was insufficient to alert them to the possibility the teacher was molesting students. Further, the court was satisfied that the principal's actions, in contacting his supervisor, directing a school counselor and social worker to interview the student and a witness, interviewing the teacher, and meeting with her mother showed that school officials did not respond with deliberate indifference.[92]

The parents of a student who was shot and killed by a classmate while riding on the school bus unsuccessfully filed suit against a county school board under the state Civil Rights Act. The Supreme Court of Arkansas affirmed that the board was not liable under the Act because it did not have the necessary custodial relationship with either the perpetrator or victim and because even though officials had knowledge of his violent tendencies during junior high school, there was no evidence of similar behavior while he was enrolled in high school.[93]

---

[90] Reese v. Jefferson Sch. Dist. No. 14J, 208 F.3d 736 [143 Educ. L. Rep. 450] (9th Cir. 2000).
[91] Denno v. School Bd. of Volusia County, 218 F.3d 1267 [145 Educ. L. Rep. 942] (11th Cir. 2000).
[92] Davis v. DeKalb County Sch. Dist., 233 F.3d 1367 [149 Educ. L. Rep. 376] (11th Cir. 2000).
[93] Rudd v. Pulaski County Sch. Dist., 20 S.W.3d 310 [146 Educ. L. Rep. 560] (Ark. 2000).

A high school student in Pennsylvania filed a civil rights action against a teacher and a school board based on the teacher's having used physical force in disciplining his disruptive or unruly behavior. A federal trial court granted the teacher's motion for summary judgment in determining that the momentary use of physical force did not shock the judicial conscience in violation of the student's right to substantive due process.[94]

In the first of three cases from New York, the mother of a second-grade student alleged title IX liability for sexual harassment on the part of a principal, teacher, and school board. A federal trial court ruled that another child's teasing, punching, and poking the girl did not constitute sexual harassment and that a single incident of sexual misconduct did not result in a denial of equal access to education.[95]

When an eighth-grade student refused to give her physical education teacher a twenty dollar bill that she found on the floor, and that he thought was his, she ran into a storage closet. After about thirty seconds, the teacher allowed the student out of the closet and, as he restrained her arm, she threw the money against his chest. While hesitating to make a "federal case" out of a brief incident, a federal trial court in New York denied the teacher's motion for summary judgment on a false imprisonment claim since it regarded his actions as an abuse of his power but granted such a motion as it did not think that he violated the student's substantive or procedural due process rights. The court added that the school board was not liable for the teacher's actions because there was no evidence that it condoned his behavior or knew that it was likely to occur.[96]

In New York, when a high school student sued his school board under title IX alleging sexual harassment by a teacher, a federal trial partially granted the board's motion for summary judgment since there were issues of fact were as to whether it was liable for negligent training and supervision. The court further declared that it was a matter for trial as to whether a school administrator was deliberately indifferent to the student's complaints.[97]

A middle school student in Georgia and her mother sought damages from a county, school board, various officials, and a custodian who alleg-

---

[94] Kurilla v. Callahan, 68 F. Supp.2d 556 [139 Educ. L. Rep. 900] (M.D. Pa. 1999).

[95] Manfredi v. Mount Vernon Bd. of Educ., 94 F. Supp.2d 447 [144 Educ. L. Rep 118] (S.D.N.Y. 2000).

[96] Bisignano v. Harrison Cent. Sch. Dist., 113. F. Supp.2d 591 [147 Educ. L. Rep. 529] (S.D. N.Y. 2000).

[97] Flores v. Saulpaugh, 115 F. Supp.2d 319 [147 Educ. L. Rep. 941] (N.D.N.Y. 2000).

edly raped her. A federal trial court partially granted the defendants' motions for summary judgment in asserting that the Violence Against Women Act pertained only to the custodian.[98] In addition, the court deemed that the board was not liable under title IX since there was no connection between its failure to place surveillance cameras in the area where the alleged incident took place and the injury.

Parents of an elementary school student unsuccessfully sued their school board and various officials for failing to control bullies who beat their son up, alleging that their failure to provide protection violated his constitutional rights. A federal trial court in North Carolina granted the defendants' motions to dismiss since it was of the view that insofar as the parents voluntarily withdrew their son from public school to attend a private school, they could not file a claim for deprivation of due process.[99]

Children filed suit under title IX against a school board following incidents of sexual and harassment by their teacher. A federal trial court in Ohio denied the board's motion for summary judgment since there were material issue of fact as to whether school officials had actual knowledge of the teacher's actions.[100] The court also rejected a similar motion on a section 1983 claim because there were material questions of fact as to whether board officials had a custom of failing to prevent sexual abuse by the teacher after receiving repeated notices suggesting that he was a pedophile.

In a second case from Ohio, a student who was seriously injured when he was struck in the face by a peer who had threatened him in the presence of the principal and a teacher sued the superintendent and school board. A federal trial court in Ohio dismissed the claim on the basis that no special relationship existed between the students involved, the board, and superintendent which created a duty to protect the injured child.[101] Further, the court maintained that insofar as the child who injured the student was a private actor rather than a governmental or school official acting under the color of state law pursuant to any stated governmental or school policies or customs, the board could not be liable.

A student in California sued a classmate and school board under title IX after he was assaulted while walking home from school because of his perceived homosexuality. The student claimed that he reported the assault to

---

[98] Sherman *ex rel.* Sherman v. Helms, 80 F. Supp.2d 1365 [141 Educ. L. Rep. 689] (M.D. Ga. 2000).

[99] Stevenson *ex rel.* Stevenson v. Martin County Bd. of Educ., 93 F. Supp.2d 644 [143 Educ. L. Rep. 856] (E.D.N.C. 1999).

[100] Massey v. Akron City Bd. of Educ., 82 F. Supp.2d 735 [141 Educ. L. Rep. 1104] (N.D. Ohio 2000).

[101] Oldham *ex rel.* Young v. Cincinnati Pub. Schs., 118 F. Supp.2d 867 [148 Educ. L. Rep. 845] (S.D. Ohio 2000).

school officials who failed to take steps to stop the harassment. A federal trial court rejected the board's motion to dismiss in noting that the educators' actions met the deliberate indifference element under title IX.[102]

In Iowa, a student and her mother sued their school board for damages resulting from her having been sexually abused by a school employee. A federal trial court granted the board's motion for summary judgment in reflecting that it was not liable under title IX since there was insufficient evidence to support a finding of deliberate indifference to the employee's conduct.[103] The court was also of the opinion that the board was exempt on the claim of negligent hiring, retention, and supervision because state law insulated it from tort liability in the performance of discretionary functions.

In Florida, a student sued his school board for damages alleging the excessive use of corporal punishment by school employees. A federal trial court held that since state remedies precluded it from acting, it lacked jurisdiction over the dispute.[104]

When an individual sued a school board claiming that his being shot by one of its police officers violated his constitutional rights, the defendants sought to have the suit dismissed based on Eleventh Amendment immunity. The federal trial court in Nevada rejected both the board's motion in indicating that it was not an arm of the state for Eleventh Amendment purposes and the employees' claims for Eleventh Amendment immunity.[105]

A school board in Illinois filed an interlocutory appeal over whether a female student who was harassed by two male peers had a private right to action against it under the state constitution's gender discrimination provision. An appellate court responded that the sole mechanism for a private recovery of damages was under the Human Rights Act which does not extend to sexual harassment in primary and secondary schools.[106]

Employee Initiated Cases

A teacher in Indiana sued her school corporation and principal under title VII and section 1983 for sexual harassment. On cross appeals, the Seventh Circuit affirmed that the teacher suffered a tangible employment

---

[102] Ray v. Antioch Unified Sch. Dist., 107 F. Supp.2d 1165 [146 Educ. L. Rep. 1036] (N.D. Cal. 2000).
[103] Gordon *ex rel.* Gordon v. Ottumwa Community Sch., 115 F. Supp.2d 1077 [147 Educ. L. Rep. 984] (S.D. Iowa 2000).
[104] Carestio v. School Bd. of Broward County, 79 F. Supp.2d 1347 [141 Educ. L. Rep. 629] (S.D. Fla. 1999).
[105] Herrera v. Russo, 106 F. Supp.2d 1057 [146 Educ. L. Rep. 710] (D. Nev. 2000).
[106] Teverbaugh *ex rel.* Duncan v. Moore, 724 N.E.2d 225 [144 Educ. L. Rep. 541] (Ill. App. Ct. 2000).

loss when the principal confiscated art supplies and gave her a poor evaluation following her rebuff of his advances.[107] The court reasoned that while the principal was not an "employer" for title VII purposes, liability could be imparted under section 1983 based on the presence of a hostile environment.

In Illinois, a former high school teacher sued his school board for sexual harassment and retaliation under title VII. A federal trial court dismissed the harassment claim as time barred and, in denying the retaliation claim, held that oral and written reprimands regarding excessive absences did not constitute adverse employment action.[108]

Where the former secretary to a superintendent of schools filed a sex discrimination action alleging violations of title VII and state law, a federal trial court in Ohio acknowledged that the existence of material issues precluded granting his and the board's motions for summary judgment.[109] In denying the motions, the court relied on the fact that the secretary submitted affidavits from nine female board employees, all of whom stated that the superintendent habitually belittled and mistreated female employees. The court contended that the superintendent's acts of sabotaging the plaintiff's computer equipment, taking her building keys, yelling at, and intimidating her was sufficiently severe or pervasive as to alter the conditions of her employment.

In California, a school employee who was suspended for thirty days for anonymously communicating information to bidders on a school district construction contract had her penalty overturned on the basis that her communication was protected by the First Amendment. The employee subsequently unsuccessfully filed a section 1983 claim against the board for improperly suspending her for engaging in protected speech. An appellate court affirmed that since the board was a governmental entity that was considered an "arm of the state" for Eleventh Amendment purposes, it was not a "person" subject to liability under federal civil rights statutes.[110]

---

[107] Molnar v. Booth, 229 F.3d 593 [148 Educ. L. Rep. 54] (7th Cir. 2000).

[108] Cross v. Chicago Sch. Reform Bd. of Trustees, 80 F. Supp.2d 911 [141 Educ. L. Rep. 662] (N.D. Ill. 2000).

[109] Plotner v. Swanton Local Bd. of Educ., 85 F. Supp.2d 747 [142 Educ. L. Rep. 343] (N.D. Ohio 2000).

[110] Kirchmann v. Lake Elsinore Unified Sch. Dist., 100 Cal.Rptr.2d 289 [147 Educ. L. Rep. 224] (Cal. Ct. App. 2000).

Conclusion

While the total number of reported cases has remained fairly constant in recent years, the proportion of constitutional torts continued to rise. In particular, there was an increase in actions for student on student sexual harassment. The assertion of immunity by school boards and their employees remained the most effective defense in tort actions.

6
SPORTS

Linda A. Sharp

Introduction

This chapter includes cases in K-12 and higher education dealing with student-athletes and coaches as well as athletic directors, facilities, and associations. The chapter does not discuss litigation pertaining to the instruction of physical education.

Eligibility

This section reviews twenty-three cases: two challenge longevity rules, two concern recruiting, five discuss academic eligibility requirements, one addresses a transfer rule, five relate to disciplinary sanctions, four involve the Fourth Amendment, one reviews salary caps for coaches, one concerns an appearance rule, one discusses eligibility of a home-schooled student to participate in varsity athletics, and one deals with disability.

Longevity

A basketball player who attended a number of different schools throughout his high school career, including a year as an exchange student in Germany, contested his being declared ineligible by the state athletic association due to his allegedly violating its Eight Consecutive Semester Rule. When the student enrolled for his senior year, officials assured him that he could play basketball but the high school association asserted that his seventh and eighth semesters of eligibility had expired while he was in Germany. The student unsuccessfully filed suit alleging that the semester rule was unconstitutional. However, the Supreme Court of Montana granted the student's request for an injunction which allowed him to play. On further review, the same court dismissed the appeal as moot since the student had completed his last season of eligibility and this issue was not capable of repetition.[1]

A league sought a writ of mandamus from the Supreme Court of Texas directing a trial court to vacate its orders requiring the league to conduct a baseball playoff game between two high schools and finding the league in contempt because it did not permit the playoff game to take place and declaring one the winner. The court decided that the trial judge abused his discretion and granted the writ of mandamus.[2] In noting that league officials determined that the team that used an ineligible player was disqualified from the state tournament, the court held that the allegation that the students would suffer immediate and irreparable harm if not permitted to play in the tournament was not enough to show a constitutional violation.

---

[1] Grabow v. Montana High Sch. Ass'n, 3 P.3d 650 [145 Educ. L. Rep. 776] (Mont. 2000).
[2] *In re* Univ. Interscholastic League, 20 S.W.3d 690 (Tex. 2000).

Recruiting

A high school sought to enjoin a state athletic association from enforcing a rule that prohibited undue influence in recruiting student-athletes on the basis that doing so violated its First Amendment right to freedom of speech. The association used the rule to try to prohibit a football coach from sending letters to students who had already been admitted to the school, advising them of spring practice. A federal trial court in Tennessee granted the school's request for a permanent injunction on the basis that the rule violated the First Amendment on its face and as applied to the letter in question. The Sixth Circuit reversed, vacated, and remanded in ruling that a section 1983 action could not be brought against the athletic association since it was not a state actor.[3] Insofar as the Supreme Court has agreed to hear this case, a discussion will ensue in next year's edition of the Yearbook of Education Law.[4]

In Florida, when the high school activities association realized that a member school violated its recruiting rules, the Commissioner declared its girls' and boys' basketball teams ineligible to participate in further championship competition. When the school and four students sought declaratory and injunctive relief, a trial court entered a temporary injunction allowing the teams to continue participating. On further review, an appellate court reversed in indicating that the temporary injunction failed at its threshold because there was no showing of a substantial likelihood of success on the merits.[5]

Academic Eligibility

Where a football player was rendered ineligible in his final year of participation due to academic deficiencies, his university unsuccessfully asked the NCAA to waive its eligibility requirements. The student-athlete then filed a declaratory action against the university and the NCAA seeking injunctive relief. A trial court issued an injunction allowing the student to play and enjoined the NCAA from imposing any penalty on the university or player for complying with its order. The court specifically enjoined the NCAA from enforcing its Restitution Rule which would have permitted it to impose penalties such as forfeitures of individual records as well as team

---

[3] Brentwood Academy v. Tennessee Secondary Sch. Athletic Ass'n, 180 F.3d 758 [136 Educ. L. Rep. 145] (6th Cir. 1999).

[4] Brentwood Academy v. Tennessee Secondary Sch. Athletic Ass'n, *cert. granted*, 528 U.S. 1153 [142 Educ. L. Rep. 34] (2000).

[5] Florida High Sch. Activities Ass'n v. Kartenovich, 749 So. 2d 1290 [142 Educ. L. Rep. 583] (Fla. Dist. Ct. App. 2000).

victories and receipts from competition. An appellate court dismissed the matter as moot but the Supreme Court of Texas, in turn, reversed and remanded.[6] The court explained that the NCAA's potential application of its Restitution Rule against the student and the university created a live controversy between him and the NCAA.

A federal trial court in Washington granted a football player's request for a temporary restraining order allowing him to continue to play on the team. The NCAA declared the player, who has a learning disability, ineligible for the 1999 season because he violated the 75/25 Rule during the 1998-99 school year. This rule provides that student-athletes shall earn at least 75% of the minimum number of hours required for satisfactory progress during the academic year and no more than 25% of their required hours during the summer. The purpose of this rule is to focus student-athletes on the considerable amount of attention that should be paid to academic work. The player had previously received two waivers from the NCAA, which acknowledged that he had a learning disability. The court granted the payer's request for a temporary restraining order but not for a preliminary injunction since it was not convinced that he could demonstrate a likelihood of success on the merits of his claims under the Americans with Disabilities Act (ADA).[7] The court judged hat the ADA did not appear to apply to the NCAA since it was neither a "place of public accommodation" nor an operator of a place of public accommodation. The court also posited that even if the ADA had applied to the NCAA, it would have had to dispense with essential eligibility criteria.

In New Jersey, another student-athlete with a learning disability challenged the NCAA's declaration that he was a nonqualifier because the special education classes that he took in high school did not satisfy its core course requirements. Further, since the high school could not show that the special education classes were the equivalent of regular classes, the NCAA Council Subcommittee on Initial-Eligibility Waivers did not excuse the core course requirements based on its judgment that the student would have been unable to succeed academically during his first year of college if he participated in athletics. The trial court had previously granted motions for summary judgment on behalf of the university and NCAA based on the inapplicability of the Sherman Act. Turning to the student's ADA and Rehabilitation Act claims, the court rejected the defendants' motions for summary judgment.[8]

---

[6] National Collegiate Athletic Ass'n v. Jones, 1 S.W.3d 83 [140 Educ. L. Rep 398] (Tex. 1999).
[7] Matthews v. National Collegiate Athletic Ass'n, 79 F. Supp. 2d 1199 [141 Educ. L. Rep. 619] (E.D. Wash. 1999).
[8] Bowers v. National Collegiate Athletic Ass'n, 118 F. Supp.2d 494 [148 Educ. L. Rep. 760] (D.N.J. 2000).

In opposition to the previous case, the court decreed, as a matter of law, that the NCAA is an operator of a place of public accommodation under title III of the ADA. The court reasoned that the NCAA does more than merely regulate the eligibility of potential college athletes since it manages and controls places of public accommodation in many senses. The court added that it could not reach a conclusion as to whether the NCAA's eligibility requirements are essential, due to a lack of evidence. As to the student's claim under the Rehabilitation Act, the court was of the opinion that since there was insufficient evidence to support the NCAA's position that it is not a recipient of federal financial assistance, a threshold requirement of the Rehabilitation Act, it could not grant the NCAA's motion for summary judgment.

A first year university football player with a learning disability sued the NCAA in alleging that its initial eligibility requirements were discriminatory and violated the ADA. The player could not participate as a "qualifier" in athletic competition because he was unable to meet the NCAA's initial eligibility requirements. After unsuccessfully seeking a waiver of the NCAA's requirements, a federal trial court in Georgia denied the payer's request for a preliminary injunction as moot because the season had ended and his participation in Division I football was no longer limited by his partial-qualifier status. The court contended that the student's only season of football which was affected by his partial-qualifier status was over and no additional relief was available since money damages are unavailable under title III of the ADA.[9]

The last matter against the NCAA by a student-athlete with a learning disability concerned a request by a plaintiff's counsel for an award of attorney fees. The plaintiff, a university football player, filed suit under the ADA to prevent the NCAA from rendering him nonqualified to compete, an action that would have prevented him from receiving an athletic scholarship. After a federal trial court in Washington granted the student's request for a preliminary injunction that allowed him to participate on the team for two years, the NCAA entered into a consent decree with the United States Department of Justice (DOJ) which called for it to reevaluate its eligibility requirements regarding athletes with learning disabilities. At issue was whether this consent decree was sufficient to characterize the plaintiff as a prevailing party in the litigation so that attorney fees could be awarded. The court denied the motion for attorney fees in maintaining that it was unable to discern whether

---

[9] Cole v. National Collegiate Athletic Ass'n, 120 F. Supp.2d 1060 [148 Educ. L. Rep. 935] (N.D. Ga. 2000).

the plaintiff's litigation was causally related to the relief he obtained. The court further observed that the evidence suggested that the consent decree would have been entered even if the plaintiff had not instituted his litigation and that his suit had no real impact on the DOJ's negotiations with the NCAA.[10]

Transfer

A foreign exchange student from Italy challenged the state high school association's denial of his request for a hardship exception that would have allowed him to participate on the varsity swimming team of the school he attended while living in Indiana with his host family. The association denied the student's request for eligibility because his exchange program did not meet the requirement of "direct, hands-on" control over the placement and supervision of students even though it satisfied the requisite standard of control when he applied for it. A trial court granted the student's request for a restraining order against the association and dismissed the eligibility suit on the ground that the recognition requirement as applied to the exchange program had no relationship to the purpose of a transfer rule that was designed to prevent recruitment and transfers for athletic reasons. On further review, an appellate panel reversed and remanded in commenting that the trial court erred by failing to apply the arbitrary and capricious standard of review properly in evaluating the challenge to the rule.[11] The tribunal was not convinced that this standard, which requires a body's actions to reach the level of willful and unreasonable decision making without any consideration of the circumstances, was met.

Discipline

The first four cases in this section deal with disciplinary actions taken due to violations of alcohol polices. In Hawaii, a high school student was suspended from school for violating a policy which prohibits the possession of alcohol while attending a school function. The student was allowed to participate in the state championships for cross-country but was suspended from school for ninety-two days. This suspension also meant that the student could not participate in athletics, which he alleged, might have affected his ability to earn a college athletic scholarship. The student and his parents rejected the option of participating in a mandatory drug and alcohol counseling program which would have resulted in a five-day sus-

---

[10] Butler v. National Collegiate Athletic Ass'n, 74 F. Supp.2d 1021 [140 Educ. L. Rep. 621] (W.D. Wash. 1999).
[11] Indiana High Sch. Athletic Ass'n v. Vasario, 726 N.E.2d 325 [142 Educ. L. Rep. 1027] (Ind. Ct. App. 2000).

pension. The federal trial court partially granted their motion for a preliminary injunction.[12] Although the court wrote that the student had no constitutional liberty or property interest in athletics, it noted that the plaintiffs were likely to prevail on the merits of their claim since there was no evidence that he actually "possessed intoxicating liquor" while at the school function. The court rescinded the disciplinary action taken against the student, including the ban from athletics, in offering that since the policy violated due process, any punishment adopted pursuant to it was invalid.

Two high school football players in Florida were suspended for thirty days from all extracurricular activities for violating their school's Zero Tolerance Policy which prohibited the consumption of alcoholic beverages off campus. On further review, an appellate court affirmed the suspensions not only since the students had no constitutionally protected right to participate in sports but also because even though school officials did not follow their procedures in the precise sequence, they substantially complied with due process.[13]

In Texas, a high school athlete challenged his being suspended from the basketball team and later the baseball team, after he received a ticket for possessing an alcoholic beverage. A trial court granted the student's request for a temporary injunction. On an interlocutory appeal, the preliminary injunction was reversed.[14] An appellate tribunal pointed out that the trial court abused its discretion by effectively awarding the student the principle relief that he sought by allowing him to play. For all practical purposes, remarked the panel, the trial court denied the school board of its right to discipline a student without affording it a trial.

A high school senior who participated in three sports challenged his suspension for one calendar year from all athletic contests after his fifth violation of the school's athletic code. The student's offenses included smoking a cigarette as well as arrests for possession of marijuana and alcohol and for disorderly conduct. A federal trial court in Wisconsin denied the student's request for a preliminary injunction in deciding that the school board did not violate his rights to due process at his hearing.[15] Even in adding that the student had a protectable property interest in athletic participation, the court was satisfied that he received appropriate due process.

---

[12] James P. *ex rel.* Robert P. v. LeMahieu, 84 F. Supp.2d 1113 [142 Educ. L. Rep. 233] (D. Haw. 2000).
[13] L.P.M. and J.D.T. v. School Bd. of Seminole County, FL, 753 So. 2d 130 [143 Educ. L. Rep. 411] (Fla. Dist. Ct. App. 2000).
[14] Friona Indep. Sch. Dist v. King, 15 S.W.3d 653 [143 Educ. L. Rep. 1106] (Tex. App. 2000).
[15] Butler v. Oak Creek-Franklin Sch. Dist., 116 F. Supp.2d 1038 [148 Educ. L. Rep. 229] (E.D. Wis. 2000).

In a university case from Illinois, where two student-athletes were involved in an administrative hearing concerning rape accusations by a fellow student, one of the athletes was expelled while the other was suspended indefinitely. When the charges turned out to be false, one of the student-athletes was acquitted and the other was never charged. The plaintiffs sued the university claiming that their due process rights were violated at an administrative hearing since they were not permitted to confront their accuser or to present their own evidence. A federal trial court in Illinois dismissed the case based on qualified immunity and the Eleventh Amendment. On further review, the Seventh Circuit affirmed that insofar as it was not established law that the plaintiffs had a property interest in their continued university education, they failed to meet their burden of showing that their constitutional rights were violated.[16]

Fourth Amendment

Three of the four Fourth Amendment cases involved drug testing. In Pennsylvania, a school board adopted a policy under which students who wished to participate in extracurricular programs or drive to or park at school had to sign a consent form subjecting them to tests for alcohol and controlled substances. Insofar as the sole motivation behind the policy was the health of students, there were no criminal sanctions or academic penalties. The testing was done through breath, urine, and blood samples. The students argued that the policy unconstitutionally violated their right against unreasonable searches and seizures under the state constitution since testing was not based on individualized suspicion and was limited to pupils in extracurricular activities and those who have driving/parking privileges. After a trial court upheld testing, an appellate panel vitiated the policy as unconstitutional on the ground that the state constitution is more protective of privacy interests than its federal counterpart.[17] The court noted that, absent a showing of special need or justification, the policy invaded students' privacy rights and that the board did not act reasonably when it promulgated its sweeping policy to conduct selective searches without articulating a single reason why the specific group it targeted required testing over that of the general school population.

In Indiana, students unsuccessfully challenged a school board's random, suspicionless, drug testing policy for participants in extracurricular activities and those who drove their own vehicles to school. The Seventh Circuit affirmed the use of the policy for participants in athletic and non-

---

[16] Lee v. Board of Trustees of Western Ill. Univ., 202 F.3d 274 (7th Cir. 2000).
[17] Theodore v. Delaware Valley Sch. Dist., 761 A.2d 652 [148 Educ. L. Rep. 985] (Pa. Commw. Ct. 2000).

athletic extracurricular activities since the board demonstrated a sufficient governmental need to test for drugs and alcohol but not for nicotine in students who drove to the campus.[18] The court wrote that while it did not agree that participants in non-athletic extracurricular activities should have been should subjected to drug testing, it was bound to uphold the policy based on stare decisis.

In a second case from Indiana, students relied on state, rather than federal, law in challenging a random drug testing policy for those who participated in extracurricular activities or who drove to school. A trial court upheld the drug testing policy but a state appellate court reversed and remanded on the basis that the state constitution provided greater protection than its federal counterpart.[19] The court posited that it was consistent with the state constitution in striking down the policy as unconstitutional since there was no correlation between drug use and the school board's need to engage in random drug tests of the majority of students.

A mandated pregnancy test gave rise to a privacy case in Pennsylvania where a high school swimmer claimed that her coach coerced her into taking one. Although the swimmer denied that she could be pregnant, the coach used her teammates to finally convince her to take four different tests, three of which came back negative. The swimmer, who eventually gave birth, and her mother brought a section 1983 action against the coach claiming that the pregnancy tests constituted an illegal search under the Fourth Amendment, that it violated the student's rights to privacy regarding personal matters, and that it violated the mother's right to familial privacy. A federal district court granted the coach's motion for summary on the basis of qualified immunity. The Third Circuit reversed and remanded on the Fourth Amendment and privacy claims.[20] As to qualified immunity, the court noted that not only is the right to privacy clearly established but also that the coach's alleged conduct was objectively unreasonable. In acknowledging that current Supreme Court precedent clearly establishes that a school official's administration of a pregnancy test constitutes an unreasonable search, the court found that the coach was not entitled to qualified immunity on the Fourth Amendment claim.

Salary Cap for Coaches

University coaches prevailed in their challenge, based on anti-trust grounds, to a NCAA rule that set a salary cap for entry level positions. After

---

[18] Joy v. Penn-Harris-Madison Sch. Corp., 212 F.3d 1052 [144 Educ. L. Rep. 866] (7th Cir. 2000).

[19] Linke v. Northwestern Sch. Corp., 734 N.E.2d 252 (Ind. Ct. App. 2000).

[20] Gruenke v. Seip, 225 F.3d 290 (3rd Cir. 2000).

a jury verdict of $22.3 million was trebled, resulting in an aggregate award of $66.9 million, the court awarded another $5.026 million as a net present value adjustment. The court then approved the NCAA's settlement offer of $54,500,000. This aspect of the case dealt with a request for approval of a revised plan of allocation of the proceeds. The federal trial court in Kansas approved the revised plan in ruling that it effectively matched each plaintiff's recovery to the strength of his or her claim because the method of allocation was well supported by expert testimony, economic theory, and factors regarding the efficient administration of the settlement fund.[21]

Appearance

A high school student from Illinois who was suspended from his basketball team because he violated a team rule governing personal appearance by receiving a tattoo unsuccessfully challenging the rule under the First and Fourteenth Amendments. After a federal trial court denied the student's request for a preliminary injunction, the Seventh Circuit dismissed the student's appeal as moot.[22] According to the court, the case lacked a live controversy since the student graduated and was no longer eligible to play high school basketball.

Home-Schooling

Where school officials granted the request of parents who home-schooled their son to allow him to play high school varsity soccer, an administrative appeal affirmed an order of the state activities commission rendering him ineligible to play for the next school year. The parents then moved to another county where the school board denied their request to permit their son to participate based on the commission's adjudication. The parents unsuccessfully sued the second board alleging that the commission and the first board discriminated against their son. Yet, the plaintiffs did not name any entity in the second county as a defendant. On further review, the Supreme Court of Appeals of West Virginia affirmed that since none of the individual defendants named in the suit resided in the county and the commission's home office was not there either, the case was without merit.[23]

---

[21] Law v. National Collegiate Athletic Ass'n, 108 F. Supp.2d 1193 [146 Educ. L. Rep. 1044] (D. Kan. 2000).

[22] Stotts v. Community Unit Sch. Dist. No.1, 230 F.3d 989 [148 Educ. L. Rep. 111] (7th Cir. 2000).

[23] Crispen v. West Va. Secondary Sch. Activities Comm'n, 525 S.E.2d 677 [142 Educ. L. Rep. 551] (W. Va. 1999).

Disability

In Kentucky, a student unsuccessfully alleged that school officials violated his rights under the Rehabilitation Act and the ADA when they placed him on "hold" status pending the receipt of a medical clearance from his doctor based on his being a hemophiliac and a carrier of the hepatitis B virus. A federal trial court granted the defendants' motion for summary judgment. On further review, the Sixth Circuit affirmed that school officials acted reasonably in attempting to ascertain whether the student's participation was a direct threat to the health and safety of others.[24] It was entirely reasonable, stated the court, for school personnel to be concerned with limiting risk of exposure to any contagion as well as limiting any injury that the student might suffer. Under the circumstances of this case, the court concluded that the officials acted appropriately when they placed the student on "hold" for three weeks while they considered how to proceed.

Equality of Programs

Gender

The first of four cases dealing with allegations of inequity in the provision of sport programs involved a university while the remaining three involved high schools. In Louisiana, female student-athletes claimed that their university intentionally violated title IX when it failed to add a varsity programs for women in soccer and softball. A federal trial court found that although the university violated title IX since women comprised 49% of the student body but only 29% of varsity athletic participants, it was not liable since this was unintentional. On appeal, the Fifth Circuit reversed on the basis that the violation was intentional.[25] The Fifth Circuit subsequently vacated its earlier judgment and denied a petition for an en banc rehearing in reiterating that university officials engaged in intentional discrimination because they treated women differently on the basis of sex by providing them with unequal athletic opportunities.[26] The court explained that its review of the record convinced it that an intent to discriminate, although fueled by chauvinist notions rather than enmity, drove officials' actions regarding athletic opportunities for females.

---

[24] Doe v. Woodford County Bd. of Educ., 213 F.3d 921 [145 Educ. L. Rep. 887] (6th Cir. 2000).

[25] Pederson v. Louisiana State Univ., 201 F.3d 388 [141 Educ. L. Rep. 126] (5th Cir. 2000).

[26] Pederson v. Louisiana State Univ., 213 F.3d 858 [145 Educ. L. Rep. 113] (5th Cir. 2000).

A civil rights organization in Michigan joined the parents of female student-athletes in suing the state's high school athletic association alleging that it excluded them from opportunities to participate in interscholastic athletics and violated title IX by subjecting them to unequal treatment. After a federal trial court rejected the association's motion for summary judgment, it granted the plaintiffs' motion for class certification[27] before denying a second motion for summary judgment.[28] Although finding that the association did not, directly or indirectly, receive federal funds, the court decided that it may be subject to title IX by using the controlling authority rationale. The court reviewed the association's history and noted that it had a de facto monopoly over interscholastic sports as evidenced by the fact that not a single high school in the state which was eligible to join was not a member. This evidence, wrote the court, revealed a genuine issue of material fact regarding the association's control over interscholastic athletics which precluded its motion for summary judgment on the title IX claim. The court also denied the association's motion for summary judgment on the equal protection claim in maintaining that it was a state actor because its actions may be "fairly attributed to the state" under either the state compulsion or symbiotic relationship test.

In Kentucky, female students alleged that the high school athletic association's failure to sanction fast-pitch softball violated title IX by diminishing their ability to compete for college scholarships. The association defended its actions on the basis of its 25% rule whereby a new sport would not be sanctioned unless at least 25% of member schools indicated a willingness to participate. While an earlier appeal was pending, the state legislature amended a statute which directed the association to require schools to offer the sport for which the NCAA provided athletic scholarships when it offers one of two similar sports. On remand, a trial court again granted the association's motion for summary judgment. The Sixth Circuit, in turn, affirmed on whether there was proof of an intentional violation of title IX, a prerequisite for compensatory damages.[29] The court was satisfied that the association had not committed an intentional violation of title IX when officials refused to adopt the plaintiffs' proposal that the intent standard should have been deliberate indifference rather than intentional discrimination.

Parents of female high school students in Virginia sued the state high school athletic league claiming that it denied their daughters equal treatment

---

[27] Communities for Equity v. Michigan High Sch. Athletic Ass'n, 192 F.R.D. 568 [144 Educ. L. Rep. 990] (W.D. Mich. 1999).
[28] Communities for Equity v. Michigan High Sch. Athletic Ass'n, 80 F. Supp.2d 729 [141 Educ. L. Rep. 646] (W.D. Mich. 2000).
[29] Horner v. Kentucky High Sch. Athletic Ass'n, 206 F.3d 685 [142 Educ. L. Rep. 728] (6th Cir. 2000).

because certain girls' sports were played in different seasons based on the division in which a school competes while the boys' seasons were uniformly scheduled regardless of division. This disparity, argued the plaintiffs, resulted in reduced opportunities to obtain college athletic scholarships and sometimes required female athletes who participated in multiple sports to give up one or more sports. A federal trial court not only denied the league's motion to dismiss but also rejected its defense of qualified immunity.[30] The court was of the view that because the league was closely analogous to a local government body which is not entitled to immunity, it could not rely on such a defense.

The first of three cases dealing with sexual harassment or abuse related to coaches and/or sport programs came from Virginia where a former student unsuccessfully sued her university and several football players that she accused of rape based on title IX and the Violence Against Women Act (VAWA). On further review, the Supreme Court, in *United States v. Morrison*,[31] affirmed the dismissal of the student's claims. The Court decreed that Congress had no authority under the Commerce Clause or the Fourteenth Amendment to enact the VAWA and it federal civil remedies for victims of gender-motivated violence. Turning to the Commerce Clause analysis, the Court pointed out that gender-motivated crimes of violence can neither be considered economic activity nor to be under Congress' regulation of interstate commerce.

In a case from Illinois, a former student-athlete unsuccessfully alleged that her basketball coach violated title IX by pursuing a sexual relationship with her that lasted through her time at the university and that his advances created a hostile environment which interfered with her educational and athletic experiences. The plaintiff also alleged that the athletic director knew of the inappropriate relationship simply because her home address on school records was the same as the coach. A federal trial court dismissed the plaintiff's complaint in discerning that current jurisprudence requires actual notice of a violation of title IX and deliberate indifference to the misconduct.[32] Here, contended the court, it is hard to imagine the circumstances under which the identical address would have come to the attention of school officials. The court added that even if the athletic director recognized the similarity, there are perfectly innocuous reasons why a student would share the same address as a coach.

---

[30] Alston v. Virginia High Sch. League, Inc., 108 F. Supp.2d 543 (W.D. Va. 2000).
[31] 120 S. Ct. 1740 [144 Educ. L. Rep. 28] (2000).
[32] Turner v. McQuarter, 79 F. Supp.2d 911 [141 Educ. L. Rep. 588] (N.D. Ill. 1999).

Where a coach allegedly had improper sexual contact with female students over the course of two decades, he was incarcerated for felony offenses including rape, indecent assault, and battery. After a female reported the coach's conduct to the principal, he told her parents that he believed the rape allegations and that the coach was a "sick man who needs help." Even so, the principal did not take appropriate steps to keep the coach from contacting the student. In the ensuing litigation, the federal trial court in Massachusetts denied the school board's motion for summary judgment under title IX in commenting that since the principal's failure to take timely and reasonable measures to end the harassment may have amounted to deliberate indifference, summary judgment was precluded.[33]

Tort

In 2000, thirty-three tort cases involved sports. The first six cases dealt with intentional torts. Of the remaining twenty-seven negligence cases, twenty-four concerned participants while the final three involved spectators.

Intentional

Fraud

A case from Indiana involved a dispute over the interpretation of a required waiver-insurance form which high school students had to complete before being able to participate in varsity football. A student-athlete filled out the information portion of the form and wrote "none" with regard to insurance coverage but did not have it signed a parent. After the student suffered a broken leg in a scrimmage, he sought to have the school's catastrophic insurance policy cover his medical costs. The student sued his school board for fraud, claiming that officials induced him to sign the waiver in return for an illusory promise of insurance coverage. A trial court partially granted the student's motion for summary judgment on the ground that there was no ambiguity in the section of the form which stated that catastrophic insurance coverage was being provided. On further review, an appellate court reversed and remanded.[34] The court agreed that while the form was unambiguous, neither the board nor the insurance company had a

---

[33] Canty v. Old Rochester Reg'l Sch. Dist., 66 F. Supp. 2d 114 [139 Educ. L. Rep. 421] (D. Mass. 1999).
[34] Tri-Central High Sch. v. Mason, 738 N.E.2d 341 [148 Educ. L. Rep. 1021] (Ind. Ct. App. 2000).

contractual obligation to pay for the student's medical expenses since the language relating to coverage was directed to parents who, by not signing it, had not accepted the offer for insurance.

Defamation

In Maryland, a high school cross-country coach who was accused of sexual abuse by two of his female athletes was suspended during an investigation and placed in a non-teaching position. Once he was cleared of all charges, the coach unsuccessfully filed a defamation action against the students and their parents as a trial court dismissed on the basis that their statements were absolutely privileged. On further review, an appellate court reversed in maintaining that whether statements in an administrative proceeding are absolutely privileged turns on two factors, the nature of the public function of the proceeding and the adequacy of the procedural safeguards.[35] The court was of the opinion that while the statements met the first factor based on the strong public interest in protecting students from the alleged sexual misconduct of teachers, the lack of adequate procedural safeguards during the investigation meant that the accusations were not absolutely privileged.

Corporal Punishment

In Georgia, a high school football player who was blinded in one eye after his coach hit him in the face with a metal weight lock allegedly as punishment for his involvement in a fight with another player unsuccessfully alleged that the coach's behavior violated his substantive due process rights. A federal trial court granted the coach's motion to dismiss on the grounds that corporal punishment cannot give rise to a substantive due process claim and that his reactive, spontaneous actions did not amount to corporal punishment. On further review, the Eleventh Circuit vacated and remanded in remarking that most of the circuit courts of appeal agreed that excessive corporal punishment, when not administered in conformity with a valid school policy, may be actionable under the due process clause if it is tantamount to arbitrary, egregious, and conscience-shocking behavior.[36] The court asserted that in considering whether behavior is arbitrary and conscience-shocking, a plaintiff must allege facts demonstrating that the amount of force used was obviously excessive under the circumstances and that it presented a reasonably foreseeable risk of serious injury.

---

[35] Flynn v. Reichardt, 749 A.2d 197 [143 Educ. L. Rep. 585] (Md. Ct. Spec. App. 2000).
[36] Neal v. Fulton County Bd. of Educ., 229 F.3d 1069 [148 Educ. L. Rep. 86] (11th Cir. 2000).

Section 1983

In the first of two cases involving hazing, when a high school football in Utah player came out of a shower, was grabbed by four teammates, forcibly bound to a towel rack with highly adhesive athletic tape, and a girl that he dated was brought in to see what they did, he complained to various school officials. The student then informed the coach that he would not apologize for complaining and no longer wanted to play on the team. The coach angrily dismissed the student from the team and the remainder of the football season was canceled. The federal trial in Utah dismissed the case as not significant enough to warrant its consideration. On further review, the Tenth Circuit reversed and reinstated the claim in stating that if proven, the coach, board, and various officials could be liable for the student's injuries.[37]

A high school wrestler filed suit alleging violations of federal civil rights and various state common-law claims. After the parties reached a settlement for $151,000, a federal trial court in Pennsylvania approved the petition for the settlement amount but reduced the amount of attorney fees sought by the plaintiff's counsel.[38] The court offered that since the attorneys sought approximately 37% of the gross recovery, an amount in excess of the presumptive lodestar of 25% applicable in that county, their performance did not warrant such fees.

In a second case from Pennsylvania, a high school wrestler, who was rendered quadriplegic on being injured at practice by an alumnus, and his parents sued the two wrestling coaches and school board under section1983 for the deprivation of his right to bodily integrity. A federal trial court denied the defendants' motions for summary judgment despite their claim that the plaintiffs failed to present sufficient evidence of the state-created danger theory of liability under section1983.[39] The court found that a reasonable jury could have concluded that the case met the four elements of the theory. First, the court noted that there was evidence that the injury was foreseeable based on the physical mismatch of the alumnus and this student and a previous injury that the latter suffered at the hands of an alumnus wrestler. Second, the court was convinced that the jury could agree that the coaches knew of the danger but were nevertheless deliberately indifferent. Third, there was evidence, according to the court, that the student was a discrete, foreseeable victim of the custom of alumni wrestling which was maintained

---

[37] Seamons v. Snow, 206 F.3d 1021 [142 Educ. L. Rep. 755] (10th Cir. 2000).
[38] Nice v. Centennial Area Sch. Dist., 98 F. Supp.2d 665 [144 Educ. L. Rep. 982] (E.D. Pa. 2000).
[39] Sciotto v. Marple Newtown Sch. Dist., 81 F. Supp.2d 559 [141 Educ. L. Rep. 698] (E.D. Pa. 1999).

and condoned by the coaches. Finally, the court was satisfied that a jury could also agree that the coaches had created an opportunity for the injury to occur by using their authority to continue the practice of inviting older, heavier, and more experienced alumni participate in wrestling practices.

Negligence

Participants

In New York, an appellate court affirmed that a school did not owe a duty of care to a student who was injured in a roller skating accident.[40] The ruled that the school was not liable since the accident did not occur on school property or within the custody and control of school authorities and that at the time of the accident, the plaintiff was in the custody and control of his mother.

· Another no duty case arose in Texas where a student who was seriously injured in an altercation in an off-campus bar with four of his university's football players unsuccessfully sued it for negligent supervision of the athletes. An appellate court affirmed a grant of summary judgment in favor of the university on the bases that its officials generally had no duty to control the conduct of third persons and that the institution did not have a special relationship with its adult students.[41]

Where two basketball players at a university were hit by a truck during a mandatory early morning conditioning run on a road which was heavily traveled and one of them was killed, a jury rendered a verdict against the driver and the university based on the negligence of the coaches. The plaintiffs appealed on the ground that the trial court erred in instructing the jury that the university owed the athletes a duty of ordinary care as the trial judge refused to treat them as having had a special relationship. The Supreme Court of Kansas affirmed that they trial court correctly explained the duty of care.[42]

Another discussion of duty owed arose in a case which dealt with informal recreation wherein a sorority member who was participating in "Greek week" social events, including volleyball, was injured when a volleyball standard disconnected from a pole and hit her in the leg causing a deep

---

[40] Ruiz v. Life Skills Sch., 700 N.Y.S.2d 456 [141 Educ. L. Rep. 289] (N.Y. App. Div. 1999).

[41] Boyd v. Texas Christian Univ., 8 S.W.3d 758 [141 Educ. L. Rep. 374] (Tex. App. 1999).

[42] Howell v. Calvert, 1 P.3d 310 [144 Educ. L. Rep. 760] (Kan. 2000).

laceration to her bone. The student unsuccessfully alleged that the university was negligent in allowing her and friends to use defective equipment and in its failure to supervise. On further review, the Supreme Court of Appeals of West Virginia affirmed in part.[43] The court ascertained that the student failed to provide enough evidence to support her claims of defective equipment and failure to supervise. At the same time, the court posited that university officials had a duty to supervise even in this recreational sport context.

In the first of two cases from New York, a high school softball player who was injured when two girls on the opposing team suddenly attacked her sued both high schools for failure to supervise. On further review of the denial of the school boards' motions for summary judgment, an appellate court reversed.[44] The court acknowledged that while school officials must provide adequate supervision, since there was no history of problems between the teams and the coaches had no actual or constructive knowledge of dangerous conduct, the educators did not breach their duty of care because the attack could not have been reasonably foreseen.

A high school wrestler unsuccessfully alleged that the school officials' failure to clean mats properly after a contestant suffered a bloody nose caused him to contract a case of herpes simplex. An appellate court in New York reversed a grant of summary judgment in favor of the board.[45] The court determined that the board was not entitled to judgment as a matter of law because it did not address the allegation that officials failed to clean the mats properly.

In Illinois, a duty case dealt with the contact sports exception to negligence liability where a student was knocked to the ground by another boy while playing killerball during recess. Although school personnel stated that killerball was prohibited, the game was played regularly during recess in the presence of playground monitors. When the injured student sued the board for failing to supervise recess properly, it filed a third-party negligence complaint against the student who injured the plaintiff. A trial granted the other's student's motion for summary judgment on the basis that the contact sports exception to negligence liability applied. On further review,

---

[43] Stevens v. West Va. Institute of Technology, 532 S.E.2d 639 [146 Educ. L. Rep. 925] (W. Va. 1999).

[44] Brown v. Board of Educ. of Glen Cove Pub. Sch., 700 N.Y.S.2d 58 [140 Educ. L. Rep. 721] (N.Y. App. Div. 1999).

[45] Joseph E.G. v. East Irondequoit Cent. Sch. Dist., 708 N.Y.S.2d 537 [144 Educ. L. Rep. 631] (N.Y. App. Div. 2000).

an appellate court affirmed that the public policy of striking a balance between the need to protect participants in sporting activities and the voluntary nature of participation in a game where physical contact is inherent and inevitable was furthered by applying the contact sports exception.[46]

The first of five cases dealing with immunity involved the death of a student who was killed by a golf cart which was used during safety presentations put on by a city's department of public safety a recreation center. While children were touring an ambulance, some of the students climbed on a golf cart which had been left unattended. When one student started the cart, it pinned another child against the side of the ambulance and he later died. In a suit against the city and the school board, the jury found the former 66% at fault and the latter 34%. On appeal, the board argued that it should have been immune from liability since the actions of officials in making policy related to field trips or in supervising students were discretionary functions. The Supreme Court of Iowa affirmed that the principal's decision as to what supervision should have been provided on the field trip was not a matter of choice since it was specifically mandated by policy.[47] The court also believed that a teacher's failure to use ordinary care in supervising the class involved judgment but not the kind that the discretionary function exception was designed to shield.

In a case from Texas, an appellate court upheld discretionary immunity where a student attended a school party at a university's aquatic center in the presence of teachers and other school employees. Even though the student could not swim, he climbed onto the diving board, other children forced him to jump into the water, and went under. The student was revived using CPR but died the following day from cardiac arrest. The deceased student's parents challenged the dismissal of their negligence claims against school employees on the basis of immunity. An appellate court affirmed that since the school employees were present within the scope of their employment and had an obligation to supervise the students, the question was whether their duty involved the exercise of judgment or discretion which would make the acts immune.[48] The court held that the statutory immunity provided to professional school employees applies to claims of failure to supervise or negligent supervision.

---

[46] Azzano v. Catholic Bishop of Chicago, 710 N.E.2d 117 [141 Educ. L. Rep. 218] (Ill. App. Ct. 1999).
[47] City of Cedar Falls v. Cedar Falls Community Sch. Dist., 617 N.W.2d 11 [147 Educ. L. Rep. 671] (Iowa 2000).
[48] Williams v. Chatman, 17 S.W.3d 694 [144 Educ. L. Rep. 775] (Tex. App. 1999).

A sixteen-year-old in Illinois drowned during a high school swimming team tryout that was supervised by a coach since the lifeguard had left the pool for a short time. As the coach watched this student, he turned his attention to another swimmer. The decedent was soon discovered at the bottom of the pool. In response to a suit filed by the student's estate, a trial court granted the school board's motion for summary judgment on the basis of immunity. An appellate court affirmed that there is absolute immunity for claims against local government units for their failure to supervise and is subject to exception only when a local public entity designates a part of public property for use as a swimming area and does so by posting a notice on the premises indicating the hours for such use.[49] The court indicated that since there was no evidence that a notice of hours was posted anywhere, the board was immune from liability.

After a high school cheerleader was practicing a "basket toss," fell and injured her elbow, she unsuccessfully sued her school board. On further review, Supreme Court of Rhode Island vacated a grant of summary judgment that had been entered on behalf of the board in declaring that it owed her a "special duty," an exception to governmental immunity.[50] The court reasoned that since the board was aware of the student and knew of her exploits, her injury was sufficiently foreseeable to trigger the special-duty doctrine. The court was also of the view that assumption of risk had to be submitted to the trier of fact.

Members of a men's soccer team at a community college who were injured when the van in which they were traveling to a game overturned contested a grant of summary judgment in favor of the school based on immunity. An appellate court in California affirmed that under the general rule, vicarious liability applies to accidents such as this where the community college district provided transportation to and from the location of an off-premises school-sponsored activity.[51] The court also pointed out that another statutory provision overrode this rule and immunized the college from liability for accidents occurring during field trips or excursions. In light of the question whether transportation to the game was such a field trip or excursion, the court judged that since the statutory language placed trips in connection with extracurricular sports programs into this narrowly defined type of activity, it was applicable.

---

[49] Dixon v. Chicago Bd. of Educ., 710 N.E.2d 112 [141 Educ. L. Rep. 213] (Ill. App. Ct. 1999).
[50] Schultz v. Foster-Glocester Reg'l Sch. Dist., 755 A.2d 153 [146 Educ. L. Rep. 256] (R.I.2000).
[51] Barnhart v. Cabrillo Community College, 90 Cal. Rptr.2d 709 [139 Educ. L. Rep. 978] (Cal. Ct. App. 1999).

In the first of three cases from New York dealing with assumption of risk, a high school cheerleader who was injured during practice challenged a grant of summary judgment in favor of her school board. An appellate court affirmed that the student assumed the risk associated with the sport of cheerleading since there was neither evidence showing that the board failed to protect her from unreasonably increased risks nor was she participating under inherent compulsion.[52]

An athlete who suffered an ankle injury after being stepped on by another runner during track practice in a high school hallway challenged a grant of summary judgment on behalf of her school board. An appellate court reversed in favor of the student in contending that although an athlete voluntarily assumes those commonly appreciated risks which are inherent in a sport, there were questions of fact as to whether the runners maintained a safe distance from each other and whether the risk of contact and falling was unreasonably increased in this situation.[53]

In New York, a student who was trying out for a position as a fast-pitch catcher who was not directed to wear a face mask suffered a concussion and a broken nose after a curve ball hit off of her glove and struck her in the face. A jury then entered a verdict in favor of the student based on her allegation that the failure to provide her with and ordering her to wear a face mask was a breach of sound coaching practice which enhanced the risk of injury normally associated with catching. On further review, an appellate court affirmed that there was evidence submitted from which the jury could have concluded that since the risk of injury was unreasonably increased, the school board had a duty to protect the student from injury.[54]

The first two of the four playground cases were from New York. Where a child was injured when he fell from a swing at an elementary school playground, his mother timely filed a notice of claim on the board but the action was commenced more that one year and ninety days after the accident occurred. A trial court allowed the board to amend its answer to respond that the action was time-barred. However, an appellate court modified this order and did not allow the board to plead the statute of limitations against the claim.[55] According to the court, since the child was under the age of eigh-

---

[52] Weber v. William Floyd Sch. Dist., 707 N.Y.S.2d 231 [144 Educ. L. Rep. 610] (N.Y. App. Div. 2000).
[53] Kane v. North Colonie Cent. Sch. Dist., 708 N.Y.S.2d 203 [145 Educ. L. Rep. 1096] (N.Y. App. Div. 2000).
[54] Zmitrowitz v. Roman Catholic Diocese of Syracuse, 710 N.Y.S.2d 453 [145 Educ. L. Rep. 760] (N.Y. App. Div. 2000).
[55] Blackburn v. Three Village Cent. Sch. Dist., 705 N.Y.S.2d 53 [142 Educ. L. Rep. 1022] (N.Y. App. Div. 2000).

teen when the cause of action accrued, it was not time-barred. Further, the court maintained that since the parent's derivative claim was not timely, it was properly dismissed.

An appellate court in New York affirmed a grant of summary judgment for a school board in a case filed by a student who was injured in a playground.[56] The court agreed that the child's sudden unforeseeable attempt to perform a "back flip" dismount from a moving swing while his teacher's back was turned was the sole proximate cause of his injuries.

In South Carolina, a nine-year-old child fell who from the school playground's monkey bars, which had been modified by a sales representative, suffered a severe fracture of her femur. At trial, the plaintiffs were not permitted to submit evidence relating to the Consumer Product Safety Commission's guidelines for playground safety or the American Society for Testing and Materials' standards for playground equipment. The plaintiffs claimed that this exclusion was erroneous. When an appellate tribunal agreed with the plaintiffs, it reversed and remanded insofar as it asserted that the exclusion of the evidence was based upon the trial court's erroneous belief that the school board had to have adopted the standards for playground safety before they would be admissible.[57] Rather, the court stated, the evidence had been proffered to establish the applicable standard of care, a necessary element of the plaintiff's case, and should have been admitted to allow the jury to assess the proper standard of care.

As three boys attempted to move a heavy tether ball pole, which was encased in a tire filled with cement, one of the children suffered a head injury which became organic brain syndrome. Although a trial court awarded the student $450,000, he and his parents appealed based on their claim that the damage award was too low. An appellate court in Louisiana affirmed that the student's behavioral problems were not all related to his injury at school since he engaged in drug and had other psychological problems.[58] In view of the fact that, at the time of trial, the student, who was then seventeen, had been drug free for one year, had not had any emotional outbursts, and was planning to enroll in art school, the court agreed that it was not an of discretion to award him $450,000 in damages.

The first two of three cases dealing with real property were litigated in Louisiana. After a university student who fell off a natatorium roof that he climbed died as a result of his injuries, his estate unsuccessfully filed suit

[56] Ascher v. Scarsdale Sch. Dist., 700 N.Y.S.2d 210 [140 Educ. L. Rep. 724] (N.Y. App. Div. 1999).
[57] Elledge v. Richland/Lexington Sch. Dist. Five, 534 S.E.2d 289 [147 Educ. L. Rep. 372] (S.C. Ct. App. 2000).
[58] Labouisse v. Orleans Parish Sch. Bd., 757 So. 2d 866 [144 Educ. L. Rep. 1082] (La. Ct. App. 2000).

claiming that the roof was an unreasonable risk of harm. The state further argued that officials were at fault for not acting to dissuade others from climbing on to the roof by planting shrubbery or installing a fence, especially in light of the fact that there had been three previous incidents there. An appellate court in Louisiana affirmed that the roof was not an unreasonable risk of harm under the statute providing liability for building defects since it properly functioned as a roof and had nothing inherently dangerous to repair or to warn others about.[59] The court also stated that since officials had no custodial duty to protect students from their own misjudgments, their obligation to provide a safe campus did not extend to protecting this individual from his deliberate act of recklessness.

A member of a booster club who sustained a torn rotator cuff as she took a shortcut to the concession stand that she was working at and slipped on the plywood sued a school board based on strict liability and negligence. On further review, an appellate court in Louisiana reversed in favor of the board.[60] The panel disagreed with the trial court's determination that the piece of plywood created an unreasonably dangerous condition since the club, not the board, was the sole creator of the condition which it could have removed or replaced. The court added that since not every imperfection is a legal defect, the board did not breach its duty to act reasonably.

In Pennsylvania, when a pedestrian who was injured in a fall at a university's ice skating rink did not immediately accept its settlement offer, officials withdrew it during closing statements during a trial on the merits. After the jury returned a verdict in favor of the university, the trial judge granted the pedestrian's motion enforce the settlement. On further review, an appellate court affirmed that an offer without time or event conditions remains open for a reasonable period of time.[61]

Where parents of high school seniors sponsored an all-night party for their children, one student injured his knee while engaging in "sumo wrestling," an activity in which the participants wore inflatable suits and bounced off of each other on a mat. The injured student then filed suit against the promoter which filed a third-party complaint against the parents' planning committee asserting claims of indemnity based on a clause in the contract. A federal trial court in Oregon granted the third-party defendants' motions for

---

[59] Robertson v. State of La., 747 So. 2d 1276 [141 Educ. L. Rep. 388] (La. Ct. App. 1999).

[60] Blackwell v. Bossier Parish Sch. Bd., 747 So. 2d 1248 [141 Educ. L. Rep. 384] (La. Ct. App. 1999).

[61] Yaros v. Trustees of the Univ. of Pa., 742 A.2d 1118 [140 Educ. L. Rep. 968] (Pa. Super. Ct. 1999).

summary judgment on the ground that the indemnity clause was inapplicable since sumo wrestling was not listed as an activity for the party.[62] Moreover, the court wrote that members of the planning committee could not be liable under the theory of respondeat superior.

In the final case involving negligence, where a high school custodian injured his neck and back while moving wrestling mats as a part of his job, he filed suit against the town since it opted out of the state's Workers' Compensation Act. After town officials admitted that they failed to provide adequate training to the custodian to perform this work safely, an arbitrator awarded him $732,000 while town officials claimed that the amount should have been $100,000 under the State Tort Claims Act. The Supreme Court of Rhode Island affirmed that since the town failed to perfect its appeal, there was no excusable neglect under the circumstances.[63] The court commented that the office administrator's failure to file the transcript order before she left for maternity leave did not satisfy the standard of excusable neglect.

Spectators

Where a spectator at a high school football game was injured after she tripped and fell, a school board filed a motion to dismiss her complaint on the basis that she had not met the statutory notice requirements. A trial court denied the motion to dismiss in finding that letters from the plaintiff to the board's insurance carrier met the statutory notice requirements. The Supreme Court of Mississippi affirmed that there was a factual issue to be explored concerning how and when the board's insurance carrier received notice of the accident.[64]

In Utah, where a business invitee was injured when a plank broke in the wooden bleachers at a football game that she was attending, she unsuccessfully sued a university for negligence. An appellate court reversed in rejecting the university's claim of latent defect immunity.[65] The court noted that immunity for governmental inspections was meant to be a narrow category which did not apply because this case involved acts of maintenance and not acts of inspection. Additionally, the court observed that latent defect immunity applied without further findings of fact regarding the type

---

[62] Harwood v. The Howard Group, Inc., 86 F. Supp. 2d 1027 [142 Educ. L. Rep. 855] (D. Or. 2000).

[63] Daniel v. Cross, 749 A.2d 6 [143 Educ. L. Rep. 580] (R.I. 2000).

[64] Smith County Sch. Dist. v. McNeil, 743 So. 2d 376 [139 Educ. L. Rep. 753] (Miss. 1999).

[65] Ilott v. University of Utah, 12 P.3d 1011 [148 Educ. L. Rep. 1067] (Utah Ct. App. 2000).

of defect. The court offered that since the plaintiff raised an issue about whether the inspection process was reasonable to discover planks prone to breakage when a heavier person stepped on one, further proceedings were warranted.

When a guest at a graduation ceremony in a school gymnasium was injured as she fell off of the side of an accessibility ramp, she alleged that school officials were negligent since they did not place a railing on the ramp, light the area, and/or warn of the drop-off. A trial court partially granted the school board's immunity defense. On further review, an appellate court in Illinois affirmed in part and reversed in part.[66] As to the main issue of whether the accessibility ramp was public property intended or permitted to be used for recreational purposes under the state immunity statute, the court discerned that there was no immunity under this law because the ramp was located outside of recreational public property.

Employment

Twenty cases dealt with employment issues. Six cases concerned contract disputes; five dealt with collective bargaining; and nine cases related to discrimination in employment.

Contract Disputes

In the first of three cases from Illinois, the constitutionality of a section of state School Code, which allowed school boards to seek waivers from certain mandates, was at issue. A board applied for a waiver from the requirement that all eleventh and twelfth grades students take daily classes in physical education, a move that was accompanied by an increase in science and foreign language courses. The teachers' union, two physical education teachers, parents, and several taxpayers unsuccessfully challenged the change as a trial court dismissed their action for lack of standing. An appeal to the Supreme Court of Illinois dealt only with the standing of the physical education teachers and taxpayers. The court wrote that the teachers did not have standing since any reduction in registrations for physical education classes was purely conjectural and even if the number of sections were diminished, such a change would not necessarily have harmed the tenured teachers who filed suit.[67] The court also remarked that the taxpayers lacked standing to bring this type of action under the statute.

---

[66] Capps v. Belleville Sch. Dist. No. 201, 730 N.E.2d 81 [145 Educ. L. Rep. 733] (Ill. App. Ct. 2000).
[67] Chicago Teachers Union, Local 1 v. Board of Educ. of Chicago, 724 N.E.2d 914 [144 Educ. L. Rep. 547] (Ill. 2000).

When a tenured physical education teacher who worked at the same high school for over twenty years lost his job because his position was eliminated, he filed suit claiming wrongful dismissal. The school board responded that it exercised its power to lay off tenured teachers and properly placed him in the category of reassigned teachers. A federal trial court in Illinois partially denied the board's motion to dismiss.[68] The court was convinced that it could not, as a matter of law, determine whether the teacher was properly dismissed since the board did not provide him with the required notice of justification for the dismissal.

The third Illinois case dealt with the disciplinary action taken against two teachers, one who taught the class in which a high school student apparently drowned and the other a coach. The student's body was not discovered at the bottom of the pool until the next day, leading to the inference that he may have returned to the pool after class and drowned since some students reported that they saw him leave the pool at the end of class. After one of the teachers was dismissed and the other was reassigned to office duty for eight months, they filed suit claiming violations of various constitutional rights. A federal trial court partially granted the school board's motion for summary judgment.[69] The court rejected the teachers' liberty interest claim since no prospective employment opportunities were foreclosed due to stigmatizing statements made in reference to their responsibility for the student's death. However, the court was of the opinion that the second teacher suffered a deprivation of a property interest in being assigned to office duties. Although the court did not agree that the second teacher's due process right was violated by removing him from his position because it was justified by concerns for student safety, it decided that since the continuation of his suspension may have violated due process, this part of the suit was not subject to dismissal.

A high school physical education teacher/ coach was fired after being arrested outside of a local night club and charged with domestic violence battery, resisting an officer with violence, and battery on a law enforcement officer. The teacher was acquitted on the reduced charges of resisting arrest without violence but the perjured himself during the trial leading to his dismissal for misconduct in office. Although an administrative law judge recommended the teacher's reinstatement, an appellate court in Florida affirmed the school board's termination of his employment.[70] The court noted

---

[68] Chandler v. Board of Educ. of City of Chicago, 92 F. Supp. 2d 760 [143 Educ. L. Rep. 822] (N.D. Ill. 2000).

[69] Townsend v. Vallas, 99 F. Supp. 2d 902 [145 Educ. L. Rep. 263] (N.D. Ill. 2000).

[70] Purvis v. Marion County Sch. Bd., 766 So. 2d 492 [147 Educ. L. Rep. 740] (Fla. Dist. Ct. App. 2000).

that since the teacher lied under oath and resisted arrest, a level of misconduct which supported the inference that his effectiveness had been impaired, the board acted on substantial evidence.

In Arkansas, when a teacher/head high school football coach was reassigned to coach at the junior high school without a reduction in his compensation, he unsuccessfully claimed that since this was a nonrenewal of his contract, the state Teacher Fair Dismissal Act came into effect. An appellate court affirmed a motion to dismiss in favor of the board on the ground that since this was an issue reassignment rather than nonrenewal, the Act was inapplicable.[71]

A school board in California dismissed a high school football coach for violating the state interscholastic governing body's rule on "undue influence," thereby causing the school's athletic program to be put on probation for one year. The coach filed suit claiming that the board violated a state law which mandates that any action taken against an employee because of a "charge or complaint" must be preceded by a notice period of twenty-four hours in order to enable the individual to request an open hearing. A trial court not only vitiated the dismissal as null and void since the board did not follow the notice provision but also awarded the coach attorney fees and costs. On further review, an appellate court largely affirmed except as to the award of fees and costs because they were not apportioned properly.[72] As to notice, the court agreed that the coach's dismissal was improper because he was not advised in writing or orally that the board intended to take personnel action against him at the meeting in which the rule violations were discussed.

Collective Bargaining

In the first of three cases from Pennsylvania, when a school board posted a vacancy for a job as a high school girls' athletic director, since it did so in such a way that only one person, the current athletic director at the high school, was eligible for the position, a union filed a grievance on behalf of an unsuccessful applicant. An appellate court rejected the board's claim that under state case law supplemental nonprofessional employee positions cannot be covered by arbitration provisions involving a professional employee collective bargaining agreement (CBA). In so doing, the court maintained that the CBA provided the arbitrator with the authority to re-

---

[71] Meadors v. Arkadelphia Public Sch., 10 S.W.3d 109 (Ark. Ct. App. 2000).
[72] Bell v. Vista Unified Sch. Dist., 98 Cal. Rptr.2d 263 [146 Educ. L. Rep. 328] (Cal. Ct. App. 2000).

solve the dispute. The court was satisfied that since the arbitrator declared that the board did not use predetermined objective criteria and seniority considerations to fill the vacancy, despite its obligation to do so, the trial court erred in vacating the award.[73]

Where a CBA provided that all extra pay positions first had to be offered to members of the bargaining unit, a union successfully filed a grievance when the school board hired a person who was not a member of the union as head football coach. On further review, an appellate court in Pennsylvania affirmed that a grievance over whether the board violated the provision in the CBA was procedurally and substantively arbitrable since there was a dispute as to how it should have been interpreted.[74]

When the Pennsylvania Labor Relations Board (PLRB) asserted that the bargaining unit which represented faculty members was the appropriate one for athletic trainers, even those without faculty status, the competing unit, which was composed of administrative personnel, unsuccessfully argued that it erred in certifying the faculty union. On further review, an appellate court affirmed in reasoning that since the PLRB determined that the athletic trainers shared an identifiable community of interest with the employees in the faculty bargaining unit, it would defer to the PLRB's judgment.[75]

Where a vacancy occurred for a principalship, an assistant principal who was a varsity basketball coach for nineteen years was advised that since he could not be both a coach and a principal, he resigned from the coaching position. When the coaching position was advertised again, and the principal was awarded the job, an unsuccessful applicant filed a grievance that was resolved in favor of the board. After a trial court reversed in favor of the applicant, the Supreme Court of Appeals of West Virginia, in turn, reversed and remanded in favor of the board.[76] At issue was whether a principal of one school may simultaneously serve as the head basketball coach in another school. The court interpreted the state statute which prohibits principals in schools with more than 170 students from being assigned to teaching duties as being inapplicable to coaching jobs.

---

[73] School Dist. of City of Erie v. Erie Educ. Ass'n, 749 A.2d 545 [143 Educ. L. Rep. 595] (Pa. Commw. Ct. 2000).

[74] Penn-Delco Sch. Dist. v. Penn-Delco Educ. Ass'n, 754 A.2d 51 [145 Educ. L. Rep. 693] (Pa. Commw. Ct. 2000).

[75] State Sys. of Higher Educ. v. Pennsylvania Labor Relations Bd., 757 A.2d 442 [146 Educ. L. Rep. 812] (Pa. Commw. Ct. 2000).

[76] Holmes v. Board of Educ. of Berkeley County, 526 S.E.2d 310 [142 Educ. L. Rep. 1085] (W. Va. 1999).

The Supreme Court of North Dakota affirmed that an elementary school teacher who was required to take a class due to the unavailability of music and physical education teachers was not entitled to additional compensation since the school board never paid for "play day" or music rehearsals.[77] The court indicated that a board committee and union negotiators agreed that such activities were never intended to be included in the definition of unavailability as contained in the CBA.

Discrimination

Gender

In Alabama, a female physical education teacher/coach complained that she was not paid as much as her male colleagues for equivalent work and was provided with unequal training facilities, schedule times for practice and games, equipment, supplies, and travel services, in violation of title IX, title VII, and the Equal Pay Act. The coach signed a release of claims which waived all equal pay claims against the school board up until the date of the release, but not for those arising thereafter. A federal trial court partially granted the board's motion for summary judgment.[78] The court dismissed the plaintiff's title IX action because she alleged disparate pay, hostile work environment, and disparate treatment solely to seek redress for gender-based discrimination in the workplace and title VII provides the exclusive remedy for employment discrimination. However, the court permitted the plaintiff's title VII claim for disparate treatment to proceed to trial.

A community college tennis coach and residence hall supervisor alleged that the school violated the Equal Pay Act (EPA) by paying her less than males in similar positions and that president violated title VII was in terminating her. When the residence hall that the plaintiff supervised was closed, she refused to accept reassignment to the only other dormitory available, a large, all-male residence hall that was difficult to supervise. At this, the college president advised the coach that her contract would not be renewed since the positions were tied. The federal trial court in Kansas partially granted the college's motion for summary judgment.[79] In dismissing the EPA claim, the court held that the coach's attorney improperly used male coaches in cross country, track and filed, and softball as her compara-

---

[77] Mandan Educ. Ass'n v. Mandan Public Sch. Dist. No.1, 610 N.W.2d 64 [143 Educ. L. Rep. 1056] (N.D. 2000).
[78] Blalock v. Dale County Bd. of Educ., 84 F. Supp. 2d 1291 [142 Educ. L. Rep. 244] (M.D. Ala. 1999).
[79] Sobba v. Pratt Community College, 117 F. Supp. 2d 1043 [148 Educ. L. Rep. 338] (D. Kan. 2000).

tors since there was evidence showing that the actual work required in these positions involved skills and responsibilities not needed in plaintiff's jobs. Even so, the court permitted the coach's title VII claim to proceed because there was a genuine issue of fact as to whether the president's proffered reason for tying the coaching and supervisory positions together was pretextual.

In Delaware, a former women's basketball coach at a university alleged that her dismissal violated titles VII and IX, section 1983, and state laws. The federal trial court granted the university's motion for summary judgment on all but the title VII claim based on its defense that the charges were not timely filed.[80] As to title VII, the court believed that no definitive employment decision was made in regard to the continuation of her contract until May 31, 1995 and she did file her charge with the EEOC within 180 days of this decision. The court was of the view that since the university's president gave the coach an indication that her contract might not be terminated if her performance changed during the year, the letter informing her that her last contract was a terminal one was subject to reversal and did not begin the statutory limitations period.

The male Coordinator of Sports Studies program in Ohio unsuccessfully claimed that he was sexually harassed by his female supervisor, the Dean of Education. On further review, the Sixth Circuit affirmed the dismissal of the Coordinator's claims.[81] Under a title VII analysis, the court pointed out that the Coordinator failed to prove that the harassment resulted in a tangible employment action or was severe or pervasive since the temporary loss of his position was not a tangible employment action. Further, the court contended that the incidents which the Coordinator alleged were not sufficiently severe or pervasive to constitute a hostile work environment.

Disability

The federal trial court in Massachusetts posited that a high school field hockey coach with a panic disorder presented a justiciable claim under the ADA after she was dismissed. In denying a school board's motion for summary judgment, the court maintained that the coach's being awarded Social Security benefits for her disability did not necessarily disqualify her from an ADA claim.[82] The court added not only that the failure of board officials to inform the coach of the reason for her dismissal at the time was

---

[80] Lamb-Bowman v. Delaware State Univ., 1999 U.S. Dist. LEXIS 19648 (D. Del. 1999).

[81] Bowman v. Shawnee State Univ., 220 F.3d 456 [146 Educ. L. Rep. 90] (6th Cir. 2000).

[82] Lemire v. Silva, 104 F. Supp. 2d 80 [146 Educ. L. Rep. 161] (D. Mass. 2000).

further evidence that the real basis for its action was discriminatory but also that in light of its claim that it relied on an independent report stating that the coach's job performance was unsuitable, she proffered sufficient evidence for a jury to find that this was a pretext.

Age

In a case from Oklahoma, an employee in a university's athletic department unsuccessfully alleged that she was dismissed due to age discrimination. On further review, the Tenth Circuit affirmed that it appeared that the plaintiff was not replaced by another, younger, person and that her duties were distributed as part of a reorganization of the athletic department.[83] The court decreed that since the plaintiff did not argue that she was treated unfavorably compared to her younger coworkers, summary judgment was proper.

First Amendment

A high school track coach who was placed on administrative leave for allegedly advocating the use of caffeine as a performance-enhancing substance unsuccessfully claimed that administrators violated his First Amendment right to speech. A federal trial court in Ohio granted the defendants' motion for summary judgment on the basis that the coach's remarks to a student-athlete concerning the use of caffeine did not address a matter of public concern.[84] The comments, reasoned the court, related to the purely private concern of the athlete's performance in a track meet.

In New York, a graduate student in theology at a Catholic university who worked as an administrative assistant in the men's soccer program wrote a paper questioning Nike's business practices in Third World countries. When the university subsequently entered into a contract with Nike requiring coaches and players to wear Nike athletic apparel, the student refused to do so and spoke out against the contract. Insofar as officials in the athletic department were not pleased with the student's behavior, he resigned from his position and later sued alleging that he was forced to resign for refusing to wear Nike athletic apparel. A federal trial court dismissed all of the student's federal civil rights claims because the university was not a state actor. The court also dismissed the student's employment discrimination charge under state law based on his claim that officials dis-

---

[83] Beery v. University of Okla., 203 F.3d.834 (10th Cir. 2000).

[84] Schul v. Sherard, 102 F. Supp. 2d 877 [145 Educ. L. Rep. 1016] (S.D. Ohio 2000).

criminated against him because his views of Catholicism were different from those of university officials in explaining that this disagreement was not grounded in plaintiff's religious beliefs but in the application of those teachings to the university's social role and business activities.[85]

A former assistant football coach at a university in Louisiana, the father of a heavily-recruited player who chose to attend another school in the state, sued the head coach and other officials for violating his First Amendment rights to familial association after he was dismissed. The coach unsuccessfully alleged that he was fired in retaliation for his son's decision to attend the rival school. On further review, the Fifth Circuit affirmed the dismissal of the constitutional claims in noting that the defendants acted objectively reasonably in dismissing the coach.[86] The court subsequently denied the coach's petition for an en banc rehearing on the basis that he did have a clearly established constitutionally protected right to familial association with his son under these circumstances.[87]

Miscellaneous

First Amendment

A school board in Texas adopted a policy which allowed a student council chaplain, elected by the student body, to deliver a prayer over the public address system before each home varsity football game. Current students and others challenged the policy as violating the Establishment Clause. During the pendency of the action, the board amended the policy to permit, but not require, a student-led prayer before each home game. A federal trial court modified the amended policy to permit a "nonsectarian, nonproselytizing prayer." Even so, the Fifth Circuit observed that the modified policy violated the First Amendment. The Supreme Court in *Santa Fe Independent School District v. Doe,*[88] in focusing on the coercive effect of the policy, affirmed that it was unacceptable to ask students to choose between attending a game or facing a religious ritual. The Court ruled that delivery of a pre-game prayer has the improper effect of coercing those present to participate in an act of religious worship.

---

[85] Keady v. Nike, Inc., 116 F. Supp. 2d 428 [147 Educ. L. Rep. 1021] (S.D. N.Y. 2000).

[86] Kipps v. Caillier, 197 F.3d 765 (5th Cir. 2000).

[87] Kipps v. Caillier, 205 F.3d 203 [142 Educ. L. Rep. 640] (5th Cir. 2000), cert. denied,120 S. Ct. 52 (2000).

[88] 120 S. Ct. 2266 [145 Educ. L. Rep. 21] (2000).

The Establishment Clause was argued in a different context where a high school's baseball booster club raised money by soliciting advertisements from local businesses that would be placed on outfield fences. When a businessman purchased an advertisement and submitted a design which included the Ten Commandments, he filed suit after school officials refused to post this sign based on their fears that it might run afoul of the Establishment Clause and also may have had a potentially disruptive effect leading to a public controversy and expensive litigation. A federal trial court in California granted the board's motion for summary judgment in discerning that posting the advertisement would have violated the Establishment Clause and that the refusal to post it was reasonable for the nonpublic forum of the baseball field. On further review, the Ninth Circuit affirmed.[89] Although not reaching the Establishment Clause issue, the court agreed that since the baseball field was a nonpublic forum open for a limited purpose, the board's rejection of the advertisement was legitimate based on its concerns regarding disruption and potential controversy.

Breach of Contract

In Illinois, a university precipitated a breach of contract action when it withdrew from an athletic conference without providing the required two years notice of its intention to do so contained in the organization's constitution. When the conference sued the university for $200,000 in liquidated damages, a trial court dismissed on the bases that the Court of Claims was the appropriate forum and the claim was barred by sovereign immunity. On further review, an appellate court affirmed not only that the university was not an independent fiscal entity for purposes of sovereign immunity but also that since it was an arm of the state, the breach of contract action had to have been filed in the Court of Claims.[90]

Property Tax

When an athletic conference unsuccessfully applied to the state department of revenue for a property tax exemption, the Director of the Department of Revenue adopted the recommendation of an administrative law judge who affirmed the denial. After a trial court reversed the Director,

---

[89] DiLoreto v. Downey Unified Sch. Dist. Bd. of Educ., 196 F.3d 958 [139 Educ. L. Rep. 865] (9th Cir. 1999).

[90] Association of Mid-Continent Univ. v. Board of Trustees of Northeastern Ill. Univ., 721 N.E.2d 805 [143 Educ. L. Rep. 324 (Ill. App. Ct. 1999).

an appellate panel in Illinois affirmed the property tax exemption on the ground that the administration of intercollegiate athletic programs is a legitimate educational activity.[91] According to court, although the athletic events arranged by the conference raised revenue for its members schools, since those funds did not alter the underlying educational character of the activity, the property tax exemption is appropriate.

Trademark

A plaintiff who owned two businesses which were engaged in selling clothing and novelty items related to University of Nebraska athletics opposed the university's opening of its own retail store to sell goods, which referred to the exact product used or produced by the athletic department such as a football signed by the players. The university attempted to register the name "Husker Authentics" in June, 1996 but its action was canceled due to improper publication. After the cancellation, in June 1997, the plaintiff successfully filed an application for the trade name "Husker Authentics" even though he did not actually use it for his business. Thereafter, the plaintiff unsuccessfully sued the university alleging wrongful use of the trade name since it used the name subsequent to registering it again after June, 1997. On further review, the Supreme Court of Nebraska affirmed that since the university had prior common law rights superior to the trade name, the trial court properly canceled the plaintiff's registration.[92]

Workers' Compensation

In a long-standing dispute from Texas, a former university football player was denied workers' compensation benefits for a serious injury he sustained in 1974 while playing in an intercollegiate contest that left him paralyzed. In 1991, the Workers' Compensation Commission granted his request for benefits. At a trial de novo, a jury decided that the plaintiff was not an employee of the university. On further review, an appellate court affirmed not only that the evidence reflected that both the player and the university intended that he was an amateur rather than a professional but also that under an NCAA policy governing intercollegiate sports there was a concerted effort to ensure that student-athletes were not employees.[93] The court concluded that the parties did not treat the financial aid which the player received as "pay" or "income."

---

[91] Big Ten Conference v. Department of Revenue, 726 N.E. 2d 114 (Ill. App. Ct. 2000).
[92] White v. Board of Regents of Univ. of Neb., 614 N.W.2d 330 (Neb. 2000).
[93] Waldrep v. Texas Employers Ins. Ass'n, 21 S.W.3d 692 (Tex. App. 2000).

Conclusion

The traditional tort claim by participants has given way in many situations to other causes of action such as Section 1983 and intentional tort claims. Employment claims continue to be prevalent, especially as related to civil rights issues. Title IX cases relating to participation issues and to sexual are also commonplace.

7

HIGHER EDUCATION

F. King Alexander & Paul W. Thurston

The authors are indebted to Matt Bills and Brian La Fratta for the contributions they made as research assistants. This chapter is dedicated to the loving memory of Elizabeth W. Alexander.

Introduction

As observed in last year's chapter on higher education, the Supreme Court heralded a new era of federalism in the United States. By force of recent precedents, the Court has apparently resurrected old issues of federalism that it thought it had resolved at least since the conservative decisions rendered by the Court in the 1930s that were intended to stifle Roosevelt's New Deal legislation leading to the famous efforts to pack the Court.

Since 1995 a series of cases has laid the groundwork for a new federalism emanating principally from the Eleventh Amendment. Yet, dicta that suggest a possibly much broader restrictive reading of the powers of Congress to legislate for the general good. Congress has taken new steps to control the scope of its power to use the Fourteenth Amendment to achieve social ends that it had assumed to be discernable and, indeed, necessary, in many circumstances.

During the last two years the Court has used many higher education cases to reassert constitutional principles found in the enhancement of the power of the Eleventh Amendment. Federalism has been the Rehnquist Court's principal theme since *United States v. Lopez*[1] wherein the Justices determined that federal legislation establishing schools as "gun-free" zones was unconstitutional. Most recently, this theme was advanced even further when the Court held that nothing in the Constitution authorizes Congress to enact a federal remedy for "gender-based" violence in *United States v. Morrison*.[2]

Early in 2000 the Court decided a case involving the applicability of the Age Discrimination in Employment Act (ADEA) which makes it unlawful for an employer, including a State, to fail or refuse to hire or to discharge any individual or otherwise discriminate against any individual dues to age. Three sets of plaintiffs filed suit under the ADEA against their state employers. The plaintiffs sought money damages for their employers' discrimination on the basis of age. When the employers sought to have the cases dismissed on the basis of the Eleventh Amendment, only one of the trial courts agreed to do so. On a consolidated appeal to the Eleventh Circuit, the court held that states are entitled to Eleventh Amendment immunity from suit by private citizens in federal court under ADEA.[3] On further review, a divided Supreme Court, in *Kimel v. Florida Bd. of Regents*,[4] affirmed that the ADEA does not abrogate the States' Eleventh Amendment immunity.

---

[1] 514 U.S. 549 (1995).
[2] 120 S. Ct. 1740 (2000).
[3] Kimel v. Florida Bd. of Regents, 139 F. 3d 1426 (1998).
[4] 528 U.S. 62, 120 S. Ct. 63) (2000).

Another Eleventh Amendment suit emerged wherein a group of Alabama state employees sought money damages under title I of the Americans with Disabilities Act (ADA). The ADA prohibits States and other employers from discriminating against qualified individuals with disabilities with regard to terms, conditions, and privileges of employment. In an opinion disposing of both cases, a federal trial court granted the state's motion for summary judgment, agreeing with it that the ADA exceeded Congress' authority to abrogate the State's Eleventh Amendment immunity. Ultimately, the Supreme Court, in *Board of Trustees of the University of Alabama v. Garrett,*[5] held that state employees were not entitled to recover money damages by reason of the State's failure to comply with title I of the ADA and are barred by the Eleventh Amendment.

Since 1995 the Rehnquist Supreme Court has significantly transformed the relationship between states and the federal government. The Court's recent rulings have led many to question the role and authority of the federal government to interfere in the operations of state governments and agencies. The significance of these changes is apparent while the extent to which these cases grant public institutions unlimited sovereign immunity remains unclear and ambiguous. In addition to these higher education cases that provide the basis for the Court to work out the new federalism doctrine, there are a large number of more mundane actions involving disputes in higher education across a variety of legal sources.

Intergovernmental Relationships

This section addresses intergovernmental relations and organizes the cases according to the locus of authority. The first sections deal with legislative and state authority before discussing cases based on specific state or local statutory claims such as freedom of information, zoning and taxation laws. The next part reviews cases dealing with jurisdiction or evidentiary matters involving topics such as venue, standing, mootness, discovery, and intervention. The last section examines a large number of federal statutory and constitutional claims that are relied upon as authority for legal redress.

---

[5] 121 S. Ct. 955 (2001).

Legislative Authority

In New York, the state attorney general sued a former president and university trustees alleging mismanagement of assets based largely on the president's salary and alleged abuse of expense accounts. The president and trustees moved to dismiss the claim, which the court denied.[6] A trial court found facts regarding the president's use of the expense account and residence at an apartment purchased by the university, including reimbursement for nearly $400,000 worth of travel and entertainment expenses over a three-year period, sufficient to permit the case to go forward.

State Authority

A state statute authorizes community colleges to apportion their board positions by population to the two public school districts which comprise the community college district. One board member moved from the district in which his seat was slated to the other district without informing the Board prior to meeting at which the matter was voted upon. When the board member refused to resign from his seat, a trial court granted the State's motion for summary judgment on the basis that he disenfranchised himself by moving from one district to another. The Supreme Court of Arkansas reversed in holding that the earlier judgment was inappropriate since there was a disputed material fact over the date of the board member's move.[7]

In Washington, a Vietnam veteran challenged a university's authority to exclude students in selected professional schools from being eligible for veteran tuition reduction program. In reversing an earlier adjudication, an appellate court maintained that the university's regulations regarding veteran tuition waiver were subject to the requirements of the Administrative Procedure Act (APA). The court also rejected the university's argument that the policy involved "fiscal process" which would have excluded it from many APA rules.[8]

Freedom of Information

In an interesting case highlighting important distinctions between public and private institutional authority, an attorney used the Freedom of

---

[6] Vacco v. Diamandopoulos, 715 N.Y.S.2d 269 [148 Educ. L. Rep. 1012] (N.Y. Sup. Ct. 1998).
[7] Parsons v. State of Arkansas, 15 S.W.3d 339 [143 Educ. L. Rep. 1096] (Ark. 2000).
[8] Hunter v. University of Washington, 2 P.3d 1022 [145 Educ. L. Rep. 514] (Wash. Ct. App. 2000).

Information Law (FOIL) to request a series of complaints made about a professor who was disciplined for having sexually harassed female under-graduates. The Court of Appeals of New York maintained that the university's disciplinary records were not subject to disclosure under FOIL.[9] In explor-ing the public or private nature of the relationship between the statutory colleges at the university, the court focused on the discretion that the legis-lature vested in its administration. The court reflected that, given the unique statutory scheme, the disciplinary records are not subject to FOIL disclo-sure.

Zoning

A college sued a city alleging that its zoning plan was invalid on a series of independent grounds. The city passed a zoning ordinance that prohib-ited more than two students from living together in a dwelling unit in locations adjacent to campus. An appellate panel in Pennsylvania upheld the ordi-nance, thereby nullifying the college's complaint. However, the court reversed in observing that the ordinance was invalid because it did not meet the notice and hearing requirements of the state code and the city's ordinances.[10]

In Wisconsin, a board of regents challenged a determination of a local county board of adjustment that a tower for the student-run radio station was not a "governmental use" under the applicable county zoning ordi-nance. After a trial court reversed, an appellate panel affirmed that governmental use is any service, function, or facility that a governmental unit is authorized by statute to provide.[11] The court added that since the board acquired a Federal Communications Commission license in its name, leased the land in its name, and allocated the construction funds, the radio tower was governmental use under the zoning ordinance.

A town in New York challenged a college's catering events and drivers' education courses for non-matriculating students based on zoning restric-tions. An appellate court rejected the town's interpretation of its zoning laws.[12] The court noted that educational institutions enjoy special treat-ment with respect to residential zoning audiences and are generally permitted to engage in activities and locate on their property facilities for such social,

---

[9] Stoll v. New York State College of Veterinary Med., 701 N.Y.S.2d 316 [141 Educ. L. Rep. 291] (N.Y. 1999).

[10] Muhlenger College v. Zoning Hearing Bd. of the City of Allentown, 760 A.2d 443 [147 Educ. L. Rep. 1044] (Pa. Comwlth. Ct. 2000).

[11] Board of Regents of the Univ. of Wis. v. Dane County Bd. of Adjustment, 618 N.W.2d 537 [148 Educ. L. Rep. 478] (Wis. Ct. App. 2000).

[12] Town of Islip v. Dowling College, 712 N.Y.S.2d 160 [146 Educ. L. Rep. 839] (N.Y. App. Div. 2000).

recreational, athletic and other accessory uses that are reasonably associated with their educational purpose.

Taxation

In a case that has significant ramifications for institutions seeking to privatize many of its educational enterprises, a college sought to annul a city board of assessment review's denial of its request for a real property tax exemption for a dormitory. The dormitory was constructed by a developed after the college leased the underlying land to the developer under a ground lease and the developer leased the dormitory back to the school under a master lease. The Court of Appeals of New York ruled that since the college owned the dormitory for taxation purposes, it was exempt from real property taxation.[13]

Eminent Domain

In Ohio the owner of an adjacent property sued a university alleging constructive takeover alleging that it took his property without proper compensation and that it violated his rights to both substantive and procedural due process and equal protection. A federal trial court granted the university's motion for summary judgment on the basis that it had not interfered with the plaintiff's property in more than a minimal way.[14]

Court of Claims

A faculty member in a neurology department at a state university testified on behalf of a claimant in a medical malpractice suit. The faculty member received no salary from the university, although he was listed as a full-time faculty member and was a employee of a not-for-profit corporation that managed clinical practice income of department members. A trial court in New York decided that since the faculty member was not a full-time salaried state employee, he was not disqualified from testifying on behalf of the client.[15] The court also remarked that the faculty member could receive compensation for his testimony.

---

[13] Colleges of Seneca v. City of Geneva, 709 N.Y.S.2d 493 [145 Educ. L. Rep. 1102] (N.Y. 2000).
[14] Levy v. Mote 104 F. Supp.2d 538 [145 Educ. L. Rep. 1045] (D.Md. 2000).
[15] Gilbert v. State of New York, 711 N.Y.S.2d 279 [146 Educ. L. Rep. 360] (N.Y. Sup. Ct. 2000).

In Illinois, an intercollegiate athletic conference sued a university for breach of contract for allegedly withdrawing from the conference without proper notice. An appellate court affirmed a grant of sovereign immunity in favor of the university since state law provides that suits against the it or one of its departments cannot be sued in circuit court; rather, suits against the state must be brought in the court of claims.[16] The court rejected the conference's argument that the university was an independent corporate and fiscal entity and not an arm of the state.

Graduates of a medical assistant's program sued a college, and an accrediting agency, claiming that the school improperly operated its medical assistant program. Following removal from a state court, the federal trial court in Maine was of the view that the action against the accrediting body was not a parallel suit against the college for the purpose of abstention.[17] The court concluded, after balancing all factors, that even if the two cases were parallel, there were no exceptional circumstances justifying a stay of the federal case in this circumstance.

In Pennsylvania, a collective bargaining agent for faculty members filed a petition in state court seeking declaratory judgment that the board of governors for higher education's proposal to add additional salary categories within an existing salary structure violated state law. A state court decreed that although the complaint did not refer to an unfair labor practice explicitly, such an allegation was implicitly included.[18] The court offered that since exclusive jurisdiction lies with the PLRB and the Association's petition for declaratory judgment should be dismissed.

An insurer brought a subrogation claim against a state university after it paid benefits to an insured patron whose car had previously collided with a university employee. On review of a ruling in favor of the insurer, an appellate court in Ohio reversed in favor of the university on the basis that the trial court lacked subject matter jurisdiction over the claim because the state's statutory waiver of immunity from suit contained an exception that included subrogation actions against state universities.[19]

Parents of a student who died in New York following surgery performed by a physician employed by his university filed a negligence action against

---

[16] Association of Mid-Continent Univ.. v. Board of Trustees of Northeastern Ill. Univ., 721 N.E.2d 805 [143 Educ. L. Rep. 324] (Ill. App. Ct. 1999).
[17] Ambrose v. New England Ass'n of Schs. & Colleges, 100 F. Supp. 2d 48 [145 Educ. L. Rep. 298] (D. Me. 2000).
[18] Association of Pa. State College & Univ. Faculties v. Board of Governors of State Sys. of Higher Educ., 744 A.2d 387 [141 Educ. L. Rep. 196] (Pa. Comwlth. Ct. 2000).
[19] Colonial Ins. Co. of Cal. v. Ohio Univ., 735 N.E.2d 946 [147 Educ. L. Rep. 273] (Ohio Ct. App. 1999).

it in federal court. A federal trial court in Pennsylvania granted the university's motion to dismiss or transfer the case.[20] The court was of the opinion that it lacked personal jurisdiction over the university because it did not have continuous and substantial contacts with the state of Pennsylvania. The court transferred the action to a federal court in New York on the basis of convenience of the parties and the interests of justice.

Jurisdiction

Administrators at a university filed an interlocutory appeal from the denial of the motion for summary judgment when they were sued by an expelled student. The Supreme Court of Texas ruled that since the summary judgment was based on the issue of immunity, an intermediate appellate court had jurisdiction over the administrators' appeal.[21]

Female employees filed an administrative charge of gender discrimination against a university and various officials. A federal trial court in Pennsylvania partially granted the university's motion to dismiss in deciding that although it had subject matter jurisdiction to hear the suit based on an early issuance of a right-to-sue letter, the institution was entitled to Eleventh Amendment immunity and the officials were not persons under section 1983.[22]

The administrator of the estate of a patient who died as a result of o disease allegedly contracted through exposure to a Human Growth Hormone sued various parties, including state universities in Virginia and Maryland for negligence and strict product liability. The Court of Appeals of New York affirmed that while the full faith and credit clause did not require the application of notice of claims provisions under Virginia and Maryland law in the dispute, they would be applied under the principles of comity.[23] Even so, the court added that the lack of a formal notice of claim required under the applicable statutes required the dismissal of the claims against the state universities.

---

[20] Gallant v. Trustees of Columbia Univ., 111 F. Supp. 2d. 638 [147 Educ. L. Rep. 93] (E.D. Pa. 2000).

[21] University of Tex. Southwestern Med. Ctr. of Dallas v. Margulis, 11 S.W.3d 186 [142 Educ. L. Rep. 555] (Tex. 2000).

[22] Seybert v. West Chester Univ., 83 F. Supp. 2d 547 [142 Educ. L. Rep. 97] (E.D. Pa. 2000).

[23] Crair v. Brookdale Hosp. Med. Ctr., 707 N.Y.S. 2d 375 [144 Educ. L. Rep. (Ct. App. 2000).

Venue

When a prospective faculty member sued a state university in Georgia for racial discrimination after she was not hired, a federal trial court denied the university's defense of qualified immunity. The Eleventh Circuit affirmed the denial in maintaining that since the appeal concerned only an examination of the circumstantial factual evidence of the case and not abstract issues of the law, it lacked jurisdiction to hear the appeal.[24]

An faculty member sued his university for breach of contract and age discrimination. On further review of the denial of the university's motion for a change of venue to the county in which the alleged facts occurred, the Supreme Court of New Jersey reversed in its favor.[25] The court held that the university was entitled to a change of venue because it was a public agency under the venue rule.

Parents of a university student in Indiana filed a section 1983 claim against it for the murder of their son, a twenty-seven year old graduate student and resident advisor, by a fellow student. After a trial court denied the university's motion to transfer the case from the county where the parents lived to the one where it was located, an appellate panel reversed in its favor.[26] The court explained that the county where the parents reside is not the preferred venue since personal representatives of estates and estates themselves are not individual plaintiffs under the statute, and the plaintiffs did not allege any individual claims separate and distinct from their son's. The count acknowledged that since the parents were not individual plaintiffs for the purpose of determining preferred venue, the county where the university is located is the appropriate venue.

An employee of a technical college challenged the denial of his request for a writ of mandamus after he was denied the opportunity to teach a course. An appellate court affirmed that the denial of the teaching license was a quasi-judicial action, which, under Minnesota law required an investigation, an application of the facts to a prescribed standard, and a binding decision.[27] Under the circumstances, the court agreed that mandamus was improper if there is an adequate remedy at law.

---

[24] Koch v. Rugg, 221 F.3d 1283 [146 Educ. L. Rep. 659] (11th Cir. 2000).
[25] Fine v. Rutgers, State Univ. of N.J., 750 A.2d 68 [143 Educ. L. Rep. 980] (N.J. 2000).
[26] Board of Trustees of Purdue Univ. v. Severson, 729 N.E.2d 1020 [144 Educ. L. Rep. 716] (Ind. Ct. App. 2000).
[27] Lund v. Minnesota State Colleges & University, 615 N.W.2d 420 [146 Educ. L. Rep. 865] (Minn. Ct. App. 2000).

Standing

The wife of a faculty member at a state university unsuccessfully filed a declaratory judgment action challenging amendments to a university's disciplinary adjudications code that were not adopted in accord with the APA after a student accused her husband of sexual harassment. The Supreme Court of Washington affirmed that since the wife was not aggrieved or adversely affected by the amendments, she lacked standing to file suit.[28]

Intervention

A former employee of a community college in Illinois filed suit alleging that he was fired without adequate due process. Eventually, the parties settled their dispute, with a condition that the settlement prohibited disclosure of the terms of the agreement. Thereafter, a newspaper sought to gain access to the agreement. After a federal trial court denied the intervention, the Seventh Circuit reversed in maintaining that the newspaper met the requirements for intervention since it had a direct and substantial interest in the subject matter of the litigation.[29]

Discovery

A taxpayer filed a mandamus action, under the Public Records to have certain documents related to this acquisition released for public inspection, following a sate university's acquisition of a private hospital. After reviewing the documents in camera, the Supreme Court of Ohio decided that most of them were not exempt from disclosure as trade secrets or intellectual property records.[30] Yet, the court did restrict public review of a list of the top patient-volume medical personnel at the hospital because it was a trade secret.

---

[28] Allan v. University of Wash., 997 P. 2d 360 [143 Educ. L. Rep. 648] (Wash. 2000).

[29] Jessup v. Luther, 227 F.3d 993 [147 Educ. L. Rep. 796] (7th Cir. 2000).

[30] State *ex rel.* Besser v. Ohio State Univ., 732 N.E.2d 373 [146 Educ. L. Rep. 378] (Ohio 2000).

Federal Issues

Eleventh Amendment Immunity

Under the Eleventh Amendment, a private individual cannot bring suit for damages against a state in federal court unless Congress has explicitly abrogated the state's immunity or the state has waived its immunity from suit. Political subdivisions of a state are not entitled to such immunity unless they are an "arm or alter ego of the state." Therefore, the central issue in many of the Eleventh Amendment cases involving colleges and universities is whether they are legitimate arms of a state making them immune from suit.

In a First Amendment claim against a community college, the federal trial court in Nebraska held that it was not an arm of the state because legislative authority clearly stated that community colleges are controlled, governed, and supported by local citizens.[31] The court concluded that since the school is not an arm of the state, it was not entitled to Eleventh Amendment Immunity.

A faculty member sued his university claiming that its affirmative action plan violated the Fourteenth Amendment and Vermont law. In response to the university's claimed that the Eleventh Amendment barred the suit, a federal trial court held that since the university was not an arm of the state, it was not immune from suit under the Eleventh Amendment.[32]

In New York, an employee of the central administration of a university filed an age discrimination suit under the ADEA against the central administration. In ruling that the central administration was an arm of the state, a federal trial court refused to permit the suit to proceed.[33]

A physician sued his college seeking to delay the submission of a report of his resignation to the National Practitioner Data Bank (NPDB) as required by the Health Care Quality Improvement Act (HCQIA). Among other issues, the college asserted was that it was entitled to Eleventh Amend-

---

[31] Griner v. Southeast Community College, 95 F. Supp. 2d 1054 [144 Educ. L. Rep. 251] (D. Neb. 2000).
[32] Honadle v. University of Vt., 115 F. Supp. 2d 468 [147 Educ. L. Rep. 949] (D. Vt. 2000).
[33] Becker v. City Univ. of N.Y., 94 F. Supp. 2d. 487 [144 Educ. L. Rep. 128] (S.D.N.Y. 2000).

ment immunity as an arm of the state. A federal trial court in Ohio held that the college was immune from suit and that the HCQIA does not create a private right of action allowing doctors to challenge a report made to the NPDB.[34]

In Tennessee, a Chapter 7 debtor sued a student assistance corporation for an undue hardship discharge of her student loans. A federal bankruptcy court asserted that since the corporation is an arm of the state, it was entitled to sovereign immunity.[35] Similarly, when a Chapter 7 debtor sued his university to discharge his debts under the undue hardship exemption. A federal trial court in Virginia reversed the Bankruptcy Court and posited that the university was entitled to Eleventh Amendment sovereign immunity.[36] The court believed that the adversary proceeding was a suit because the debtor sought to have a federal court dispossess the state of an asset in its possession and that the state had not waived its immunity.

An author sued a university in Texas alleging violations of the Copyright Act when it published his book. On review of the denial of the university Eleventh Amendment immunity defense, the Fifth Circuit remanded the case with instructions to dismiss because under the Copyright Remedy Clarification Act, Congress attempted to abrogate states' sovereign immunity and required them to submit to suits in federal court.[37]

In Colorado, a former faculty member brought section 1983 claim in state court against a board of trustees of state colleges alleging due process and equal protection violations. The board removed the case to federal court and asserted a sovereign immunity defense. The Tenth Circuit held that by removing the case to federal court, the board waived its immunity defense because it effectively consented to the suit.[38] Even so, the court affirmed a dismissal in favor of the board because it is not a person for section 1983 purposes.

A tenured faculty member in New York sued a state university under the Equal Pay Act (EPA). The university unsuccessfully moved to dismiss the claim on the basis of Eleventh Amendment immunity, which the trial court denied maintaining that the EPA abrogated the its Eleventh Amendment immunity. On remand following *Kimel*, a federal trial court noted that since the EPA was not an unconstitutional substantive addition to the protections

---

[34] Brown v. Medical College of Ohio, 79 F. Supp. 2d 840 [141 Educ. L. Rep. 581] (N.D. Ohio 1999).

[35] Seay v. Tennessee Student Assistance Corp., 244 B.R. 112 [141 Educ. L. Rep. 173] (Bankr. E.D. Tenn. 2000).

[36] University of Va. v. Robertson, 243 B.R. 657 [141 Educ. L. Rep. 157] (W.D. Va. 2000).

[37] Chavez v. Arte Publico Press, 204 F.3d 601 [142 Educ. L. Rep. 36] (5th Cir. 2000).

[38] McLaughlin v. Board of Trustees of State Colleges of Colo., 215 F.3d 1168 [145 Educ. L. Rep. 239] (10th Cir. 2000).

of the Fourteenth Amendment, it was a valid abrogation of the state's Eleventh Amendment immunity.[39]

In Ohio, a university employee who was discharged for catering a wedding reception while on paid medical leave unsuccessfully sued claiming that this violated the Family and Medical Leave Act (FMLA). A federal trial court dismissed the case for lack of subject matter jurisdiction on the basis of Eleventh Amendment immunity. The Sixth Circuit affirmed that finding that the FMLA did not validly abrogate the States' Eleventh Amendment immunity.[40]

Sovereign Immunity

As reflected by a case from Texas, state entities are immune from suit unless they consent to suit or waives such immunity. A former faculty member and sued his university for allegedly breaching their settlement agreement over his wrongful dismissal. On further review of the denial of the university's plea that it was entitled to immunity, an appellate court affirmed that it waived immunity since it accepted the faculty member's performance under the agreement.[41]

A former patient sued two doctors at a university medical center alleging malpractice. A state statute provided immunity from personal liability for governmental employees for acts occurring within the course and scope of employment. The Supreme Court of Mississippi concluded that since the doctors were employees under the Act, they were immune from suit.[42]

Title IX

Female students filed a title IX class action suit against a university in Louisiana seeking to require officials to offer intercollegiate women's soccer and fast pitch softball teams. A federal trial court found violations of title IX but determined that they were unintentional. The Fifth Circuit reversed on the basis that the trial court abused its discretion by decertifying the class,

---

[39] Anderson v. State Univ. of NY, 107 F. Supp. 2d 158 [148 Educ. L. Rep. 143] (N.D. N.Y. 2000).
[40] Sims v. University of Cincinnati, 219 F.3d 559 [146 Educ. L. Rep. 53] (6th Cir. 2000).
[41] Texas A&M Univ.—Kingsville v. Lawson, 28 S.W.3d 211 [147 Educ. L. Rep. 1119] (Tex. App. 2000).
[42] Sullivan v. Washington, 768 So. 2d. 881 [147 Educ. L. Rep. 1148] (Miss. 2000).

since the plaintiffs met the burden of numerosity by establishing that numerous future female students would have been interested in participating in intercollegiate softball and soccer. The court added that since the university accepted federal funding, it waived it Eleventh Amendment immunity. As to the merits of the title IX dispute, it affirmed that the university violated title IX since there was clearly an interest in both sports, officials failed to determine the level of interest in participation in female athletics, and there was tremendous disproportionality in the number of men and women participating in intercollegiate athletics.[43]

A female student sued her college alleging that officials breached their fiduciary duty and violated title IX when she was sexually harassed by a professor. On further review of a judgment in favor of the student, the Supreme Court of New Hampshire affirmed that the university breached its fiduciary duty to the student.[44] The court remanded the title IX issue for further proceedings.

In Minnesota, a former student sued a university and one of her professors under title IX for their having engaged in a sexual relationship. The federal trial court in Minnesota held that the professor's sexual advances were not actionable under title IX. The court added that even if the even if the professor's advances were actionable, the student could not recover under title IX since there was no showing that university officials responded to actual knowledge of harassment with deliberate indifference.[45]

A female physician sued a medical school and its parent institution under title IX and similar state and city laws alleging sexual harassment during her medical schooling. A federal trial court in new York granted the school's motion for summary judgment on the basis that harassment during the doctor's internship was not actionable under title IX because, as an employee, she should have filed suit under Title VII. However, the court was of the view that even though several of the claims occurred off campus, they were actionable because there was a sufficient nexus between the off-campus behavior and the on-campus environment.[46]

In Illinois, a former basketball player brought Title IX sexual harassment suit against her university for the alleged sexual harassment by her former basketball coach. The student alleged that her coach engaged in a pattern of sexual harassment during her participation on the basketball team. A

---

[43] Pederson v. Louisiana State Univ., 213 F.3d 858 [145 Educ. L. Rep. 113] (5th Cir. 2000).
[44] Schneider v. Plymouth State College, 744 A.2d 101 [141 Educ. L. Rep. 183] (N.H. 1999).
[45] Waters v. Metropolitan State Univ., 91 F. Supp. 2d 1287 [143 Educ. L. Rep. 551] (D. Minn. 2000).
[46] Crandell v. New York College of Osteopathic Med., 87 F. Supp. 2d 304, 320 [142 Educ. L. Rep. 875] (S.D.N.Y. 2000).

federal trial court in Illinois held that the university's notice was insufficient to impute liability on the university since the common address could indicate a number of possibilities other than discrimination.[47]

Whistleblower Protection Act

The former chair of a chemistry department sued his university under the Texas Whistleblower Act for retaliation alleging that officials took adverse employment action against him after her reported various s by faculty members. After a trial court rejected the university's claim that the faculty member failed to initiate a grievance prior to filing suit, an appellate panel affirmed that by making his grievances known to the senior administration and by filing his claim pursuant to the university's policy on the ethical use of research funds he, in essence, initiated his action under the university's grievance procedure as required by the Act.[48]

Family Educational Rights and Privacy Act

After the Supreme Court of Ohio issued a writ directing a university to release records of a student's disciplinary infraction,[49] the federal government challenged this as a violation of the Family Educational Rights and Privacy Acy (FERPA). A federal trial court in Ohio ruled not only that the Department of Education had the right to intervene but also that since the student records were within the scope of FERPA, they were protected from public disclosure.[50]

Sherman Act

Students who lived in an off-campus fraternity house claimed that a university's newly-adopted policy requiring all students to live on campus and buy a meal plan violated the Sherman Antitrust Act. A federal trial court in New York rejected the students' argument that the university had a mo-

[47] Turner v. McQuarter, 79 F. Supp. 2d 911 [141 Educ. L. Rep. 588] (N.D. Ill. 1999).
[48] University of Houston v. Elthon, 9 S.W.3d 351 [141 Educ. L. Rep. 926] (Tex. Ct. App. 1999).
[49] The Miami Student v. Miami Univ., 680 N.E.2d 956 [119 Educ. L. Rep. 219] (Ohio 1997).
[50] United States v. Miami Univ., 91 F. Supp. 2d 1132, 1148 [143 Educ. L. Rep. 522] (S.D. Ohio 2000).

nopoly since there were more than 100 colleges with which it competed for students.[51] The court stated that prospective students who did not find the university's housing policy appealing were free to attend different schools.

Patent

Two faculty members and their university sued a company for patent infringement, copyright infringement, fraud, and unjust enrichment. Previously, a trial court determined that while the faculty members, on their own initiative, invented a reformulated vitamin product, the company secretly patented the invention. On remand, the federal trial court in Colorado held that the faculty members were the true and sole inventors of the product and that the company was liable to the faculty members and university for fraud and unjust enrichment for secretly patenting the product.[52]

Higher Education Act

A student debtor sued a state higher education authority alleging that its garnishment of his salary violated the Higher Education Act (HEA). A federal trial court in Alabama granted the debtor's request for summary judgment since the plain language of the HEA prohibited any withholdings greater than a total of ten percent.[53] The court noted that since the HEA's prescriptions on garnishment amounts limited the amount of garnishment to twenty-five percent, the authority was required to return the wages it unlawfully garnished from the debtor.

Participation in Financial Assistance Programs

The president and founder of a private post-secondary educational institutional in Puerto Rico appealed a decision by the federal Department of Education (DOE) prohibiting it from participating in federal student financial assistance programs. After the federal trial court dismissed the school's

---

[51] Hamilton Chapter of Alpha Delta Phi v. Hamilton College, 106 F. Supp. 2d 406 [146 Educ. L. Rep. 693] (N.D.N.Y. 2000).
[52] University of Colo. Found. v. American Cyanamid Co., 105 F. Supp. 2d 1164 [146 Educ. L. Rep. 1005] (D. Colo. 2000).
[53] Green v. Kentucky Higher Educ. Assistance Auth., 78 F. Supp. 2d 1259 [141 Educ. L. Rep. 564] (S.D. Ala. 1999).

motion for a temporary restraining order, the First Circuit reversed on the ground that the pro se motion should have been liberally construed.[54] The court held that if liberally construed, the motion was also a complaint against the Secretary of Education, challenging his action.

In the companion case, the president/founder sued the DOE, the Secretary, and officials seeking money damages for the alleged unlawful termination of the institution's eligibility for federal student aid. The federal trial court in Puerto Rico granted the DOE's motion for summary judgment in favor of the DOE. The First Circuit Court affirmed that there were no material issues of fact and that even if there were, the plaintiff named the wrong defendants.[55]

Federal Appellant Procedure

An employee of a private university in California challenged the dismissal of his suit alleging breach of contract, tort claims, and discrimination based on age, religion, race, and national origin in connection with his being denied a promotion. The Ninth Circuit affirmed on the basis that the employee failed to comply with the Federal Rule of Appellant Procedure.[56]

Constitutional Law Decisions

State Action

A female former student at a public military college in South Carolina filed a section 1983 action against various parties including two upperclass students alleging gender discrimination in violation of her right to equal protection. The federal trial court granted the defendants' motion for summary judgment on the basis that they were not state actors.[57]

In New York, a former graduate assistant sued his university and Nike alleging that their contract, which required coaches and players there to wear Nike clothing exclusively, violated section 1983. A federal trial court

---

[54] Instituto De Educacion Universal Corp. v. United States Dep't of Educ., 209 F.3d 18 [143 Educ. L. Rep. 474] (1st Cir. 2000).
[55] Ruiz Rivera v. Riley, 209 F.3d 24 [143 Educ. L. Rep. 480] (1st Cir. 2000).
[56] Han v. Stanford, 210 F.3d 1038 [143 Educ. L. Rep. 781] (9th Cir. 2000).
[57] Mentavlos v. Anderson, 85 F. Supp. 609, 620 [142 Educ. L. Rep. 322] (D.S.C. 2000).

dismissed the claim because there was no state action since the university and Nike are private actors and mere financial assistance was not sufficient to make a private actor's conduct state action.[58]

A faculty member brought First Amendment free speech and section 1983 claims against a state university and two of its administrators relating to an investigation of a sexual harassment grievance brought against him by two of his students. The Supreme Court of Kansas affirmed a dismissal in favor of the university in reasoning that the faculty member lacked a viable section 1983 claim against the university because the statute only applies to persons acting under color of state law.[59] The court dismissed the First Amendment claim based on sovereign immunity.

Equal Protection

A former employee brought a section 1983 action against the president of a university in Texas and other officials alleging political affiliation discrimination and equal protection violations. The university had a policy requiring all employees to obtain university permission before engaging in outside employment. After the employee was elected Constable, he unsuccessfully sought permission for outside employment from university officials. On further review of a trial court's denial of the university's motion for summary judgment, the Fifth Circuit reversed.[60] The court held that the employee failed to assert any credible evidence proving political affiliation discrimination. The court remarked that the university did not violate the employee's right to equal protection because, just as with others, he was denied permission to take the other job because he was a full-time employee.

Due Process

The owner of an adjacent property sued a university alleging a taking of his property in violation of the Ohio Constitution and the Fifth and Fourteenth Amendments. The owner argued that by publishing maps and plans with his property shown as part of the university's future expansion and maps showing his property as part of the university's parking lot as well as failing to place physical barriers between his property and the university's parking lot, the university constructively took his property without due process. A federal trial court in Ohio entered a judgment in favor of the

---

[58] Keady v. Nike, 116 F. Supp. 2d. 428 [147 Educ. L. Rep. 1021] (S.D.N.Y. 2000).

[59] Goldbarth v. Kansas State Bd. of Regents, 9 P.3d 1251 [147 Educ. L. Rep 703] (Kan. 2000).

[60] Dudley v. Angel, 209 F.3d 460 [143 Educ. L. Rep. 486] (5th Cir. 2000).

university in determining that at most the taking was only minimal.[61] The court found that because the faculty and students only periodically traversed his property and that the owner was able to lease his property, which evidenced that it had some economic viability, the interference was minimal at best.

A former faculty member in Utah brought a section 1983 claim against his former department chairperson and an assistant general counsel for his alleged constructive dismissal without due process after a subordinate accused him of sexual harassment and retaliation. The Tenth Circuit affirmed a grant of summary judgment in favor of the university officials on the ground that since the faculty member failed to show that he had a property right in his job that was protected by due process.[62]

In Georgia, a former employee brought a section 1983 action against the president of a college and its board of regents alleging a violation of due process for terminating him for sexual harassment without providing him an opportunity for a name-clearing hearing. After a federal trial court rejected the president's motion for summary judgment based on qualified immunity, the Eleventh Circuit reversed in his favor.[63] The court ruled that the employee could not have filed his section 1983 action in federal court since he had adequate state remedies to clear his name.

A faculty member in Oregon filed a section 1983 action against other faculty members alleging that he was retaliated against for exercising his right to speak out publicly against feminist criticism of male writers in American literature. On further review of a grant of summary judgment in favor of the defendants, the Ninth Circuit held that because the plaintiff was denial of a promotion, merit pay, and salary constitute denials of governmental benefits, the faculty members involved with these decision were not entitled to qualified immunity.[64] The court indicated that since the faculty member had a clearly established constitutional right to speak out on matters of educational policy, the state could not take such adverse employment actions against him in response to his speech.

The estate of a college student in an abusive relationship who was murdered filed a section 1983 action against the college and various officials alleging violations of the deceased's substantive due process rights, negligence, and wrongful death. The federal trial court in New Jersey ruled not

---

[61] Cook v. Cleveland State Univ., 104 F. Supp.2d 752 [145 Educ. L. Rep. 1056] (N.D. Ohio 2000).

[62] Lighton v. University of Utah, 209 F.3d 1213 [143 Educ. L. Rep. 753] (10th Cir. 2000).

[63] Cotton v. Jackson, 216 F.3d 1328 [145 Educ. L. Rep. 648] (11th Cir. 2000).

[64] Hollister v. Tuttle, 210 F.3d 1033 [143 Educ. L. Rep. 777] (9th Cir. 2000).

only that the Eleventh Amendment barred action against the state and college but also that the efforts of school officials to help her did not create an affirmative duty to protect the student.[65]

First Amendment Speech

Faculty members at public colleges and universities in Virginia challenged the constitutionality of a state statute that prohibits state employees from accessing sexually explicit material on computers owned or leased by the state. On further review of a grant of summary judgment in favor of the faculty members, an en banc panel of the Fourth Circuit reversed on the basis that the statute did not infringe on the First Amendment or academic freedom rights of the faculty members.[66] The court declared that if there is a right to academic freedom, it belongs to the universities and not individual faculty members.

In another public concern case, a faculty member at a junior college in California sued the college president and vice president alleging that they fired her for the exercise of her First Amendment free speech rights. A federal trial court granted the defendants motion for summary judgment on the basis of qualified immunity. The Ninth Circuit affirmed, but on the different ground that since the faculty member denied writing the letters for which she was allegedly punished, there was no First Amendment cause of action.[67]

A taxpayers association unsuccessfully sued a public university in California alleging that a faculty member's anti-smoking work was an unlawful use of public funds in violation of the free speech clause of the First Amendment. An appellate court affirmed that since state-supported lobbying of legislative bodies on partisan matters is permissible to the extent that the state had a clear legislative agenda opposing first and second hand smoking, the state authorized the university to play a part in promoting a smoke-free society.[68]

In Pennsylvania, a student-run newspaper at a university filed a section 1983 claim to enjoin the enforcement of a Pennsylvania law that prohibits businesses from advertising alcoholic beverages in newspapers published

---

[65] Nannay v. Rowan College, 101 F. Supp. 2d 272 [145 Educ. L. Rep. 392] (D.N.J. 2000).
[66] Urofsky v. Gilmore, 216 F.3d 401 [145 Educ. L. Rep. 582] (4th Cir. 2000).
[67] Wasson v. Sonoma County Junior College, 203 F.3d 659 [141 Educ. L. Rep. 995] (9th Cir. 2000).
[68] Californians for Scientific Integrity v. Regents of the Univ. of Cal., 97 Cal. Rptr. 2d 501 [144 Educ. L. Rep. 1014] (Cal. Ct. App. 2000).

by, for, or in behalf of any educational institution. The Third Circuit affirmed the denial of the newspaper's request for an injunction since it had not shown a likelihood of success on the merits of its claim.[69]

A faculty member in Colorado filed a section 1983 claim against his junior college district claiming that his dismissal violated his First Amendment free speech rights. The faculty member argued that his allegedly inappropriate classroom conduct and comments, including profanity was protected by the First Amendment. The Tenth Circuit affirmed a judgment in favor of the faculty member.[70] The court rejected the college's argument on appeal that the question of whether the faculty member's dismissal was related to its legitimate pedagogical concerns was a question of law that the trial judge erroneously submitted to the jury. The court ruled that since the college had not raised this issue at trial, it waived its right to do so on appeal.

The state coordinator of the Knights of the Ku Klux Klan (KKK) in Missouri sued a public university and the general manager of its nonprofit public broadcast radio station alleging that it violated the organization's First Amendment rights by denying its application to underwrite a radio program. The Eighth Circuit affirmed a grant of summary judgment in favor of the university because its underwriting of programming did not create a public forum.[71]

Students and non-students at a public university in Texas challenged their being prevented from distributing political leaflets outside of the university's all-purpose center. A federal trial court entered a declaratory judgment for the plaintiffs on the ground that the property was a public forum; however, the court held that because the plaintiffs were impermissibly blocking access to the center, the university did not violate their constitutional rights. The Fifth Circuit affirmed that while university officials could place reasonable time, place, and manner restrictions on a traditional public forum, they could not limit the content of the speech.[72] The court added that even though the plaintiffs had a constitutional right to distribute flyers in this area, university officials had the right to prevent them from blocking access to the center.

Faculty members whose bonuses were less than average brought suit under section 1983 against a state university and officials alleging First Amendment free speech violations because they were outspoken on the

---

[69] Pitt News v. Fisher, 215 F.3d 354 [145 Educ. L. Rep. 173] (3d Cir. 2000).
[70] Vanderhurst v. Colorado Mountain College Dist., 208 F.3d 908 [143 Educ. L. Rep. 456] (10th Cir. 2000).
[71] Knights of the Ku Klux Klan v. Curators of the Univ. of Mo., 203 F.3d 1085 [141 Educ. L. Rep. 1001] (8th Cir. 2000).
[72] Brister v. Faulkner, 214 F.3d 675 [145 Educ. L. Rep. 154] (5th Cir. 2000).

issue of faculty salaries. A federal trial court in Indiana granted the university's motion for summary judgment. On further review, the Seventh Circuit ruled that while the statue university was entitled to Eleventh Amendment immunity, summary judgment was precluded since the faculty members raised material issues of fact as to whether their raises had been reduced because they were outspoken on the matter of pay raises.[73]

A fraternity member who was convicted of violating an anti-hazing statute unsuccessfully challenged the law as overly broad and vague and violating his First Amendment rights. The Maryland Court of Special Appeals disagreed and affirmed the conviction.[74] The court held that because the statute only proscribed the very limited form of conduct, namely that which recklessly or knowingly subjects a student to the risk of serious bodily injury that is already illegal under other criminal statutes, it was not overly broad. As to the violation of freedom of speech claim, the court held that hazing is not protected speech and even if it were, the government has a sufficient interest in preventing bodily harm to its citizens to justify a slight infringement of speech.

First Amendment Association

In South Carolina, a faculty member unsuccessfully sued his college alleging that officials violated his First Amendment right of by canceling a course he was going to teach due to his affiliation with a labor organization. An appellate court affirmed that evidence supported the finding that the course was canceled because the faculty member deceived college officials as to his involvement with the organization and its involvement with the course.[75]

A fraternity chapter in Pennsylvania challenged the denial of its claim that the university's withdrawal of its recognition as a student organization after a drug raid led to the arrest of several members violated its rights to freedom of association. The Third Circuit affirmed a grant of summary judgment in favor of the university since the chapter's large size, lack of selectivity in recruiting members, and the open, public nature of its activities precluded an intimate association claim.[76] The court also noted that while association

---

[73] Power v. Summers, 226 F.3d 815 [147 Educ. L. Rep. 434] (7th Cir. 2000).

[74] McKenzie v. State of Md., 748 A.2d 67 [143 Educ. L. Rep. 273] (Md. Ct. Spec. App. 2000).

[75] Greer v. Spartanburg Technical College, 524 S.E.2d 856 [141 Educ. L. Rep. 1179] (S.C. Ct. App. 1999).

[76] Pi Lambda Phi Fraternity v. University of Pittsburgh, 229 F.3d 435 [147 Educ. L. Rep. 915] (3d Cir. 2000).

for the purpose of engaging in activities protected by the First Amendment is covered under the right to expressive association, they failed to show that it engaged in any such activity.

The former chancellor of a university in Puerto Rico filed a section 1983 action against the university, its president, and chair of its board of trustees alleging political discrimination and due process violations. The federal trial court in Puerto Rico entered summary judgment for the defendants on the basis that since the chancellor was an at-will employee and thus had no property interest in continued employment.[77]

First Amendment Religion

Taxpayers sought to invalidate a political subdivision's bond issue that was designed to benefit a private, religious university. A federal trial court in Tennessee held that since the university was pervasively sectarian, the issuance of tax-exempt bonds and loaning the proceeds to the university violated the Establishment Clause.[78]

Discrimination in Employment

Americans with Disabilities Act

In 2000 one of the most important of the year cases was brought to the United States Supreme Court by a group of Alabama state employers, seeking money damages under title I of the Americans with Disabilities Act of 1990 (ADA), 42 U.S.C. § 12112(a), which prohibits the States and other employers from "discriminat[ing] against a qualified individual with a disability because of th[at] disability in regard to terms, conditions, and privileges of employment."

In *Board of the Trustees of the University of Alabama v. Garrett*,[79] the Supreme Court held that under the structures of the Eleventh Amendment, state employees were not entitled to recover money damages by reason of the State's failure to comply with title I of the ADA. The Court pointed out

---

[77] Ramos-Biaggi v. Martinez, 98 F. Supp. 2d 171 [144 Educ. L. Rep. 945] (D.P.R. 2000).
[78] Steele v. Industrial Dev. Bd. of the Metro. Gov't of Nashville & Davidson County, 117 F. Supp. 2d.693 [148 Educ. L. Rep. 287] (M.D. Tenn. 2000).
[79] 121 S. Ct. 955 (2001).

that the Eleventh Amendment provides that "the judicial power of the United States shall not be construed to extend to any suit in law or equity, commenced or prosecuted against one of the United States by Citizens of another State, or by Citizens, or Subjects of any Foreign State." Although the Amendment applies only to suits against a State by citizens of another State, cases law has extended its applicability to suits by citizens against their own States.[80]

During the year 2000, ADA cases involving higher education were abundant. In Oregon, a paraplegic student sued her college and its administrators for failure to accommodate her disabilities during an overseas educational program. On cross-motions for summary judgment, the federal trial court denied the college's motion on the basis that there were sufficient grounds to advance the suit.[81]

In Illinois, a state employee sued under the Pregnancy Discrimination Act and the ADA alleging that university officials failed to accommodate her efforts to have children because she was fired when her medical care for infertility caused her to miss a great deal of work. After a federal trial court denied the university's motion to dismiss based on Eleventh Amendment immunity, the Seventh Circuit reversed in its favor.[82] The court acknowledged that since title I of ADA does not enforce the Fourteenth Amendment and that the Eleventh Amendment and associated principles of sovereign immunity block private litigation against an arm of the state such as a university.

After filing for Chapter 7 bankruptcy, a former instructor at a college in Indiana unsuccessfully sued it for discrimination and retaliation under the ADA. The Seventh Circuit affirmed a grant of summary judgment in favor of the college since there was no evidence that officials deviated from the even-handed application of objective criteria in not renewing the plaintiff's contract.[83]

In a second case from Indiana, an electrician at a state university filed suit claiming employment discrimination under ADA. A federal trial court

---

[80] See Kimel v. Florida Board of Regents, 528 U.S. 62 (2000); College Savings Bank v. Florida Prepaid Postsecondary Education Expense Bd., 527 U.S. 666 (1999); Seminole Tribe of Fla. v. Florida, 517 U.S. 44 (1996); Hans v. Louisiana, 134 U.S. 1, 15 (1890).

[81] Bird v. Lewis & Clark College, 104 F.Supp.2d 1271 [146 Educ. L. Rep. 178] (D. Or. 2000).

[82] Erickson v. Board of Governors of State Colleges and Universities for Northeastern Illinois Univ., 207 F.3d 945 [143 Educ. L. Rep. 84] (7th Cir. 2000).

[83] Cable v. Ivy Tech State College, 200 F.3d 467 [141 Educ. L. Rep. 73] (7th Cir. 1999).

granted the university's motion for summary judgment since the electrician failed to demonstrate that he was disabled in accordance with criteria set forth in ADA.[84]

A discharged worker sued a state university and various individual employees alleging violations of his constitutional right of freedom of speech and violations of ADA. The federal trial court held that the Eleventh Amendment barred suit for damages against the state of Kansas and its agencies in federal courts.[85]

In Iowa, a dismissed medical student sued a university alleging discrimination on account of his disability by failing to provide reasonable accommodations in testing. On further review of a grant of summary judgment in favor of the university, the Eighth Circuit affirmed that the student failed to meet the burden of showing that the requested accommodations were actually related to his dyslexia.[86]

Title VII

Generally

In Virginia, a faculty member who was denied tenure unsuccessfully filed suit under title VII, alleging gender, national origin, and religious discrimination. The faculty member sent a letter to the EEOC to investigate his claim months after the denial of tenure, but did not file suit until after the 300 day statute of limitations had passed. On further review of the dismissal of the faculty member's claim, the Fourth Circuit court affirmed that since the plain language of the title VII provided that the verification of an unsworn charge must occur within the 300 day period, he failed to comply with the law.[87]

National Origin

In Illinois, a faculty member of East Indian origin sued a university's board of trustees for discrimination based on his race and ethnicity and retaliation when he was not hired as dean of a business college. After a

---

[84] Hawkins v. The Trustees of Indiana Univ., 83 F.Supp.2d 987 [142 Educ. L. Rep. 121] (S.D.Ind.1999).

[85] Brin v. Kansas, 101 F. Supp.2d 1343 [145 Educ. L. Rep. 658] (D. Kan. 2000).

[86] Stern v. University of Osteopathic Med. & Health Sci., 220 F.3d 906 [146 Educ. L. Rep. 108] (8th Cir. 2000).

[87] Edelman v. Lynchburg College, 228 F.3d 503 [147 Educ. L. Rep. 803] (4th Cir. 2000).

federal trial court overturned a jury verdict that university retaliated against the applicant due to lack of sufficient evidence, the Seventh Circuit, in turn, reversed and allowed the jury's decision to stand.[88]

Religion

In Georgia, a temporary faculty member sued a university claiming discrimination based on her religion when she was refused a permanent appointment. On appeal, the Eleventh Circuit affirmed that the plaintiff was not discriminated against in any way.[89]

Similarly, a former employee sued his religious college in Tennessee for religious discrimination. The Sixth Circuit affirmed that since the college qualified as a religious institution, it was entitled it a title VII exemption from claims of religious discrimination.[90]

A faculty member in Louisiana, a Russian born Jewish male, sued his university and his department alleging discrimination based on religion and national origin when he was denied a pay raise. After receiving a favorable judgment from a lower court, the Fifth Circuit reduced the amount of the earlier ruling for the plaintiff from $75,000 to $25,000.[91]

Sexual Harassment

An assistant professor in Florida sued the state board of regents for sexual harassment and retaliation alleging that a senior faculty member made sexual advances toward her. The Eleventh Circuit held the there was not enough evidence to support a sexual harassment claim against the accused faculty member and that the university had not retaliated since officials had sufficient non-discriminatory reasons to support their adverse employment actions against the plaintiff.[92]

The coordinator of sports studies in Ohio unsuccessfully sued his university and immediate supervisor, the dean of education, alleging sexual harassment, discrimination, and retaliation. The Sixth Circuit affirmed that

---

[88] Mathur v. Board of Trustees of S. Ill. Univ., 207 F.3d 938 [143 Educ. L. Rep. 77] (7th Cir. 2000).

[89] Palmer v. University of Ga. Bd. of Regents, 208 F3d 969 [143 Educ. L. Rep. 467] (11th Cir. 2000).

[90] Hall v. Baptist Memorial Health Care Corp., 215 F.3d 618 [145 Educ. L. Rep. 216] (6th Cir. 2000).

[91] Rubenstein v. Administrators of Tulane Educ. Fund, 218 F.3d 392 [145 Educ. L. Rep. 924] (5th Cir. 2000).

[92] Gupta v. Florida Bd. of Regents, 212 F.3d 571 [144 Educ. L. Rep. 822] (11th Cir. 2000).

the coordinator did not suffer materially adverse employment action and there was no evidence supporting the claim of a hostile work environment.[93]

Race

As in earlier years, many cases involved title VII racial discrimination claims. An African-American custodial worker in Minnesota unsuccessfully filed suit against a university challenging a three-day suspension and subsequent dismissal for sleeping on the job on the ground that it was racially motivated. On further review of a judgment absolving the university of racial discrimination, the Eighth Circuit affirmed that the plaintiff failed to establish a prima facie case of retaliation and university officials offered evidence that their decision was not racially motivated.[94]

An African-American, and former faculty member in Alabama, sued his university claiming that he received a lower salary because of his race and that officials retaliated against him in various ways, including his dismissal, for seeking redress. A federal trial court granted the university's motion for summary judgment on the ground that officials rebutted any claim of rebuttal by stating that their action was in response to the faculty member's having embezzled university funds.[95]

In Mississippi a faculty member filed a title VII action against his university after his department was closed and he was repeatedly denied other employment on another campus. The faculty member alleged that officials intentionally discriminated and retaliated against him by not allowing alternative employment. After a trial court held that the faculty member was entitled to an award of $300,000 for mental anguish, the Fifth Circuit reduced the damages to $10,000.[96]

A white employee sued a university in California alleging that his dismissal was racially motivated. A federal trial court held not only that the employee failed to establish the necessary qualifications for a discrimination action against the institution but also that mere allegations of anti-white animus were insufficient to demonstrate pretext.[97]

---

[93] Bowman v. Shawnee State Univ., 220 F.3d 456 [146 Educ. L. Rep. 90] (6th Cir. 2000).
[94] Scroggins v. University of Minn., 221 F.3d 1042 [146 Educ. L. Rep. 655] (8th Cir. 2000).
[95] Gibbons v. Auburn Univ. at Montgomery, 108 F. Supp.2d 1311 [146 Educ. L. Rep. 1052] (M.D. Ala. 2000).
[96] Vadie v. Mississippi State Univ., 218 F. 3d 365 [145 Educ. L. Rep. 906] (5th Cir. 2000).
[97] Maurey v. University of S. Cal., 87 F. Supp.2d 1021 [142 Educ. L. Rep. 946] (C.D. Cal. 1999).

In Illinois, an unsuccessful applicant for a position as dean sued a board of trustees and individual search committee members alleging unlawful racial discrimination in violation of the equal protection clause. A federal trial court granted the university's motion for summary judgment absolving it and members of the search committee of discriminatory intent.[98]

The Sixth Circuit ruled in favor a university in Ohio when a former vice president sued it for racial and national origin discrimination and violations of free speech. The court ascertained that the university was immune from the discrimination claims under the Eleventh Amendment and that the vice president's speech was not entitled to First Amendment protections because the university had a significant interest in making certain that his internal comments were accurate and not disruptive.[99]

Gender Discrimination

In the first of two cases from Kansas, a female faculty member who was also a Native American filed suit against her university and department chair alleging gender and race discrimination and retaliation in violation of title VII. A federal trial court denied the university's motion for summary judgment on the basis that genuine issues of material fact existed as to the gender discrimination and retaliation claims.[100] However, the court also ruled that the faculty member failed to establish a prima facie case of race discrimination and that the department chair was entitled to qualified immunity on the gender discrimination claim.

A female faculty member in Kansas sued her university alleging sexual discrimination and retaliation when she was denied promotion and tenure. After a jury entered a verdict in favor of the plaintiff on her retaliation claim, a federal court ruled that since the university was entitled to summary judgment, she did not have a right to an adjunct appointment, front pay, or recovery of attorney fees.[101]

In New Mexico, a female faculty member sued the state board of regents when she was denied tenure in claiming that she was punished in retaliation for filing an earlier sex discrimination claim against members of the univer-

---

[98] Butt v. Board of Trustees of E. Ill. Univ., 83 F. Supp.2d 962 [142 Educ. L. Rep. 106] (C.D. Ill. 1999).

[99] Johnson v. University of Cincinnati, 215 F.3d 561 [145 Educ. L. Rep. 187] (6th Cir. 2000).

[100] Annett v. University of Kan., 82 F.Supp.2d 1230 [141 Educ. L. Rep. 1118] (D. Kan. 2000).

[101] Aquilino v. University of Kan., 109 F.Supp.2d 1319 [146 Educ. L. Rep. 1081] (D. Kan. 2000).

sity community. A federal trial court denied the university's motion for summary judgment on the ground that the plaintiff's claim, that she was discriminated against her on the basis of sex, was reasonable.[102]

A female faculty member who was denied tenure unsuccessfully filed suit claiming sexual discrimination under the Missouri Human Rights Act (MHRA) as well as title VII and IX. A federal trial court granted the university's motion for summary judgment on the basis that the MHRA claims were time-barred and that the plaintiff failed to establish a prima facie case of sex discrimination under titles VII and IX.[103]

Employees

Non-tenured Faculty

First Amendment Speech

A suspended faculty member in Michigan obtained a preliminary injunction gaining reinstatement after he was suspended for seven months due to the use of profane language in the classroom and the university sought to extend the suspension another four months on the basis of a student complain. In ordering the faculty member's reinstatement, the court decreed that his actions were protected by the First Amendment.[104]

Discrimination

A former faculty member at a private college filed suit for wrongful failure to renew his contract, defamation, and libel. Officials at the college claimed that their actions were based on the faculty member's having been relieved of duty as a priest due to his homosexuality and identifying himself as a priest in an article he wrote to a newspaper. The federal trial court in Connecticut granted the college's motion for summary judgment on the

---

[102] Lee v. New Mexico Bd. of Regents, 102 F.Supp.2d 1265 [146 Educ. L. Rep. 129] (D.N.M. 2000).

[103] Tapp v. St. Louis Univ., 78 F.Supp.2d 1002 [141 Educ. L. Rep. 548] (E.D. Mo. 2000).

[104] Bonnell v. Lorenzo, 81 F. Supp. 2d 777 [141 Educ. L. Rep. 731] (E.D. Mich. 1999).

basis that it was sufficiently affiliated with the Catholic Church to invoke protections under the Free Exercise and Establishment Clauses.[105] However, the court also decided that since genuine issue of fact remained as to the nature of the faculty member's responsibilities, it could not grant the college's motion for summary judgment on that issue.

In the first of two cases from New York, an assistant professor of Italian ancestry whose contract was not renewed brought suit under section 1981 and title VII, alleging discrimination on the basis of national origin. The plaintiff also brought a Labor Relations Management Act claim based on his union's refusal to pursue his grievance. A federal trial court partially granted the university's motion for summary judgment.[106] The court was satisfied that the university did not violate its dismissal procedures and that the union did not breach its duty of fair representation. As to the title VII claim, the court found that since the only possible discriminatory action that fell within the statute of limitations was the decision by university officials not to rescind the professor's notice of termination, the case could go forward.

An assistant professor who was denied promotion unsuccessfully brought claims under the ADA and the state human rights law. An appellate court in New York affirmed that both claims were barred by the statute of limitations and that since the denial of promotion was not an ongoing violation, the statute of limitations prevailed.[107]

In Iowa, a private college sought review of, and the National Labor Relations Board (NLRB) cross-petitioned for the enforcement of, a finding that the college committed an unfair labor practice by refusing to extend a contract to an adjunct instructor and others who formed a committee to address issues of concern to adjunct faculty members. The Eighth Circuit held that the NLRB failed to establish a prima facie case showing that the instructor's conduct was the motivating factor behind a dean's refusal to extend his contract.[108] The court added that the instructor's behavior at a meeting provided legitimate reasons for the non-renewal of his contract.

A faculty member unsuccessfully filed a discrimination case based on title VII against a university, alleging sexual harassment, constructive discharge, and retaliation. The federal trial court in Nebraska granted the

---

[105] Hartwig v. Albertus Magnus College, 93 F. Supp. 2d 200 [143 Educ. L. Rep. 836] (D. Conn. 2000).

[106] Commodari v. Long Island Univ., 89 F. Supp. 2d 353 [143 Educ. L. Rep. 210] (E.D. N.Y. 2000).

[107] Martinez-Tolentino v. Buffalo State College, 715 N.Y.S.2d 554 [149 Educ. L. Rep. 240] (N.Y. App. Div. 2000).

[108] Carleton College v. National Labor Relations Bd., 230 F.3d 1075 [148 Educ. L. Rep. 114] (8th Cir. 2000).

university's motion for summary judgment since the faculty member was unable to establish the occurrence of any sexually harassing incidents within the 300 day statute of limitations.[109] The court dismissed the retaliation claim because the actions that the faculty member complained of, including exclusion from a meeting, and the publication of her complaint and the Dean's response to other members in the department, did not constitute adverse employment actions, since they did not produce a tangible change in her working conditions leading to a material disadvantage.

Contract Bargaining

When officials at a community college imposed a limit on total teaching hours, a faculty union filed a grievance protesting the limitation. When the state employment relations commission found that the overload hours were a a permissive subject of bargaining, it confirmed the college's determination. On further review, an appellate court in Michigan reversed in determining that the limit was a mandatory subject of bargaining.[110] The court reasoned that although overtime is outside of a normal work relationship, restricting it directly affected a bargained for distribution process.

Breach of Contract

A former faculty member unsuccessfully filed suit in federal court alleging breach of contract. Subsequently, a state trial court granted the university's motion for summary judgment on the basis of issue preclusion. The Supreme Court of Nevada affirmed that issue preclusion did bar the claim, explaining that it applies even if the causes of action are different as long as the same fact issues are present.[111]

In New York, a faculty member unsuccessfully sued his university for breaching their employment agreement. An appellate court affirmed in favor of the university both since the complaint did not identify a specific contractual term that was breached and the claim involved an administrative decision reviewable only under statutory guidelines.[112]

---

[109] Schwebach v. Board Regents of the Univ. of Neb., 112 F. Supp. 2d 908 [147 Educ. L. Rep. 147] (D. Neb. 2000).
[110] Grand Rapids Community College Faculty Ass'n v. Grand Rapids Community College, 609 N.W.2d 835 [143 Educ. L. Rep. 1039] (Mich. Ct. App. 2000).
[111] LaForge v. State, 997 P.2d 130 [143 Educ. L. Rep. 641] (Nev. 2000).
[112] Risley v. Rubin, 708 N.Y.S.2d 377 [144 Educ. L. Rep. 629] (N.Y. App. Div. 2000).

Dismissal During Contract Period

An adjunct faculty member whose employment was terminated just prior to the start of a fall term due to his refusal to resolve a grade dispute with a student to the university's satisfaction unsuccessfully sued for wrongful discharge. The Supreme Court of Oklahoma affirmed that while the faculty member was not an at will employee at will, he had an implied contract that gave either party the right to terminate the contract for any reason prior to the first class of the semester being taught.[113]

Denial of Tenure

Tenure Review Process

When a faculty member claimed that colleagues falsely accused him of unethical publishing practices during his tenure review proceess, a trial court granted the defendants motion for summary judgment on the basis of intracorporate immunity. On further review, the Supreme Court of Virginia reversed in maintaining that the issue was a matter of qualified privilege.[114] The court noted that the privilege attaching to such communications is qualified and may be overcome by a showing of maliciousness.

As an assistant professor was in the process of applying for tenure, his chair learned of allegations against him, questioned him without warning, and he was denied tenure. The faculty member the unsuccessfully filed suit claiming that university officials violated the state government data practices act by failing to provide him with a fair warning about the questioning. An appellant court in Minnesota affirmed a dismissal in favor of the university in deciding that while the state data practices act prohibits the release of data classified as private without proper authorization, which requires a fair warning, a public employee's description of an incident that occurred during the course of employment is not private data.[115]

Two faculty members who were invited to submitted applications for tenure never had their documents reviewed and their were subsequently not renewed. The faculty members filed a breach of contract claim and were awarded $1.1 million in damages. An appellate court in Illinois was of the view that since the faculty members' submission of tenure applications quali-

---

[113] Dixon v. Bhuiyan, 10 P.3d 888 [147 Educ. L. Rep. 1106] (Okla. 2000).
[114] Larimore v. Blaylock, 528 S.E.2d 119 [144 Educ. L. Rep. 430] (Va. 2000).
[115] Kobluk v. University of Minn., 613 N.W.2d 425 [146 Educ. L. Rep. 418] (Minn. Ct. App. 2000).

fied as petition for tenure review under the university's bylaws, the university breached their by not following through on the process.[116] Yet, in discerning that since there was no evidence that the faculty members would have been granted tenure if the process had been completed, the court remanded with instructions to the university to complete the process fairly, including not allowing any of the faculty members who were involved in the initial decision to participate in the review.

Procedural Issues

A faculty member who was denied tenure sued the university, arguing that officials did not follow proper procedure in that the provost, rather than the president, made the final decision. On further review of a grant of summary judgment in favor of the university, the Supreme Court of Oregon reasoned that the issue presented an important and unresolved state law issue.[117]

In Wisconsin, a faculty member who was denied tenure sought a writ of mandamus to compel the university to provide him with a formal notice of his right to seek judicial review of the tenure denial. On further review of a dismissal in favor of the university, an appellate court affirmed that while formal notice to seek review is only required in contested cases, it was not necessary here since this was not a contested decision.[118]

Contract Issues

A faculty member who was denied tenure filed suit alleging breach of contract and negligent misrepresentation on the basis that university officials did not consider his entire teaching record in making its decision. The Supreme Court of Washington affirmed a grant of summary judgment in favor of the university.[119] The court was convinced that the full record was considered and that written documentation of tenure evaluations is not necessary under the employment manual.

---

[116] Hentosh v. Herman M. Finch Univ., 734 N.E.2d 125 [148 Educ. L. Rep. 429] (Ill. App. Ct. 2000).
[117] Matthews v. Oregon State Bd. of Higher Educ., 220 F.3d 1165 [146 Educ. L. Rep. 112] (9th Cir. 2000).
[118] Collins v. Policano, 605 N.W2d 260 [141 Educ. L. Rep. 333] (Wis. Ct. App. 1999).
[119] Trimble v. Washington State. Univ., 993 P.2d 259 [141 Educ. L. Rep. 917] (Wash. 2000).

Where a professor of Russian Language who was denied tenure unsuccessfully filed a breach of contract claim, his university responded that its acted based on the fact that it had no need to continue the Russian program. An appellate court in New York affirmed a grant of summary judgment in favor of the university.[120] The court reasoned that the faculty handbook, which was the contract between the parties, specifically addressed tenure as it related to the continuance of academic programs.

A tenure track faculty member challenged her denial of tenure on a variety of legal grounds including breach of contract, intentional infliction of emotional distress, interference with contractual relations and prospective advantage, breach of an implied covenant of good faith and fair dealing, breach of an implied-in-fact employment contract, conspiracy and retaliation, and discrimination under the District of Columbia Human Rights Act. The District of Columbia Court of Appeals affirmed a grant of summary judgment for the university on all counts.[121]

Discrimination

A faculty member in Missouri who was denied tenure unsuccessfully filed suit claiming gender discrimination. The Eight Circuit affirmed that the university's reasons for the denial, such as failure to publish in top-tier journals, all of her publications being co-authored, and outside critique of her publication record, were not pretexts for gender discrimination.[122]

In Minnesota, a faculty member who was appointed under an agreement that tenure was contingent upon completion of a doctoral degree, challenged the dismissal of his case when he was denied tenure since he had not completed his degree. The Eighth Circuit affirmed that the plaintiff's title VII racial discrimination suit was time barred and that the university was immune from suit in federal court.[123]

A faculty member in Puerto Rico who was denied tenure filed suit against her university alleging due process violations and quid pro quo and hostile environment sexual harassment. On further review of a grant of summary judgment in favor of the university, the First Circuit affirmed that the faculty member failed to establish that the university engaged in unfair procedures.[124]

---

[120] Roklina v. Skidmore College, 702 N.Y.S.2d 161 [141 Educ. L. Rep. 1158] (N.Y. App. Div. 2000).

[121] Paul v. Howard Univ., 754 A. 2d 297 [145 Educ. L. Rep. 702] (D.C. 2000).

[122] Lawrence v. Curators of the Univ. of Mo., 204 F.3d 807 [142 Educ. L. Rep. 50] (8th Cir. 2000).

[123] Cooper v. St. Cloud State Univ., 226 F.3d 964 [147 Educ. L. Rep. 462] (8th Cir. 2000).

[124] Hernandez-Loring v. Universidad Metropolitana, 233 F.3d 49 [149 Educ. L. Rep. 30] (1st Cir. 2000).

At the same time, since it was of the view that material issues of fact remained about the sexual harassment claims, the court reinstated these charges.

In a second case from Puerto Rico, a faculty member who was denied tenure unsuccessfully filed a discrimination claim against the university in state court on the basis of race and national origin. The faculty member subsequently filed a substantially similar suit in federal court that the university moved to dismiss and the court converted the motion into one for summary judgment. On further review, the First Circuit affirmed that the conversion was harmless because the faculty member had an opportunity to respond to the materials the decision was based on but failed to respond.[125]

When a faculty member in New York was denied tenure, he unsuccessfully filed a claim of racial discrimination against the university. A federal trial court commented that the plaintiff failed to establish a prima facie case of discrimination but even if he had done so, university officials offered non-discriminatory reasons for the denial of tenure.[126]

In Kansas, a female faculty member who was denied promotion and tenure sued the university, claiming sex discrimination and retaliation for filing an administrative charge. A federal trial court ruled that the plaintiff failed to show that the university's reasons for not promoting her, namely deficiencies in teaching, were a pretext for discrimination.[127] However, the court also asserted that since material questions of fact existed as to the retaliation claim, that part of the case should proceed.

Retaliation
A faculty member who was denied tenure in New Mexico unsuccessfully filed suit claiming that it was in retaliation for exercising of her First Amendment rights. The Tenth Circuit affirmed that the since plaintiff's speech, criticisms of the internal nature of the university and did not affect the community, they did not involve matters of sufficient public concern to merit protection.[128]

---

[125] Boateng v. Interamerican Univ., 210 F.3d 56 [143 Educ. L. Rep. 768] (1st Cir. 2000).

[126] Grant v. Cornell Univ., 87 F. Supp. 2d 153 [142 Educ. L. Rep. 864] (N.D. N.Y. 2000).

[127] Aquilino v. University of Kan., 83 F. Supp. 2d 1248 [142 Educ. L. Rep. 155] (D. Kan. 2000).

[128] Clinger v. New Mexico Highlands Univ., 215 F.3d 1162 [145 Educ. L. Rep. 233] (10th Cir. 2000).

In Texas, a faculty member who was denied tenure unsuccessfully filed suit claiming that the university based its decision on her having reported a colleague's sexually harassing conduct. An appellate court affirmed that while the faculty member engaged in protected activity, she could not show a causal connection between that activity and the denial of tenure.[129]

Tenured Faculty

Breach of Contract

In Louisiana, a faculty member made an oral agreement with the president of a university to be in charge of a new honors program. When the president subsequently resigned, the faculty member unsuccessfully challenged the new president's refused to recognize the oral agreement. An appellate court affirmed a grant of summary judgment on behalf of the university on the ground that since the administrative position as head of the new program was an at will employment relationship, there was no basis on which relief could be granted.[130]

A faculty member sued her university alleging breach of contract was breached due to alleged violations of the faculty handbook, including refusing to recognize her joint teaching appointment and requiring her to vacate her office. Although a faculty grievance panel found in the plaintiff's favor, the federal trial court for the District of Columbia denied the motion for judgment on the basis of estoppel.[131] The court reasoned that since the prior proceeding was not before a court, it was of no preclusive effect.

Dismissal For Cause

A state board of regents challenged a finding that its termination of the contract of a tenured faculty member who sexually harassed a student was not supported by clear and convincing evidence. Although finding some legal error with the lower court's decision, the Supreme Court of Tennessee affirmed that it was not enough to warrant a reversal.[132] The panel noted not only that the trial court was entitled to grant deference to the live testimony since that is one of the purposes of a trial but also that the university had the opportunity to present live testimony but chose not to do so.

---

[129] Marsaglia v. University of Tex., El Paso, 22 S.W.3d 1 [145 Educ. L. Rep. 1113] (Tex. App. 1999).

[130] McJamerson v. Grambling State Univ., 769 So. 2d 168 [148 Educ. L. Rep. 522] (La. Ct. App. 2000).

[131] Breiner-Sanders v. Georgetown Univ., 118 F. Supp. 2d 1 [148 Educ. L. Rep. 751] (D. D.C. 1999).

[132] Wells v. Tennessee Board of Regents, 9 S.W.3d 779 [141 Educ. L. Rep. 933] (Tenn. 1999).

In Pennsylvania, a faculty member who was dismissed for sexually harassing students unsuccessfully filed a breach of contract action. The faculty member challenged a grant of summary judgment in favor of the university on the basis that the trial court improperly deferred to the findings of the university. An appellate court affirmed that the record contained substantial evidence of serious misconduct by the faculty member which supported the university's decision to terminate his contract.[133]

Denial of Due Process

In the first of two cases from Pennsylvania, a tenured faculty member who alleged that he was denied the benefits of tenure unsuccessfully filed suit under section 1983 claiming that his university's grievance procedures denied him due process. The Third Circuit affirmed a grant of summary judgment in favor of the university since the faculty member's failure to avail himself of the university's grievance process precluded a showing that he was denied procedural due process.[134]

A faculty member in Pennsylvania who was dismissed unsuccessfully sued his university alleging violations of due process, claiming that his tenured professorship was a property interest entitled to protection. The Third Circuit affirmed that the faculty member's property interest in tenure is not a fundamental interest since it is a state created contract right which bears little resemblance to the property interests that have been deemed fundamental under the Constitution.[135]

Denial of Benefits

A tenured faculty member unsuccessfully filed a breach of contract claim against his university, claiming that officials failed to provide him with a salary and teaching responsibilities. An appellate court in Illinois affirmed in favor of the university in explaining that no evidence was offered to show that the university breached any contractual obligations since the faculty member's contract did not provide for a guaranteed salary or promise him teaching assignments.[136]

---

[133] Murphy v. Duquesne Univ. of the Holy Ghost, 745 A.2d 1228 [142 Educ. L. Rep. 383] (Pa. Super. Ct. 2000).

[134] Alvin v. Suzuki, 227 F.3d 107 [147 Educ. L. Rep. 468] (3d Cir. 2000).

[135] Nicholas v. Pennsylvania State Univ., 227 F.3d 133 [147 Educ. L. Rep. 485] (3d Cir. 2000).

[136] Kirschenbaum v. Northwestern Univ., 728 N.E.2d 752 [144 Educ. L. Rep. 595] (Ill. App. Ct. 2000).

Discrimination

When a faculty member filed gender and age discrimination claims against her university after she was denied tenure, a federal trial court in Texas ruled that the Eleventh Amendment barred the age discrimination claim.[137] The court added that the discrimination claim based on a failure to promote was time-barred under title VII since the suit was not instituted within three hundred days of non-promotion.

All Employees

Grievances

In Minnesota, a former university vice president sought judicial review by means of writ of certiorari of the university's decision to terminate her employment. An appellate court agreed with the university's argument that the case was not subject to judicial review because the vice president had failed to exhaust the university's grievance procedures.[138]

A dean filed a petition for judicial review of his university's refusal to grant him back pay in an employment dispute. After a trial court ruled that the dean was entitled to back pay, an appellate panel in Tennessee reversed in favor of the university.[139] The panel concluded that the trial court lacked subject matter jurisdiction to hear the case because it was brought under the state's uniform administrative procedures act which limited judicial review to contested cases and that this was not a contested action because the dean was a member of the administration.

Union Certification

A state faculty association sought to amend its certification to include athletic trainers, both with and without faculty status. When the state labor board approved the amendment, the state system of higher education challenged the decision in arguing that non-faculty trainers should not be included in the same bargaining unit as the faculty trainers. An appellate court affirmed in favor of the association.[140] In noting its deference to the findings

---

[137] Lowery v. University of Houston - Clear Lake, 82 F. Supp.2d 689 [141 Educ. L. Rep. 1090] (S.D. Tex. 2000).

[138] Stephens v. Board of Regents of the Univ. of Minn., 614 N.W.2d 764 [146 Educ. L. Rep. 494] (Minn. Ct. App. 2000).

[139] Dishmon v. Shelby State Community College, 15 S.W.3d 477 [143 Educ. L. Rep. 1100] (Tenn. Ct. App. 1999).

[140] State Sys. of Higher Educ. v. Pennsylvania Labor Relations Bd., 757 A.2d 442 [146 Educ. L. Rep. 812] (Pa. Commw. Ct. 2000).

of the labor board, the court declared that since the statutory requirement of the appropriateness of a bargaining unit requires that the employees have an identifiable community of interest the labor board did not err by comparing the similarity between the job duties of the faculty and non-faculty trainers.

Administration and Staff

Collective Bargaining

An organization of graduate employees challenged the state labor relations board's dismissal of its petitioned requesting certification as the collective bargaining representative for teaching assistants and graduate assistants at a state university. The board dismissed the petition on the basis that the state educational labor relations statute permits only educational employees, defined as excluding students, to organize as a union. An appellate court in Illinois reversed and remanded in favor of the organization in positing that the state board improperly applied the appropriate test for whether the graduate assistants were students and whether their positions were significantly connected to their status as students.[141]

Due Process

The former director of a research institute in Texas whose contract was terminated on the basis of her failure to broaden the institute's funding sued the administrators who dismissed her claiming that she was fired in retaliation for her earlier complaints about funding. On further review of the denial of their motion for summary judgment, the Fifth Circuit reversed in favor of the defendants.[142] The court held not only that the director received both notice and an opportunity to be heard but also that her speech, which was made as an employee, was not a matter of public concern. Subsequently, the Fifth Circuit denied the director's request for an en banc rehearing but maintained that her speech was not a factor in her dismissal and that she would have been released even if she had not engaged in such speech.[143]

---

[141] Graduate Employees Org. v. Illinois Educ. Labor Relations Bd., , 733 N.E.2d 759 [147 Educ. L. Rep. 651] (Ill. App. Ct. 2000).
[142] Gerhart v. Hayes, 201 F.3d 646 [141 Educ. L. Rep. 465] (5th Cir. 2000).
[143] Gerhart v. Hayes, 217 F.3d 320 [145 Educ. L. Rep. 654] (5th Cir. 2000).

In Mississippi, an employee at a community college unsuccessfully challenged the denial of her request for disability benefits. An appellate court reversed in favor of the employee since her due process rights were violated when two members of the initial review board that denied her claim subsequently sat on the appeals committee that reached the same result.[144]

A Caucasian custodian at a university challenged his being discharged after he had an altercation with a senior African-American custodian. A federal trial court in Ohio granted the university's motion for summary judgment since the custodian was informed of his pretermination hearing and had an opportunity to speak at it but chose not to do so.[145] As to the discrimination claim, the court wrote that the custodian failed to show a prima facie case because he was unable to demonstrate that he and the senior custodian were similarly situated.

In Pennsylvania, a discharged college financial aid office employee brought suit alleging violation of due process under section 1983 on the basis of the lack of a termination hearing and deprivation of the liberty interest of reputation, and breach of contract on the grounds of the absence of just cause. A federal trial court granted the college's motion for summary judgment in noting that even though a for-cause dismissal provision in an employment contract may be a protected property interest, it did not have statutory authority to enter into a non-at-will employment contract with The court added that since the employee lacked a property interest, he was not entitled to a hearing.

Retaliation

When a former employee filed a retaliation claim against his university alleging that he was dismissed for exercising his First Amendment right to free speech, a federal trial court in Illinois rejected its motion to dismiss on the basis that he stated a prima facie case of retaliation. The Seventh Circuit denied the university's motion for an immediate interlocutory appeal because the dispute did not involve the necessary element of presenting an abstract legal issue.[146]

---

[144] Flowers v. Public Employees Retirement Sys. of Miss., 748 So. 2d 178 [141 Educ. L. Rep. 402] (Miss. Ct. App. 1999).
[145] Hardman v. University of Akron, 100 F. Supp. 2d 509 [145 Educ. L. Rep. 341] (N.D. Ohio 2000).
[146] Ahrenholz v. Board of Trustees of the Univ. of Ill., 219 F.3d 674 [146 Educ. L. Rep. 64] (7th Cir. 2000).

In a second case from Illinois, a researcher who was discharged unsuccessfully brought a retaliation claim against his university, alleging that he was released in response to his suggestion to administrators that it was necessary to report human test subjects' overexposure to radon to authorities. An appellate court reversed in favor of the researcher since his allegations established a violation of a mandated public policy of protecting lives of citizens from radioactive material.[147]

The curator of a museum sued her university claiming that officials violated her First Amendment rights after she filed work-related grievances against her director. On cross motions for summary judgement, a federal trial court in Iowa ruled that the curator's grievances not only touched on matters of public concern but were protected by the First Amendment since they were not disruptive.[148]

Discrimination

When a former employee sued a university in New York under the ADA, it unsuccessfully sought a stay pending arbitration. The Second Circuit affirmed that a provision in the operative collective bargaining agreement providing for arbitration of such claims, in lieu of filing suit in federal court, was not enforceable because the agreement was negotiated by a union and it could not waive an employee's right to a federal forum.[149]

A former employee of a community college claimed wrongful discharge in violation of state employment discrimination statutes. The Supreme Court of New Jersey ruled that the former employee could not maintain an action for wrongful discharge because it was irrelevant that university officials did not learn of his bribery conviction until after his employment was terminated.[150]

In the first of three cases Ohio, a university challenged a determination that it unlawfully discriminated against mentally retarded applicants for custodial positions because it required an examination. An appellate court modified a decision in favor of the applicants in requiring the university

---

[147] Stebbings v. University of Chicago, 726 N.E.2d 1136 [144 Educ. L. Rep. 575] (Ill. App. Ct. 2000).

[148] Milman v. Prokopoff, 100 F. Supp.2d 954 [145 Educ. L. Rep. 354] (S.D. Iowa 2000).

[149] Rogers v. New York Univ., 220 F.3d 73 [146 Educ. L. Rep. 75] (2d Cir. 2000).

[150] Cedeno v. Montclair State Univ., 750 A.2d 73 [144 Educ. L. Rep. 282] (N.J. 2000).

create a plan on how mentally retarded applicants may obtain jobs on campus.[151] The court added that since the applicants were classified as handicapped under state law, they were entitled to reasonable accommodations such as temporary job coaching.

A quality control engineer who resigned from her position sued her university under title VII on the basis of national origin discrimination and on the basis of public policy alleging that she was dismissed because she was a homosexual. A federal trial court in Ohio granted the university's motion for summary judgment in ruling that it was immune from suit based on the Eleventh Amendment, that she failed to establish a prima facie case of discrimination under title VII, and that she failed to establish any violations of state public policy.[152]

In Ohio, a custodial worker who sustained an arm injury that limited her to light duty work unsuccessfully sued her university alleging that her dismissal was discrimination on the basis of disability when she was rejected for a job as a clerical worker since there were no such vacancies. An appellate court affirmed that while an assignment to a vacant position might have been a reasonable accommodation, since there were no vacant positions, putting the worker on an indefinite leave of absence was not required by the law.[153]

A research assistant who was discharged unsuccessfully sued her university under the ADA alleging discrimination and retaliation. The federal trial court for the District of Columbia granted the university's motion for summary judgement on the basis that the researcher failed to establish that she was disabled for the purposes of the ADA and that her dismissal was a justified response to her behavior problems.[154]

In Massachusetts, a female university employee of West Indian ancestry who resigned her position filed suit under title VI and VII, and section 1981 alleging discrimination on the basis of race, gender, color, and national origin. The federal trial court partially granted the university's motion for summary judgment.[155] The court denied the employee's title VI claim because the purpose of the federal financial assistance that the university

---

[151] Miami Univ. v. Ohio Civil Rights Comm'n, 726 N.E.2d 1032 [143 Educ. L. Rep. 360] (Ohio Ct. App. 1999).

[152] Das v. Ohio State Univ., 115 F. Supp. 2d 885 [147 Educ. L. Rep. 975] (S.D. Ohio 2000).

[153] Scott v. University of Toledo, 739 N.E.2d 351 [149 Educ. L. Rep. 245] (Ohio. Ct. App. 2000).

[154] Weigert v. Georgetown Univ., 120 F. Supp. 2d 1 [148 Educ. L. Rep. 888] (D. D.C. 2000).

[155] Joseph v. Wentworth Inst. of Tech., 120 F. Supp. 2d 134 [148 Educ. L. Rep. 911] (D. Mass. 2000).

received was not to provide employment. The court rejected the title VII claims as time-barred in the absence of continuing violations and was no evidence of discharge, constructive or otherwise. The court permitted the section 1981 claim, which dealt with a failure to promote, since university officials did not produce requested information that hampered the employee's ability to argue her claim, to proceed.

A former tennis coach and residence hall supervisor at a community college alleged that the school violated the Equal Pay Act (EPA) by paying her less than males in similar positions and that president violated title VII was in terminating her . The federal trial court in Kansas partially granted the college's motion for summary judgment.[156] In dismissing the EPA claim, the court held that the coach's attorney improperly used male coaches in cross country, track and filed, and softball as her comparators since these positions were not comparable since there was evidence showing that the actual work required in these positions involved skills and responsibilities not needed in plaintiff's jobs. Even so, the court permitted the coach's title VII claim to proceed because there was a genuine issue of fact as to whether the president's proffered reason for tying the coaching and supervisory positions together was pretextual.

In Oregon, a former residence services supervisor unsuccessfully sued a university for unlawful employment practices, alleging discrimination on the basis of disability and intentional infliction of emotional distress. An appellate court in Oregon affirmed a grant of summary judgment in favor of the university on the discrimination claim because the employee could not meet the essential functions of the job since she was unable to continue employment in her position on a full time basis.[157] As to the intentional infliction of emotional distress claim, the court agreed that it should have failed because the employee did not comply with state law and notify university officials in a timely fashion of her intention to bring suit.

Reduction in Force

Employees whose positions were terminated under a university's reduction in force (RIF) rules challenged their validity and application primarily alleging that they were treated differently from other categories of employees. An appellate court in the District of Columbia affirmed the dismissals

---

[156] Sobba v. Pratt Cmmunity College, 117 F. Supp. 2d 1043 [148 Educ. L. Rep. 338] (D. Kan. 2000).
[157] Flug v. University of Ore., 13 P.3d 544 [149 Educ. L. Rep. 261] (Or. Ct. App. 2000).

since university officials had the statutory authority to manage its personnel and their interpretation of the RIF rules was reasonable.[158] The court added that the employees were unable to demonstrate that other groups of employees were treated more favorably than they were.

Denial of Employee Benefits

When a state university reduced retirement health care benefits, faculty members a breach of contract action. A trial court dismissed the contract claims on the basis of sovereign immunity, but allowed a claim based on vested rights to go forward. On further review, The Supreme Court of Arkansas reversed in favor of the university in finding that since sovereign immunity applied, the suit should have been dismissed.[159]

In North Dakota, a university adopted an early retirement program whereby certain employees may be eligible for a payment of their final salary if they retire. Believing that the payments were not wages, when the university did not withhold taxes from the payments, and after an audit by the Internal Revenue Service, it was required to submit the non-withheld taxes. But was denied a subsequent refund. When both parties filed motions for summary judgment, the federal trial court partially granted the motions.[160] The court determined that payments to administrators were taxable as wages since the administrators were at-will employees with no property interest in their positions and the payments were based on length of service. However, as to tenured faculty, the court held that the payments were not taxable as wages but rather payment for the purchase of property, namely their tenure rights.

When a university terminated unemployment benefits for workers who were on strike, it did so based on a state labor law statute that prohibits payment of benefits during periods of academic recess if an employee has a reasonable assurance of a job during the following academic term. Employees unsuccessfully challenged this denial in claiming that they were on strike, not in recess. The Court of Appeals of New York reversed in favor of the employees.[161] The court reasoned that since the collective bargaining agreement at issue had expired, a question of fact remained over whether the employees were reasonably assured of returning to work the following term.

---

[158] Harrison v. Board of Trustees of the Univ. of the District of Columbia, 758 A.2d 19 [147 Educ. L. Rep. 194] (D.C. 2000).

[159] Arkansas Tech Univ. v. Link, 17 S.W.3d 809 [144 Educ. L. Rep. 1070] (Ark. 2000).

[160] North Dakota State Univ. v. United States, 84 F. Supp. 2d 1043 [142 Educ. L. Rep. 222] (D. N.D. 1999).

[161] *In re* Goodman, 709 N.Y.S.2d 884 [145 Educ. L. Rep. 748] (N.Y. 2000).

Tort Liability

Negligence

Bodily Injury

The parents of a pedestrian filed a wrongful death action against a city, state, and university stemming from the death of their son as he was walking along an area of a city park that passed through a university campus after he fell to his death from a cliff when the ground beneath him gave way. The Supreme Court of Rhode Island affirmed a dismissal in favor of the defendants since the deceased was a trespasser who should not have been on the road since it was closed at the time of the accident.[162]

The operator of a restaurant at a Maine college campus who slipped and fell on snow and ice on the fire lane adjacent to the residence hall where she lived and unsuccessfully sued college officials based on their failure to maintain the fire lane in a reasonably safe condition. The First Circuit affirmed a grant of summary judgment in favor of the college and the officials because it was immune from liability under the governmental immunity provisions of state law.[163]

Other Negligence Claim

A parent sued a university research foundation and school board for sexual of her son by a counselor hired by the latter to administer a program to identify students who would not traditionally enter college but showed potential to succeed in college. The counselor, who was not an employee of a school district, met with the student behind close doors on a regular basis for a period of six months. A trial court in New York dismissed claims of negligent hiring against the foundation because there was no proof that its officials had any prior knowledge of the counselor's conduct.[164]

---

[162] Cain v. Johnson, 755 A. 2d 156 [146 Educ. L. Rep. 259] (R.I. 2000).
[163] Campbell v. Washington County Technical College, 219 F. 3d 3 [146 Educ. L. Rep. 47] (1st Cir. 2000).
[164] Murray v. Research Found. of State Univ., 707 N.Y.S.2d 816 [144 Educ. L. Rep. 620] (N.Y. Sup. Ct. 2000).

Qualified Immunity

The Fifth Circuit denied a petition for an en banc rehearing where the dismissal of an assistant football in Louisiana coach because of his son's decision to attend another college, led to a suit for damages for allegedly violating his familial rights. The court affirmed that since the head coach's action in dismissing the assistant coach was objectively reasonable, he was entitled to qualified immunity.[165]

Sovereign Immunity

When two former employees, both non-Native Americans, of a community college unsuccessfully brought charges of racial discrimination with the EEOC and the state human rights commission, they filed suit in the federal trial court in South Dakota. When the college failed to answer the complaint and a default judgment was entered, the court rejected its arguments based on lack of subject matter jurisdiction and immunity. On further review, the Eight Circuit reversed in favor of the college since it enjoyed sovereign immunity.[166]

Defamation

A former department chair unsuccessfully sued other faculty members for defamation after he survived a no confidence vote by department members. An appellate panel in New York affirmed that the trial court properly granted the defendants' motion for summary judgment since common interest qualified privilege applied.[167]

Intentional Infliction of Emotional Distress

A jury awarded a female employee who sued her university for intentional inflection of emotional distress for sexual harassment and intimidation on the job $5,000 in punitive amages from a fellow worker and $500,000 against the university. On appeal, the Supreme Court of North Carolina affirmed that punitive damage liability of an employer under a theory of

---

[165] Kipps v. Caillier, 205 F.3d 203 [142 Educ. L. Rep. 640] (5th Cir. 2000).
[166] Hagan v. Sisseton Wahpeton Community College, 205 F.3d 1040 [142 Educ. l. Rep. 701] (8th Cir. 2000).
[167] Anas v. Brown, 702 N.Y.S. 2d 732 [142 Educ. L. Rep. 450] (N.Y. App. Div. 2000).

vicarious liability cannot exceed the punitive damage liability of the employee.[168]

Workers' Compensation

The Supreme Court of Rhode Island modified a grant of summary judgment in favor of a university that denied an employee's claim for disability retirement benefits under its pension plan.[169] The court held that the plan required that the employee be given credit for time that he was not performing duties because of disability for which he was receiving workers compensation and that the additional hours of service brought him to the fifteen-year service requirement so as to make him eligible for disability pension.

In the first of two cases from New York, an appellate court affirmed that an employer - employee relationship existed between a university and a research assistant.[170] The court found that there was substantial evidence to support the Worker's Compensation Board's decision that such an employment relationship existed.

An appellate court in New York affirmed a compensation award to a university employee who suffered severe headaches caused by exposure to carbon monoxide at her work place.[171] The court agreed that the Workers' Compensation Board provided substantial evidence supporting its determination that headaches were causally related to carbon monoxide exposure, thereby constituting a compensable accidental injury.

Invasion of Privacy

A university and various officials sued a former faculty member for invasion of privacy as a result of his actions in creating websites and e-mails which gave the impression that they belonged to the officials and directing e-mail recipients to visit the websites that he created. An appellate court in

---

[168] Watson v. Dixon, 532 S.E. 2d 175 [146 Educ L. Rep. 555] (N.C. 2000).

[169] Perry v. Johnson & Wales University, 749 A. 2d 1101 [143 Educ. L. Rep. 963] (R.I. 2000).

[170] Semus v. University of Rochester, 710 N.Y.S. 2d 128 [145 Educ. L. Rep. 757] NY App. Div. 3 Dept. 2000).

[171] Rich v. Pace Univ., 703 N.Y.S. 2d 565 [142 Educ. L. Rep. 470] (N.Y. App. Div 2000).

Indiana affirmed a permanent injunction in favor of the university on the basis that the faculty member invaded the privacy of the officials.[172]

Insurance Coverage

After the settlement of wrongful death and action battery claims against a university that was filed by participants in a radioisotope experiment, its excess liability insurer sought a declaratory judgment as to its indemnity obligations. A federal trial court in Tennessee granted the insurance company's motion for summary judgment since the university's failure to provide timely notice prejudiced the company by preventing it from conducting a timely investigation of the underlying facts of the case.[173]

Contract Liability

Contract Terms

A temporary employee unsuccessfully sued a college for breach of contract and petitioning for reclassification as a contract employee. An appellate court in California affirmed a grant of summary judgment in favor of the college.[174] The court reasoned that the relevant statute did not provide for automatic reclassification as a contract employee merely because the employee exceeded full time due to substitute assignments.

In Ohio, a faculty member unsuccessfully sued a university on the basis of promissory estoppel and breach of contract. On further review, an appellate court affirmed that the parol evidence rule precluded the introduction of evidence of an oral agreement that varied the terms of the faculty member's written contract which was clear and unambiguous.[175]

---

[172] Felsher v. University of Evansville, 727 N.E.2d 783 [143 Educ. L. Rep. 1008] (Ind. Ct.App. 2000).

[173] United States Fire Ins. Co. v Vanderbilt Univ., 82 F. Supp. 2d 788 [142 Educ. L. Rep. 83] (M. D. Tenn. 2000).

[174] Balasubramanian v. San Diego Community College Dist., 95 Cal. Rptr.2d 837 [143 Educ. L. Rep. 985] (Cal. Ct. App. 2000).

[175] Kashif v. Central State Univ., 729 N.E.2d 787 [144 Educ. L. Rep. 698] (Ohio Ct. App. 1999).

A landlord who leased space to a university in New York sued state entities and officials seeking a declaration that a state statute eliminating appropriations for rental payments under an expired lease on the school's relocation unconstitutionally impaired its contract rights. After a federal trial court agreed that the statute violated the Contract Clause, the Second Circuit vacated and remanded.[176] The court decided that the state law breached a contract, an action that was distinct from an impairment of a contract, since the obligation to pay remedies still remained.

Contract Liability

In New York, a former employee unsuccessfully sued a state university for breach of covenant of good faith and fair dealing and violating an overtime compensation statute. The Second Circuit affirmed that the employee could not file suit since a covenant of good faith and fair dealing arises out of the existence of a contract and he was employed pursuant to a state statute rather than a contract.[177] The court was also of the opinion that the university was statutorily exempt from the overtime statute.

Alaska sued a post-secondary vocational school for breach of contract based on its failure to refund tuition to students after closing two of its campuses. The Supreme Court of Alaska affirmed an ordered directing the school to reimburse tuition.[178]

An unsuccessful bidder on a state university contract unsuccessfully challenged the rejection of his bid on the basis that it was non-responsive. The Supreme Court of Alaska affirmed that the university's rejection was not arbitrary and capricious, but rather, reasonable based on the omissions in the bidder's bid.[179]

---

[176] TM Park Ave. Assocs. v. Pataki, 214 F.3d 344 [145 Educ. L. Rep. 147] (2d Cir. 2000).
[177] Kim v. Regents of the Univ. of Cal., 95 Cal.Rptr.2d 10 [143 Educ. L. Rep. 602] (Cal. Ct. App. 2000).
[178] American Computer Inst. v. State of Alaska, 995 P.2d 647 [142 Educ. L. Rep. 1055] (Alaska 2000).
[179] Aloha Lumber Corp. v. University of Alaska, 994 P.2d 991 [142 Educ. L. Rep. 527] (Alaska 1999).

Sovereign Immunity

A faculty member who was removed from an administrative position sued the university for breach of contract. The Supreme Court of New Mexico affirmed the denial of the university's motion for summary judgment on the basis of sovereign immunity.[180] The court reasoned that since the state statute governing sovereign immunity only extended immunity to actions not based on written and the suit alleged a breach of his written contract, the state was not entitled to sovereign immunity.

Conclusion

Litigation in higher education, if not a growth industry, is at least ro-bust. The causes of action are diverse and the significance of the cases beyond the contesting parties range from marginal to major. As indicated in the introduction to this chapter, higher education is a significant battle zone for defining the parameters of the new federalism, calibrating the limitations upon congressional authority to pass federal legislation, and setting bound-aries to Eleventh Amendment immunity. Much of the detail of this new federalism is being worked out in these cases. One is struck in the totality of these cases by the broad deference that courts give to institutions of higher education institutions and the difficulties that plaintiffs have in winning their suits. The extent to which this generalization is based upon changing judicial philosophies or changing practices by higher education institutions will need to be examined by specific substantive areas of higher education law.

---

[180] Handmaker v. Henney, 992 P.2d 879 [141 Educ. L. Rep. 901] (N.M. 1999).

8
STUDENTS IN HIGHER EDUCATION

Brad Colwell

Introduction

During 2000, almost one hundred cases involved students in higher education. This chapter reports on disputes from all levels of federal courts, including a Supreme Court case on student fees as well as a variety of other litigation on issues ranging from discrimination to discipline to bankruptcy. The remainder of the chapter reviews state cases examining typical issues of tort and contractual liability.

Admission

Recently, a number of rejected applicants challenged universities' uses of affirmative action in admissions processes. A federal trial court in Georgia ruled that only one plaintiff had standing to challenge a university's use of race in its admissions process.[1] The other applicants appealed to the Eleventh Circuit[2] which vacated and remanded for further consideration in light of *Texas v. Lesage*.[3] On remand, the trial court determined that *Lesage* did not impact its original decision since neither of the remaining plaintiffs who lacked standing could show they were otherwise academically qualified to compete for admission with minority applicants.[4]

Title VI

Three white females in Georgia sued alleging that the use of racial and gender preference in the final phase of a university's admissions process violated title VI and the Equal Protection Clause.[5] Reasoning that the legal analyses for title VI, title IX, and equal protection were identical, a federal trial court held that the use of racial and gender bonus points in the admissions process must pass a strict scrutiny analysis. The court reviewed the Supreme Court's opinion in *Bakke*[6] and post-*Bakke* cases before declaring that under the present set of facts, university officials did not identify exactly how the goal of diversity would be achieved. According to the court, basing racial preferences upon an unquantifiable and unlimited goal is "racial balancing," would not have met strict scrutiny. Utilizing the same

---

[1]   Tracy v. Board of Regents of the Univ. Sys. of Ga., 59 F. Supp.2d 1314 [138 Educ. L. Rep. 355] (S.D. Ga. 1999).
[2]   Tracy v. Board of Regents of the Univ. Sys. (Tracy II), 208 F.3d 1313 [144 Educ. L. Rep. 69] (11th Cir. 2000).
[3]   528 U.S. 18 [139 Educ. L. Rep.791] (1999) (holding that a university's race-based admissions policy violated equal protection and federal statutes).
[4]   Tracy III, 2000 WL 1123268 (S.D.Ga. 2000), reh'g denied (2000).
[5]   Johnson v. Bd. of Regents of the Univ. Sys. of Ga., 106 F. Supp.2d 1362 [146 Educ. L. Rep. 717] (S.D.Ga. 2000).
[6]   Regents of the Univ. of Cal. v. Bakke, 438 U.S. 265 (1978).

analysis, the court also rejected the use of bonus points for gender in the university's admissions process. Finally, the court noted that the three applicants should have been admitted because university officials could not show that they would have made the same decision absent the forbidden considerations.

Conversely, the Ninth Circuit adjudicated a title VI racial discrimination suit brought by rejected applicants to a law school in Washington.[7] The court, relying on *Bakke*, affirmed that it is permissible for university admissions programs to consider race for other than remedial purposes and that educational diversity is a compelling interest that meets strict scrutiny analysis.

A case from Texas involved an appeal by rejected law school applicants who claimed that they were discriminated against on the basis of race. In extended litigation consisting of numerous appeals, a federal trial court found that the applicants failed to establish that they would have been offered admission to law school under a constitutional system and entered a permanent injunction prohibiting any consideration of race, for any purpose, in the law school admission process. On further review, the Fifth Circuit affirmed that the rejected applicants had no reasonable chance of being offered admission under a race-blind admission system.[8] At the same time, the court reversed the permanent injunction barring the use of race as an admission criteria since this conflicted with Bakke.

In Michigan, in response to a suit filed by rejected applicants, university officials, in trying to satisfy strict scrutiny, argued that race conscious admissions policies are constitutional because of the educational benefit of a diverse student body and to remedy past discrimination. A federal trial court concluded that diversity constitutes a compelling interest in higher education justifiying the use of race as an admissions criteria.[9] In examining the university's current admission policy, the court discerned that it was permissible to utilize bonus points for race.

---

[7] Smith v. Univ. of Wash., Law Sch., 233 F.3d 1188 [149 Educ. L. Rep. 347] (9th Cir. 2000).
[8] Hopwood v. State of Texas, 236 F.3d 256 [150 Educ. L. Rep. 51] (5th Cir. 2000) (Hopwood III).
[9] Gratz v. Bollinger, 122 F. Supp.2d 811 [149 Educ. L. Rep. 451] (E.D. Mich. 2000).

Readmission

A law student who was expelled for disciplinary misconduct unsuc-cessfully sued his university for refusing his request for readmission. An appellate court in Oklahoma affirmed the rejection of the student's claim for negligence against the university since officials had no duty to readmit him.[10] Further, the court rejected the student's due process claim, stating that there was no property interest in admission to law school.

Tuition and Fees

Student Fees

In 2000, the Supreme Court examined *Board of Regents of the University of Wisconsin v. Southworth,*[11] a case filed by students who alleged that a mandatory activity fee violated their First Amendment rights of free speech and association by subsidizing ideological and political speech of organiza-tions with which they disagreed. Reversing two lower court actions, the Court upheld the constitutionality of the activity fee in rejecting an analogy to unions and bar associations that do not require members to pay fees supporting speech with which they disagree and directed that the fee must be allocated on a viewpoint neutral basis. The Court remanded the question of a student referendum as a viewpoint neutral method of fee allocation.

Three other federal cases directly related to the issue of student refer-enda in Southworth. On remand, the Seventh Circuit, in turn, remanded to a trial court but suggested that it would appear that a "majority rules" basis for funding would only advance certain viewpoints.[12] A federal trial court in Wisconsin ruled that there was standing for new plaintiffs who were current students since the previous students had graduated.[13] In a separate opin-ion, the court was of the view that objective criteria for distribution of funds must be in place since it was incumbent to allocate the scarce financial resources on some acceptable neutral principle. Insofar as there were no

---

[10] Mason v. State *ex. rel.* Bd. of Regents of the Univ. of Okla., 23 P.3d 964 (Okla. Ct. App. 2001).
[11] 529 U.S. 217 [142 Educ. L. Rep. 624] (2000).
[12] Southworth v. Board of Regents of the Univ. of Wis. Sys., 221 F.3d 1339 [148 Educ. L. Rep. 572] (7th Cir. 2000).
[13] Fry v. Board of Regents of the Univ. of Wis. Sys., 132 F. Supp.2d 740 (W.D. Wis. 2000).

criteria, the court commented that "[d]ecision[s] as to who receive funding in what amounts are left to the complete discretion of the student officials on student government committees."[14] Insofar as it maintained that a direct democratic referendum sacrificed viewpoint neutrality, the court enjoined the university from distributing fees until it adopted a viewpoint neutral policy.

Tuition and Waivers

Every year, students challenge university policies or actions relating to residency as they relate to eligibility for in-state or out-of-state tuition. For example, in New Jersey, a law student objected to his school's refusal to treat him as an in-state resident. An appellate court affirmed that a domicile is a permanent home from which a student does not intend to move that once determined, remains the same until replaced by a new domicile.[15] The court considered three elements in evaluating whether a change of domicile occurred: physical establishment of an abode in a particular state, intent to make home permanent or at least stay indefinitely, and intent to abandon the previous domicile. The court also pointed out that state law requires a student be a resident for twelve months prior to enrollment in order to be considered for in-state tuition. The court affirmed the dismissal of the student's complaint since the evidence showed that he worked out of state for three years, paid taxes out of state, and did not intend to return to his parents' in-state home.

Two other appellate courts addressed cases concerning residency policies and tuition. An appellate court in Maryland upheld an equal protection challenge filed by a student who claimed that a university policy established an irrational classification between in-state and out-of-state students.[16] In rejecting the university's motions to dismiss, the court reviewed the policy at issue wherein "financially independent" students' residence was determined by their own residency status while a "financially dependent" students' residence was decided, without exception, solely by those person(s) providing the support. Here the student was a state resident whose financial support came from parents who divorced and left the state. The court agreed that this policy was unconstitutional since its application would have been inconsistent with the notion of providing a tuition benefit to bona fide state residents.

---

[14] Fry v. Board of Regents of the Univ. of Wisc. Sys., 132 F. Supp.2d 744, 749 (W.D. Wis. 2000).

[15] Lipman v. Rutgers, 748 A.2d 142 [143 Educ L. Rep. 288] (N.J. Super. Ct. App. Div 2000).

[16] Frankel v. Board of Regents of the Univ. of Md. Sys., 761 A.2d 324 [148 Educ. L. Rep. 966] (Md. Ct. App. 2000).

In the second case, the court addressed tuition waivers. A law student who was a Vietnam veteran challenged a university's policy that excluded professional degrees from a veteran's free tuition.[17] While state law provided tuition waivers for Vietnam veterans, at issue was the university's administrative policy that limited the waiver to bachelors and masters degrees. An appellate court in Washington reversed in favor of the student in agreeing with his argument that the university's degree stipulation was subject to the rule-making provisions of the Administrative Procedures Act. The court maintained that since the requirements restricted the right of Vietnam veterans to receive the statutory benefit of the tuition waivers, they should have been subject to the notice and comments procedures.

Collection Costs and Refunds

A federal trial court in New York addressed whether a community college's assessment of a thirty percent collection fee for delinquent accounts was clearly articulated in its student handbook. The handbook authorized the college to recover "any and all association collection costs" on a delinquent account. The court denied the college's motion for summary judgment on the basis that it was an issue of fact whether this fee constituted a deceptive practice.[18]

In a dispute over a tuition refund, a student and his mother brought a breach of contract suit against a college regarding its policy for individuals who withdraw before the end of an academic year.[19] While the handbook policy provided for a proportional refund of prepaid tuition based on the number of weeks left in an academic year, a footnote in the policy said that it was currently under review and that students should check future tuition bills for more information. Over the summer, the college changed the policy to afford students a much smaller refund. In reversing an earlier judgment, the Supreme Court of Vermont indicated that the proportional refund was in effect at the time the contract was formed with the student. As such, the court rejected the college's attempt to reserve unlimited power to modify the policy since any unilateral modification of the contract had to be supported by additional consideration.

---

[17] Hunter v. University of Wash., 2 P.3d 1022 [145 Educ. L. Rep. 514] (Wash. Ct. App. 2000).
[18] Alexson v. Hudson Valley Comm. College, 125 F. Supp.2d 27 [150 Educ. L. Rep. 222] (N.D.N.Y. 2000).
[19] Reynolds v. Sterling College, 750 A.2d 1020 [144 Educ. L. Rep. 314] (Vt. 2000).

Bankruptcy

Again this year, numerous cases surrounded issues facing former students who have accumulated significant school loans that they cannot afford to repay and are trying to discharge their debts in bankruptcy. Congress addressed the issue of student loans and bankruptcy when it enacted the Bankruptcy Reform Act of 1978. As part of this Act, 11 U.S.C. § 523(a)(8) provides that a student is not discharged from a debt for an educational loan "unless excepting such debt from discharge . . . would impose an undue hardship on the debtor .... ."[20] Typically, former students who seek to discharge their loans attempt to accomplish this by filing either for Chapter 7 or Chapter 13 bankruptcy.

According to a bankruptcy court in Ohio, a hearing to consider the dischargeability of a debt is an "adversary proceeding" which follows formal rules of conduct and may be requested by either the creditor or the debtor. During a discharge proceeding, the court observed that a creditor has the initial burden of establishing the existence of the debt and that it is excepted from discharge. The court added that if a creditor meets this burden, then the debtor must show that the debt qualified for discharge due to undue hardship.[21]

Undue Hardship

While section 523(a)(8) does not define what constitutes "undue hardship," bankruptcy courts have fashioned three tests in reviewing what comprises an undue hardship: totality of the circumstances,[22] the Brunner test,[23] and the Johnson test.[24] A bankruptcy court in Massachusetts adopted

---

[20] 11 U.S.C. § 523(a)(8) provides, in relevant part, "(a) A discharge under...this title does not discharge an individual debtor from any debt....(8) for an educational benefit overpayment or loan made, insured, or guaranteed by a governmental unit, or made under any program funded in whole or in part by a governmental unit or nonprofit institution . . . unless excepting such debt from discharge under this paragraph will impose an undue hardship on the debtor and the debtor's dependents."

[21] *In re* Ledbetter, 254 B.R. 714, 716 [148 Educ. L. Rep. 388] (Bankr. S.D. Ohio 2000).

[22] *See In re* Kopf, 245 B.R. 731 (Bankr. D. Me. 2000).

[23] Brunner v. New York State Higher Educ. Servs., Corp., 831 F.2d 395 [42 Educ. L. Rep. 535] (2nd Cir. 1987).

[24] Penn. Higher Educ. Assistance Agency v. Johnson (*In re* Johnson), 5 B.C.D. 532 (Bankr. E.D. Pa. 1979). This test consists of a review of income, education, employment status, skills, and access to transportation; then a debtor's expenses; and finally either a bona fide effort to repay or pass the "policy" test.

the totality of the circumstances test in evaluating whether the student loan debt constituted an undue hardship.[25] Under this test, the court reviewed past, present, and reasonably reliable future financial resources; reasonable living expenses of debtor and debtor's dependents, and other relevant facts or circumstances particular to the debtor's case that would have prevented the debtor from a minimal standard of living. The court ruled that even though the debtor lived on a tight budget, he still enjoyed amenities of life and had a monthly financial surplus. Further, the court ascertained that it does not constitute a hardship just because loan repayments precluded the debtor from purchasing life insurance or preparing for retirement.

A second line of cases utilized the *Brunner* test in examining undue hardship. Under this test, a debtor has the burden to show whether he or she cannot maintain a minimal standard of living for himself or herself and dependents if forced to repay the loan, whether additional circumstances exist indicating that this state of affairs is likely to persist for a significant portion of the repayment period, and whether a debtor has made good faith efforts to pay.

Bankruptcy courts in Montana and Oklahoma applied the *Brunner* test. In Oklahoma, the court focused on the third prong of the test and a debtor's good faith effort to repay loans. In granting a part of the debtor's discharge request, the court focused on two key factors: even with the debtor's monthly financial surplus it was not possible to pay off all the loans, and his current financial circumstances, caring for his ill mother, were the result of factors beyond his control.[26] In refusing to discharge all of the debtor's outstanding student loans since they were not consolidated, the court reviewed his ability to repay each one and explained that only six of thirteen loans were dischargeable.

The same bankruptcy court in Montana denied three separate requests for student debtors to discharge student loans in bankruptcy.[27] In each case, the court focused on the second prong of the *Brunner* test and whether the likelihood that the current financial situation will persist. The court acknowledged that each debtor was in an "unenviable financial position at this time [emphasis added]," but there was no evidence indicating the debtors' conditions would persist.[28] Further, the court remarked that it takes more than "mere financial difficulty" to discharge a loan; it takes financial hard-

---

[25] *In re* Dolan, 256 B.R. 230 [149 Educ. L. Rep. 555] (Bankr. D. Mass. 2000).

[26] *In re* Hollister, 247 B.R. 485 (Bankr. W.D. Okla. 2000).

[27] *In re* Marsh, 257 B.R. 569 (Bankr. D. Mont. 2000), *In re* Hatfield, 257 B.R. 575 (Bankr. D. Mont. 2000), *In re* Gettle, 257 B.R. 583 (Bankr. D. Mont. 2000).

[28] *In re* Gettle, 257 B.R. at 590.

ship plus other extenuating circumstances. In one case, the court went so far as to deny a discharge to a physically-challenged debtor because she had the ability to function in her occupational pursuits with therapy and proper medication.[29]

Educational Loan and Payments

A student from New York who was allowed to attend class even though he had yet to pay his tuition later declared bankruptcy and sought to discharge the amount of tuition that he owed the university on the basis that there was no loan. Insofar as section 523(a)(8) does not define an educational loan, the Second Circuit relied upon a common law definition that defines one as a contract whereby one party transfers money or its equivalent to another that the latter agrees to repay.[30] The court affirmed that the debt could be discharged since it was borne from the debtor's failure to pay tuition and became a past due account, not an agreement by the university to exchange funds or extend credit.

In Massachusetts, a law student declared bankruptcy and sought to have his loans discharged as an undue hardship. At issue was whether spousal income or future financial interest in a will or trust constituted resources for a court to consider when evaluating the ability to pay off the loans. The court cited well-established law supporting the proposition that the section at issue requires the judiciary to consider spousal income in considering undue financial hardship.[31] As to the will, the court wrote that creditors may reach property interests in satisfaction of obligations, if the present owner has more than a mere expectancy interest in the property.

Sovereign Immunity

Sovereign immunity under the Eleventh Amendment is a defense that public universities are raising with increased regularity in attempts to deny jurisdiction to federal courts that are reviewing bankruptcy suits filed by former students. Even so, Eleventh Amendment sovereign immunity is not absolute since Congress may abrogate it or a state can waive it.

A student who sought to discharge his student loans under Chapter Seven filed an adversary proceeding against a public university.[32] A federal trial court in Virginia contended that since an adversary proceeding constituted a lawsuit, the university was entitled to Eleventh Amendment immunity.

---

[29] *In re* Hatfield, 257 B.R. at 583.
[30] *In re* Renshaw, 222 F.3d 82 [146 Educ. L. Rep. 675] (2nd Cir. 2000).
[31] *In re* Dolan, 256 B.R. 230 [149 Educ. L. Rep. 555] (D. Mass. 2000).
[32] University of Va. v. Robertson, 243 B.R. 657 [141 Educ. L. Rep. 157] (W.D. Va. 2000).

In a similar case, a public university in Washington asked a bankruptcy court to deny jurisdiction based on sovereign immunity against a student's bankruptcy action.[33] The court was satisfied that Congress intended to abrogate states' sovereign immunity when it enacted Section 106 of the Bankruptcy Code, but after *Seminole Tribe*,[34] the Ninth Circuit observed that Congress did not have the power to act. Here the court ruled that the state agreed to waive its right to sovereign immunity as a condition to accepting federal funds.

A federal bankruptcy court in Missouri explored the issue of what constitutes a "waiver" of immunity.[35] In granting a university's motion for summary judgment, the court decreed a state can effectuate a waiver in three ways: by state statute or constitutional provision, by participating in a federal program, or by enlisting the jurisdiction of the federal courts. The court added that since a state must knowingly agree to a waiver, mere participation in a federal program is insufficient unless it is made unambiguously clear that doing so would be to exercise a waiver of immunity.

Health Education Assistance Loans

One case dealt with that discharge of a special type of educational loan: Health Education Assistance Loans (HEAL Loans). A bankruptcy court in Ohio considered whether it was unconscionable to have a student repay his HEAL Loans. The court defined unconscionable as equating to "shockingly unfair, harsh or unjust,"[36] a higher standard than the undue hardship provision for traditional educational loans. Most important, the court determined that instead of adopting a rigid test at what is unconscionable, it would look at the totality of the circumstances and in so doing held that the loan was nondischargeable since the debtor made no attempt to repay the funds.

---

[33] *In re* Huffine, 246 B.R. 405 (Bankr. E.D. Wash. 2000).
[34] Seminole Tribe of Fla. v. Florida, 517 U.S. 44 (1996).
[35] *In re* Janc, 251 B.R. 525 (Bankr. W.D. Mo. 2000).
[36] Rodgers v. Ohio College of Podiatric Med., 250 B.R. 883, 887 [145 Educ. L. Rep. 1070] (Bankr. S.D. Ohio 2000).

Constitutional Rights

Right to Privacy

In two separate opinions, a federal trial court in Illinois reviewed a suit filed by student athletes at a university who were videotaped in various states of undress without their knowledge or consent. The students sued the university and others after the tapes were made available for public purchase on the Internet. In the first case, the judge found for the defendants, computer service providers, stating that under the Communications Decency Act of 1996 they were immune from any state law cause of action that would have rendered them liable for information originating from a third party.[37] About a month later, the same court noted that university officials were entitled to qualified immunity because there was no clearly established constitutional right in relation to the specific facts. Although recognizing a constitutional right to privacy, the court posited that knowledge alone of a disclosure of personal matters by a private party is not actionable.[38]

Right of Association

The Third Circuit evaluated the constitutionality of a university policy in Pennsylvania that allowed officials to strip a fraternity chapter of its right as a registered student organization after an act of misconduct by some of its members. The court affirmed that the fraternity chapter did not have First Amendment rights of intimate or expressive association.[39] In making comparisons to a family unit, the court rejected the right to intimate association due to the fraternity's size, membership criteria, and openness to the public. The court also judged that the fraternity could not be considered an expressive organization because it did not take positions on political, cultural, or social events of importance.

---

[37] John Does 1 Through 30 v. Franco Productions, 2000 WL 816779 (N.D.Ill. 2000).
[38] Does, 2000 WL 968827 (N.D. Ill. 2000).
[39] Pi Lambda Phi Fraternity v. University of Pittsburgh, 229 F.3d 435 [147 Educ. L. Rep. 915] (3rd Cir. 2000).

Discipline

In *Missouri v. Horowitz* the Supreme Court explored the federal procedural due process rights of a student was dismissed for academic reasons and recognized that there was a difference "between the failure of a student to meet academic standards and the violation by a student for valid rules of conduct."[40] Consequently, courts have invoked different standards of protection when addressing nonacademic and academic sanctions.

Academic Dismissal

Typically, courts will not interfere in the academic evaluations of students. This judicial standard was affirmed when a student in a physician assistant program was dismissed for academic shortcomings. An appellate court in New York agreed that in the absence of bad faith or statutory or constitutional violations, an evaluation of a student's academic capabilities is "beyond the scope of judicial review."[41] Even so, many students filed causes of action against professors and universities alleging various causes of action after they did not meet certain academic standards.

Due Process

In *Horowitz* the Court reasoned that since students dismissed from public institutions for academic reasons were entitled to notice of faculty dissatisfaction and possible dismissal, the dismissal decision must be careful and deliberate. Yet, as reflected by a case from Arkansas, a formal hearing is not required. The Eighth Circuit affirmed that the suit of a pharmacy student who was dismissed for not making sufficient progress was properly dismissed since a formal hearing was not required.[42]

---

[40] Board of Curators of the Univ. of Mo. v. Horowitz, 435 U.S. 78, 86 (1978). See also Nussbaum v. University of Tex. Med. Branch at Galveston, 2000 WL1864048, 3 (Tex. App. 2000) (stating that "[S]tudents dismissed for 'disciplinary' reasons have a protected liberty interest requiring procedural due process [while those] dismissed for 'academic' reasons do have the same protections; their cases are reviewed under far less stringent standard . . . ").
[41] Ratigan v. Daemen College, 710 N.Y.S.2d 267 (N.Y. App. Div. 2000).
[42] Richmond v. Fowlkes, 228 F.3d 854 [147 Educ. L. Rep. 848] (8th Cir. 2000).

The Tenth Circuit resolved two cases from New Mexico dealing with the academic dismissals of medical students. In the first, the court relied extensively on *Horowitz* in discerning that the due process clause "does not require that a student dismissed from a state medical school for academic reasons be given a hearing."[43] The court was convinced that university officials went far beyond what was constitutionally necessary by providing the dismissed student three opportunities to improve her academic performance.

In a second case, the Tenth Circuit quickly rejected the disability claims of a dismissed medical student because she failed to articulate any particular major life activity that was affected by her depression.[44] The court also decided that the student did not allege a property or liberty interest in her continued enrollment in school.

An appellate court in Wisconsin affirmed a dismissal in favor of a university in commenting that the judiciary should not intervene on behalf of a doctoral student who twice failed his preliminary examination.[45] The court indicated that the student could not articulate a legitimate entitlement, other than a unilateral expectation to continue his academic program. The court concluded that solely because a student may have been evaluated differently from others did not mean the evaluation was arbitrary.

In Delaware, where a graduate student was dismissed for poor academic performance due to a grade in an advanced seminar course, the faculty had a personal dislike of him and desired that he leave the program. After his dismissal, the federal trial maintained that even though academic decisions should be afforded deference, faculty should not be allowed to insulate their actions based on their apparent dislike for a student under "the guise of an 'academic decision.'"[46] The court characterized the faculty's decision as one made in "bad faith" since course grading standards were changed for a class the student was enrolled in and because he was never informed that poor professional demeanor was a basis for dismissal from the program.

---

[43] Trotter v. The Regents of the Univ. of N.M., 219 F.3d 1179, 1185 [146 Educ. L. Rep. 68] (10th Cir. 2000).

[44] Dixon v. Regents of the Univ. of New Mexico, 242 F.3d 388 (10th Cir. 2000), cert. denied, 121 S. Ct. 1361 (2001).

[45] Reidinger v. Board of Regents of the Univ. of Wis. Sys., 622 N.W.2d 770 (Wis. App. Ct. 2000), reh'g denied (2001).

[46] Leonard v. University of Del., 2000 WL 1456295, 7 (D. Del. 2000).

Breach of Contract

Three state courts addressed breach of contract claims brought by dismissed medical students who failed to pass mandatory examinations. The Supreme Court of Mississippi acknowledged that the student-university relationship is contractual in nature and that the terms of the contract may be derived from a student handbook, catalogue, or other statement of university policy.[47] Even so, the court rejected a rigid interpretation of terms of the contract, asserting that universities have an implicit right to modify academic degree requirements, even if it is not specifically set forth in student handbooks.

In New York, a federal trial court relied on a similar analysis in ascertaining that there is an implied contractual relationship between students and universities with the terms supplied by bulletins and handbooks.[48] The court was of the view that a student did not meet the terms of his handbook when he failed an examination and did not notify the university before participating in clinical rotations. Further, the court explained that while the student was treated differently from peers, it was solely because the others had passed the mandatory examination.

Where a jury found that a private university arbitrarily dismissed a fourth-year student for poor academic performance, an appellate court in Florida conceded that the relationship between a university and a student "is solely contractual in nature,"[49] the terms of which are to afford students protection. Additionally, the court wrote that any damages from a breach of contract were those that naturally result and could reasonably be expected when the contract was made. Ultimately, the court reversed on the ground that it was appropriate for the jury to consider the possibility of lost future earnings and so rejected the university's argument that it should only compensate the student for lost tuition.

When a law school's modification of its policy on academic standing during the middle of a term had a negative consequent impact on a student, he sought further review. An appellate court in Washington affirmed that since the handbook included a provision reserving the university's right to amend its academic rules at any time, the change was acceptable since it not made in an arbitrary fashion and students had timely notice because the amendment had been discussed for over a year.[50]

---

[47] University of Miss. Med. Ctr. v. Hughes, 765 So.2d 528 (Miss. 2000).
[48] Babiker v. Ross Univ. Sch. of Med., 2000 WL 666342 (S.D.N.Y. 2000).
[49] Sharick v. Southeastern Univ. of the Health Sciences, 780 So. 2d 136, 138 [152 Educ. L. Rep. 448] (Fla. Dist. Ct. App. 2000).
[50] Ishibashi v. Gonzaga Univ., 2000 WL 1156899 (Wash. Ct. App. 2000).

Racial Discrimination

A federal trial court in New York adjudicated a title VI claim brought by an African-American female who was forced to take a leave of absence from her social work program after complaining of racial discrimination during an internship. Utilizing the Supreme Court's three-part test from *McDonnell Douglas*,[51] the court decreed that the university's actions were prompted by the student's unsatisfactory performance in her internship rather than discrimination.[52] Insofar as the student could not substantiate her claim that the university's decision was pretextual, the court was satisfied that officials did not retaliate against her.

Nonacademic Disciplinary Action

In following the lessons from *Horowitz*, courts usually do not afford deference for nonacademic sanctions. For instance, an appellate court in Kentucky remarked that "courts are permitted to review the college's [disciplinary] decision to determine whether it was improper or arbitrary."[53] If a student who is expelled or suspended for disciplinary reasons can show a liberty or property interest,[54] then due process requires officials to provide the individual with notice of the charges and an opportunity for a hearing, if the charges are in dispute.

Due Process

In Kentucky, a student at a private college was expelled for possession of a weapon in his residence hall after security officers summoned him to an administrator's office, with no prior notice of the meeting, no legal counsel, and no opportunity to cross-examine witnesses. In fact, the letter of expulsion was prepared before the meeting. In reversing a grant of summary judgment in favor of the college, an appellate court contended that a state statute provided that both public and private state institutions must establish policies whereby all students are ensured due process.[55] Consequently, the court ruled that the student did not receive a fair hearing since he neither received notice of charges nor an opportunity to respond.

---

[51] *See* McDonnell Douglas v. Green Corp., 411 U.S. 792 (1973) (establishing a three part test for discriminatory retaliation: a plaintiff must first establish a "prima facie" case of retaliation, the burden the shifts to the defendant to offer a legitimate and non-retaliatory reason for its action, and if the defendant(s) meet this burden, then the plaintiff must produce sufficient evidence to find the defendant's reasons are a pretext for discriminatory retaliation).

[52] McKie v. New York Univ., 2000 WL 1521200 (S.D.N.Y. 2000).

[53] Trzop v. Centre College, 2000 WL 1134505 (Ky. Ct. App. 2000).

[54] *See* Lee v. Board of Trustees of W. Ill. Univ., 202 F.3d 274 (7th Cir. 2000) (holding that students did not have a property interest in continued education at a university since such a property interest must arise from state law).

[55] Trzop v. Centre College, 2000 WL 1134505 (Ky. Ct. App. 2000).

A graduate of a public university in Virginia alleged due process violations after his degree was revoked for misconduct that occurred while he was a student. Among other allegations, the former student claimed that he was unaware that revocation of his degree was a possible sanction for his misconduct. According to a federal trial court, the plaintiff had to receive sufficient notice, which includes notice of the charge and the possible sanction that might have been imposed.[56] The court added that a university could violate procedural due process if it deviates significantly from its own procedures, upon which a student relied to his detriment.

In Virginia, a federal trial court addressed two separate suits filed by different students stemming from the same altercation with a third student. When a university's judiciary committee adjudged the two students guilty of misconduct and ordered their expulsion, an appeals board rejected this recommendation and ordered a new hearing at which they were again declared guilty. Ultimately, the university president modified the sanction and increased the discipline. In the first case, the court offered that the Eleventh Amendment provided immunity to all university defendants who were sued in their professional capacities.[57] The court also pointed out that university officials violated procedural due process when they fail to notify a student of all of the claims brought against him before the judiciary committee. In the second case, the court held that the other student was entitled to notice and hearing since he had a liberty interest in his reputation and a property interest in continued enrollment.[58] The court concurred with the student's claim of supervisory liability since university officials were aware that the student-run disciplinary committee might not have been competent.

Fair Hearing

In Delaware, when a university dismissed a graduate student for using patients' records without their consent during his academic dismissal hearing, he alleged due process concerns about the hearing since one of the faculty members in his program was on the panel. The federal trial court noted that the student had to show that the professor was actually biased and that having mere information about the case was not enough to constitute a conflict.[59] The court agreed that there could be a conflict since the

---

[56] Goodreau v. The Rector and Visitors of the Univ. of Va., 116 F. Supp.2d 694 [148 Educ. L. Rep. 191] (W.D. Va. 2000).

[57] Tigrett v. Rector and Visitors of the Univ. of Va., 97 F. Supp.2d 752 (W.D. Va. 2000).

[58] Smith v. Rector and Visitors of the Univ. of Va., 115 F. Supp.2d 680 [147 Educ. L. Rep. 966 (W.D. Va. 2000)

[59] Leonard v. University of Del., 2000 WL 1456295 (D. Del. 2000).

professor had personal knowledge about the facts of the case and had previously voted in a faculty meeting to pursue further action against the student. The court also ruled that the university violated a covenant of good faith and fair dealing with the student.

When a student at a university in New York was suspended for telling a series of lies to his professors to gain a competitive academic advantage, a federal trial court upheld the sanction since neither the hearing nor the result was arbitrary.[60] The court judged that university officials followed established procedures by considering the student's prior acts of misconduct when discussing the severity of the sanction, especially since the prior offense dealt with his dishonesty.

Breach of Contract

In response to his appeal, a university official modified an undergraduate's expulsion for sexual misconduct to allow him to return to classes if ultimately acquitted of the accompanying criminal charges. When the student was acquitted, he challenged a notation on his transcript indicating a nonacademic suspension and grades of "WF" in those classes he could not complete due to the disciplinary sanction. Although recognizing the contractual nature of the student-university relationship, the Court of Claims of Ohio was of the opinion that since the letter modifying the sanction did not make any reference to the expungement of the student's records or adjustment of his grade point average, he was not entitled to the relief that he requested.[61]

A student at a university in Maryland who was expelled for murder after completing his academic program was later denied his diploma by the university. Restating the contractual relationship between the university and student, an appellate court reviewed a handbook provision that provided that a student will not receive a degree based solely on the completion of course work and that all outstanding charges of misconduct must be resolved before being allowed to graduate. Consequently, the court affirmed that the university's actions were not arbitrary, especially since the student remained subject to its policies.[62]

---

[60] Bhandari v. The Trustees of Columbia Univ., 2000 WL 310344 (S.D.N.Y.)
[61] Cornett v. Miami Univ., 728 N.E.2d 471 [143 Educ. L. Rep. 1034](Ohio Ct. Cl. 2000).
[62] Harwood v. Johns Hopkins Univ., 747 A.2d 205 [142 Educ. L. Rep. 980] (Md. Ct. Spec. App. 2000).

In New York, a student brought a breach of contract suit against a community college, claiming that his removal from a classroom for being disruptive was a form of discipline that required all of the procedural protections of the student handbook. A federal trial court rejected the college's motion for summary judgment in observing that a jury should consider whether the student's removal constituted an expulsion to which the contractual disciplinary procedures would apply.[63]

Academic Misconduct

A federal trial in Virginia reviewed the case of a student who filed suit claiming constitutional and common law tort violations after he was expelled for cheating on an in-class examination. In positing that cheating is a disciplinary matter, not an academic sanction, the court rejected the student's claim that he was negatively impacted by a delay in assigning him a faculty advocate since this was not necessary for due process.[64] The court dismissed the student's defamation claim because the letter of sanction that he received was not "published" outside of the university.

Residence Halls

Three cases addressed residence hall policies regarding mandated on-campus housing or objections to co-educational halls. Two cases dealt with whether universities created monopolies by requiring students to live on campus. Students who lived in an off-campus fraternity house claimed that a university's newly-adopted policy requiring all students to live on campus and buy a meal plan violated the Sherman Antitrust Act. A federal trial court in New York rejected the students' argument that the university had a monopoly since there were more than 100 colleges with which it competed for students.[65] The court stated that prospective students who did not find the university's housing policy appealing were free to attend different schools.

In the other case, Orthodox Jewish students in Connecticut challenged a university's policy that all unmarried students less than twenty-one were to reside in co-educational residence halls. The plaintiffs unsuccessfully alleged that the policy tied their educational attainment to the purchase of an unrelated housing service in violation of the Sherman Antitrust Act. The Second Circuit rejected the students' argument that the uniqueness of the

---

[63] Hudson Valley Community College, 125 F. Supp.2d 27 [150 Educ. L. Rep. 222] (N.D.N.Y. 2000).

[64] Cobb v. Rector and Visitors of the Univ. of Va., 84 F. Supp.2d 740 [142 Educ. L. Rep. 195] (W. D. Va. 2000).

[65] Hamilton Chapter of Alpha Delta Phi v. Hamilton College, 106 F. Supp.2d 406 [146 Educ. L. Rep. 693] (N.D.N.Y. 2000).

education that they were receiving compelled them to buy something that they might not have in a competitive market. In affirming a dismissal in favor of the university, the court noted there are many universities of superb quality and that the students could have gone elsewhere if they were dissatisfied with the school's rules.[66] The court also rebuffed the plaintiffs' Fair Housing Act claim on the basis that it only protects those seeking inclusion, not exclusion, into a residence.

An appellate court in New York affirmed the motion to dismiss a complaint against a university and its policy of permitting classmates or married couples with children to live in campus housing.[67] Where two unmarried females were denied permission to live in residence halls with their partners who were students, the court agreed that they failed to establish that the policy had a disparate impact on homosexuals since it had the same impact on non-married, heterosexual students as it had on non-married, homosexual students.

Federal Statutes

Title IX

Congress enacted title IX as part of the Education Amendments Act of 1972 to proscribe gender discrimination in education programs or other activities receiving federal financial assistance. Title IX claims include both quid pro quo and hostile environment sexual harassment. Regarding hostile environment harassment, the federal trial court in Minnesota reasoned that a female graduate student failed to show she was subjected to "unwanted sexual advances" by a faculty member.[68] The court, in focusing on the power disparity between the individuals, wrote that the student could not rely on a potential power disparity. The court was not convinced that there was a power disparity since the student did not have the accused faculty member as her advisor and was no longer taking his classes.

In the first of three federal cases from New York, a female medical student alleged numerous acts of sexual harassment against faculty members and medical residents.[69] In adopting a totality of the circumstances or cumu-

---

[66] Hack v. President and Fellows of Yale College, 237 F.3d 81 [150 Educ. L. Rep. 347] (2nd Cir. 2000).

[67] Levin v. Yeshiva Univ., 709 N.Y.S.2d 392 [146 Educ. L. Rep. 837] (N.Y. App. Div. 2000).

[68] Waters v. Metropolitan State Univ., 91 F. Supp.2d 1287 [143 Educ. L. Rep. 551] (D. Minn. 2000).

[69] Crandell v. New York College of Osteopathic Med., 87 F. Supp.2d 304 [142 Educ. L. Rep. 875] (S.D.N.Y. 2000).

lative approach in reviewing the existence of a hostile environment, the court partially denied the school's motion to dismiss in rejecting its argument that each act of misconduct should be treated individually.

Two federal trial courts in New York addressed substantially similar issues concerning whether victims of sexual harassment can allege both section 1983 and title IX causes of action. In the first, a court struck down a female student's section 1983 claims for equal protection violations against a university.[70] In deciding that the section 1983 claims against the university were subsumed under title IX, the court relied on notion that Congress intended title IX to be the exclusive remedy for claims of sexual misconduct against non-individual defendants and was meant to preclude Section 1983 claims. However, the court did not strike down the section 1983 claims against the professor on the ground that title IX does not afford an adequate remedy since the statute does not permit suits against individual plaintiffs. About five months later, the same court, in a case with similar facts, adopted the same holding as in the previous action.[71]

Sexual Misconduct

In *Gebser v. Lago Vista Independent School District*,[72] the Supreme Court found that a private litigant can only collect damages under title IX if an appropriate official at an educational institution has actual knowledge of the harassment and responds with deliberate indifference. In attempting to clarify *Gebser*, a federal trial court in New York maintained that an educational institution did not need actual knowledge of every incident for liability to attach.[73] According to the court, an educational institution should have enough knowledge of the harassment that it reasonably could have responded with remedial measures. The court concluded that misconduct occurring off-campus is sufficient to support a title IX claim and that an alleged victim needs only report it to someone with authority to take corrective measures and not necessarily follow an institution's official route for reporting sexual harassment.

---

[70] Cinquanti v. Tompkins-Cortland Community College, 2000 WL 949460 (N.D.N.Y.).
[71] Hayut v. State Univ. of N.Y., 127 F. Supp.2d 333 [150 Educ. L. Rep. 682] (N.D.N.Y. 2000).
[72] 524 U.S. 274 [125 Educ. L. Rep. 1055] (1998).
[73] Crandell v. New York College of Osteopathic Med., 87 F. Supp.2d 304 [142 Educ. L. Rep. 875] (S.D.N.Y. 2000).

Athletic Opportunities

The Fifth Circuit, on rehearing, addressed a case filed by female athletes in Louisiana who claimed that they were denied equal opportunities to in intercollegiate athletics, scholarships, and other resources. The court indicated that the plaintiffs had standing to challenge the university's failure to field teams for certain sports and should not have had to prove they had the athletic ability to make the teams.[74] However, the court also commented that no plaintiff had standing to challenge equity surrounding existing varsity teams since none of them were current varsity team members. In conceding that the case was not moot as it related to monetary relief, the court determined that the university waived its Eleventh Amendment immunity by accepting federal funds under title IX. Lacking immunity, the court overturned an earlier judgment and decided that university officials arguably acted with deliberate indifference to the condition of athletic programs for females.

Violence Against Women Act

In *United States v. Morrison*,[75] the Supreme Court affirmed an en banc ruling of the Fourth Circuit[76] that the Violence Against Women Act (VAWA) was unconstitutional on the basis that it cannot be sustained by section 8 of the Commerce Clause or Section 5 of the Fourteenth Amendment. The Court, in explaining that the civil remedy section of VAWA was invalid, rejected the argument that the Act regulated activity that substantially affected interstate commerce in rebuffing the concept that every violent crime affects interstate commerce. If this were the case, suggested the Court, then Congress would have had the uthority under the Commerce Clause to regulate any crime that impacts transportation, employment, production, or consumption. The Court also rejected the Fourteenth Amendment argument since the section at issue was a remedy against individual criminals and not against public officials.

---

[74] Pederson v. Louisiana State Univ., 201 F.3d 388 [141 Educ. L. Rep. 126] (5th Cir 2000), vacat'g on reh'g, 213 F.3d 858 [145 Educ. L. Rep. 113] (5th Cir. 2000).
[75] 120 S. Ct. 1740 [144 Educ. L. Rep. 28] (2000).
[76] Brzonkala v. Virginia Polytechnic and State Univ., 169 F.3d 820 [136 Educ. L. Rep. 15] (4th Cir. 1999).

Disability Laws

Congress enacted the Americans with Disabilities Act (ADA) and the Rehabilitation Act to address discrimination against individuals with disabilities. Insofar as both statutes apply to federally funded educational institutions, courts frequently adjudicate discrimination claims under these statutes using the same legal analysis.[77]

A federal trial court in Virginia granted a university's motion for summary judgment when a student claimed that he was disabled within the definition of the ADA and the Rehabilitation Act.[78] In order to establish a prima facie case under the ADA, the court pointed out that the student had to prove that he had a disability, was otherwise qualified, and was denied a benefit solely because of his disability. Under the ADA, the court was of the view that a disability is defined as a physical or mental impairment that substantially limits one or more of the major life activities of such individual, a record of such an impairment, or being regarded as having such an impairment. The court noted that even though learning is a major life activity, since attending school is not, the student had to show that his disability substantially limited his ability to learn.

In New Jersey, the federal trial court addressed whether a student-athlete was otherwise qualified. A prospective college athlete with a learning disability claimed that universities stopped recruiting him after they learned he may not have been an academic "qualifier" under the regulations set forth by the National Collegiate Athletic Association (NCAA). At issue was whether the student was a qualified and whether he was denied eligibility due to his disability. The court denied the university's motion for summary judgment since factual issues existed regarding whether it stopped recruiting the student because of his lack of athletic skill or because of his disability.[79] In this same case, the court addressed whether the defendants were recipients of federal funds. The court rejected the NCAA's motion for summary judgment because there was a factual issue regarding whether it was an indirect recipient of federal financial assistance. However, the court granted the ACT/Clearinghouse's motion for summary judgment on the basis that it was a contractor with the federal government. The court asserted that since the ACT/Clearinghouse only entered into a compensatory contractual relationship and did not receive a federal subsidy, it was not a recipient of federal financial assistance.

---

[77] Bird v. Lewis & Clark College, 104 F. Supp.2d 1271 [146 Educ. L. Rep. 178] (D. Ore. 2000).

[78] Betts, II v. Rector and Visitors of the Univ. of Va., 113 F. Supp.2d 970 [147 Educ. L. Rep. 573] (W.D. Va. 2000).

[79] Bowers v. National Collegiate Athletic Ass'n., 118 F. Supp.2d 494 [148 Educ. L. Rep. 760] (D.N.J. 2000).

The Eighth Circuit examined the issue of accommodation for students with disabilities. In so doing, the court reviewed the Rehabilitation Act, which requires making reasonable accommodations when a student with a disability would otherwise be denied meaningful access to a school unless doing so would fundamentally alters its nature or constitutes an undue burden. The court affirmed that a university in Iowa provided the exact accommodations called for by the student's expert witness.[80]

In Colorado, the federal trial court considered whether the Eleventh Amendment provided immunity to educational institutions against ADA and Rehabilitation Act claims.[81] The issue was borne out of a Supreme Court holding that another act of Congress exceeded its authority by abrogating sovereign immunity for ADA claims.[82] The court pointed out that it was clearly the intent of Congress to abrogate States' sovereign immunity to suit under both the ADA and the Rehabilitation Act and that both were valid congressional acts.

Torts

University Duty

Two state courts examined what duty, if any, universities had to suicidal students. In the first, the Supreme Court of Iowa affirmed that there was no special relationship that would give way to a duty owed to a student that committed suicide.[83] The court stated that Section 323 of the Restatement (Second) of Torts provides that a defendant must have put a plaintiff in a worse situation than if the defendant had never acted. The court was of the opinion that while university officials took no affirmative action to increase the risk of suicide, the former student's suicide was an intervening act that precluded their responsibility for his death.

In Rhode Island, the parents of a young man who died of a self-inflicted wound sued a university and its campus security for failing to act reasonably after they put them on notice that their son was suicidal. Campus

---

[80] Stern v. University of Osteopathic Med. and Health Sciences, 220 F.3d 906 [146 Educ. L. Rep. 108] (8th Cir. 2000).

[81] Werner v. Colorado State Univ., 135 F. Supp.2d 1137 [152 Educ. L. Rep. 712] (D. Colo. 2000).

[82] Kimel v. Florida Bd. of Regents, 528 U.S. 62 [140 Educ. L. Rep. 825](2000) (modifying the test for determining the validity of congressional abrogation of Eleventh Amendment immunity and holding that Congress exceed its authority to do so as applied to the Age Discrimination in Employment Act).

[83] Jain v. Iowa, 617 N.W.2d 293 [147 Educ. L. Rep. 320](Iowa 2000).

security did not detain the young man or consult a mental health professional after locating him on campus. In denying its motion for summary
judgment, a trial court ascertained that campus security had an obligation
under state law to certify persons who, if left unsupervised, would be in
danger of serious harm due to a mental disability.[84]

Where a graduate student sued her university after she was sexually
assaulted in the parking lot of her off-campus internship site, the Supreme
Court of Florida wrote that since school officials undertook the responsibility to assign her to a mandatory and approved internship location, they
assumed a duty to act reasonably in doing so.[85] The court declared that it
was a jury's responsibility to determine reasonableness, especially when
university officials had knowledge that the location of the internship was
dangerous.

The Supreme Court of Nebraska examined a university's responsibility
in the face of the foreseeable criminal activity. A husband and wife who were
students at a university filed suit after a third student stabbed the husband
during an altercation. The court observed that university officials owed a
landowner-invitee duty to their students to take reasonable steps to protect
against foreseeable acts of violence on its campus.[86] The court decreed that
while the acts of the accused student were foreseeable, the case had to be
remanded for a new trial to consider whether university officials failed to
take reasonable steps to discharge their duty.

A student actor who was accidentally stabbed during a theatrical performance sued the directors, two drama club faculty advisors, and the
university. At issue was whether the faculty advisors were acting in their
faculty capacities for purposes of the university's respondeat superior liability. The Supreme Court of Texas decided that the university could be
liable since the faculty members were not independent contractors or volunteers but were acting in their paid capacity on its behalf when the injury
occurred.[87] The court concluded that just because the advisors did not
receive additional compensation for their services did not mean they were
not acting on behalf of the university.

---

[84] Frizzell v. Town of Little Compton, 2000 WL 33159170 (R.I. Super. 2000).
[85] Nova Southeastern Univ. v. Gross, 758 So. 2d 86 [144 Educ. L. Rep. 1097]
(Fla. 2000).
[86] Sharkey v. Board of Regents of the Univ. of Neb., 615 N.W.2d 889 [146
Educ. L. Rep. 1103] (Neb. 2000).
[87] Bishop v. Texas A&M Univ., 35 S.W.3d 605 [150 Educ. L. Rep. 970] (Tex.
2000).

Where a student in Minnesota sued a university for injuries she suffered when she fell on ice as she exited a building, an appellate court affirmed that a jury verdict against it was not unreasonable.[88] The court agreed that while the university owed a duty to clear dangerous situations from its property, and was entitled to a reasonable time after the storm's end to do so, enough time had elapsed for someone to have removed the ice.

Alcohol

Parents of a fraternity member unsuccessfully brought a wrongful death suit after their son died of consuming large amounts of alcohol as part of a "big brother" fraternity event. A trial court granted motions of summary judgment in favor of the national and state chapters of the fraternity as well as a fellow fraternity member. The Supreme Court of Iowa affirmed that there was no special relationship between the national or state fraternity and the deceased member because no chapter funds were used to purchase the alcohol and its consumption was neither coerced nor a part of any initiation ritual. Further, the court contended that a fellow fraternity brother who allowed the deceased to "sleep it off" did not assume a duty to continuously monitor the deceased. The court summarized its position by stating that a fraternity "is not a custodial institution and its members, as adults, are free to make choices about their use and abuse of alcohol."[89]

Defamation

When a university in Washington denied a student teacher a certificate of moral fitness that was required by the state department of education after being informed of his alleged acts of sexual misconduct, he sued the college of education and officials for defamation, breach of contract, and invasion of privacy. On further review, an appellate court reversed on the basis that communications between and among university personnel was not "published" for the purpose of defamation.[90] The court also court acknowledged that since any university communication made to the state department of education was outside of its corporate structure, it was subject to a claim of defamation. The court also rejected the former student's invasion of privacy claim because he waived his right to object since he subjected himself to the

---

[88] Frykman v. Univ. of Minnesota-Duluth, 611 N.W.2d 379 (Minn. Ct. App. 2000).

[89] Garofalo v. Lambda Chi Alpha Fraternity, 616 N.W.2d 647, 654 (Iowa 2000).

[90] Doe v. Gonzaga Univ., 992 P.2d 545 [141 Educ. L. Rep. 359] (Wash. Ct. App. 2000).

requisite rules for teacher certification. As to the breach of contract claim, the court declared since state law, rather than the university's student handbook, governed the certificate of moral fitness, it was not liable.

Sports/Recreational Injury

The Supreme Court of Kansas rejected a request to create a special duty between a university and its athletes in a case where a basketball player was killed and another was critically injured while participating in a mandatory physical conditioning session. The plaintiffs appealed on the basis that the trial court erred in instructing the jury that the university owed them a duty of ordinary care since they did not share a special relationship. The court affirmed that they trial judge correctly explained the duty of care.[91]

A appellate court in New York affirmed a grant of summary judgment in favor of a university where an athlete filed suit against it after he was injured when he ran into a bench during lacrosse practice.[92] In a brief opinion, the court posited that the university was not liable since bench was an open and obvious condition that could have been readily observed by an individual who was employing the reasonable use of his senses.

In a second case from New York, a student who was injured during a game of tackle football organized by two competing residence halls unsuccessfully sued his college claiming that he was injured by a tackle that involved an unforeseeable flagrant infraction. An appellate court affirmed a grant of summary judgment in favor of the college on the ground that the student assumed the risk of injury because he was aware that being tackled in a violent manner is an inherent part of football.[93]

Fraud

A former student sued a technical college for fraud and breach of contract, alleging that officials made numerous misrepresentations about her academic program. The college argued that its contractual relationship with the student was included in one document, that it did not breach those terms, and that parol evidence could not be admitted to alter those terms.

---

[91] Howell v. Calvert, 1 P.3d 310 [144 Educ. L. Rep. 760] (Kan. 2000).
[92] Cherry v. Hofstra Univ., 711 N.Y.S.2d 898 (N.Y. App. Div. 2000).
[93] Glazier v. Keuka College, 713 N.Y.S.2d 381 (N.Y. App. Div. 2000).

Affirming a directed verdict in favor of the college, an appellate court in Texas rejected the idea that only one document contained all of the binding agreements between students and the college.[94] The court agreed that even though an implied contract did exist, the student failed to submit proof that its terms required the college to perform the acts about which she complained.

Educational Malpractice

A student who was dismissed for academic reasons claimed that his law school committed educational malpractice and breach of contract because he received inadequate legal instruction. An appellate court in Oklahoma affirmed a grant of summary judgment in favor of the university on the basis that there was no cause of action for educational malpractice against a private educational institution.[95] The court was of the view that such a tort would have violated the public policy that provides educational institutions broad discretion in academic matters such as student evaluation with which the judiciary should not interfere. The court sounded a different tone regarding a breach of contract claim when it stated that an institution's brochures, handbooks, and policies may well have formed the basis of a contractual relationship between the school and the student. However, in explaining that the contractual language must be a specific agreement of a particular service beyond the notion of receiving an adequate education, the court ultimately dismissed this claim since the student only produced general policy language that provided for an adequate education.

Statute of Limitations

In the only case specifically discussing a statute of limitations for tort actions, the Supreme Court of Oklahoma was asked to interpret the Governmental Tort Claims Act as it applied to a student who was injured from chemical exposure. The Act provided, in part, that any claim would be denied if not approved by a political subdivision within ninety days after the claim was submitted, unless the date of denial is extended by written agreement. Although the student did not hear from the university within ninety

---

[94] Villarreal v. Art Institute of Houston, 20 S.W.3d 792 [145 Educ. L. Rep. 804] (Tex. Ct. App. 2000).
[95] Bittle v. Oklahoma City Univ., 6 P.3d 509 [146 Educ. L. Rep. 870] (Okla. Civ. App. 2000).

days, she received a letter from the Attorney General months after the deadline stating that the claim was denied as of the effective date of that letter. In reversing on behalf of the student, the court ruled the letter served to extend the deadline and that she had 180 days from the date of that letter to commence a suit.[96]

Immunity

Where a state university and its employees were sued by a former student and employee alleging numerous state tort violations, a trial court granted the employees' motion for summary judgment on the basis that the state constitution provided them and the state absolute immunity. On further review, the Supreme Court of Alabama reversed in favor of the plaintiff.[97] The court held that since the plaintiff alleged that the employees exceeded their scope of statutory authority and acted willfully and maliciously in their individual capacities, they were beyond the protection of absolute immunity. Additionally, the court declared that absolute immunity did not apply to employees in their official capacities when a plaintiff is seeking injunctive or declaratory relief.

A student who was enrolled in a motorcycle safety course at a community college in Connecticut sued it after he was injured during the training. In response, the state's community college board of trustees raised the defense of sovereign immunity. The student argued that state statute allows a cause of action where a state employee's negligent conduct caused the personal injury provided the state owned and insured the vehicle. An appellate court rejected the student's interpretation of the statute, stating reasoning it required the employee's negligent operation of the vehicle.[98] The court pointed out that since the student operated the vehicle at the direction of the state employee, his injury was not subject to the exception.

In a second case involving sovereign immunity, a university claimed such a defense when sued by a former student after one of its officials mistakenly informed a prospective employer that he had not earned enough academic credits to graduate.[99] The student unsuccessfully argued that the university's negligent use of tangible property, namely computers, consti-

[96] Carswell v. Oklahoma State Univ., 995 P.2d 1118 [142 Educ. L. Rep. 1078] (Okla. 1999).
[97] Matthews v. Ala. A&M Univ., 2000 WL 681055 (Ala. 2000).
[98] Pannoni-Barron v. State of Conn. Bd. of Trustees of Comm. Tech. Colleges, 28 Conn. L. Rep. 77 (Conn. Super. Ct. 2000).
[99] Prairie View A&M Univ. of Texas v. Mitchell, 27 S.W.3d 323 (Tex. Ct. App. 2000).

tuted a waiver of sovereign immunity. An appellate court in Texas rejected the student's argument that the university should have been liable because the use or misuse of information does not have a tangible quality within the meaning of the statute.

In New Jersey, a public university tried to claim the protection of the state's Charitable Immunity Act against a suit brought by a student who was injured after falling down a staircase in its amphitheater.[100] Reversing in favor of the student, an appellate court noted that even though the university was a nonprofit institution, since the legislative intent was for the Charitable Immunity Act to apply solely to private charities, the university should have defended itself under the state's Tort Claims Act.

Conclusion

Overall, this was a bit of a lean year for cases involving students in higher education as there were about fifty fewer reported actions. Even so, in many ways, this year was typical of the types of cases reported in prior years. It was particularly interesting to see that some new trends were starting to develop within the traditional higher education areas. For example, although students have always attempted to discharge their student loans in bankruptcy, public universities are becoming more aggressive and alleging a sovereign immunity defense in attempts to deny the federal courts jurisdiction over such disputes.

A number of unexpected trends also developed this year. For instance, it was surprising to observe the decline in the number of reported cases concerning title IX gender equity in college athletics as well as in those concerning traditional constitutional issues such as freedom of religion and Fourth Amendment search and seizure. Another surprising trend was the number of cases surrounding the financial aspects of schooling involving student fees, tuition waivers, and, of course, bankruptcy. Despite some of these new trends, there were still numerous cases on the usual issues of tort, contract, discrimination, and academic/nonacademic sanctions. In the end, this was a good year for clarifying legal issues and providing clues to future legal trends.

---

[100] O'Connell v. State of New Jersey, 762 A.2d 696 [149 Educ. L. Rep. 566] (N.J. Super. Ct. App. Div. 2000).

9
FEDERAL AND STATE LEGISLATION

David L. Dagley

Introduction

This chapter chronicles statutes related to education at the K-12 and collegiate level, passed in 2000 by the United States Congress and the legislative bodies of the fifty states.

Federal Legislation

The Second Session of the 106th Congress demonstrated increasing interest in legislation related to the state function of education. However, few of the education-related bills that were proposed actually passed. This section briefly describes federal bills that were passed in 2000.

Credit Enhancement Initiative to Assist Charter School Facility Acquisition

Federal legislation in 2000 included a consolidated appropriations bill for education.[1] Notable in this bill was a subpart related to charter schools[2] that provides three one-time grants to eligible entities to permit them to demonstrate innovative credit enhancement initiatives to assist charter schools in addressing the cost of acquiring, constructing, and renovating school facilities.

International Academic Opportunity Act

The 106th Congress passed the International Academic Opportunity Act[3] which established a grant program for undergraduate students of limited financial means to study abroad. To be considered for grants of up to $5,000, a student must be in good standing, a citizen or national of the United States, accepted into a study abroad program approved for credit by the student's home institution, and currently receiving Pell Grants under title IV of the Higher Education Act of 1965.

---

[1] L. 106-554. 114 Stat. 2763.
[2] 114 Stat. 2763A-57.
[3] P.L. 106-309, 114 Stat. 1078.

Children's Health Act of 2000

The Children's Health Act of 2000[4] increased appropriations for pediatric research in a broad array of diseases and medical conditions including autism, traumatic brain injury, juvenile arthritis, diabetes, and asthma. The law not only continues the Healthy Start program but also contains provisions to revise and extend graduate medical education programs in Children's Hospitals.

Acts Related to Native American Education

Two laws passed by Congress in 2000 have implications for Native American communities and institutions including colleges and schools. The first law amended the Higher Education Act of 1965, purportedly to simplify the process of submitting funding applications by American Indian colleges and universities as well as Alaska Native and Native Hawaiian institutions.[5] This provision prohibits Native institutions from receiving funds from Section 316(d) and Section 317 and concurrently receive funding from other provisions of Part B of the Higher Education Act. The second provision, the Tribal Self-Government Amendments of 2000,[6] represents yet another policy change by the federal government with respect to Native Americans. Its stated purpose is to establish and implement permanent tribal self-government within the Department of Health and Human Services and to permit the orderly transition from Federal dominance to self-determination. This act may have implications for all human service providers on tribal land.

State Legislation

The remainder of the chapter discusses new education laws that were passed by the states. Topic groupings are used to provide a sense of the different types of matters with which legislatures are dealing and the different approaches that they have adopted on these questions.

---

[4] P.L. 106-310. 114 Stat. 1101.
[5] P.L. 106-211. 114 Stat. 330.
[6] P.L. 106-260. 114 Stat. 711.

Accountability and School Reform

Accountability and reform of schools figured prominently in the 2000 legislative year. Legislation involving accountability and school reform showed a decided emphasis on the use of punishments over incentives. This is a trend continued from previous years. Six states passed comprehensive accountability packages. Georgia enacted the A-Plus Education Reform Act of 2000[7] which includes an anti-nepotism provision requiring a public vote and personal abstention on personnel votes where a candidate for employment is related to a board member.[8] A separate provision created local school councils to provide advice to principals and school boards on a variety of educational matters including the school's calendar, conduct code, curriculum, budget priorities, and preparation and distribution of information profiling the school.[9] The legislation also authorized an early intervention program to permit state intervention in under-performing schools.[10]

Kansas required the State Board of Education to prepare a strategy for identifying, developing, and implementing a mastery of basic skills reading program for grades kindergarten to three. The strategy must include the identification of state standards, a plan for monitoring pupil progress, and the means to be used in determining mastery. The strategy must also include plans for restructuring the school day, additional school days, summer school, or individualized instruction.[11]

Minnesota specified the components of what it calls the Profile of Learning which is required of local schools in choosing graduation requirements.[12] This statute requires local selection of the means of assessment, to supplement the existing statewide student assessment, and requires the Commissioner of Education to post each individual school's standards for graduation on a website.

Pennsylvania passed accountability legislation detailing that a school district with a history of low test scores will be placed on an educational empowerment list;[13] districts on the list are subject to state-imposed benchmarks and timetables for improvement. South Dakota directed its State Board and Department of Education to develop standards and practices to ensure that students entering the K-12 educational system are ready to learn; that

---

[7] 2000 Ga. Laws H.B. 1187, No. 2.
[8] 2000 Ga. Laws H.B. 1187, No. 2, sec. 6.
[9] 2000 Ga. Laws H.B. 1187, No. 2, sec. 10.
[10] 2000 Ga. Laws H.B. 1187, No. 2, sec. 15.
[11] 2000 Kan. Sess. Laws 138, sec. 9.
[12] 2000 Minn. Sess. Law Serv. 500 (West).
[13] 2000 Pa. Laws 44, no. 16, sec. 8.1.

by the third grade all children have reading, mathematics, language, science, and technology skills; and that by the twelfth grade students will have learned educational and personal skills sufficient to make them responsible members of society.[14]

Virginia passed seven acts related to its accountability program, the Standards of Learning assessment program. One requires students who do not pass literacy and other parts of the test to attend summer school.[15] Another authorizes the use of computerized tests.[16] A third requires the scheduling of a review of standards,[17] and a fourth calls for the review to occur every seven years.[18] A fifth requires coordination of the testing schedule with regional superintendents of schools.[19] A sixth act breaks the United States history examination into three portions.[20] The seventh specifies that the state is not required to release tests as minimum competency tests if doing so would breach security.[21]

Two states focused on planning as a means of improvement. California amended existing legislation related to the public school accountability program by requiring an action plan to allow increased numbers of school days and permit certificated employees to contract for up to twelve months.[22] Utah gave school community councils the role of developing plans listing a school's most critical need, a recommended course of action to meet the need, a specific list of programs, practices, materials, or equipment the school will need to have a direct impact on students, and how the school intends to enhance or improve academic excellence.[23]

Six states modified their student testing laws. Alabama changed a statute on student assessment, requiring the State Board of Education to cease testing eleventh and twelfth graders with nationally-normed achievement tests; it instead requires the provision of assessment and remediation to help students to prepare for the state graduation examination.[24] Arizona delegated the authority to decide which grades between three and twelve take standardized achievement tests to its State Superintendent of Public Instruction.[25] Nebraska reinstated a statewide system for the assessment of student learning and for reporting the performance of school districts.[26]

---

[14] 2000 S. D. Laws 65, sec. 1.
[15] 2000 Va. Acts. 684.
[16] 2000 Va. Acts 1061.
[17] 2000 Va. Acts 710.
[18] 2000 Va. Acts 662.
[19] 2000 Va. Acts 653.
[20] 2000 Va. Acts 677.
[21] 2000 Va. Acts 750.
[22] 2000 Cal. Legis. Serv. 190 (West).
[23] 2000 Utah Laws 59, sec. 5.
[24] 2000 Ala. Acts 753.
[25] 2000 Ariz. Legis. Serv. 398 (West).
[26] 2000 Neb. Laws LB 812.

Oklahoma modified its testing program by administering a norm-referenced test in the third grade to continue until a criterion-referenced test is constructed.[27] In the same legislation, Oklahoma also required test results to be disaggregated by ethnic group and gender and setting standards to evaluate which schools are low-performing. Utah changed the name of its program of statewide testing to "Utah Performance Assessment System for Students (U-PASS)."[28] In response to concerns about test security, Virginia authorized its Attorney General to investigate breaches of security for tests required by the State Board of Education, to bring actions, and to obtain a civil assessment of $1,000 against wrongdoers or permit the State Board to suspend or revoke an offending employee's certificate.[29]

Reporting information about how schools are performing continued as an element of accountability. Arizona added class size to the information required on school district report cards.[30] Colorado created a report card for grading all public schools including charter schools.[31] Colorado provided highly prescriptive language about what items are to be included in its report card and the rubric for grading schools. Delaware required the Secretary of Education to submit to the Governor and General Assembly an annual educational outcome report, including data on the numbers of students enrolled in twelfth grade at the beginning and end of the year, who have dropped out, and who have transferred.[32] Utah added the requirement to report last year's, as well as the current year's, criterion reference test scores on the district report card.[33]

Three states addressed the competency of new teachers as a focal point for accountability. Arizona specified that proficiency examinations for teacher licensure shall consist only of a professional knowledge test and a subject knowledge test.[34] Colorado added a teacher-testing requirement based upon standards set by the State Board.[35] Additionally, Colorado required teacher education programs to have 800 hours of supervised field-based experience for teachers in training.[36] Washington created a Professional Standards Board charged with establishing assessment policies to ensure that new educational practitioners have the knowledge to be competent and establishing a prospective teacher assessment system for basic certification.[37]

---

[27] 2000 Okla. Sess. Laws 306.
[28] 2000 Utah Laws 219, sec. 1.
[29] 2000 Va. Acts 634.
[30] 2000 Ariz. Legis. Serv. 76 (West).
[31] 2000 Colo. Legis. Serv. 107 (West).
[32] 72 Del. Laws 430, sec. 1 (2000).
[33] 2000 Utah Laws 224, sec. 5.
[34] 2000 Ariz. Legis. Serv. Ch. 97 (West).
[35] 2000 Colo. Legis. Serv. 251 (West).
[36] *Ibid.*
[37] 2000 Wash. Legis. Serv. 39 (West).

While most states continued to layer on more requirements, three states experimented with the waiver of requirements. Arizona permitted the State Superintendent of Public Instruction to issue waivers of state statutory requirements[38] in conformance with the Education Flexibility Partnership Act.[39] California added a provision setting conditions for waiver of state statutes.[40] Colorado permitted the State Board of Education to grant waivers of state laws or regulations except those related to public school finance and to the provision of services to exceptional children.[41] In their applications for waivers, Colorado school boards must demonstrate that the waiver would enhance educational opportunities and quality within their districts and that the costs of the waived requirements severely limited opportunity.

Of the variety of accountability approaches adopted in 2000, only four states added incentives to help foster improvement. Alabama established the Governor's Academic Achievement Program to provide financial rewards to public schools and local school boards that improve their academic status.[42] Colorado created a school performance grant fund for improving academic performance.[43] The fund is to be created from excess revenues that would normally be refunded in the next fiscal year unless voters approve a revenue change in accordance with the state constitution.[44] Delaware created an award program beginning in 2002 to recognize school programs demonstrating superior performance in the state's accountability program.[45] In an enlightened move designed to encourage the state's best teachers to work where they are needed most, Florida provided a stipend of $1,000 to $3,000 for master teachers who transfer to under-performing schools or to alternative schools for violent youth.[46]

Athletics

Four states enacted legislation impacting the operation of state athletics associations. Florida addressed the situation where a student's GPA falls below 2.0 and would normally not be eligible for participation. In order

---

[38] 2000 Ariz. Legis. Serv. 166 (West).
[39] 20 U.S.C. 5891.
[40] 2000 Cal. Legis. Serv. 464 (West).
[41] 2000 Colo. Legis. Serv. 245 (West).
[42] 2000 Ala. Acts 766.
[43] 2000 Colo. Legis. Serv. 389 (West).
[44] Colo. Const, art. X, sec. 20.
[45] 72 Del. Laws 294, secs. 51, 52 (2000).
[46] 2000 Fla. Sess. Law Serv. 301, sec. 3 (West).

to participate in interscholastic sports, Florida now requires a performance contract between the failing student, his or her parents, and the state activities association.[47] The same bill adds the requirement that home schooled students participating in interscholastic sports must represent the public school they would have attend if not home schooled.

Both Hawaii and Illinois passed gender equity provisions. The Hawaii legislation prohibits discrimination in athletics based on sex.[48] Illinois' legislation reinstated a provision requiring gender equity in interscholastic athletics.[49]

Indiana created a nine-member panel to serve as a hearing review board concerning the application and interpretation of state athletic association rules. When a student's parent disagrees with a decision of the state athletic association director, an aggrieved student-athlete may receive a hearing before the board.[50]

Attendance

Five states changed their compulsory attendance laws to strengthen their application and provide greater coordination between school officials and officers of the courts. Connecticut raised the mandatory school attendance age from sixteen to eighteen, with parents retaining the ability to provide consent for the student to withdraw at age sixteen or seventeen.[51] Delaware withdrew a provision declaring students truant if they are absent without valid excuses for more than three days during the school year.[52] In addition, Delaware mandated that each student and parent be notified at the beginning of each school year of the requirements for school attendance, including procedures and penalties for truancy.[53] The legislation mandates truancy conferences and an appeals process.

Georgia extended compulsory attendance requirements to students in alternative schools but specified that the provision should not be construed to require a local board to enroll a student in an alternative school in lieu of suspension or expulsion.[54] Ohio amended its compulsory attendance law to define a "chronic truant" as a student who misses school without a legitimate excuse seven or more consecutive days, ten or more school days in a month, or fifteen or more school days in a year.[55] This legislation identifies

---

[47] 2000 Fla. Sess. Law Serv. 121 (West).
[48] 2000 Haw. Sess. Laws 229, sec. 1.
[49] 2000 Ill. Legis. Serv. P.A. 91-792 (West).
[50] 2000 Ind. Acts P.L. 15-2000, sec. 1.
[51] 2000 Conn. Legis. Serv. P.A. 00-157 (West).
[52] 72 Del. Laws 346, sec. 6 (2000).
[53] 72 Del. Laws 346, sec. 14 (2000).
[54] 2000 Ga. Laws H.B. 114, No. 1.
[55] 2000 Ohio Legis. Serv. 861 (Baldwin).

a chronic truant as an "unruly child," sufficient to provide juvenile court jurisdiction. A juvenile court may order attendance at an alternative school and press criminal charges against a parent. Mississippi added sheriffs, deputy sheriffs, and municipal law enforcement officers to school attendance officers as those authorized to investigate all cases of truancy and to file petitions in youth court.[56]

Two states addressed school attendance problems through drop-out prevention programs. Arizona instituted a drop-out prevention program by allocating $50,000 to the State Department of Education to provided targeted assistance for high school students who do not perform well on the AIMS (Arizona Instrument to Measure Standards) test.[57] Arizona also created a study committee to consider whether dual enrollment would serve as a means of increasing retention for high school students.[58] Kentucky directed its State Board of Education to establish a strategy to address the school drop-out problem and provide technical assistance to school districts.[59]

Two states made minor changes related to the enrollment of students. Maryland added blood tests for lead poisoning to the immunization requirements for school admission.[60] Wyoming permitted students to enroll in part-time preschool programs to meet compulsory attendance requirements.[61]

Buildings and Grounds

During the 2000 legislative year, nine states adopted legislation related to school buildings and grounds. Arizona amended its school facilities law to permit the use of funds for the relocation and placement of portable school buildings.[62]

California adopted four pieces of legislation in this category beginning with extending the Leroy F. Greene School Facilities Act of 1998 to provide supplemental grants for the demolition and replacement of single story buildings with multi-story buildings.[63] California also extended to 2007 the time in which relocatable school buildings could be used if the structure in question was in use prior to May 1, 2000.[64] Additionally, California changed a

---

[56] 2000 Miss. Laws 397.
[57] 2000 Ariz. Legis. Serv. 377 (West).
[58] 2000 Ariz. Legis. Serv. 136 (West).
[59] 2000 Ky. Acts 452, sec. 2.
[60] 2000 Md. Laws 677.
[61] 2000 Wyo. Sess. Laws 60, sec. 1.
[62] 2000 Ariz. Legis. Serv. 158 (West).
[63] 2000 Cal. Legis. Serv. 458 (West).
[64] 2000 Cal. Legis. Serv. 747 (West).

requirement that schools be constructed only on lands owned by school authorities by permitting their erection on leased lands, with certain conditions.[65] Finally, California permitted the Department of General Services to issue stop-work orders when construction work is not being performed in accordance with existing law and would compromise the structural integrity of the building.[66]

Connecticut added video surveillance equipment to the list of permissible expenditures under a grant program for general improvements to school buildings.[67] Iowa directed the state treasurer to release bonds for school buildings.[68] Maine required its State Board of Education to conduct a study and create a plan to address the needs for improved and new school facilities.[69] Maryland added the requirement of questions related to the diversity of the board of directors of interested contractors to the pre-qualification questionnaire administered by county boards of education for soliciting school construction bids.[70] Maryland also created a Solar Energy Pilot Program to provide grants to assist school districts in construction or remodeling school buildings to utilize solar energy systems.[71]

New Jersey established a facilities rehabilitation fund for vocational education facilities.[72] Utah prohibited any higher education entity or any part of one from submitting a proposal to provide architectural or engineering services to school boards.[73] The same legislation prohibits school boards from contracting with higher education entities or any part of one for architectural or engineering services. It is unclear whether a university faculty member acting as an independent consultant is considered a "higher education entity" under this prohibition. Washington permitted local school boards to serve as their own general contractors in the construction of school facilities, by designating a construction manager and obtaining approval from a newly-created project review board.[74]

---

[65] 2000 Cal. Legis. Serv. 530 (West).
[66] 2000 Cal. Legis. Serv. 463 (West).
[67] 2000 Conn. Legis. Serv. P.A. 00-220, sec. 15 (West).
[68] 2000 Iowa Legis. Serv. 186 (West).
[69] 2000 Me. Legis. Serv. 789 (West).
[70] 2000 Md. Laws 208.
[71] 2000 Md. Laws 300.
[72] 2000 N.J. Laws 72, sec. 58.
[73] 2000 Utah Laws 21.
[74] 2000 Wash. Legis. Serv. 209 (West).

Curriculum Requirements

In specifying curriculum requirements for their schools, state legislatures continued to address concerns about patriotism and character, altered graduation requirements, and added a potpourri of curricular subjects. Three states passed United States flag legislation. Idaho now directs all schools to display the United States flag, recite the Pledge of Allegiance, and sing the National Anthem without compelling individual students to participate.[75] Kentucky directed the State Board of Education to develop a program of instruction related to the United States flag.[76] Utah required an instructional program within public schools about the history, etiquette, customs, and use of the flag of the United States.[77] Utah elementary students are required to recite the Pledge of Allegiance daily; secondary students must recite it once each week. Schools must post notice of the right not to recite the Pledge in a conspicuous place, and students may be excused from reciting by parental written request.

Arizona adopted legislation requiring the teaching of character education, highlighting at least six of the following character traits: truthfulness, responsibility, compassion, diligence, sincerity, trustworthiness, respect, attentiveness, obedience, orderliness, forgiveness, and virtue.[78]

Two states adopted legislation related to the review of instructional materials. California permitted school boards to review instructional materials to consider when they are obsolete and to bring the results of the review to a public meeting.[79] Florida permitted its textbook commission to conduct an independent inquiry into the accuracy of instructional materials.[80]

Two states addressed graduation requirements and the type of diplomas offered; four awarded diplomas to veterans who had dropped out of high school. Connecticut increased graduation requirements for the Class of 2004 and thereafter to twenty credits.[81] Effective 2004, Delaware created three separate diploma tracks: Standard Diploma, Academic Diploma, and Distinguished Achievement Diploma.[82] Both Florida and Maryland permitted the awards of high school diplomas for veterans whose education was interrupted by World War II.[83] West Virginia directed county boards to

---

[75] 2000 Idaho Sess. Laws 468, sec. 1.
[76] 2000 Ky. Acts. 235, sec. 1.
[77] 2000 Utah Laws 155, sec. 1.
[78] 2000 Ariz. Legis. Serv. 313 (West).
[79] 2000 Cal. Legis. Serv. 461 (West).
[80] 2000 Fla. Sess. Law Serv. 291, sec. 9 (West).
[81] 2000 Conn. Legis. Serv. P.A. 00-156 (West).
[82] 72 Del. Laws 294, sec. 56 (2000).
[83] 2000 Fla. Sess. Law Serv. 225, sec. 1 (West). 2000 Md. Laws 587.

award high school diplomas to veterans of World War I, World War II, the Korean conflict, and the Vietnam conflict.[84] Wisconsin permitted the award of high school diplomas to veterans age 65 or older, who left high school before receiving a diploma, to join the United States armed forces during a war period and served on active duty under honorable conditions.[85]

Two states added to their state's school holiday schedule. Georgia permitted the observance of Veteran's Day, by closing schools on November 11th each year.[86] Maryland made President's Day an official school holiday.[87]

The remainder of this section lists the various acts passed by legislatures related to their curricula. Alaska required every school with a majority of students who are Alaska Natives to establish a Native language curriculum advisory board charged with recommending a language curriculum to the local school board.[88] Arizona amended its statute requiring a curriculum on environmental protection, by specifying the purposes of the curriculum and the activities that shall occur in the curriculum.[89] Georgia required the State Board of Education to develop a rape prevention and personal safety education program and add it to the core curriculum by the start of the 2000-2001 school year.[90] Illinois encouraged public and private elementary and secondary schools to use alternatives to dissection such as computer technology in teaching;[91] the provision permits schools to excuse students from participating in dissection but requires parents to be notified when dissection is to be used or when their children may be expected to observe, perform, or participate in dissection.

New York required the Regents to make suitable curricular materials available to all elementary schools to aid in the understanding and acceptance of children with disabilities.[92]

Rhode Island required the Department of Elementary and Secondary Education to develop curricular materials on genocide and human rights issues including the period of transatlantic slave trade, the great hunger period in Ireland, the Armenian genocide, the Holocaust, and the Mussolini fascist regime.[93] Utah made it mandatory for school boards to develop and implement programs integrating technology into the curriculum, instruction, and student assessment.[94] Utah also ordered the State Board of Education,

---

[84] 2000 W. Va. Acts 35 (West).
[85] 1999-2000 Wis. Legis. Serv. 73 (April 12, 2000) (West).
[86] 2000 Ga. Laws H.B. 68, No. 1.
[87] 2000 Md. Laws 293.
[88] 2000 Alaska Sess. Laws Sec. 4, Ch. 29.
[89] 2000 Ariz. Legis. Serv. 146 (West).
[90] 2000 Ga. Laws H.B. 171, No. 1.
[91] 2000 Ill. Legis. Serv. P.A. 91-771 (West).
[92] 2000 N.Y. Laws 265.
[93] 2000 R.I. Pub. Laws 511, sec. 1.
[94] 2000 Utah Laws 59, sec. 4.

in consultation with local boards and superintendents, to establish core curricula, defined as the basic knowledge, skills, and competencies each student is expected to acquire or master while advancing through the public schools.[95] Washington established the World War II Oral History Project to assist the Superintendent of Public Instruction in developing a curriculum to be used in grades K-12.[96]

Employment

In 2000, legislatures addressed a wide array of concerns related to employment. Changes occurred in tenure law, certification requirements, and contract rights; however, the greatest amount of legislative activity in this topic area concerned responses to the shortage of teachers and administrators, with various approaches utilized.

One approach to dealing with teacher shortages was to ease the way for out-of-state teachers to become certified either through reciprocity arrangements or providing special status to out-of-state teachers. Arizona granted in-state residency status for one year to out-of-state teachers to permit them to take courses for recertification; this residency status does not extend to other family members.[97] California amended its requirements for obtaining administrative or teaching certificates by permitting certification of experienced, out-of-state teachers;[98] it also gave in-state residency status to teachers with emergency certificates who are taking classes to obtain certification.[99] Colorado authorized the State Department of Education to issue licenses to out-of-state teacher, administrative, and special services license holders to increase the pool of teachers in the state.[100] Kentucky authorized reciprocity in certification for teachers with out-of-state certificates and certificates from the National Board of Professional Teaching Standards.[101] Massachusetts created a temporary certificate for persons with at least three years teaching experience out-of-state who have not passed the certification testing requirements.[102] Michigan permitted acceptance of licensure of speech and language therapists from the American Speech and Hearing Association in lieu of a speech and language teaching certificate.[103] Okla-

---

[95] 2000 Utah Laws 301, sec. 1.
[96] 2000 Wash. Legis. Serv. 112 (West).
[97] 2000 Ariz. Legis. Serv. Ch. 322.
[98] 2000 Cal. Legis. Serv. 703 (West).
[99] 2000 Cal. Legis. Serv. 949 (West).
[100] 2000 Colo. Legis. Serv. 247 (West).
[101] 2000 Ky. Acts 257, sec. 1.
[102] 2000 Mass. Adv. Legis. Serv. 284, sec. 1 (Law. Co-op.).
[103] 2000 Mich. Legis. Serv. P.A. 387 (West).

homa permitted holders of the teaching certificate from the National Board for Professional Teaching Standards to be granted a state teaching certificate without any additional requirements.[104]

Two states increased the pool of educator candidates by authorizing alternative paths to certification. Colorado created an exemption for administrative licensure by authorizing local boards of education to contract with any person to serve as an administrator based on qualifications that it sets.[105] Massachusetts specified that no teacher may be hired who is not certified unless he or she passes a state teachers test;[106] this provision seems to authorize teachers to by-pass certification by simply taking a test.

Eight states addressed teacher shortages by providing incentives such as loans, loan-forgiveness, or scholarships to classroom teachers. California encouraged the development of more teachers by creating a loan assumption program for teachers who are willing to serve populations of low-income families, low-performing schools, or schools already having a high percentage of teachers on emergency credentials.[107] To another existing loan assumption program for educators, California added the provision that the loans are not eligible for repayment until the person teaches for a full-time academic year.[108] California also added a third student loan assumption program for persons willing to train for subject areas experiencing shortages.[109] Florida created a student fellowship loan program to provide $6,500 per year for two years for rising college juniors who are willing to train to become associate teachers.[110] Maine established the Educators for Maine Program to provide financial assistance for students who demonstrate an interest in pursuing a career in Maine in education and for teachers and speech pathologists seeking advanced degrees.[111]

Maryland reenacted the Maryland Teacher Scholarship.[112] Mississippi extended for another year a program that provided housing loans for teachers who render service and buy a home in a geographic area where there exists a critical shortage of teachers;[113] this provision was set for automatic repeal effective July 1, 2001. New York established the Teachers of Tomorrow Teacher Recruitment and Retention Program, to target teacher shortage areas;[114] the program provides grants to school boards to develop programs

---

[104] 2000 Okla. Sess. Laws 232.
[105] 2000 Colo. Legis. Serv. 237 (West).
[106] 2000 Mass. Adv. Legis. Serv. 227, sec. 6 (Law. Co-op.).
[107] 2000 Cal. Legis. Serv. 583 (West).
[108] 2000 Cal. Legis. Serv. 460 (West).
[109] 2000 Cal. Legis. Serv. 371 (West).
[110] 2000 Fla. Sess. Law Serv. 301, sec. 53 (West).
[111] 2000 Me. Legis. Serv. 783 (West).
[112] 2000 Md. Laws 490.
[113] 2000 Miss. Laws 321.
[114] 2000 N.Y. Laws 62.

and offers cash awards for individuals who enter teacher training programs. Oklahoma asked the Regents for Higher Education to establish a loan repayment program for secondary level mathematics and science teachers.[115] Wisconsin established a student loan program to attract persons into training programs for becoming teachers of the visually impaired or blind.[116]

Two states called on retired teachers to alleviate staffing shortages. Kentucky permitted the appointment of retired teachers and administrators in critical shortage areas.[117] Massachusetts permitted school boards to hire retired teachers as classroom teachers or mentors without penalty from retirement compensation;[118] the additional time in service does not add to creditable service in the retirement system.

Five states responded to the shortage of teachers by requiring the studying, planning, or restructuring of the teaching profession. Florida created the Florida Mentor Teacher School Pilot Program to provide a model to reform and improve the current structure of the profession.[119] Kentucky authorized a program to encourage persons to enter the profession.[120] Nebraska created the Teacher Salary Task Force and charged it to study how to compensate teachers for what they know and how they perform, alternative pay scales, and appropriate compensation levels to attract and retain teachers.[121] South Dakota called for a study to gather demographic data about the public education workforce to assist in planning staffing needs in coming years.[122] West Virginia created a statewide task force on teacher quality to address strengthening of the profession, teacher salaries, and the means of assuring an adequate supply of teachers.[123]

Only one state specifically addressed the retention of new teachers as a means of easing the shortage. Minnesota established the New Teacher Project, for the improved retention of first and second year teachers;[124] the project anticipates the use of one-to-one mentoring, intensive summer orientation, workshops, peer review, mutual observation between new and experienced teachers with training in classroom management techniques, cultural diversity, and reading strategies.

---

[115] 2000 Okla. Sess. Laws 242.
[116] 1999-2000 Wis. Legis. Serv. 144 (May 9, 2000) (West).
[117] 2000 Ky. Acts 498, sec. 3.
[118] 2000 Mass. Adv. Legis. Serv. 114, sec. 6 (Law. Co-op.).
[119] 2000 Fla. Sess. Law Serv. 301, sec. 59 (West).
[120] 2000 Ky. Acts 527, sec. 1.
[121] 2000 Neb. Laws LB 1399.
[122] 2000 S. D. Laws 75, sec. 3.
[123] 2000 W. Va. Acts 100 (West).
[124] 2000 Minn. Sess. Law Serv. 489, art. 6, sec. 42 (West).

Two states changed their tenure laws. Alabama's Teacher Accountability Act removed tenure for principals, replacing it with performance-based contracts and providing for hearing procedures for principals whose are not renewed;[125] the accountability act also adds "failure to perform duties in a satisfactory manner" to the statutory grounds for cancellation of teacher . Connecticut added language to its teacher tenure statute to specify that if the cause of dismissal is incompetence, it must be based upon an evaluation of the teacher using guidelines established in a separate evaluation statute.[126]

Seven states altered their law related to educator certification. In certificate revocation actions, Connecticut placed the burden of production and proof on the State Board of Education, to prove by a preponderance of the evidence, that an action is appropriate.[127] Florida substantially amended its teacher certification requirements to include demonstration of mastery of general knowledge, subject area knowledge, professional preparation and educational competence.[128] Graduation with a bachelors or higher degree, and fingerprints and criminal background checks are also required for certification in Florida. Local boards in Florida are permitted to hire teachers with alternative certificates, with full certification to be achieved by obtaining additional training where competency has not yet been shown. Hawaii amended its certification requirements to require prospective school administrators to now have five years, rather than one year, experience as a teacher.[129] Iowa amended its law certification of para-educators to specify that applicants for certification carry the burden of proof that requirements for licensure have been met.[130]

Michigan added specific requirements for certification as a guidance counselor, including holding a teaching certificate with a counseling endorsement, completion of a prescribed program at the masters level, or five years experience as a counselor in another state, and passing an examination created by the State Department of Education.[131] Additionally, Michigan specified that the State Superintendent of Public Instruction controls rulemaking about teacher licensure and certification.[132] Oklahoma required the teachers of honors courses to be certified in the subject areas of the courses.[133] Tennessee permitted teachers in private schools with valid teach-

---

[125] 2000 Ala. Acts 733.
[126] 2000 Conn. Legis. Serv. P.A. 00-13 (West).
[127] 2000 Conn. Legis. Serv. P.A. 00-220, sec. 7 (West).
[128] 2000 Fla. Sess. Law Serv. 301, sec. 19 (West).
[129] 2000 Haw. Sess. Laws 31, sec. 1.
[130] 2000 Iowa Legis. Serv. 96 (West).
[131] 2000 Mich. Legis. Serv. P.A. 288 (West).
[132] 2000 Mich. Legis. Serv. P.A. 497 (West).
[133] 2000 Okla. Sess. Laws 215.

ing certificates to receive professional licenses in a manner equitable to public school teachers.[134] In separate legislation, Tennessee defined a professional license as a teaching license received after satisfactory completion of three year as an apprentice teacher along with positive evaluations from a local education agency.[135]

Six states adopted legislation related to evaluation or professional development of educators. California appropriated $1 million to pay for a training program for administrators to learn how to evaluate teachers;[136] the governor vetoed this appropriation with the expectation that it would be reconsidered during the annual budget process. Idaho established requisite evaluation procedures for educators with different requirements for different types of employment.[137] Louisiana amended an existing teacher evaluation statute to permit its State Department to withhold state minimum foundation funds if a local school district does not have in place an evaluation program for each certificated employee.[138] Ohio mandated that teachers whose contracts were not expiring to receive one evaluation per year and that teachers whose contracts were expiring to receive one preliminary and one final evaluation before their contracts expire.[139] Florida listed legislative findings on what effective educators are able to do.[140] The list contains sixteen items that might show up later on school board evaluation instruments including, for example, the ability to "recognize signs of tendency toward violence and severe emotional distress in students and apply techniques in crisis intervention."[141] Florida also required professional development plans for school personnel to be based upon data related to student performance.[142] Finally, Washington adopted a faculty awards endowment program, to provide awards for individuals or groups, or to provide faculty development activities.[143]

Three states offered direction regarding professional and ethical standards. Kentucky gave the Education Professional Standards Board the authority to certify teachers of exceptional children with communication disorders.[144] Delaware created a Professional Standards Board to control the requirements for the award and revocation of teacher certificates; the law provides for a three-tiered licensure system and requires annual educa-

---

[134] 2000 Tenn. Pub. Acts 635, no. 1.
[135] 2000 Tenn. Pub. Acts 903, no.3.
[136] 2000 Cal. Legis. Serv. 935 (West).
[137] 2000 Idaho Sess. Laws 66, sec. 1.
[138] 2000 La. Sess. Law Serv. 38(X) (West).
[139] 2000 Ohio Legis. Serv. 298 (Baldwin).
[140] 2000 Fla. Sess. Law Serv. 301, sec. 7 (West).
[141] 2000 Fla. Sess. Law Serv. 301, sec. 7 (k) (West).
[142] 2000 Fla. Sess. Law Serv. 301, sec. 48 (West).
[143] 2000 Wash. Legis. Serv. 127 (West).
[144] 2000 Ky. Acts 375, sec. 1.

tor evaluations.[145]   Utah directed the State Board of Education to establish basic ethical conduct standards for public education employees who provide education-related services outside their regular employment to their current or prospective public school students.[146]

Other employment-related provisions passed by state legislatures in 2000 follow. Arizona permitted faculty and staff of educational institutions to use other identification numbers besides their social security numbers.[147] California extended the protections of the state's Whistleblowers Protection Act to employees of school districts and community colleges[148] while amending its personnel records law to permit these same employees to inspect their own personnel files and to require that they be advised when derogatory material is introduced into their files.[149] California also altered its school labor law to require employees to either join representative organizations or pay the organization a faire share service fee.[150] Florida amended the duties of school superintendents to require a principal's recommendation to nominate teachers for employment.[151]   Illinois required that the determination, after an evaluation, that contract renewal for a principal be made 150 days prior to the expiration of the principal's current performance-based contract.[152] Louisiana backed away from a commitment to make average pay for teachers and other personnel equal to the regional average pay for teachers and other personnel;[153] now the pay will be an amount set by the legislature. Maryland prohibited the printing of an employee's social security number on any type of identification card.[154] Mississippi permitted librarians to count years of employment in a public library for placement on school districts' salary schedules.[155]

Nebraska adopted a master teacher program, providing annual salary bonuses of $5,000 for teachers receiving certification from the National Board of Professional Teaching Standards.[156] South Dakota directed that stipends of $1,000 from the state department and $1,000 from local school districts be paid for recipients of the National Board for Professional Teaching Stan-

---

[145] 72 Del. Laws 294, sec. 2 (2000).
[146] 2000 Utah Laws 276, sec. 1.
[147] 2000 Ariz. Legis. Serv. Ch. 264.
[148] 2000 Cal. Legis. Serv. 531(West).
[149] 2000 Cal. Legis. Serv. 886 (West).
[150] 2000 Cal. Legis. Serv. 893 (West).
[151] 2000 Fla. Sess. Law Serv. 301, sec. 5 (West).
[152] 2000 Ill. Legis. Serv. P.A. 91-728 (West).
[153] 2000 La. Sess. Law Serv. 23 (2X) (West).
[154] 2000 Md. Laws 328.
[155] 2000 Miss. Laws 433.
[156] 2000 Neb. Laws LB 1399.

dards teaching certificate.[157] Utah entitled educators who successfully defend themselves against claims arising from alleged errors or omissions during the performance of their duties to attorneys fees and costs.[158] West Virginia authorized a personal leave bank, separate from other personal leave, for caregivers who provide for the needs of a spouse, child, or parent.[159]

Finance and School Business

This section lists legislative provisions related to school finance that were passed other than appropriations. Arizona amended its procurement law to permit progress payments and the award of attorneys fees.[160] Illinois permitted local school boards to access Medicaid funds if they offer early periodic screening and diagnostic services for Medicaid-eligible children.[161] Indiana permitted the donation of proceeds from riverboat gambling to public school endowment corporations.[162] Iowa extended authority for parent-teacher organizations and booster clubs to conduct bingo games and raffles for the benefit of schools in its licensing law for games of chance.[163] The provision also requires that, if a licensee derives ninety percent or more of its income from bingo, raffles, or games of chance, at least seventy-five percent of net receipts must be distributed to an unrelated entity for educational, civic, public, charitable, patriotic, or religious use. In another act, Iowa required all school corporations self-insured dental plans to maintain excess loss coverage and contract with third party administrators, if the yearly claims exceed more than one percent of the school corporation's general fund budget.[164]

Kentucky required local district superintendents to appoint school finance officers who will be required to complete forty-two hours of continuing education every two years.[165] Maine directed its State Board of Education to develop a model comprehensive school budgeting procedure with specified cost centers and more cooperation between the state and local agencies;[166] the budget must be submitted by referendum to voters for approval. Mississippi amended its prior requirements on the sale of surplus property by sealed bid only to permit the sale of surplus property other than

---

[157] 2000 S. D. Laws 89, sec. 1.
[158] 2000 Utah Laws 226, sec. 1.
[159] 2000 W. Va. Acts 112 (West).
[160] 2000 Ariz. Legis. Serv. 233 (West).
[161] 2000 Ill. Legis. Serv. P.A. 91-842 (West).
[162] 2000 Ind. Acts. P.L. 15-2000. Sec 1.
[163] 2000 Iowa Legis. Serv. 140 (West).
[164] 2000 Iowa Legis. Serv. 222 (West).
[165] 2000 Ky. Acts 389, sec. 1.
[166] 2000 Me. Legis. Serv. 710 (West).

real property and buildings by public auction.[167] Ohio revised its revenue code to classify booster clubs as charitable organizations.[168] South Dakota prohibited school boards from transferring funds from the general fund to the capital outlay fund.[169] Washington permitted student groups to conduct fund-raising activities for charitable purposes such as disaster relief.[170]

Governance and School Leadership

This section lists legislative actions related to school board organization, governance, and leadership. Arizona changed the requirements for creating a unified school district by permitting more than one common school district to join with a high school district.[171] Florida passed the Educational Governance Reorganization Act of 2000, which takes effect in 2003, to establish a seamless academic system between kindergarten through graduate school.[172] The legislation sunsets the Board of Regents, the State Board of Community Colleges, and various divisions of the State Department of Education, in favor of the Florida Board of Education with appointed chancellors of K-12, community colleges, and career preparation, and state universities. Florida also waived the sovereign immunity of school readiness coalitions, entities involving multiple service agencies including faith-based child care providers.[173]

Illinois added to the powers and duties of the State Board of Education the responsibility for supervising adult education and adult literacy programs.[174] In another act, Illinois introduced a no-nepotism provision for assistant regional superintendents.[175] Indiana permitted school corporations to appoint one or more assistant or deputy school treasurers.[176] Indiana also allowed its State Board of Education to count teacher aides as teachers for the purpose of meeting state pupil-teacher ratio requirements, when hardship is shown.[177] Iowa raised the lower dollar limit, from $1,500 to $2,500 at which school directors are prohibited from having a personal interest in a public contract.[178] In addition, Iowa directed its Department of Education to

---

[167] 2000 Miss. Laws 481.
[168] 2000 Ohio Legis. Serv. 3181 (Baldwin).
[169] 2000 S. D. Laws 77, sec. 1.
[170] 2000 Wash. Legis. Serv. 157 (West).
[171] 2000 Ariz. Legis. Serv. 211 (West).
[172] 2000 Fla. Sess. Law Serv. 321 (West).
[173] 2000 Fla. Sess. Law Serv. 149 (West).
[174] 2000 Ill. Legis. Serv. P.A. 91-830 (West).
[175] 2000 Ill. Legis. Serv. P.A. 91-765 (West).
[176] 2000 Ind. Acts P. L. 15-2000, sec. 2.
[177] 2000 Ind. Acts P.L. 15-2000, sec 3.

study the feasibility of initiating new school district reorganization and incentives for sharing resources.[179] The legislation also directs the state athletic and activities associations to submit any information about the elimination of sports-related barriers to reorganization.

Louisiana required the renewal applications for propriety schools to be treated like new applications although approval will now be for two years instead of one.[180] Maine provided for shared service agreements between two or more school boards to provide for alternative educational programs.[181] Massachusetts intervened directly in a school-closing dispute and prohibited the school committee in the city of Woburn from closing a public school there unless it votes to build a new school on the same lot or obtain a 2/3 vote of its members or the city council.[182]

Michigan changed its law on school board organization to specify that if a local board does not internally fill vacancies in its membership within thirty days, then an intermediate board is authorized to do so.[183] In other legislation, Michigan outlined the authority of school boards to receive, own, enjoy, and transfer gifts of real or personal property.[184] Minnesota specified that school board members begin their four -year term of office on the first Monday in January.[185] Minnesota also added significantly to its education code with respect to adult basic education including funding and requirements for a performance tracking system.[186] Mississippi required school board members to have at least a high school diploma and to spend at least one full day, without compensation, in a school they represent.[187] Mississippi also directs school board members to participate in training to be offered by community colleges, universities and organizations other than the Mississippi School Board Association.[188]

---

[178] 2000 Iowa Legis. Serv. 200 (West).
[179] 2000 Iowa Legis. Serv. 146 (West).
[180] 2000 La. Sess. Law Serv. 63(X) (West).
[181] 2000 Me. Legis. Serv. 683 (West).
[182] 2000 Mass. Adv. Legis. Serv. 116, sec. 1 (Law. Co-op.).
[183] 2000 Mich. Legis. Serv. P.A. 48 (West).
[184] 2000 Mich. Legis. Serv. P.A. 231 (West).
[185] 2000 Minn. Sess. Law Serv. 467 (West).
[186] 2000 Minn. Sess. Law Serv. 489 (West).
[187] 2000 Miss. Laws 461.
[188] 2000 Miss. Laws 610.

Parental and Student Rights

This section lists legislative requirements related to parental or student rights. Indiana placed restrictions on the use of information received by an official recruiting representative of the armed forces of the United States concerning the education and career opportunities of students.[189]

Maine prohibited the posting of personal student information and directory information on an internet web-site without written approval of a pupil's parents.[190] Maryland prohibited the printing of a student's social security number on any type of identification card.[191] Michigan forbade state or local agencies, including school districts, from delivering or causing to be delivered an envelope or package on the outside of which personal information is placed or is visible through the window of the envelope.[192] Prohibited personal information includes a person's social security number, driver's license number, or state identification number.

New York prohibited public or private schools, colleges, and universities from identifying students by social security number through posting or public listing of grades, on course rosters, or on student directories.[193] Utah forbids state and local education agencies from requiring infant or pre-school in-home literacy or other education or parenting programs without obtaining parental permission in each individual case;[194] this law does not prohibit Department of Children and Family Services home visits or court-ordered visits. In its juvenile law, Virginia specified that in a proceeding involving custody or the termination of parental rights, the records of minors relating to attendance, transcripts, or grades are material shall be received as evidence.[195]

Program Development

The states continued to use a programmatic approach to address particular problems. The dominant program areas involved the basic skills of reading and mathematics, although a resurgence was noted in vocational-technical education and the arts.

The largest volume of program-related legislation occurred in reading. Alabama created a tutoring program for students with below-average scores

---

[189] 2000 Ind. Acts P.L. 15-2000, sec. 4.
[190] 2000 Me. Legis. Serv. 595 (West).
[191] 2000 Md. Laws 328.
[192] 2000 Mich. Legis. Serv. P.A. 1 (West).
[193] 2000 N.Y. Laws 214.
[194] 2000 Utah Laws 274, sec. 1.
[195] 2000 Va. Acts 558.

in reading and other subjects.[196] Alabama also budgeted over $10 million to continue the Alabama Reading Initiative.[197] Colorado funded learning improvement grants to assist in the development of programs to enhance literacy and reading comprehension skills of early elementary grade students.[198] Colorado also created the Read to Achieve Program to fund grants for intensive reading programs for second, third, and fourth graders who are performing below grade level.[199] Maryland funded grants to promote literacy for organizations promoting literacy through well-child visits in health care settings.[200] South Dakota established the Advanced Reading Enhancement Program to assist and strengthen the teaching and learning of reading in grades one and two;[201] additionally, the State Education Department was directed to develop a comprehensive statewide program focused on reading and writing. Utah funded a Reading Performance Improvement Scholarship Program to assist elementary teachers to return to school to obtain an endorsement in reading.[202]

Mathematics programs were boosted by two legislatures. Kentucky called for the development of the Kentucky Early Mathematics Testing Program, a website based program to lower the number of high school graduates who require remediation.[203] Maryland created the Maryland Academic Intervention and Support Program in the Department of Education to provide academic intervention for students who have demonstrated deficiencies in mathematics as well as reading; the program funds local plans submitted according to State Board criteria.[204]

Two states funded specialized programs in the arts. Louisiana created the Center for Creative Arts at the Riverfront Center in New Orleans to succeed the joint agreement between the state and Orleans Parish School Board and to sustain a creative arts high school for tenth, eleventh, and twelfth graders.[205] Utah created the Arts in Elementary Schools Pilot Program to expand the offering of music, visual art, dance, and theater in the elementary grades.[206]

Four states addressed the needs of early childhood. In a statute authorizing the Department of Children's Affairs to study and report to the Governor

---

[196] 2000 Ala. Acts 804.
[197] 2000 Ala. Acts 594.
[198] 2000 Colo. Legis. Serv. 378 (West).
[199] 2000 Colo. Legis. Serv. 373 (West).
[200] 2000 Md. Laws 492, 493.
[201] 2000 S. D. Laws 75, sec. 2.
[202] 2000 Utah Laws 341, sec. 1.
[203] 2000 Ky. Acts 258, sec. 2.
[204] 2000 Md. Laws 492, 493.
[205] 2000 La. Sess. Law Serv. 60(X) (West).
[206] 2000 Utah Laws 234, sec. 1.

and Legislature methods of coordinating the delivery of services to children, Alabama created the Office of School Readiness in the Department of Children's Affairs.[207] Maryland created the Judith P. Hoyer Early Child Care and Education Enhancement Program to provide grants for interagency collaboration in providing better early childhood programs.[208] New Hampshire created the Parents as Teachers Program in rural Sullivan County, because of the high risk factors for children in that locale.[209] New Jersey established a commission on early childhood education to approve statewide standards for early childhood programs and develop standards for appropriate facilities.[210]

Four states passed legislation related to vocational and technical education. New Jersey funded apprenticeship programs for vocational schools and community colleges in urban areas.[211] Pennsylvania adopted a matching grant program to assist area vocational technical schools to purchase equipment for courses in automotive technology, diesel technology, precision machine technology, heat and air conditioning, printing, dental assisting, electronics, and building trades;[212] the state will match $2 for every $1 provided by local vocational technical schools. Rhode Island established the Vocational Technical Equity fund, to provide $500 for each student enrolled in career and technical education programs.[213] Washington directed the Superintendent of Public Instruction to support career and technical student organizations by providing a program staff officer to help foster their development in local school districts.[214]

Other miscellaneous programmatic approaches taken by legislatures are described now. California permitted the delivery of programs before school;[215] together with summer school, these programs will now be designated "supplemental instructional programs." For schools with fifty percent or more of its students qualifying for free and reduced lunch, Illinois added breakfast to the child nutrition program.[216] Iowa added to accreditation standards the requirement that all public and accredited nonpublic schools must adopt policies on health, media, and guidance services, although the existence of those services is not required for accreditation.[217]

---

[207] 2000 Ala. Acts 613.
[208] 2000 Md. Laws 680.
[209] 2000 N.H. Laws 140:1.
[210] 2000 N.J. Laws 138, sec. 1.
[211] 2000 N.J. Laws 72, sec. 64.
[212] 2000 Pa. Laws 44, no. 16, sec. 10.
[213] 2000 R.I. Pub. Laws 55, art. 20, sec. 2.
[214] 2000 Wash. Legis. Serv. 84 (West).
[215] 2000 Cal. Legis. Serv. 72 (West).
[216] 2000 Ill. Legis. Serv. P.A. 91-843 (West).
[217] 2000 Iowa Legis. Serv. 177 (West).

Kentucky created the Center for Middle School Academic Achievement to improve content knowledge and instructional practices of middle school teachers through professional development.[218] To address declines in geography literacy, Kentucky also established a Geography Education board.[219] Further, Kentucky ordered the employment of a librarian in every library media center in every elementary and secondary school to promote literacy and technology in the curriculum and to facilitate student achievement and life-long learning.[220] Louisiana required local school boards to have policies to provide placement for students in foster care and to prohibit the denial of enrollment for such children.[221] New Hampshire created the Granite State Scholars Program to benefit highly qualified state residents and to encourage them to pursue post-secondary education.[222] Wisconsin amended its study abroad program to permit grants of an amount less than $2,000.[223]

School Choice

Two states, Colorado and Vermont, adopted new charter school legislation in 2000. As in the prior year, most choice-related legislation amended existing charter school legislation with six states addressing limitations on enrollment, financial reporting and budgeting requirements, and governance changes.[224]

Colorado created a new type of charter school that will operate within an existing local school building when a school board has failed to provide adequate educational opportunities as measured by receiving an "F" on the grade card.[225] When a local school fails, a charter school is authorized to take over the building. If the school receives a "D" on the report card, the charter school and local board may agree to operate the building jointly. If a charter school within a school is graded "F" or "D" for a third year, the local board may issue a request for proposals for a replacement charter school.

Vermont adopted a public high school choice provision for grades 9-12.[226] Under this law, students are permitted to attend any public high school within the high school choice region. Transfers are limited to three percent

---

[218] 2000 Ky. Acts 527, sec. 3.

[219] 2000 Ky. Acts 259, sec. 1.

[220] 2000 Ky. Acts 339, sec. 1.

[221] 2000 La. Sess. Law Serv. 39(X) (West).

[222] 2000 N.H. Laws 70:2.

[223] 1999-2000 Wis. Legis. Serv. 152 (May 10, 2000) (West).

[224] Besides the states listed below, Florida also made minor amendments to its charter schools laws. 2000 Fla. Sess. Law Serv. 306 (West).

[225] 2000 Colo. Legis. Serv. 107, part 3.

[226] 2000 Vt. Laws 150.

of the students for the first three years but this allotment is permitted to grow to five percent of the students thereafter.

The remainder of this section lists the various amendments to existing charter school legislation. In one bill, Arizona made several amendments to its law related to charter schools.[227] First, when a sponsoring school board is out of compliance with state requirements on maintaining uniform financial records, a charter school may transfer to another sponsor. Second, the misappropriation of charter school funds was made a Class 4 felony. Third, resumes of charter school employees must now be placed on file and made available for inspection by the public. Finally, a provision making school boards not liable for acts or omissions in their charter schools was repealed.

California passed six acts amending its charter school law. First, California extended the life of charter schools serving at-risk students in Los Angeles County before 1997, permitting them to continue to operate until June 30, 2003.[228] Second, California made charter schools in default to the revolving loan fund responsible for their own default, making it no longer the responsibility of the chartering authority.[229] A third provision permits charter schools to enter into liability insurance risk pooling agreements.[230] A fourth change allows loans from the revolving loan fund to no longer be limited to one year; rather, the limitation is placed on the dollar amount to $250,000.[231] In a fifth provision, California supplied procedures for unsuccessful applicants for renewal of charter schools. In situations where a charter school was not granted a renewal by its chartering agency, California permitted the charter school to appeal by submitting an application for renewal under procedures pertaining to denial of the original petition to establish a charter school.[232] Finally, California required chartering authorities to file reports with the state retirement system on behalf of their charter schools.[233]

Colorado authorized charter schools to expend capital reserve funds for the planning and inspection of school buildings.[234] Delaware restricted enrollment in charter schools by limiting the number of children who are offspring of charter school founders to five percent of the total charter school student population.[235] Hawaii added another twenty-five charter

---

[227] 2000 Ariz. Legis. Serv. 90 (West).
[228] 2000 Cal. Legis. Serv. 19 (West).
[229] 2000 Cal. Legis. Serv. 586 (West).
[230] 2000 Cal. Legis. Serv. 14 (West).
[231] 2000 Cal. Legis. Serv. 429 (West).
[232] 2000 Cal. Legis. Serv. 160 (West).
[233] 2000 Cal. Legis. Serv. 466 (West).
[234] 2000 Colo. Legis. Serv. 147 (West).
[235] 72 Del. Laws 312, sec. 1 (2000). 72 Del. Laws 316, secs. 1, 2 (2000).

schools in its New Century Charter Schools program.[236] Massachusetts amended its existing charter school law to set limits on the percentage of pupils in the state who attend charter schools.[237] New Jersey modified its charter school law to permit charter schools in the same public school district and that are not operating on the same grade levels to petition to consolidate.[238]

School Safety

School safety again led all topical areas for the number of pieces of legislation passed last year, with seventy-eight legislative acts in 2000. Dominant methodologies included criminalizing more acts, increasing penalties for existing criminal acts, requiring more policy responses by local school boards, and demanding more collaboration between schools and the law enforcement community. Criminal background checks for school employees continued to be added while some states began to back away from "zero-tolerance" laws on expulsion.

Nine states passed new criminal laws or increased penalties for existing criminal acts. Alabama made making a bomb threat a Class C felony.[239] Arizona edited existing criminal law about causing a disruption, trespassing, or threatening damage to an educational institution;[240] the law now requires the element of knowledge, namely that a miscreant knowingly caused a disruption, trespassed, or threatened damage. California amended existing law on hate crimes and required the State Board of Education to revise its human relations curriculum to combat bias on basis of race, color, religion, ancestry, national origin, disability, gender or sexual orientation (not including pedophilia).[241] California also allocated $150,000 to assist school board personnel in the identification and determination of hate violence on school campuses.[242] To an existing statute prohibiting sex offenders from entering a school building without the superintendent's permission, Illinois added a proscription that registered sex offenders could not knowingly reside within 500 feet of school property where students under age 18 attend.[243] Massa-

---

[236] 2000 Haw. Sess. Laws 187, sec. 3.
[237] 2000 Mass. Adv. Legis. Serv. 227, sec. 2 (Law. Co-op.).
[238] 2000 N.J. Laws 142, sec. 1.
[239] 2000 Ala. Acts 113.
[240] 2000 Ariz. Legis. Serv. 226 (West).
[241] 2000 Cal. Legis. Serv. 955 (West).
[242] 2000 Cal. Legis. Serv. 959 (West).
[243] 2000 Ill. Legis. Serv. P.A. 91-911, sec. 5 (West).

chusetts created the crime of criminal harassment including acts on the telephone, by email, or by Internet postings, punishable by two-and-one-half years imprisonment or $1,000 fine or both.[244]

Michigan permitted courts to put restraining orders on persons convicted of the offenses of riot, incitement to riot, unlawful assembly, or civil disorder on or within 2,500 feet of a public community college, public college, or university, and to require individuals to reimburse the institution for expenses incurred.[245] Mississippi made it illegal to locate a strip club, or any establishment where public displays of nudity are present, within one quarter of a mile of a church, school, kindergarten, or courthouse, punishable by a $10,000 fine or one year of imprisonment.[246] Mississippi also made the adult use of tobacco on school property punishable by a warning on first occurrence, a $75 fine on the second occurrence, and a $150 fine on the third occurrence.[247] Missouri made trespass of a school bus a Class A misdemeanor.[248] Tennessee reauthorized local governments to establish school safety zones with speed limits that shall not be less than 15 miles per hour;[249] if a local government fails to set a speed limit, then speeds in excess of 15 miles per hour in the safety zone will be seen as prima facie guilt of reckless driving.

Another legislative response to public concerns about school safety in nine states was to articulate state policy on school safety and set up partnerships and violence prevention programs. For example, Florida created a Partnership for School Safety and Security which is charged with evaluating school safety programs and creating an electronic clearinghouse of school safety and security information, as well as providing technical assistance to schools and fostering coordination among schools, law enforcement agencies, and crisis intervention teams.[250]

Idaho announced a legislative requirement that safe public schools are required and that unsafe or unhealthy conditions must be abated.[251] If local school boards cannot provide adequate funds to meet this requirement, then the legislature authorized the use of lottery proceeds for this purpose. Idaho then required schools to participate in the Idaho School Safety Program once a school is identified as unsafe.[252] Maine required the

---

[244] 2000 Mass. Adv. Legis. Serv. 164 (Law. Co-op.).
[245] 2000 Mich. Legis. Serv. P.A. 51 (West).
[246] 2000 Miss. Laws 558.
[247] 2000 Miss. Laws 626.
[248] 2000 Mo. Legis. Serv. 60.
[249] 2000 Tenn. Pub. Acts 967, no. 3.
[250] 2000 Fla. Sess. Law Serv. 235, sec. 3 (West).
[251] 2000 Idaho Sess. Laws 219, sec. 1.
[252] 2000 Idaho Sess. Laws 334, sec. 2.

Commissioner of Education to provide technical assistance to school administrative units as they seek to prevent violence;[253] the violence-prevention program must emphasize conflict resolution, peer mediation, and early identification and response to signs of violence. Massachusetts established a commission to study alternative education programs for disruptive students.[254] Missouri established a pilot program for middle school aged students using military training and motivation methods with four-weeks residence at a national guard armory;[255] the same legislation also permits the sharing of records of students pre-adjudicated as delinquent with the juvenile justice system.

New York passed the Safe Schools Against Violence in Education Act, a comprehensive law which requires teachers to report acts of violence, reinforces their right to remove disruptive students from their classrooms, calls for the adoption of a conduct code and school safety plans, directs the Commissioner of Education to implement a reporting system, provides competitive grants for school violence prevention programs, and requires training in school violence prevention and intervention for certification as a teacher or administrator.[256] Also, in its health education curriculum, New York required the incorporation of violence prevention.[257] Oklahoma authorized school boards to contract with nonprofit agencies and community-based service provides for assistance in addressing school violence through an emphasis on prevention.[258] Pennsylvania directed the Secretary of Education to establish the position of Safe Schools Advocate for each school district of the First Class;[259] the Advocate will monitor acts of violence and the possession of contraband in schools and will act on behalf of victims of violence. Washington directed its state schools for the blind and for the deaf to address safety concerns relating to child abuse and neglect, to increase communications with parents, to adopt training programs for staff, to provide adequate staff, and to deny admission to adjudicated sex offenders.[260] In another move aimed at safety for student-age citizens, Washington created a graduated drivers licensing system for youthful motorists by introducing an intermediate license for drivers aged sixteen to eighteen who have successfully driven for six months with an instructional permit.[261]

---

[253] 2000 Me. Legis. Serv. 781 (West).
[254] 2000 Mass. Adv. Legis. Serv. 227, sec. 8 (Law. Co-op.).
[255] 2000 Mo. Legis. Serv. 60A.
[256] 2000 N.Y. Laws 181.
[257] *Ibid.*
[258] 2000 Okla. Sess. Laws 34.
[259] 2000 Pa. Laws 672, no. 91, sec. 3.
[260] 2000 Wash. Legis. Serv. 125 (West).
[261] 2000 Wash. Legis. Serv. 115 (West).

Besides articulations of state policy, twelve legislatures directed local school boards to add to their own policy statements. Alaska schools were charged with creating, collaboratively with parents, written school disciplinary and safety programs which include procedures and standards related to student behavior. Once disciplinary and safety programs are in place, teachers are to be protected from adverse employment actions arising from the lawful enforcement of the programs. Teachers in Alaska are also not to be found liable for civil damages resulting from enforcement of the disciplinary program, unless their act or omission is intentional or exhibits gross negligence.[262]

Arizona required that policies be in place to create alternative education programs for students in which suspension or expulsion is not available.[263]

Delaware called for the notification of students and parents of provisions prohibiting the making of false statements, disturbing school, or destroying school property, and the consequences for violating these provisions;[264] this legislation also mandates the reporting of crimes perpetrated in schools. Florida directed school boards, by 2002-2003. to adopt policies creating schools within schools to reduce anonymity of students in large schools.[265] Kentucky ordered local boards to adopt student disciplinary codes to be put in student handbooks and delegated to local school principals the responsibility of implementing those codes.[266] Missouri passed legislation mandating the adoption of student behavior policies.[267] New Hampshire required each school board to adopt a pupil safety and violence prevention policy that must address harassment, set reporting requirements, identify consequences, and provide for training of school personnel.[268] Oklahoma permitted local school boards to adopt dress codes including school uniforms.[269]

Utah required local school boards to develop comprehensive emergency response plans to prevent and combat violence in school settings, to

---

[262] 2000 Alaska Sess. Laws Sec. 2, Ch. 114.
[263] 2000 Ariz. Legis. Serv. 82 (West).
[264] 72 Del. Laws 368, sec. 1 (2000).
[265] 2000 Fla. Sess. Law Serv. 235, sec. 4 (West).
[266] 2000 Ky. Acts 452, sec. 4.
[267] 2000 Mo. Legis. Serv. 60.
[268] 2000 N.H. Laws 193-F:3.
[269] 2000 Okla. Sess. Laws 232.

coordinate plans with local law enforcement, and to provide inservice training for employees related to the plan.[270] Vermont required independent private schools to implement plans for responding to student misbehavior while requiring public schools to report attendance data, drop-out rates, and discipline reports to the Commissioner.[271] In the same legislation, Vermont made provisions for alternative schools programs and increased fines for weapons in schools and making false public alarms. Virginia directed local boards to adopt and revise policies on student searches.[272] Wyoming permitted safety drills to be used in lieu of fire drills to organize a response to any potential threat to health and safety of students.[273]

Another method of dealing with school safety concerns was to foster greater cooperation between schools, the law enforcement community, and the courts. Ten states adopted legislation in this area. Colorado amended its public records law to authorize information-sharing between schools and other service agencies and law enforcement;[274] information to be shared includes information related to incidents that rise to the level of a public safety concern, including truancy and disciplinary records maintained by school authorities. Florida school systems must provide instructional personnel to juvenile justice facilities and provide access to justice system personnel to the school district's database on student records.[275]

Iowa ordered area education agencies to provide educational services at juvenile justice facilities.[276] Additionally, Iowa required peace officers to make reasonable efforts to identify parents and school of attendance of students who violate alcohol-related laws, and give parents and schools notice of the offense.[277] Iowa also called for the sharing of juvenile court, social service, and child records, with public school officials for use in connection with their official duties and the support and protection of children and families.[278] Maine permitted the disclosure of educational records of pre-adjudicated juveniles to criminal justice agencies.[279] Minnesota amended statutory language requiring the disclosure of information to the juvenile justice system by schools, to now exclude home schools from the

---

[270] 2000 Utah Laws 119, sec. 1.
[271] 2000 Vt. Laws 108.
[272] 2000 Va. Acts 684.
[273] 2000 Wyo. Sess. Laws 89, sec. 1.
[274] 2000 Colo. Legis. Serv. 106 (West).
[275] 2000 Fla. Sess. Law Serv. 137 (West).
[276] 2000 Iowa Legis. Serv. 131 (West).
[277] 2000 Iowa Legis. Serv. 138 (West).
[278] 2000 Iowa Legis. Serv. 133 (West).
[279] 2000 Me. Legis. Serv. 595 (West).

requirement.[280] Missouri permitted the sharing of records of students pre-adjudicated as delinquent with the juvenile justice system.[281]

New York required juvenile courts to provide notice to schools of enrollment of juvenile persons sentenced for crimes.[282] Oklahoma authorized school boards to request disciplinary and nondirectory educational records from schools a student formerly attended to ascertain safety issues and ensure full disclosure by the student upon enrollment.[283] Virginia gave authority to school resource officers to enforce school board rules and codes of student conduct.[284] Also, Virginia added violation of drug laws on school property to the list of offenses a law enforcement officer may report to a school principal.[285] Washington called for education records to be released upon request to the Department of Social and Health Services for students under jurisdiction of the juvenile courts.[286] Further, Washington gave juvenile courts the authority to order children to attend school, set forth minimum attendance requirements including the allowable number of suspensions, and to not consume controlled substances or alcohol.[287]

Nine states added requirements for criminal background checks for school personnel or child care facilities. Alabama added a criminal background check for license holders for child and adult care facilities as well as for employees and volunteers for child and adult care facilities.[288] Arizona changed its law related to criminal background checks for teachers, by requiring that fingerprint records be kept until the teacher is age ninety-nine or two years after the teacher's death.[289] Idaho added a criminal history check for new employees.[290] To the existing criminal background check requirements for new school employees, Illinois added the reporting requirement for enumerated drug and criminal offenses, including all felonies in the last seven years and crimes that would be a felony had they occurred in Illinois.[291] Kansas added a criminal history records check as a requirement for initial employment in Kansas schools.[292] The record check must be conducted by the Kansas Bureau of Investigation and paid for by the school board. Insofar as criminal records are confidential, the legislation provides

---

[280] 2000 Minn. Sess. Law Serv. 451 (West).
[281] 2000 Mo. Legis. Serv. 60A.
[282] 2000 N.Y. Laws 214.
[283] 2000 Okla. Sess. Laws 186.
[284] 2000 Va. Acts 785.
[285] 2000 Va. Acts 611.
[286] 2000 Wash. Legis. Serv. 88 (West).
[287] 2000 Wash. Legis. Serv. 61 (West).
[288] 2000 Ala. Acts 775.
[289] 2000 Ariz. Legis. Serv. 208 (West).
[290] 2000 Idaho Sess. Laws 310, sec. 1.
[291] 2000 Ill. Legis. Serv. P.A. 91-885, sec. 20 (West).
[292] 2000 Kan. Sess. Laws 138, sec. 1.

for criminal and civil penalties as well as removal from office for school officials who disclose the criminal history. School boards in Kansas may offer provisional to applicants, pending completion of the criminal background check.

Kentucky imposed criminal background checks for school volunteers.[293] Mississippi required a criminal background check of school employees paid by the applicant;[294] the law provides for a hearing before a school board to explain mitigating circumstances. New York ordered fingerprinting and criminal background checks for all prospective school employees in all school districts except those with a population of 1 million or more.[295] South Dakota called for criminal background investigations of prospective school employees.[296] South Dakota also permitted local school boards to refuse to employ persons who have been convicted of crimes involving moral turpitude but prohibited them from employing persons who have been convicted of a crime of violence, a sex offense, or the crime of narcotic trafficking.[297]

Eight states addressed school safety concerns through student exclusions. To existing legislation related to procedures concerning student discipline, Arizona inserted language providing for the readmission of pupils excluded for more than ten school days.[298] California clarified the authority of county boards to review decisions of local school boards related to student expulsions;[299] this authority includes the power to order the local board to expunge records of students. Florida mandated the one year expulsion and referral for criminal prosecution of a student who makes a threat or false report involving school personnel.[300] Mississippi amended the powers and duties of local school boards related to the suspension or expulsion of misbehaving students so that they may now also change a student's placement to alternative school or a homebound program.[301] Ohio permitted school superintendents to expel students for one year for making bomb threats.[302] Utah removed a local superintendent's authority to provide a lesser penalty than expulsion for one year for students who bring firearms to school.[303] To the statute requiring expulsion for bringing weapons on school property, Virginia added a definition of school property, to include "any real property owned or leased by the school board, or any

[293] 2000 Ky. Acts 336, sec. 1.
[294] 2000 Miss. Laws 587.
[295] 2000 N.Y. Laws 180.
[296] 2000 S. D. Laws 76, sec. 1.
[297] 2000 S. D. Laws 76, sec. 2.
[298] 2000 Ariz. Legis. Serv. 277 (West).
[299] 2000 Cal. Legis. Serv. 147 (West).
[300] 2000 Fla. Sess. Law Serv. 235, sec. 4 (West).
[301] 2000 Miss. Laws 559.
[302] 2000 Ohio Legis. Serv. 2701 (Baldwin).
[303] 2000 Utah Laws 336, sec. 1.

vehicle owned or leased by the school board, or operated by or on behalf of the school board."[304] Wisconsin permitted the early reinstatement of expelled students, if the student meets conditions set down by the expulsion hearing and the superintendent then grants early reinstatement.[305]

Four states enacted legislation concerning the administration of medication to students. Illinois amended a provision permitting only certified school nurses to administer medication to children, now permitting such administration by registered professional nurses even if they do not have certificates from the State Board of Education.[306] Maine required the Commissioner of Education to adopt rules for the administration of medication to students by unlicensed personnel and to require local boards to have policies on this subject and to provide for training of unlicensed personnel.[307] Michigan changed its law on administration of medication to children to permit licensed professional nurses to administer medication without another adult present;[308] previously, the law required all adults to have another adult present to administer medication. Michigan also permitted students to use asthma inhalers with written approval from a physician is provided and the school principal has received a copy of the approval;[309] the principal must notify teachers of the approval. The statute also provides immunity for damages for school personnel who do not let students use inhalers, because of a reasonable belief that the student has not met the requirements for approval. In a third act, Michigan changed existing law related to consequences for violent acts in schools to provide wider discretion in the use of exclusions to include suspensions and permanent expulsions.[310] Wisconsin permitted school employees or volunteers to administer an epinephrine autoinjector to any pupil who appears to be experiencing a severe allergic reaction if the individual calls the emergency telephone number "911;" this provision provides immunity unless an act constitutes a high degree of negligence.[311]

Other miscellaneous acts related to school safety follow. Iowa provided immunity from civil or criminal liability for nonpublic and public school corporations for reporting violence and threats against school employees or students on school property or during school activities when such reports are made in good faith.[312] Michigan raised the standard for removal of

---

[304] 2000 Va. Acts 523.
[305] 1999-2000 Wis. Legis. Serv. 128 (May 9, 2000) (West).
[306] 2000 Ill. Legis. Serv. P.A. 91-719 (West).
[307] 2000 Me. Legis. Serv. 669 (West).
[308] 2000 Mich. Legis. Serv. P.A. 9 (West).
[309] 2000 Mich. Legis. Serv. P.A. 10 (West).
[310] 2000 Mich. Legis. Serv. P.A. 230 (West).
[311] 1999-2000 Wis. Legis. Serv. 126 (May 9, 2000) (West).
[312] 2000 Iowa Legis. Serv. 163 (West).

liability in civil actions arising from the use of corporal punishment to willful acts.[313] Further, Michigan removed any expectation of privacy in school lockers and required local and intermediate school boards to adopt policy on searches of school lockers;[314] likely to produce litigation is the provision that permits law enforcement officers to assist school personnel in searches and that any evidence obtained shall not be inadmissible because the search violated this section. Michigan prohibited any school, after December 31, 2004, from purchasing, storing, or using free-flowing elemental mercury or using any instrument that contains mercury.[315] Minnesota raised the limit from thirty to fifty-five inches above grade, where bleachers must have no more than four inches of space between bleachers, or safety nets must be installed.[316] New York passed a comprehensive child reporting act for school personnel.[317]

Students with Disabilities

Legislatures departed from past practice and passed much less legislation related to the provision of services to students with disabilities. This section lists five such acts passed in 2000. Delaware permitted schools to establish alternative assessments for children with disabilities who cannot participate in the state assessment of achievement.[318] Louisiana passed legislation stipulating that no local school board or service provider is obligated to repair or replace assistive technology devices that are lost, stolen, damaged, broken, destroyed, or otherwise misused by a child, parent, or guardian.[319] Louisiana also raised the age students may be served at the Louisiana Special Education Center and Cerebral Palsy Center from twenty-five to thirty two.[320] Maine extended for two more years, until June 2002, the identification of "emotional disability" as a disability for which special education is required.[321] Mississippi created a recognition program for schools doing well at including children with disabilities in academic and extracurricular activities.[322]

---

[313] 2000 Mich. Legis. Serv. P.A. 461 (West).
[314] 2000 Mich. Legis. Serv. P.A. 87 (West).
[315] 2000 Mich. Legis. Serv. P.A. 376 (West).
[316] 2000 Minn. Sess. Law Serv. 417 (West).
[317] 2000 N.Y. Laws 180, sec. 12.
[318] 72 Del. Laws 294, sec. 55 (2000).
[319] 2000 La. Sess. Law Serv. 67(X) (West).
[320] 2000 La. Sess. Law Serv. 15(X) (West).
[321] 2000 Me. Legis. Serv. 721 (West).
[322] 2000 Miss. Laws 317.

Technology

The states continued their efforts to implement the use of technology in schools. Yet, the volume of legislation in this area was not as great as might have been expected, with only fifteen states adopting technology-related legislation. Alabama created the Office of Information Technology within the executive branch to provide for the administration of programs and student technology services for public schools and public institutions of higher education.[323]

California provided additional funds for computers to supplement the Digital High School Education Technology Grant Act of 1997.[324] Colorado incorporated the Colorado Institute of Technology, through the universities, state colleges, and community colleges, to foster the creation of telecommunications and technology-related education programs.[325] Delaware funded Technology Block Grants for local and charter schools to support maintenance and replacement of technology equipment and personnel to maintain the equipment.[326] Florida established an on-line high school for developing and delivering on-line and distance learning education across the state;[327] this legislation forms a Board of Trustees appointed by the Governor and grants duties and powers to the Board of Trustees similar to other local school boards in the state.

Illinois created the Arthur F. Quern Information Technology Grant Program which provides $2,500 maximum for qualified students pursuing additional certification or a degree in an information technology field at a degree-granting institution.[328] Iowa gave authority to school corporations to hire information technology specialists when ten percent of the budget for technology uses is taken up by with consultants for services.[329] Maryland required each county or board of trustees of county libraries to adopt and implement policies and procedures to prevent minors from having access to child pornography via the Internet and to submit their policies and procedures to the State Superintendent of Education for review;[330] as written, the required policies apparently need not proscribe adult pornography.

Minnesota added to its public record law to require the disclosure of data in electronic form except that information must not be provided in a

---

[323] 2000 Ala. Acts 715.

[324] 2000 Cal. Legis. Serv. 78 (West).

[325] 2000 Colo. Legis. Serv. 6 (West).

[326] 72 Del. Laws 450, sec. 1 (2000).

[327] 2000 Fla. Sess. Law Serv. 224 (West).

[328] 2000 Ill. Legis. Serv. P.A. 91-711 (West).

[329] 2000 Iowa Legis. Serv. 83 (West).

[330] 2000 Md. Laws 9, sec. 1.

format other than how it is stored.[331] In addition, Minnesota required guaranteed access to telecommunications to all schools, including nonpublic schools, but excluded home schools from this provision.[332] North Carolina transferred the Office of Information Technology Services from the Department of Commerce to the Governor's Office.[333] Under this law, local government agencies, including schools, are not required to comply with competitive bidding laws when they work through the Office of Information Technology Services for technical programs, services, or , including procurement. Ohio authorized public school officials to loan computer equipment to pupils attending nonpublic schools within their districts or to their parents.[334]

Oklahoma directed the Virtual Internet School in Oklahoma Network (VISION) Pilot Program to concentrate on developing web-based instructional programs in mathematics.[335] South Dakota established the Office of Educational Technology within the Department of Education and Cultural Affairs to assist local school boards in using educational technology.[336] Utah permitted local school boards to purchase computers from Utah Correctional Industries without following competitive bidding procedures.[337]

Transportation

Nine states passed legislation concerning transportation of schoolchildren in 2000. Alabama required all new school buses to be equipped with crossing control arms.[338] Colorado changed the definition of school buses to include contracted vehicles and those vehicles used on school-sponsored activities.[339] Connecticut removed the defense of sovereign immunity in personal injury actions arising from pupil transportation to and from school.[340] Idaho added two provisions related to school bus drivers. First, school bus drivers are now required to have commercial driving licenses.[341] Second, school bus drivers with diabetes mellitus may obtain a waiver from a local board of trustees to obtain their drivers' licenses.[342] Indiana required

---

[331] 2000 Minn. Sess. Law Serv. 468 (West).
[332] 2000 Minn. Sess. Law Serv. 489, sec. 8 (West).
[333] 2000 N.C. Sess. Laws 174, no. 3.
[334] 2000 Ohio Legis. Serv. 2797 (Baldwin).
[335] 2000 Okla. Sess. Laws 304.
[336] 2000 S. D. Laws 75, sec. 4.
[337] 2000 Utah Laws 76, sec. 1.
[338] 2000 Ala. Acts 701.
[339] 2000 Colo. Legis. Serv. 7 (West).
[340] 2000 Conn. Legis. Serv. P.A. 00-133 (West).
[341] 2000 Idaho Sess. Laws 469, sec. 81.
[342] 2000 Idaho Sess. Laws 426, sec. 2.

that the name of each school corporation be displayed on school buses.[343] Minnesota required local school boards to officially approve the safety of individual bus stops.[344] New York prohibited standing passengers in school buses, with a phase-in provision permitting twenty percent of riders to stand in 2001, fifteen percent of riders to stand in 2002, ten percent of riders to stand in 2003, then five percent in 2004.[345] South Dakota permitted local school boards to allow nonprofit civic organizations to use their buses and other vehicles to transport persons to activities in the public interest.[346] Tennessee made it a Class A misdemeanor, punishable by a $250 to $1,000 fine, for a vehicle to fail to stop upon approaching a school bus.[347]

Higher Education

It is not unusual, from year to year, for legislatures to pass laws concerning the governance structure of higher education institutions and to target specialized programs within the academy for funding. It is unusual, however, for legislatures to involve themselves in the management of universities, a legislative practice now commonly utilized for K-12 education. This year saw more new statutes directing the internal affairs of universities as well as a marked increase in the volume of higher education-related legislation.

Seven states passed legislation about governance, membership on a board, or the role of trustees. Arizona added a second student member to its university's Board of Regents.[348] In the same bill, Arizona added a procedural requirement that required the Board of Regents to provide ten days notice and a hearing before raising tuition. California increased from one to two the number of student members on the Governor's Board of community colleges.[349] Illinois permitted the membership of a student on the university board of trustees to continue past 2001.[350] Maryland required the University System of Maryland to adopt and submit a mission statement to the higher education commission and update the statement every four years.[351]

---

[343] 2000 Ind. Acts P.L. 15-2000, sec. 1.
[344] 2000 Minn. Sess. Law Serv. 426 (West).
[345] 2000 N.Y. Laws 19.
[346] 2000 S. D. Laws 86, sec. 2.
[347] 2000 Tenn. Pub. Acts 663, no. 2.
[348] 2000 Ariz. Legis. Serv. 128 (West).
[349] 2000 Cal. Legis. Serv. 390 (West).
[350] 2000 Ill. Legis. Serv. P.A. 91-778 (West).
[351] 2000 Md. Laws 542.

Minnesota empowered The University of Minnesota's Board of Trustees to set the Chancellor's compensation, but only within the approved salary range.[352] Ohio clarified that university trustees are responsible for creating a job classification plan for unclassified employees and that rule making related to these employees is not subject to the approval of the state personnel board.[353] Tennessee permitted its Higher Education Commission to review and approve or disapprove proposals by higher education institutions to establish a physical presence at any location other than its main campus.[354]

Three states enacted legislation relating to open meetings and open records laws (sunshine laws) or the manner in which trustees meetings are conducted. California extended provisions of open meeting laws to state university student body organizations and made it a misdemeanor for such groups to fail to meet these requirements.[355] Illinois added a provision requiring that at all meetings of university board of trustees time must be allotted, subject to reasonable constraints, for members of the public and employees of the university to make comments or ask questions of the board.[356] Iowa amended its public records law relating to universities to make it permissible to disclose to a parent or guardian of a student under age twenty-one information related to a violation of federal, state, or local law, or institutional rule or policy governing the use of alcohol or controlled substances.[357]

Five states pushed increased collaboration between K-12 and university communities in the delivery of programs. Hawaii created a Running Start Program to allow eligible high school students to enroll in university courses for college credit while still in the eleventh and twelfth grades.[358] Iowa required the creation of an individual program of study for each student, to be developed jointly by a secondary school, a post-secondary school, and employer, no later than the beginning of the student's senior year in high school.[359] Michigan required community colleges and universities to cooperate with secondary schools in the delivery of career and technical preparation programs, to teach trade, occupations, or vocational education to eligible high school age students.[360] New Mexico established learning center districts as collaborative efforts between school and community college districts, to assist in workforce development and to help

---

[352] 2000 Minn. Sess. Law Serv. 453 (West).
[353] 2000 Ohio Legis. Serv. 1635 (Baldwin).
[354] 2000 Tenn. Pub. Acts 836, no. 3.
[355] 2000 Cal. Legis. Serv. 330 (West).
[356] 2000 Ill. Legis. Serv. P.A. 91-715 (West).
[357] 2000 Iowa Legis. Serv. 162 (West).
[358] 2000 Haw. Sess. Laws 236, sec. 2.
[359] 2000 Iowa Legis. Serv. 15 (West).
[360] 2000 Mich. Legis. Serv. P.A. 258 (West).

unserved or underserved populations to receive post-secondary education.[361] Oklahoma expressed its legislative intent that education, vocational technical education, and higher education entities coordinate calendars to produce a common spring break period.[362]

Three states legislated intellectual property issues for the academic community. Arizona required Arizona State University to obtain information regarding revenue derived from patents on drug discovery and report that information to the state's political leadership.[363] California weighed in on copyright issues by prohibiting any business, agency, or person from preparing, causing to be prepared, giving, selling, transferring, or otherwise distributing or publishing any contemporaneous recording of an academic presentation.[364] Ohio expanded the field of places where a university claims an interest in intellectual property produced by employees, by adding "any facility" to the list of "any experiment station, bureau, laboratory, or research facility."[365]

Two states passed legislation related to property control and ownership. Alabama ordered two-year colleges to dispose of surplus property by donating it to local public high schools, middle schools, and elementary schools.[366] The Alaska Legislature authorized the University of Alaska to select and have conveyed to it 250,000 to 260,000 acres of land that had been conveyed to the state by the Alaska Statehood Act.[367] From this acreage, the University is obligated to create a demonstration forest.[368]

Nine states addressed tuition and fees for post-secondary institutions. Alaska established a Higher Education Savings Trust to secure obligations to participants and beneficiaries under a postsecondary education savings program operated by the University of Alaska to provide participants with a method of saving for college.[369] Colorado prohibited the charging of a separate fee for student organizations in post-secondary institutions;[370] in addition, student fees may not be used for political causes except through an affirmative authorization from a student or a student's parent. To a provision authorizing the payment of tuition for dependents of deceased or disabled police and firefighters, Colorado added payment for room and board

---

[361] 2000 N.M. Laws 105, sec. 2.
[362] 2000 Okla. Sess. Laws 232.
[363] 2000 Ariz. Legis. Serv. Ch. 332.
[364] 2000 Cal. Legis. Serv. 574 (West).
[365] 2000 Ohio Legis. Serv. 858 (Baldwin).
[366] 2000 Ala. Acts 689.
[367] P.L. 85-508, 72 Stat. 339.
[368] 2000 Alaska Sess. Laws Sec. 5, Ch. 136.
[369] 2000 Alaska Sess. Laws Sec. 4, Ch. 3.
[370] 2000 Colo. Legis. Serv. 103 (West).

charges.[371] Florida amended provisions delineating the powers of the Board of Regents to identify a prescriptive fee schedule by, for example, setting the application fee at thirty dollars and the identification card fee set at fifteen dollars.[372] Florida also permitted the waiver of student fees for persons who supervise interns for the university system.[373]

Louisiana amended the powers and duties of university management boards to put a cap on tuition increases of $250.[374] Additionally, Louisiana authorized Louisiana State University to charge a student fee of $150 for the promotion of academic excellence.[375] Maine passed legislation requiring state post-secondary education institutions to absorb the reduction in tuition revenues resulting from tuition waivers and indicating that the institutions may not request additional general fund monies to offset the reduction in tuition revenues.[376] Maryland provided an exemption from tuition for foster care recipients.[377] Mississippi established the Mississippi Prepaid Affordable College Tuition (MPACT) Program.[378] New Mexico ordered community college boards to award all other scholarships that are available before granting any lottery tuition scholarships.[379] Oklahoma helped students taking multiple advanced placement tests in one year, by providing financial assistance for the payment of test fees.[380]

Three state legislatures called for more consultation and coordination within universities or between universities and other entities. Kentucky directed its state universities to align their programs in speech-language pathology and teacher education to increase the number of students obtaining licensure as speech-language pathologists.[381] South Dakota ordered its State Board and State Department of Education to work with colleges of education to examine teacher and administrator preparation programs and to report strengths, deficiencies, and recommendations for improvement.[382] Minnesota required the State Board to consult with representatives from faculty and administration of post-secondary institutions that have teacher preparation programs in reviewing rules related to program approval.[383]

Three states enacted laws concerning general studies courses to facilitate easier transfer between institutions. California directed community

---

[371] 2000 Colo. Legis. Serv. 352 (West).
[372] 2000 Fla. Sess. Law Serv. 215, sec. 1 (West).
[373] 2000 Fla. Sess. Law Serv. 215, sec. 2 (West).
[374] 2000 La. Sess. Law Serv. 4(2X) (West).
[375] 2000 La. Sess. Law Serv. 100(X) (West).
[376] 2000 Me. Legis. Serv. 774 (West).
[377] 2000 Md. Laws 506.
[378] 2000 Miss. Laws 391.
[379] 2000 N.M. Laws 52, sec. 3.
[380] 2000 Okla. Sess. Laws 312.
[381] 2000 Ky. Acts 375, sec. 2.
[382] 2000 S. D. Laws 75, sec. 6.
[383] 2000 Minn. Sess. Law Serv. 469, sec. 6 (West).

colleges to construct a transfer core curriculum that fully articulates with core curricula with institutions in the California State University and University of California systems and to provide students with copies of the transfer core curriculum.[384] California also encouraged transfers from community colleges to universities by requiring the former to provide information on financial aid and academic requirements to students who wish to transfer.[385] Colorado authorized the delivery of basic skills courses at community colleges and two state colleges while calling for the administration of basic skills placement or assessment tests in English and mathematics at those institutions.[386] Tennessee ordered its Commission on Higher Education to develop a university core program within the current system of sixty hours of instruction in general education and pre-major courses in order to make it easier for students to transfer credit between institutions.[387]

Concerns about student safety became generalized to the university community as well as to K-12 settings. Florida authorized the Board of Regents to construct student conduct codes along with specifying the range of penalties for misconduct.[388] Illinois directed each university board of trustees to authorize its police department to create a distinct badge which displays the university's name and a badge number.[389] Kentucky required its post-secondary institutions to develop housing and security policies for safe residence facilities for students with disabilities.[390] In addition, Kentucky placed a duty on its post-secondary institutions to maintain a log of criminal activity on campuses and to report to the campus community crimes and threats to safety to students and employees.[391] Tennessee directed on each institution of higher education having probable cause that a student has committed a Class A misdemeanor or any of the five categories of felonies to report such probable cause to an appropriate law enforcement officer;[392] the legislation does not define an appropriate law enforcement officer.

Other miscellaneous acts by the legislatures related to higher education follow. California established a distance learning policy in establishing goals

---

[384] 2000 Cal. Legis. Serv. 187 (West).
[385] 2000 Cal. Legis. Serv. 588 (West).
[386] 2000 Colo. Legis. Serv. 308 (West).
[387] 2000 Tenn. Pub. Acts 795, no. 3.
[388] 2000 Fla. Sess. Law Serv. 215, sec. 6 (West).
[389] 2000 Ill. Legis. Serv. P.A. 91-883 (West).
[390] 2000 Ky. Acts 191, sec. 1.
[391] 2000 Ky. Acts 190, sec. 2.
[392] 2000 Tenn. Pub. Acts 542, no. 1.

and principals for the use of technology in postsecondary education.[393] Colorado made all information related to prepaid tuition expense fund and college savings programs as well as proprietary information of the trust fund administration confidential and privileged.[394] Connecticut added language to its higher education law to permit colleges or programs in naturopathic medicine to include within their curricula didactic and clinical training necessary to qualify for accreditation.[395]

Florida named the football field at Florida State University "Bobby Bowden Field at Doak S. Campbell Stadium;" this takes effect on the first day following Coach Bowden's retirement.[396] Florida prohibited university and community college direct support organizations, such as foundations, from making political contributions unless done so by a roll-call vote of their governing boards.[397] Florida authorized the creation of colleges of law at Florida International University and Florida A&M University; the legislation provides for duties of the Board of Regents, accreditation requirements, and that the admission process shall not include preferences on the basis of race, national origin, or sex.[398] Illinois called for informed consent for research experiments at the University of Illinois medical school to be in the native language of a participant or read to an individual who cannot read or has difficulty reading.[399] Louisiana required all actions against faculty and staff of LSU Medical School alleging administrative or supervisory negligence and arising out of discharge of duties to be brought only in the parish where the medical care was actually provided.[400]

Michigan passed two statutes related to alcohol permits for universities. The first law permits an award of Class B hotel licenses to universities having a hospitality program.[401] The second statute permits an award of liquor licenses to universities operating conference centers.[402] Michigan also established a military school.[403] Minnesota required boards at the University of Minnesota, state colleges, and universities to select at least two

---

[393] 2000 Cal. Legis. Serv. 467 (West).
[394] 2000 Colo. Legis. Serv. 70 (West).
[395] 2000 Conn. Legis Serv. P.A. 00-52.
[396] 2000 Fla. Sess. Law Serv. 374 (West).
[397] 2000 Fla. Sess. Law Serv. 267 (West).
[398] 2000 Fla. Sess. Law Serv. 259 (West).
[399] 2000 Ill. Legis. Serv. P.A. 91-861 (West).
[400] 2000 La. Sess. Law Serv. 127(X) (West).
[401] 2000 Mich. Legis. Serv. P.A. 166 (West).
[402] 2000 Mich. Legis. Serv. P.A. 344 (West).
[403] 2000 Mich. Legis. Serv. P.A. 338 (West).

primary designers for construction projects and to conduct a public meeting to select the finalist.[404] Tennessee repealed a provision which permits university faculty members with tenure who have been dismissed or suspended for cause to obtain de novo review in a chancery court.[405]

Conclusion

The 2000 legislative sessions saw a slight decrease in the involvement of the law makers with education compared to the 1999 sessions as there was approximately ten percent less total legislation. Concerns about school accountability and school safety again dominated the thoughts of legislators with more than twenty-five percent of the school-related legislation representing these categories. Legislation about charter schools filled in more details regarding the contours of their authority in states where they were already established. Decidedly less legislation created new charter schools.

Of the variety of accountability approaches adopted in 2000, there were again more sticks than carrots, indicating a tendency by the legislatures to value punishment over rewards as a policy tool. Notably absent among the categories this year was the category of Training Programs. In 1998 and 1999, sixteen and thirty-nine, respectively, legislative acts were passed that created specialized training programs for teachers or administrators, rewarded incentives for teachers who received advanced training or directed the creation of staff development programs. In 2000, such enlightened legislative viewpoints were rare.[406] Together, these trends in punishment-oriented accountability legislation and the dearth of training program legislation indicate at worst a collective mean-spiritedness by legislatures toward education and cynicism about their roles in educational leadership. At best, these trends indicate an inorance about how humans are motivated toward individual excellence and how organizations are led to improve. Added to this commentary is the observation that employment law in education was dominated by reactions to teacher shortages. Whether these disparate observations connect to portray a coherent educational policy is left open to question.

One remarkable change in law making during the 2000 legislative year, compared to previus years, was the increased volume of legislation related

---

[404] 2000 Minn. Sess. Law Serv. 384 (West).
[405] 2000 Tenn. Pub. Acts 588, no. 1.
[406] *See* text for footnotes 143, 156, 157, and 188 *supra*, for solitary examples.

to higher education. Historically, universities, and to a lesser degree, community colleges, have functioned with little direct involvement from legislatures compared to K-12 schools. Last year's total of higher education-related legislation quadrupled the amount of such laws passed only two years earlier. Higher education legislation historically focused on the creation of governing boards and funding programs within universities, reflecting the traditional view that, like church property, universities were sanctuaries from the crown. In 2000, a growing body of legislation reached directly into the academy and directed how programs should be administered. This change perhaps indicates a growing view among legislators that universities are nothing more than an extension of K-12 education. If this observation is correct, then this may mark the beginning of the end for universities as we have known them.

10

EDUCATION RELATED

Scott Ellis Ferrin, J.D., Ed.D.
Rick Alan Griffin, J.D.

Introduction

This chapter summarizes key decisions of the United States Supreme Court and other jurisdictions from the year 2000. In this education-related chapter, cases are highlighted that do not necessarily arise in school settings but whose factual patterns and results may have implications for educators and their attorneys. This chapter is best read as a supplement that requires reference to subject matter chapters that touch on cases arising in educational settings.

Fourteenth Amendment—Equal Protection

Under the Omnibus Consolidated Rescissions and Appropriations Act of 1996,[1] Congress prohibited funding of any organization that:

> initiates legal representation or participates in any other way, in litigation, lobbying, or rule making, involving an effort to reform a Federal or State welfare system, except that this paragraph shall not be construed to preclude a recipient from representing an individual eligible client who is seeking specific relief from a welfare agency if such relief does not involve an effort to amend or otherwise challenge existing law in effect on the date of the initiation of the representation.[2]

The Act was aimed at Legal Services Corporations (LSCs), non-profit entities that provide legal services to low income recipients, and was intended to limit their activities, especially challenges to federal legislation on behalf of indigent clients. The Supreme Court, in *Legal Services Corp v. Velazquez*,[3] with Justice O'Connor's dissent joined by Chief Justice Rehnquist and Justices Scalia and Thomas, held that the restriction imposed on LSCs was unconstitutional viewpoint discrimination. *Velazquez* may have a great impact on the vitality of legal services to low income and minority litigants in education law, social services, and welfare issues. Of course, this still does not necessarily raise the funding of LCSs back to previous levels, but is an important development and may impact the type and quality of legal representation provided to low income parents and students.

In 1999 in *Chicago v. Morales*,[4] the Supreme Court struck down Chicago's Gang Congregation Ordinance, which prohibited "criminal street gang members" from loitering in public places. The case was of some interest in light

---

[1] Section 504, 110 Stat. 1321-53 (1996).
[2] Legal Servs. Corp. v. Velazquez 121 S. Ct. 1043, 1047 (2001).
[3] *Id.* at 1043.
[4] 527 U.S. 41 (1999).

of anti-loitering rules in public schools with their attendant suspensions such as one challenged in *Wiemerslage v. Maine Township High School District 207*,[5] wherein a student received a three day suspension for talking with friends in a school's "no loitering area."

In January of 2000, a federal trial court in Cincinnati, Ohio struck down an ordinance banning persons who had been convicted of a drug abuse or related crimes from "drug exclusion zones."[6] The City Council enacted the ordinance in expressly pointing out that certain areas had significantly higher incidences of conduct associated with drug abuse activity. The Council also noted that those arrested for drug abuse often returned to the same areas since they had proven lucrative for drug-abuse activity. Even though these facts served as the basis for a laudable plan to confront a challenging problem, the court held that such a scheme was unconstitutional since it violated the plaintiffs' fundamental rights of association and travel. While these rights are not explicitly enumerated in the Constitution, the court decided that they were basic, fundamental, and necessary concomitants to the entire Bill of Rights and that the ordinance was insufficiently narrowly tailored to respond to the City's interests while protecting the basic rights of the plaintiffs. In light of *Johnson,* educators may wish to be careful of over-reaching, even for laudable aims, when their policies too broadly infringe on fundamental rights.

Disabilities

In *Board of Trustees of the University of Alabama v. Garrett,*[7] the Supreme Court took another step to reinforce its new vision of states' rights under the Eleventh Amendment. *Garrett* amounts to a declaration that Congress did not abrogate the sovereign immunity of states under Title I of the Americans with Disabilities Act (ADA). As such, Garrett and other recent actions indicate that Congress, no matter how explicit its intention to do so, may not abrogate sovereign immunity absent some sort of balancing and proportionality test.

In *Garret* a registered nurse who returned to work after having had to take a substantial leave of absence due to breast cancer, sought monetary damages under Title I of the ADA after she was forced to resign from her position as a director at the University of Alabama Hospital in Birmingham. At about the same time, a security officer for the Alabama Department of Youth who suffered from chronic asthma and sleep apnea requested a reassignment so that he could work during the day in an environment that would

---

[5] 29 F.3d 1149 (7th Cir. 1994).

[6] Johnson v. City of Cincinnati, 119 F. Supp.2d 735 (S.D. Ohio 2000).

[7] 121 S. Ct. 955 (2001).

minimize his exposure to cigarette smoke and carbon monoxide, both of which exacerbated his condition. When the officer's requests went unanswered, he also sued the state for money damages under Title I of the ADA. In both cases the state unsuccessfully raised the defense of Eleventh Amendment sovereign immunity. A federal trial court granted summary judgment for both petitioners on the ground that the ADA exceeded Congressional authority to abrogate Eleventh Amendment immunity. After the Eleventh Circuit reversed, the Supreme Court agreed to hear an appeal to resolve a conflict among the circuits.

Writing for the majority, Chief Justice Rehnquist reversed the Eleventh Circuit on the basis that the Eleventh Amendment bars ADA damage claims. The Court explained that the Fourteenth Amendment does not require states to make special accommodations for the disabled as long as their actions towards such individuals are rationally related to legitimate governmental purposes. The Court commented that since the ADA's legislative record failed to identify a pattern of "irrational state discrimination" against state employees who are disabled, the ADA does not abrogate Eleventh Amendment immunity protections. Yet, according to the Court, even a positive finding under this standard would not necessarily have violated the Fourteenth Amendment. The Court went on to determine that if the states are going to be compelled to provide the disabled with special accommodations, such a legal requirement must come from positive law and not the Equal Protection Clause of the Fourteenth Amendment. The Court also reflected that Congressional enforcement power under the Fourteenth Amendment applied only to state violations and not to local governments such as cities or counties.

In a concurring opinion, Justice Kennedy, joined by Justice O'Connor, agreed that the state did not violate equal protection. Even so, in reviewing whether Congress could compel a state to act, the concurrence argued that the Court should have addressed "whether the States can be subjected to liability in suits brought by . . . private persons seeking to collect moneys from the state treasury without the consent of the State."[8]

Justice Breyer, writing for Justices Stevens, Souter, and Ginsburg, dissented on the ground that the Court, "through its evidentiary demands, its non-deferential review, and its failure to distinguish between judicial and legislative constitutional competencies, improperly invades a power that the Constitution assigns to Congress"[9] and that Congress had the authority to apply the ADA to the states. The dissent further argued that the Court erred in maintaining that the Fourteenth Amendment did not authorize Con-

---

[8] *Id.* at 968.
[9] *Id.* at 975.

gress to review local governmental violations because its substantive obligation applied to both state and local governments.

Garrett has the potential to have a great effect on public education in suits based on the ADA and a host of other federal civil rights statutes since it leaves many questions unanswered. For example, it is uncertain how *Garrett* will affect reasonable accommodation cases under Section 504 of the Rehabilitation Act. Equally unclear is how *Garrett* will impact upon teachers and staff members with disabilities who are covered by the ADA. In *Garrett* the Court sufficiently eliminated federal private suits for money damages against the states in finding, despite the fears of the dissent, that there really was not any pattern of state discrimination in the ADA's record and thus no legislative intent to apply Title I to the states. Although the Court posited that protections are still available for the disabled under state law, *Garrett* is a setback for the disabled and their advocates.

Search and Seizure

This section provides some broad contours of recent search and seizure cases resolved by the Supreme Court. Although these cases may not be directly applicable to school settings, they can inform administrators and their attorneys regarding current trends on this important issue.

In *Illinois v. McArthur*,[10] the Court, with Justice Stevens as the lone dissenter, asserted that a police officer's refusal to allow an individual to enter his residence without a police officer until a search warrant was obtained was a "reasonable seizure" that did not violate the Fourth Amendment. The seemingly-paradoxical question begged by *McArthur* is that if the police lack probable cause to search a residence or constitutionally-protected space, whether it is permissible to detain a citizen or homeowner outside of his or her home while awaiting a search warrant. Evidently, there is no paradox for most of the Supreme Court.

Eastern Associated Coal Corporation v. United Mine Workers of America[11] was filed by an employee who was fired from his job driving heavy machinery on highways because he failed a valid drug test. A unanimous Supreme Court, with Justice Scalia filing a concurrence that was joined by Justice Thomas, upheld an arbitration award ordering the driver's reinstatement pursuant to a collectively bargained grievance procedure. The Court was of the view that even public policy considerations such as safety in the Omnibus Transportation Employee Testing Act and Department of Transportation regulations implementing the Act did not preclude an award

---

[10] 121 S. Ct. 946 (2001).
[11] 121 S. Ct. 462 (2000).

allowing the reinstatement of an employee who tested positive on a drug test. The implications are surprisingly powerful regarding drug testing of school bus drivers and the power of collectively bargained arbitration or grievance rights to allow employees to avoid even important safety regulations. This outcome may also have a slight impact on drug testing cases of students who participate in extracurricular activities even in the absence of individualized suspicion.

In *City of Indianapolis v. Edmond*,[12] the Supreme Court wrote that establishing drug interdiction check points in the city violated the Fourth Amendment. Edmond was a class action suit that was filed after city officials set up drug interdiction checkpoints that were much like DUI stops to deter drunk driving. The Court, with Chief Justice Rehnquist and Justices Thomas and Scalia dissenting, observed that such suspicionless searches violated the Fourth Amendment. In its analysis, the Court briefly reviewed the legal basis for suspicionless searches:

> The rule that a search or seizure is unreasonable under the Fourth Amendment absent individualized suspicion of wrongdoing has limited exceptions. For example, this Court has upheld brief, suspicionless seizures at a fixed checkpoint designed to intercept illegal aliens . . . and at a sobriety checkpoint aimed at removing drunk drivers from the road . . . . The Court has also suggested that a similar roadblock to verify drivers' licenses and registrations would be permissible to serve a highway safety interest . . . . . However, the Court has never approved a checkpoint program whose primary purpose was to detect evidence of ordinary criminal wrongdoing.[13]

Edmond seems to signal that the Court continues to maintain a healthy vigilance over extending the practice and scope of searches in many settings that are not based on individualized suspicion. There are obvious current implications for schools and on the ongoing conflict between the circuits regarding whether all students participating in extracurricular activities can be subject to random drug testing.

Somewhat related to search and seizure issues is the Supreme Court's upholding of the *Miranda* Warning. In *Dickerson v. United States*,[14] the Court, with Justices Scalia and Thomas dissenting, the Court affirmed that since the *Miranda* Warning-based approach to the admissibility of a confession was constitutionally based, it could not be overruled by Congress. Congress, subsequent to *Miranda*, established a rule that the only criteron

---

[12] 121 S. Ct. 447 (2000).
[13] *Id.* at 454.
[14] 120 S. Ct. 2326 (2000).

for admissibility of evidence was the voluntariness of a confession. Once again, the Court declared that separation of powers does not allow Congress much latitude in statutorily abrogating its constitutional law decisions. *Dickerson* at least marks an enduring contour line regarding searches and gathering evidence against infractions in many settings, including perhaps schools. *Dickerson* might be an indication that new novel forms of search in schools, including random drug testing, infrared scanning, and security cameras will be carefully scrutinized. Moreover, it does seem to be a signal that this Court will continue to be vigilant of separation of powers, and parenthetically, the Fourth Amendment.

The Supreme Court has also reviewed what constitutes a search while slightly expanding and clarifying zones of individuals' reasonable expectations of privacy. In *Bond v. United States*,[15] with Justices Scalia and Breyer dissenting, a defendant sought to suppress evidence that originated from a Border Patrol Agent's "manipulation" of his carry-on bag on a bus. As an Agent entered a bus in Texas to check of the documentation status of passengers, he squeezed the soft luggage in the overhead rack. Discovering that a brick-like shape seemed to be inside of the petitioner's bag, the Agent conducted a search that led to the discovery of a "brick" of methamphetamine. The Court, in reversing two earlier judgments sustaining the Agent's action, decided that this manipulation was an impermissible Fourth Amendment search. The Court specifically pointed out that just exposing the bag to public view did not remove the petitioner's reasonable expectation of privacy in its contents and that its physical manipulation, as opposed to a visual inspection without a touching, was an intrusive search. Even though *T.L.O. v. New Jersey*[16] lowered the standards for initiating a search in a school so that probable cause is not required, Dickerson may help administrators be aware of the contours of what constitutes a search and to define expectations of privacy.

The Court also provided guidance on *"Terry"* or limited suspicion searches that may be justified with some quantum of suspicion less than probable cause under limited circumstances. After police in the Miami-Dade area received an anonymous telephone call reporting that a young black male wearing a plaid shirt at a bus stop was carrying a concealed weapon, they came upon three black males and searched a sixteen-year-old was wearing a plaid shirt. The search led to the discovery that the sixteen-year-old possessed a concealed weapon which he sought to exclude from the evidence against him as unconstitutionally obtained. In *Florida v. J.L.*,[17] a unanimous Court, with Chief Justice Rehnquist joining Justice Kennedy's

---

[15] 120 S. Ct. 1462 (2000).
[16] 469 U.S. 325 (1985).
[17] 120 S. Ct. 1375 (2000).

concurrence, found for the youth on the basis that an anonymous tip in and of itself is not sufficient cause for a search, even if it is a limited pat down. Under the *Terry* rubric, police officers are generally within constitutional constraints in conducting a carefully limited search of the outer clothing of a person for a weapon if an officer observes the individual engaged in unusual conduct that causes the officer, in light of his or her experience and training, to believe that criminal activity may be imminent and the person is likely to be armed and "presently dangerous."[18] In this instance, since the officers did not observe any conduct justifying a limited weapons search, the Court ascertained that there were insufficient indicia of reliability to justify the search.

J.L. helps illuminate what constitutes suspicion to initiate a *Terry* stop search based on a lower standard of suspicion in *Illinois v. Wardlow*.[19] On seeing a caravan of police cars enter an area of Chicago known for heavy narcotics trafficking, a suspect fled into an alley, leading officers to believe that they had reasonable suspicion to perform a *Terry* stop, pat down search for a weapon. When the police discovered a concealed .38 special caliber pistol on the suspect, he was arrested on a weapons charge. A state court in Illinois reversed the conviction because it was unconvinced that running away was sufficient reasonable suspicion to support a *Terry* stop. On further review, the Supreme Court decided that the actions observed by the police were sufficient to justify the search. In an part concurrence and part dissent, Justice Stevens, joined by Justices Souter, Ginsburg and Breyer, argued that a search must be based on a totality of the circumstances and emphasized that there should be no bright line test that an individual fleeing to avoid an interaction with police is not enough, in and of itself, to support a search, even a limited one. Prudence seems to dictate that care should be taken in making bright line guidelines for training educators about searches.

In *Wal-Mart Stores v. Goodman*,[20] the Supreme Court of Alabama examined a private entity's liability for a search and/or detention. *Goodman* was couched as a malicious prosecution in connection with the detention and prosecution of an alleged shoplifter at a Wal-Mart store. Although the facts surrounding the alleged shoplifting are not without their nuances that may not be clearly in favor of the accused shoplifter, a jury awarded the plaintiff $3,000,000 in compensatory and $600,000 in punitive damages. The Supreme Court of Alabama reduced the amounts to a lower, but still significant, amount while upholding punitive damages in a three to one ratio to the compensatory damages. The court permitted such damages because, among other things, the store provided unhealthy incentives for its security em-

---

[18] Terry v. Ohio, 392 U.S. 130 (1968).
[19] 120 S. Ct. 673 (2000).
[20] 2000 WL 1868437 (Ala.2000)

ployees whose job evaluations, raises, and chances for promotions were based on the number of apprehensions that they made. In fact, the security employee, in her ninety day evaluation before this incident, had been informed that she was below average in her apprehensions and needed to increase her number of apprehensions. The security employees even wrote on an evaluation form that she would improve the number of her monthly apprehensions.

Goodman illustrates the potential dangers in such an incentive arrangement. Private schools, and universities, as well as public educational institutions would be well advised to ensure that any security personnel, or "resource officers" not be evaluated too directly based on number of apprehensions or searches or other activities that may implicate constitutional and other rights of students and potential claimants.

Firearms Related

The Supreme Court considered cases dealing with the enhancement of penalties and sentences based on the presence or absence of factors such as firearms or hate crimes. In *Lopez v. Davis*,[21] the Court reasoned that the Bureau of Prisons could deny a prisoner entry into an early release program for individuals completing a drug treatment program if an offense was a felony that included possession or use of a firearm. There were some complexities of statutory construction and ultra vires at issue but the important point, in brief, is that the Court continues to support sentence-enhancing and early release sanctions based on the presence of a firearm. This is an example of zero tolerance for adults at a time when the American Bar Association, among others, has called for the end of zero tolerance laws for weapons and drugs in schools.

In *Castillo v. United States*,[22] defendants were convicted of offenses including using or carrying a firearm during the commission of a violent crime. The relevant federal statute read that use of a firearm in any crime of violence shall affect an accused's sentence: "[i]n addition to the punishment provided for such crime . . .be sentenced to imprisonment for five years . . .and if the firearm is a machine gun . . . to imprisonment for thirty years."[23] When a jury determined that the defendants violated the statute in the commission of their other crimes, the judge invoked a mandatory thirty year prison sentence because the weapons were machine guns.

---

[21] 121 S. Ct. 714 (2001).
[22] 120 S. Ct. 2090 (2000).
[23] 18 U.S.C.§ 924 (c)(1)

The salient issue was whether the having a firearm, in the form of a machine gun, was an element of the crime which needed to be argued before and resolved by a jury or was a sentencing factor within a judge's discretion. A unanimous Supreme Court reversed in noting that the history, structure, and context of the statute supports the interpretation that whether a firearm is a machine gun is a separate element of the crime. This seems appropriate as a fact issue, especially with the great jeopardy a defendant runs in terms of severity and length of sentencing. Further, *Castillo* can be viewed as background for zero tolerance laws regarding weapons in schools.

Another type of sentence enhancer is hate crime legislation. The Supreme Court considered such a statute in *Apprendi v. New Jersey*[24] where an individual who shot bullets into the home of an African-American family was arrested and admitted that while he did not know the people personally, he did not want blacks in his neighborhood.[25] The defendant pled guilty to possession of a firearm for an unlawful purpose and unlawful possession of a prohibited weapon. A judge, guided by the state's preponderance of the evidence standard, in acknowledging that the defendant acted with purpose to intimidate the victim based on particular characteristics, increased his maximum sentence under the state's hate crime statute. An appellate tribunal and the Supreme Court of New Jersey affirmed. The Supreme Court reversed and remanded, with Justices O'Connor, Rehnquist, Kennedy, and Breyer dissenting. The Court decreed that any element that may increase a criminal penalty beyond the prescribed statutory maximum must be submitted to a jury under the standard of beyond reasonable doubt. The Court added that the hate crime statute at issue, which allows an increase in the maximum prison sentence based on a judge's reliance on preponderance of evidence that a defendant's purpose was to a intimidate victim based on particular characteristics, violated due process. *Apprendi* may impact on similar penalty enhancer laws for crimes that take place on school property by raising misdemeanors to a felonies and so increase potential punishments.

First Amendment

In *Hill v. Colorado*,[26] pro-life advocates challenged the constitutionality of a criminal statute designed to protect those entering health care facilities for family planning services. The plaintiffs charged that the statute as infringed on constitutionally protected speech under the First Amendment since it prohibits any person from knowingly approaching within eight feet

---

[24] 120 S. Ct. 2348.
[25] *Id.* at 2351.
[26] 120 S. Ct. 2480 (2000).

of another near a health care facility without the other individual's consent. The Supreme Court, with Justices Scalia, Thomas, and Kennedy dissenting, upheld the statute as not being an unconstitutionally overbroad prior restraint on speech. Rather, the majority considered the statute to be a permissible, narrowly-tailored time, manner, and place restriction on speech.

The implication for schools is that divisive issues have been moving to the sidewalks around schools. The statute in *Hill* may be a tool considered by states to ensure that students are not harassed by adults or others as schools become the focus of speech actions and demonstrations.

Another case that was couched in the First Amendment, focusing on , was the much publicized *Boy Scouts of America v. Dale*.[27] The plaintiff, an assistant scoutmaster for the Boy Scouts who was expelled from the private, not-for-profit, organization after he publicly proclaimed that he was gay sought reinstatement and damages in arguing that New Jersey's public accommodations statute prohibited discrimination on the basis of one's sexual orientation. A state court granted the Boy Scouts' motion for summary judgment on the ground that the group was not a public accommodation since it was a "distinctly private group exempted from coverage under New Jersey's law."[28] An appellate court reversed and remanded in not only declaring that the Boys Scouts were covered by, and violated, the law but also in rejecting the First Amendment claims of intimate and expressive association. The Supreme Court of New Jersey affirmed that the state had a compelling interest to eliminate discrimination and that the public accommodation law abridged "no more speech than is necessary to accomplish its purpose."[29]

On further review, the Supreme Court, in an opinion by Chief Justice Rehnquist, reversed in ruling that the law could not be used to force the Boy Scouts to readmit the plaintiff because doing so would have violated their First Amendment right of expressive association and free speech. The Court explained that "[t]he forced inclusion of an unwanted person in a group infringes the group's freedom of expressive association if the presence of that person affects in a significant way the group's ability to advocate public or private viewpoints."[30] However, the Court did make clear that this was not an absolute freedom, but one that could be overridden by regulations designed to bring to pass a compelling state interest or interests "'unrelated to the suppression of ideas, that cannot be achieved through means significantly less restrictive of associational freedoms.'"[31]

Justice Stevens, writing for the dissent that also included Justices Souter, Ginsburg, and Breyer, rejected the Court's position that the law violated the

---

[27] 120 S. Ct. 2446 (2000).
[28] *Id.* at 2450.
[29] *Id.*
[30] *Id.* at 2451.
[31] *Id.*

Boy Scout's First Amendment freedoms of association and free speech. The dissent argued that the law neither imposed any serious burden on the Scout's "collective effort" or "shared goals" nor did it force them to "communicate any message that it [did not] wish to endorse."[32]

As in *Hurley v. Irish-American Gay, Lesbian and Bisexual Group of Boston*[33] and *California Democratic Party v. Bill Jones*,[34] the Court seems to be establishing that First Amendment protections of speech and association allow an organization the right to "choose the content of its own message" and that a state cannot simply modify such speech via public accommodation laws. One of the issues raised by *Dale* is the stance in the future in schools that have special relationships with Cub and Boy Scouting, including Boy Scout days, Scout food drives, and other functions. As part of their position, the Boy Scouts made clear why they were not a public accommodation covered by the statute, but rather a private association with freedom of association rights. Following that reasoning, the relationship that some schools share with the Boy Scouts and their charitable and other enterprises may change.

During its 2001-2002 term, the Court will hear oral arguments in yet another important case involving the First Amendment. In *Ashcroft v. Free Speech Coalition*[35] the Court will review *Free Speech Coalition v. Reno*[36] and the constitutionality of the Child Pornography Prevention Act of 1996 (CPPA).[37] The CPPA makes illegal any depiction that "appears to be" or "conveys the impression" of being child pornography even if no child is used or harmed in its production. The Ninth Circuit struck down portions of the statute that outlawed the appearance or impression of child pornography as an unconstitutionally vague limitation on protected First Amendment speech. In also writing that the government could not justify criminal prosecution when no actual children were involved in the depictions, the court severed these portions of the CPPA so that its other protections could remain in effect.

In *Ashcroft*, the Supreme Court is likely to address whether the CPPA constitutes a prior restraint on speech, whether it is unduly broad, and whether there is a sufficient state interest to allow criminalization of the appearance or impression of child pornography. It is worth keeping in mind that the Court has had difficulty defining obscenity and that it has struck down other statutory schemes intended to remove obscene images from the

---

[32] *Id.* at 2460.
[33] 515 U.S. 557 (1995)
[34] 120 S. Ct.2402 (2000)
[35] *cert. granted*, 121 S. Ct. 876 (2001).
[36] 198 F.3d 1083 (9th Cir. 1999).
[37] 18 U.S.C.A. § 2256(8)(B).

Internet and other media as unconstitutionally vague. Even so, it is possible that the Court may apply a different nexus between a governmental interest and the danger or harm to children. The theory behind the CPPA is that children may be harmed or victimized because of the responses of pedophiles to pornography apparently depicting children. The Ninth Circuit offered that "[t]he premise behind the Child Pornography Prevention Act is the asserted impact of such images on the children who may view them. The law is also based on the notion that child pornography, real as well as virtual, increases the activities of child molesters and pedophiles."[38]

Educational agencies and state licensing boards that certify teachers seem to believe they are justified in treating educators who access what may appear to be child pornography differently, and more severely, than those who access obscene or pornographic images of adults. If this is done in practice, it is based on the real world experience of educators, law enforcement, and child protection officers as well as others who deal with the potential risk to students from adult pedophiles with access to school children. *Ashcroft* bears watching as the Court considers whether there is a practical difference in terms of the type of speech and the danger involved in apparent child pornography as compared to obscenity or pornography in general. The question is whether the Court's historic difficulty in defining obscenity and free speech will lead it to affirm the Ninth Circuit's judgment or whether the protection of children and the potential danger that the CPPA seeks to avoid will be seen as a narrowly drawn and appropriate use of legislation.

Jurisdictional and Immunity Issues in Statutes and Regulations

Insofar as federal statutes, from civil rights enactments to the Equal Educational Opportunity Act to the Individuals with Disabilities Education Act are important to educational agencies, this section highlights ongoing developments at the Supreme Court involving limitations and immunity under the Commerce Clause and the Eleventh Amendment vis-a-vis states in suits by their own citizens to enforce federal laws. This area, with its shifting map of federal versus state authority and immunity, may become one of the more radical alterations in current school law presaged by this year's Supreme Court cases.

Following serious crude oil spills during the 1960s, Congress and Washington state passed stringent laws regulating oil tankers. More recently,

---

[38] Free Speech Coalition v. Reno 198 F.3d 1083, 1089 (1999).

after the Exxon Valdez disaster in 1989, Congress passed the Oil Pollution Act of 1990 while Washington established an agency to promulgate and enforce "best achievable protection" against oil spills. Whether Washington could develop its own language preparation policies in this arena was the issue in *United States v. Locke*.[39] The newly promulgated state standards required all licensed deck officers and the vessel master of a tanker operating in Washington to be proficient in English and to speak a language understood by all subordinate officers and unlicensed crew members. A unanimous Court decided that the regulation's imposition of an English language proficiency requirement was preempted by the federal Ports and Waterways Safety Act. The Court posited that although other provisions of the Washington code could remain in effect, the English language requirement was unenforceable because the area was pre-empted by a federal statutory scheme.

Even though *Locke* did not occur in an educational setting, it may be interesting because the Court struck down a state language policy statute as pre-empted by federal law. This may be noteworthy in light of the current spate of state English Only laws and statutes outlawing bilingual education in states such as California, Utah, and Arizona. Whether these laws will be affected over time by Locke, especially in light of the federal Native American Languages Act which encouragws the use of Native American languages for instruction remains to be seen.

In *Food and Drug Administration v. Brown & Williamson Tobacco Corporation*,[40] the Court removed control over tobacco and its advertising from the Food and Drug Administration (FDA) as lacking jurisdictional authority in its enabling legislation. In 1996 the FDA claimed authority to regulate tobacco since nicotine is a "drug" and cigarettes were devices for its delivery. The FDA then promulgated regulations regarding advertisement and labeling of tobacco products and their promotion to adolescents and children. The major aim of these regulations was to limit tobacco use by adolescents in an effort to limit the effects of the nation's leading cause of premature death. Most adult smokers, according to the FDA, became smokers when they were minors.

The Supreme Court held that the FDA lacks the authority to regulate tobacco products since doing so would lead to internal inconsistencies in the legislation that established it because Congress has considered, and rejected, bills to provide the DRA with the power to regulate tobacco products. The Court pointed out problems with the jurisdiction such as the required removal of all tobacco products for mislabeling since they were

---

[39] 120 S. Ct. 1135 (2000).
[40] 120 S. Ct. 1291 (2000).

drug conveyance devices. The Court also recognized that under its regulatory scheme, the FDA is required to evaluate whether a drug is safe for its intended use, and that tobacco, and its attendant nicotine, can not be determined to be safe.

In terms of its effect on schools, the FDA's regulations, among other provisions to protect children from tobacco advertising, would have prohibited any outdoor advertising of tobacco products within 1,000 feet of any public playground or school. Justice Breyer wrote a sharply worded dissent that was joined by Justices Stevens, Souter and Ginsberg. The dissent believed that the Act establishing the FDA was completely consonant with regulation of tobacco products on several grounds, but stressed:

> First, tobacco products (including cigarettes) fall within the scope of this statutory definition, read literally. [Defining FDA's jurisdiction to regulate articles other than food that affect the structure or any function of the body.] Cigarettes achieve their mood-stabilizing effects through the interaction of the chemical nicotine and the cells of the central nervous system. Both cigarette manufacturers and smokers alike know of, and desire, that chemically induced result. Hence, cigarettes are "intended to affect" the body's "structure" and "function," in the literal sense of these words. Second, the statute's basic purpose--the protection of public health--supports the inclusion of cigarettes within its scope. See United States v. Article of Drug ... Bacto-Unidisk ... is to be given a liberal construction consistent with [its] overriding purpose to protect the public health. . . . Unregulated tobacco use causes [m]ore than 400,000 people [to] die each year from tobacco-related illnesses, such as cancer, respiratory illnesses, and heart disease."
> . . . . . Indeed, tobacco products kill more people in this country every year than ... AIDS, car accidents, alcohol, homicides, illegal drugs, suicides, and fires, combined.[41]

Kimel v. Florida Board of Regents,[42] arose only incidentally in an educational setting since several of the plaintiffs were employees of a state university. Yet, *Kimel's* ramifications may go beyond higher education as the case highlights the ongoing struggle on the Court over newly announced limits on Congress' ability to abrogate the sovereign immunity of states vis-a-vis the Eleventh Amendment. The outcome of this struggle may have a profound impact on the vitality of several federal civil rights statutes affecting education.

---

[41] *Id.* at 135.
[42] 120 S. Ct 631 (2000).

Kimel joined three cases, two of which were against state universities, Alabama State University, Florida State University, and the Florida Department of Corrections. The plaintiffs sued their employers alleging violations of their rights under the Age Discrimination in Employment Act of 1967 (ADEA) which makes it unlawful for an employer, including a state, "to fail or refuse to hire or to discharge any individual or otherwise discriminate against any individual . . . because of such individual's age."[43] The states sought to have the claims dismissed on the ground that the Eleventh Amendment gave them right to avoid the application of the ADEA in this type of setting based on sovereign immunity.

The substantive facts and allegations of the plaintiffs were not addressed since the case came to the Supreme Court on motions to dismiss. *Kimel* is important as another in the line of recent cases that declare a new understanding of the Eleventh Amendment. Writing for the majority in what appears to be a plurality, Justice O'Connor was joined by Chief Justice Rehnquist and Justice Scalia. Justice Stephens filed a partial concurring and partial dissent which was joined by Justices Souter, Ginsburg, and Breyer. Justice Thomas, joined by Justice Kennedy, concurred in part and dissented in part. The plurality of opinions and dissents here underscores the continuing controversy on the Court over the Eleventh Amendment's reach and Congressional authority to abrogate states' sovereign immunity. The importance of this debate is that it may come to impact nearly all federal civil rights legislation grounded in Fourteenth Amendment equal protection values, especially those statutes applicable to public schools, colleges, and universities.

Briefly put, the central issues and analyses, with no definitive attempt to address each point of concurrence or dissent, follows. The majority maintained that although the Eleventh Amendment declares that "[t]he judicial power of the United States shall not be construed to extend to any suit in law or equity, commenced or prosecuted against one of the United States by Citizens of another State, or by Citizens or Subjects of any Foreign state," it does not mean exactly that. In other words, for the majority, the Eleventh Amendment, in its plain language, does not seem to bar suits by citizens against their own states, as opposed to those by citizens of other states or countries. However, the majority contended that "the Court has long understood the Eleventh Amendment to stand not so much for what it says, but for the presupposition which it confirms."[44] The majority understands that the Eleventh Amendment "does not provide for federal jurisdiction over suits against nonconsenting States."[45] The issue for the majority is whether Congress validly abrogated states' sovereign immunity.

---

[43] 29 U.S.C. § 623(a)(1).
[44] 120 S.Ct. 631, 640 (2000)
[45] *Id.*

The dispositive issue in such cases used to be whether there was a clear Congressional intent to abrogate sovereign immunity and subject states to suits for damages from private citizens. This was a stringent standard: "Congress may abrogate the States' constitutionally secured immunity from suit in federal court only by making its intention unmistakably clear in the language of the statute."[46] The majority of seven justices uncovered clear Congressional intent to abrogate states' sovereign immunity. Yet, Justice Thomas, joined by Justice Kennedy, did not even discern Congressional intent in the ADEA to abrogate sovereign immunity, clearly signaling how far they are willing to go to limit the application of federal statutes to states.

According to the rest of the majority, and the dissenters, the ADEA clearly passes the stringent intent to abrogate test. Yet, the majority now seeks a test to evaluate whether Congress "acted pursuant to a valid grant of constitutional authority."[47] In *Seminole Tribe of Florida v. Florida*,[48] the Court already indicated that Congress lacks authority under Article I of the Constitution to abrogate states' sovereign immunity. This article had been understood somewhat differently in the past. Article I reads, among other sweeping provisions, that Congress has "[p]ower to . . . regulate Commerce with foreign Nations, and among the several States, and with the Indian Tribes." This issue has now been settled, for the time being, by a slender majority comprised of Chief Justices Rehnquist and Justices O Connor, Scalia, Thomas. and Kennedy. Now, in Kimel, the Court dealt with Congress' power to abrogate a state's sovereign immunity under Section 5 of the Fourteenth Amendment, according to which "Congress shall have power to enforce this article by appropriate legislation."

The issue, for the new majority, is whether the ADEA is appropriate legislation and thus a valid abrogation of states' sovereign immunity. In order to make such an evaluation, this new majority used a "congruence and proportionality" test in *Florida Prepaid Postsecondary Education Expense Board v. College Savings Bank*.[49] This test was used to consider whether, over strong dissents from four Justices, the Fourteenth Amendment's provision for "appropriate legislation" to protect against deprivations of property without due process of law, here alleged patent infringement by the state, did not provide Congress with authority to abrogate states' sovereign immunity under the Patent and Plant Variety Protection Remedy Verification Act. The majority also did not agree that the Patent Clause provided such

---

[46] Dellmuth v. Much, 491 U.S. 223, 228 (1989).
[47] 120 S. Ct. 631, 640 (2000).
[48] 517 U.S. 44 (1996).
[49] 527 U.S. 627 (1999).

authority. The Court cited its 1997 decision in City of Boerne v. Flores,[50] for the provenance of the "congruence" test regarding the "appropriateness" of legislation pursuant to section 5 of the Fourteenth Amendment: "[t]here must be a congruence and proportionality between the injury to be prevented or remedied and the means adopted to that end."[51] This test and analysis seems relatively subjective. Even so, the majority was of the opinion, in fairly strong language, that

> " . . .it is clear that the ADEA is 'so out of proportion to a supposed remedial or preventive objective that it cannot be understood as responsive to, or designed to prevent, unconstitutional behavior.'"[52]

The dissent, led by Justice Stephens, took issue with the majority's basic foundational concepts regarding Congressional power to authorize federal remedies against state agencies that violate federal laws. The dissent obviously considered Congressional power to be more extensive than the majority did in regulating the American economy, which includes outlawing discrimination in the workplace even against public employers. The dissent was not convinced that either the Eleventh Amendment or sovereign immunity places any limit on that power. In other words, for the dissent, Congressional power to authorize remedies against state agencies is coterminous with its right to impose such statutory obligations on states in the first place. The dissent disagreed with the majority's novel application of the "ancient judge-made doctrine" of sovereign immunity as a freestanding limitation on Congressional power necessary to protect states' "dignity and respect" from the national government. The dissent argued that the Framers "did not . . . select the Judicial Branch as the constitutional guardian" of states' interest in being protected from the federal government. Such protection was intended to derive from the normal operation of the legislative process itself. In concluding, the dissent wrote that "[i]t is the Framers' compromise giving each State equal representation in the Senate that provides the principal structural protection for the sovereignty of the several States"[53] and "despite my respect for stare decisis, I am unwilling to accept *Seminole Tribe* as controlling precedent. First and foremost, the reasoning of that opinion is so profoundly mistaken and so fundamentally inconsistent with the Framers' conception of the constitutional order that it has

---

[50] 521 U.S. 507 (1997).

[51] *Id.*, at 520.

[52] Kimel 120 S. Ct. 631, 647 (2000), citing *City of Boerne*, 521 U.S. at 507, 532 (1997).

[53] *Kimel, id.* at 651.

forsaken any claim to the usual deference or respect owed to decisions of this court."[54]

This issue will continue to be important as the Court imposes a new view of federalism and the Eleventh Amendment on the older understandings of Constitutional law, comity, and practice. The Court, which seems willing to continue to grant certiorari to allow the new majority to continue to explore this area, may accept more cases to elucidate the reach of this new understanding of sovereign immunity.

Certainly, many of the civil rights statutes that apply to educational settings are, or may be, influenced as the majority applies its new and vague "congruence and proportionality" standard to evaluate whether federal legislation is "appropriate legislation" under section 5 of the Fourteenth Amendment and whether the legislation can validly abrogate states' sovereign immunity rights. Certainly, the next appointment on the Court will be important if that Justice helps to settle or overturn the current majority's view of sovereign immunity as well as its principles of federalism and comity.

An important question can be raised over just how far Eleventh Amendment immunity encroaches on the entire basis of the ADEA and other civil rights statutes. A partial answer may be offered by a case from the Ninth Circuit, *Katz v. Regents of the University of California.*[55] In *Katz*, in a relatively unusual twist, the plaintiffs sought to have the court rule that the state could not be sued because of *Kimel's* declarations regarding the Eleventh Amendment and its sovereign immunity vis-a-vis the ADEA. In so doing, the plaintiffs tried to negate an adverse judgment in a federal trial court where they unsuccessfully argued that the state waived sovereign immunity:

> The case is unusual, for it is the state that asserts that it has waived its immunity and the plaintiffs who assert that the state has not. We agree with the state that it has waived its immunity by consenting to the prosecution of this case through trial and by expressly waiving any Eleventh Amendment defense in this case.[56]

The plaintiffs argued that in light of *Kimel*, since there was no basis for federal subject matter jurisdiction, the adverse decision against them was null. The court refused to agree that *Kimel* entirely removed the statutory jurisdictional basis for age discrimination against state agencies. Instead, the court interpreted *Kimel* merely to say that a state cannot be compelled to submit to the jurisdiction of federal courts under the ADEA but that a state

---

[54] *Id.*
[55] 229 F.3d 831 (9th Cir.(Cal.) (2000).
[56] *Id.* at 833.

may waive its sovereign immunity by defending a case in federal court. The question thus becomes whether such a waiver effected a waiver of all claims to sovereign immunity under the ADEA in the future. Although the Ninth Circuit's language may be termed dicta since it was not central to the outcome, it remarked that California could waive Eleventh Amendment immunity on a case-by-case basis.

Torts

Educational entities, from primary schools to universities, deal with athletic injuries and the potential for personal injury suits based on multiple theories of tort, negligence, and even medical malpractice from team doctors. The basic rule has been that under well-accepted assumption of the risk doctrine, players accept the risks of possible injury from contact associated with their sports. Yet, it is possible to render players liable for malicious or willful misconduct that extends beyond the contact and conduct normally associated with a sport.

In November of 2000, the Supreme Court of Rhode Island, in a case of first impression, held that ordinary negligence is not the standard of care required for athletic participants.[57] Rather, the court ascertained that wilful or reckless conduct may subject a participant to liability.

At issue was whether a male base runner could be liable for injuries to the knee of a female second baseman in a co-ed softball game. As the male slid into the base, he extended his leg and injured the knee of the second baseman. The runner unsuccessfully moved for summary judgment on the basis that the second baseman's claim was precluded by assumption of risk. The court noted that the second baseman who sued the runner for "negligently, recklessly or wantonly" causing her injuries could also seek recompense for injuries under a recklessness or wantonness standard even though she could not sue for mere negligence. Specifically the court observed that:

> [I]f she can prove the runner slid into her knee deliberately or in reckless disregard of creating an unreasonable risk of injury to her, then she can seek to hold him liable for allegedly executing a so-called forbidden "take-out slide." In baseball and softball parlance, this is a maneuver in which the base runner attempts to take the infielder out of the play by sliding "into a fielder, attempting to off-balance that player and prevent his [or her] making a play." . . . Although this softball league permitted sliding, some evidence available to the motion justice indicated that take-out slides were

---

[57] Kiley v. Patterson, 763 A.2d 583 (R.I. 2000).

against the rules. Still other evidence suggested that Patterson may have acted willfully or recklessly when he slid into Kiley's knee. [58]

This opinion may provide general background for educators on the importance of dealing with, and striving to prevent, injuries from reckless student-athletes. Although assumption of risk generally precludes suit against athletic participants and educational institutions, since some behaviors may be deemed willful or wanton, they may open the door to liability. The prevalence of coaching and practices of "take out slides" on all levels of schooling may become problematic. Other actions and conduct in athletic events may also be raised to this standard. In light of this judgment, educators would be well-advised to be vigilant regarding coaching and the type of play and practice that coaches and physical education instructors advocate as well as the standards of sportsmanship that they teach.

Parental Rights

In *Troxel v. Granville,*[59] the Supreme Court dealt with parental rights. When an unmarried couple with two daughters separated, the father often brought them to visit him in the residence he shared with his own parents. After the father committed suicide, the mother chose to limit the grandparents visitations to one short period per month. When the grandparents petitioned for extended visits, a trial court granted their request but was reversed on appeal. The Supreme Court of Washington affirmed in favor of the mother on the basis that the state statute at issue was overly broad.

The Supreme Court affirmed that the statute granting the grandparents extended visitation rights violated the Fourteenth Amendment because it was overly broad. It reasoned that "'the [liberty] interest of parents in the care, custody, and control of their children—is perhaps the oldest of the fundamental liberty interests recognized,'" by the Supreme Court.[60] The Court added that the trial judge erred by ignoring the traditional presumption that a fit parent will act in the best interest of his or her child and by not at least applying some special weight to the mother's wishes. In so doing, the Court agreed that the trial judge violated the mother's right to make decisions concerning the care, custody, and control of her children.

Troxel further supports the traditional common law presumption that parents and not grandparents, friends, or school administrators possess

---

[58] *Id.* at 584.
[59] 120 S. Ct. 2054 (2000).
[60] *Id.* at 2060.

primary authority to determine what is in the "best interest" of a child. The result also supports the notion that the Court is likely to strike down state action to the contrary as a violation of a parent's Fourteenth Amendment rights.

Employment–Age Discrimination

In *Reeves v. Sanderson Plumbing Products*,[61] the Supreme Court clarified the standards of proof for a prima facie case of age discrimination, perhaps making it somewhat easier to prosecute such an action successfully. When an employee in Mississippi who worked for a plumbing products company was fired after more than forty years on the job, he filed suit that claiming that his employer violated the ADEA since he was dismissed due to his age. Company officials responded that the employee was dismissed because he failed to maintain accurate attendance records. A federal trial court refused to grant the company's motion for judgment as a matter of law and sent the matter to the jury with instructions that if the employee's attorney failed to prove that age was a determinative or motivating factor in his dismissal, it had to return a verdict in favor of the company.[62] The jury found in favor of the plaintiff, awarding him $70,000 in damages.

On further review, the Fifth Circuit reversed, in positing that besides providing evidence for a prima facie case and to refute the company's nondiscriminatory explanation for the dismissal, the employee also had to prove that his firing was motivated by his age. The Supreme Court agreed to hear an appeal to resolve the conflict among the circuits over whether a plaintiff with a prima facie case of discrimination and sufficient evidence for a reasonable jury to reject an employer's nondiscriminatory explanation for dismissal has presented a case "adequate to sustain a finding of liability for intentional discrimination."[63]

A unanimous Supreme Court, in an opinion by Justice O'Connor, reversed in favor of the employee in commenting that a prima facie case and sufficient evidence of pretext was sufficient for a trier of fact to uncover unlawful discrimination and that a plaintiff did not necessarily have to provide a court with additional independent evidence of discrimination. The Court was also of the view that such evidence will not always be adequate to sustain a jury's determination of liability. Although supporting the Court's overall judgment, Justice Ginsburg, in a separate concurrence, would have simply reversed on the ground that the Fifth Circuit erred in "plainly" and

---

[61] 120 S.Ct. 2097 (2000).
[62] *Id.* at 2104.
[63] *Id.*

"erroneously" requiring a plaintiff to provide additional evidence to sustain his prima facie case in assisting a finder of fact in evaluating whether a defendant's explanation for dismissal was false.

Conclusion

This chapter was designed to illuminate areas of concern to educators from cases that they and their attorneys may not have noticed or read because they did not arise in school settings. It is worth recalling that the Supreme Court continues to shape First and Fourth Amendment disputes in ways that affect practices in educational settings. This chapter also dealt with other important areas, with perhaps none as significant as the Court's continuing development of a new jurisprudence regarding the jurisdictional basis of sovereign immunity in underlying suits to enforce federal civil rights and other statutes. The cases that shed light on the Court's thinking in these areas merit careful scrutiny by educators and their attorneys.

11
INTERNATIONAL LAW

AUSTRALIA

Mary Keeffe-Martin, Katherine Lindsay, Doug Stewart

Introduction

This Chapter highlights legal issues in Australia concerning inclusion of students with disabilities. The Chapter also analyses determinations of anti-discrimination tribunals which addressed issues in enrollment and placement, assessment, suspension, and exclusion. While the number of complaints of disability discrimination in education is growing in Australia as the practice of inclusion is extended more broadly in private and public education sectors, the annual total of decisions in this area is still very modest by American standards. Further, developments in the jurisprudence of tribunals and courts are, on the whole, piecemeal and slow in Australia.

Equal access to education for students with disabilities has become a key concern throughout the common law world, including in the United Kingdom[1], the United States,[2] and Australia.[3] One of the areas of policy and legal interest has been the entrenching of non-discriminatory enrollment and placement policies and practices for these students. In Australia, education statutes in the States and Territories contain no legal requirement for the implementation of inclusion policies for students with disabilities. However, State education departments have produced bona fide inclusion policies which are not clear responses to existing legislative duties. Additionally, there are no statutory requirements directing that all students with disabilities are to be educated alongside their able peers. Absent constitutional protection in the form of a bill of rights or the benefit of general educational legislative protection, students with disabilities in Australia rely on two frameworks in seeking equal access to education: policies and practices of educational authorities and the provisions of disability discrimination statutes at the state and federal level.

Students with disabilities in Australia rely on the willingness of school authorities and administrators (principals) to maintain and administer inclusion policies. Inclusion policies which exist without legislative sanction are inherently liable to change and amendment and, as such, alone are insufficient to protect the interests of students with disabilities. Where educational authorities do not accede to the desires of students with disabilities to access mainstream educational environments, the provisions of Commonwealth and State disability discrimination statutes are invoked through their complaint-based mechanisms, with varying outcomes. What continues to

---

[1] N. Harris & K. Eden (2000) Challenges to School Exclusion. London: Routledge and Falmer.

[2] A.G. Osborne (1999) Students with Disabilities. In C.J.Russo (Ed) The Yearbook of Education Law.

[3] See K Lindsay "The Application of Anti-Discrimination Laws to Education" in I.M. Ramsay & A. R. Shorten Education and the Law, Sydney: Butterworths, 1996.

prove problematic in Australia, among other difficulties, is the limited level of knowledge of school principals in the management of inclusion policies and practices in order to eschew unlawful discrimination as proscribed by State and Commonwealth legislation. All schools, government and non-government alike, are subject to some anti-discrimination legislation.[4] However, implementing adequate policies and procedures depends on the commitment of school administrators who, in many instances, lack the level of legal knowledge sufficient to meet their responsibilities in this area.

The Legislative Framework: The Disability Discrimination Act

In 1992, the Commonwealth government enacted the Disability Discrimination Act 1992 (Cth),[5] the objects of which are:

(a) to eliminate, as far as possible, discrimination against persons on the ground of disability in the areas of ... education ... ; and

(b) to ensure, as far as practicable, that persons with disabilities have the same rights to equality before the law as the rest of the community; and

(c) to promote recognition and acceptance within the community of the principle that persons with disabilities have the same fundamental rights as the rest of the community.[6]

The 1992 Act conforms in general terms with the other Commonwealth laws against unlawful discrimination on the grounds of sex and race in areas of public life including education. The Act declares that it is unlawful for an educational authority to discriminate on the ground of disability in the enrollment, treatment, exclusion, or expulsion of a student with a disability or to subject a student to a detriment in education. The Act provides that it is unlawful to refuse or fail to accept a person's application for admission as a student or in the terms or conditions on which it is prepared to admit the person as a student; by denying the student access, or limiting the student's access, to any benefit provided by the educational authority; or by expelling the student; or by subjecting the student to any other detriment.[7]

---

[4] Disability Discrimination Act (1992) (Cth) governs all educational authorities. Complaints may be made by Australians from any State or Territory jurisdiction. Each State and Territory also has its own legislation, but in some jurisdictions, complaints may be limited to government sector schools (eg under Anti-Discrimination Act 1977 (NSW).
[5] See M. Conley Tyler "The Disability Discrimination Act 1992: Genesis, Drafting and Prospects" (1993) 19, 1 Melbourne Univ. L. Rev. 211-228.
[6] Section 3 (a) to (c). Disability Discrimination Act (1992) (Cth).
[7] Section 22 Disability Discrimination Act (1992) (Cth).

At the same time, in recognition that students with disabilities may require services or facilities which are not required by able students, the Act introduces the concept of unjustifiable hardship to balance the notion that educational authorities are required to make reasonable accommodation for students' disabilities, providing:

This section does not render it unlawful to refuse or fail to accept a person's application for admission as a student at an educational institution where the person, if admitted as a student by the educational authority, would require services or facilities that are not required by students who do not have a disability and the provision of which would impose unjustifiable hardship on the educational authority.[8]

Unlike American statutes, discrimination is statutorily defined in Australian law as including both direct (disparate treatment) and indirect (disparate impact) discrimination. These definitions have proved difficult to interpret as some judges have criticized them as "highly complex and artificial."[9] According to the statute, direct discrimination[10] occurs when:

> . . . a person ("discriminator") discriminates against another person ("aggrieved person") on the ground of a disability of the aggrieved person if, because of the aggrieved person's disability, the discriminator treats or proposes to treat the aggrieved person less favourably than, in circumstances that are the same or are not materially different, the discriminator treats or would treat a person without the disability.[11]

Indirect discrimination[12] occurs when:

> . . . a person ("discriminator") discriminates against another person ("aggrieved person") on the ground of a disability of the aggrieved person if the discriminator requires the aggrieved person to comply with a requirement or condition :
>
> (a) with which a substantially higher proportion of persons without the disability comply or are able to comply; and
>
> (b) which is not reasonable having regard to the circumstances of the case; and
>
> (c) with which the aggrieved person does not or is not able to comply.

---

[8] Section 22 (4).
[9] See IW v City of Perth (1997) 71 ALJR 943 per Brennan CJ and McHugh J.
[10] Section 5.
[11] Significantly, in Australia the burden of proof remains on the complainant ("aggrieved person") throughout the litigation process.
[12] Section 6.

In relation to the proof of "unjustifiable hardship" the Commonwealth Act provides:[13]

> For the purposes of this Act, in determining what constitutes
> unjustifiable hardship, all relevant circumstances of the par
> ticular case are to be taken into account including:
>
> (a) the nature of the benefit or detriment likely to accrue or
> be suffered by any persons concerned; and
>
> (b) the effect of the disability of a person concerned; and
>
> (c) the financial circumstances and the estimated amount
> of expenditure required to be made by the person claiming
> unjustifiable hardship; ...

Under the Commonwealth and most State statutes, disability is defined
extremely broadly and includes a total or partial loss of the person's bodily
or mental functions as well as the presence in the body of organisms capable
of causing disease, designed to protect among others, students who are
HIV positive. The definition also covers disabilities which cause persons to
learn differently from others.[14]

Case Law

Finney v Hills Grammar School;[15] Hills Grammar School v Finney[16]

Few discrimination complaints in Australia proceed beyond a tribunal
hearing to the superior courts. Where they do so, this is the result of an
unsuccessful conciliation process which is compulsory under Australian
anti-discrimination statutes. *Finney* is an exception and provides important
contemporary guidance on the application of disability discrimination legislation to enrollment processes. In *Finney*, a dispute which significantly
concerned complaints of unlawful discrimination against a private sector
school, the school officials appealed against a decision of the Human Rights
and Equal Opportunity Commission to the Federal Court of Australia.[17] The

---

[13] Section 11.
[14] Section 4 Disability Discrimination Act (1992) (Cth).
[15] Human Rights and Equal Opportunity Commission No H 98/60.
[16] Human Rights and Equal Opportunity Commission No H 98/60; Hills
Grammar School v Human Rights and Equal Opportunity Commission [2000]
FCA 658.
[17] The complaint of discrimination in Finney was made under the
Commonwealth disability discrimination statute. This choice of jurisdiction
was required as the state anti-discrimination statute was expressed not to apply
on this ground to "private educational authorities." This is a significant
anomaly in New South Wales law which is not reflected in all state statutes.

legal issues arose from the refusal of school officials to enroll the complainant, Scarlett Finney, and their claim that accommodating her disability would
have caused an unjustifiable hardship.

There was no issue that the child was a person with a disability. Scarlett
Finney was born in 1992 and her parents sought to enroll her in 1997 in the
kindergarten section of a school situated in suburban Sydney. In their letter
of application, the parents indicated that since their daughter had spina
bifida, she required a school with physical arrangements adequate to meet
her needs including level walkways and wheel chair accessibility.

The school held an interview with the parents and Scarlett. Some months
later, school officials informed the parents that they could not offer Scarlett
a place in the kindergarten class for 1998 based on their belief that the school
could not meet her "special needs." A letter from the officials indicated that
they did not have adequate resources to look after Scarlett in the manner
that she required and in a way that was suitable for her needs. The refusal
led Scarlett's parents to file a complaint with the Human Rights and Equal
Opportunity Commission claiming unlawful discrimination on the ground of
disability. At the hearing, during the latter part of 1999, the parties accepted
that the actions of school officials constituted direct discrimination. Even
so, the officials sought to justify their discriminatory behavior through reliance on the provisions of section 22(4), maintaining that the accommodation
of Scarlett's needs would have amounted to an "unjustifiable hardship."

The school's argument of justifiable hardship was premised on the fact
that Scarlett would be likely to spend her whole school career of thirteen
years at Hills Grammar, including kindergarten, primary, and secondary education and that the need to accommodate her would extend over that period.
The parents presented counter evidence that they and Scarlett were attracted and heartened by the fact that the school's prospectus contained a
statement that it admitted persons with disabilities. The parents also indicated that on account of their religious beliefs, there were few private schools
in the area to which they would send their daughter. Importantly, the evidence given to the Tribunal by Scarlett's parents indicated that she required
little in the way of support and that she was an independent child even to
the extent of being able to walk, albeit with some difficulty. In addition,
Scarlett was able to attend to her own toileting although due to a level of
incontinence she did require catheterization that could be carried out by a
visiting nurse or a school aide. This evidence was supported by evidence
from teachers at her local government school which indicated that Scarlett's
special needs were not extensive.

The school's approach to the issue of the assessing Scarlett prior to
enrollment was particularly inept, being heavily reliant upon stereotyping of
persons with spina bifida and without an independent assessment of her

actual needs. For example, school officials expressed grave concerns to the parents about how Scarlett would fit in. In particular, one of the major concerns was a need for assistance with toileting. The parents consistently informed school authorities that a nurse, parents, or family friends would be available to assist in this function. Another concern expressed by school authorities related to mobility problems and how Scarlett would manage to move around the school. Officials also argued that it would be necessary to get the approval of the School Board as well as the staff who would be teaching Scarlett.

In giving his evidence, the school principal relied heavily on financial evidence of school debt levels, the percentage of government funding, and school fees to underscore the unjustifiable hardship claim. The principal testified that the school had a debt of just over $5m and that the interest was subsidized by Commonwealth government grants to around 35% with the remainder being subsidized by parents. The principal further indicated that the school had enrolled students with a range of physical and intellectual disabilities and that appropriate teacher training and modified curriculum arrangements in addition to specialist visits were made in order to meet their needs. However, the school had never enrolled a student with spina bifida. The principal reported that teachers trained and willing to accept the additional responsibility for someone with spina bifida, special toilet facilities, accessibility to areas of the school, a full-time special integration aide, special transport on occasions such as school excursions, and modifications to the curriculum and school buildings would all be required.

In reaching his judgment, the Hearing Commissioner in the Human Rights and Equal Opportunity Commission made the following findings of fact from the extensive evidence: the teachers at the school were willing to accept responsibility of teaching and supervising Scarlett; only minimal additional training for the teaching staff would be required; catheterization would be needed only once a day and could be performed by a Community nurse; further, it was likely that Scarlett would be able to catheterise herself in the future; there would be no need for a new toilet to be built; there was likely no need for a full-time integration aide and the two aides currently in the school could assist her; there was no evidence that she had an intellectual disability and so did not need any assistance; adequate assistance could be provided for Scarlett around the school, in classrooms, and on excursions; only minimal curriculum changes would be needed; government funding was available to assist the school in accommodating her needs; although the school had a debt it could still utilize surplus operating funds to modify the school or employ additional staff; while the estimate of $1m to modify the school was accurate, Scarlett did not, in fact, require the modifications argued by the school.

As a matter of law, the Hearing Commissioner found that the complainant proved direct discrimination by the school in terms of the Disability Discrimination Act. With specific reference to the unjustifiable hardship defense argued by the school, the Commissioner noted:

> . . . the concept of hardship connotes much more than just hardship on the respondent. The Objects of the Act make it clear that elimination of discrimination as far as possible is the legislation's purpose. Considered in this context, it is reasonable to expect that the school should have to accept some hardship in accepting Scarlett's enrollment. It is clear from the evidence that this would have occurred, as Scarlett required services and facilities not required by other students. The nub of the issue is whether such hardship was unjustifiable . . . . I find the defence of unjustifiable hardship has not been made out by the school . . . . In making this finding I do not accept many of the conclusions which the School drew in the process of making its decision.[18]

The school sought judicial review in the Federal Court of Australia on the ground that the Commissioner misinterpreted relevant sections of the Disability Discrimination Act and made "other errors of fact and law which led to an improper exercise of the power conferred on the Commission."[19] Tamberlin, J., rejected the school's appeal in writing:

> I am satisfied that no reviewable error of law or principle is shown in the reasons for decision of the Commissioner . . . . The decision canvassed the essential issues, carefully setting out the competing considerations, and disclosed the application of the weighing process involved in reaching the Commission's conclusion.
>
> The reliance of school authorities on the unjustifiable hardship defense brought into focus the balancing which the legislation requires between the rights and interests of the individuals and groups involved in the complaint. As indicated above, this required the Commissioner to consider:
>
> (a) the nature of the benefit or detriment likely to accrue or be suffered by any persons concerned;
>
> (b) the effect of the disability of a person concerned; and
>
> (c) the financial circumstances and the estimated amount of expenditure required to be made by the person claiming unjustifiable hardship.

---

[18] Human Rights and Equal Opportunity Commission No H98/60 at p.40.
[19] Hills Grammar Sch. v. Human Rights and Equal Opportunity Comm'n N794 of 1999 at p.2.

In *Finney*, the following issues were comprehensively addressed and the judgment was not disturbed on appeal. As to Scarlett Finney, the school provided opportunities not available at the government school which she attended after the refusal of enrollment at Hills Grammar School. Further, the multidisciplinary approach at the private school would enhance the management skills required by Scarlett in operating within the timetable of multiple teachers and classroom environments. As to Scarlett's family, her attendance at Hills Grammar School would see a reduction in daily travelling time to and from school as well as the advantages offered by a non-denominational education in an independent school setting. As to the school, the changes required to accommodate Scarlett would improve the school for all students as would the additional funding and teacher training. Further, the quality of life of the community is enhanced by the inclusion of all members of society.

A significant issue was the costs to the school that were to be incurred in the involvement of extra staff, teacher training, and modifications to buildings to widen some doorways and to modify an existing toilet block. The Hearing Commissioner held that the principal and others in the school not only had stereotypical attitudes in respect of Scarlett but allowed these to influence their decision to reject her application for enrollment. In particular, he decided that the principal overgeneralized the characteristics of a person with spina bifida to the extent of arguing from a worst case scenario that included the construction of lifts and pathways as well as widening doorways and providing toilets in every block of buildings. The Commissioner was also critical of the lack of expert information in the school's submission. He pointed out that Scarlett did not receive a formal educational assessment and no expert was approached for advice or information regarding her needs. The Commissioner added that the principal negatively prejudged her educational requirements and then exaggerated these to give credibility to the refusal to enroll Scarlett.

On the basis of the detailed findings in the hearing which were not overturned on appeal, it may be argued that the school failed precisely because it lacked adequate processes to assess students with disabilities individually in order to determine Scarlett's actual needs, accommodations and hardships. The principal and his staff might have negotiated on a more open basis with Scarlett's parents, sought expert advice from guidance officers, physiotherapists and occupational therapists comprehensively to assess Scarlett's needs. The case demonstrates clearly that the assertion of unjustifiable hardship by institutions is subject to the forensic scrutiny of the courts and may be difficult of proof.

Hoggan v State of New South Wales[20]

Unlike *Finney*, Daniel Hoggan's complaint against a state government educational authority concerned discrimination on the ground of disability in the context of suspension and expulsion. Like *Finney*, the complainant was successful in establishing unlawful direct discrimination on the ground of disability. *Hoggan* has a complex factual background. In his opinion, the hearing Commissioner referred in detail to a range international human rights principles underpinning anti-discrimination legislation and to case law from other common law jurisdictions, including Canada and the United States, undoubtedly reflecting the continuing globalization of law, especially in the broad area of human rights. In essence, Daniel's case highlights attitudes, assessment, and due process in relation to suspension and expulsion of students with disabilities.

Daniel Hoggan, who was born in December, 1984, suffered a brain injury at seven months of age. Due to his injuries, Daniel has epilepsy, impaired vision, and some intellectual disability. He also became prone to behavioral disorders that manifested themselves as flares of temper and aggression. Daniel commenced school in 1990 in a special education setting attached to a government school in New South Wales; he attended school there for four years. At the start of 1994, Daniel's guardians, Mr. and Mrs. Purvis, wished to have him educated in a "non-segregated setting." Yet, Daniel was not placed in another government school on a part-time basis until November and was enrolled full-time from the beginning of the school year in 1996.

During the second half of 1996 Mr. Purvis attempted to enroll Daniel for 1997. The school did not automatically accept the application. After a series of case meetings that did not involve either of his guardians, the school integration committee that was formed to assess Daniel's application for enrollment, decided not to support it. At a meeting with his guardians, school officials raised a number of obstacles to Daniel's enrollment and suggested that he re-enroll in the special education setting. Despite the arguments of his guardians that Daniel would receive a more appropriate education in a non-segregated classroom setting, the principal informed them that their application was declined.

In December, 1996, after an appeal to the principal was also declined, Mr. and Mrs. Purvis lodged a complaint with the Human Rights and Equal Opportunity Commission.[21] At that same time, the Superintendent for the school district wrote to Daniel's guardians indicating that it had not com-

---

[20] Alex Purvis on behalf of Daniel Hoggan v The State of New South Wales (Department of Education) (unreported) HREOC No.98/127, Nov. 2000. See M Keeffe-Martin (2000) 5, 2 Australia and New Zealand J.l of L. and Educ. 74.
[21] Unlike Finney, Hoggan might have been resolved under state anti-discrimination legislation which applies to public educational authorities.

plied with the Department of Education's policy on enrollment of children with disabilities. As a result, in January, 1997 a conciliation meeting was arranged by the Disability Discrimination Commissioner between Daniel's guardians, the school, and Education Department representatives. The parties agreed that the school would reassess Daniel's application.

After further meetings including that of a reconstituted school integration committee, the parties agreed that Daniel would attend the school for a one-day trial in to assess his needs more comprehensively. At staff and union meetings at the school there was strong support to reject Daniel's application. Teachers were of the view that inclusion of Daniel was not appropriate and that his education needs should be met in a special education unit at another school. By this time, the matter of Daniel's integration had clearly become an issue of industrial significance. Despite opposition, the principal accepted the application and began preparation for Daniel's attendance, including the construction of a special toilet and bathroom. He also undertook several further tasks to facilitate Daniel's integration, including the appointment of a school case management committee, seeking funding to provide for a teacher's aide and for a casual support teacher to assist Daniel, and preparation of a statement of the difficulties associated with Daniel's integration at the school. The difficulties encompassed the fact that there was no formal assessment of Daniel's motor skills or his level of visual impairment. This caused the principal to have concerns for Daniel's safety in participating in what might loosely be termed the more hazardous curriculum subject areas such as science and sport.

Daniel eventually started school in April, 1997 but was suspended for one day sixteen days later for violence against staff. At a subsequent case management meeting, it was pointed out that the effect on other children and staff of Daniel's presence varied from class to class. It was also noted that there had been difficulty in getting appropriate learning materials, from the Distance Education section of the New South Wales Department of Education. It became evident that Daniel was becoming socially isolated in the playground.

One month later Daniel was again suspended from school, this time for two days, for kicking a fellow student and for vocally abusing his teacher's aide. Through May, June, and July, Daniel became increasingly vocally abusive and physically aggressive with other students and staff. He was again suspended for two days on 30 July. His behavior continued to deteriorate and he was suspended for thirteen days, later reduced to seven days, in early September for kicking another student and again on 18 September for twelve school days for punching a teacher in the back. Apart from a one day trial, Daniel did not return to school after September 1997.

During the period of his attendance at the school it is reported that the principal spent, on average, "7 hours per week in providing the structure and strategies to support Daniel's education at this school."[22] The school, in collaboration with the District Education Office, prepared a number of options including studying at home through distance education but continued to argue strongly for the need to have Daniel enrolled in the special education setting at another local school. In November, the teachers' union conducted another meeting at which a motion rejecting Daniel's enrollment at the school on the grounds of safety and his special needs was passed. At this meeting staff argued that Daniel must enroll at the Special School where teachers and resources more suited to his educational requirements were available. The results of the staff meetings might lead to serious questions about its commitment to inclusion.

Three major Education Department policies and a School policy were relevant to Daniel's case: the statewide Special Education Policy which advocates inclusion of students with disabilities; the Student Welfare Policy and the Procedures Concerning Suspension, Exclusion and Expulsion of Students from School; and the School Discipline Policy which had been modified in order to meet Daniel's specific disabilities, especially his behavioural difficulties. [23]

The ultimate decision to exclude Daniel from school occurred after extensive consultations between educational authorities. What is notable about this process was the regular exclusion of Daniel's guardians from the discussions about his welfare. Daniel's guardians maintained their view that integration was the best solution for Daniel and appealed the exclusion decision to the New South Wales Assistant Director General for Education. This appeal was rejected with the provision that alternative arrangements for Daniel would be negotiated.

In early March, 1998 Daniel's guardians lodged a second complaint of discrimination on his behalf with the Human Rights and Equal Opportunity Commission. The basis of the complaint was that Daniel's suspensions, his exclusion, and his treatment while at the High School constituted less favourable treatment pursuant to sections 5 and 22 of the Commonwealth Disability Discrimination Act.[24]

At his hearing, Commissioner Innes held that Daniel was a person with a disability within the terms of section 4 of the Act. The particular disabilities were identified as:

(a) an intellectual disability that manifests in unusual individual man

---

[22] HREOC No. 98/127, Nov. 2000 at 22.

[23] Id. at 27

[24] Id. at 51.

nerisms and disturbed behaviour such as rocking, humming, swear
ing, and at times aggressive behaviour such as hitting or kicking;

(b) an intellectual disability that affects Daniel's thought processes,
perception of reality, emotions, and results in disturbed behaviour;

(c) an intellectual disability which results in Daniel learning differently
from a person without the intellectual disability;

(d) a visual disability;

(e) epilepsy; and

(e) a past disability, namely severe encephalopathic illness.

This list highlights the breadth of the definition of disability contained
in Australian legislation.

Importantly for the finding of unlawful discrimination, the Commissioner
ruled that even though Daniel's medical reports were on file at the school
and available to those concerned, the principal and teaching staff lacked an
understanding of his various disabilities. As Commissioner Innes stated,
"staff at [the school] had a very poor knowledge of the nature of Daniel's
disabilities and the implications of those disabilities. This lack of understanding is a fundamental issue in this case."[25] He was of the view that
although there was considerable information available on Daniel's condition at the time of his first application for enrollment, the principal should
have sought further and more detailed professional advice in order to more
fully understand his impairments. Moreover, the imprecise information and
processes involved were seen to have negatively influenced the second
application for enrollment. As the Commissioner noted, "both Daniel and
the staff . . . would have benefited if a valid means of assessment had been
found, as it would have provided a benchmark from which progress could
have been gauged."[26] This statement has echoes of *Finney* in which stereotyping took the place of actual knowledge in the school's assessment of the
student's needs.

The issue of staff preparedness is of fundamental importance in implementing inclusion policies. In relation to teacher preparation at Daniel's
school, the hearing Commissioner acknowledged that only some staff had
taken advantage of the opportunity to receive training prior to his enrollment. There was evidence that staff who were connected with Daniel's
program attended a single session of a one day staff training program. Yet,
the focus of that training was on providing information concerning the nature of Daniel's disabilities rather than of reasonable accommodation in the
mainstream educational setting. Despite this inauspicious background to

---

[25] HREOC No. 98/127, Nov. 2000 at 53-54.
[26] Id. at 54.

Daniel's enrollment at the school, the Commissioner decided that Daniel did appear to have benefitted educationally from the experience and that the "activities he carried out (although at a very different level) were following the thrust of the curriculum."[27] As to Daniel's social interaction, the Commissioner was satisfied that a measure of social integration had commenced during his time at school. Significantly, there was a finding that the special education setting promoted by the teachers and the school would not have provided a superior educational or social environment for the complainant.

In addressing the legal issues, the Commissioner accepted the fundamental truth of the complainant's argument that "the objectives of the [Disability Discrimination] Act are to promote equality of opportunity for people with disabilities."[28] The Commissioner also noted that "in the context of education, avoiding discrimination on the grounds of disability means that children with disabilities should have access to mainstream regular schools. It is accepted that segregation is discriminatory."[29] The Commissioner further indicated that while mainstreaming was not an issue in the present case, comments from a previous tribunal[30] supported the proposition that "in the area of disability the principle of mainstreaming is generally accepted" and that it "represents a clear rejection of the practice of exclusion which has historically characterised policy approaches towards disability."[31]

The Commissioner confirmed that subjective intent to discriminate is not an element of proof of direct discrimination under Australian law. Thus, proof of subjective knowledge of Daniel's impairments on the part of staff was unnecessary. As to the causation element of proof, the Commissioner made a significant assertion that "Daniel's behaviour occurs as a result of his disability [and that his] behavior is so closely connected to his disability that if I find that less favourable treatment has occurred on the ground of Daniel's behavior then this will amount to discrimination on the ground of his disability."[32] Based on the evidence, the Commissioner ruled in favor of the complainant that "it is clear that Daniel's exclusion from [the school] was on the ground of his disability."[33] According to the Commissioner, the school's acts, including the expulsion, while arguably in Daniel's best interests, still amounted to less favorable treatment in breach of sections 5 and 22 (2) of the Disability Discrimination Act. The comparator chosen by the Commissioner in considering less favorable treatment was a student with-

---

27 Id. at 57.
28 Id. at 74.
29 Id.
30 Dalla Costa v The ACT Department of Health (1994) EOC 92-633.
31 Supra, note 19 at 74.
32 Id. at 77.
33 Id. at 83.

out Daniel's disabilities in the same year level at his school; this evidence revealed that no student in this category suffered expulsion.

The Commissioner addressed the role of the significant people in Daniel's life in stating that his guardians had not taken responsibility for his comprehensive assessment at the time of enrollment. This responsibility related directly to the guardians' desire to pursue inclusive education for Daniel. Further, the Commissioner did not uphold a complaint concerning an effective orientation programme for Daniel at the school. However, the Commissioner was convinced that the Education Department's failure to adjust its Welfare and Discipline policy to accommodate Daniel's particular needs amounted to a detriment in contravention of the Act. The Commissioner commented on the inflexibility of the policy under which Daniel was ultimately excluded from school as contributing to the discrimination which he experienced."[34]

In relation to standard of teaching, the Commissioner observed that, in practice, Daniel was taught mainly by teacher's aides, reflecting directly on the evidence presented about the attitudes of staff to inclusion at the school. As such, the Commissioner determined that this differential standard of teaching constituted a detriment. Moreover, as the school had made only limited efforts to make training available to Daniel's teachers, this constituted a detriment under section 22 of the Act as was the failure of the school, and particularly the principal, to seek assistance of experts in special education or behavior.[35] Additionally, the Commissioner reasoned that the school's failure to follow Departmental exclusion policy resulted in further detriment to Daniel as he had received no formal school after expulsion. In his concluding remarks, Commissioner Innes commented that this

> ...was an example of the long and arduous route which people must travel to obtain redress for discrimination against them. It reinforces the need, particularly in the area of disability discrimination complaints, to find broader solutions to policy and systemic issues than the individual private inquiry process. The case is also unfortunate in that whilst many people . . . made genuine and unstinting efforts to make Daniel's placement . . . a success, it was unsuccessful. In the main this lack of success was not due to lack of commitment, but to misguided decisions based on inflexibility and a lack of specialist information.[36]

This statement is highly instructive for those who would implement inclusion policies, especially for students with behavioral disabilities. Inclu-

---

[34] Id. at 87.
[35] Id. at 88.
[36] Id. at 96

sion, in practice, relies critically upon flexibility and knowledge of the needs of the individual students as well as individual and institutional commitment to inclusion or integration.

I. v. O'Rourke and Corinda State High School and Minister for Education for Queensland[37]

In the final case, *I. v. O'Rourke and Corinda State High School and Minister for Education for Queensland*, the Queensland Anti-discrimination Tribunal uncovered a violation of the State's anti-discrimination legislation.[38] As identified earlier, there is considerable similarity between the drafting of State and Commonwealth anti-discrimination statutes. The main purpose of the Queensland Act is to "promote equality of opportunity for everyone by protecting them from unfair discrimination in certain areas of activity, including work, education and accommodation."[39] As is the case of all Australian anti-discrimination statutes, exemptions are included which constrain the operation of the statutes.[40] Unlike Commonwealth legislative initiatives which address one ground of discrimination only, State and Territorial statutes tend to cover a range of grounds or attributes of discrimination. In Queensland, the Anti-Discrimination Act provides protection on the basis of thirteen grounds,[41] which include disability (called "impairment"). Of the areas of prohibition, education is included along with employment and the provision of goods and services.[42] Both direct and indirect discrimination are prohibited.[43] The statute provides that a person's motive for discriminating is irrelevant.[44]

"I's" case involved three complaints, two which unsuccessfully charged unlawful indirect discrimination. A third, successful, complaint alleged unlawful direct discrimination. In essence, the case considered the practical issues associated with schools achieving the legislative requirements for reasonable accommodation of students' disabilities, including physical and intellectual impairments. In addition, it should be noted that the school, in responding to "I's" complaints, addressed the needs of students with various impairments for many years as officials acquired considerable experience managing the needs of students in wheel chairs.

---

[37] I v. O'Rourke and Corinda State High School and Minister for Education for Queensland [2001] Queensland Anti-Discrimination Tribunal 1 (QADT) (31 January 2001).
[38] Anti-Discrimination Act 1991(Qld)
[39] Id. § 6. (1)
[40] Id. Parts 4 and 5.
[41] Id. § 7(1).
[42] Id. § 37.
[43] Id. § 9.
[44] Id. § 10 (3)

The complainant "I" was born with multiple disabilities in October, 1979. She has spastic quadriplegia, a severe intellectual disability, lacked independent mobility, and requires a wheelchair and assistance for toileting and eating. Although there were suggestions at the hearing of earlier complaints, "I" was in her final year at the government secondary school when the alleged acts of discrimination occurred.

As part of her school studies at Corinda High School, "I" was enrolled in the subject, Tourism, which required students to undertake an excursion to a tourist destination. The school refused to permit "I" to attend a one-day excursion to an island resort (Tangalooma) off of the coast from Brisbane. The school arranged an alternative excursion to a local shopping center for "I" and other students who, for a variety of reasons, were not able to attend the excursion to the island resort.

School officials imotially informed "I's" parents that she would be able to attend the excursion. However, the situation changed after the school had investigated the arrangements for boarding and alighting from the vessel, The Tangalooma Flyer, the normal means of transport to the island. The school's investigations indicated that "I" would have to be lifted aboard the vessel by means of a forklift and the ship's management would not be responsible for any mishap. Alternative means of transportation for "I" were also considered. One option was to take another vessel to the island; this was rejected as unsatisfactory since it landed some distance away from the resort, would have involved transporting "I" across a considerable distance of rough terrain in a four wheel drive vehicle, and would have reached the resort well after the start of the program. The other major alternative was hiring a helicopter; the school rejected this as too expensive. Significantly, "I's" parents were not given an opportunity to consider this transportation option.

In considering "I's" complaint of direct discrimination on the ground of impairment, the Queensland Anti-Discrimination Tribunal found that she had experienced "less favorable treatment." In reaching this result of unlawful discrimination, the President of the Anti-Discrimination Tribunal considered the position of comparable students. Evidence indicated that students in wheel chairs in the tourism class had undertaken the excursion to Tangalooma in previous years. Moreover, the President noted that the school had adduced insufficient expert evidence in support of its argument for a high level of concern over potential risks to the health of the complainant undertaking the excursion.[45]

The underlying facts concerning allegations of indirect discrimination arose from attendance at two formal school events. The first concerned a

---

[45] Id. at 20-21.

school senior ball. Dance is a very popular extra-curricular offering at the school and the annual ball is a well-attended event by all students, including those in wheel chairs. About three hundred students attend the ball each year. The second event where indirect discrimination was alleged was the annual graduation dinner. On both occasions, "I's" parents expressed their concern and opposition to the venues which the school had selected. Their concerns were associated with wheel chair access, availability of suitable toilets, and the privacy associated with toileting. In relation to both events, the school appointed a committee of staff to examine potential venues. The principal specified criteria in respect of choice of venue as requiring a capacity for at least 300 people on the dance floor; needing to be more attractive than the school hall; being available on a Saturday evening; having indoor toilets so as to ensure privacy, security, and no access to alcohol; being reasonably inexpensive; and having access for people with disabilities.

The school committee identified a range of possible venues that were inadequate in one or more of the criteria established by the principal. The result was that acceptable venues used in previous years were selected for the dance and the dinner. The school dance took place at a local club which had limited wheel chair access. In order to overcome this problem and to meet the concerns of the complainant's parents, the school purchased a "stair climber for power wheel chairs" and used it successfully. In addition, two staff members looked after "I" at the dance, helping her with toileting and eating. Even so, her parents alleged that "I" was treated differently from other students, claiming that the use of the stair climber was neither a dignified nor a safe means of accessing the club.

The school's formal graduation dinner took place on a converted barge on the Brisbane River. "I's" parents were concerned about the choice of this venue as it had difficult ramp access and lacked privacy in toilets for people in wheel chairs. The parents were also concerned about the safety of their daughter in the event of an accident on board. In this instance, a member of the ship's crew, specially trained in shipboard safety was assigned to assist in looking after "I" during boarding and was to be on hand in case of a safety emergency. The problem of privacy of toileting was overcome by having senior students at the school make a portable toilet and appropriate screens. The problem of access was met by the school's purchasing two ramps that were used successfully to assist "I" in gaining safe access to the boat.

In rejecting the claim of unlawful indirect discrimination in relation to the dance at the club or the dinner aboard ship, the President of the Anti-Discrimination Tribunal considered the issue of unjustifiable hardship to the school in the provision of alternative venues for "I:"

> . . . The respondents (the school and its representatives) are not the owners of the venues and therefore are not in a position to

install the special facilities. The only alternative for the respondent were (sic) to arrange the formal functions at venues which would be at considerable cost and disruption to all of the other students. The evidence demonstrates . . . [that the school is] constantly on the lookout for more suitable venues but these have not been found to date. In weighing up the benefit to the complainant against the detriment to the respondent and all others concerned in relation to the school formal/ball and the graduation dinner I am of the view that the supplying of special services and facilities would impose unjustifiable hardship on the respondents.[46]

"I's" case highlights the serious tension which may arise when the perspectives of parents and the policies and practices of school authorities do not coincide completely. This tension is also demonstrated *Hoggan*. The resolution of the complaints of indirect discrimination against Corinda High School by the Queensland Tribunal demonstrates that in considering efforts at reasonable accommodation, a court will not demand that a school find a venue solely on the basis on the needs of a student with a disability. The range of criteria established by the principal, which included wheelchair access, addressed a range of needs and interests. The court's role in disability discrimination cases always involves a delicate balancing of the rights and interests of the parties by reference to the statutorily-defined criteria. This difficult work was aided in "I's" case by the clear evidence adduced by the school of its policies, practices, and identification of students needs, evidence which was not forthcoming in *Hoggan* and *Finney*.

Conclusion

In Australia, anti-discrimination legislation at the Commonwealth, State, and Territorial levels is being used increasingly to ensure the rights of children with disabilities are both recognized and protected. Current educational practice for disabled children, wherever feasible and consistent with their best interests, is to include them in mainstream schooling settings. However, as *Finney, Hoggan*, and *"I"* amply demonstrate, there are still great difficulties in making equal educational opportunities a reality for many children with impairments. Equal opportunity means providing choices and it is certain that Australian tribunals will continue to reject educational policies, procedures, and practices that are in any way exclusionary or do not provide students with the opportunities enjoyed by their non-disabled peers.

---

[46] Id. at 33.

CANADA

Anwar (Andy) N. Khan

Introduction

This year's chapter deals with some important questions to which the judiciary, particularly the Supreme Court of Canada, have provided definitive answers. The issues have arisen in Constitutional Law, Administrative Law, Collective Bargaining Law, and Criminal Law.

Constitutional Law

In last Year's chapter, this author wondered whether, in the new century, provincial governments would enjoy legislative autonomy, particularly over funding of education, so that the perception that the public or separate school boards may have had that they, and not the provincial government, enjoy reasonable autonomy can be settled. The author also wondered whether the focus will be on educational equality and equity, in particular, secular, non-discriminatory and non-denominational morality and ethics in schools; and whether there is any justification for public funding of only Roman Catholic or Protestant schools. Over the past year the Supreme Court of Canada provided definite answers.

The Supreme Court of Canada cannot rewrite the Constitution. Even so, the Court's powers of interpretation are wide enough to give new meanings to old phraseology. Insofar as section 93 of the Constitution Act 1867 protects denominational schools, absent its amendment or abolition, the Supreme Court's discretion of interpretation can only go up to a certain limit. Under this section, each province has exclusive jurisdiction to legislate with respect to education; it also cannot prejudicially affect rights or privileges affecting denominational schools enjoyed by a particular class of persons by law in effect at the time of Confederation in 1867.

The basic principles of section 93, ruled to the Supreme Court of Canada, "are religious freedom and equitable treatment. This approach recognizes that provinces may alter their education systems but prevents an expansion of the original purpose of section 93. The rights guaranteed by section 93 do not replicate the law of 1867 verbatim."[1] In two cases, the Court laid down the foundations of provincial autonomy to be applied during the new cen-

---

[1] Ontario English Catholic Teachers' Ass'n v. Ontario (Attorney General) [2001] SCC 15. Hereunder referred to as The Ontario Case.

tury. This section analyzes these developments and superior court cases dealing with constitutional matters.

Education and the Constitution

The constitutional demarcation of educational functions in the provinces means that Canadian law may seem peculiar. To some extent that is true. As the Supreme Court of Canada has cogently observed, "[i]n many countries, education issues are matters of public policy, to be decided by democratic debate. In Canada, we are in the rather unusual position of having certain education rights constitutionally entrenched in s. 93 of the Constitution Act 1867. This state of affairs is the product of our history, stemming from what this Court has referred to as 'a solemn pact resulting from the bargaining which made Confederation possible.'"[2]

Provincial Parliamentary Control and Funding of Schools

The perplexing question whether, under the Canadian Constitution, school boards enjoy reasonable autonomy from provincial control, especially over funding, has been answered by the Supreme Court of Canada in two land mark decisions: *Public School Boards' Association of Alberta v Alberta (Attorney General)*[3], and *The Ontario English Catholic Teachers' Association Ontario (Attorney General)*. [4]

The Alberta Case arose out of provincial legislative amendments which centralized funding and gave more financial powers and discretion to the provincial government. Prior to enacting the amendments, education in Alberta had dual funding sources: both the provincial government and local education boards funded secondary and primary education.

On review from the Alberta Court of Appeal, the Supreme Court of Canada was asked to evaluate the constitutionality of Alberta's legislative amendments that introduced a new school funding scheme. Under the new funding formulae, the provincial government was enabled to centralize the control and funding of primary and secondary education by pooling all revenues distributing them to school boards in a provincial-wide per-student amount multiplied by the number of students enrolled in each board's jurisdiction. Only separate denominational school boards could opt out of the fund and continue to requisition taxes directly from ratepayers. However, denominational schools could not retain an amount less than or greater than the allotment they would have received from the fund. Further, if a

---

[2] Iacobucci, J., in The Ontario Case, Id.
[3] [2000] 2 SCR 409. Hereunder referred to as The Alberta Case.
[4] *Supra*, Note 1.

board opts out and has a surplus, it was to be returned to the fund. In short, the new scheme imposed spending restrictions on school boards by strengthening ministerial control over school board senior staff and created the Alberta School Foundation Fund. The main aim, as the courts recognized, was a cost-cutting measure to reduce overall funding to education and to address discrepancies in school resources. The public school boards claimed that since separate school boards could opt out of the scheme, while they could not, this was discriminatory.

The school boards and their associations challenged the constitutionality of the scheme based mainly on their claim that they had a constitutional right to reasonable autonomy. They also charged that they were discriminated against by the new legislative scheme and, as the constitution guarantees equivalent rights to public and separate school boards, the new scheme violated the constitutional mirror of equality.

The Supreme Court rejected the boards' allegation that they had constitutional reasonable autonomy because they are a form of municipal institution that are delegates of provincial constitutional jurisdiction. The Court also decided that the amendments were fair and non-discriminatory.

In the author's opinion, two things become clear from the unanimous judgment in this case. First, while the Supreme Court cannot rewrite the Canadian Constitution, it has confirmed the gradual and incremental erosion by provincial governments of the perceived autonomy of school boards, so that in the Twenty-First Century their full autonomy cannot be sustained. Second, while the special status of separate schools may shield them from a good deal of provincial interference, public schools have nowhere to hide. This means that the case will encourage provinces to further reduce school boards' independence. The Director of the Public School Boards' Association of Alberta was reported to have commented that the provinces would continue down a road that could lead to the dismantling of local boards.

If further evidence was needed that the Supreme Court was on the side of Provincial Parliaments and not school boards, it came in The Ontario Case where the question was whether provincial legislation that created a new governance and funding model for all school boards was constitutional. This legislation was passed in part to address a disparity of revenues between boards by allocating funds on a per-pupil basis, including the removal of their ability to set property tax rates for education while centralizing taxation powers in the hands of the Minister of Finance.

The Supreme Court upheld the legislation as constitutional on the basis that it did not prejudicially affect the right of separate schools to financial management and control. Section 93 allows the provincial government to manage its denominational rights or privileges or a non-denominational aspect necessary to deliver denominational elements of education. Insofar as the new legislation affected only secular aspects of education and did not interfere with aspects of financial management and control necessary to provide denominational elements of education, the Court did not think that it conflicts with section 93. The rules apply to all schools alike and impartially. Therefore, the court was convinced that the rules of fair and equitable funding were not breached.

Two important consequences flow from this case. First, since, under the Canadian Constitution, denominational school boards have neither a right to independent taxation nor an absolute right to management or control, public school boards can definitely not have that right. Therefore, school boards, subject to the limited constitutional protection provided by section 93, have no constitutional status. Second, the design of public school system is vested in the provincial parliament; and school boards have no say in the policy matters of that design. Section 93 of the Constitution Act, although giving effect to the historic compromise that was reached regarding education in Canada at the time of Federation in 1867, provides limited denominational rights and will be construed restrictively.

One aspect that remains solid in Canadian constitutional law is that secular education is not guaranteed in every province. However, the special funding, where applicable, is strictly limited to two types of denominational schools. In order to remove this privilege, the Constitution would have to be amended. When the Constitution was patriated in 1982, and, emulating the American Bill of Rights model, the Canadian Charter of Rights and Freedoms was entrenched in the Constitution, section 29 which specifically states: "Nothing in this Charter abrogates or derogates from any right or privilege guaranteed by or under the Constitution of Canada in respect of denominational, separate or dissentient schools." Without this guarantee, some provinces would not have accepted the Constitution Act 1982.

Security of the Person and Fundamental Justice

In *K.L.W. v Winnipeg Child & Family Services,*[5] the issue before the Supreme Court of Canada was the Child and Family Services Act of a province which provides for the warrantless apprehension of a child by the Child and Family Services Agency, or a peace officer, as long as there are reasonable and probable grounds to believe that a child is in need of protection. This Act was challenged on the basis that it infringed on Section 7 of the Charter of Rights and Freedoms which guarantee a person's life, liberty, or security except in accordance with the principles of fundamental justice. In this case, the Agency apprehended the newborn son of an appellant Agency because she was an alcoholic who neglected her four other children.

---

[5] [2000] 2 SCR 519.

The Court, by a majority of five-to-two, sustained the statutory provisions. The Court held that since the section 7 analysis is a contextual, the rights of parents and children must be balanced in light of the rights of children to life and health and the state's duty to protect them, and that the underlying philosophy and policy of the legislation must be kept in mind when determining its constitutional validity. The majority said that the state must be able to take preventive action to protect children and should not always be required to wait until a child has been seriously harmed before being able to intervene. While the interests at stake in cases of apprehension are of the highest order, particularly because the impact that state action involving the separation of parents and children may have on their lives, the court was of the opinion that the procedural protections laid down in criminal cases cannot be imported in the current context. To the argument that a distinction should be made between emergency and non-emergency situations (this argument was accepted by a minority of two judges), the Court responded that requiring prior judicial authorization in non-emergency situations, assuming that they can be distinguished from emergency situations, may impede pro-active intervention by placing the burden on the sate to justify intervention in situations of arguably non-imminent, yet serious, danger to a child. Conceding that the bond of love and support between parents and their children is crucial and should not be disrupted by the state, the Court declared that children are vulnerable and depend on others for their emotional, physical and intellectual well being and development. Thus, the Court concluded that protecting children from harm is one of the state's responsibilities which is accepted in every civilized society.

Minority Language Education Rights

In *Arsenault-Cameron v Prince of Edward Island*,[6] the Supreme Court of Canada reiterated that the purpose of the constitutional provision in minority language educational rights is to redress past injustices and provide the official language minority with equal access to high quality education on its own language in circumstances where community development will be enhanced. In this case the Minister of Education, overruling a French Language Board which was willing to establish a French school for the linguistic minority, proposed bussing students to an adjoining school district approximately thirty kilometers (about eighteen miles) and a fifty-seven minutes bus ride away. The trial judge, on an application of the minority parents, found that the plaintiffs' rights to minority language facilties was violated because the school offered by the provincial government was not reasonably accessible. The Court of Appeal allowed the provincial

---

[6] [2000] 181 DLR (4th) 1.

government's appeal. The Supreme Court of Canada restored the trial judge's decision. Other developments in this area of the law are as follows.

Under section 23 of the Canadian Charter of Rights and Freedoms, citizens of Canada whose first language is that of the English or French linguistic minority population of the province in which they reside have the right to have their children receive primary and secondary school instruction in that language in that province. This applies wherever the number of children in the province is sufficient to warrant such instruction out of public funds.

The Supreme Court of Canada had previously ruled that language rights cannot be separated from a concern for the culture associated with the language and that the constitutional provision was meant to correct, on a national scale, the historically progressive erosion of the two official language groups. Further, the provision was designed to give effect to equal partnership of the official language groups in the context of education.[7] The Court also noted that it is important to understand the historical and social context of the situation to be redressed, for example the reasons why the system of education was not responsive to the actual needs of the official language minority.[8] This is why the courts have to interpret the constitution provision "purposively, in manner consistent with the preservation and development of official language communities in Canada."[9]

In the most recent case on the subject, *Noella Arsenault-Cameron et al v. Prince Edward Island*,[10] the Supreme Court of Canada clarified another point. The Court decreed not only that representatives of the official language community have the right to a degree of governance of the facilities but also that this right of management and control is independent of the existence of a minority language board. The Court further asserted that identifying what is required involves a determination of the appropriate services, in pedagogical terms, for the number of students involved and an examination of the costs of the contemplated services and that the services provided to the education of minority students need not be identical to the ones provided to the majority. The Court was of the view that minority students can be treated differently, if necessary, based on their particular circumstances and needs, in order to provide a standard of education equivalent to that of the official language majority. However, the Court advised that a province has the duty to actively promote educational services in the minority language and to assist in determining potential demand and that a province cannot avoid its constitutional duty by citing insufficient proof of numbers, especially if it is not prepared to conduct its own studies or to

---

[7] *See, e.g.*, Mahe v. Alberta [1990] 1 SCR 342.
[8] For example, *see, e.g.*, re Public Act (Manitoba) [1993] 1 SCR 839.
[9] R v Beaulac [1999] 1 SCR 768.
[10] [2000] 1 SCR 3.

obtain and present other evidence of known and potential demand. Nevertheless, the Court was believed that the government should be given wide discretion in selecting the institutional means by which to meet its obligations.

Simple Possession of Child Pornography and Freedom of Expression

An important issue arose in the British Columbia Court of Appeal.[11] The accused was charged, under the Canadian Criminal Code, with possession of child pornography and child pornography for the purposes of distribution or sale. The accused challenged to the constitutionality of the statutory provision under the first count, claiming that it infringed his guarantee of freedom of expression under section 2(b) of the Canadian Charter of Rights and Freedoms. This section lays down:

> Everyone has the following fundamental freedoms: freedom of thought, belief, opinion and expression, including freedom of the press and other media and communication.

The prosecution argued that while simple possession of child pornography infringed freedom of expression, it was justified in a free and democratic society, under section 1 of the Charter which provides:

> The Canadian Charter of Rights and Freedoms guarantees the rights and freedoms set out in it subject only to such reasonable limits prescribed by law as can be demonstrably justified in a free and democratic society.

A trial court maintained that since punishment for the simple possession of child pornography went beyond the reasonable limits, the statute was unconstitutional. The British Court of Appeal, by a majority of two to one, dismissed the prosecution's appeal on the basis that the criminal provision in question was too broad. The court stated that a child's age was under eighteen (instead of say fourteen), that the detrimental effects of prohibition of simple possession of pornography on freedom of expression and personal privacy are substantial, that the subsection captures a vast range of materials, a significant portion of which cannot be shown to pose a danger to children, and that criminalizing of a simple possession of pornographic material, without its further transmission or dissemination is too far-reaching in its effects on a constitutional guarantee.[12] The Chief Justice

---

[11] R. v Sharpe [2000] 1 WWR 241.
[12] The Prosecution awaits word on whether the Supreme Court of Canada will hear its appeal.

of British Columbia, in his dissent, pointed out that parliament did not go so far beyond what was necessary and that the provision should not have been struck down.

This author strongly disagrees with the majority's analysis since Justices should be much more sensitive to the issue of pornography and its harmful effects and consequences. To this end, the author offers that as far as freedom of expression is concerned, no freedom or right can be absolute or unlimited. The dominant factor should be the protection of children from exploitation and . This is an overriding consideration, which should be paramount. In support of this contention, some conflicting non-Canadian authorities can be cited.

While First Circuit[13] upheld the Child Pornography Protection Act's prohibition on possession of child pornography, the Ninth Circuit struck down parts of the same statute.[14] In 1990, the United States Supreme Court upheld an identical Ohio statutory provision that possession laws are an essential element of a successful enforcement strategy against production and distribution.[15] Similarly, in England, the Protection of Children Act 1978 and the Criminal Justice Act 1988 (both amended by the Criminal Justice and Public Order Act 1994) outlaw child pornography; however, like in Australia, the upper age is sixteen.

Administrative Law

Judicial Review for Procedural Breaches or Excess of Jurisdiction

Two cases confirmed the principles on which judicial review should be granted. Two years earlier, the Supreme Court of Canada provided a summary of the jurisprudence on the standards of review.[16] In recent years, the courts have recognized that the level of judicial scrutiny of decisions made by tribunals moves along a continuum ranging from patent unreasonableness at one end (maximum deference) to correctness at the other end (no deference). The level of scrutiny to be applied to any specific decision is determined by a 'functional and pragmatic' approach which aims at determining the extent to which the Legislature intended that the courts should review an issue. The cases identify a number of factors which must be

---

[13] United States v Hilton, 167 F.3d 61 (1st Cir. 1999).
[14] But *see* Free Speech Coalition v. Reno, 198 F.3d 1083 (9th Cir. 1999), *cert. granted sub nom. Ashcroft v. Free Speech Coalition*, 121 S. Ct. 876 (2001). (striking down portions of the Child Pornography Prevention Act of 1996.
[15] Osborne v Ohio, 495 U.S. 103 (1990).
[16] Pushpanathan v Canada [1998] 1 SCR 982.

considered in evaluating the appropriate level of review. These include the existence of a right of appeal and the scope of that right; the presence of a privative clause and the language of that clause, the nature of the judgment being challenged, and, the role or function performed by a tribunal when making the decisions being challenged.

These principles were applied in the two cases.[17] In the first, *Baker v School Board for District 7 – Burin*,[18] after two referenda on the issue of school reforms, the Constitution of Canada was amended in 1997 to allow for elected school boards in Newfoundland on non-denominational bases. The new Schools Act set up 10 boards with one for francophones. Each board was divided into zones and districts. The Act provided that a board could close a school, but only after the parents of students affected have been given an opportunity to make representations to the board.

In one district of a zone it was clear that one school would have to be closed. A consultant's report, which was prepared after public meetings in communities within the district, recommended that St. Bernard's All Grades School be closed. Further consultations took place and a program specialists' report was prepared while the board continued to conduct public meetings. When the final decision was made to close the school at a full board meeting, it was reached in a closed session which parents were not allowed to attend. Further, the program specialists' report was not brought to the board's attention. In addition, two trustees were disqualified because they had children in the school to be closed. The applicants took the case to court contending that deliberately keeping the specialists' report from the trustees violated the board's policy, the statute, and the common law of procedural fairness.[19] The plaintiffs also raised other procedural defects such as that the board ignored school closure guidelines which provided for voting on restructuring should take place not less than sixty days after it was introduced.

The Newfoundland Supreme Court granted the judicial review application and held that the board violated its own School Closure Guidelines. The Court reasoned that the board violated its own school closure guidelines in

---

[17] A third case also was decided where a teacher's dismissal was involved. The Supreme Court applied the same principles in that case too and decided that the standard of patently unreasonable error should be applied: Syndicat de l'enseignement du Grand-Portage v Morency, [2000] 2 SCR 913. For further details see below.

[18] The Supreme Court of Canada, during the year under review, confirmed, by dismissing the appeal from the Newfoundland Court of Appeal - 183 DLR (4th) 224, the amendment of the Constitution, whereby a single school system regardless of religious affiliation was introduced: Hogan v Newfoundland (Attorney-General) [2000] SCCA No. 91

[19] 178 DLR (4th) 155.

voting on the restructuring draft less than sixty days after it was introduced and by failing to have specialist' report presented to it. The Court indicated that these violations infringed the principles of procedural fairness at common law. The court added that the two trustees were wrongly disqualified because having children in the affected schools was not a conflict of interest. As such, the Court quashed the board's action and awarded costs to the plaintiffs.

In *British Columbia College of Teachers v Trinity Western University,*[20] the Supreme Court confirmed a grant of judicial review. The College of Teachers refused to approve the application of a teacher training certificate's validation made by a Christian private college on the ground that it followed discriminatory practices against homosexual staff and students. The Christian college, in its "List of Practices That Are Biblically Condemned," included "sexual sins including premarital sex, adultery, homosexual behaviour and viewing of pornography." All members of its community were required to sign an agreement to refrain from such activities. The Court, in dismissing the appeal, reasoned that the College of Teachers took matters into account that were irrelevant and beyond their competence under the Teaching Profession Act. In any case, the Court posited that freedoms of religion and conscience coexist with the right to be free from discrimination based on sexual orientation. The Court further ascertained that the requirement that students and staff adopt the Christian standards may have created unfavorable differential treatment, but that one must consider the true nature of the undertaking and the context in which this occurs since a distinction should be made between belief and conduct. The end result was that judicial review was granted because the College of Teachers exceeded its authority under the statute.

The minority Justice stated that it was not patently unreasonable for the College to deny accreditation on the ground that the compulsory Community Standards of the teachers college discriminated against homosexuals and bisexuals. This Justice reflected that it becomes obvious when the audience perceiving public school teachers includes homosexuals and bisexual students, parents, colleagues, and staff, students with homosexual and bisexual relatives and friends, and also adolescents exploring their sexual identities. The dissenting Justice remarked that judicial review should not have been granted because the decision of the Teachers' College, refusing validation on the grounds of discrimination on sexual orientation, was reasonable and within the ambit of its statutory powers and jurisdiction.

---

[20] [2001] SCC 31.

Judicial Deference to University Committees

The Ontario Court of Appeal, overturning an earlier judgment, found that a university committee's action in student examinations, even if it does not completely follow its rules of assessment, should be given maximum judicial deference since it involves academic standards, a matter at the core of the internal governance of a university.[21] The court explained that since a university examination committee is in a much better position to balance the need to maintain appropriate academic standards while ensuring that students are treated fairly, the judiciary should interfere only if such a committee's interpretation of the policy is patently unreasonable.

Here the university's grading practices policy stipulated that after an instructor announced the methods of evaluation for a course, they could not be changed without the consent of at least a majority of the students. A post-graduate dentistry student complained unsuccessfully to the faculty's appeals committee that when he failed the written examination that was not specified before the course commenced, he was asked to repeat the course. Even so, the faculty appeals committee permitted the student to sit for another written examination. The committee said that the result of the examination, together with the student's performance in the other components of the course, should be used to consider whether he met the minimum standards. The student's request for further review by the university's appeal committee was rejected on the ground that the faculty's appeal committee provided an adequate relief by appropriately addressing concerns about prior notice. Yet, the university appeals committee directed that the student should take the new written examination within six months. The student instituted .

The trial court allowed the student's application on the basis that the university had not followed its policy of giving notice in advance that there would be a written examination. As such, the court ordered the results of the written examination to be expunged from the student's record and directed officials to grant him the post-graduate diploma in orthodontics. However, on the University's appeal to the Court of Appeal, the trial judge's order was overruled.

The court applied some previous cases dealing with university's autonomy in decision making[22] to come to the conclusion that maximum deference should be have been given to the university-wide appeals committee because it performs a function that goes to the core of the internal

---

[21] Hayat v University of Toronto, 181 DLR (4th) 496.
[22] *See. e.g.*, King v University of Saskatchewan, [1969] SCR 678; Paine v University of Toronto, (1981) 131 DLR (3d) 325; Ross v New Brunswick School District No 15, [1996] SCR 825.

governance of a university. In this case, according to the court, the committee was anxious to maintain appropriate academic standards through appropriate methods of evaluation while providing fair and objective evaluation. The court noted that any problem associated with fair and adequate notice of the examination disappeared when the university committee gave the student up to six month to prepare for a new test. The court acknowledged that the judiciary should interfere only if a university committee's interpretation of its policy was patently unreasonable, which in this case it was not. Thus, the court restored the decision of the university appeal's committee in a move that will bring a sigh of relief in many university staff tearooms!

Assessment of Education Rates and Self-designation of Religious Belief

An interesting and novel point of law arose in a case from Saskatchewan.[23] Under provincial law, property owners could designate the school portion of their property taxes either to the Protestant (minority) or the Roman Catholic (majority) schools. Neither the Canadian Constitution, the Canadian Charter of Rights and Freedoms, nor the provincial legislation define the key terms or phrases Roman Catholic, Protestant, "religious faith," or "membership in a religious faith." Further, no statute specifies the procedure for evaluating whether an individual is a Protestant, Roman Catholic, adheres to a religious faith, or is a member of a religious faith.

One majority school board objected to, and made application, to the Board of Review to examine some ratepayers' options for minority schools based on its allegation that they were not members of the minority religious faith. The board further charged that the assessment roll, based solely on the ratepayers' written statements, was in error. The Board of Revision issued notices of hearing of the review appeal. It appears that this would have been a first because even though the law does not define important religious terms, the Board of Revision was willing and ready to take up the Herculean and inquisitional task of deciding the ratepayers' religious beliefs and affiliations, presumably by an intrusive and invasive inquiry into the religious faith and practices of each ratepayer.

Before that unprecedented proceedings could commence, ratepayers applied to a court asking that the Board of Review be prevented from embarking on the issue because no one, except they themselves, can decide what their religious beliefs, practices, or affiliation were. A trial court, in

---

[23] Buhs et al. v. Board of Revision of the Rural Municipality of Leroy et al., 178 DLR (4th) 322.

granting the application, agreed that the Board of Review lacked jurisdiction to conduct an inquisition into the personal religious beliefs or practices of ratepayers, or otherwise consider whether an individual was a member of the minority religious faith. The court accepted the ratepayers' contention that their declarations of school support were determinative and that as long as they were authentic and accurately recorded, they were unchallengeable on the basis of any inquiry into their religious faith or affiliation.

The court maintained that the terms and phrases in statutes originated at a time in Canada's history when the identification of an individual as a Protestant or Roman Catholic was not problematic. The court went on to declare that the categories of Protestant and Roman Catholic are themselves far from unambiguous, even among Christian believers since many of them would not accept either description. The court gave the example of some Church of England members who believe themselves to be the reformed Catholic Church in England and would be uncomfortable with the designation Protestant. Similarly, many in the churches of the Byzantine and Pre-Chalcedonian Traditions do not like being described as Roman.

The court discerned that the legislative intent is that the questions of membership in religious faith should be left to the subjective determination of an individual. Otherwise, the court feared that an intensively insensitive invasive inquiry would have to be conducted to determine someone's religious faith. Therefore, the court was satisfied that it should be left to each ratepayer individually to identify which school would receive his or her rates.

Criminal Law

One case under the Canadian Young Offenders Act 1985, *F.N. v R. & Roman Catholic School Board for St. John*[24] which reached the Supreme Court of Canada is worth discussing. At issue was the confidentiality of young offenders trials. The Youth Court in one city began routine distribution of its weekly Youth Court Docket to local school boards disclosing the names, dates, and places of trials of young people. The appellant unsuccessfully claimed that this administrative practice violated his right of non-disclosure.

On a further and final appeal, the Supreme Court of Canada, in allowing the appeal, held that while it is an important constitutional rule that judicial activities be open to the public and that their proceedings be accessible to all those of interest, the public concern for confidentiality in such circumstances outweighs the public interest in openness. The Court thus asserted

---

[24] [2000] 1 SCR 880.

that the practice violated Parliament's restrictions on openness because disclosure was not authorized by a judge, distribution was not limited to the board responsible for the appellant's school, and the information was distributed for school purposes and not for purposes related to the administration of justice. The court further determined that school boards should not consider themselves government agencies responsible for the supervision of care of young persons in trouble with the law since this function should be left to the appropriate authorities. In so ruling, the Court cited the United Nations Standard Minimum Rules for the Administration of Juvenile Justice, also known as the "Beijing Rules," to support its view of protection of privacy of young offenders. These include the following:

8.1 The juvenile's right to privacy shall be respected at all stages in order to avoid harm being caused to her or him by undue publicity or by the process of labeling.
8.2 In principle, no information that may lead to the identification of a juvenile offender shall be published.

Collective Agreements and Employment

Redundancy

Syndicat de l'enseignement du Grand-Portage v Morency,[25] reached the Supreme Court of Canada in an appeal over a collective agreement and redundancy of teachers. In this case, after conducting numerous consultations with parents, teachers, and other stakeholders a school board adopted a new course grid for the ensuing year. Under the new grid, some teachers were reassigned to different levels of teaching. Later in the year, after completing the evaluation of its staffing needs, the board laid off two teachers. In their grievance, the teachers alleged that the board had not evaluated its needs and surpluses by field of study in accordance with their collective agreement. An arbitrator dismissed the grievance on the grounds that the board had full discretion in evaluating its teacher staffing needs, that laying the two teachers off was not unreasonable or invalid, and that it had not violated the collective agreement.

On an application of the union for judicial review, the trial court, quashing and invalidating the arbitrator's award, allowed the application. The board sought further review at the Quebec Court of Appeal which dismissed. However, the Supreme Court of Canada, on appeal by the board, reversed the Court of Appeal and confirmed the arbitration award.

---

[25] [2000] 2 SCR 913.

The Court reasoned that the appropriate standard of judicial review in such cases involving an arbitration award remains that of patently unreasonable error. Here the Court was convinced that it was clear from reading the arbitrator's award that it contained no errors justifying the intervention of the superior courts. In the future, when negotiating terms and conditions of a collective agreement, teachers' unions will have to be extremely careful as to what they agree to.

Removal of Principals from Teachers' Bargaining Unit

A case which reached the Ontario Court of Appeal[26] involved a trickier problem. In a protest over provincial legislation making substantial changes in education finance, program delivery, school board management, and the collective bargaining rights of teachers, teachers and their unions engaged in an industrial action, including the withdrawal of their services. The government, rather cleverly, hastily passed another legislative amendment which removed principals and vice-principals from teacher bargaining units and from statutory membership in their unions. Consequently, the unions challenged the amendment on the grounds that it contravened the guarantee of freedom of association in section 2(d) of the Canadian Charter of Rights and Freedoms, and that it was enacted for punitive reasons, namely in retaliation for participation in the teachers' protests and strikes. A trial judge dismissed the application on the bases that the amendments were not introduced in reprisal and that they did not no infringe on the constitutional freedom of association.

On further review, appeal, the Court of Appeal strongly and unanimously affirmed. The court was of the opinion that the burden rested on the applicants to prove that reprisal was the motive of the amendments. According to the court, the judiciary should not render legislation invalid only on the basis of extrinsic evidence. The court pointed out that in his speech at the provincial Parliament, the Minister did not criticize the principals or vice-principals for leaving their schools during the strike, not for participating in any other aspect of the protest. The court was thus of the view that rather than reflecting an intention to punish, these statements explicitly indicated a desire to remove the source of conflict of interest resting on principals and vice-principals which the government perceived to have operated to the detriment of the public interest during the protest against the amended statute.

---

[26] Ontario Teachers' Fed'n et al v. Attorney General of Ontario, [2000] Docket C29509.

The court also affirmed that removing principals and vice-principals from trade union membership is not unconstitutional since there is no such right of association in Canada. In regard to the freedom of association point, it is submitted that the interpretation previously given by the Supreme Court of Canada, and naturally followed by the subordinate courts, that the Canadian Constitution or the Canadian Charter of Rights do not give any protection to employees to form a trade union or be members of a trade union flies in the face of international standards and treaties. This provision had been criticized by the International Labor Organization and laughed at by many academics. However, as the law stands at the moment, the subordinate courts have no discretion to depart from the Supreme Court's restrictive interpretation of the guarantee of freedom of association. Many people in Canada hope that, one day soon, the Supreme Court will change its mind on the rights of employees to form, and be members of, a trade union, so that these are encompassed in the guarantee of freedom of association.

Conclusion

With the continuing and progressive evolution of the law of education in Canada, particularly in view of the cases reaching higher courts under the Canadian Constitution Act 1982, many areas of the law, including some novel or even obscure points, are being clarified. After the entrenchment of fundamental rights and freedoms in the Canadian Constitution in 1982, an interesting interplay between legislatures and judiciary is developing - in common with the American system. More and more detailed examinations of many aspects of education law are being conducted. Thus, the role of the courts has increased considerably. In many ways, since the judges are still struggling with this new role that is being thrust upon them, there are many disagreements between judges and various levels of courts. This author submits that this is a healthy developments because if all issues are debated openly, educational policies and decisions will be made transparently and temperately.

EUROPE

Prof. Dr. Jan De Groof, Hilde Penneman

Student Grants

The Right to Student Grants: Definition of the Problem

As to establishing conditions for the mobility of students, non-discrimination for access to education in another Member State is only a first step. Once access is achieved, other questions arise which are related to the conditions under which one can take part in education; this is a sensitive issue relating to the financial conditions surrounding education. In some countries, the system of financial support for students is very advanced while others have scant provisions or subject the awarding of financial support to limiting requirements. The question of the extent to which nationals of one Member State can appeal for student grants from another Member State has given rise to great controversy.[1]

The Right to Student Grants for Different Categories of Students

Children of European Community Workers/Self-Employed Persons

According to Article 12 of Regulation 1612/68, children of an European Community (EC) national who is conducting or has conducted work within the territory of another Member State "under the same conditions as the nationals of that same Member State are granted the right to general education, apprenticeship training and professional training. This also includes the right to any awarded education grants."[2]

The question of whether the right to a student grant remains in effect if a child goes to study in a Member State other than the one in which his or her parents are migrant workers was posed in the *Carmina di Leo*.[3] Article 12 of Regulation 1612/68 states that a child must be a resident in the state where the migrant parent-worker performed labor. Germany and the Netherlands also argued this before the court. In addition, they contended that the purpose of the Article, as evident from the preamble to the regulation, is the "integration" of the migrant worker and his family in the receiving Member

---

[1] M. Verbruggen, "Access to Education and Student Grants." *T.O.R.B.,* 1992-1993, at 282.

[2] R. Van de Ven, "Toward European Education Financing," *NTOR,* 1992, p; 161-162.

[3] CoJ., 13 November 1990, case 308/89, Carmina di Leo, *Jur.,* 1990, p. 4204.

State and that studies in another Member State did not contribute to this end. The court rejected this argument and decided that equal treatment of children of migrant workers is not dependent on where education is received. The court wrote that if children of nationals of a receiving Member State have the opportunity to study in another Member State while retaining their student grants, then the children of migrant workers must have that opportunity as well.

The question remained as to whether the children of migrant workers can claim student grants for living costs. While a student grant can be considered a social benefit for migrant workers themselves, if this benefit is not conferred by a receiving Member State, then the parents have to finance the study. In *Bernini*,[4] the court held that student grants awarded by a Member State to the children of workers forms a social benefit in the sense of Article 7, paragraph 2, of Regulation 1612/68, when the worker continues to provide for the support of his child. In Bernini, the court maintained that a child can call upon Article 7, paragraph 2, to obtain a student grant under the same conditions as those which apply to children of national workers and in particular without that a further condition as to his residence can be set. This led to an end of the domicile requirement in Carmina Di Leo. After Bernini, Article 12 of Regulation 1612/68 is no longer necessary for the financially dependent child of a migrant worker. The court confirmed this reasoning in *Meeusen*.[5]

Spouses of EC Workers/Self-Employed Persons

Article 12 of Regulation 1612/68 only grants rights to children of EC migrants in the area of education. This raises the question of which financial claims the spouse of an EC migrant who, after all, does not fall under the persons covered by Article 12 of Regulation 1612/68, can derive from EC law in the framework of access to education. With regard to access to education, if a spouse has the nationality of one of the Member States, then on the basis of Article 12 (formerly Article 6), 149 and 150 of the EC Treaty, the spouse has the right to equal treatment with regard to access to education in the receiving Member State. On this ground, the spouse has the right to equal student grants as far as enrollment fees and tuition fees are concerned.[6]

Student-Workers

An EC national who goes to work in another Member State procures a number of rights as a result of Article 39, paragraph 2, formerly Article 48, of

---

[4] CoJ., 26 February 1992, case *31/90,(* Bernini) *Jur.* 1992.

[5] CoJ., arrest van 8 June 1999, case 337/97 (Meeusen).

[6] CoJ., 13 July 1986, case *152/82* (Forcheri), *Jur.* 1983, p. 2335.

the EC Treaty. In this way, Article 39 forbids discrimination with regard to employment, pay, and other terms of employment. The rights of migrant workers are further addressed in Regulation 1612/68 Article 7, paragraphs 2 and 3 which confer the right to the same social and tax benefits as the national workers; they also receive education at vocational schools and rehabilitation centres under the same conditions.

A further issue is whether a student who works can benefit from a basic grant. In *Lair*,[7] the court decided that since student grants for living costs are a "social benefit" in the sense of Article 7, paragraph 2, of Regulation 1612/68, a student could appeal for such a grant even when a worker goes to study.[8] The broad scope of the interpretation of the concept "social benefit" was also made evident in *Matteuci*,[9] a case which involved an Italian woman, who while working in Belgium, requested a grant for the purpose of taking a course in Germany. In acknowledging that the grant was a "social benefit," the court relied on a bilateral treaty between Belgium and the Federal Republic of Germany. According to the court, the fact that the grants were provided not by Belgium but by the Federal Republic of Germany did not take away from the fact that workers from other Member States also had to be treated equally with regard to the request for grants. The provision of Article 10 (formerly Article 5), paragraph 2 of the EC Treaty, under which Member States have to abstain from all measures which could jeopardize the realization of the objectives of that treaty also has bearing on bilateral treaties between Member States.

"Regular" Mobile Students

In *Wirth*, the court ruled that a grant that partly includes living expenses falls beyond the sphere of action of EC and that this could it be a matter in casu of an anomaly under Article 12 Regulation 1612/68. The court added that Member States are free to consider and, if necessary, to change the regulations regarding student grants for education taken abroad.[10] After all, the court had already explained that support for students for living expenses falls under the "education policy" which is not within the scope of authority of the EC's institutions and which, under the social policy, since the special provisions of the Treaty do not determine otherwise, falls under the competence of the Member States.[11]

---

[7] CoJ., 21 uni. 1988, case 39/86,(Lair) *Jur.* 1988, at 3161.
[8] Article 7 paragraph 3 is however not applicable to university education: the term trade school is more limited than professional training..
[9] C.o.J., 27 September 1988, (Mateucci), *Jur.,* 1988, p.. 5589.
[10] C.o.J., judgement of 7 December 1992, case 109/92, (Wirth), *Jur.* 1993, p. 6447.
[11] Lair, *Supra.7* r.o. 15.

Non-Nationals of Member States

Students who are not nationals of a Member State and who are not covered by EC law cannot call upon it in order to claim grants.

Remainder Category

One might wonder whether students could not derive rights from the treaty provision regarding the freedom of movement of services 49 and 50, formerly Articles 59 and 60, of the EC Treaty. Article 50, formerly Article 60 of the EC Treaty, declares that services are normally carried out for a fee. Yet, as outlined above, there is usually no commercial price for services in public education.[12] While private education with a profit motive is a different matter, there is, in general, no question of an appeal to equal treatment in the matter of student grants because such students are more likely to fund their studies themselves.

Foreign Students in Belgium

The non-discrimination principle of Article 12, formerly Article 6, of the EC Treaty applies only to registration fees and not for the actual grants meant, for example, to cover living costs. In this way, one cannot request additional enrollment fees because of the fact that one comes from abroad. Pursuant to Article 2 of the Law of 19 July 1971 with regard to the awarding of student grants, these grants are limited to Belgian students. The Royal Decree of 1 February 1978 expanded the award potential to foreign students such as the children of nationals of Member States who call upon Article 12 of EC Regulation 1612/68 if one parent works in Belgium; every other foreigner who resides in Belgium with his or her family or married partner must be in the country for two years from the last submission date for study grant, namely 31 October.[13]

In order to receive a student grant, one must attend a school that is organized, subsidized, or recognized by the Flemish Community. In principle, only students who study at a Flemish institution of higher education can receive a study grant in the Flemish Community. Students from the Flemish Community who study in the French-language region of the nation must submit their requests to the French Community. Students who study in the German language region can receive student grants from the Flemish Community for higher studies in the German medium of communication if they meet certain legal requirements or can turn to the French Community.

---

[12] See Humbel
[13] Y. Jorens, "EEA student in the European Union" in *Student and Law: Judicial and social guide for students in higher education*, Leuven, Acco, 1999, p. 427 and B. Vermeulen, "Access to Education within Europe," Utrecht, Dutch Centre for Foreigners, 1997, at 95-96.

The principle is that one requests a student grant in the region in which one attends class. Flemish students who wish to study abroad must take care when it comes to their student grants since they can receive them only by exception. The Royal Decree of 1 February 1978 creates the following exceptions.

The first exception is for Belgians who live abroad with their families and receive education there. Insofar as they can call on Article 12 of Regulation1612/68 regarding the freedom of movement of workers, they qualify for student grants in the countries where they live. It is only if one falls beyond the range of application of the Regulation that one qualifies for a grant from the Flemish Community for studies abroad. Flemish students who study abroad only qualify if there is no equivalent in Belgium for the studies they wish to take abroad. If a student goes abroad in the framework of the Erasmus/Socrates program, Lingua, Comett II, and Tempus under a grant from the Flemish Community, then he or she student can combine these with an EU grant. Agreements have been made with a number of countries for the purpose of retaining the right to student grants. For example, the GHENT agreement was signed with the Netherlands whereby studies there are considered equal to those in the Flemish Community.

Right of Residence for Students

Background

On 28 June 1990, the Council made a decision in the domain of right of residence in the EC for the first time in more than fifteen years. This involved three: Directive 90/364 on the right of residence, Directive 90/365 on the right of residence for workers and self-employed persons who have ceased their professional activity, and Directive 90/366 on the right of residence for students. The last was later nullified by the Court of Justice and replaced by Directive 93/96.[14]

---

[14] Directive 90/366, *Pb.* 1990,L.180, p.30. This directive was declared null and void by the Court in the judgement of 7 July 1992, case 295/90, *Jur.* 1992 p. 4193, because it rested on unjust legal grounds (Article 308 (formerly Article 235) EC Treaty). The Court likewise determined that the consequences of the directive would stay in effect until the implementation of a directive based on just grounds. On 29 October 1993, the proper directive was laid down RI. 93/ 96.

Definition

A distinction is made between pupils and students.[15] In the decree of the Council and the European Parliament, which established the Socrates program, the term students refers to persons who are registered at a university to pursue higher education, regardless of discipline, with the aim of obtaining a recognized title or diploma, including a doctorate. University is understood to mean all sorts of institutions of higher education which issue qualifications or titles of this level, regardless of their appellation in the Member States.[16] What also should be taken into account is a broader definition, used in the context of social security of migrant workers, wherein student refers to every person other than a worker or self-employed person or a member of that person's family who is regularly enrolled at an institution recognized by the national bodies of a Member State for the purpose of studying there or receiving professional training and who is insured in the framework of a social security system that is specially applicable to students.

Pursuant to Article 1 of Directive 93/96, Member States grant the right of residence to every student who is a national of a Member State and who does not yet have this right on the basis of another provision of EC law as well as to a student's spouse and children in their care when a student has met the following three conditions (Article 1 Directive 93/96): making a guarantee to relevant national authorities that he or she has sufficient income resources to prevent his or her becoming a charge of the welfare system of the host country, being enrolled in a recognized institution for the purpose of professional training as primary activity, and having health insurance which covers all risks in the receiving Member State.

The right of residence is limited to the duration of an educational program and is established by the issuance of a residence permit of a national of a Member State. The period of validity for a residency permit can be limited to the duration of an educational program or one year if the duration of the study is longer than one year, in which case the permit can be renewed annually.

---

[15] All persons enrolled at a school as such: This definition is in the decision of the European Parliament and the Council for the establishment of the community action programme Socrates (Article 2), as well as the definition of "school:" all types of institutions for school education, including general, professional and technical education, as well as, by exception, non-school educational institutions for the promotion of measures, namely the exchange of pupils for the purpose of learning languages *Pb.* L 87 of 24 April 1995.

[16] Decision 819/95/EC of the European Parliament and the Council of 14 March 1995 to establish the community action programme Socrates, *Pb* L 87 of 20.4.1995.

The Spouse and Children in the Care of a Student

The spouse and children in the care of a national of a Member State who has a right of residence in the territory of a Member State pursuant to Directive 93/96 have the right to carry out any work throughout the entire territory of that Member State, whether paid employment or not, even if they are not nationals of a Member State. The following conditions must be met to have a right of residence.

1. Ensuring that a student has sufficient income; this can be met by means of a statement or other equivalent manner. The most obvious method is for a student to show that he or she works in the receiving Member State or that his or her parents or other solvent third parties declare that they will provide the student with the necessary means.

2. Enrollment in a recognized professional training program; the term professional training should be broadly interpreted to include every form of education that prepares a student for a specific profession, trade, or occupation, or which provides special competence to practice such a profession, trade, or occupation, regardless of the age and educational level of a pupil and even if a program includes a number of general subject matters. Professional training and university education fall under this term. Further, the directive prescribes that enrollment must be at a recognized educational establishment for professional training. It must be assumed that this means that an educational establishment has obtained authorization from its national authorities to provide education and/or to award diplomas recognized by the relevant Member State.

3. Professional training as primary activity: the directive sets no absolute requirements with regard to the minimum amount of time that must be dedicated to study should one wish to obtain a right of residence. All that is required is that a student's primary activity is professional training. It is therefore irrelevant whether full-time or part-time study is involved as long as a student's primary activity is study. The question then arises as to where the minimum lies with regard to the time spent on study below which there is no claim to a right of residence. Likewise, the question arises as to what extent a student actually has to study in order to obtain or retain his right of residence. To the letter of the directive, it could be stated that the right of residence also falls to an EC student who is enrolled in recognized education or training that demands a large number of hours per week by virtue of the curriculum but who does not make a single real study effort.

4. Health insurance: this must be of such a nature that it covers all risks in the host country, a vague standard which probably means that an individual must be insured for the same risks as nationals in comparable situations and that minimal insurance is insufficient. The weak point of this condition

is the enormous diversity of health insurance systems in the various Member States since each has its own system with its own degree of coverage for risks and accompanying financial costs. That is why, in negotiations, considerable controversy has arisen about the requirements which health insurance must meet.

4. Student grants or loans: the Member State in which a student resides should have to pay subsidies for living expenses to students who stay there on the basis of Directive 93/96.

5. Entry and residence in the framework of Community education programs: EC programs such as Socrates and Leonardo do not provide a right of residence to a student who completes part of his or her professional training in another Member State in the context of such a program. Such a student, as an EC national, will, in general, be able to derive the right to entry and residence from Directive 93/96; during a stay at a host institution, a student remains enrolled at his or her own institution but is not prevented from also being enrolled at the host institution and receiving professional training as the primary activity. Under such a condition, a student does not pay tuition to the host institution and retains the grant awarded by the Member State. Further, a student usually has a mobility grant to cover the extra costs of a stay abroad such that the requirements as set forth by Article 1 Directive 93/96 will have been met.

European Citizenship and Right of Residence

The Maastricht Treaty established European citizenship. Further, for the benefit of EU citizens who do not yet have this right on the basis of the freedom of movement, the Treaty also established a right to entry to and residence in the territory of another Member State. Insofar as citizenship is a vague concept with which various elements are associated, a question arises as to what should be understood by European citizenship.

A first initiative can be found in the verdict of the Court of Justice in *Cowan*[17] regarding the free movement of services. In this case, the Court established not only that potential receivers of prohibited services were subject to discrimination but also that they were protected by the non-discrimination ban. Insofar as everyone is a potential receiver of services, the Court expanded the potential discrimination ban to all EU citizens. This judgement, which is considered to be the first practical application of European citizenship, could also imply a general right of entry to and residence in the territory of other Member States for all EU citizens.

---

[17] CoJ., 2 February 1989, 186/87, (Cowan), *Jur.,* 1989 at 195.

The Maastricht Treaty did not go as far. Article 18, formerly Article 8A, declares that "Each citizen of the Union has the right to travel and to reside freely on the territory of the Member States, subject to the limitations and conditions set forth by this Treaty and the provisions for the implementation thereof." As such, since it can be assumed that the Treaty does not have an unlimited right to freedom of residence in mind, it can be further assumed that this is a matter of a "stand still clause." The limitations that exist today remain in force but no new limitations may be introduced and changes can only establish further liberalization of the movement of persons.

The great reticence on the part of Member States to grant non-working nationals of other Member States the right to reside on their territories is primarily inspired by financial considerations. The fear is that those not actively engaged in the economy and without sufficient income or health insurance would go to countries where the social security system is most advantageous for them.

The Right of Residence as a Student in Belgium

Directive 93/96 EC, which introduces a right of residence for EU students, was converted in Belgian law by the Royal Decree of 22 February 1995. This modified the law of 15 December 1980 on entry to the territory, residence, establishment, and deportation of aliens, the Aliens Act,[18] and the Royal Decree of 22 February 1995 modifying the Royal Decree of 8 October 1981 on entry to the territory, residence, establishment, and deportation of aliens, the Aliens Royal Decree. Under this change, an EC student refers to every foreigner who is a national of a Member State of the EC and who comes to Belgium for professional training at a recognized educational establishment as his or her primary activity. An EC citizen who comes to Belgium to study has the right to remain for more than three months if he or she meets the conditions set forth in Article 55, section 1, of the Aliens Royal Decree, in particular that a student is enrolled in an educational establishment that is organized, recognized, or subsidized by the government in order to have professional training there as his or her primary activity. An eligible professional training programs is one which prepares a student to practice a professions. This category is very broad since it includes higher education, whether university level or not and, in principle, higher secondary education. On the other hand, save for exceptional cases, primary and lower secondary education are excluded.

---

[18] *B.S.* 31 December 1980.

The procedure to grant a student residence corresponds to that which is applicable to other EC aliens. Under Article 41 of The Alien Act, a right to entry in the Kingdom is granted to a student with an identity card or a valid national passport. On arrival, a student must report to the local authority administration and register in the alien register. A student then receives both a certificate of enrollment B, which is valid for three months from the date of issue, and a document in accord with "appendix 19" of the Royal Decree as evidence that he or she has submitted a request for residence as a student pursuant to Article 55, section 2, of the Aliens Royal Decree. A student has three months to demonstrate that he or she meets all of the conditions to stay in Belgium. In practice, a student must be able to present evidence of enrollment at an educational institution, of financial resources, and of health insurance. If a student is able to present these documents before the three-month term lapses, then the local authority administration gives him or her the residency permit of a national of a Member State of the EC. If a student does not submit any supporting documents before the deadline, then the local authority administration gives him or her a document in accordance with the model of appendix 14 with the Royal Decree which is a denial of a request for residence with an order to leave the territory. If the supporting documents are insufficient, the stay is denied and the student receives an order to leave the territory.[19]

A residency permit is valid for the period of the education or training without the possibility of exceeding one year. If the period of the education or training is longer than one year, a residency permit may be renewed annually on the condition that all requirements continue to be satisfied.[20] Although a student and his or her family must report to the local authority administration for registration and for issuance of a residence permit, it appears that this does not take place systematically in practice and this is sometimes forgotten.

In addition to these special conditions, all EU nationals/students must meet general conditions in order to be allowed to study in Belgium. In this way, entry and residence for an EC national can be denied for reasons of public order, public safety, or public health. Yet, Article 43 of the Aliens Act does identify four important limitations: the reasons may not be invoked for economic purposes; the measures of public order and safety must be exclusively founded on an individual's personal behavior except that a record of criminal convictions is not a sufficient reason for such measures; the expiration of the document that granted entry to and residence in Belgian territory

---

[19] Article 55, § 3, Aliens Act.
[20] Article 55, § 4, Aliens Act.

can in itself not justify deportation; and only diseases and ailments mentioned in the schedule to this law can justify denial of entry to the territory or refusal to issue the first residence permit.

European Policy: Positive Integration

Mobility Programs

The Erasmus Program

The Erasmus Program, the European Community Action Scheme for the Mobility of University Students, has been in effect since 1987. The Program's objective is to promote European cooperation in higher education and thereby encourage mobility of students and teachers. The target is to have 10% of the EC's students spend a period of study in another Member State. Attempts to reach this goal include providing financial support for international student exchanges. As per 1 January 1995, the Erasmus Program was integrated in a new community action scheme called Socrates.[21]

The Socrates Program

The Socrates action scheme encourages cooperation between Member States in the area of school education (Comenius: partnerships between schools), higher education (Erasmus encourages student mobility), the promotion of knowledge of languages (Lingua), improving teachers' skills, and the exchange of information and experiences (Eurydice, Aron, and Naric). Socrates is aimed at pupils, students, teachers, university administrative personnel, instructors, children of migrant workers, persons with a traveling occupation, and gypsies. With respect to the Erasmus Program, Socrates has new elements. This enrichment of study programs through innovative elements is geared toward promoting the virtual mobility of students. For the groups of universities, three new curricular activities were provided: European modules based on socio-economic, cultural and historic structures of the Member States, the European integration and comparative aspects; education modules offered in a foreign language and especially in the language in which education is least provided in Europe; and courses at a high level (Master) in certain specialized fields.

The most innovative and most debatable aspect of the Program is the institutional contract between the Commission and each institution that proposes international cooperative activities for the purpose of obtaining a

---

[21] Decision *819/95* of the European Parliament and the Council of 14 March 1995, *Pb.* 1995

subsidy from the Commission. The transition from the Interuniversity Co-operation Programs in the framework of the Erasmus Program to the institutional contract stirred a commotion in the university world which feared that the bottom-up approach would have been discouraged by this contract since it introduces top-down approach. It is indeed the case that the responsibilities of the institutions must make proposals with regard to the cooperation activities that make up part of a strategy to be followed within the institution. Still, one needs to take into consideration the fact that the strategy of university responsibilities must be established on the basis of democratic decision-making. The contract forms a solid basis on which every university can outline a European policy. Yet, the Commission was aware that the transition would not take place without a struggle and chose not to bring the contract into effect until after an extensive information campaign in 1997/1998.

The Thematic Networks

The thematic networks, referring to the disciplinary or multidisciplinary dimensions of education, were formally established in 1996. In 1997 and 1998, two new calls were granted to renew or submit files and to expand the actions in some new areas. The objective of these thematic networks was to offer each institution of higher education the opportunity to establish a forum to study the development of education and training and to promote the European dimension and quality of the education. In point of fact, the thematic networks must make it possible to evaluate the quality of European cooperation and to stimulate pedagogical reform and discussions regarding the improvement of teaching methods. In principle, faculties and departments of higher education were involved along with scholarly and professional organizations in order to ensure a great impact on the institutional level, both intradisciplinary and interdisciplinary.

To date, of the forty-three thematic networks that have been recognized, twenty-one deal with academic educational programs in the areas of economic, social, and philanthropic sciences as well as science and technology. Seventeen networks deal with education and training in women's studies, art, law, teacher training, tourism, free time, and biotechnology. Five networks are geared toward encouraging human and social values. On average, each network has 117 institutions for higher education. The success of the thematic networks lies in their originality and the Commission's break from earlier actions. What is important is the emphasis which is placed on the European cooperation that should become a medium to reflect on the content of education. The thematic networks must form a cohesion factor within higher education.

The Lingua Program

The Lingua Program for the promotion of knowledge of foreign languages in the EC includes four actions.[22] Action 1 introduces measures to promote refresher training for teachers of foreign languages. Action 2 involves measures to promote learning foreign languages at the university level and for the development of basic training for teachers of foreign languages. Action 3 seeks to promote knowledge of foreign languages for use in business affairs and the economic world. Action 4 is designed to promote the expansion of the exchange within the Community of young people in professional, vocational, or technical education. These exchanges are organized in the framework of projects between educational establishments.

Eurydice

Eurydice is the European education information network whose goal is the production and sharing of information about education systems and reforms as well as about research results and innovations in the field of education.

Naric

Naric is the network of national information centers for academic recognition which are responsible for providing information to institutions and citizens about higher education systems. Naric also deals with qualifications in view of promoting the recognition of such qualifications in other countries for academic and, in many cases, professional purposes.

Arion

Arion includes study visits for education policy makers.

The Tempus Program

The primary goal of Tempus, the Trans-European Mobility Program for University Towns (1990-1995), was to establish and promote international cooperation in higher education between the European Union (EU) and the Central and East European countries, the new independent states of the former Soviet Union and Mongolia.

The Comett II Program

The Comett II Program forms the second phase of the program regarding cooperation between universities and companies with regard to education in the field of technology.

---

[22] Decision L 239 of the Council of 28 July 1989, *Pb.* 16.08.1989.

The PETRA Program

PETRA (1988-1994) was the EC action program for the professional training of young people in their preparation for life as adults and in professions. PETRA was designed to supplement and to support the policy measures of the Member States in order to increase the level and quality of the initial professional training.[23]

The Eurotecnet Program

The aim of the Eurotecnet program (1990-1994) was to promote innovation in the fields of initial and further professional training in order to take into account current and future technological changes as well as their consequences for employment, labor, and required qualifications and skills.[24]

The FORCE Program

FORCE (1991-1994) was designed to develop further professional training. It had the aim of improving the supply and quality of further professional training for the benefit of workers and companies by means of innovation and the exchange of experiences.[25]

The Leonardo da Vinci Program

The Leonardo da Vinci[26] Program (1995-1999) aimed at developing a European dimension in professional and technical training and to improve the quality, the innovative capacity, and the accessibility of professional training systems and facilities in participating countries. This program subsidized transnational partnership projects, transnational exchanges, transnational studies, and analyses.

The da Vinci Program was geared toward everyone, regardless of whether an individual worked as well as for those who were responsible for initial and further professional training. The program had four parts. Part 1 provided support for the improvement of the professional training systems and facilities in Member States. These transnational trial projects not only had bearing on cooperation in the field of the improvement of initial and further professional training but also supported job counseling and career choice guidance, the promotion of equal opportunities for men and women, and the improvement of the quality of professional training facilities for

---

[23] Decision of the Council of 1 December 1987, *Pb* L. 346 of 10.12.1987 and Decision of the Council of 21 July 1991, *Pb*. L214 of 2.8.1991.

[24] Decision of the Council of 18 December 1989, *Pb.,* L393 of 30 December 1989.

[25] Decision of the Council of 29 May 1990, *Pb.* L.156 of 21.06.1990.

[26] Decision of the Council of 6 December 1994, *Pb.* L 340 of 29.12.1994

those who have difficulty entering the job market. The da Vinci Program provided EC support to transnational apprenticeship programs for young people in initial professional training, for working young people, and for transnational programs for teacher exchange programs.

Part 2 offered support for improving professional training actions, partly by cooperation between universities and companies for the benefit of companies and employees. The transnational trial projects had bearing on innovation in professional training in order to take into account technological changes and their influence on work and required qualifications and skills. The program also supported transnational cooperation in the field of investments in the further education of workers, the transfer of technological innovations in the framework of cooperation between the business world and universities, and the promotion of equal treatment for men and women in the field of professional training. The da Vinci Program provided community support to transnational apprenticeship and exchange programs between companies and universities or educational institutions and the transnational exchange of education officials.

Part 3 provided support for the development of knowledge of languages as well as the dissemination of innovations in professional training. In the framework of this part, support was made available for cooperation with a view to improving knowledge of languages by establishing and implementing transnational trial projects and exchange programs, developing knowledge by means of questionnaires and analyses, and through the exchange of comparable data in professional training. This part also aimed at disseminating innovations in professional training by means of multiplier projects and transnational exchange programs. These exchange programs were carried out by Cedefop, the European Center for the Development of Professional Training.

Part 4 offered guidance measures involved in the promotion and follow-up of the program via the establishment of a cooperative network between countries participating in it and by means of screening, follow-up, and evaluation measures.

Education and Training: Teaching and Learning; Transition to a Cognitive Society

1996 was declared the European year for education and schooling for young and old. The goals set for the year were the advancement of personal development and initiative, the integration of people in professional life and society, their participation in demographic decision-making process, and their ability to adapt to what they come up against economically, technologically, and socially. In connection with this, the Commission took a first initiative by publishing the White Paper on Education and Training.[27]

The White Paper aims to strengthen education and training policy in relation to the challenges of the information society, economic globalization, and rapid scientific and technical progress. In order to best take advantage of these developments, the Commission introduced a number of action directives that led to the development of the principle of subsidiarity in the sense that actions complement national policy. Insofar as the acquisition of new and further knowledge is an absolute priority, the Commission proposed that the skills which are not rated in the form of a diploma will be recognized by the further development of a European system for the recognition of technical and professional skills. In addition, the Commission proposed that schools and businesses be brought closer together through the formation of training centers, the promotion of mobility, and the approval of a European students statute.[28] Another objective concerns solving the problem of exclusion by avoiding having marginalized groups in the population such as young people without diplomas, older employees, long-term unemployed, and women returning to the workforce who have no chance in the labor market due to their lack of knowledge and skills. In order to achieve this goal, the Commission proposed making extra European financial means available to give these groups a second chance in educational institutions. The next objective was the thorough command of several languages by introducing a class label which will be granted to schools who best develop language teaching. Further, the Commission set the goal of holding out the prospect of advantages in the area of tax benefits and administration for companies that invest in training their personnel. The Council, in response, underlined the great benefit of the discussions on the White Paper that have made it possible to give a meaning to the concept of a "Community of Knowledge."[29]

Mobility Obstacles and Possible Solutions: The Green Paper

The removal of the obstructions to free movement of people is, since the Treaty of Rome, one of the fundamental objectives of the European construction process and is one of the basic conditions for the existence of

---

[27] COM (95) 590.

[28] *See* J. de Groof & H. Penneman, "The Legal Status of Pupils in Europe," London, Kluwer Law International, 1998.

[29] Conclusions of the Council of 22 September 1997 on the announcement concerning The White Paper "teaching and learning. Towards a cognitive society," *Pb.*, C 303 of 04/10/1997, p. 0008.

a real Europe of the people. Yet, mobility still runs into too many obstacles since capital, goods, and services move around more easily within the EC than people. Hindrances are found in the implementation of EC teacher training and research programs which have been diminished. Obstacles to mobility particularly harm young people from lower or middle class backgrounds and the unemployed. According to the Treaty founding the EC, action must be taken to promote mobility in education, training, and research. It is in the framework of this task that the Commission drafted a Green Paper[30] on transnational mobility, a discussion of which follows.

Obstacles

Problems Related to the Right of Residence

It is possible that some students cannot make a claim to Directive EEC 93/96 because they are not following a course at a "recognized institution" within the meaning of the Directive. Some people also want to move to other Member States to follow a course of study. Thus, it must be examined whether individuals can be qualified as employees within the spirit of Article 39, formerly article 48, of the EC treaty. It is not always easy to examine each case individually and determine whether an activity pursued by a person shows the essential characteristics of an employment position. "Interns" and "researchers" can be described as employees in the spirit of Article 39 of the EC Treaty if, during a specific time for the benefit of another person and under this person's guidance, they have carried out duties for which they have received payment. Moreover, it is not ruled out that a person receiving training can lay claim to the right of residence in the framework of a service as intended in EEC Directive 73/148 of 21 May 1973. Those concerned can also be service providers such as a teacher who teaches in an occupational training center during a limited period and receives payment for doing so or a service receiver such as a person who follows training and pays a set price. Finally, a person who cannot lay claim to the right of residence can always appeal under EEC Directive 90/364 under which a right of residence can be obtained if sufficient means are available and an all-risk sickness insurance has been taken out. Even so, it is possible that a person does not fall into any of the categories such as when he or she cannot prove that he or she has sufficient means to be eligible for EEC Directive 90/364.

---

[30] European Union Bulletin Supplement *5/96* and COM (96) 462 def.

Due to a lack of a specific framework of rights, interns on work placements in companies in Member States run up against serious problems since they are neither students nor are recognized as employees or as unemployed. Sometimes they do not even have the chance of transnational mobility. Yet, all EU citizens have the right to stay in another Member State for three months as a tourist or as a receiver of services as identified in EEC Directive 73/148 as long as they possess identity documents or a passport. A person who wishes to prolong a stay abroad after three months must apply to the government of the Member State for a residence permit and should confirm that he or she carries out paid work or can give proof of registration in an educational institution and has sufficient means of support, including health insurance. As its first line of action, the Green Paper proposes the recognition of the status of trainees and voluntary workers on placements.

National Differences for Research Trainees
Mobile researches who have received a Community mobility scholarship, a Marie Curie scholarship, do not have the same status in every country. Member States pass on to researchers their own systems of charging National social differences as to security contributions and direct taxation for research trainees. These researchers are mostly treated as employees but may have student or self-employed status. These differences in the treatment of researchers and the scholarships which they are granted have consequences on two levels.

The first consequence concerns the useful effect of EC funds for research. When the EC awards scholarships, whether via an institution or directly to a student, the implementation of each Member State's system has a direct influence on the amount of the EC scholarship which will finally be used for research after a recipient has handed over the obligatory charges in compliance with the law of the receiving Member State.

The second consequence concerns the attractive character of the EC scholarships which are awarded in the framework of common research projects. A decision in connection with the mobility of researchers risks being significantly influenced by considerations of a financial nature while the choice of a host establishment basically should be made based on community considerations. The maintenance of these differences could lead to candidates delaying the submission of applications for community scholarships with a view to carrying out research in other Member States and that a brain drain could be set in motion. The present situation of the researchers with a community scholarship must be improved upon and solutions must be sought which will lead to changes in specific areas, chiefly in labor law and fiscal law under the national policies.

Obligatory Charges: Direct Taxation and Social Security Contributions

In many Member States, since scholarships and other allowances are considered income, they are subject to income tax. In other Member States, these amounts become payment of expenses and are not considered taxable income. The danger exists that the income of wage earners who make use of the right of double mobility is taxed.

In international tax law, a tax charge is based on the criterion of the fiscal place of residence. People who remain in one state, meaning that their fiscal place of residence is situated there, are generally obliged to declare their income regardless of whether they come from this state or from a foreign source. Non-residents are, on the other hand, generally only taxed on income they received in the State. This competition in the law to levy taxes can lead to double taxation which can be avoided by applying international agreements. There still remain cases of double taxation. Normally, students are exempt from taxes in a receiving country on amounts they receive from overseas which are intended to cover their expenses. An exemption does not apply when a scholarship is paid by a receiving State, an institution, or a company which is established there. Further, a scholarship can be taxed in a receiving State under conditions set down in national law. The decree of the Danish Fiscal Court of 12 June 1991 judged as illegal the attempt of the Ministry of Economic Affairs to add the Erasmus scholarship to the income of students and consider it as their pay; in Denmark students normally receive pay. In this way, a candidate would be assessed in a higher tax bracket. As a result of this decree, Denmark has implemented a tax exemption for mobility scholarships including the Erasmus scholarships and in so-doing acknowledged that a scholarship is not a salary but is intended to cover costs for travel and stay.

Recognition, Certification, and Validation

The validation of work placements and training periods remains problematic. In non-regulated professions, there are no legal obstacles to mobility; Yet, insufficient understanding of foreign qualifications is a great hindrance. In 1985, the EC ordered a number of actions to improve the comparability, transparency and recognition of skills and qualifications. This is still one of the aims of the Leonardo da Vinci Program.

Territoriality of National Scholarships

In many Member States, students lose the right to a national scholarship or financial support if they carry out their studies in another state of the EC. These scholarships are merely awarded for studies which are followed in the country which grants the scholarship. This situation puts those with modest incomes, who cannot support the cost of foreign study for their children, at a disadvantage. In line of action 5, the Green Paper proposes removing territorial restrictions on grants and national financing.

Socio-Economic Obstacles

Job protection: An employee or intern who is going to undergo training/work placement in another country is not always guaranteed his job upon return.

Insufficient financial support: The extraordinary development of the mobility in the framework of the Erasmus Community program demonstrates the enthusiasm which exists for the student exchange. The limitation of the amounts awarded has, until now, resulted in some selected students receiving no access to mobility. The support is also insufficient for researchers because most maintain their homes in their countries of origin, often making their mobility costs very heavy. The situation is bad for the unemployed who, after no more than a three-month stay abroad, lose their rights. For young people who have finished their studies, the situation is even more difficult.

Administrative Obstacles Resulting from the Organization of School and University

Timetable of the school and academic year: The timetable of the academic year is sometimes determined on a national level and at other times by a training structure itself. A problem can arise when the timetable of a Member State of origin does not correspond with that of the receiving Member State.

Examinations: Students who take part in a mobility plan find themselves no longer in the country of origin when their examinations are being held or because of their absence cannot turn up for the exams in their original education institution, thus causing problems in obtaining a diploma.

No replacement during absence: In most cases, teachers are not replaced during their mobility with the result that when they return, they have to catch up with the backlog in material.

Not knowing a language remains an obstacle to mobility. The greatest mobility is concentrated in the triangle Germany/France/United Kingdom. The learning of fewer diffuse languages is a guarantee for a better dispersal of the streams of students and for a greater diversity in the exchanges. At the beginning of the 1996-97academic year, test projects were launched to that end so that Socrates-Erasmus students who went to Portugal, Greece, Italy, Denmark, or Finland received intensive linguistic preparation.

Practical Obstacles

At least six obstacles often impede high quality mobility. Sometimes they are so great that the demoralized participants do not set out or go back to their country of origin without having profited from the mobility possibilities on offer. These obstacles are before departure lack of information concerning the training and housing; lack of host companies; affordable rents for accommodations; additional insurance for accidents, repatriation, and/ or civil responsibilities; family problems; and bank and exchange costs of the less well-off or individuals who are handicapped especially have problems with these practical obstacles.

Lines of Action

These lines of action fill in the grey zones of the EC, to verify the extent of change of the EC regulations by Member States and to examine which actions must be taken to encourage Member States to do so. The nine assumed lines are not exhaustive. Line of action 1 is intended to address the status of trainees on placements and voluntary workers in the EC. Line of action 2 concerns equal treatment for all EC grant-aided research trainees. Line of action 3 seeks to ensure social protection for everyone benefiting from transnational mobility as part of training. Line of action 4 calls for creating a European area of qualifications. Line of action 5 seeks the removal of territorial restrictions on grants and national financing. Line of action 6 is designed to improve the situation of nationals of third countries who are legal residents in the EC with regard to training. Line of action 7 address reducing socio-economic obstacles. Line of action 8 aims to reduce linguistic and cultural obstacles. Line of action 9 hopes to improve information available and administrative practices. More details can be found in the document of the EC itself.[31]

A few questions have arisen from the actions in the Green Paper.[32] The fact that no mention is made of the level on which the above-mentioned actions should take place is problematic. The competence problem is still the weak point in European education policy. It is still unclear how far the EC can go and where the jurisdictions of the Member States are misunderstood. A discussion of the lines of action remains fruitless without the indications of the correct authorities which can take measures or elaborate further.

---

[31] Supplement of the European Union *5/96* " Education, Training, Research: the obstacles to transnational mobility ".

[32] M. Verbruggen, "The Commission's Green Paper' Education, Training, Research: the obstacles to transnational mobility: content and comment," *EJELP,* 1997, at 41.

The correct terminology still causes a problem. The Green Paper contains definitions concerning the people involved such as pupils, students, researchers, and teachers. These definitions are still used in the texts of the European Council but this does not mean that they can be considered EC definitions. Further, these terms should be dealt with carefully because it is possible that in a national context they mean something else. In addition, it can clearly be deduced from the obstacles laid out in the Green Paper that mobility already functions adequately. Most problems are of a practical, administrative, or psychological nature. The biggest problem for volunteers and researchers is that their statute in the different Member States in the social as much as the fiscal area varies a great deal since they are neither economically active nor students. The Green Paper is nevertheless a very useful instrument as a discussion paper for the formation of a real European Education Policy in the EU.

Future Perspectives

Development of New Work Procedures for European Cooperation in Education and Training

In its resolution,[33] the Council stressed the need for a coherent approach of EC action in education and training. The cooperation could be intensified via the realization of a structured framework for political discussions and activities in the coming years. Future activities in education and training could be organized around a progressing agenda of three priority subjects: the role of education and training in employment policy; development of education and training of a high quality at every level; and promotion of mobility, including the recognition of qualifications and period of study segments. Other relevant subjects which can be cooperated upon would be examined, keeping in mind the relevant political developments in the coming years.

New Subjects Contributing to the Development of High Calibre Education

Quality care cannot, in any way, be considered to be a new concept in education legislation.[34] The standard of education was usually used as a

---

[33] *Pb.* C 008 of 12/01/2000, p. 0006-0007.
[34] European J. for Educ. L. & Pol'y, J. of the European Ass'n for Educ. L. &

norm in the earliest organic education laws. In some Member States of the EU, an independent primary school could, historically, be adopted under an adoption contract and make a claim for subsidy. Other laws[35] provided systems of patronage for independent secondary schools, provided they agreed to be subject to inspection. Consequently, non-official schools obtained conditional subsidies and recognition even though they had not entered into a contract with local authorities, provincial, or national governments.

Educational historians have shown how decent education provisions could not be guaranteed without government intervention and even the inveterately, liberal authors of the Constitution pointed out from the very early days the danger of charlatans and speculators who misused the freedom they enjoyed. The principle by which a government which is providing funding enforces quality, soundness, efficiency, and legal security is elevated to a constitutional standard in a number of countries,[36] but could chiefly be anchored in the education laws, although in most countries it still remained a rather static and dormant concept. This is why an inspectorate was set up and demands written in regarding structure, curriculum, teaching materials, and school equipment while the skill diplomas and the approval or sanctioning of certificates has been geared to this from way back. Only in more recent times have legislatures written quality care into statutory instruments in more explicit terms, fearlessly drawing the card of international screening and applying the test of international indicators.

The search for a balance between freedom and the responsibility of the governing bodies or administrative authorities of schools, universities, and other higher education institutions on the one hand, and the driving, guiding role of the government on the other hand, continued to be a decisive factor in the debate and in decision-making even though not, it is true, with any great uniformity. Some constitutional courts designated the prime importance of "decent educational provision" as the guideline for government intervention[37] albeit with respect for the school governing bodies' own visions on the form and content of education.[38] The demand for good quality education was proclaimed as a matter of public interest.[39]

Pol'y, Kluwer, The Hague, 1997, Vol., no. 1-2.
[35] Especially art. 32.
[36] Especially art. 208 of the Dutch Constitution.
[37] Judgment of the Court of Arbitration, no. 25/92, 2 April 1992, *Moniteur belge*, 14 May 1992.
[38] *See, e.g,* Judgment of the Court of Arbitration, no. 18/93, 4 March 1993, *Moniteur belge*, 24 March 1993; Judgment of the Court of Arbitration, no. 25/92, 2 April 1992, *Moniteur belge*, 10 June 1992.
[39] Judgment of the Court of Arbitration, no. 73/96, 11 December 1996, *Moniteur belge*, 10 January 1997.

In the majority of European countries, legislators have also explicitly taken up the option of basing organization, rationalization, and curricula on quality criteria. Quality standards at macro and micro levels are also being erected or have been the subject of recent judgements,[40] including those on the admission or exclusion of pupils, contentious issues surrounding exams,[41] and staff charters. Further legal refinement of quality care needs to be promoted, as a right, as something to which a pupil or student is entitled. This is another reason why comparative Education Law can be inspiring and the young democracies are showing a major degree of maturity in this respect. The quality of government intervention is, for that matter, best evaluated in terms of the efforts it makes to promote quality in the school, university or other higher education institution. This is known in the jargon as "remote steering" or "steering at a distance." Meanwhile, government, ministers and representatives of school governing bodies will do no small service by putting the quality debate on compulsory education and higher education high on the agenda from a European perspective.

The following ideas apply mainly to higher education. A recent comparative and pan-European study[42] advances the view that the pragmatic austerity policies in England and the Netherlands only produced a more or less coherent government strategy after the event. Similarly, quality care, as a measure, seems, after the event, to fit in neatly with the response which politicians are being forced to formulate as an up-to-date vision of university autonomy, partly due to pressure from the social-economic environment. The fact that most governments do not allow themselves to be carried away by the higher and higher bids of and explosion in quality agencies, which sometimes have a flavor of commercialism, but use government instruments for this, plus the unadulterated techniques of peer review and visitation committees, can be said to be healthy. At the same time, it has become clear that it has not been the universities which have taken the lead in making quality care explicit. The reform of universities, as evident from the volumes of the Flemish historian Hilde de Ridder Simoens, has usually been a laborious process, not spurred on by the universities.

Quality care is intrinsically associated with the definition of academic autonomy: a university as a place which governs itself. Anglo-Saxon writ-

---

[40] Judgment of the Court of Arbitration, no. 42/96, 2 July 1996, *Moniteur belge*, 17 July 1996. See also law mentioned in J. De Groof & P. Mahieu, *De school komt tot haar recht. De uitoefening van rechten in het onderwijs*, Antwerp, 1994.

[41] On the contribution of a jury from an educational institution to get the student to improve the quality of his work 'in his own interests': judgment of the Council of State, no. 39.179, 7 April 1992, *R.A.C.E.*, 1992.

[42] J. De Groof, G. Neave, & J. Svec. *Democracy and Governance in Higher Education*, Kluwer Law International, 1998.

ers, in particular, make a distinction between the mechanisms of strict control, the supervising role, and evaluation of output at a distance. Some models offer an original and balanced account of the various supervisory techniques, including process and product control. There is not a single voice of authority which still defends the paring down of government supervision to the mere verification of whether administrative and budgetary procedures are being observed to the letter (and in the area of personnel policy, official basic regulations continue to be vital, for quality among other things). However, what education institutions have to face is that the product depends on a sound process. They also have to be prepared to answer the question, which is being asked throughout Europe, whether in exchange for quasi-autonomy in the process area, their freedom as far as the delivery of products is concerned is not being restricted too much.

There is increased consensus on implementing quality care as a principle of proper administration to be enforced on educational institutions, on the one hand, and on the need to investigate the excessive and over detailed nature of existing regulations to be enforced on the government, on the other hand. This need for screening, including the in-built restraining character with respect to the European principle of mobility and non-discrimination, concerns, in the first instance, the legal position of various echelons of staff, not to serve corporate interests, but to command better opportunities for quality in freedom.

Would it be bold to say that the current and anticipated regulations on quality care in national education systems are only a snapshot of a particular moment in time, that the balance which leaders are aiming for will shift, and on the following three points to be going on with:

a) The objection professed almost unanimously up to now to positive, and if necessary, also negative, sanctioning opportunities in the area of quality control; this is unsustainable in the long-term. Incentive funding should indeed be afforded more opportunities.

b) Quality evaluation touches all aspects of the running of an institution and so is not confined to the mission but also includes management and administration, their transparency and cohesion. This need not conflict with the position of the Dutch education lawyer, ex-Secretary of State for Education and vice-chancellor Professor J. Cohen, who started from the premise that what is seductive about a university is, in some sense, the gentle and controlled chaos which can operate there, certainly in an institution where freedom is the greatest good and the "unpredictable" must be cherished.

c) One of the most ambitious powers of the EU which has gone almost unnoticed will, from now on, be quality care and its European dimension. Member States ought to include this dimension in their national policies. It leads to institutions stressing their distinctive features more forcefully to a degree of ranking of innovative and enterprising educational institutions, even though power and prestige usually speak for themselves. It also requires minimum standards for evaluation techniques to guarantee comparability. Even so, all strategies for quality in higher education will have to boast a partnership between autonomous institutions and a dynamic government. They are, as it were, "sentenced to each other," tied together in service of the community. The Council Recommendation on European Co-Operation in Quality Assurance in Higher Education was formally adopted in Autumn 1998 and refers rightly as foundation to the following principles:

The free movement of goods, persons, services and capital as per Article 6 of the EC Treaty and the contribution to education and training of quality as well as the flowering of the cultures of the Member States is in Article 3.q of the Treaty. For education and training, Articles 149 and 150 state that the EC's role is to encourage co-operation between Member States and, if necessary, to support and supplement their actions while fully respecting the responsibility of the Member States for the content of teaching and the organisation of education and training systems and their cultural and linguistic diversity.

The Recommendation respects the diversity of European education and training systems and builds on voluntary co-operation and adaptation. Community action in the field could have an added value insofar as the advantages of co-operation at the European level, especially in quality assessment and quality assurance, cannot be achieved by one Member State alone or a single group of Member States without establishing links to all of the others. The pace of change in this area makes permanent exchange of experience and full information on all developments in the Member States necessary in order to keep up. As this exchange would draw on Europe's overall problem-solving capacity, it could build up momentum and give a substantial and effective boost to the quality of European higher education. Further, the Recommendation lays particular emphasis on the advantages of European co-operation in quality assessment and quality assurance in helping Member States to meet the new quality-demands on education systems. Permanent observation and comparison of the impact of the legal and institutional frameworks on performance will help to avoid possible undesired side-effects of quality assurance procedures in the different Member States and contribute to increasing effectiveness. Co-operation will also make it easier to develop strategies for innovation in higher education systems.

Self-assessment is mostly the major positive output in the whole process of evaluation. Yet, self-analyses of the weaknesses illustrates the need of a transparent definition of quality. For instance, on the output side, it must be decided what the expected level of knowledge will be for students.

Such an assessment needs an independent external evaluation that is not to be limited to peers but should also be accessible to the stake holders, the social, economic, cultural environment and, of course, the clients.

In the long term this question of what is assessed handles the item of the competence to change, the competence to improve. The greatest danger for educational institutions is self-evidence. "Cambridge versus Cambridge:" Cambridge (United States) thinks it can change the world, Cambridge (United Kingdom) thinks it is the world. What ought to be included in this assessment is first, the specific missions, specific aims of a particular educational institution. Review can indeed assess the denominational factor, the specificity of the educational institution. How the contribution to regional development will be laid down in most charters of educational institutions, how this is expressed, is realized into practice. A second aspect of assessment is that all of an educational institution's tasks should be included, research, teaching, and scientific public service. The different missions of educational institutions cannot be split up. The distinction between university, academy, and institute covering one or more disciplines is another interesting aspect. The third element of assessment of educational institutions comprises the presence of an interface between educational institutions and the environment. This might ask, for example, whether there is an application of basic knowledge into technology or whether educational institutions could be assessed and classified on such following items as the number of graduates who enjoy training in non-European institutes in the United States or Asia or who are connected with prestigious research institutes, or the number of academics, staff member of an institute, who graduated in such an institute or in other European universities and who obtained their Ph.Ds. and made their careers there, or which contribution(s) of an educational institutions are recognized by international networks.

According to French law, assessment is organised by four actors: the CMU, or board of universities, which assesses the approval and promotion of professors; the research council on scientific research of a university; the ministry on degrees and programs; and the inspector general on the management of the institutions. The concern ought to be expressed that this could lead to a fragmentation of techniques of quality assessment. An integrated concept is needed including product and process analysis. Down to the process of research, for instance, is the question of how boards of educational institutions will stimulate young brilliantly talented researchers.

Quality control of the second generation consists in reaching academic standards. The standards express the level of achievement expected or required by students according to a variety of types and will include professional and academic contents. In the last visitation of the commission in the Flemish community of Belgium, rectors were upset. It was the first time, through a visitation-commission, that this subject of standards, main aims, main purposes of certain level of higher education, was touched. Until that moment, rectors thought this was only the concern of primary and secondary education. Yet, it unavoidably will be the second generation of discussions on quality in higher education as to standards and basic achievements of knowledge.

Another question addresses who is responsible after assessment of educational institutions. Will a minister have the means to implement recommendations from visitation commissions as in French, British. and most European systems, or to implement improvement plans as in the Dutch system? This question was answered in different ways in the Danish and the Dutch legislation. According to Danish law, a minister will not be obliged to implement the findings of external evaluation because there is a complete autonomy of the institutions. Under the Dutch convention, a minister will bare the overall responsibility; the inspectorate will monitor the improvement plans and its effects. The Flemish system fosters co-responsibility, a dialogue between universities and the minister. In case of systematic neglect that is not random or coincidental of more than one year, there will be coercive and remedial recommendations.

Taking into account the hierarchy of this kind of recommendations (advisable, desirable, coercive), one must again consider the British system. In case of systematic neglect of such kind of coercive recommendations and a confirmed lack of quality, institutes could be financially penalized. In legal terms, this question also touches the principle of equal treatment of students. Further, it might violate the principle of competition on equal terms between higher education institutions. In case of a positive assessment, additional resources for free use by an institution, as in Australia, will improve the prestige of the higher education institution and have a far reaching positive influence. This question of responsibility will bare heavy consequences also on the accountability of the States but also for the students, the users. It is not inconceivable that students go to the court if a basic minimal requirement of quality is not achieved since such a possibility is already stipulated in Russian Law.

School Safety

Satisfactory quality education is not possible without having an atmosphere of openness and security at school in which pupils/students can be educated and teachers can educate without fear of intimidation, bullying, or ill-treatment. It is also necessary to take measures as much at the level of the

Member States as at the European level.[43] Increasing security at schools can include strategies to avoid and fight intimidation, bullying, and ill-treatment. It is clear that while school safety unmistakeably falls under the authority of the Member States, the European dimension in this area can provide additional value. It can, therefore, be very useful to exchange information and learn from each other's experiences in the area of safety at school and that, if one wants to profit from both cases, one has to do this in a structured way.

Future Perspectives Concerning European Higher Education Policy

The Sorbonne Declaration

In the Sorbonne Declaration of 25 May 1998, the education ministers of the four largest European countries expressed their aspirations for a joint basic structure for higher education to imprve the external recognition of education and promote student mobility. The core ideas were higher education in the context of lifelong learning with a widespread credit system; an open European area for higher learning where mobility is self-evident; two main cycles in higher education, undergraduate and graduate which must be internationally comparable; international recognition, broadening the function and society's recognition of the undergraduate level; a short, more professionally oriented, cycle and a longer, scientifically oriented cycle preparing for a doctorate at the graduate level; at least one semester of study abroad at each level; and more teacher mobility and more university cooperation.[44]

The Bologna Declaration

The European education ministers, in a follow-up forum to the Sorbonne Declaration, signed a joint declaration on 19 June 1999 in Bologna named "The Open European Education Area." The Bologna Declaration formulated two important objectives indicating the need to increase the comparison of the systems of higher education in Europe and urging the strengthening of the competitive strength of the systems.

---

[43] P. Akkermans, J. De Groof, H. Penneman. "Education Law and Policy in an Urban Society" Kluwer International, 1997, in Yearbook of the European Association for Education Law and Policy.

[44] P. Henderikx. " The Sorbonne Declaration: Looking Outside," *Thema*, 1999 at 23.

At this time there is still no mention of an unequivocal identification and recognition in Europe and beyond of the degrees which the European systems of higher education grant in national contexts. This recognition is a condition in bringing about the "Europe of knowledge" to provide access to students without obstacles to the educational institutions within Europe, the so-called open European education area, and to guarantee citizens free traffic to the open European labor market. The second consideration in the Bologna Declaration relates to the discovery that the systems are increasingly in competition, especially with the United States. According to the Declaration, European institutions should have to supply recognized titles not only to confront this competition but also to be better able to play an effective part in the international educational market.

The most important intention mentioned in the Bologna Declaration is undoubtedly the goal of the education ministers to arrange national higher education systems in the coming decade into a system essentially based on two cycles, undergraduate and graduate. In this new system, access to the second cycle will require successful completion of a first cycle's studies, lasting a minimum of three years. The degree awarded after the first cycle shall also be relevant to the European labor market as an appropriate level of qualification. The second cycle should lead to a master's and/or doctoral degree as in many European countries. The majority of EU countries already offer two cycles of undergraduate and graduate higher education or are preparing similar schemes. Based on a study carried out in preparation for the Bologna Declaration, it appears that "only a few countries in the EU/EEA area do not seem to have or do not seem to be experimenting with two-tier curricula in at least part of their higher education system, namely Greece, The Netherlands, and, to a certain extent, Spain."[45]

The imminent expansion of the EU with the admission of new Member States points to the need for a variety of solutions while strengthening, rather than diluting, the European project. The search for this balance is already making itself felt in the EU and must continue to contribute to an escalation of the finality of Europe. Culture and education, universities and colleges of further education have a special role to play in this respect. In particular, centers in Eastern and Central Europe invariably refer to improving the cohesion of the European higher education area as one of the four roads to the development of European universities as well as strengthening quality in higher education, restructuring the universities, and changing the system of financing European universities in social integration. Concern

---

[45] A. Van Staa, "The Bologna Declaration: new labels or an Anglo-Saxon education scheme in the Netherlands? *Thema,* 1999, at 25.

about the need to put the economic approach to education into perspective, expressed polemically as functionality versus spirituality, and the continuing need for diversity within unity (uniformity versus authenticity?) were factors borne in mind by the reading of the Sorbonne and Bologna Declarations by an undoubtedly important and select group of ministers.

The document, *Trends in Learning Structures in Higher Education*, partly initiated by the Confederation of EU Rectors' Conferences and the Association of European Universities (CRE), and produced in preparation for the Bologna meeting, starts with the assertion that there are even more systems of higher education than countries in Europe. On the other hand, a number of different trends affect the structure of degrees and qualifications in Europe. There is particular interest in the recent reforms in Germany and Austria which introduced new bachelors/masters curricula on a voluntary basis and in Italy and France where the existing curricula are being reorganized into first degree and postgraduate levels.

It needs to be said again that there is no Europe-wide model[46] for the organization of higher education and there is no need for such a model. Each country must work out for itself the best structures to meet future challenges. The OECD monograph, *Redefining Tertiary Education*,[47] also confirmed that the crucial issue is not whether a system has a unitary or binary structure and that the diversity of learning structures need not mean that there is a huge gulf between different learning trajectories. This is also true at an international level. It would not be worthwhile trying to develop uniform systems across Europe. Further, it is unclear how the adoption of a two-level system of bachelors and masters degrees across Europe could be realized in the context of Articles 149 and 150 of the EU Treaty. The implementation of the convergence principle[48] has to remain in conformity with the responsibility of the Member States. Reference is regularly made to an Anglo-Saxon or American model. However, no where is there such a huge discrepancy between the quality of universities and personal and social development opportunities as in the United States.

---

[46] P. Scott, Unified and Binary Systems of Higher Education in Europe, in A. Burgen, (ed.), *Goals and Purposes of Higher Education in the 21ˢᵗ Century, Higher Education Policy Series 32*, London 1996, p.49.

[47] OECD, Paris, 1998.

[48] *See, e.g.*, K. Lenaerts, Subsidiarity and Community Competence in the Field of Education, in the first Report of the European Education Law and Policy Association, J. De Groof (ed.), *Subsidiarity and Education, Aspects of Comparative Education Law*, Leuven-Amersfoort, 1994, at 117 ff.

In a number of countries, people have started to reflect on the progress and outcomes of courses, the best way to structure higher education courses, and the co-ordination of academic courses. This includes the debate around the naming of diplomas and minimum study periods to attain diplomas. One cannot avoid looking at this from an international perspective as a new generation of initiatives for voluntary convergence and internationalization of the educational systems in each of the Member States.

Comparability of degrees has to be based on proven, not just claimed, academic quality. The credibility of the quality control and inevitable claim to "an enhanced European dimension in quality assurance and evaluation"[49] would seem to be more effective than "harmonisation" that is difficult to achieve. As soon as Article 149 was ratified, it was predicted that one of the most urgent tasks of the EU would be the promotion of quality care. There are convergences in this area, too, but educational research also indicates that the context of each individual educational institution is still a decisive factor in quality analysis.

Transferability of credits is even more important. The establishment of a generally accepted and applied system of credits requires agreement, a fortiori in relation to the non-university sector, on objectives and levels, "readability and comparability," and the awarding of credits as a means of quantifying minimum effort.

Complete agreement needs to be reached about the fundamental features that constitute a university. There needs to be complete clarity on admissions requirements for higher education such as twelve years in primary and secondary education, not counting any time spent in school before the age of six, and on whether a possible professional bachelor's qualification, following three years of education outside of a university, counts the same as an academic bachelor's degree for admission to postgraduate courses.

The following brief considerations may be added here. Contrary to Article 149.3 of the EU Treaty, which held out the prospect of special collaboration with the Council of Europe, the activities of the Council do not figure in several recent strategic documents. Nevertheless, collaboration with the Council of Europe does seem to be important, as does incorporating these results into the legal order of the EC. It would be relevant here to investigate what progress has been made on, for example, the Recommenda-

---

[49] But not necessarily "accreditation." The eagerly worded appeal for 'accreditation agencies' to be set up, independent of national and European authorities and working along subject lines, as outlined in *Trends and Issues in Learning Structures in Higher Education in Europe,* in preparation for the Bologna Declaration, does not tally with the primacy of the academic authorities' powers to recognise objective standards themselves, individually and jointly.

tion of the Committee of Ministers on Access to Higher Education,[50] including the provisions on admissions (point 4) and student progress (point 5) and the extent to which the Convention on the Recognition of Qualifications concerning Higher Education in the European Region[51] is already aiming to fulfil a number of the objectives of the Sorbonne and Bologna Declarations, albeit by means of a simpler request for the recognition of the equivalence of a diploma issued in another Member State.[52] This would mean an application, as it were, of the general principle of community trust in implementing Article 10 of the EC Treaty, in particular, the recognition of a diploma of a subject of a different member State by evaluating such a diploma carefully and on equal terms as upheld by the Court of Justice in a judgment of 7 May 1991 in the case of *Vlassopoulou*,[53] in accordance with a transparent technique and making it enforceable before the Court of Justice.

At the same time, it is important to avoid disadvantages that may arise from proposed intergovernmental cooperation to achieve basic objectives to establish the European area of higher education and to promote the European system of higher education in the world. In federal regimes, this kind of platform is known as the hird level, namely any voluntary inter-state consultation separate from federal authorities, usually with a view to voluntary harmonization or even unification. Thus, it is important to prevent European institutions from being weakened and to avoid the emergence of diverse education areas among Member States and the creeping in of a fast track/slow track Europe, or, despite statements to the conrary, the direct or indirect mortgaging of the autonomy of the university sector. It is highly questionable whether an international arrangement for accreditation of courses and educational institutions would be compatible with the competences of national governments and the autonomy of universities.

---

[50] *Recommendation* no. R (98) 3, dated 17 March 1998
[51] *Council of Europe, European Treaties, ETS no. 165, Lisbon, II.IV.1997.*
[52] See in particular: Section III (Basic principles related to the assessment of qualifications) and Section IV (Recognition of qualifications giving access to higher education). Section V contains a number of regulations on Recognition of periods of study. The key article, Article IV.I, provides: "Each Party shall recognise the qualifications issued by other Parties meeting the general requirements for access to higher education in those Parties for the purpose of access to programmes belonging to its higher education system, unless a substantial difference can be shown between the general requirements for access in the Party in which the qualification was obtained and in the Party in which recognition of the qualification is sought."
[53] COJ, case C-340/89, *Jur 1991, p. 1 2384/2385.*

Conclusion

Compatible credit systems, understandable degree structures, increased European dimensions on quality assurance, and a more European labor market are structural improvements since they contribute to better learning opportunities for all. This is the essential message of the Bologna Declaration. Further, national governments need to make sure that the remaining obstacles, which are still entrenched in national social security systems, are removed. National governments should be invited to report to European institutions on this from time to time.

The Bologna Declaration also contains an appeal for more practical and democratic educational administration.[54] "Flexibilisation" is currently the key word used for the reform of educational organizations, training programs, student profiles, and personnel policies. These are not really objectives, as such, but merely instruments serving a real objective, the university's ability to innovate. Knowledge management requires a more daring form of innovation than educatonal technology, for instance. The innovative post in higher education needs to unleash a real revolution on many fronts.[55] Even so, it remains to be seen whether European universities are able to take a pioneering role in this regard on the international level.

---

[54] For information on European concepts in this area, *see* J. de Groof, G. Neave, J. Svec, *Democracy and Governance in Higher Education, 1997,* Dordrecht, in: *Council of Europe monograph series of the Legislative reform programme,* Strasbourg.
[55] I. Nonaka & H. Takeuch, *The Knowledge Creating Company,* Oxford University Press, 1996.

HIGHER EDUCATION IN GREAT BRITAIN

Dennis J. Farrington

Introduction

This chapter provides an update on the legal issues which are currently engaging the attention of university and college administrators in Great Britain. It has been a busy year for both the United Kingdom (UK) Parliament and the new Scottish Parliament. The year 2000 saw the UK Parliament enact the Human Rights Act 2000, the Regulation of Investigatory Powers Act 2000, the Freedom of Information Act 2000, and complex Orders bringing into force the provisions of the Data Protection Act 1998, which has itself undergone some changes. All of these measures are expected, in due course, to have a far-reaching effect on higher education activities across a range of subject matters. The Scottish Parliament, exercising its new powers over education, voted to abolish tuition fees for all Scottish-domiciled students and suspended payment of tuition fees from session 2000/01, planning to introduce a new graduate endowment scheme (essentially deferred tuition fees) from session 2001/02. The Scottish Parliament also passed a Regulation of Investigatory Powers Act and is now debating a Freedom of Information Bill. In light of all of these activities, this chapter looks at the effects of UK legislation, English, and European case law on higher education in Great Britain.

Status of Institutions

Following the enactment of the Teaching and Higher Education Act 1998, which imposed tighter regulation on the use of the word "university" as a noun or adjective in an institutional title, there inevitably have been disputes about institutions which used the titles in the past but do not meet the new criteria. One such college is the entirely respectable Liverpool Institute of Higher Education, which does not meet the new criteria for the continued use of its adopted name, Liverpool Hope University College, principally because it does not have the power to award degrees. It had used the title for some time. In correspondence between the Institute and the relevant government department, officials indicated that an interval would be allowed in order for it and other institutions to adjust to the new provisions which would effectively mean the dropping of the use of "University College" in their titles. The Institute applied for judicial review of the date of commencement for the coming into force of the relevant provisions under the Teaching and Higher Education Act 1998 (Commencement No. 4 and Transitional Provisions) Order 1998. The Institute alleged not only that by failing to provide adequate time for compliance with the Act, the provision thwarted the intention of Parliament but also that it suffered from substantive unfairness, an of power, and breach of the principle of proportionality.

The application for judicial review was dismissed. The reference to an interval was designed to give the college and other institutions in a similar position time to stop using the offending phrase. The court found that the institution had been fairly treated.[1]

Revised Powers for Higher Education Corporations

The higher education corporation (h.e.c.) was one of the new types of corporations set up in the UK education reforms of the 1980's and 1990's. Broadly, a higher education institution conducted by an h.e.c. is expected to operate in much the same way as a university established by Royal Charter. However, as a statutory corporation, a h.e.c.'s powers would be limited to those prescribed in its enabling statute.

Among the powers that h.e.c's could reasonably expect to exercise, so as to be on a "level playing field" with universities, more so after many of the institutions conducted by them gained university title following the enactment of the Further and Higher Education Act 1992 and corresponding Scottish legislation, was the establishment of "arms length" companies. These companies would be able to exploit the fruits of research and the like generated by the conducted institutions. Universities have established such companies for many years, principally to avoid putting their charitable status as risk. A National Audit Office report in 1998 indicated that universities are charities that cannot provide services with a view to profit without jeopardising their charitable status. In such cases, the establishment of companies to undertake commercial opportunities is not uncommon and profits from such companies may be covenanted to allow a university to benefit from such activity without paying tax. Moreover, the Funding Councils issued guidance in 1996 on procedures and controls to be put in place to secure that such companies conducted their business at arms length from universities and other higher education institutions and without risk to public funds.

Section 41 Teaching and Higher Education Act 1998 inserted section 125A into the Education Reform Act 1988 to put beyond doubt that an h.e.c. is a charity which is an exempt charity for the purposes of the Charities Act 1993. However, whether h.e.c.'s as the legal entities conducting the new universities could actually do what older universities have done in this respect has been questioned in the past. Section 124(2)(f) Education Reform Act 1988 formerly gave an h.e.c. power to form or take part in forming a body

---

[1] R v. Secretary of State for Educ. and Employment, ex parte Liverpool Hope Univ. College[2000] Ed CR 330; [2000] ELR 579.

corporate for carrying on any such activities. The activities in question arise from the powers of the h.e.c. in section 124(1) to provide higher and further education, and "to carry out research, publish the results of the research or any other material arising out of or connected with it in such manner as the corporation think fit." In order to carry on activities under the corporation's section 124(1) powers, it has the power to conduct an educational institution.

Further, an h.e.c. has power in section 124(2) to do anything which appears to it to be "necessary or expedient" for the purpose of or "in connection with" the exercise of its powers in section 124(1). These derivative powers include supply of goods and services, acquisition and disposal of land and other property, and entering into contracts including employment . Section 124(f) did not specifically permit an h.e.c. to take a financial stake in companies which it or others might wish to establish in order to commercialise research findings or sell teaching materials, such as to exploit the opportunities offered by the Internet.

Paragraph 15 of Schedule 9 Learning and Skills Act 2000 makes a significant change to the powers of an h.e.c.. Section 124(2)(f) of the 1988 Act now reads "to subscribe for or otherwise acquire shares in or securities of a company for the purpose of carrying on any such activities." An h.e.c. therefore no longer has the statutory power to form a body corporate, not being a company, to carry on its various activities, but can set up and/or participate in the affairs of a company for these purposes. Removing the power to set up any other form of body corporate presumably prevents an h.e.c. from establishing an incorporated college or a company limited by guarantee without shares or securities.

There remains the question whether the activities of an arms length company are "for the purpose of" carrying on the activities pursuant to the powers set out in section 124(1). Essentially this has to be "necessary or expedient" or "in connection with" the exercise of those powers. The activity might be "necessary" for the purpose of avoiding conflict with charitable status. It might be "expedient" for the same reason or in order to allow those managing the activity a greater degree of commercial freedom than that which a public body can reasonably expect will satisfy its auditors. It might be "connected with" in the same sense as appears in section 18 Further and Higher Education Act 1992 in respect of further education corporations.

European Union Law

European Union (EC) Directives co-ordinating procedures for the award of public supply contracts provide that there should be regular review of the list of public authorities in their Annexes. The representative body for UK universities, the Committee of Vice-Chancellors and Principals (re-titled Universities UK from February 2001) informed the Treasury that the Directives did not apply to all universities and that reference to universities in the Annexes should be deleted. However, the Treasury suggested a different wording, which did not satisfy the University of Cambridge. It then sought a judicial review of the Treasury's decision. The English High Court (Queen's Bench Division) referred to the European Court of Justice a number of questions concerning interpretation of the Directives.

The Directives provided that contracting authorities included bodies governed by public law, defined as, first, established in the public interest, not having a commercial character; second, a separate legal person; third, financed mostly by the State or other public bodies, subject to management supervision by those bodies, or having a managerial or administrative board appointed by the State or other public bodies. The University of Cambridge met the first two conditions. As to the third, the relevant factor was the extent of public financing since the other two alternatives did not apply. Public financing included grants for teaching as well as research and tuition fees but not other income. The European Court of Justice decided that whether a university met the requirement for financing "mostly" by the State or other public bodies must be determined annually by reference to the budgetary year in which the procurement procedures commence, even if the figures are then provisional.[2]

European Court of Human Rights Law

Now that the Human Rights Act is in force, UK courts and tribunals are expressly required to take decisions of the European Court of Human Rights (ECHR) which sits in Strasbourg into account. Consequently, decisions of the ECHR relevant to the higher education are now of direct interest in Great Britain. There is, for example, a number of such cases relating to freedom of information within a range of possible interpretations (the "margin of appreciation" doctrine of the Court). The jurisprudence of the Court in relation to the conduct of disputes about civil rights and obligations is also relevant.

Before the Human Rights Act came into force, it was necessary for UK citizens to take any complaint of infringement of their rights under the European Convention for the Protection of Human Rights and Fundamental Freedoms (1950, as amended) against the UK government direct to the Court in Strasbourg. During 2000 there was one such case of interest, arising from a decision of the English Court of Appeal and relating to the Visitorial juris-

---

[2] R v. HM Treasury ex parte Univ. of Cambridge [2000] CMLR 1359; [2000] All E R (EC) 920; [2001] CEC 30; [2000] 1 WLR 2514.

diction. The case was complex because it also involved a counter-claim by a university against a student for unpaid fees. In this account this complication has been ignored.

The Visitor, a system of dispute resolution by HM the Queen, senior bishops of the Church of England or other notables or dignitaries, based on the medieval concept of the university as a closed community, and excluding the ordinary courts, is now almost totally confined to England. Like other oddities of the UK constitution, it continues to exist despite misgivings that it may be outdated. In particular, doubts have been expressed about its compatibility with Article 6(1) of the Convention which includes provision for a fair trial of civil rights and obligations by an independent and impartial tribunal established by law. The UK government appears to have accepted that the jurisdiction is obsolete but that as an ancient common law arrangement its abolition can only be achieved through primary legislation, which is not yet on the horizon. However, a challenge to the jurisdiction under the provisions of Article 6(1) has been awaited.

When a student H failed his MA degree at the University of East Anglia, he had had several extensions to the time allowed for submission of his dissertation. After H's internal appeals failed, he petitioned the Visitor (HM The Queen in Council, the Visitorial function being carried out by The Lord President of the Council) complaining of bias in the marking process and collusion between the examiners. The Visitor declined the petition, giving no reasons. H sought judicial review of the Visitor's decision both on this ground and that the Lord President, a long-standing Conservative MP, in the period coming up to the 1997 General Election did not want to damage the university's reputation which might affect its status as a major local employer. The university provided the court with a comprehensive rebuttal of H's claim.

The Court of Appeal dismissed H's renewed application for leave to apply for judicial review. The court held that even if it could be argued that reasons should have been given, there was nothing that could have led the Visitor to exercise discretion in H's favour. There was not even the remotest suspicion of political bias on the part of the Lord President. The court pointed out that the merits of H's petition had been fully dealt with by the university and there was nothing to justify a judicial review of the Visitor's decision. The court ruled that H's further argument under Article 6 of the Convention was not justiciable since the Human Rights Act 1998 was not then in force and that, in any event, he failed to demonstrate a true argument in relation to the Article and it would not be appropriate to investigate the matter further. The court also dismissed a further argument concerning pro-university bias in the wording of part of the University's Royal Charter.

The ECHR, Second Section, declared that H's attempt to challenge the decision of the University and Visitor under Article 6(1) of the Convention was inadmissible. The court found, by its unanimous, but unreasoned decision, that the application was not compatible with the provisions of the Convention since the proceedings did not involve the determination of a civil right or of a criminal charge against the applicant within the meaning of Article 6(1). In this the Court appeared to be applying its own jurisprudence concerning matters which relate to the exercise of professional judgment, when there are doubts as to whether a "right" is at issue.[3]

This decision has been greeted with some scepticism in the academic press. Given that there is a contractual background to the relationship between student and institution, one could assume that civil rights were in issue. However, university bodies and Visitors are making public law decisions, albeit the court will not intervene where there is a Visitor. H's complaints were in essence about public law functions. The ECHR has not offered a definitive explanation of what constitutes a dispute about an individual's civil rights and obligations, where Article 6(1) is relevant, and public law disputes, where it is not. The issue remains complex and undecided in the English courts.

Student Cases in Domestic Law

Apart from Hanuman's case, the domestic courts have been relatively busy dealing with applications from disappointed students who are not subject to the Visitorial jurisdiction. That is, generally speaking, all of the "new" universities (former polytechnics) and the Universities of Oxford and Cambridge are civil corporations. The leading cases in 2000 are from Cambridge and two new universities.

In the first case, P was a Ph.D. student at the University of Cambridge since 1992 (the normal length of a full-time UK PhD being 3-4 years). In 1999, since she had failed to make adequate progress, the University's Board of Graduate Studies terminated her registration. P claimed unfairness on a number of grounds, the most significant of which were that University officials refused to inform her of the existence and identity of a senior member of her Faculty who provided an opinion on reports she had submitted and whose comments were instrumental to the Board's decision. The University further refused to disclose another report so as to enable her to comment and make representations. The court found that this was not an 'anxious scrutiny' case in the sense of *R v. Secretary of State for the Home Department ex*

---

[3] R v. Visitor to the Univ. of East Anglia ex parte Hanuman, [1999] Ed CR 781 (CA); Hanuman v. UK [2000] ELR 685; [2000] Ed Law 232.

parte Bugdaycay[4] dealing with immigration. The court's task, as it saw it, was to ensure that P was considered in the fair and proper way that the seriousness of the circumstances required. The court would not interfere in pure academic judgement. According to the court, withholding the reports was not unfair, since "[t]here are sound and obvious reasons why reports to those who have to make academic judgements of this type should remain confidential, thus enabling the reporters to express themselves frankly in the knowledge that what they have to say will not be made available to the subjects of the reports."[5]

The extract from the opinion of the court in Persaud is interesting, not the least because it appears to run contrary to the express provisions of the Data Protection Act 1998, in force from 1 March 2000. This Act, which implements a European Directive but also derives from the Data Protection Act 1984, passed to partially fulfil the requirements of the Council of Europe's Data Protection Convention of 1981, effectively grants access by an individual to all material held by reference to her or him in a computer or structured manual file, with very few exceptions. Opinions expressed on individual students in circumstances akin to those in Persaud would appear to be disclosable to her without question. In addition, the withholding of the information appears to be less than fair in all the circumstances. It is an open question whether disclosing it would have made any difference to the outcome for P.

Another case illustrates the reluctance of the English courts to become involved in university-student disputes, in particular since changes in judicial rules now encourage parties in most types of litigation to seek to settle their differences by mediation and other forms of alternative dispute resolution. C was a final year student who was due to submit a dissertation as part of her assessment. On the night before the dissertation was due, C's father's computer, on which she was preparing it, crashed, and she had not made a backup. Instead, C submitted a clearly plagiarised document. After the university's academic bodies failed C's dissertation, she retook her finals and was awarded a third class degree, the highest award the regulations permitted 'normally.' Although a governor's appeal body referred the matter back for reconsideration, the academic body affirmed its decision. When the

---

[4] [1987] AC 514; [1987] 2 WLR 606; [1987] 1 All ER 940; [1987] Imm AR 250; (1987) 84 LSG 902; (1987) 137 NLJ 199; (1987) 131 SJ 297 (HL)
[5] R v. University of Cambridge ex parte Persaud, [2000] Ed CR 635.

case eventually reached the Court of Appeal, it required the parties to attempt to settle the matter by mediation. The court noted that C's action based on contract raised issues of academic judgement on the part of the appeal body, and repeated that the courts would not become involved in adjudicating in this area.[6]

As illustrated by the case of N, the courts are willing to intervene where a student has not been treated fairly. N sought to appeal her second year assessment by reference to extenuating circumstances, including, eventually, an allegation of sexual harassment by her tutor. The court decided that N should have been informed of material placed before the Committee considering her case. While the underlying issue related to academic judgement, the matters central to the internal appeal related not to the objective assessment of N's work but to the extenuating circumstances.[7]

Staff Cases in Domestic Law

Staff of UK universities and colleges enjoy all of the statutory rights normally accorded to employees. Academic staff have, in addition, some statutory rights peculiar to their status as academics. Disputes between staff and institutions which cannot be resolved internally end up in front of an employment (formerly "industrial") tribunal. Appeals from these tribunals on points of law go first to the Employment Appeal Tribunal and thereafter to the higher courts. The years 1999 and 2000 saw a number of cases arising under the employment provisions of the Disability Discrimination Act 1995. Essentially, these require employers not to discriminate unreasonably against prospective and existing employees who are disabled for the purposes of the Act. This protection is effected by obligating employers to provide "reasonable adjustments" in the workplace to accommodate those who are, or who become, disabled. The definition of disability is complex and the case law is developing relatively slowly.

The process starts with selection of applicants for interview. R, who was disabled within the meaning of the 1995 Act, applied for several academic posts at Manchester Metropolitan University and advised that he was registered disabled. When R was not short-listed for any position, he claimed unlawful discrimination on ground of disability contrary to the Act. The Employment Tribunal dismissed the application on the ground that since no consideration whatsoever was given to R's disability, it was irrel-

---

[6] R v. University of Lincolnshire and Humberside ex p Clark, [2000] 1 WLR 1988; [2000] 3 All ER 752; [2000] Ed CR 553; [2000] ELR 345; COD 293 (2000); NLJ 616 (2000); (2000) 144 SJLB 220.

[7] R v. Chelsea College of Art and Design ex parte Nash, [2000] ELR 686; [2000] Ed CR 571.

evant. Further, the court observed that R's failure to be shortlisted was based solely on his insuitability for the posts on the basis of the information given in his application form. In respect of a claim under the duty to make reasonable adjustments, the court rejected R's claim that a duty arose. On appeal, the Employment Appeal Tribunal dismissed R's appeal under the first head. The Appeal Tribunal also agreed that the university had no prior notice of a claim for reasonable adjustment and no evidence was produced to support it. The court concluded that mentioning a disability was not sufficient to put the matter in issue.[8]

The next step in the process is job interviews. M, a profoundly deaf applicant for a post at Sheffield Hallam University which he had notified of his disability, was interviewed without benefit of a sign interpreter. An Employment Tribunal accepted that the university should have made appropriate arrangements for the interview, provision of an interpreter being a 'reasonable adjustment' in the language of the Disability Discrimination Act 1995.[9]

What happens during the course of employment is illustrated by a case involving the University of Huddersfield. H was disabled for the purposes of the Disability Discrimination Act 1995. When, in 1990, H was interviewed for a technician post at the university (then Huddersfield Polytechnic), he notified officials of his need to move around and to rest during the working day but did not advise them of his need for personal physiotherapy nor that his condition was degenerative. Even so, officials made adjustments to accommodate H's notified requirements. In 1995, when H unsuccessfully applied for transfer to a post in another workshop, he did not indicate that he was unhappy with the facilities in the other workshop. Following a reorganisation, H was required to transfer to that workshop. H objected to the transfer, not because he allegedly needed privacy for personal physiotherapy but since he felt it was a demotion. When H refused to supervise students, ostensibly on health and safety grounds, he was suspended. H complained that his health had deteriorated and that the university had made no assessment. Instead of taking up an offer of assessment, H complained to the Employment Tribunal, alleging discrimination contrary to the Act and the university's failure to make reasonable adjustments. The tribunal declared that although the suspension constituted less favourable treatment, this was not based on H's disability but on his refusal to perform his contractual duties. The tribunal added that there was no failure on the university's part to make reasonable adjustments since H had never in-

---

[8] Rudzki v. Manchester Metropolitan Univ., (1999) EAT/640/99.
[9] Murphy v. Sheffield Hallam Univ., (1999) 40 EOR/DCLD 11.

formed it of the need for any, other than those made in 1990. On appeal against the second finding, the Employment Appeal Tribunal, dismissing the appeal, held that this was essentially a question of fact for the tribunal. In addition, the court was of the view that university officials had no knowledge of H's need for privacy and could not be presumed to have been aware of this need.[10]

Most cases of personal injury are settled before ever reaching court. One case which was not settled involved West Lothian College in Scotland where R was employed as a welfare nurse. R claimed damages on the basis of vicarious liability after suffering a nervous breakdown comprising severe anxiety and depression, panic attacks and loss of confidence and self-esteem resulting from the conduct of her colleagues. The College argued that a nervous breakdown was not a recognised psychiatric illness and that R's averments (Scots term for pleadings) were not sufficient to establish that her colleagues ought to have foreseen that their actions would result in a psychiatric illness. Dismissing R's action, the court asserted that R had not pled any disorder recognised as a psychiatric illness or had been required to be treated by a psychiatrist and that nothing in her averments which could establish that her colleagues ought to have foreseen that R was under a material risk of sustaining a psychiatric disorder in consequence of their behaviour, as opposed to feeling unsatisfied, frustrated, embarrassed and upset. In fact, the court maintained that suffering these and related emotions was a normal part of human experience. The court posited that it was only if they were liable to be suffered to such a pathological degree as to constitute a psychiatric disorder that a duty of care to protect against them could arise and that was not a reasonably foreseeable occurrence by an ordinary person unless there was some specific reason to foresee it in a particular case.[11]

Moving on from discrimination, there have been two important cases dealing with the contractual and fiduciary obligations of employees towards their institutions. In the first, involving the London School of Economics and Political Science (LSE), P was employed as a communications supervisor who was responsible for commissioning work from and subsequently sanctioning payments to E, a telecommunications engineer. Allegations were made that P and E conspired to defraud LSE through P sanctioning overcharging by E, alternatively that E misrepresented the fairness of his charges and PO was negligent in overseeing the charges. The amount alleged to be overcharged was £220,000 (about US$330,000). It was also alleged that P, in breach of contract, received secret payments amounting to £9875 (about

---

[10] Hanlon v. University of Huddersfield, [1999] Disc LR 82 (EAT).
[11] Rorrison v. West Lothian College, 2000 SCLR 245; 1999 Rep LR 102; 1999 GWD 27-1296 (Court of Session, Outer House).

US$14,100) from other suppliers which LSE were entitled to recover on the basis that P held them as a constructive trustee. There was no evidence of corrupt payments or that work charged for by E had not been carried out and although a police investigation had taken place, no criminal charges were brought. The court ruled that there was no evidence of a conspiracy to defraud LSE and that even if P had breached his duty to use reasonable care and skill by not ensuring that minor telecommunications work was put out to tender, there was no demonstrable or provable loss to LSE. Further, the court was convinced that P's receipt of money from the other contractors was a breach of his fiduciary duties and he was liable to LSE to the limit of the 'secret payments' in the amount of £9875. The court dismissed claims of overcharging against both P and E.[12]

In a case involving the University of Nottingham, university officials sought an account of profits or damage for alleged breach of fiduciary duty and breaches of contract by its former employee F, a clinical embryologist in relation to work done at various clinics abroad. F joined the university in 1985 and in 1991 became scientific director of Nurture (N) a self-funding institution providing treatment as an infertility clinic. N was intended to bring the university to the international forefront of teaching and research in the field. F had also been working in private clinics before he became a full-time employee of the university and as N became more successful, the range of these increased. Some research work vital to the success of N had to be done abroad as it was not permitted in the UK. N's equipment was often used on visits to foreign clinics but the costs were borne by the clinic concerned. In 1996, F was the university's highest paid employee. The university then varied his contract relating to pay and F resigned. On F's departure, the university recovered documents and computers, one of which revealed detailed information about his work abroad.

The university claimed not only that F breached of his duties under his employment contract and certain fiduciary obligations but also that he induced other staff to break their employment by encouraging them to work abroad and receiving remuneration for doing so. F had a standard clause in his contract requiring appropriate consent for outside work. F contended that the university suffered no loss from his breach of contract for failing to obtain its prior consent and therefore no damages should be awarded for breach of contract.

The court found that F breached his contract by failing to obtain the requisite consent for his paid outside work but as no loss had been suffered by the university, there would be no award of damages. The court also

---

[12] London School of Economics and Political Science v (1) Pearson and (2) Evans, unrep. QBD 20 June 2000.

stated that F breached his fiduciary duty by receiving payment for directing other staff to work outside the university for his own interests and it was entitled to an account of F's profits therefrom.[13]

Finally, the rules relating to transfer of employees from one legal entity to another are impacting on higher education institutions which "hive off" some of their functions. In a case involving the University of Oxford, H was employed to set, mark and moderate GCSE and A-level examinations for the Delegacy of Local Examinations. The activities of the Delegacy were transferred to the Associated Examining Board in 1995. H was informed prior to the transfer that the university intended to transfer his contract of employment to the Board and he objected to becoming the Board's employee, under Regulation 5(4A) of the Transfer of Undertakings (Protection of Employment) Regulations 1981 as amended. It was common ground that the transfer would have involved a substantial and detrimental change in H's working conditions. After the transfer H brought a wrongful dismissal action in that the purported transfer constituted constructive dismissal. The university's application to have the action struck out as disclosing no reasonable basis of claim was rejected at first instance, the judge rejecting its argument that under the Regulations any liability for alleged breach of H's contract had been transferred to the Board. However, the Board were permitted to be joined to the proceedings. Rejecting the appeal, the Court of Appeal held that H was entitled to treat his contract of employment as terminated by the university, by serving notice of his objection under Regulation 5(4A) and to seek compensation for wrongful dismissal as against the university.[14]

---

[13] University of Nottingham v. (1) Fishel (2) Nottacor Twenty Nine Limited (formerly Nurture Limited), [2000] ICR 1462; [2000] IRLR 471; [2000] Ed CR 505; [2000] ELR 385.

[14] Humphreys v. Chancellor, Master and Scholars of the University of Oxford [2000] 1 All ER 996; [2000] 1 CMLR 647; [2000] ICR 405; [2000] IRLR 183; [2000] Ed CR 246 (CA).

GREAT BRITIAN K-12

Neville Harris

Introduction

The Government's push towards improved standards of education and greater social inclusiveness continues to dominate much of the developmental planning and strategic implementation of policy in relation to school education in England and Wales. The School Standards and Framework Act 1998 reforms, discussed in previous *Yearbooks*, are firmly in place and consolidated and the long-anticipated statutory reform in the area of special educational needs and disability[1] is due to come into operation from September 2001. In 2000, the incorporation of the European Convention for the Protection of Human Rights and Fundamental Freedoms 1950 into national law, and the hugely important court ruling in *Phelps v London Borough of Hillingdon*,[2] shifted the focus of Education Law back to the rights of the individual within the education system even more strongly than was occurring in the 1980s.[3] The former has contributed significantly to the growing 'rights culture' affecting relationships between service providers and citizens, although both areas of development have opened up new opportunities for legal challenge.

The discussion in this chapter is divided into three principal parts. First, there is an analysis of the new human rights legislation. Second, there is a discussion of Phelps and its implications. Third, there is a review of other case law developments. The chapter ends with some concluding remarks.

Human rights

Incorporation

On October 2, 2000 the Human Rights Act 1998 came into effect in England and Wales. Its significance in the short, medium, and long-term for the development of Education Law has been the subject of considerable discussion.[4] On the basis of the limited case law to date, it seems most likely that the Act's impact will be relatively small in terms of guaranteeing new substantive rights or extending those based on previous legislation or com-

---

[1] Special Educational Needs and Disability Act 2001.
[2] [2000] ELR 499, House of Lords.
[3] *See* N. Harris, Law and Education: Regulations, Consumerism and the Education System (London: Sweet and Maxwell, 1993).
[4] *See e.g.,* A. Bradley, 'Scope for Review: The Convention Right to Education and the Human Rights Act 1998' [1999] E.H.R.L.R. 395-409; H. Mountfield, 'The Implications of the Human Rights Act 1998 for the Law of Education' (2000) 1(3) Education Law Journal 146-158.

mon law principles and that only a thin veneer of additional protection has been provided for individual rights in relation to procedural and due process issues in some areas of decision making. Even so, the Act has compelled the judiciary to widen their juristic techniques. The 1998 Act incorporates the key articles of the European Convention for the Protection of Human Rights and Fundamental Freedoms 1950 into national law but does so in a way that ensures that courts will have to take account of the jurisprudence of the European Court of Human Rights (ECHR) (and the European Commission of Human Rights which, until two years ago, was, in effect, the first tier in the redress procedure established by the Convention). The underlying assumption seems to be that judges in England and Wales need guidance from the Strasbourg judgments in applying the more open-textured and less precise terminology of the Convention and in adopting the teleological approach to interpretation that the ECHR practices.

This is not to say that the Convention has, in the past, been ignored by the courts in England and Wales; from time to time the Convention and other international human rights instruments have been cited in legal argument and judgment. It has been calculated that the Convention was referred to in over 650 English cases between 1964-1999.[5] Indeed, in the period between the enactment of the Human Rights Act 1998 and the run-up to October 2, 2000, the courts were anticipating the incorporation of the Convention in their approach to human rights arguments that were already being advanced. Human rights protagonists hope that over time the courts will establish new benchmarks for human rights protection. So far, while most judges seem reasonably comfortable with Convention law, they have adopted, certainly in the field education litigation, a fairly cautious and perhaps even conservative approach, being particularly wary of over-stepping their remit and blurring the separation of powers within the constitution. It should be noted that the 1998 Act requires legislation in the United Kingdom (UK) to be construed in a way that is compatible with the Convention; does not enable the courts to strike down primary legislation on the grounds of incompatibility; but empowers them to make a declaration that such legislation is incompatible with the Convention, which would put political pressure on the Government to seek reform.[6]

---

[5] S. Grosz, J. Beatson QC and P. Duffy QC, Human Rights (London: Sweet and Maxwell, 2000), p. 3.

[6] Human Rights Act 1998 ss 3-5. Not much political pressure seems to have been brought about by a UN report on human rights in education in the UK, published in 2000: UN Commission on Human Rights, Economic, Social and Cultural Rights, Report submitted by Katarina Tomasevski, Special Rapporteur on the right to education, Mission to the United Kingdom 18-22 October 1999, E/CN.4/2000/6 Add.2

The appeal of human rights is, of course, their universality. One of the principal themes of the chapter on England and Wales in last year's Yearbook was inclusion, reflecting the Labour Government's drive to improve school standards for all children and to tackle problems such as truancy, exclusion from school, poor literacy and numeracy and gaps in early years education. To see human rights, or more precisely the European Convention, as some kind of panacea for these problems would, however, be mistaken. In general, the rights and protections the Convention offers are far from absolute (an exception being the Article 6 right to a fair trial in relation to criminal charges or the determination of civil rights and obligations[7]). A state's economic integrity is not threatened by the Convention: thus in the field of education the duty (Article 2 of Protocol 1) to safeguard the individual's right to education and, in doing so, to recognize the right of parents to have their children educated in accordance with their religious and philosophical convictions, not only provides a low threshold of protection but leaves the allocation of resources within the state's more or less absolute autonomy. The state is given a "margin of appreciation" which means that the effect of Convention rights may to some extent vary from state to state in accordance with national priorities and traditions.

This becomes more problematic once one moves away from the area of personal integrity such as torture or inhuman or degrading treatment (Article 3, the subject of several cases involving in school[8]), slavery or servitude (Article 4), incarceration (Article 5) or perhaps even the right to life (Article 2) – and into the more esoteric fields of freedom of expression (Article 10) or respect for private and family life (Article 8). But, in relation to the right to education there are two important factors. First, the Convention does not (unlike, for example, the UN Convention on the Rights of the Child) attempt to define what is meant by education; in other words, it is silent as to the minimum level of provision or as to the aims or content that could properly constitute an "education" for the purposes of the Convention. The ECHR has, however, identified a right of access to institutions providing education, a right to be educated in the national language (or languages) and the right to receive official recognition of studies completed as within the ambit of this right.[9] Further, it is clear that the duty to respect parents' religious and philosophical convictions as regards the education of their children applies to all aspects of education, "not only to the content of the curriculum and the manner of its teaching, but to other factors such as the organizing and

---

[7] *See* Millar v Dickson; Payne v Heywood; Stewart v Same; Tracey v Same, July 24, 2001, Privy Council, The Times Law Report July 27, 2001, per Lord Bingham.

[8] (1982) 4 EHRR 293.

[9] Belgian Linguistics Case (1979-80) 1 EHRR 252.

financing of public education (but see below), and matters relating to internal administration such as discipline."[10] Second, the Court itself observed that the scope of the right to education is not fixed but may be dictated by prevailing economic or social conditions at the time or in the particular place.[11] In any event, the UK entered a reservation which states that the principle of adherence to parents' religious or philosophical convictions in relation to the right to education is accepted by it only so far as is compatible with the provision of efficient instruction and training and the avoidance of unreasonable public expenditure.

The cases on education that have come before the Commission or ECHR have produced results which have had only a limited influence on the educational system in England and Wales. Probably the only major effect was the banning of in state schools in 1987[12] followed the ruling in Campbell and Cosans v UK[13] when it was held to be unlawful not to respect children's parents' philosophical opposition to which was in use at the school; the parents had kept the children away from school because of their opposition to this punishment. The court has also ruled on the lawfulness of itself.[14] It is arguable that when introducing compulsory sex education in secondary schools in England and Wales the UK Government could have relied on the Court's majority opinion in *Kjeldesen, Busk Masden and Pedersen v. Denmark*[15] to avoid giving individual parents an opt-out on the grounds of religion or philosophical convictions; but it chose not to do so, although gave parents a right to withdraw their children only from sex education not comprised in the National Curriculum, in other words excluding withdrawal from the science curriculum covering purely biological aspects of human reproduction.[16] In any event, the more prescriptive regime regulating the

---

[10] Citing Campbell and Cosans op cit, Kjeldesen, Busk Masden and Pedersen v Denmark (1979-89) 1 EHRR 711 and Valsamis v Greece (1997) 24 EHRR 294.
[11] Note 9 supra.
[12] Education (No 2) Act 1986, s 47. The ban has since been extended to all schools via the School Standards and Framework Act 1998 s 131: see R v H [2001] 2 FLR 431 per Rose LJ at para [10].
[13] (1982) 4 EHRR 293.
[14] Article 3. Costello-Roberts v United Kingdom [1994] ELR 1; see also the Commission decision in Warwick v United Kingdom (1986) A9471/81 and the court's decision in A v United Kingdom (1998) 27 EHRR 611 and Tyrer v United Kingdom (1980) 2 EHRR 1.
[15] (1979-80) 1 EHRR 711.
[16] Education Act 1996, ss 356(9), 403, 404, 405.

content of sex education introduced under the Learning and Skills Act 2000 would have necessitated the introduction of this right.[17]

In general, the time and expense involved in taking a case to Strasbourg and awaiting a decision have deterred litigants. It was in order to combat these problems that the Government first proposed its Human Rights Bill, to "bring rights home."[18] One area in which there was considerable but under-utilized potential for human rights challenges concerned equal treatment. Article 14 of the Convention provides for the enjoyment of Convention rights to be secured without discrimination on any ground such as sex, race, color, language, religion, political, or other opinion and so on. There have been a number of education cases before the UK courts where equality issues were in question and the possibility of arguing Article 14 could have made a difference. One example would be *Sikander Ali*[19] where the fact that the law failed to prevent the disadvantage in relation to school choice to Asians in the Manningham area of the city of Bradford resulting from school catchment areas (zones) might, in a similar instance, be considered worth challenging on the basis of a lack of racial equality under Article 14 (particularly as a claim of breach of the Race Relations Act 1976 failed in that case).[20] Article 8's duty not to interfere with an individual's private and family life, seems to offer less potential in the education; as the Court commented in *Costello-Roberts v. United Kingdom*, "the sending of a child to school necessarily involves some degree of interference with his or her private life."[21]

---

[17] Almost all of the 2000 Act is concerned with further education: see chapter by Denis Farrington in this volume. The law on sex education in schools is amended by section 148 of the 2000 Act, including a new power for the Secretary of State to issue guidance designed to secure that when sex education is given in school, pupils 'learn the nature of marriage and its importance for family life and the bringing up of children' and 'they are protected from teaching and materials which are inappropriate having regard to the age and the religious and cultural background of the pupils concerned'. Governing bodies and head teachers must have regard to this guidance, which can be accessed on the web at: http//:www.dfee.gov.uk.

[18] Lord Chancellor, Rights Brought Home, Cm 3782 (London: The Stationery Office, 1997)

[19] R v. Bradford Metropolitan Borough Council ex p Sikander Ali [1994] ELR 299.

[20] This is particularly so given the Court of Human Rights' conclusion that the state may not regulate access to an educational institution in a discriminatory way: Belgian Linguistics Case (1979-80) 1 EHRR 252 at 257.

[21] [1994] ELR 1 at p. 12.

Human Rights in Decisions of the Courts in England and Wales

The 'Assisted Places' Scheme

Many of the human rights arguments pursued in the run-up to October 2, 2000 and thereafter have been somewhat exploratory. For the most part they have tended to form an adjunct to the other, main grounds of challenge. For example, in *R v. Secretary of State for Education and Employment ex p Begbie*[22] a girl had been attending a private (independent) school, in what was, in effect, its junior department, with the assistance of state aid under the "assisted places" scheme. Prior to the 1997 general election, the Labour Party made statements indicating that if elected to power it would abolish this scheme for new entrants to primary or secondary schools, but that in schools running beyond primary school age ("all-through" schools, where the primary and secondary stages of education were linked) pupils due to move from primary to secondary stages and already in receipt of assistance might be able to continue to receive support. The new Secretary of State for Education and Employment gave a similar indication by letter following the general election. The Education (Schools) Act 1997 implemented the abolition arrangements, to be phased in. They included a discretion to continue a child's entitlement when reasonable to do so in the circumstances. When Ms. Begbie was, in the event, denied support when joining the secondary stage of her schooling, she mounted a legal challenge. The Court of Appeal refused to hold the politicians to their pre-election and other promises under the general public law doctrine of "legitimate expectation," nor did they find the Secretary of State to have committed an of power, although Peter Gibson LJ did comment that "the way the Secretary of State dealt with the proper concerns of parents like Ms. Begbie reflects no credit whatsoever on him."[23]

Although the case was resolved prior to October 2, 2000, the Court of Appeal dealt fully with the human rights argument put forward by Miss Begbie's distinguished counsel. He had argued that to deny Ms. Begbie her assisted place would prejudice her right to education under Article 2 of Protocol 1 and that even before the Human Rights Act 1998 came into force the Convention should inform the exercise of discretion. Peter Gibson LJ[24] did not, however, believe that the Convention put the state under an obligation to fund education at a private school when education was available in the state sector. He referred to the ECHR's ruling in Belgian Linguistics (No. 2) where it was concluded that the Contracting Parties to the Convention

---

[22] [2000] ELR 445.
[23] Id. para [62].
[24] Id. para [72].

"do not recognize such a right to education as would require them to establish at their own expense, or to subsidise, education of any particular type or particular level."[25]

Special Educational Needs

Legal challenges to cases concerning special educational needs still occur in great number partly because there is a right of appeal to the High Court against judgments of the special educational needs tribunal; partly since the legislation gives local education authorities fairly wide discretion which they tend to exercise with one eye firmly on their budgets; and partly due to the fact that a reasonably large number of parents understand the importance to their child's future of decisions on special educational needs and provision, especially with regard to school placements. This is an area that is ripe for human rights challenges even though the Convention has been viewed as subjugating individual education rights to the more collectively-orientated responsibilities of the state, particularly given the need for the state's careful management of limited resources.

The Commission of Human Rights addressed three cases in which it was argued that there was a breach of Article 2 Protocol 1 (philosophical convictions) where a child with special educational needs was educated in a special school. The parents believed in inclusive education for their child but the Commission upheld the power of the state to determine such matters in the light of all the circumstances, even in acknowledging that the growing weight of opinion favored inclusive education.[26] Probably the most influential Strasbourg case in this field, again one of the Commission rather than Court, is *Simpson v United Kingdom in 1989.*[27] The courts in England and Wales have already placed considerable reliance upon Simpson.

Simpson concerned a boy with special educational needs who, due to his dyslexia, wanted the fees for his attendance at a private special school to be met by the local education authority which maintained that his needs could be met in one of its own secondary schools and at a much lower cost. He claimed a breach of Article 2 of Protocol 1. The Commission responded that it recognized that there must be a wide measure of discretion left to the appropriate authorities as to how to make the best use possible of the resources available to them in the interests of disabled children generally and that while these authorities must place weight on parents' and pupils' views,

---

[25] (1979-80) 1 EHRR 252 at p 281.
[26] PD and LD v United Kingdom (1989) 62 D.R. 292; Graeme v. United Kingdom (1990) 64 D.R. 158; Klerks v. Netherlands (1995) 82 D.R. 41. See also Cohen v United Kingdom (1996) 21 E.H.R.R. CD 104.
[27] (1989) 64 DR 188.

it cannot be said that the first sentence of Article 2 of Protocol 1 requires the placing of a dyslexic child in a private specialized school, with fees paid by the State, when a place is available in an ordinary school which has special teaching facilities for disabled children. The Commission also made an important point about Article 6(1), holding that the right not to be denied an education was not in the nature of a 'civil right' but was a 'public law' right with no analogy in private law. Thus, the procedures under statute for challenging decisions concerning the education right were not subject to the fair trial provisions of Article 6.

The Article 6 point in Simpson was adopted by the Court of Appeal in a case in July 2000, *R v. London Borough of Richmond ex p JC*,[28] arising from an appeal to a local education appeal committee against its choosing not to admit a child to a school selected by his parents.[29] The parents also argued that there was a breach of Article 8. The court concluded that the argument that proper account was not taken of all the health issues relating to the child and his mother when denying them their choice of school was "untenable;" in any event, the class size limit that was imposed by law and which affected the authority's ability to meet everyone's choice was found to be "necessary in a democratic society."[30]

Returning to the question of the extent to which Article 2 of Protocol 1 confers any choice to parents concerning the education of children with special educational needs, this matter was considered further in a case that was resolved in May 2000: *H v. Kent County Council and the Special Educational Needs Tribunal*.[31] Here again the court gave full consideration to the human rights argument despite the fact that the Human Rights Act 1998 was not in force. The principal issue was whether the tribunal, on appeal against a local education authority's refusal to conduct a statutory assessment of a ten year old girl's special educational needs, had made an error of law in allegedly failing to take account of the evidence from various witnesses, including two experts on behalf of the girl and in not providing adequate reasons for acting. The court accepted that the justification offered by the tribunal were inadequate an so quashed its decision. The court dismissed the human rights argument that the local education authority's refusal to make a statutory assessment and the tribunal's choice not to order

---

[28] [2001] ELR 21 per Kennedy, L.J., at para [59].
[29] It was also adopted by Newman J., in early 2001: The Queen (on the application of B) v. Head Teacher of Alperton Community School and Others; The Queen v. Head Teacher of Wembley High School and Others ex parte T; The Queen v. The Governing Body of Cardinal Newman High Sch and Others ex parte C [2001] ELR 359.
[30] Note 28 *supra*, at para [87], per Ward LJ, referring to Article 8(2).
[31] [2000] ELR 660.

an assessment gave rise to a breach of Article 2 Protocol 1. Grigson J accepted the findings of the Commission in Simpson and the referred to Belgian Linguistics (No. 2) cited above.

In *L v. Hereford and Worcester County Council and Hughes*[32] the special educational needs tribunal decreed that a placement in one of three mainstream schools suggested by a local education authority, preferably involving additional support, would meet the needs of their child, a nine year old girl with cerebral palsy. The parents argued that the placement was contrary to their religious and philosophical convictions for the purposes of Article 2 of Protocol 1. Yet, since this point had not been raised before, the tribunal the court refused to entertain it. This dispute pre-dated the Human Rights 1998. Had it been made subsequently, the court should have taken it on board because, as noted above, the court itself is now bound by the Act to act consistently with the Convention.[33]

Parental Ballots on Selection of Pupils

Outside the area of special educational needs, human rights points were argued in two other cases. In *R v. Secretary of State for Education and Employment ex parte RCO*,[34] the complainants were parents who were excluded by the relevant regulations from voting on parental ballots to consider whether a school should retain a selective admissions system (in other words, whether it should select pupils by their academic ability and thus be classed a "grammar school"). The parents asserted that this infringed on their human rights. The parents also regarded it as unfair that the regulations excluded them because their child already attended the school while enfranchised parents had a child who attended one of the school's feeder schools. Scott Baker, J., explained that the regulations merely reflected Parliament's intention as expressed in the primary legislation, the School Standards and Framework Act 1998, and that since the court had no constitutional power to strike down any part of an Act of Parliament, he would not declare the regulations unlawful due to unfairness or irrationality.[35] There were subsidiai y human rights arguments based on Article 2 of Protocol 1 and also Article 8 which also pre-dated October 2, 2000. The judge took a hard line, refusing to consider the arguments at all. He wrote, in effect, that the court's jurisdiction over claims of breach of the Convention could not operate retrospectively.[36]

---

[32] [2000] ELR 375.
[33] Human Rights Act 1998, ss 3, 6 and 7.
[34] [2000] ELR 307.
[35] Id. at 312A-D.
[36] Id. at 313F-G.

School Transport Costs

R v. Carmartheshire CC ex parte White[37] concerned a child who was attending a school where she was bullied and felt stressed. When the girl's parents withdrew her from the school and had her admitted to another school, further from her home, the local education authority refused to meet the costs of transporting her to her new school on the grounds that the nearer school was suitable and it was reasonable for her to attend classes there. There was also a suggestion that the child's stress was induced by the parent's irrational dislike of the previous school. The court held that the suitability of the arrangements for attendance at a school was a matter for the local education authority to assess rationally, taking account of the stress caused by alternative arrangements. A further point concerned Article 2 of Protocol 1: counsel for the parents argued that the girl could not benefit from her education (and thus from her education right) unless she was free from psychiatric problems and stress which was not the case at the school she had been attending. Tomlinson, J., remarked that the Article was concerned with "effective education" and that the Convention is at one with English jurisprudence, so far as concerns this issue. In his view, the local education authority had been concerned with the ability of the child to receive an effective education at that school.

The Right to Education and Asylum Applicants

In December 2000 the Court of Appeal resolved an important human rights-based appeal brought by a Polish couple who were asylum applicants. The couple argued that the refusal of their asylum application, thereby forcing them to return to Poland, would result in damage to their daughter's educational progress to such an extent that she would suffer a denial of her right to education under the Convention: *Holub and Holub v. Secretary of State for the Home Department.*[38] Since coming to the UK at the age of eight, the child had made such good progress at school that, by the age of fourteen, she was well on course to secure university entrance at eighteen. The parents claimed that if their daughter returned to Poland she would need to resume her education where she left off and would not catch up. The Secretary of State responded that the girl was intelligent enough to catch up quickly and would not be denied an education. The court noted that the Secretary of State, while having to consider the educational implications of granting asylum, was not obliged to take a view on whether the Article 2 Protocol 1 right was infringed. However, the court declared that as the Hu-

---

[37] [2001] ELR 172, decided July 20, 2000.
[38] [2001] ELR 401.

man Rights Act 1998 had only been in force for a short time, it should refrain from laying down any principles of more general application unless it had to. In the event, the court did not consider that the evidence showed that the girl's right to education would be denied. Poland had a well developed system of education and the court said it was not enough simply to say that the girl would receive a better education in the UK. The court endorsed a view of the right to education under the Convention as connoting a right of access to educational institutions; a right to official recognition of academic qualifications obtained; and a right to an effective (but not the most effective) education, which, to be meaningful, meant that the education was required to reach a minimum standard.

What amounts to a "minimum standard" is, of course, open to argument in individual cases. Here the court clearly accepted that the girl would receive a minimum standard. The court was not convinced that the girl would have been denied an effective education had the family returned to Poland and so refused her parents' appeal. The notion of "effective education" is surely set for further legal argument and judicial analysis, especially in the light of common law developments discussed below.

The Duty of Care and the Performance of Educative Duties

No education case has attracted more attention in recent years, both inside and beyond the UK, than the long-awaited ruling of the *House of Lords in Phelps v. London Borough of Hillingdon in July 2000.*[39] The Court of Appeal's judgment in *Phelps*[40] was discussed in the previous Yearbook. The House of Lords overturned that action and confirmed that a teacher or other educational professional may owe a duty of care at common law towards a child and his or her parents with regard to the child's education. Thus, it follows that where an educator fails to meet the required standard of care,[41] he or she and the employer may be liable in damages for harm suffered if the usual other ingredients of the tort of negligence (breach of the duty of care, causation) can be proved. Where, as in *Phelps* itself, an educational psychologist was called in specifically to advise in relation to

[39] Phelps v. London Borough of Hillingdon; Anderton v. Clwyd County Council; G v. London Borough of Bromley; Jarvis v Hampshire County Council [2000] ELR 499. The judgment can be accessed via http://www.lcd.gov.uk/.
[40] [1998] ELR 587.
[41] Namely the standard of an ordinarily competent and skilled member of that profession acting in accordance with practice accepted by a responsible body of professionals in that field: Bolam v Friern Hospital Management Committee [1957] 1 WLR 582.

the assessment and future provision for a specific child, and it is clear that the parents and the teachers can be expected to follow that advice, a prima facie a duty of care will arise.

Phelps may be of assistance to former pupils who suffered psychological consequences such as low self-esteem or depression or have under-achieved at school, with resultant damage to their long term career prospects, provided that these problems can be shown to causally linked to the teacher or other professional's failure of duty. Miss Phelps was a dyslexic who made slow progress at school. The House of Lords maintained that since the educational psychologist employed by the local education authority failed to diagnose Miss Phelps' condition despite its discernible signs, the local education authority was vicariously liable. The question of whether local education authorities could be directly, as opposed to vicariously, liable was left fairly open. According to Lord Slynn, an authority would not be directly liable for the way it established arrangements to meet its statutory duties towards, say, children with special educational needs, but might be so if it employed professionals who were not qualified or competent to undertake their duties.[42]

In reaching its judgment on the duty of care and liability, the House of Lords acknowledged, but was not swayed by, policy arguments against permitting such claims to be brought, which have influenced the courts in the United States.[43] The arguments include the risk that vexatious claims might be brought perhaps many years after the child had left school; the cost to local education authorities in defending such claims; the possible development of a defensive approach to educational practice in order to avoid suits; and the unfairness of singling out a particular professional among a number responsible for a child's education. There is also a general issue of policy in English tort law as to whether the existence of a duty is fair, just, and reasonable.

Phelps, like the previous case of *X* (Minors),[44] confirms that local education authorities and their employees cannot be liable for actions taken under statutory powers since otherwise their statutory functions would be unduly hindered. However, since a duty of care may be owed in respect of other, general professional duties, liability is possible. It should be noted

---

[42] At p. 521D-H.

[43] *See* generally, R.E. Rains, 'A primer on special education law in the United States - Part 3: remedies for misdiagnosis or misplacement of special education students' (1998) 10(4) Education and the Law 205-224. Peter W. v. San Francisco Unified Sch. Dist., 60 Cal. App. 3d 814 (Cal. Ct. App. 1976). Donohue v. Copiague Union Free Sch. Dist., 407 NYS2d 874 (N.Y. App. Div. 1978).

[44] X (Minors) v. Bedfordshire County Council (and linked cases) [1995] ELR 404, House of Lords.

that the House of Lords confirmed that "'a failure to mitigate the adverse consequences of congenital defect are capable of being 'personal injuries to a person.'"[45] Consequently, damages claims such as those in Phelps can proceed as personal injury cases, which has certain advantages to litigants such as the possibility of pre-proceedings discovery of documents.[46] Damages could be based on the failure to diagnose a congenital condition and to take appropriate action resulting in a child's reduced level of achievement, reduced employment prospects and depressed earnings.

Negligence claims are not straightforward, especially in this context. Showing that a teacher fell below generally accepted standards within the profession may be difficult in a field where professional practices vary and fault might be difficult to prove. Moreover, school records might not be adequate and recollections some time after the event might be unreliable. Thus, evidence to support a negligence claim may be inadequate. Above all, perhaps, establishing a causal connection between the alleged negligence and the alleged loss and assessing any damages might be problematic. Lord Clyde stressed that "these possible difficulties should not be allowed to stand in the way of the presentation of a proper claim."[47] Lord Nicholls distinguished cases where there is "manifest incompetence or negligence comprising specific, identifiable mistakes," such as where a teacher "carelessly teaches the wrong syllabus for an external examination," from a more general claim that a child did not receive an adequate education or was not properly taught where a range of external factors that contribute to performance.[48]

The question of which other areas of educational practice might be within the scope of the duty of care has been the subject of much debate. Lawyers are understandably keen to adopt a broad interpretation of the *Phelps* and *X* (Minors) rulings. There seems to be acceptance that the teachers' duty to prevent bullying among pupils is in any event within the ordinary duty of care to safeguard not only a pupil's physical well-being but also his psychological and emotional well-being.[49] There is a Scottish case to that effect[50] and now a High Court judgment in England by Garland, J., in November 2000.[51] Although finding that a school had no legal responsibility for the consequences of failing to deal with bullying that occurred outside school,

---

[45] Note 39 *supra*, at page 529.
[46] This had been the issue in Anderton (note 39).
[47] At 537F.
[48] At 532A-D.
[49] As Lord Browne Wilkinson confirmed in X (Minors) v. Bedfordshire County Council [1995] ELR 404 at 450H-451A, referring to Van Oppen v. Trustees of the Bedford Charity [1990] 1 WLR 235.
[50] Scott v. Lothian Regional Council (unreported), September 29, 1998, Ct of Session.
[51] Bradford-Smart v. West Sussex County Council [2001] ELR 138.

Garland, J., implicitly acknowledged that there could be liability on the part of the education authority if the bullying occurred in school. Another case, before Manchester County Court, resulted in an award for psychological harm due to verbal bullying at school.[52]

Other Case Developments

School Choice/Admissions

The introduction of class size limits for five, six, and seven year olds in state maintained primary schools via the School Standards and Framework Act 1998 is intended to raise standards of education by lowering pupil-teacher ratios. Yet, one of the direct consequences of the limit is that parental choice is likely to be restricted. The limit has been set at thirty.[53] This means that a school which might have admitted ninety-six pupils across three classes of thirty-two now has to turn away six pupils. Prior to the introduction of this limit, the position in relation to the selected school was basically that unless the admission of a pupil in excess of the admission number set by the admission authority for the school would prejudice the provision of efficient education at the school or the efficient use of resources, a pupil had to be admitted. Moreover, even if a pupil's admission was incompatible with these factors, there was still a duty to admit the child if the reasons put forward by the parents outweighed the prejudice to efficiency.[54] This is still the position in relation to older pupils;[55] but where the class size limit applies the law now states that prejudice must be taken to arise from an admission if the class size limit would be exceeded.[56] At the same time, there are very limited exceptions to this.[57] Further, an appeal panel hearing an appeal by a parent for a school place which has been denied because admission would exceed the class size limit must only uphold the appeal if the decision was not one which a reasonable authority would make in the circumstance of the case, or that the child would have been offered a place if the admission arrangements as published had been properly implemented.[58]

---

[52] C v. Trafford Borough Council, October 25, 2000, Holman J.

[53] School Standards and Framework Act 1998, s 1.

[54] Education Act 1996, s 411(2), (3)(a); R v. South Glamorgan Appeals Committee ex p. Evans (1984) 10 May (CO/197/84) (unreported).

[55] School Standards and Framework Act 1998, s 86(2), (3). For the exception, see s 87 (pupils twice or more often excluded from school within prescribed period).

[56] Id. s 86(4).

[57] See DfEE, Code of Practice, School Admissions (London: DfEE, 1999) paras A.35-A.36.

[58] School Standards and Framework Act 1998, Schedule 24 para 12.

In *R v. South Glamorgan Education Appeal Committee ex parte Bryant*[59] the court held that the admission appeal committee correctly applied the criteria for class size limit cases. The new limit applied to appeals in respect of admission from September 1999. The class size limit of thirty would affect seven year olds from the school year 2001/02, and local education authorities were entitled to take it into account for children to be newly admitted in September 1999.[60]

There is no right of appeal against an admission appeal action but an application may be made for judicial review on public law grounds such as error of law, unfairness, and/or unreasonableness. In *R v. London Borough of Richmond ex parte JC*,[61] referred to above in the discussion on human rights, the court considered the effect of the new statutory arrangements. The parents expressed a preference for a place for their child at a school attended by their child's cousin, with whom the child had a relationship akin to a fraternal bond. The parents explained that their child had a hole in the heart and set out various other social factors underlying their choice. There were eighty-eight applicants for whom the school was their first choice, but only sixty places. When the parents were not allocated a place for their child, they appealed and put forward various specialist reports relating to their child (including one from a speech therapist) to support their claim. The appeal was dismissed and the parents applied for judicial review.

In the High Court, one of the issues raised by the parents was that the appeal committee had not taken account of the further evidence submitted prior to the appeal. Kay, J., wrote that while appeals against admission actions would normally take the form of a re-hearing, that was not the case with appeals governed by the new criteria for resolving class size limit cases. In the latter case, the hearing was a review that had to be examined on the basis of the information provided at the time of the decision against which the appeal was made, so generally later material should not be admitted. Kay, J., also explained that the burden of proof lay with the parents to establish grounds for exceeding the class size limit (above). The Court of Appeal subsequently upheld Kay, J's., opinion but was somewhat more favourably disposed than he was to the admission of further evidence at the appeal committee stage.

---

[59] [2000] ELR 602.
[60] Education Act 1996, Schedule 33 para 11A (replicated in the School Standards and Framework Act 1998, Schedule 24 para 12 (above)); and the Education Act 1996 (Infant Class Sizes) (Modification) Regulations 1998 (S.I. 1998 No. 1971).
[61] [2001] ELR 21 (Court of Appeal); [2000] ELR 565 (Queen's Bench Division).

One particularly important matter highlighted by the Court of Appeal was the granting of legal aid to children. Parents generally bring these kinds of legal challenge in the name of their child because the ch'ld's means are independently assessed. Children invariably have no resources, irrespectively of their parents' wealth, and state legal aid is unlikely to be refused on income or capital grounds a alone. Further, costs are not enforced against a losing legally-aided applicant. JC was brought in the child's name. Kennedy LJ commented that while in some "exceptional cases" it might be appropriate for the child to apply for judicial review, generally in admission appeal cases the challenge should be brought by the parents. He asserted that "the only reason why the application is made in the name of the child is to obtain legal aid, and to enable the parents to protect themselves in relation to costs. That I regard as an . Our legal system works on the basis that those who seek a remedy should expose themselves in relation to costs."[62] He also warned that using that device in the future might lead to a refusal of judicial review.

Of the other cases on school admissions, arguably the most important were two arising from actions by adjudicators who exercise jurisdiction (in England only) under the School Standards and Framework Act 1998. The office of adjudicator is new. The status of adjudicators has yet to be clarified by the courts; they appear not to be judicial figures (since they are appointed by the Secretary of State for Education and Skills[63] not the Lord Chancellor) but their work is monitored by the Council on Tribunals. Under section 89, which covers the statutory procedure for determining admission arrangements, any proposed variations to the arrangements during the course of the year which are necessitated by a major change of circumstances must, unless they fall within a description of variations to be prescribed, be referred to an adjudicator. An adjudicator is then to consider whether variations should be introduced and, if so, whether in their proposed, or a modified, form. Under section 90, parents may raise objections which may be referred to an adjudicator who must determine the matter or, in any cases prescribed by regulations,[64] refer the objection to the Secretary of State. Both the adjudicator and the Secretary of State, when acting under the section, may make modifications to the admission arrangements and must publish their judgment on the objection and the reasons for it. The decision on the objection is binding on the admissions authority.

---

[62] [2001] ELR 21 at para 31.
[63] School Standards and Framework Act 1998 s 25.
[64] Education (Objection to Admission Arrangements) Regulations 1999 (S.I. 1999 No. 125).

In *R v. Downes ex parte Wandsworth London Borough Council*[65] an adjudicator reduced the proportion of pupils who could be selected for admission on ability grounds to three secondary schools in Wandsworth. He found that the admission arrangements were not in the best interests of local children and ordered that the percentages be cut from 50% to 25% in relation to two of the schools and from 32% to 25% in relation to the other. A local junior school, which wanted partial selection to be replaced by a different admission system, and by the parents of child attending one of the primary schools, who preferred the previous admission arrangements, brought objections. The court pointed out that the school had no right to have its objections considered by the adjudicator since they related to the principle of partial selection itself. Yet, the court considered that it was not clear that the adjudicator considered whether the change to the selection arrangements might be so fundamental as to bring about a significant change in the character of the school; if they had made such a change by virtue of section 103 of the 1998 Act, the adjudicator would have had no jurisdiction.

In the other adjudicator case, *R v. The Schools Adjudicator ex parte Metropolitan Borough of Wirral*,[66] the issue was whether the adjudicator acted lawfully in overturning admission arrangements after consulting with a range of interested parties who had broadly supported them. The local education authority operated both grammar and all-ability schools. The admission arrangements it adopted were intended to assist parents who wanted a place at one of the authority's grammar schools but who, if their child did not perform well enough in tests, ran the risk of being a low priority for a place at a preferred all-ability school. The arrangements, therefore, enabled these parents to have two first choices, a grammar school and an all-ability school. The head teacher of an all ability school objected to this on the ground that it put these parents at an unfair advantage over parents who simply selected an all-ability school. The adjudicator agreed and imposed different arrangements. The court concluded that the adjudicator acted lawfully since he tried to produce a fair system overall.

Another school admissions case concerned a mother's challenge to a local education authority which wrongly informed her that she had a place for her child at the school of her first choice: *R v. Birmingham City Council ex parte L.*[67] The mother only discovered the error after she purchased a new school uniform for her child. The mother refused the authority's offer of a rehearing of her appeal and compensation for expenses. The court refused to overturn the action on the basis that the authority acted reasonably. Also,

---

[65] [2000] ELR 425.
[66] [2000] ELR 620.
[67] [2000] ELR 543.

the court indicated that the ambiguity in the letter of decision sent to the mother should have alerted her to the potential error and defeated any claim that its contents created a legitimate expectation in her favor.

One final admission case worthy of mention is *R v. Rotherham Metropolitan Borough Council ex parte LT*[68] in the Court of Appeal. There has long been a potential conflict between the statutory duty on admissions authorities not to discriminate between school place applicants merely on the basis that they do not live in the authority's area,[69] on the one hand, and the fact that school catchment areas or zones are a legitimate means of prioritizing admission applications in relation to a particular school,[70] on the other. Here the applicant lived in Nottinghamshire but wanted a place at a school in a neighbouring authority, Rotherham. The school had a catchment area but the applicant did not live in it and was denied a place. The eastern boundary of the catchment area followed the Rotherham local education authority boundary. The court held that catchment are boundaries had to be drawn rationally and suggested that if they coincided exactly with the local education authority boundaries it might run contrary to what Parliament had intended. The court was satisfied that the catchment area was not unlawful merely because it coincided to some extent with the authority boundary.

Exclusion from School

The total number of permanent school exclusions in England was over 10,000 in 1998-99. Even so, this represented a fall for the first time in several years. These figures do not include private schools. Among the exclusion cases in courts in the past year was one concerning whether the exclusion of a child from a private school was amenable to judicial review. Established case law holds that this is not the case[71] and that a remedy must be sought under the law of contract rather than on public law grounds. However, in *R v. Muntham House School ex parte R*,[72] the status of the school, which was a residential facility catering to pupils with emotional and behavioral difficulties, was in question. A child was permanently excluded from the school since his behavior made it impossible for the staff to maintain any appropriate relationship with him; he also made a death threat to a teacher. It was also contended that the school placement itself was not viable. Richards J

---

[68] [2000] ELR 76.
[69] Currently found in the School Standards and Framework Act 1998 s 86(8) but dating back to the Education Act 1980 s 6(5).
[70] R v. Greenwich London Borough Council ex p. Governors of the John Ball Primary School (1989) 88 LGR 589, per Lloyd LJ at 599.
[71] *See* in particular R v. Fernhill Manor School ex p. A [1994] 67.
[72] [2000] ELR 287.

noted that although the school was not classifiable as an independent school for statutory purposes, since it was not funded by the public sector and its decisions did not have the public law character necessary to make it amenable to judicial review.

Another case arose from a head teacher's investigation of an alleged theft of a handbag from a school classroom which resulted in his excluding a pupil permanently: *R v. Headteacher and Independent Appeal Committee of Dunraven School ex parte B.*[73] The court reiterated the duty on the school's governing body to review whether the head teacher's order should stand and the appeal panel to which a parent (or pupil, but only if aged eighteen or over) may appeal against a governors' action, to disclose to the appellants, and enable them to comment on, documentary evidence on which the decision-maker relied in reaching a judgment. The Court of Appeal quashed the decision while putting forward some guidance as to the conduct of an investigation by a head teacher. The court wrote that while a head teacher was not in the same position as a police officer governed by the statutory guidance on interrogation contained in the Police and Criminal Evidence Act 1984, he or she still has a duty to conduct a fair, non-oppressive investigation.

Finally, in *R v. Independent Appeal Panel of Sheffield City Council ex parte N,*[74] a boy was excluded from school following an alleged sexual assault on a girl pupil. The police investigated and a prosecution was pending. Meanwhile, an appeal was bought against the exclusion with the appeal panel finding that in the absence of a final ruling on the prosecution by the criminal court, it should not assume that the boy was guilty and should satisfy itself as to whether he committed the alleged conduct. As such, the panel ordered the boy's reinstatement. The victim of the alleged assault was so upset that she remained away from school and applied for judicial review of the panel's action. Moses, J., indicated that the best approach for an appeal panel in such a situation, which he indicated was likely to be repeated in future cases, was for it to accept that since it could not uncover the truth or otherwise of the charge, it should consider whether it was in the best interests of all concerned for the pupil to be excluded. He added that "[i]t seems to me that a panel is making all sorts of difficulties for itself in attempting to decide the issue of guilt or innocence with its hands tied behind its back."[75]

---

[73] [2000] ELR 156.
[74] [2000] ELR 700.
[75] Id. at para (6).

A book based on research highly critical of the current school exclusion appeal arrangements in England was published in March 2000.[76] Among the major concerns were deficiencies in training of panel members and the inexpert way in which panels handled the participation of children and young people in the hearings. The researchers also detected a degree of "unconscious bias" in favor of schools by appeal panels and called for improvements to the system.

Special Educational Needs

Decisions by the authorities on educational provisions for children with special educational needs continues to generate disputes and consequent litigation. Having already considered human rights and common law negligence issues arising in this context, this chapter now turns to the substantive issues concerned with the Education Act 1996 Part IV, as supplemented by regulations[77] and a code of practice.[78] The legislation lays down an elaborate framework of rights and duties concerning children with special educational needs and an appeal process involving a special educational needs tribunal and further appeal to the High Court. Local education authorities and schools have a duty to ensure that children's special educational needs are met. There is also a duty, soon to be strengthened under the Special Educational Needs and Disability Act 2001, to ensure a child with special educational needs is educated in a mainstream rather than special school unless that is incompatible with the wishes of the parents.[79] For most children with special educational needs, provision is made by the school as part of its normal functions; but for some the provision required is specified in a 'statement' which is the equivalent of an American Individualized Education Plan. A statement must be developed if the local education authority considers, following an child's assessment, that the student has special educational needs.[80] The form of the statement is prescribed by the regulations. The parents must be consulted over the contents of the statement and given an opportunity to express a preference for a school to be named in the statement; the preference must be upheld unless the school is unsuitable for the child or his or her attendance there would prejudice the education of other children who attended or the efficient use of resources.[81]

---

[76] N. Harris and K. Eden, with A. Blair, Challenges to School Exclusion (London: RoutledgeFalmer 2000).
[77] Currently the Education (Special Educational Needs) Regulations 1994 (S.I. 1994 No. 1047) and the Special Educational Needs Tribunal Regulations 1995 (S.I. 1995 No. 3113) (to be replaced in September 2001).
[78] The current code, made under the 1996 Act s 313, will be revised shortly.
[79] Id. ss 316 and 317.
[80] Id. s 324(1).
[81] Id. Sch 27 para 3.

The effect of a statement is that a local education authority must ensure that the specified provision is delivered. A statement does not need to name a school for a child to attend, but if it does, then the school must admit the child.[82] In the recent case of *R v. Chair of Governors and Head teacher of A and S School ex parte T*[83] the court held that the duty applies even if a school is not in the local education authority's area. Parents who lived in Southwark expressed a preference for a school in Lewisham to be named in the statement but had their request denied. Southwark was prepared to pay for the child's education at the Lewisham school, but the school did not want to take him. Jackson J reasoned that the duty on a school named in a statement to admit a child was mandatory irrespective of the authority in whose area it is situated. This case could precipitate disputes between neighboring local education authorities over provisions for children with special educational needs. It means one authority can bind another authority's school to take a child.

A further issue relating to children placed in schools outside of a local education authority's area was resolved in the House of Lords in *B v. London Borough of Harrow and Others.*[84] The family lived in the London Borough of Harrow and the child, who had Rett syndrome, was placed in one of its special schools. The mother later argued that the child's needs were not being met and wanted her placed in a school in neighboring Hillingdon. Harrow refused to support this move on the basis that it would make it more difficult for it to manage a co-ordinated response to the girl's needs and would cost too much. The tribunal agreed that a placement at the school in Hillingdon would not be compatible with "the efficient use of resources." A question arose as to whose resources fell to be considered for this purpose: the sending authority's (Harrow's) or those of the receiving authority (Hillingdon). The House of Lords held that the relevant resources were those of the sending authority thereby enabling account to be taken by the authority which had responsibility for the child (the sending authority) of the additional cost that educating a child outside the borough would generally involve.

L v. Hereford and Worcester County Council and Hughes[85] was mentioned above in connection with the human rights arguments advanced in support of the appeal relating to a nine-year old girl with cerebral palsy whose parents wanted a private school to be named in her statement at an annual cost of £44,000. The local education authority proposed any one of three mainstream schools where the cost of educating the child would be

---

[82] Id. s 324(5).
[83] [2001] ELR 274.
[84] [2000] ELR 109.
[85] [2000] ELR 375.

less than half that amount. The High Court considered an argument by the parents that the tribunal should not have accepted the local education authority's plan that the girl should be placed in a mainstream school with additional support on the grounds that it was contrary to the parents' wishes. On this point Carwath, J., observed that the local education authority's primary duty was to ensure that proper and appropriate provision was made for the child; and a secondary duty was to ensure mainstream education unless the parents objected. He stated that if the parents objected, the secondary duty went but not the first. He also declared that if the authority considered a mainstream school appropriate for the statement it would fulfil its primary obligation by arranging for her to be educated there. The local education authority sought further review by the Court of Appeal[86] which confirmed that in respect of the primary duty, the local education authority had to consider in detail the kind of provision the child required, adding that the it had to take account of parental wishes under the general principle applicable to all areas of education decision-making.[87] The case nevertheless adds further weight to the view that parents do not have a simple veto over mainstream placements.

Conclusion

In relation to the schools sector, the types of education dispute most likely to find their way into the courts in England and Wales continue to be those concerned with access to a particular type of provision, whether in respect of general choice of school, provision for children with learning difficulties, or a place at a school from which a child has been excluded. The contentious nature of these issues is recognized by the existence of an initial right of appeal to a specialist appeal panel or tribunal. The Human Rights Act 1998 has added a new dimension for public law challenges to these appeal bodies' decisions or those of the original decision-maker, usually a local education authority or school governing body. However, the courts have treaded cautiously to date and human rights arguments have had little impact on their rulings. Even so, these are early days. Meanwhile, Phelps has created opportunities for common law negligence claims and in the process has shifted the balance of rights yet further in the direction of the ordinary citizen and away from the increasingly regulated (despite the Government's commitment to a reduction) education system.

---

[86] L v. Worcestershire County Council and Hughes [2000] ELR 674.
[87] Education Act 1996 s 9.

NEW ZEALAND

Paul Rishworth

Introduction

Education-related litigation in New Zealand was sparse in 2000-2001. Even the generally fertile field of employment law spawned little activity. But, as always, this does not mean that there were no developments in education law. First, there has been significant legislative change. The Labour-Alliance Coalition Government, elected in late 1999, entered its second full year of office and, after enacting the first year's reforms, foreshadowed in last year's *Yearbook*, now has a fresh Education Amendment Bill before Parliament. This is certain to be enacted before the close of 2001. Second, as to litigation, the New Zealand tradition of finding mediated solutions to education disputes still continues. This means that issues that might, in other countries, be the subject of extensive litigation often end in ad hoc settlements or successful mediation. Even these can, in some cases, contribute something to the corpus of education law: especially where a mediated result embodies an official position on the part of a public agency such as the Human Rights Commission or Privacy Commission. This will have implications for other education providers who may face proceedings before the relevant Commission.

The following account of developments in 2000-2001, therefore, deals with recent and pending legislative and policy reforms, as well as with such litigation as has occurred, including, where significant, that which was resolved by mediation.

Elementary and Secondary Education

School funding

Public education at primary and secondary level in New Zealand is, and always has been, free, consistent with article 13 of the International Covenant on Economic, Social and Cultural Rights.[1] The funds are provided from central government revenue raised through direct and indirect taxes. School funding is not, as in some North American jurisdictions, derived from municipal property taxes. This has meant that New Zealand has been immune from some of the difficulties and disparities that can arise as between wealthy and poor school districts.

Yet, there are disparities nonetheless. The schools in wealthier areas have long been the high-performing ones, reflecting the heightened degree of community interest in education in these areas, as well as available finan-

---

[1] 21 UNGAOR Supp (No 16) at 49, UN Doc A/6316 (1966), 993 UNTS 3, entered into force Jan. 3, 1976.

cial support. In lower socio-economic areas, schools struggle for resources, whether by way of parental involvement or financial help. The major reforms of 1989, described in the 1999 Yearbook, exacerbated some of these problems. Each school community has since then been required to elect a Board of Trustees to run its school within the parameters of national guidelines, and this new regime has had its least success in the poorer areas. Further, in a time of economic stringency when government funding for education has fallen below perceived needs, public schools increasingly look to their parent constituency for extra assistance. This is least forthcoming in lower socio-economic areas.

A growing practice in schools has been to levy "voluntary contributions" from parents, with a fixed "fee" per student being collected each academic year. The expectation is that all parents will pay the fee, although there is no legal requirement to pay it since, by section 3 of the Education Act 1989, primary and secondary education is free.

In practice, the success rate for schools in extracting the fee varies in proportion to the relative wealth of a community. Middle and upper class areas now charge and collect fairly significant fees, ranging up to around $500 per student per year, while schools in lower socio-economic areas ask for a much smaller sum, if any, and expect a lower collection rate. The difference can be very significant in terms of funds for extra equipment such as computers or staff.

At least once a year the question of school fees, and school tactics in collecting them, receives publicity. In previous years, some schools have made access to extra-curricular activities, attendance at the annual school ball, for example, conditional on the fee being paid. This has raised serious legal issues, not yet explored in litigation, about what the "core" of free education actually is. In 2000 the debate surfaced again when Auckland's leading state school, Auckland Grammar School, sent parents of newly enrolled students a letter requesting a $500 fee to perfect their enrolment, without making it clear that the payment was voluntary. The Ministry of Education directed school officials to make it clear that payment was optional.

Payment of Teacher Salaries

Teacher salaries are set nationally through a bargaining process involving the relevant unions and the Crown, and until the early 1990s were uniformly paid directly to teachers from a centrally-administered payroll. This had the effect that individual school boards, although legally the "employers" of teachers, were neither negotiating nor paying salaries and the combined amount of salaries did not feature in a school's budget.

In1992 a change was made. The National Government amended the law so as to allow school boards to opt for "bulk funding" of teachers' salaries. Schools which so opted had the salary component of their operating requirements made available for them to deploy themselves. The amount of bulk funding was calculated pursuant to a staffing formula which served to make some, although not all, schools somewhat better off. Many schools therefore transferred to this system, becoming "bulk funded schools." School leaders found that bulk funding afforded them flexibility to staff their school in a manner that could make funds available for other purposes, even for additional staff. At various times in the 1990s, schools were also offered extra funding as an incentive to become bulk-funded, since it was government policy to encourage the transition.

The teacher unions were critical of bulk funding since they saw it as placing incentives on schools to replace experienced and expensive teachers with junior ones in order to generate savings for other essential purposes. This, the unions pointed out, really only served to produce funds that ought to have been provided by government in the first place. On the other hand, bulk funding had vigorous supporters in the community as it signified a devolution to schools of important decision-making powers, giving local administrators more options to be creative in deploying their operational budgets. Bulk funding therefore appealed to the entrepreneurial spirit of many principals and boards who saw it as a way to advance the educational missions of their schools.

Indeed, the availability of bulk funding almost became a symbol of the different political approaches of New Zealand's two principal political parties. The Labour Party, in opposition throughout the 1990s, had been a vigorous opponent of bulk funding, enjoying strong historic and current links with the union movement. Many of its key personnel, including those who would go on to hold the offices of Prime Minister, Attorney-General, and Minister of Education, were formerly university or secondary teachers. It was little surprise, having regard to their opposition, that the incoming Government's first education law reform, sections 7-10 of Education Amendment Act 2000, included removal of the option of bulk funding.

Enrolments and School Zoning

Another central pillar of the 1989 reforms was the notion that a student could apply to attend any school. This was seen to provide incentives for excellence in school administration, since schools would have to perform well in order to attract students and attendant funding. To some extent this was borne out, but the principle impact of the reform was that the already successful schools were flooded by applications. The 1989 legislation dealt with this problem by requiring schools that were at capacity to implement an "enrolment scheme," setting out the criteria on which they would select among applicants. The selection criteria were left to individual schools, subject only to the requirement that the anti-discrimination law could not be breached. While geographical proximity to a school could be a factor in enrolment schemes, it need not be decisive. Many school leaders established schemes that simply set out the various factors they would consider but reserved the final decision on enrolment was up to themselves. This approach left many disappointed applicants very unsatisfied and there were some well publicised cases of students who could not gain access to a school that was down their street or even literally over their back fence. There were various criticisms, including the complaint that the good schools could select students to enhance their academic and sporting reputations. This made it very difficult for nearby schools which felt that they were being denied the students who could make a difference in performing their own educational mission.

Throughout the 1990s enrolment schemes were the subject of controversy and a degree of legislative tinkering, but the Education Amendment Act 2000 has now changed the whole regime completely. Under the new law, every school is required to designate a geographic "home zone," with reference to surrounding streets, such that it is possible to say whether a given address is within a zone. All students within a zone are entitled to enrol in a particular school. If there are then spare places, the following applies. When more applications are received than there are places for, selection is made according to a statutory list of priority. First, applicants for any "special programs" run by the school, such as students with disabilities; next, siblings of enrolled students; next, siblings of former students; then, children of employees of the school board, and finally, all other applicants. If there are more applicants in any category than there are places, selection is by way of ballot.

This regime was in place for selections into the 2001 school year; in New Zealand school years are also calendar years. While the reforms were generally popular, some difficulties emerged. The principle difficulty was that there was some evidence of fraud in enrolment applications to the top schools, with parents giving false addresses or else maintaining a temporary address within the zone for the purpose of gaining enrolment. In order to deal with these issues, the Education Amendment Bill presently before Parliament is being amended to provide that students enrolling dishonestly or with temporary addresses assumed for enrolment purposes will have their enrolments annulled within one month.

The effect of the new law has been to return to the era of rigid school zoning which has a concomitant effect on real estate prices within the zones of desirable schools. When the home zones were being settled in mid-2000, there was considerable community interest in where the lines were to be drawn.

Discrimination in School Enrolment Applications

The Human Rights Commission made an interesting determination in 2001 in respect of the old enrolment scheme regime. For reasons explained below, even though the underlying enrolment law has now been changed, the determination continues to have implications for private schools.

The case arose as follows. Between 1991 to 1999, a considerable number of schools included, as one of the factors they would consider in selection of students, an applicant's "connection" to a school through having a parent or grandparent who was a past student there. This practice raised serious questions about discrimination on two bases. First, a scheme employing that criterion could operate in an indirectly discriminatory manner against new immigrants who were obviously unable to gain the benefit of the "parental connection" factor. Second, it arguably constituted discrimination on the grounds of "family status," a concept defined in the Human Rights Act 1993 as including the characteristic of "being a relative of a particular person." The argument ran that a student whose mother was not an past student of a school was discriminated against on the ground of being a relative of her mother, that is, of a "particular person" who was "not an old-girl." However, there were various problems with this interpretation of the law along with the pragmatic concern that if the Human Rights Act precluded consideration of a parental connection with a school, then it must equally have prevented consideration of sibling connections. This would mean that schools were acting unlawfully when favouring the brothers and sisters of existing students. Yet, that type of preference seemed innocuous and most New Zealanders would have been astonished to learn that human rights law ruled out any preference for keeping families together at one school.

Over the years, indeed right from the very outset of the enrolment scheme regime in 1991, there were criticisms of schools that employed the "parental connection" criterion. It seemed to some a rather unprincipled preference and students who were refused selection understandably resented the fact that a lack of parental connection to the school may have counted against them. Even so, because the factor was only one of many that schools claimed to have considered, it was difficult for rejected applicants to show that the lack of a parental connection was a decisive factor.

Against this background, it was somewhat odd that the Human Rights Commission came out strongly, in March 2001, against the legality of parental connection as a criterion employed in the enrolment scheme of Hamilton

Girls' High School. The complaint against the school related to its enrolment procedures for 1999, so the case apparently took two years to advance to the stage of a determination by the Commission. At the same time, it was not as if the issue was new to the Commission, for complaints about school enrolment criteria had been coming in fairly constantly since 1992. Moreover, since that law had, by March 2001, been changed to preclude any sort of selection other than balloting, this seemed a case of closing the stable door after the horse had not merely bolted but been cremated.

The ruling has had the incidental effect of raising serious questions for private schools. Private schools operate largely outside the Education Act 1989 once they have been registered under section 35A of that Act. Their enrolment decisions are affected by neither the old law nor the new. However, private schools are nevertheless subject to the Human Rights Act 1993 and hence are bound not to discriminate on the stated grounds when dealing with applications to enrol. As such, the Human Rights Commission's March 2001 determination has implications for them since it suggests that they, too, will act unlawfully if they prefer applicants with a parental connection to the school. Yet private schools are known to prefer the sons and daughters of past students since it can be important to them to maintain inter-generational family links with their school. This can facilitate fund-raising and endowments, as well-heeled families may see some benefit accruing to future generations of the family from their donations of time and money. If the Human Rights Commission is right in its apparent reading of the Human Rights Act, then consideration of "parental connection" is equally unlawful in a private school. Further, it would be direct discrimination, permitting no defense of "good reason" as is available in the case of indirect discrimination. It seems unlikely, then, that this will be legally tested and the status quo will probably continue for private schools because, even without having to ask, most private schools will simply know who among its applicant pool are the sons or daughters of past pupils. Thus, parental connection will not be an explicit factor, but will operate sub silentio in a manner that cannot easily be proved. Also, a private school is more likely to contest the Human Rights Commission's interpretation of the relevant statutory provision.

The Human Rights Commission's March 2001 determination that Hamilton Girls High School acted unlawfully, in 1999, in considering parental connection, means that the issue of compensation for the non-admitted complainant remains on the table. Although the ruling came two years too late to secure an applicant's admission to the school but she is reported to be seeking a public apology and $5000 legal costs. If these are not forthcoming from the school willingly, then the student's remedy is to take proceedings before the Complaints Review Tribunal, the body that adjudicates on unmediated Human Rights Act complaints. The Human Rights Commission can, and probably will, take the case to the Tribunal on her behalf. The Tribunal has power to award damages for violations of the Human Rights Act.

Constitution of School Boards

Until 2000 boards of trustees of state schools had the option of deciding whether to have a student representative. The Education Amendment Act 2000 removed the option: all school boards must now have a student representative.

Teacher Registration

Insofar as the Teacher Registration Board (TRB) has the statutory function of registering teachers, most schools are legally required to employ registered teachers. The exceptions are some parts of the early childhood education sector, and Kura Kaupapa Maori language immersion schools. These exceptions owed their existence to concerns over the availability of suitably qualified registered teachers to staff schools in those areas. The pending Education Amendment Bill will extend registration requirements to teachers in these institutions.

The TRB has been in litigation in two reported cases. In *Richardson v. Teacher Registration Board*,[2] a teacher fabricated a story about a student's suicide attempt and her own urgent intervention to save the child's life. The TRB canceled the teacher's registration on the grounds that she was neither of "good character" nor "fit" to be a teacher, the statutory criteria. On the teacher's appeal, the District Court affirmed the TRB's decision. In particular, the Court ruled that the TRB did not predetermine the matter by making a preliminary judgment that the principal's application to have R's registration canceled raised a prima facie case against the teacher. Further, the Court was satisfied that the TRB's investigation and hearing on the matter was full and fair.

In *C v. Teacher Registration Board*,[3] after Mrs. C committed the criminal offense of dishonesty while employed by a school board in a non-teaching capacity, the TRB cancelled her registration. The District Court, on appeal, remitted the matter back for further consideration, holding that the Board failed to look at the facts "in the round" and had too much attention to the previous conviction. The question of good character for registration purposes was, said the judge, to be examined on a "forward looking" basis.

---

[2] District Court, Wellington, [2000] DCR 595.
[3] District Court, Wellington, [2000] DCR 803.

Proposed Structural Reforms

The pending Education Amendment Bill would establish an Education Council which would subsume the teacher registration functions. It will have wider membership, including four to be elected from the teacher constituency, three to be nominated (one each by the primary and secondary teacher unions, and one by the School Trustees Association), and four to be appointed by the Minister. The Council will have statutory functions including developing a code of ethics for teachers, dealing with misconduct and incompetence by teachers, determining standards for teacher registration and qualifications, co-ordinating a system of police-vetting of all teachers and all others employed in schools, and to promote and sponsor research.

Closing a loophole in the present scheme of things, whereby schools might simply facilitate the departure of errant teachers from their own employ, employers will henceforth be required to immediately report both serious teacher misconduct and incompetence to the Education Council. There are offences of failing to report. In addition, the Council would be able to receive competence complaints made by any person. Further, all criminal convictions must be reported by teachers to the Council within seven days, where the offence is punishable by three months or more imprisonment.

School Reporting Requirements and Early Interventions

The new Bill overhauls school reporting requirements, emphasizing the non-financial as much as the financial. Reporting templates and internet technology will be used to make the process more simple. Schools will be required to develop school plans, in consultation with their communities. School plans and reports will replace the "Charters," which were the centrepiece of the 1989 reforms. Charters were statements of a school's objectives, to be developed after consultation with school communities and with special reference to Maori in the community. Plans will serve the same role, but must be updated annually. This will probably serve to make them less anodyne and more informative than Charters.

A recurring problem under the present regime has been how to deal with non-performing and mis-managed schools. The threshold for intervention by the Ministry has been set quite high, such that a poorly performing school that meets its reporting obligations may be immune from intervention. The proposed new law deals with this by conferring powers upon the Ministry to request specific information about a school so as to assess its performance, appoint a specialist advisor to the school, require the school to develop an action plan to deal with a problem, and appoint a limited purpose manager to control specific functions on behalf of the school. Insofar as these are all laudable aims, it is interesting to reflect how in this area, as in others, the pendulum is starting to turn back to more heavy monitoring and potential involvement by central authorities.

Same-Sex State Schools

Many New Zealand state schools are single-sex establishments. The highest performing boys and girls schools are in this category. The ability to establish and maintain a single-sex state school is presently preserved from the impact of anti-discrimination law by two provisions: the first in section 3A the Education Act 1989 which provides that no boy may be enrolled at a designated girls' school and vice versa; the second is in section 58 of the Human Rights Act 1993 which provides that educational institutions do not breach the Human Rights Act if they are maintained for students of one race, sex or religion, one type of disability, or a certain age group.

The Government is proposing, in the new Education Bill, to repeal section 3A but to leave section 58 intact. The Government's stated reason is that a single-sex school will thenceforth be entitled to admit students of the other sex if it chooses to do so. It must be said, however, that this option is already available to schools in terms of section 3A, since it explicitly recognizes that the designation of a school as a single sex school may be changed. A number of schools have made this change over the past few years.

Principals of state single sex schools are reported to be fearful of the effects of the repeal of section 3A since they see section 58 of the Human Rights Act as insufficient comfort. They view the proposed legislation as a step toward changing the nature of their schools against their will. But they need not worry: section 58 is enough to make it plain that the anti-discrimination provisions of the Human Rights Act do not mandate a change from single-sex schools to co-education. To the extent that girls are reported to perform better at single-sex schools, there is no significant lobby group seeking to alter the status quo. The more interesting story is why the Government wishes to maintain the provision in section 58 for separate racial schools, which, in other countries, seem anachronistic if not invidious. In New Zealand, the reason for this aspect of section 58 is that there are a number of venerable old Maori schools which are generally seen as a good thing. No doubt the intention was to preserve them from the suggestion that they act unlawfully in refusing entry to non-Maori applicants. Still, the effect of a statutory immunity for schools established for particular races is to signal that a "whites-only" school is a legal possibility. In practice, of course, any such state school is most unlikely, and a private school of that type would face insurmountable hurdles in getting registered in terms of the statutory criteria.

Health Education

Health Education includes information about sexuality. Existing legislation gives schools and principals discretion whether to exclude sexuality education from a school's health education program. The new Education Amendment Bill would remove this discretion, putting the topic on the same footing as all other national curriculum elements. Parents would still have the right to remove their children from classes teaching sexuality education, for that right is guaranteed under a section of the Education Act 1964 that is not to be repealed. The Human Rights Commission, in its submission on the proposed new law, criticizes the fact that parents may opt their children out of health education at all, contending that this is contrary to article 10(h) of the International Convention on the Elimination of all Forms of Discrimination against Women, which guarantees women: "Access to specific educational information to help ensure the health and wellbeing of families, including information and advice on family planning."[4]

School Boarding Hostels

A case in 1997, about the expulsion of a male student from a boarding hostel for theft, included a judicial finding that the operation of a boarding hostel by a state school board was not properly conceived as a "public function," meaning that the provisions of the New Zealand Bill of Rights Act 1990 did not apply to the relationship between student and hostel.[5] There was, in United States terms, no "state action." Regardless of whether that was a correct decision, the new Education Amendment Bill will authorize the making of regulations to govern hostels and to ensure the safety of students who board in them. This embryonic governmental attention to the standards in hostels may lead future courts to decide that a state school's boarding hostel, should it choose to operate one, now has the character of a "public" rather than private function. That being the case, the Bill of Rights would apply to hostel authorities in their dealings with students.

State Funding of Religious Schools

The 1999 Yearbook outlined the position of private, including religious, schools seeking public funding. In summary, private schools may seek integration into the state system, under an agreement with the Minister of Education that allows them to retain their "special character," which may be

---

[4] 34 UNGAOR Supp No 46 at 193, UN Doc A/34/46, entered into force September 3, 1981.
[5] McGuinn v. Board of Trustees of Palmerston North Boys High Sch. [1997] 2 NZLR 60.

religious or philosophic such as Montessori, Steiner, and so on. This is a generous and inclusive accommodation of religious values in the public education system, driven in its inception by a crisis in the funding of private Catholic schools during the 1960s and 1970s.

An amendment that became operative in late 1998 deserves mention.[6] This amendment was designed to plug a perceived gap by allowing the Minister to decline to enter into negotiations an integration agreement with a private school that applies for integration. The amendment adds that the Minister is entitled to consider, among other factors relevant to whether to so decline, "the nature, character, and capacity of the existing network of schools" (emphasis added). Further, according to sections 5 and 6 of the PSIA, the Minister may decline to accept applications to negotiate integration agreements from schools in particular geographic areas.

The interesting thing about these amendments is that they reveal implicit assumptions about the underlying theory of integrated schools. They suggest that there is no conception that religious parents have any sort of right to establish religious schools and to receive the benefits of public funding. It is now clear that the mere presence of perfectly good state schools in the area, with spare capacity, can be enough to defeat the aspirations of religious parents for a publicly-funded religious education for their children.

Treaty of Waitangi and Maori Educational Aspirations

Last year's Yearbook reported on a High Court case about school closure, in which the judge rejected the claims of a Maori community that a rural school should be exempted from the normal criteria for closure. The claim was that the school was teaching in the Maori language and should be allowed to continue to do so, even if other indicators supported closure. The disappointed plaintiffs also took their complaint to the Waitangi Tribunal, a body established under the Treaty of Waitangi Act 1975 with jurisdiction to hear complaints that the Government has acted, or proposes to act, inconsistently with the principles of the Treaty of Waitangi. The Treaty of Waitangi is the treaty made in 1840 whereby the English Crown acquired sovereignty in New Zealand, with promises to the Maori tribes to protect and preserve their "rangatiratanga," or chiefly authority, over their property and other "taonga," or treasured possessions. It is accepted that the Maori language itself is a taonga, and so the argument before the Tribunal was that the Government, in considering school closures, was required to have regard to and act consistently with an obligation to preserve and enhance the viability of the Maori language. In other words, the argument

---

[6] Private Schools Conditional Integration Amendment Act 1978, section 3 (substituting new sections 5 and 6 in the principle Act).

was to maintain the school. On 31 March 2000 the Tribunal issued its decision, concluding that:

Our analysis of the evidence and submissions presented in the claim leads to the conclusion that, despite the Crown's commitment to the goal of improving the education of Maori children, the closure of Mokai Primary School was not undertaken consistently with the principles of the Treaty of Waitangi. In brief, the 'good governance' that is required of the Crown, and that is demonstrated by its attention to protecting taonga and enhancing tino rangatiratanga by reasonable means, was not evident in the chain of events that culminated in the school's closure. The nature of the prejudice this has caused the claimants is such that we recommend that Mokai Primary School be 'reopened' with more intensive support from the Crown than was available in the past. We also recommend that the Crown clarify its policies and processes for intervening (by closure of other means) in the government of schools in difficulty.[7]

This is a good illustration of the dialogical approach to resolution of Maori claims in relation to governmental initiatives. The Tribunal may make recommendations but they are not binding on the Government. In this case, the Minister of Education publicly expressed reservations about the Tribunal's action, but undertook to look afresh at the closure in light of the judgment. The school has not so far been reopened, but it is understood that discussions are continuing between the Ministry and the claimants, both about the particular school and as to the wider implications of the Tribunal Report for dealing with Maori language education.

Tertiary Education

Age Discrimination in Employment

The Human Rights Act 1993 introduced a prohibition on age discrimination, but did so in a manner that ensured its impact on mandatory retirement would not arise until 31 January 1999. From that date on, the understanding has been that mandatory retirement at age 65, or any age, is unlawful.

A special savings provision in the Act provided that if an employment contract that was in force on 1 April 1992 specified a retirement age, then that provision would remain in effective as long as that the retirement age was re-affirmed or varied in writing after 1 April 1992. Relying on this section, the University of Otago contended in 2000 that all its staff were subject to mandatory retirement at age 65 since their current employment still con-

---

[7] The quotation is from the Tribunal's Press Release on Claim Wai 46, The Mokai Primary School Claim, dated 31 March 2000.

tained the same clause, requiring retirement at 65, as had been in the 1992 contract. In *Fogelberg v Association of University Staff of New Zealand*,[8] the High Court of New Zealand held against the University, reasoning that the "savings" provision in the Act did not apply. According to the Court, all staff were on new, albeit with the same term about retirement at age 65 having being carried over from the 1992 contract. The Court maintained that being new, the "savings provision" in the Act did not apply, because it "saved" only the mandatory retirement clauses in the contracts that existed in 1992. The Court thus concluded that since the clauses in the current contracts were unlawful and unenforceable, the 953 university employees at Otago were therefore not subject to mandatory retirement. Other universities in New Zealand had already accepted that this was the position in relation to their own staff.

Government Ownership Interest and Financial Accountability

For some years, the Government has been concerned with the implications of the potential financial failure of a public tertiary education provider. The questions of ownership of public educational institutions, and of ultimate responsibility for their financial failure, have been seen as complex ones. Yet, whatever the law might be, there is little doubt that creditors would see government as a guarantor, if not itself directly responsible. Against this background, the Government was concerned to minimize the risk of institutional failure. Accomplishing this goal requires the legislation of powers to acquire information and to intervene when judged necessary.

At present, the Minister has little or no statutory authority to intervene in the governance of tertiary institutions. The new Bill will tackle this issue in a variety of ways, beginning with a requirement for Tertiary Education Institution Councils to monitor their Chief Executive's performance, and to ensure that their institution operates in a financially responsible manner.

Ultimately there is power for a Minister to dissolve a council and appoint a commissioner in its place. These proposals are controversial, for they are seen to threaten institutional autonomy. It remains to be seen whether, or in what form, they are enacted.

Conclusion

The themes in education law in New Zealand for 2000-2001, legislative and structural reform, are likely to continue next year. The new Coalition

---

[8] Elias, C.J., High Court, Dunedin, September 8, 2000.

Government has a clear Parliamentary majority and is intent on significant reforms. On the other hand, there seems to have been something of a hiatus in contentious litigation, especially in the area of student rights. Whether this is an emerging trend should be revealed over the next few years. However, it appears that this year's lull was only a temporary aberration. After all, in a small jurisdiction of 3.8 million people, there will always be relatively few cases. Thus, one should not attribute too much significance to there being a period in which there are no such cases.

SOUTH AFRICA

Izak Oosthuizen

Introduction

This chapter focuses on significant developments in Educational Law in South Africa by analyzing cases from the year 2000 which had a major bearing on education in South Africa. The chapter commences with a discussion and an evaluation of the continuing trend towards decentralization of power in South African education before reviewing some of the significant effects which the South African Constitution has on contemporary education.

Decentralization of Power

One of the significant directives in South Africa is the decentralization of power whereby the statutory authority vested in local schools and their governing bodies is continually being amplified. Decentralization of power to various stakeholders, of whom the parents of learners form a very significant part, is one of the national directives for education in South African.[1] The principle of decentralization of power is rooted in democracy since it is enshrined as a constitutional value in section 7 of the South African Constitution.[2]

During the year 2000 the trend to empower the governing bodies of local schools was fixated on the South African educational scene not only in terms of legislation but also in the courts. Key cases in this regard are *Governing Body, Tafelberg School v. Head of Cape Education Department*[3] wherein a governing body's powers to handle a learner's disciplinary mat-

---

[1] Section 4(m) of the National Education Policy Act determines as follows: "The policy contemplated in section 3 shall be directed toward ensuring broad public participation in the development of education policy and the representation of stakeholders in the governance of all aspects of the education system." A natural consequence of this directive, is the statutory role of governing bodies in the governance of public schools in South Africa. Section 16(1) of the South African Schools Act determines that the "governance of every public school is vested in its governing body". In terms of section 23 of this Act, a governing body has to be a body for school governance with representation from the parents of learners of a specific school (which have to constitute the majority of members on the governing body); the principal of the school; educators teaching at the school; non-educating staff members from the school; learners from grades 8 to 12; co-opted members if necessary.

[2] "7(1) This Bill of Rights is a cornerstone of democracy in South Africa. It enshrines the rights of all people in our country and affirms the democratic values of human dignity, equality and freedom."

[3] Governing Body, Tafelberg Sch. v. Head of Cape Educ. Dep't, 2000(1)SA 1209(C).

ters with regard to expulsion were the point of contention; *Gordon Harrison and King Edward High School v. The Minister of Education and Training and The Director-General of Education, Kwa Zulu-Natal,*[4] wherein the governing body's powers with regard to the recommendation of educator appointments came into contention; and *Laerskool Hartswater v. LUR vir Onderwys, Noord-Kaap*[5] *(Hartswater Primary School v MEC for Education. Northern Cape)* which, although ultimately settled outside of court, saw a governing body's powers with regard to the recommendation of educator appointments come into contention.

Expulsion of a Learner

In Governing Body, *Tafelberg School v. Head of Cape Education Department,* the applicant was the governing body of the Tafelberg School, a public school for handicapped learners situated at Sea Point in Cape Town. The respondent was the head of the Western Cape Department of Education[6] within whose area the school resorts. The minor was a fourteen year old boy and a learner at the school who was accused of having stolen a computer hard drive at school. From the affidavit of the school's governing body's disciplinary committee, it appeared that the learner had taken two screw drivers to school which he used to unscrew the hard drive of one of the computers in the Technical Drawing room which he put in his school bag, removed from the classroom, and took home. When the theft of the hard drive was discovered the next day and the news was spread that the police had been requested to investigate the matter, the learner admitted to having stolen the hard drive. The boy also conceded that he understood that his conduct amounted to theft and that it was wrong. When the matter came before the disciplinary committee of the school's governing body, it recommended the learner's expulsion.

Under section 3(2) of the South Africa Schools Act,[7] such a recommendation must be forwarded to the Head of the local Provincial Department who must decide whether to permit the learner to be expelled. Here the boy's

---

[4] Gordon Harrison and King Edward High Sch. v. The Minister of Educ. and Training and The Director-General of Educ., Kwa Zulu-Natal, case number 4295/98 of 11.09.2000 (N).

[5] Laerskool Hartswaterv LUR vir Onderwys, Noord-Kaap, case 864/CC of 3.10.2000 NC) (Hartswater Primary Sch. v. MEC for Educ., Northern Cape

[6] Western Cape is one of the provinces of the Republic of South Africa.

[7] In terms of Regulation 3(2) of the Western Cape Regulations Relating to Serious Misconduct of Learners, the expulsion of learners has to be handled as follows: "Where a governing body recommends to the Head of Department that a learner be expelled, such a learner shall not be allowed to attend the school, pending a decision by the Head of Department in this regard."

father submitted a letter to the respondent trying to influence him in his son's favor. The Head determined that the learner should be re-admitted to school conditionally with the provision that if he were to commit an offence again, appropriate measures would be taken.

The applicant was of the opinion that the respondent's decision against the expulsion of the learner was unduly influenced by the letter. Consequently, the applicant filed suit against the Head of Department[8] on the ground that the it had not been afforded the opportunity to react to the allegations made in the letter.[9] In its affidavit, the applicant charged that it had not had the an opportunity to consider and respond to the allegations made in the letter. As such, it claimed that this not only constituted a breakdown in the respondent's general duty to act fairly but that he also did not observe the principles of natural justice.[10] The respondent contended that he was not obliged to afford the applicant an opportunity to respond to the contents of the letter.[11] The court ruled in favor of the applicant, holding that since the respondent was probably influenced by the father's letter, his decision was to be set aside.[12] The court referred the matter back to the Head so that he could properly reconsider his earlier action setting aside the applicant's recommendation for expulsion.

Appointment of a Principal

In *Gordon Harrison and King Edward High School v.The Minister of Education and Training and The Director-General of Education, Kwa Zulu-Natal*, the statutory powers of a public school governing body to recommend a candidate, Mr. Harrison, for a post as principal, were scrutinized. Mr. Harrison was teaching in Swaziland[13] when he applied for the vacant post of

---

[8] Western Cape Education Department.

[9] "At no time before making his decision did the respondent afford the applicant an opportunity to consider or respond to the representations" – the applicant's affidavit.

[10] Moreover, and this being the case, it is my view that, in the circumstances, the applicant enjoyed a legitimate expectation that, before the respondent permitted new and further representations from the parents to influence him in his decision, he would afford the applicant a reasonable opportunity to consider and respond to them – the applicant's affidavit.

[11] "I was not obliged to give the applicant an opportunity to respond to the representations of the learner's parents" – the respondent's affidavit.

[12] 'After careful consideration/review of the relevant information submitted, I have decided, in terms of reg. 3(4) of the Regulations Relating to Serious Misconduct of Learners at Public Schools in the Province of the Western Cape and the disciplinary procedures that must be followed in such cases, that (the learner) must be re-admitted to Tafelberg High School with the provision that, should he again commit an offence, appropriate action will be taken against him."

[13] Swaziland is adjacent to the Republic of South Africa.

principal at King Edward High School, Natal,[14] in 1998. Mr. Harrison was recommended by the school's governing body for the vacant post of principal in June 1998. The second respondent, the Provincial Director of Education, refused to appoint Mr. Harrison, as he was deemed not to be a "serving educator"[15] as promulgated in the Regulations of the then Educator's Employment Act of 1994.[16] King Edward High School then contested the action of the second respondent. The court ordered the Provincial Director to appoint Mr. Harrison to the post of headmaster at King Edward High School and to pay the applicants' costs. The court's main rationale was vested in the fact that all the prescribed steps in Mr. Harrison's application for the job as principal, including the recommendation for his appointment, had been completed before the Regulations were published on 17 April 1998.

Appointment of an Educator

In *Laerskool Hartswater v. die LUR vir Onderwys, Noord Kaap*,[17] a school filed a motion to enforce a governing body's recommendation to fill a vacant post. A Member of the Provincial Executive Council for Education and respondent, Mr. Moraladi, refused to appoint a candidate recommended by the governing body of Primary School Hartswater even though the vacancy was properly advertised. Mr Balt applied for the vacancy, was interviewed by the Governing Body, and recommended for the post, all in good order and in terms of the statutory specifications. Yet, the respondent did not want to appoint Mr. Balt since it believed that the gender composition on Hartswater's staff was not equitable.[18] During the course of negotiations, the respondent yielded that it would confirm Mr Balt's appointment if he were willing to pay for his own resettlement expenditure. Mr. Balt rejected the offer on the basis that the Department was obliged to pay for this expense.[19] The dispute was resolved out of court with Mr. Balt's

---

[14] Natal is one of the 9 provinces of the Republic of South Africa.

[15] In terms of section 6(2)(b) of the Regulations published on 17 April 1998, "only serving educators shall be eligible to apply for Post Level 2 and higher post level vacancies."

[16] The Educators Employment Act of 1994 has since been repealed by the Employment of Educators Act, No.76 of 1998.

[17] Laerskool Hartswater v. die LUR vir Onderwys, Noord-Kaap, case

[18] The purpose of section 2 of the Employment Equity Act, No.55 of 1998 "is to achieve equity in the workplace by implementing affirmative action measures to redress disadvantages in employment experienced by designated groups, in order to ensure their equitable representation in all occupational categories and levels in the workforce" (author's emphasis). In terms of section 1 of the act, designated groups are defined as "black people, women and people with disabilities."

[19] In terms of Regulation 90 of the Regulations Regarding the Terms and Conditions of Employment of Educators, resettlement expenditure is payable to educators on appointment.

being appointed and the Department of Education paying for resettlement costs and legal fees.

Legislation

The trend of decentralization not only had an effect on the outcome of various cases but was also one of the main issues in the Education Amendment Act of 2000.[20] The Education Amendment Act of 2000 significantly altered the content in the disciplinary code and procedures for educator misconduct in the Employment of Educators Act of 1998. One of these changes was that the authority was delegated to school principals to deal with certain acts of misconduct[21] of educators.[22] If an educator engages in misconduct, a principal has the authority to impose a sanction of counseling, a verbal warning, a written warning, and/or a final written warning. Even though counseling and written and verbal warnings have been part and parcel of the principal's duties in the past, they have never before been elevated to statutory status.

The Constitutionalization of South African Education

One of the main stimuli for major changes in South Africa in recent years has undoubtedly been the introduction of the Constitution of South Africa in 1996. One author described the result of this change as having created "a paradigm shift of magnitude that is still difficult to grasp."[23] Now, only five years after the introduction of the Constitution, its unmistakable influence

---

[20] Education Laws Amendment Act, No.53 of 2000.

[21] According to section 18(1) of the Act "Misconduct refers to a breakdown in the employment relationship¼."

[22] Examples of misconduct in this regard are when he/she absents himself/herself without a valid reason or permission; when he/she conducts himself/herself in an improper, disgraceful or unacceptable manner; when he/she incites others to unlawful conduct; when he/she refuses to obey security regulations; when he/she intimidates fellow employees, learners or students; when he/she performs poorly for reasons other than incapacity; when, in the course of duty, he/she endangers the lives of himself or herself or others by disregarding set safety rules or regulations; when he/she sleeps on duty without permission; when he/she displays disrespect towards others in the workplace or demonstrates abusive or insolent behavior; when he/she fails to carry out a lawful order or routine instruction without just or reasonable cause.

[23] Maree, L.M. 1995. Education under the New Constitution. Pretoria: Via Afrika; p.i.

on South African education has become crystal clear. Apart from the fact that the content of the Constitution should be seen as one of the driving forces behind the decentralization of power in education, it has even been more of a driving force in actions relating to the constitutionality of which was revisited in *Christian Education South Africa v. Minister of Education*;[24] the possible closure of public primary schools which was discussed in *Federation of Governing Bodies of South African Schools (Gauteng) Palm Pre-Primary School v. Member of the Executive Council for Education, Province of Gauteng*;[25] age level requirements for admission to public pre-primary schools as addressed in *Doreen Harris v. Minister of Education*;[26] and subsidies for private schools which were at issue in *Excelsior High, Phoenix College, Liberty Community College and the Association of Independent Schools for Black Children v. Member of the Executive Council for Education (Gauteng), the Superintendent General of the Gauteng Department of Education and the Minister of Education.*[27]

Corporal Punishment

The question with regard to the infliction of corporal punishment in a private[28] Christian school was revisited during 2000. As background, it is useful to refer to the fact that Christian Education South Africa (CESA) filed a suit in the South African Supreme Court[29] in 1999 at which time it unsuccessfully challenged the constitutionality of the prohibition of corporal punishment in Christian private schools. CESA contended that section 10 of the South African Schools Act[30] was inapplicable to Christian private schools since parents gave their written consent for the infliction of corporal punishment on their children. CESA was strongly in favor of corporal punishment since it deemed the practice to be a "vital part of Christian religion;" it also argued that the prohibition interfered with its Constitutional right to freedom of religion and to a cultural life of their own. The Court

---

[24] Christian Educ. South Africa v. Minister of Educ., 2000(4) SA 757(CC).
[25] Federation of Governing Bodies of South African Sch. (Gauteng) Palm Pre-Primary Sch. v. Member of the Executive Council for Educ., Province of Gauteng (case29093/2000) (T).
[26] Doreen Harris v. Minister of Educ. (case 30218/2000 dated 19.1.2001) (T).
[27] Excelsior High, Phoenix College, Liberty Community College and the Ass'n of Indep. Schs. for Black Children v. Member of the Executive Council for Education (Gauteng), the Superintendent General of the Gauteng Dep't of Educ. and the Minister of Educ. (case 00/21268 of 2000.11.24).
[28] Maree, L.M. 1995. Education under a new Constitution. Pretoria: Via Afrika; p.i.
[29] Christian Educ. South Africa v. Minister of Educ. of the Government of the Republic of South Africa 1999(3) SA 608 (SE).
[30] Section 10(1) of the South African Schools Act stipulates:"No person may administer ".

held that in a Christian private school is not only unlawful under the South African Schools Act but is also unconstitutional.

In 2000 CESA appealed the judgment of the Supreme Court to the Constitutional Court of South Africa. Judge Sachs dismissed the appeal. The first reason that the Judge gave was that Section 39 of the Constitution[31] affirms that international law is to be regarded as an important interpretative tool when interpreting the Bill of Rights. In other words, he wrote that South Africa is bound by those international Conventions that it has signed, namely, the Convention Against Torture and other Cruel, Inhuman or Degrading Treatment of 1987 and the United Nations Convention on the Rights of the Child of 1989. Both of these conventions prohibit corporal punishment to ensure that children are not be subjected to violence and degrading punishment. Judge Sachs also posited that the whole matter should be evaluated against the background of what is to be regarded as reasonable and justifiable in an open and democratic society based on human dignity, freedom, and equality.[32] After having applied the limitation clause of section 36 of the Bill of Rights,[33] the Judge held that when all of these factors are weighed together, the scales come down firmly in favor of upholding the generality of the law in the face of the appellant's claim for a constitutionally compelled exemption.

In *Federation of Governing Bodies of South African Schools (Gauteng) Palm Pre-Primary School v. Member of the Executive Council for Education, Province of Gauteng*[34] the Gauteng government's intention to close all pre-primary schools in the province as of the beginning of 2001 was at issue. Insofar as the pre-primary schools in the province of Gauteng[35] cost about R48 million a year, the respondent chose to close them schools to save money. The first applicant, the Federation of Governing Bodies of Schools, claimed that the government's proposed action was not preceded by the

---

[31] "When interpreting the Bill of Rights, a court, tribunal or forum must consider international law".

[32] Section 39(1) of the Constitution determines: "When interpreting the Bill of Rights, a court, tribunal or forum must promote the values that underlie an open and democratic society based on human dignity, equality and freedom."

[33] In terms of section 36 of the Bill of Rights, the general application of the Bill of Rights may be limited to the extent that such a limitation is reasonable and justifiable in an open and democratic society based on human dignity, equality and freedom, taking into account all relevant factors, including the nature of the right; the importance of the purpose of the limitation; the nature and the extent of the limitation; the relation between the limitation and its purpose; and less restrictive means to achieve the purpose.

[34] Federation of Governing Bodies of South African Sch. (Gauteng) Palm Pre-Primary Sch. v. Member of the Executive Council for Educ., Province of Gauteng (case29093/2000) (T)

[35] Gauteng is one of the 9 provinces in South Africa.

obligatory prior consultation with the Gauteng Education and Training Council as was required by section 15 of the Gauteng Policy Act.[36] The government responded that since its acting to close the pre-primary schools was based on policy, it was unnecessary for it to consult the Gauteng Education and Training Council. The government also claimed that the existence of pre-primary schools in Gauteng gave way to an imbalance in the educational system since the pre-primary schools provided mainly for the historically advantaged white children of Gauteng. Therefore, the government was satisfied that its choice to close the pre-primary schools was motivated by the necessity for the State to fulfill its Constitutional obligation of converting equality into educational practice.

The application succeeded. Among the ratio decedendi for the court's judgment was not only that the inequalities in education have to be addressed since Constitutional obligation rests on the State to pursue equal treatment of all children in South African but also that the Constitution[37] regulates State action in an orderly manner. As such, the court declared that organs of the State such as Departments of Education must act within the framework which the statutory enactments, regulations, rules and the Constitution itself impose. Thus, the court directed the government to consult with stakeholders such as the Federation before closing the schools.

Age Requirements

Doreen Harris v. Minister of Education involved a dispute over age requirements for admission to an independent school. At issue was King David Primary, a private school that falls under the auspices of the SA Board of Jewish Education. Talya Harris, who was born on 11 January 1995, was enrolled at a pre-primary school in Johannesburg in 1998. After Talya spent three years in the pre-primary school and was obviously well-prepared to commence with grade 1, her parents enrolled her at the King David Linksfield

---

[36] Section 15(1) of the Gauteng Education Policy Act, 12 of 1995 declares that the Member of the Executive Council must consult with the Gauteng Education and Training Council and, if appropriate, the relevant specialist Advisory Council prior to determining education policy; introducing education-related legislation in the Provincial Legislature; and issuing education-related regulations.

[37] Section 33(1) of the Constitution of South Africa determines that "everyone has the right to administrative action that is lawful, reasonable and procedurally fair". Section 33(3) stipulates that national legislation must be enacted to give effect to these rights, and must impose a duty on the state to give effect to the rights in subsection (1) and (2)."

Primary School as of January 2001. Consequently, Talya's parents applied for her admittance to the school. Although the board indicated that it wanted to admit Talya to the school, it was prohibited from doing so since she was eleven days too young in light of the statutory requirement that "A learner must be admitted to grade 1 if he or she turns seven in the course of that calendar year. A learner who is younger than this age may not be admitted to grade 1."[38]

The respondent contended with three arguments. First, since scholars below the age of seven years tend to clog the educational system as a result of high failure and repetition rates and this carries financial implications for the government, there is a need for a general rule that scholars must turn seven in the year in which they enter grade 1. Second, since there are no educational sound criteria to determine school readiness, it is not possible to provide for exceptions to the general rule. Third, the age requirement of seven years is based on sound educational principles.

The applicant contended that this notice was invalid and unconstitutional for two reasons. First, the applicant claimed that the notice was unconstitutional because it constituted unfair discrimination under section 9 of the South African Constitution. Section 9 prohibits the refusal to grant a child admission to school based on age.[39] The applicant further contended that discrimination was unfair since a psychologist's report indicated not only that the learner was ready for school but that also suggested that it

---

[38] In terms of the National Education Policy Act, No. 27 of 1996, the following government notice was promulgated by the Minister of Education: Age Requirements for Admission to an Independent School in Government Gazette No. 20911 of 18 February 2000 as amended in the Government Gazette No. 21103 of 17 April 2000.

[39] Section 9(3) of the South African Constitution reads: The state may not unfairly discriminate directly or indirectly against anyone on one or more grounds, including race, gender, sex, pregnancy, marital status, ethnic or social origin, color, sexual orientation, age, disability, religion, conscience, belief, culture, language and birth (author's emphasis). Section 95 adds: Discrimination on one or more of the grounds listed in subsection (3) is unfair unless it is established that the discrimination is fair.

could very well be to the detriment of the child not to be admitted to grade 1.[40] Second, the applicants alleged that the notice was unconstitutional because it did not serve "in the best interests"[41] of the child insofar as she was well-prepared and mature for school.

Judge Coetzee ruled that the Department of Education's notice was unconstitutional. He first posited that under section 9(5) of the South African Constitution,[42] the Department of Education was not able to discharge the onus in proving that the discrimination against Talya was fair. Rather, he maintained that under this section, the onus was on the Department of Education to prove that the discrimination was fair. Second, he offered that in light of the report from the school psychologist, as well as the fact that Talya had spent three years in pre-primary school, it was clear that under section 28(2) of the South African Constitution, her best interests were not deemed to be of paramount importance.

As to the fundamental rights stipulated in sections 9 and 28 of the South African Constitution, the court ascertained that the rights in the Bill of Rights could only be limited on the grounds of section 36.[43] The court identified three issues that could be taken into consideration in this regard. The first factor that the court examined was financial. In other words, the

---

[40] Ms Rosenthal, a psychologist, stated that "it must be noted as a matter of extreme importance in the issue of readiness that while it may not be in child's best interests to enter school before he/she is ready to cope with the demands of school, the practice of delaying school entry when a child is ready for school, also has many adverse consequences which are well-documented in literature. Motivation is a crucial aspect of all learning and a child who has completed a minimum of three years of pre-school and who can be deemed "ready" in every way, may begin the new school year with the anticipation of learning to read and write. For some children the failure to realize this expectation can result in a marked loss in motivation, since the purpose of schooling becomes somewhat meaningless to the child. Such child could well become disrupted and bored at school, to the extent that when she/he enters school, that initial momentum and enthusiasm have already been lost and as a result the child's entire early primary schooling is negatively tainted by his/her disappointment".

[41] Section 28(2) of the South African Constitution indicates that a child's best interests are of paramount importance in every matter concerning the child.

[42] Discrimination on one or more of the grounds listed in subsection (3) is unfair unless it is established that the discrimination is fair.

[43] 36. (1) The rights in the Bill of Rights may be limited only in terms of law of general application to the extent that the limitation is reasonable and justifiable in an open and democratic society based on human dignity, equality and freedom, taking into account all relevant factors, including the nature of the right; the importance of the purpose of the limitation; the nature and extent of the limitation; the relation between the limitation and its purpose; and less restrictive means to achieve the purpose.

(2) Except as provided in subsection (1) or in any other provision of the Constitution, no law may limit any right entrenched in the Bill of Rights."

court observed that since private schools, such as King David Primary School, are funded entirely with private funds, admitting the learner would have had no financial implications for the State. Second, as to the alleged connection between age and failure rate, the court was unable to uncover evidence to prove that the age requirements defined in the official notice would have had any effect, negatively or positively, on the failure rate or that there was any evidence of a correlation between a grade 1 age requirement of seven years of age and a lower failure rate. Third, the court examined an overview of the worldwide trend with regard to age requirements for school admission and pointed out that the minimum age of seven for school entrance was applicable to less than a third of the countries world wide.[44] Having considered these arguments and the possibility of limiting Talya's fundamental rights, as stipulated in sections 9 and 28, Judge Coetzee concluded that since the respondent failed to discharge the onus resting on it to prove that the limitation of Talya's rights in terms of the Constitution was justified, there was no reason why she should not have been admitted to the school.

Subsidies to Private Schools

In *Excelsior High, Phoenix College, Liberty Community College and the Association of Independent Schools for Black Children (AISBC) v. Member of the Executive Council for Education (Gauteng)*, the Superintendent General of the Gauteng Department of Education and the Minister of Education, the first three applicants were private secondary schools in the province of Gauteng. The fourth applicant (AISBC) was a voluntary organization comprising of schools providing education to black learners from a low-income background.

The nub of the matter was vested in the question of whether the formula for subsidies to private schools, as determined by the Gauteng Department of Education, was fair. The formula was a fixed one for subsidizing private schools on the basis of the annual per capita expenditure. The total announced by the Department during April 2000 consisted of a fixed amount of R3598[45] per capita per year, regardless whether a school was primary or secondary. However, the application of the formula as communicated to the

---

[44] Judge Coetzee: "On the available evidence it appears that the age of seven or above applies in less than a third of countries world wide. More than two thirds of countries have five or six years as their school entry age."
[45] At the present exchange rate R3598 amounts to about US $450.

schools during November of 1999 was at variance with the announcement of April 2000 since the earlier method of application clearly differentiated between primary and secondary schools. The November 1999 formula favored secondary schools. The applicants also contended that it was common cause that a secondary school's per capita expenses are higher than those of a primary school.

The court held that this was a clear case where the Department breached the constitutional rights of the applicants by making the change without due consultation. Judge Cameron contended that it basically boiled down to the fact that the respondents had breached the rules of natural justice pertaining to legitimate expectations. He explained that the government policy was altered in a way that could harm the applicants' rights without their being given a change or an opportunity to make representations to the decision maker. Consequently, the court set Department of Education's aside.

Conclusion

Rautenbach and Malherbe[46] state that one of the objectives of the South African Constitution is to lay the foundations for a democratic and open society in which government is based on the will of the people. At the same time, the citizens, as the people of the country, are protected by the Constitution against the violation of Government power. In order to be able to identify the effect of the Constitution on education, it is of particular significance to take cognizance of the protective function of the Constitution. Further, it is especially concerning its protective function that the magnitude of the Constitution's effect on education practice in South Africa is becoming clearer every day. The democratic values of democracy and equality are emphasized not only in contemporary court cases and legislation but also in the manifestation of specific human rights such as the right to basic education, the rights of the child, the right to just administrative justice and fair procedures, the right to human dignity, and the right to fair labour practices pertaining to education. All of these rights are constantly being amplified in various courts throughout South Africa.

---

[46] Rautenbach, I.M. & Malherbe, E.F.J. 1998. What does the Constitution say? Pretoria: Van Schaik.

TABLE OF CASES

CASES BY JURISDICTION

This section organizes cases by jurisdiction, presenting federal cases first. Following the U.S. Supreme Court cases are the circuit cases and district cases for states within each circuit. State court cases follow the federal cases.

FEDERAL CASES

United States Supreme Court

Board of Curators of the Univ. of Mo. v. Horowitz / 257
Cleveland Bd. of Education v. Loudermill / 22
College Savings Bank v. Florida Prepaid Postsecondary Education Expense Bd. / 218
Dellmuth v. Muth / 114, 337
Hans v. Louisiana / 218
Kimel v. Florida Bd. of Regents / 196, 218, 268
Kipps v. Caillier / 240
Legal Services Corp. v. Velazquez / 322
McDonnell-Douglas v. Green Corp. / 260
Regents of the Univ. of Cal. v. Bakke / 247
Santa Fe Indep. Sch. Dist. v. Doe / 51
Seminole Tribe of Fla. v. Florida / 218, 255
Terry v. Ohio / 328

District of Columbia

Breiner-Sanders v. Georgetown Univ. / 230
Equal Employment Opportunities Comm'n v. St. Francis Xavier Parochial Sch. / 10
Harrison v. Board of Trustees of the Univ. of the District of Columbia / 238
Paul v. Howard Univ. / 228
Weigert v. Georgetown Univ. / 236

First Circuit

Boateng v. Interamerican Univ. / 229
Campbell v. Washington County Technical College / 239
Hernandez-Loring v. Universidad Metropolitana / 228
Instituto De Educacion Universal Corp. v. United States Dep't of Educ. / 211
Rivera v. Riley / 211

Maine

Doe v. School Admin. Dist. No. 19 / 56
Greenleaf ex rel.. Greenleaf v. Cote / 63
Hinkley v. Baker / 147
Kopf, In re / 252
Ridge v. Cape Elizabeth Sch. Dist. / 9

Massachusetts

Boston's Children First v. City of Boston / 46
Canty v. Old Rochester Reg'l Sch. Dist. / 57
Comfort ex rel.. Neumyer v. Lynn Sch. Comm. / 46
Dolan, In re / 253, 254
Lemire v. Silva / 13

Puerto Rico

Santiago v. Fajardo / 20
Velez Cajigas v. Order of St. Benedict / 12

Second Circuit

Brewer v. West Irondequoit Cent. Sch. Dist. / 47
Gant ex rel. Gant v. Wallingford Bd. of Educ. / 69
Gordon v. New York City Bd. of Educ. / 4
Hack v. President and Fellows of Yale College / 264
Renshaw, In re / 254
Rogers v. New York Univ. / 235
Tenenbaum v. Williams / 60, 148
The Good New Club v. Milford Cent. Sch. / 53
TM Park Ave. Assocs. v. Pataki / 243

STATE CASES

Seybert v. West Chester Univ. / 202
State Sys. of Higher Educ. v. Pennsylvania
  Labor Relations Bd. / 232
Uniontown Area Sch. Dist. v. Pennsylvania
  Labor Relations Bd. *ex rel.* Uniontown
  Area Educ. Ass'n / 88
West Perry Sch. Dist. v. Pennsylvania Labor
  Relations Bd. / 81

Rhode Island

Cain v. Johnson / 239
Frizzell v. Town of Little Compton / 269
Kiley v. Patterson / 340
Perry v. Johnson & Wales Univ. / 241
Schultz v. Foster-Glocester Reg'l Sch. Dist. /
  137

South Carolina

Aughtry v. Abbeville County Sch. Dist. No. 60
  / 145
Elledge v. Richland/Lexington Sch. Dist. No. 5
  / 136
Etheredge v. Richland Sch. Dist. No. 1 / 138
Greer v. Spartanburg Technical College / 216
Mentavlos v. Anderson / 211

South Dakota

AFSCME-Local 1025 Sioux Falls Sch.
  Maintenance and Custodial Workers v.
  Sioux Falls Sch. Dist. / 82
Wuest v. Winner Sch. Dist. 59-2 / 21

Tennessee

Bowden v. Memphis Bd. of Educ. / 39
Canipe v. Memphis Schs. Bd. of Educ. / 25
Dishmon v. Shelby State Community College /
  232
Seay v. Tennessee Student Assistance Corp. /
  206
Steele v. Industrial Development Bd. of the
  Metro. Gov't of Nashville & Davidson
  County / 217
United States Fire Ins. Co. v Vanderbilt Univ. /
  242
Wells v. Tennessee Bd. of Regents / 230

Texas

Bishop v. Texas A&M Univ. / 269
Enriquez v. Khouri / 147
Friona Indep. Sch. Dist. v. King / 70
Hankins v. P.H. / 70
Lopez v. Trevino / 33
Marsaglia v. University of Tex., El Paso / 230
McGilvray v. Moses / 23
Moldt v. Tacoma Sch. Dist. No. 10 / 40
Prairie View A&M Univ. of Texas v. Mitchell /
  273
Stratton v. Austin Indep. Sch. Dist. / 18
Texas A&M Univ.—Kingsville v. Lawson / 207
University of Houston v. Elthon / 209
University of Tex. Southwestern Med. Ctr. of
  Dallas v. Margulis / 202
Villarreal v. Art Institute of Houston / 272
Weslaco Fed. of Teachers v. Texas Educ. Agency
  / 36
Williams v. Chatman / 141

Vermont

Honadle v. University of Vt. / 205
Milton Educ. and Support Ass'n v. Milton Bd.
  of Sch. Trustees / 89
Reynolds v. Sterling College / 251

Virginia

Larimore v. Blaylock / 226
University of Va. v. Robertson / 206, 254

Washington

Allan v. University of Wash. / 204
Cloud *ex rel.* Cloud v Summers / 59
Doe v. Gonzaga Univ. / 270
Evergreen Freedom Found. v. Washington Educ.
  Ass'n / 80
Hunter v. Univ. of Wash. / 198, 251
Ishibashi v. Gonzaga Univ. / 259
McCormick v. Lake Washington Sch. Dist. / 33
State v. Avila / 71
State v. J.M. / 71
Trimble v. Washington State. Univ. / 227
Tunstall *ex rel..* Tunstall v. Bergeson / 67

West Virginia

Wisconsin

Wyoming

Index

M

mainstreaming / 358
malicious prosecution / 45, 328
malpractice / 66, 127, 143, 200, 207,
 246, 272, 340
mediation / 99, 303
medical services / 111
mentally retarded / 100
methodology / 96, 99
mootness / 103, 197

N

National Collegiate Athletic Association /
 267
National Education Policy Act / 474, 482
negligence / 127-141, 149, 157, 171-176,
 180-181, 249, 304, 308, 317, 444-
 446, 453-455
nonrenewal / 184
notice / 94, 103, 113, 116, 127, 133-135,
 141-142, 170, 177-178, 181-184,
 190, 251, 257-261, 268

O

occupational therapy / 97, 111
otherwise qualified / 121, 267

P

parental ballots on selection of pupils /
 433, 442
parental consent / 94, 99
parental rights / 296, 321, 341
parochial school / 9, 11, 93-94
participants / 62, 157, 165-168, 171,
 174-176, 180, 192, 242, 314, 405
physical education / 32, 37, 82, 140, 151,
 159, 182-183, 186
playground / 55, 132, 136, 142, 175, 178-
 179, 355
privacy rights / 16, 61
private school / 35, 152, 350, 353, 439,
 451, 454, 462-463, 466-468, 473,
 479, 481-484
procedural safeguards / 172
property interests / 13, 18, 231, 254

Q

qualified immunity / 148-150, 165-166,
 170, 194, 203, 213-214, 222, 239-
 240, 256

R

race discrimination / 222
racial / 203, 221-222, 228-229, 240, 245-
 248, 260, 466
rape / 286
real property / 200, 297, 307
reasonable accommodation / 236, 348,
 357, 360, 363
reasonableness / 269
recruiting / 157-160, 216, 267, 296
reduction in force / 194, 237
Rehabilitation Act of 1973 / 2, 121
reimbursement / 48, 91-94, 100, 104,
 113-117, 125, 198
related services / 91-92, 106, 111-113,
 292
residence halls / 245, 263-264, 271
retaliation / 3-4, 14, 22-23, 55, 72, 100,
 110, 150, 154, 189, 194, 209, 213,
 218-229, 233-236, 260, 380
retirement / 10, 22, 27, 32-38, 85-86,
 234, 238, 241, 253, 289, 300, 317,
 469, 470
right to privacy / 166, 245, 256

S

safety / 25, 63, 134, 137, 140, 149, 168,
 176-179, 183, 273-275, 286, 301-
 312, 316, 325-326, 334, 355-356,
 362, 428, 467, 478
same sex / 55
school choice / 275, 299, 433, 438, 447
school districts / 49, 92, 120, 198, 279,
 283-284, 292, 296, 298, 307, 458
school grounds / 50, 127-128, 134
school property / 25, 61-64, 71, 127-129,
 174
school setting / 98, 220, 353
school transport costs / 433, 443
search and seizure / 274, 321, 325-326
section 1983 / 3, 5, 7, 12, 14, 99, 105-
 106, 114, 125, 157, 160, 166, 173,
 187, 192, 202-203, 206, 211-217,
 231, 234, 265